W9-AZY-277

Special Edition

Using

Using
MICROSOFT®
Word 97

Best Seller Edition

que®

Using

Special Edition

Using

MICROSOFT®

Word 97

Best Seller Edition

que®

Bill Camarda

Special Edition Using Microsoft Word 97

Library of Congress Catalog No.: 97-68763

ISBN: 0-7897-1398-5

99 98 97   6 5 4 3 2 1

Interpretation of the printing code: the rightmost double-digit number is the year of the book's printing; the rightmost single-digit number, the number of the book's printing. For example, a printing code of 97-1 shows that the first printing of the book occurred in 1997.

Contents at a Glance

Introduction

Table of Contents

III | Getting the Word Out: The Internet, Intranets, Electronic Files, and Hard Copy

Credits

PRESIDENT
Roland Elgey

SENIOR VICE PRESIDENT/PUBLISHING
Don Fowley

PUBLISHER
Joseph B. Wikert

GENERAL MANAGER
Joe Muldoon

MANAGER OF PUBLISHING OPERATIONS
Linda H. Buehler

PUBLISHING DIRECTOR
Karen Reinisch

EDITORIAL SERVICES DIRECTOR
Carla Hall

MANAGING EDITOR
Thomas F. Hayes

ACQUISITIONS MANAGER
Cheryl D. Willoughby

ACQUISITIONS EDITOR
Lisa Swayne

PRODUCT DIRECTOR
Rick Kughen

PRODUCTION EDITOR
Rebecca Mounts

EDITORS
Kate Givens
Sydney Jones
Tom Stevens
Brian Sweany

COORDINATOR OF EDITORIAL SERVICES
Maureen A. McDaniel

WEBMASTER
Thomas H. Bennett

PRODUCT MARKETING MANAGER
Kourtnaye Sturgeon

ASSISTANT PRODUCT MARKETING MANAGER
Gretchen Schlesinger

TECHNICAL EDITORS
Kyle Bryant
David Garratt
Curtis Knight
Brad Lindaas
Nadeem Muhammed
Verley and Nelson
Colleta Witherspoon

SOFTWARE SPECIALIST
David Garratt

ACQUISITIONS COORDINATOR
Travis Bartlett

SOFTWARE RELATIONS COORDINATOR
Susan D. Gallagher

EDITORIAL ASSISTANT
Jennifer L. Chisholm

BOOK DESIGNERS
Ruth Harvey
Kim Scott

COVER DESIGNER
Sandra Schroeder

PRODUCTION TEAM
Erin M. Danielson
Trey Frank
Nicole Ruessler
Sossity Smith
Lisa Stumpf
Donna Wright

INDEXER
Ginny Bess
Cheryl Jackson

Composed in *Century Old Style* and *ITC Franklin Gothic* by Que Corporation.

To my wife, Barbara, and my son, Matthew. You bring me joy beyond words.

About the Authors

Bill Camarda's most recent computer books include *The Cheapskate's Guide to Bargain Computing* (Prentice Hall PTR), *Windows Sources Word 97 for Windows SuperGuide* (Ziff-Davis Press), *Inside Microsoft Word for Windows 95* (New Riders Publishing), and *Inside 1-2-3 Release 5* (New Riders Publishing). He has more than 15 years experience writing about technology for users at all levels of expertise, and for corporate clients such as IBM, AT&T, MCI, Bell Atlantic, NYNEX, and Digital.

Joseph Lowery has been writing about computers and new technology since 1981. He is the co-author of *HTML 3.2 Manual of Style* published by Ziff-Davis Press and a contributor to Que's *Microsoft Office 97 Small Business Edition 6-in-1*. Joseph is currently developing the Web site for the MCP Office 97 Resource Center as well as other sites for a variety of clients, including a managed health care organization, a stock market research firm, and a bar. Joseph and his wife, the dancer/choreographer Debra Wanner, have a daughter, Margot, who hogs the computer.

Elaine Marmel is President of Marmel Enterprises, Inc., an organization which specializes in technical writing and software training. Elaine spends most of her time writing and is the author of several books on *Word for Windows, Word for the Mac, Quicken for Windows, Quicken for DOS, 1-2-3 for Windows, Lotus Notes,* and *Excel.* Elaine also is a contributing editor to *Inside Peachtree for Windows*, a monthly magazine published about Peachtree for Windows, an accounting package.

Elaine left her native Chicago for the warmer climes of Florida (by way of Cincinnati, OH; Jerusalem, Israel; Ithaca, NY; and Washington, D.C.) where she basks in the sun with her PC and her cats, Cato and Watson. Elaine also sings in the Toast of Tampa, an International Champion Sweet Adeline barbershop chorus.

Dedication: To my cousin, Ruth Bronstein (1925-1997), for all the joy and laughter you shared with me. You lit the lives of all those you touched, and I dedicate this work to you in an attempt to provide you, in the only way I can, with your own piece of immortality. You'll live on always in my memory, and I don't have the words to express how much I'll miss you.

Bill Ray is a Microsoft Certified Solution Developer, and Product Specialist. He is a Senior Consultant for the Center for Professional Computer Education (CPCE, Inc.) of Shelton, CT, a Microsoft Authorized Technical Education Center and Microsoft Solution Provider Partner. His responsibilities at CPCE include the design and implementation of customized solutions using Microsoft Office applications in the corporate marketplace. Bill is also a co-developer of CPCE's Word for Windows Productivity Pack, which is a customizable set of macros and templates for improved office productivity. Bill holds an M.A. in Music Education from Teachers College, Columbia University, and an M.S. in Computer Science from Union College. Bill can be reached via CompuServe (**71101,3402**) or the Internet (**wgray@cpce.com**).

Acknowledgments

Thanks to everyone at and around Que who made this book possible. That especially includes the three folks I've worked with most closely: my acquisition editor, Lisa Swayne, my development editor Rick Kughen, and my production editor, Rebecca Mounts. Patient, supportive, and fun to work with—what more could you want?

Kudos also to my copy editor Sydney Jones, my tech editors, Kyle Bryant, David Garratt, Curtis Knight, Brad Lindaas, Nadeem Muhammed, Verley and Nelson, and Colleta Witherspoon, and my indexers Ginny Bess and Cheryl Jackson, who have worked tirelessly to make this book as accurate, readable, and convenient as possible.

Thanks to my contributing authors, who produced terrific work on terrifying deadlines: Elaine Marmel, Joe Lowery, and Bill Ray.

Thanks to the marketing, public relations, and sales teams that partner with editorial to consistently make Que #1—and are going to sell lots of copies of this book <grin>!

Most important, thanks to *you* for choosing this book. I sincerely hope you'll find it to be a trusted companion as you work with Word for years to come.

We'd Like to Hear from You!

QUE Corporation has a long-standing reputation for high-quality books and products. To ensure your continued satisfaction, we also understand the importance of customer service and support.

Tech Support

If you need assistance with the information in this book or with a CD/disk accompanying the book, please access Macmillan Computer Publishing's online Knowledge Base at:

http://www.superlibrary.com/general/support

Our most Frequently Asked Questions are answered there. If you do not find the answer to your questions on our Web site, you may contact Macmillan Technical Support by phone at **317/581-3833** or via e-mail at **support@mcp.com.**

Also be sure to visit QUE's Desktop Applications and Operating Systems team Web resource center for all the latest information, enhancements, errata, downloads, and more:

http://www.quecorp.com/desktop_os/

Orders, Catalogs, and Customer Service

To order other QUE or Macmillan Computer Publishing books, catalogs, or products, please contact our Customer Service Department:

Phone: 800/428-5331
Fax: 800/835-3202
International Fax: 317/228-4400

Or visit our online bookstore:

http://www.mcp.com/

Comments and Suggestions

We want you to let us know what you like or dislike most about this book or other QUE products. Your comments will help us to continue publishing the best books available on computer topics in today's market.

Rick Kughen
Product Director
QUE Corporation
201 West 103rd Street, 4B
Indianapolis, Indiana 46290 USA
Fax: 317/581-4663 E-mail: rkughen@que.mcp.com

Please be sure to include the book's title and author as well as your name and phone or fax number. We will carefully review your comments and share them with the author. Please note that due to the high volume of mail we receive, we may not be able to reply to every message.

Introduction

This book has one goal: to make you the most productive Word user on the block. You'll find a relentless focus on productivity here:

- What's the fastest, easiest way to get the job done?
- How can you streamline and automate all those annoying tasks you've been doing by hand?
- How can you do more with Word than you ever thought possible?

Even if you're experienced with Word, you'll be amazed at how much more it can do for you—and how easily, if you know how. Here are some examples. You probably know about some of these features, but you're a rare and special Word user if you know how to use all of them:

- Word can automatically format your document for you.
- Word can automatically fix hundreds of common spelling mistakes.
- If your document is a page too long, Word can automatically shrink it to fit.
- Word can automatically apply numbered headings throughout your document, and keep them up-to-date.
- Word can automatically summarize your document for you.
- Built-in Word wizards can automate virtually all the formatting and organization required by resumes, memos, and many other documents.
- Word can automatically insert large blocks of text for you—even formatted text.
- If you give Word a list of words and phrases, Word can automatically build an index reflecting every reference to them.
- Word can compare two drafts of a document and show you everything that has changed.
- Word can automatically add a numbered caption to every graphic or table in your document.

There are dozens more examples, but you get the point. The time you invest in learning Word's productivity features can pay extraordinary dividends. And *Special Edition Using Microsoft Word 97, Best Seller Edition* will help you every step of the way. ■

Who Should Read This Book?

This book has been carefully designed to benefit virtually *any* Word user:

- If you've been around the block a few times with Word, you'll appreciate the focus on productivity—on better ways to do the job.
- If you're an experienced Word user, but you're new to Word 97, you'll appreciate the detailed coverage of Word's powerful new features—*especially* the practical, step-by-step coverage of using Word for Web and intranet publishing.
- If you're completely new to Word, first of all, welcome aboard! *Special Edition Using Microsoft Word 97, Best Seller Edition* will help you quickly learn the skills and good habits it might otherwise take you years to learn.
- If you're using Word in a business setting, you'll welcome this book's extensive practical business examples. You'll also appreciate its detailed coverage of business features such as managing revisions, integrating Excel worksheets, and creating mass mailings (and e-mailings).
- If you use Word to write books or other long documents, you'll like this book's practical, hands-on coverage of powerful features like outlining, tables of contents, indexing, master documents, footnotes, and cross-references.

■ Finally, if you're interested in using Word's powerful Visual Basic for Applications (VBA) language, you'll appreciate the extensive coverage at the back of the book, including three never-before-published real-world business solutions created with VBA.

How This Book Is Organized

Special Edition Using Microsoft Word 97, Best Seller Edition is organized in seven sections.

Part I: Word Basics: Get Productive Fast

You'll start with a quick introduction to Word 97's new and improved interface and formatting features. The emphasis, of course, is on productivity and new Word conveniences, plus old shortcuts you might not have noticed before. If you're new to Word, odds are you need to get productive in a hurry. Section I delivers the quick-start basics you need right now.

Part II: Building Slicker Documents Faster

In Section II, you'll learn how to make the most of Word's bread-and-butter document development tools, including styles, templates, and AutoText. Most Word users, even experienced ones, only scratch the surface of these tools. You'll find plenty of real-world scenarios and examples that show exactly how to get the biggest bang for the buck from these powerful tools.

Part III: Getting the Word Out: The Internet, Intranets, Electronic Files, and Hard Copy

In Section III, you'll learn many ways Word can help deliver your message to the widest possible audience. You'll find extensive, hands-on coverage of using Word to create Web pages, Web sites, and corporate intranets. You'll also find detailed coverage of print and print merge techniques—and you'll discover how Word can help you make the most of fax and e-mail technology.

Part IV: The Big Document: Powerful Tools and Strategies

Next, you'll focus on Word's core features for streamlining complex documents, including outlining, master documents, tables of contents, captioning, indexes, footnotes, endnotes, and cross-references. Again, you'll find plenty of case studies and practical examples to show *when* you should use these features—and *how* to use them most quickly and effectively.

Part V: The Visual Word: Making It Look Even Better

Documents are growing more visual every year. Section V shows how to use Word's powerful design and graphics tools to build documents that are highly visual—and highly effective. In Chapter 19, "Word Desktop Publishing," for instance, you'll find two case studies: one that builds a newsletter from the Newsletter Wizard, and another that builds it manually, using a variety of tools, including text boxes, drop caps, borders and shading, and so on. After that, you'll learn how to adapt Word (and other) clip art to your personal needs and how to use Word 97's enhanced drawing tools—even if you're no artist.

Part VI: The Corporate Word

If you use Word in a corporate setting, or if you're responsible for managing Word, Section VI is aimed at *you*. Discover practical, easy ways to leverage Word business features such as revision marking, annotations, and integration with Microsoft Office. Chapter 28, "Installing and Configuring Word in a Network Environment," focuses on security, networking, Windows NT 4.0/95 cross-platform, and other critical issues that are left out of most Word books. Look there for all-new coverage of the important summer revision to Office 97, which helps overcome the biggest obstacle to corporate acceptance of Word 97: file format incompatibility.

Part VII: The Power of Visual Basic for Applications

Finally, Section VII takes an exceptionally close look at Visual Basic for Applications (VBA). You'll learn all the basics of working with the VBA development environment, writing code, and adapting recorded macros. But that's just the beginning. You'll walk through the construction of three complete VBA applications, each designed to solve real problems, and each annotated to carefully explain how and why they were built the way they were. Of course, you'll find all three applications on the accompanying CD-ROM.

How This Book Is Designed

Here's a quick look at a few structural features designed to help you get the most out of this book. You'll find a roadmap at the beginning of each chapter—a convenient preview of what you'll learn. You'll also find:

T I P Tips—*plenty of them*—are designed to point out especially quick ways to get the job done, or good ideas and techniques you might not discover on your own.

N O T E Notes offer a little more insight into features or issues that may be of special interest—without distracting you from the meat-and-potatoes answers you're looking for. ■

CAUTION

Cautions, as you'd expect, warn you away from those few sharp edges that still remain in Word after more than a decade of sanding and polishing.

ON THE WEB

When you come across an On the Web reference, you'll know that you can find out more—or perhaps get some free resources—at the specified Web site. For instance, **www.microsoft.com/office/ork/appa/appa.htm** connects you to free copies of the tools and utilities associated with the Microsoft Office Resource Kit.

Often, when a subject is covered in greater detail elsewhere in the book, you'll find a marker like this, which points you to the location where the topic can be found.

▶ **See** "Creating a Hyperlink Within a Document," **p. 527**

TROUBLESHOOTING

While it's rare that you'll get yourself in deep trouble with Word, it's *not* so rare for a feature to work differently than you might expect—in other words, for it *not* to do what you wanted. At times like those, you need answers fast. That's why nearly every chapter in this book ends with a Troubleshooting section. Troubleshooting problems appear in bold, and the solutions appear in regular print.

What's on the CD-ROM?

Like many computer books nowadays, this one has a CD-ROM bound into the inside back cover. But when it comes to the CD-ROM (and many other aspects of this book), you'll find that *Special Edition Using Microsoft Word 97, Best Seller Edition* has one important advantage.

Unlike many Word 97 books, this one was published several months *after* Word 97 and Office 97 were introduced. As a result, the CD-ROM incorporates shareware, freeware, software, graphics, and other tools that simply didn't exist when many other Word 97 books were published.

Because most Word 97 users also work with other Office 97 programs, including Excel, PowerPoint, Access, and Outlook, you'll also find extensive Office 97 resources on this disk.

Conventions Used in This Book

Like contemporary political conventions, Que's Special Edition typographical conventions are designed to be completely *predictable*—so it's easy to understand what you're reading, and what you're supposed to do.

For example, you'll often read about key combinations such as Ctrl+B, Word's shortcut for boldfacing text you've selected. Ctrl+B means hold down the Control key, press B, and then release both keys.

Also, when you're instructed to select a menu item, you'll find the menu name and item have one letter underlined. For example, to display Word's Print dialog box, select File, Print.

You'll occasionally run across a few other types of formatted text, as follows:

■ Internet addresses are specified in boldface, for example, **www.microsoft.com**. If a Web address must continue on the following line due to page width restrictions, the address will be divided at the backslash. This indicates that the same Web address continues on the following line due to page width restrictions, but you should treat it as one line of text, without pressing Enter or entering spaces. You can see this in the following example:

http://www.yahoo.com/headlines/970803/business/stories/ups_6.html

- Terms introduced and defined for the first time are formatted in *italic*, as in the following example:

A *toolbar* is a set of buttons that perform related tasks.

- Text formatted in boldface may also represent type that should be entered verbatim, as in the following example:

You can tell users to run Setup using a command line such as

setup.exe /q1 /b1

- Finally, text formatted in "typewriter" type represents code listings, such as Visual Basic for Applications program listings, as in the following example:

```
Sub Macro7()
'
' Macro7 Macro
' Macro recorded 07/10/97 by Bill Camarda
'
    Selection.Font.Bold = wdToggle
End Sub
```

That's all you need to know to get the most out of this book. Now fire up your copy of Word, and let's see what it can do. ●

Word Basics: Get Productive Fast

CHAPTER 1

Word: Take the Controls

by Bill Camarda

Welcome to Word 97, the most powerful, most popular version of Word ever.

This quick-start chapter will help you start leveraging Word's power—fast. First, you'll make yourself at home with Word 97's souped-up interface. You'll discover better ways to navigate Word and your documents—even long documents that were once unwieldy. You'll discover just how much you can do with one click or a simple keyboard shortcut.

After that's squared away, you'll review the basics of creating and editing documents with Word. All the fundamentals are here, but again you'll find the focus on shortcuts to supercharge your productivity. ▪

How to use the Word 97 interface

Discover the toolbar buttons, keyboard shortcuts, and new navigation tools that help you get the job done faster.

Choosing the right document view

Learn how to make sure you're viewing your document in the most efficient way possible.

Where to find Help

Understand the Word Help system and how to get answers fast.

The basics of editing

Learn more efficient ways to cut, paste, copy, and move text.

Saving your documents

Learn quick ways to save documents, and how to save documents in different locations or formats.

Opening your documents

Learn the fastest ways to retrieve documents you use often—or only occasionally.

Finding your documents

Walk through Word's powerful Find tools, and learn how to locate any document.

Quick Tour of the "Cockpit"

Typically, the easiest way to start Word 97 in Windows 95 or Windows NT 4.0 is to click Start, Programs, Microsoft Word. Word opens with a new blank document ready for editing. In Figure 1.1, you can see the basic Word 97 interface with each of its components marked.

FIG. 1.1
The Word 97 interface is replete with shortcuts for editing and navigation.

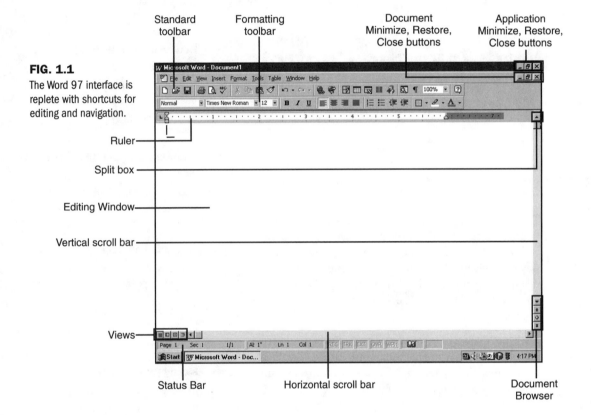

In the next few sections, you'll take a closer look at each important element of the Word interface.

Toolbars: Usually the Fastest Way to Get the Job Done

In Word, there's little you can't do by clicking a single button. In fact, sometimes the hardest part is finding the right button to click. If you're not sure what some of Word's button icons mean, position your mouse pointer over the icon and a ScreenTip will appear, displaying the button's name.

Part

I

Ch

1

 TIP Occasionally you might prefer to start using a keyboard shortcut in place of a toolbar button. Here's an easy way to learn more of the keyboard shortcuts associated with Word toolbar buttons: tell Word to display the keyboard shortcut whenever it displays a ScreenTip. To do so, select View, Toolbars, Customize; then choose the Options tab and check Show Shortcut Keys in ScreenTips.

Word comes with well over a dozen toolbars, each containing a series of buttons designed to perform common related tasks. For example, Word's Drawing toolbar contains a series of tools for drawing, coloring, and manipulating lines, shapes, and text. You can display most of Word's toolbars any time you want, by selecting View, Toolbars. A cascaded list appears. Check the toolbar you want. Table 1.1 lists the toolbars you can display using View, Toolbars.

Table 1.1   Word Toolbars Available from Choosing View, Toolbar

Toolbar Name	What it Does
Standard	File management and editing
Formatting	Font (character) and paragraph formatting
AutoText	Insertion and management of boilerplate text
Control Toolbox	Insertion and management of ActiveX controls
Database	Control of Word database tables and external queries
Drawing	Graphics, image management, text boxes, and text-based graphics (WordArt)
Forms	Electronic forms
Picture	Insertion and manipulation of clip art
Reviewing	Tracking reviewers' changes
Tables and Borders	Table and cell creation, formatting, manipulation, and sorting
Visual Basic	Running and working with Visual Basic macros
Web	Accessing Web resources; creating documents to be published on the Web
WordArt	Creating text-based graphics

Other toolbars, such as Header and Footer, automatically appear when you're performing the tasks they're designed to assist and won't appear at any other time.

 TIP In Chapter 26, "Customizing Word," you'll learn how to create new toolbars and move buttons among toolbars—creating a toolbar that is perfectly designed for your needs.

Standard and Formatting Toolbars Word clusters the most commonly used tasks on two Word toolbars that always appear unless you choose to hide them: the Standard toolbar, and the Formatting toolbar.

The Standard toolbar (see Figure 1.2) contains basic file management and editing tools, along with one-button shortcuts for common tasks like inserting tables, columns or drawings.

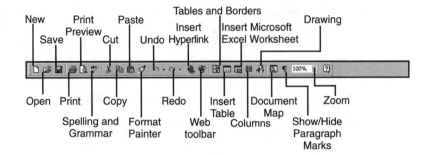

FIG. 1.2

The Standard toolbar organizes many of Word's most common file management and editing tools.

The Formatting toolbar (see Figure 1.3) contains shortcuts for formatting text, aligning paragraphs, bullets and numbering, indentation, and borders and highlighting.

FIG. 1.3

The Formatting toolbar gives you one-button access to the most important elements of font (character) and paragraph formatting.

Using the Ruler

Word's Ruler (see Figure 1.4) displays by default, providing an easy, "hands-on" way to control margins, indents and tabs. You'll take a closer look at using the Ruler to control indents and tabs in Chapter 2, "Quick and Effective Formatting Techniques," and margins in Chapter 3, "More Day-to-Day Productivity Tools."

FIG. 1.4

You can control margins, indents, and tabs by clicking and dragging elements of the ruler. To see which element does what, point to it; a descriptive ScreenTip will appear.

Moving Around Fast, with the Scroll Bars

As with most Windows applications, Word provides a vertical scroll bar that enables you to rapidly move throughout a document. To move to a specific location, click the scroll box and drag it up or down. As you drag the scroll box, Word will display a ScreenTip showing the page number you've scrolled to. To move up or down by one screen, click anywhere in the vertical scroll bar above or below the scroll box.

 TIP If you use Word heading styles to identify your document's headings, Word provides even more useful ScreenTips, displaying the headings as you move past them (see Figure 1.5). This way, you don't even need to know the page number you're looking for—just the subject matter.

FIG. 1.5

As you scroll through a document that uses heading styles, Word displays a ScreenTip showing the names of the headings you pass.

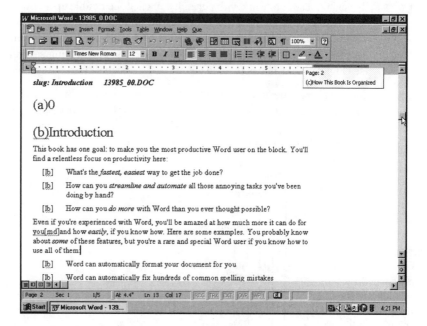

Word also provides a *horizontal scroll bar* that enables you to move from left to right in a document. You'll find this most useful when you're working in documents wider than your editing window, such as documents formatted horizontally in *landscape orientation*.

If your document is only slightly wider than your window, you might find it more comfortable to display all your text at the same time, rather than scrolling horizontally back and forth. One way to do this is to choose View, Online Layout. Word's document views will be discussed later in this chapter.

 TIP If you have a Microsoft IntelliMouse, you can also scroll through a document by rolling the wheel between the left and right mouse buttons.

Document Browser: Browse Any Way You Like   At the bottom of the vertical scroll bar, you'll find a powerful new tool for moving around your document: Word's *Document Browser* (see Figure 1.6). Document Browser enables you to jump quickly between document elements.

FIG. 1.6

With Document Browser, it's easy to move to the preceding (or next) page.

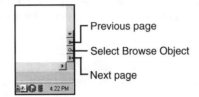

By default, it's set to work with *pages*. If you click the double up-arrow button, you move up one page, and if you click the double down-arrow button, you move down one page. However, you can use Document Browser to move among many other document elements as well. Click the Select Browse Object ball, and Word displays icons representing several document elements (see Figure 1.7). Choose the one you want. The double-arrows turn blue.

You can always check to see which element the Document Browser is set to search for. Position the mouse pointer on one of the double-arrow buttons to display a ScreenTip. When you want to revert to browsing by Page, click Select Browse Object and choose Page; the double-arrows become black again.

FIG. 1.7

When you click the Select Browse Object ball, Word enables you to choose the document element you want to browse.

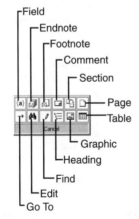

TIP   What if it's not enough to view the next or preceding document element: you want to move ahead or back by *several* elements? Or, what if you want to browse for an element that Select Browse Object doesn't control? Use Word's Go To dialog box: press F5 to display it. Go To is covered in detail in Chapter 3, "More Day-to-Day Productivity Tools."

Get the Best View of Your Document

There's more than one way to look at anything, especially your Word documents. Word lets you choose the right view for whatever purpose suits you at the moment, including editing speed, previewing, or document organization, to name a few. You can navigate and edit your document in any of these four Word views:

 ■ Normal view

 ■ Online Layout view

 ■ Page Layout view

 ■ Outline view

The fastest way to choose your view is by clicking a view button at the left of the horizontal scroll bar, near the bottom of the screen.

 Working in Normal View   Normal view, shown in Figure 1.8, is Word's default setting. It represents a trade-off between accuracy and speed. In Normal view, you see your document much as it will appear when printed, with some significant exceptions. For example, you won't see any imported images (and if you try to use Word's drawing tools, you're switched automatically into Page Layout view). If your document consists of multiple columns, Normal view displays a single column instead.

FIG. 1.8

A two-column document is displayed in Normal view. Only one column appears, and graphics are missing.

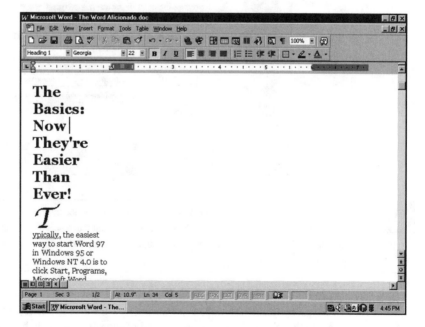

Occasionally, even Normal view will be too slow. For example, you may be using a relatively slow computer to edit an extremely long, complex document. One option is to display the contents of your document in Draft Font. You'll see virtually no text formatting, but Word will run noticeably faster. To do this, first make sure you're in Normal view. Then select Tools, Options, View, and check the Draft Font check box.

 Working in Page Layout View   Page Layout view (see Figure 1.9) shows your document exactly as it will appear when you print it, with all headers, footers, images, columns, and other elements in place. The trade-off is that Page Layout view is slower, because Word, Windows, and your computer must work harder to display all those elements.

FIG. 1.9

In this figure, the document is displayed in Page Layout view. Note that all elements are in their proper place, including text boxes, graphics, and drop caps.

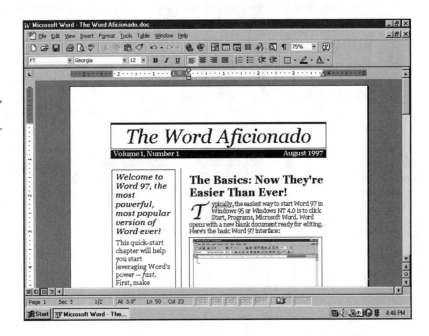

 If you find that Page Layout view runs too slowly, yet you need to see accurate page layouts, there is a compromise: keep the layout, but hide the images. To do this, first make sure you are in Page Layout view. Next, select Tools, Options, View. Check the Picture Placeholders check box, and clear the Drawings box.

 Working in Online Layout View   Online Layout view, new in Word 97, makes text easier to read *on-screen*, instead of faithfully reproducing how it will look when printed. For example, it wraps text to the width of your screen, instead of allowing it to stretch beyond the screen's borders. If your text is smaller than 12-point type, Online Layout view also enlarges it to look like 12-point type on-screen, as you can see in Figure 1.10. Online Layout view also turns on the Document Map, covered shortly in the Document Map section.

FIG. 1.10
Online Layout view enhances your document's appearance for viewing on-screen.

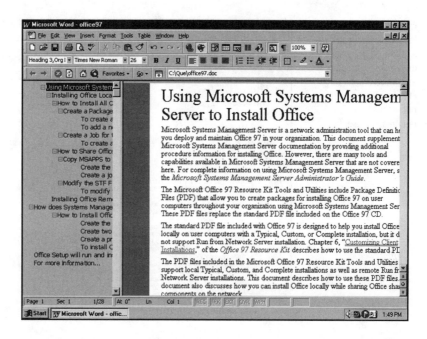

 Working in Outline View   Outline view (see Figure 1.11) displays the outline structure embedded in your document, so you can quickly see (and change) the way your document is organized. You won't see much of a difference between Outline view and other views unless you've used Word Heading Styles or Outline Levels to establish distinctions between levels of text. But if you do use these features, you'll have exceptional control over your document—control that's available in no other way. (For a close look at what you can do in Outline view, see Chapter 14, "Outlining: The Best Way to Organize a Document.")

> **T I P**   If you haven't used Heading Styles, you can often add them quickly using Word's AutoFormat feature, as discussed in Chapter 7, "Automating Your Documents: AutoCorrect, AutoFormat, AutoText, and AutoSummarize."

Document Map   If your document includes any elements that Word can use as mileposts throughout your document, you'll also find the new Document Map feature valuable. To display the Document Map, choose View, Document Map.

> **T I P**   Document Map also displays automatically whenever you switch to Online Layout view.

With Document Map (see Figure 1.12), you can see both your document's text and a map of your document at the same time. Click an element on the map, and you move to that location—just as you would if you clicked a hyperlink on a Web page.

FIG. 1.11

In Outline view, you can see exactly how your document is structured and move around large chunks of your document with remarkable ease.

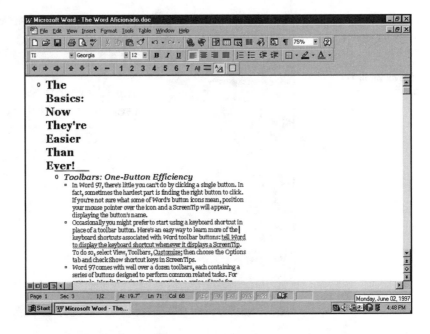

FIG. 1.12

Document Map enables you to quickly move to any location in your document.

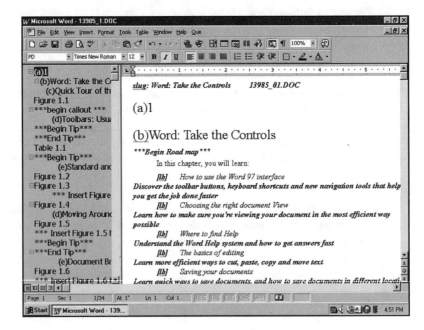

Seeing More of Your Document

Every new version of Word seems to put more interface "in your face." Some people find it just too much: all those buttons seem to get in the way of their work. If you're one of those people, you'll appreciate knowing that you can hide as much of the Word interface as you like. You can even hide all of it if you want.

Hiding Some Interface Elements   Much of Word's interface can be hidden or displayed via the View menu. For example, selecting View, Ruler toggles Word's Ruler on or off. Selecting View, Toolbars displays a cascaded list of all available Word toolbars; you can then clear the ones you want to hide.

Other interface elements can be hidden using Word's Options dialog box. Choose Tools, Options, to display this dialog box; then display the View tab (see Figure 1.13).

FIG. 1.13

The View tab of the Options dialog box enables you to show or hide scroll bars and the status bar.

Next, you can clear any or all of the following check boxes: Vertical Scroll Bar, Horizontal Scroll Bar, or Status Bar check boxes.

Working with a Blank Screen   Of course, the minimalist pièce de résistance is hiding Word's interface completely. It's easy: choose View, Full Screen. Your document editing window expands to cover the entire screen, except for a small Close Full Screen button you can click to return to the previous Word interface.

N O T E   Many long-time WordPerfect for DOS users find themselves at home with the full-screen interface, which somewhat resembles the original bare WordPerfect interface. ▪

Zooming in on What You Want to See

By default, Word displays your text at full size in Normal view: 100%. However, you may occasionally want to change this. For example, to view the intricate details of a drawing, you might want to zoom in to 200% or more, or to see most or all of a page in Page Layout view, you might want to zoom out to 50% or less. Word makes this easy, with the Zoom drop-down box in the Standard toolbar (see Figure 1.14).

N O T E The Zoom drop-down list has different options depending on the view you have selected. ■

FIG. 1.14

Use the Zoom drop-down box to specify how much you want to enlarge or reduce your document on-screen.

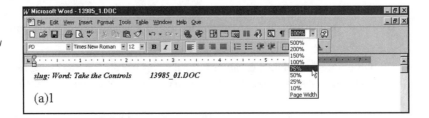

You can click the down-arrow next to the Zoom drop-down box and choose among Word's built-in ratios: 10%, 25%, 50%, 75%, 100%, 150%, 200%, 500%, and Page Width, which ensures that all your text fits horizontally on your screen. (Page Width saves you the trouble of trying to figure out how much to reduce your document to see all of its text.)

Sometimes you may want to specify an exact proportion not included on Word's drop-down list. For example, many people find their documents easier to edit if the type is enlarged to 110% or 120%. To specify an exact proportion, click inside the Zoom drop-down box and enter the value you want. Any whole digit between 10% and 500% will work.

None of the changes you make in Zoom affect the way your document will appear when printed or published online.

Tracking Your Progress with the Status Bar

Often, you'll want to know exactly where you are in your document, or on your page—especially if you're working in Normal view, where your location on the page isn't always apparent. You can always get this information—and more—from the Word *status bar*. You'll find the status bar at the very bottom of the Word screen, just above the Windows 95/NT 4.0 taskbar (see Figure 1.15).

Tracking Where You Are The location information section of the status bar tells you what page and section you're in, and how many pages are in your entire document. If you have more than one section, and you've told Word to start numbering new sections with page 1, Word will tell you both the correct page number *within* the section and the number of the page in the overall document. (See Chapter 3 to learn about document sections.)

Location information also tells you where you are on a given page. The information is provided *vertically* by inches and line numbers; and horizontally by *columns*, with each character of text on the line counted as one column. (Don't confuse this column numbering with Word's ability to create multiple-column documents such as newsletters.)

Location information

Current and total
pages in document

Track Changes

Vertical location
on page

Overtype

Status information

Line number
on page

Spelling and
Grammar

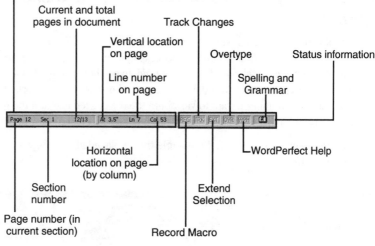

FIG. 1.15
The status bar includes
information about
where you are in your
document, as well as
information about what
mode you're in—that is
how Word currently is
behaving.

Horizontal
location on page
(by column)

WordPerfect Help

Section
number

Extend
Selection

Page number (in
current section)

Record Macro

 T I P To go to a new location, double-click anywhere in the location information area of the status bar; the
Go To dialog box will open.

Tracking Your Current Mode   Most of the time, you'll work in Word's standard editing mode,
but some tasks require you to be in another mode. For example, when you ask Word to track
changes in your document, you're in Track Changes mode. Any active modes are displayed in
the status bar; grayed out modes are inactive:

Abbreviation	Description
REC	A macro is currently being recorded.
TRK	Revisions are currently being tracked.
EXT	A text selection is currently being extended.
OVR	Word is currently overtyping (replacing text as you type over it).
WPH	WordPerfect Help is turned on (for people making the transition from WordPerfect).

At the far right of the status bar, the Spelling and Grammar Status animated icon appears.
When it resembles a pencil writing in a book, Word is busy displaying your current keystrokes.
When you stop momentarily, the icon changes to display a large red X over the book, indicating
that Word is checking your grammar and spelling. (See Chapter 4, "Making the Most of Word's
Proofing Tools," for detailed coverage of Word's automated spelling and grammar checker.)

Viewing Two Parts of the Document at the Same Time: The Split Box

Think of the split box as Word's version of a split-screen TV; it enables you to be in two places in your document at the same time. For example, if you change one clause of a contract, you might want to view another clause at the same time, to see how it should be edited. Or if you're creating a cross-reference (as is covered in Chapter 18, "Footnotes, Bookmarks, Cross-References, and Hyperlinks"), you might want to view both the referenced text and the place where you're inserting the reference.

The split box is a tiny beveled rectangle that is placed above the vertical scroll bar (see Figure 1.16).

FIG. 1.16

The split box is directly above the vertical scroll bar.

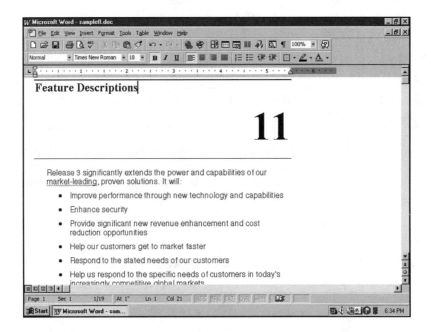

To split the screen by using the split box:

1. Place your mouse pointer on the split box.

2. Click and drag the mouse pointer down to the location in the editing window where you want your screen to split. A split pointer appears (see Figure 1.17).

3. Release the mouse button. The document is now displayed in two separate windows.

You can navigate and edit in either window. Your edits appear in both windows, because you are still working on only one document. When you no longer want a split screen, click and drag the split pointer above the top of the editing window, and your screen will return to normal.

FIG. 1.17
Drag the split pointer up or down to control where your document is split.

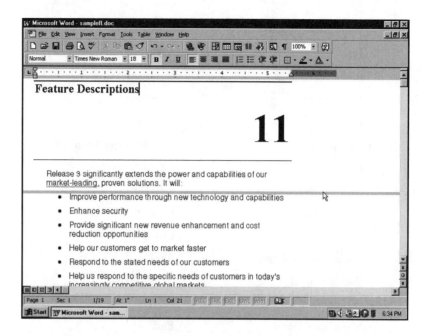

Keyboard Shortcuts: Getting the Job Done Even Faster

So far, we've focused primarily on shortcuts that involve clicking or dragging elements of the Word interface, such as toolbar buttons and scroll bars. But many people prefer to work from the keyboard whenever possible—and often, even confirmed mouse users will find Word's 250+ keyboard shortcuts faster and more powerful than its mouse shortcuts.

Word's keyboard shortcuts fall into several categories, including navigation, file management, editing, selecting text, viewing the document, inserting document elements, formatting, proofing, outlining, and several more. You may find the keyboard shortcuts for navigating your document, as listed in Table 1.2, to be especially handy.

Table 1.2 Keyboard Shortcuts for Navigating Your Document

Task	Keyboard Shortcut
Go to a specific location	Arrow keys
Display the Go To window	F5 or Ctrl+G
Go to previous insertion point	Shift+F5 or Alt+Ctrl+Z
Beginning of document	Ctrl+Home
End of document	Ctrl+End
Top of window	Ctrl+PageUp

continues

Table 1.2   Continued

Task	Keyboard Shortcut
Bottom of window	Ctrl+PageDown
Next screen	PageDown
Previous screen	PageUp
Next page	Alt+Ctrl+PageDown
Previous page	Alt+Ctrl+PageUp
Next paragraph	Ctrl+Down
Previous paragraph	Ctrl+Up
Previous window	Ctrl+Shift+F6
Beginning of column	Alt+PageUp
End of column	Alt+PageDown
Beginning of line	Home
End of line	End
Next line	Down arrow
Previous line	Up arrow
Left one word	Ctrl+Left
Right one word	Ctrl+Right

You'll find additional keyboard shortcuts mentioned throughout this book wherever they're especially useful.

 The Word Help system contains a complete list of Word keyboard shortcuts, which you can reach as follows:

1. Choose Help, Contents and Index.
2. In the Contents tab of the Help Topics dialog box, double-click Reference Information.
3. Double-click Keyboard Guide.
4. Double-click Shortcut Keys.

Using Shortcut Menus

Word provides shortcut menus that bring together all the options you're most likely to need while editing your document. You'll find different choices in Word's shortcut menus depending on what you're doing. For example, if you've selected text, Word's shortcut menus include choices for cutting, copying, pasting, or formatting that text. On the other hand, if you're working within a table, you'll find options to insert rows, delete cells, and format table borders. To view a shortcut menu, right-click in the editing window. You can see a typical shortcut menu in Figure 1.18.

FIG. 1.18
The shortcut menu that appears when you right-click ordinary text.

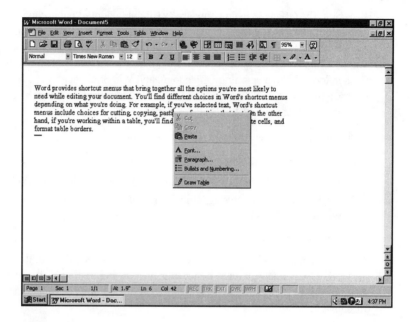

Help When and Where You Need It

In Word, online Help comes in many shapes and forms. In the previous tip, you've seen one way to access Word Help—through the front door, so to speak, through Help, Contents and Index. However, Word (and the other Office 97) programs also provide a side door shortcut to the answers you need: the *Office Assistant*.

The Office Assistant: Answers to Plain English Questions   With the Office Assistant, you can ask questions in plain English, and Office will point you to where it thinks you're most likely to find the answers. Office Assistant isn't perfect. Sometimes, you'll still have to rummage around in the Help System's Index or Find tabbed dialog boxes because Office Assistant's suggestions prove to be irrelevant, but well over half the time, Office Assistant will point you in the right direction, so it's usually worth a try.

To use Office Assistant:

1. Press F1, or click the Office Assistant icon at the far right of the Standard toolbar. (You can also choose Microsoft Word Help from the Help menu.)
2. In the What Would You Like to Do? text box, enter your question.

3. Click Search. Office Assistant displays a list of the Help pages it finds most relevant to your question.

4. Click the one you would like to view, or enter a different question and search again.

By default, the Office Assistant appears as Clippit, a dented paperclip with raised eyebrows. If you prefer not to have your PC look scornfully at you all day long, you might choose a different personality for the Office Assistant. If you've installed all of Office Assistant's personalities, you have several choices, including Power Pup, Scribble the Cat, Mother Nature, The Genius (an Einstein look-alike), a spinning Office logo, and Will Shakespeare. Choose what you will, but be aware that Mother Nature and the Genius are four times as large as the others, and might conceivably affect your system's performance.

To change the personality of your Office Assistant:

1. Display Office Assistant.

2. Right-click your current Assistant, and click Choose Assistant on the shortcut menu.

3. Click Next to move among Office's multiple Assistant personalities, until you find the one you want.

4. Click OK.

Office Assistant doesn't just answer your questions; it sits quietly in the background watching you work. Occasionally, it has a better idea for how to handle a task you've performed. To see what tips Office Assistant may have for you, right-click the Assistant, and choose See Tips from the shortcut menu.

"What's This?" Explains it All to You   If you ever see something on the Word interface that you don't understand, use Word's "What's This" feature to find out what it is. Press Shift+F1, or choose What's This from the Help menu, and your mouse pointer changes to a question mark (see Figure 1.19). Click whatever you are interested in, and Word will display an explanation. When you're done with What's This, press Esc, and your mouse pointer returns to normal.

 T I P   Not sure how a block of text is formatted? Click the What's This mouse pointer on it, and Word will show a detailed description of all the direct formatting and styles you've applied.

FIG. 1.19
The What's This pointer can explain any element of the Word interface, including formatting of specific text.

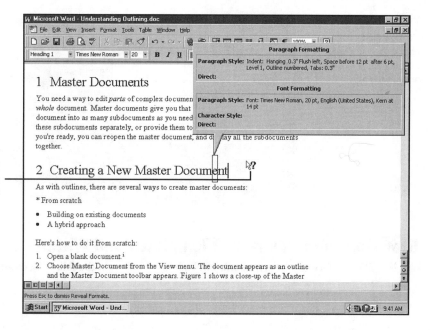

A question mark will appear next to your mouse

Creating New Documents

Now that you've completed your tour of the Word interface, it's time to get to work. In the rest of this chapter, you'll learn the basic techniques you need to create, open, edit, and save Word documents. Then, in Chapter 2, "Quick and Effective Formatting Techniques," you'll build on what you learn here, understanding how to *format* the text you've created.

Let's start with creating a new document. As you've already seen, Word opens with a blank document already displayed, ready for editing. Any time you want to create a new blank document, the quickest ways to do it are to click the New button on the Standard toolbar, or to use the keyboard shortcut Ctrl+N.

Choosing a Template That Has Already Done the Work for You

Often, you'll want to create a new document that already includes some text or formatting. For example, you might want to create a memo that follows a standard format, with a standard memo header and *To, CC, From, Date* and *Re,* lines already included and formatted. You can do that by choosing a *template*—a pattern that Word uses to build a new document.

In Chapter 6, "Templates, Wizards, and Add-Ins," you'll learn about templates in detail. For now, here's how to create a document based on a template already built into Word:

1. Choose File, New. The New dialog box opens (see Figure 1.20).
2. Click the tab corresponding to the type of template you are seeking.
3. Double-click the template of your choice.

FIG. 1.20

The New dialog box organizes all of Word's built-in templates and any you create.

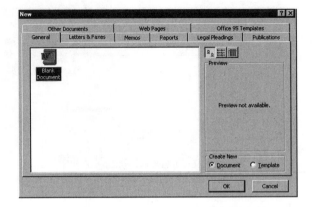

Browsing Word's Library of Templates and Wizards

Word offers an extensive library of built-in templates in the following categories:

- Letters & Faxes
- Memos
- Reports
- Legal Pleadings
- Publications
- Web Documents
- Other Documents (by default, this category includes only résumés).

Word's templates and wizards for most categories of printed documents offer three consistent approaches to document formatting: *Contemporary, Elegant,* and *Professional.* By choosing one of these approaches and using it in all your documents, you can have the benefits of consistent professional design without the expense.

If you don't want your documents to potentially look exactly the same as those of another Word user, you can change fonts and other aspects of the base styles these documents are built upon (see Chapter 5, "Styles: The Foundation of Automated Documents"). If you're careful, you can establish a distinctive, high-quality set of design standards for your business with remarkably little effort and expense.

If you installed Word 97 over an existing copy of Word 95, the New dialog box might also list several exceptionally useful Word 95 templates and wizards which were *not* included with Word. These include powerful wizards to create agendas, awards, calendars, and other types of documents.

TIP If you installed Word 97 in a separate folder, you'll have to copy the templates from Word 95's Template folder into the one used by Word 97. (The location of these folders will vary depending on your installation.) After you copy them, Word 95's templates and wizards appear as options in the New dialog box. When you use them for the first time, the templates convert to Word 97 format. (That's why you should keep a copy in Word 95 format, instead of simply moving the templates. Otherwise, after they are converted, you won't be able to use them in Word 95.)

Basic Editing

To enter text in a new or existing document, just start typing in the editing window. If the text doesn't appear, make sure that Word is the active application by clicking anywhere in the Word window.

A blinking vertical line, the *insertion point*, is displayed in your document at the location where your text will appear. As you type, your words are placed to the left of the insertion point. The insertion point moves to the right. You can move the insertion point by clicking elsewhere in the editing window.

Selecting Text

In Word, you can manipulate text in virtually any way imaginable—but before you do any of that, you have to select it. There are several ways to do that. If you're new to Word, you might try them all out to see which seems most comfortable. If you're an experienced Word user, you already select text dozens of times a day. Now might be a good time to see if you can do it more efficiently.

Mouse Shortcuts The most basic way to select text is with the mouse, as follows: Click where you want your selection to start; then drag the mouse to where you want the selection to end, and release the mouse.

You can drag the mouse in any direction. If you drag it across, you select text on the same line. If you drag it up or down, you can select many lines.

Selecting text this way is simple, and it's especially convenient if the text you're selecting doesn't fit simple boundaries, such as parts of two overlapping paragraphs, or several consecutive words. However, if you are selecting a specific word, line, sentence, paragraph, or the entire document, other alternatives might be quicker.

Mouse Shortcuts for Selecting Text To select the current word, double-click in it; to select the current paragraph, triple-click in it. To select the current line, click at the left edge of the screen, outside your margin. You will know you are in the right place when your mouse pointer faces your text). You can then extend your selection to multiple lines by dragging the mouse pointer up and down.

Keyboard Shortcuts Often, the easiest way to select a precise block of text is with a keyboard shortcut. Table 1.3 lists several convenient keyboard shortcuts for selecting text.

Table 1.3 Keyboard Shortcuts for Selecting Text

Extend Selection	Keyboard Shortcut
To select the entire document	Ctrl+A
To beginning of document	Ctrl+Shift+Home
To end of document	Ctrl+Shift+End
To top of window	Ctrl+Shift+PageUp
To bottom of window	Ctrl+Shift+PageDown
Down one page	Shift+PageDown
Up one page	Shift+PageUp
Down one paragraph	Ctrl+Shift+Down
Up one paragraph	Ctrl+Shift+Up
Current sentence	F8, F8, F8
Up one line	Shift+Up arrow
Down one line	Shift+Down arrow
To beginning of line	Shift+Home
To end of line	Shift+End
Left one word	Ctrl+Shift+Left
Right one word	Ctrl+Shift+Right
Current word	F8, F8
Left one character	Shift+Left arrow
Right one character	Shift+Right arrow

In addition, the keyboard shortcut F8 begins extending a selection; you can then continue extending the selection with the mouse, or any other way you choose.

 TIP If you need to select large blocks of copy in a document that contains Heading Styles or Outline Numbering, do so in Outline view. There, double-clicking a heading selects all the contents subordinate to it; you can then cut, copy or paste all those contents at once. See Chapter 14, "Outlining: The Best Way to Organize a Document," for more tips on cutting and pasting in Outline view.

Cut, Copy, and Paste

The heart of word processing—what first made it superior to the typewriter 20 years ago—is the ease with which you can *cut, copy,* and *paste.* Using Word, you can move text around at will, until you're satisfied with its content and organization. To cut, copy, or paste text (or other document elements, such as graphics), first select it. Then, use any of the mouse, menu, or keyboard shortcuts shown in Table 1.4.

Table 1.4 Methods for Cutting and Pasting in Word

To Do the Following:	Via Menu	Via Keyboard Shortcut	Via Standard Toolbar
Cut	Edit, Cut	Ctrl+X	✂
Copy	Edit, Copy	Ctrl+C	📋
Paste	Edit, Paste	Ctrl+V	📋

TIP Have you ever wanted to collect several blocks of text and deposit them all in the same place? Most people cut one block of text, go to the new location, paste it, and then go looking for the next. In Word, there's a faster way: the Spike. To cut text *(or anything else)* into the Spike, select it, and press Ctrl+F3. Repeat the process for anything else you want to cut into the Spike. Then click where you want to paste the Spike's contents, and press Ctrl+Shift+F3.

You can also insert the Spike's contents without emptying the Spike. Type the word **spike** and press F3. This works because the Spike is an AutoText entry in disguise; see Chapter 7, "Automating Your Documents: AutoCorrect, Auto Format, AutoText, and AutoSummarize," for more on AutoText.

Drag and Drop: When to Use It

In the real world, if you want to move something, you don't cut it and paste it somewhere else. You pick it up, and put it down where you want it. You can do the same thing with Word's *drag-and-drop* feature. Select the text you want to move. Then left-click inside the area you've high-lighted, and drag the text to the insertion point where you want it to appear.

TIP In Word, if you right-click and drag the text to a new location, Word displays a shortcut menu asking whether you want to move, copy, link or hyperlink the text. For copying text, you might find this even quicker (and more intuitive) than using the Copy toolbar button. And it's an especially quick way to create hyperlinks.

▶ **See** "Creating a Hyperlink Within a Document," **p. 527**

N O T E   You can cut, copy, or paste within the same Word document. Or you can cut, copy, or paste among open Word documents via the Window menu. You can also cut, copy, or paste to and from other Windows programs. For example, you might want to copy worksheet data from an Excel report into an executive summary created in Word. ■

▶ **See** "Integrating Excel and Word," **p. 754**

Using Word's Undo and Redo Capabilities

 With all this cutting, pasting, dragging, and dropping, you've had plenty of opportunities to make a mistake. It's time to discuss Word's Undo feature. Undo reverses the effects of an action and returns your document to the way it was before you performed the action. In many programs, Undo resembles an antidote: it can save your life, but you must take it immediately. Word Undo stores not one, but 100 actions, so you have more time to realize you've made a mistake. There are several ways to invoke Undo. The keyboard shortcut Ctrl+Z and the menu selection Edit, Undo will each undo your last action. So will the Undo button on the standard toolbar. However, if you want to undo several actions at the same time, you must use the toolbar button:

1. Click the down arrow next to the Undo toolbar button. A list of your most recent actions appear.
2. Select all the actions down to the one you want to undo. (You can't pick and choose; you have to undo all of them.)

You can imagine that certain types of changes take quite a bit of memory to store. One example is finding and replacing blocks of text that occur repeatedly through a large document. In some cases, Word warns you that it cannot store Undo information if you go through with a change you've requested. If you're sure you won't need to undo actions you've already performed, you can go ahead. After you've made the change, Word again starts tracking new changes that can be undone.

CAUTION

One important thing Undo doesn't undo is a file save. When you save over a previous file, the old file is gone for good. In addition, Word only undoes actions that change the contents of a document. It wouldn't, for example, undo a switch to Page Layout view or retrieve a document that you've just sent via e-mail.

Saving Your Documents

 Now that you've learned the basics of editing your document, let's discuss saving it. Often, you'll merely want to save your existing document in its existing location, and Word provides three quick ways to do so. You can click the Save button on the Standard toolbar, or use the Ctrl+S keyboard shortcut. You can also choose File, Save.

Sometimes, however, you'll want to make changes in the way you save a file. In particular, you may want to save a file to a different location on your computer or on your network. Or you may want to save it in a different format, so it can be used by people who run software other than Word. In each case, you use the Save As dialog box (see Figure 1.21). To display it, choose File, Save As.

FIG. 1.21
The Save As dialog box enables you to save files to different locations or in different formats.

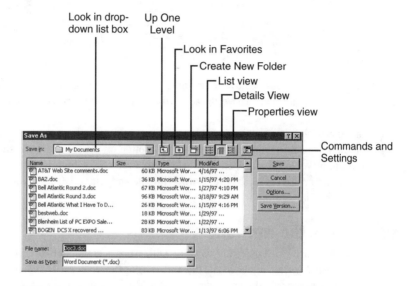

Look in drop-down list box
Up One Level
Look in Favorites
Create New Folder
List view
Details View
Properties view
Commands and Settings

N O T E The Save As dialog box is also displayed when you save a file for the first time because you must specify a name and location for the file. By default, Word expects that you will save your file in the My Documents folder. Word also inserts the first word or phrase of your document in the File Name text box, guessing that these words might be your document's title. If Word has made correct assumptions, all you need to do is click Save to store the file. ■

Saving to a Different Location

Word's Save As dialog box gives you extensive control over where you save your files. Save a copy of your file in a different folder or drive as follows:

1. Click anywhere in the Save In drop-down list box. A list of available drives and resources is displayed (see Figure 1.22).

2. Click the drive or resource where you want to store your file. A list of existing documents and folders already stored on that drive is displayed.

3. If you want to store your file in one of the subfolders, double-click it; repeat the process until you arrive at the folder you want.

4. Make sure the file name and file format are correct, and click Save.

FIG. 1.22

You can choose a folder, drive, network, or Internet FTP resource from the Save In drop-down list box.

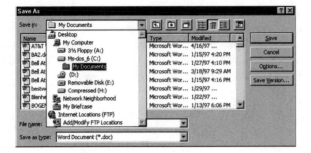

N O T E If you are using Save As to save an existing file in a new location, Word makes a second copy of your existing file; the earlier version remains where you originally stored it. ■

Sometimes, the only change in file location you want to make is to go up one level in your folder structure. Or, you may want to move around on the same drive instead of choosing a different drive. In this case, click the Up One Level toolbar button to display the next higher level folder or drive. From there, browse the file and folder lists until you find where you want to save the file.

Saving Across the Network

More and more Word users are working with Word across a network. If your computer connects to a networked folder at startup and assigns that folder a drive name, this mapped network drive appears in the list of drives under My Computer in the Save In drop-down list box. Choose the mapped drive as you would any other drive; find the folder within that drive if necessary, and click Save to save the file.

If the network drive or folder where you want to save the file is not a mapped drive, but you have unrestricted access to it, you can reach it through Network Neighborhood:

1. Click inside the Save In drop-down list box.
2. Click Network Neighborhood. Word displays a list of computers accessible to you on the network.
3. Double-click the computer where you want to store the file.
4. After that computer's name appears in the Save In drop-down list box, browse for the drive and folder where you want to store the file.
5. Make sure the file name and format are correct, and click Save.

In certain instances, you may be asked to provide a password when you attempt to access a computer or drive. For example, if you are attempting to access a drive on Windows NT Server for the first time during a session, you may be asked for a password. Enter your password, or if you don't have one, speak to your network administrator about getting access.

N O T E If you don't have access to a computer on the network, it may not even appear on the list of computers in Network Neighborhood. ▦

Creating a New Folder Occasionally, you will want to save a file in a folder that doesn't exist yet. To create a new folder within your current folder, click the Create New Folder button. The New Folder dialog box is displayed; enter the name of your new folder and click OK. The folder now appears within your current file and folder list. To save your file in the new folder, first double-click it to open it, and then click Save.

Saving in a Different Format

What if you want to save a file for use by someone who works with a different brand of processor, or with an older version of Word? Or what if you want to save the file in a format that can be imported into a desktop publishing program like Quark XPress? Or what if you want to send your document as text-only e-mail, or publish it to the Internet or your company intranet as an HTML (Hypertext Markup Language) file? In each case, you'll need to save your file in a different format.

To choose a format other than Word, display the Save As dialog box, and click in the Save as Type drop-down list box. Scroll to the file type you want to use and click it. If the file name uses a different extension (as will be the case unless you are saving to an older version of Word for Windows or DOS, or to WordPerfect), Word automatically changes the name in the File Name text box. Click Save to save the file.

Table 1.5 lists the file formats available in Word.

Table 1.5   File Formats Available as Save As Options

Format	Notes
Document Template	Saves files as a Word template for creating other similar files.
Text Only	Eliminates all formatting; converts line, section and page breaks to paragraph marks; uses the ANSI character set. Useful if you're uncertain about your file's ultimate destination.
Text Only with Line Breaks	Useful if you plan to upload the file to an e-mail system that expects regular line breaks.
MS-DOS Text	Eliminates formatting but uses the DOS extended ASCII character set; useful for converting files for use in non-Windows applications.
MS-DOS Text with Line Breaks	Similar to MS-DOS Text; however, this format also converts line, section, and page breaks to paragraph marks.

continues

Table 1.5 Continued

Format	Notes
Rich Text Format (RTF)	A Microsoft standard file processing data in text file format. RTF preserves most, but not all, Word formatting.
Unicode Text	A text file that supports the international character set Unicode.
MS-DOS Text with Layout	A text file format that attempts to mimic a formatted document through the use of additional spaces in place of indents, tab stops, tables, and other formatting elements.
Text with Layout	Similar to MS-DOS Text with Layout, except does not support DOS extended ASCII character set.
Word 2.x for Windows	Saves to Word 2.x for Windows format.
Word 4.0 for Macintosh	Saves to Word 4 for Macintosh format.
Word 5.0 for Macintosh	Saves to Word 5 for Macintosh format.
Word 5.1 for Macintosh	Saves to Word 5.1 for Macintosh format.
Word 6.0/95	Saves to Rich Text Format but with a .DOC file extension.
WordPerfect 5.0 for DOS	Saves to WordPerfect 5.0 for DOS format.
WordPerfect 5.1 for DOS	Saves to WordPerfect 5.1 for DOS format.
WordPerfect 5.x for Windows	Saves to WordPerfect 5.x for Windows format.
WordPerfect 5.1 or 5.2 Secondary File	Creates a WordPerfect 5.1 or 5.2 Secondary File.
Microsoft Works 3.0 for Windows	Saves to MS Works 3.0 for Windows.
Microsoft Works 4.0 for Windows	Saves to MS Works 4.0 for Windows.
HTML	A document for publishing on the World Wide Web or a corporate intranet.

A Closer Look at Word File Conversions It's unlikely, but you might need a file converter that isn't on this list. In this case, you have several options. In some cases, the converter you need is available in the Microsoft Office 97 Resource Kit, or free from Microsoft's Web site.

ON THE WEB

You can find these converters at **http://www.microsoft.com/office/ork/appa/ appa.htm#ORKappaC2**:

- Windows Write 3.0 or 3.1 (Write32.cnv)
- RFT-DCA (Rftdca32.cnv)
- Lotus Ami Pro 3.x (Ami332.cnv)
- WordStar 3.3-7.0 for MS-DOS and WordStar for Windows 1.0-2.0 (import only)
- WordStar 4.0 or 7.0 for MS-DOS (export only) (Wrdstr32.cnv)
- Microsoft Word 4.x, 5.x, and 6.x for MS-DOS (Doswrd32.cnv)

If you need to convert a file that isn't on this list, you may need a third-party file converter such as Dataviz Conversions Plus or Inso ImageStream 97.

What if you need to view or work with a file someone else has sent? First, note that Word can open files in a few formats that it cannot use to save files, notably WordPerfect 6.x for Windows and Lotus 1-2-3.

If you merely need to view the contents of a file, try Quick View, which comes with Windows 95 and Windows NT 4.0. (It's an optional component; you might have to run your Windows 95 or Windows NT 4.0 setup program to install it.) A third-party product, Inso Quick View Plus, supports over 200 file formats, most of which aren't included in Quick View. Unlike the free Quick View, Quick View Plus enables you to print files.

> **TIP** What if you need the text from a file right now; you can't afford to wait for a third-party product to arrive, and you can live without the formatting? Or what if you have a file that you can't even identify? Try Word's Recover Text from Any File filter, available through the File, Open dialog box. You'll learn how to use File, Open and Word's document filters in the next section.

Finally, it's important to note that Word's built-in file conversions aren't always perfect. For example, Microsoft has posted a five page report on the limitations of the Word filter for saving documents to WordPerfect 5.x (Knowledge Base Article Q157085). Many of these limitations are minor; for example, Word's decimal table cell alignments are converted to WordPerfect right-aligned paragraphs, and centering codes may have to be individually repositioned. Taken together, however, they mean you can't assume that what you see in Word is what you get in WordPerfect.

Worse, if you convert a file to WordPerfect and then reopen the WordPerfect file in Word to see what it looks like, you'll see apparent problems that wouldn't actually appear when your recipient opened the file in WordPerfect.

Ideally, you should double-check the results of any file conversion in the program you've converted to. In the real world, however, you may not have access to that program. At minimum, do your best to give your file's recipient enough time to check the file and make any necessary adjustments to it.

See Chapter 28, "Installing and Configuring Word in a Network Environment," for coverage of Word's built-in macro for converting many files at the same time.

 If you want to save a file to HTML, don't bother scrolling through the list of file types in the File, Save As menu command; just choose File, Save As HTML.

Understanding Word's AutoRecover Feature

By default, Word will store AutoRecover information about your document every 10 minutes. This AutoRecover information may help Word restore your files in the event your system crashes or there is a power failure. It's important to understand that AutoRecover information isn't a substitute for regularly saving your file; in fact, Microsoft has changed the name of this feature from Automatic Save to emphasize this. You should still save regularly, for two reasons. First, if you save regularly, your saved file may contain more up-to-date information than the AutoRecover file. Second, AutoRecover files aren't foolproof; they can't always be used to generate reliable, complete files.

If you're concerned about the stability of your system, you can tell Word to create AutoRecover files more often. Conversely, if you find that Word slows down to create AutoRecover files too often, you can tell Word to create them less often. The schedule Word uses to create AutoRecover files is set in the Save dialog box, shown in Figure 1.23.

FIG. 1.23

The Save tab of the Save dialog box, where you can control AutoRecover settings, as well as other file-saving behavior, such as how Word creates backup files.

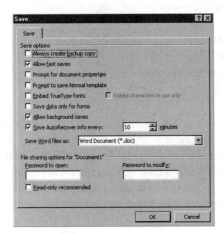

To change the frequency of AutoRecover:

1. Choose Tools, Options.

2. Click the Save tab.

3. Enter a new setting from 1 to 120 minutes in the Save AutoRecover Info Every scroll box.

Creating Automatic Backups

If you want, every time you save your file, Word can rename the previously saved version with the .BAK extension, ensuring that you always have a fairly recent backup of your work. This, too, is controlled from the Save tab of the Options dialog box. Check the Always Create Backup Copy check box.

When you use this feature, Word disables *fast saves*, so your saves will be somewhat slower, especially if you are working with long documents.

> **N O T E** Fast Saves are fast for the same reason it's faster to throw your clothes on the chair than hang them in the closet. With Fast Saves, Word doesn't actually put the changes where they belong; it simply makes a list of the changes that will be integrated the next time Word saves normally. When the list gets very long, Word does a normal save to put things back in order. ■

> **CAUTION**
> If you're using Fast Saves, turn them off before you forward a Word file to someone for use in another program, such as a desktop publishing program. Other software may not understand Word's Fast Save "to-do lists."

Retrieving Your Documents

 You can retrieve and open any saved document by clicking the Open button on the standard toolbar, using the keyboard shortcut Ctrl+O, or choosing File, Open. Each of these steps opens the Open dialog box, shown in Figure 1.24.

Look In drop-down list box   Search the Web
    Look in Favorites
    Add to Favorites
    List view
    Details view
    Properties view
    Preview

FIG. 1.24
You can retrieve any file from the Open dialog box.

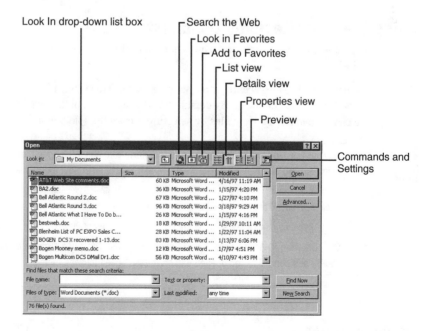

Commands and Settings

After it's open, browse the drives and folders as you've just learned how to do; select the file you want to open, and click Open.

By default, Word's Open dialog box only displays .DOC files—the files it expects to be Word files. If you can't find a file where you expect it to be, it may be there but have a different extension. To find out, click in the Files of Type drop-down box and select All Files (*.*). Word now displays all files in the current folder, not just DOC files.

If you know the extension of the file you want to open, you can choose to display only files of a specific type. If the file uses an extension Word recognizes, such as .WPS for Microsoft Works files, you can select the extension from the Files of Type drop-down box. Otherwise, enter the extension in the File Name drop-down box, using the * wildcard. For example, to display all files with the extension .RPT, enter ***.RPT**

You can open many files at the same time. Display the Open dialog box and browse to the folder you want. Press and hold Ctrl while you click each file you want to open. When they are all selected, click Open.
If you want to open several files listed consecutively in the same folder, press and hold Shift; then choose the first and last files you want. Word automatically selects all the files in between.

Increasingly, the files you want may be found on the World Wide Web. If you have installed Microsoft Internet Explorer 3.0 or higher, you can look for a file on the Web from inside the Open dialog box. Click the Search the Web button; Internet Explorer opens and displays a Microsoft-owned Web page where you can specify a search and the search engine you would like to use. Next, click Search, and the Web search engine you've chosen returns a list of pages containing the information you want.

Using the Most Recently Used List

Sometimes, you won't have to go anywhere near the Open dialog box; there are faster ways to find what you need.

If you've used the file recently, it may appear on the Most Recently Used file list that appears at the bottom of the File menu. By default, Word keeps track of the last four files you work with; you can reopen one of these files by selecting it from the File menu.

You might want Word to keep track of more than four files. Word can track up to nine files, though on some computers only seven or eight may display neatly. To change the number of files Word tracks:

1. Choose Tools, Options.

2. Click the General tab.

3. In the Recently Used File List scroll box, select the number of files you want to track, from 0 to 9.

4. Click OK. Word begins tracking the new number of files. (Of course, Word won't immediately display additional files you opened earlier; it hasn't been tracking them.)

Using the Windows 95/NT 4.0 Documents List Windows 95 and Windows NT 4.0 each keep track of the last 15 documents you work with. This includes all files you may have used: Excel worksheets, compressed ZIP files, text files, or anything else. If you primarily use Word, you may find that all the Word files you've worked with for the last few days are automatically being tracked by your operating system. To open one, click Start on the Taskbar; then click <u>D</u>ocuments. The list of files appears. Click the one you want to open.

CAUTION

If Word is already open, the file opens into Word. However, if Word is not open, and if you have two versions of Word on your computer, and if Windows currently associates the .DOC file type with a different version of Word, that version of Word will open. Because no other version of Word recognizes Word files without a special filter, you're likely to see gibberish. This is typically a problem only if you've installed an older version of Word after installing Word.

Quick Access to Your Favorite Files (Favorites Folder)

What if you often work on the same set of files, but it's inconvenient to store them all in the same folder? For example, imagine that you commonly work on three documents for the same client: a monthly sales report, an operations update, and an invoice. You may need to store all your sales reports in one location, all your operations updates in another, and all your invoices in a third location—perhaps even on another computer or server.

Word provides an easy way of accessing all those files at the same time: the *Favorites* folder. Here, you can store shortcuts to all the files you use most often. The files are still actually stored where they belong, but you only have to look in one place to retrieve them.

Here's how to create a shortcut in the Favorites folder:

1. Display the Open dialog box.
2. Browse to the location containing the file for which you want to create a shortcut.
3. Select the file.
4. Click the Add to Favorites button.
5. From the shortcut menu, click A<u>d</u>d Selected Item to Favorites. (Notice that you're also given the option of adding the entire folder to Favorites.)

Now that you have a favorite, here's how to open it:

1. Display the Open dialog box.
2. Click Look in Favorites.
3. Browse to the file you want.
4. Select the file.
5. Click <u>O</u>pen.

N O T E If you use Microsoft Explorer, your Favorites folder already contains shortcuts to any Web sites you've marked as Favorites. It also contains any Favorites shortcuts you've created in other Microsoft Office programs. ▨

T I P What if you expect to work on the same document *constantly* for a long period of time? Say you're writing a book, for instance. You can create a shortcut to that document on your Windows 95 or NT 4.0 desktop. After you do, you can double-click the shortcut to open Word and your document at the same time. To create the shortcut:

1. From Windows Explorer, right-click the file you want to create the shortcut for.

2. Select Create Shortcut from the shortcut menu that appears. This creates a new Shortcut file.

3. Select the Shortcut file you created. Its name will begin with the words "Shortcut to..."

4. Right-click and then select Cut from the shortcut menu.

5. Display the Windows Desktop by minimizing Windows Explorer and any other open programs.

6. Press Ctrl+V to paste the shortcut icon on your desktop.

Finding the File You're Seeking

Until now, we've assumed that you know the name and location of the file you want to open, but that's not always the case. How often have you scratched your head and wondered, Where did I put that file? What did I call it?

For those times, Word provides extraordinarily powerful file search features, all completely integrated into the Open dialog box.

Performing a Basic Search

You've already seen that you can use Files of Type in the Open dialog box to have Word search for all files of a specific type in the current folder. Word's other basic search features work much the same way.

If you want to search for all files in a specific folder containing specific text, you can enter that text in the Text or Property drop-down list box, and click Find Now. To search for a phrase (multiple adjacent words), surround the phrase with quotation marks.

To search for files by the dates they were last modified, click the Last Modified drop-down list box, and choose one of the following options: today, last week, this week, last month, this month, and any time.

When you're finished with a search, click New Search. Word will revert to its default settings, displaying every .DOC file in the current folder.

Word's basic search features are quick and easy to use; they may be all you need for most of your file searches, but they have some significant limitations. First of all, they'll only search for files in the current folder (and don't automatically search subfolders). That means you still have to know in which folder to look.

Searching for Files Using Advanced Find

Word's Advanced Find feature can search subfolders, but that's just the beginning of what it can do. Most impressively, it can search for an extraordinary collection of document properties and attributes. For example, imagine that you're reviewing the past year's work and you'd like to know which projects took the longest to complete. You might use Advanced Find to search for all Word files that had a "total editing time" of more than 20 hours. Or, if you're looking for reports that contain embedded audio comments, you could search for documents where the "Number of multimedia clips" is at least "1."

To use Advanced Find, first display the Open dialog box, and click Advanced. The Advanced Find dialog box opens (see Figure 1.25). Advanced Find works as follows: you first establish criteria for your search, one at a time. When the criteria are what you want them to be, click Find Now. Word searches for the files, displaying the result in the Find dialog box.

FIG. 1.25

The Advanced Find dialog box allows you to search multiple folders based on a wide variety of document elements and properties.

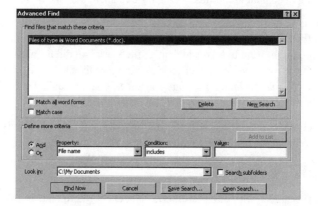

By default, Advanced Find begins with one criterion already established: it assumes you want to find only Word documents, that is .DOC files. If you have something else in mind, click Delete to eliminate that criterion. You can use Advanced Find to locate any kind of file, even files that aren't intended to be opened in Word.

You add criteria using the Property and Condition drop-down boxes and the Value text box. Choose a Property from the drop-down list of more than 100 properties and document elements Word can search for. Depending on the property, Word may display a list of available choices in the Condition drop-down list box. For example, if you're searching for documents based on the number of pages they contain, your Condition choices will include arithmetical conditions, such as equals and more than. After you've set the Condition, you need to specify a value.

Here are two examples of how the criteria you set in the Find Files That Match These Criteria window corresponds to what Word actually searches for.

If you set the criterion Comments Include the Words Smith, Word searches the Properties associated with every document, returning all files that contain the word Smith in the Comments property. (The Comments box may be found in the Summary tab of the Properties dialog box.)

If you set the criterion Last Saved by Is not Walker, Word searches for the Last Saved By property, which you can find in the Statistics tab of the Properties dialog box. If the name stored there does not include "Walker," Word will include the file in its listings. (Note that Word bases Last Saved By information on the name stored in the User Information tab of the Tools, Options dialog box.)

N O T E As you've just seen, many of the properties Word can search for are Document Properties stored in each document's Property Sheet. Briefly, every document in Windows 95 and Windows NT 4.0 has a property sheet that contains information about the document. Word extends these basic property sheets, using them to track document summary information, statistics, and many other types of information. Some Document Properties, like the author's name, are tracked automatically. Others, such as comments associated with a document, are added manually via the Properties dialog box, available by choosing File, Properties. ▪

▶ **See** "Using Document Properties to Simplify Document Management," **p. 824**

Before you finalize a search criterion, you need to take one more step, which relates to the breadth of the search you want. In some cases, you are designing criteria to find many files; for example, you might want to take a look at all the work you did for a specific client last month. In such cases, you may want each criteria to add more files to the list that Word provides. In other cases, you may be looking for one specific file. Then, you'll want to design your searches as narrowly as possible, ideally to return only that one file.

To create a broader search, click the Or button to the left of the Property drop-down list box. Word then returns files that meet either this criteria or the other criteria that you include. To create a narrower search, click the And button. Then, Word only displays files that meet this criteria and the others.

When you're satisfied with one search criterion, click Add to List, and Word places it beneath the other criteria in the large window at the top of the dialog box. You can then add other criteria until you're satisfied. Then, click Find Now, and Word displays the files you've requested.

Refining Searches Even More Word searches are not case-sensitive. If you ask for documents containing the name Walker, you might also receive documents about assistive devices for babies and senior citizens. If you want a case-sensitive search, however, you can get one; check the Match Case check box. On occasion, you might like to search for a word but you can't recall which variation of the word you used. For example, you're not sure if you used a verb in the past or present tense. If you check Match All Word Forms, Word locates files that use any form of the word you select. (This feature works with all text criteria but not with file names.)

Troubleshooting File Searches

It's easy to make a mistake in designing a search, and get results that aren't quite what you wanted—or an error message. If that happens, check your search with these troubleshooting questions:

■ Did you forget to add one of your criterion to the list by clicking <u>A</u>dd to List?

■ Are your values OK? Word may not care if you were brought up right, but it will care if you incorrectly spell a Keyword or other search Val<u>u</u>e.

■ Are your *Ands* and *Ors* correct? *Order matters.* These two similar-looking searches will return different results:

Author includes the words **Stewart**.

Creation date today.

OR: Keywords includes the words **Jones**.

Creation date today.

OR: Keywords includes the words **Jones**.

And Author includes the words **Stewart**.

In the previous first search, a file created last year whose Keywords include Jones will be found. In the second search, Word first locates files created today and files with the keyword Jones, but then eliminates all of those files except the ones authored by Stewart.

■ Are any of your search criteria mutually contradictory? Have you asked for files created after June 1st and before February 24th? No such files exist, of course, and Word usually flags the mistake with an error message. More subtly, have you asked for files that could exist, but are unlikely to? For example, have you asked for files saved on certain dates by someone who was on vacation at the time, or files created today that have been edited for more than 20 hours?

From Here...

In this chapter, you've toured the Word interface, discovering many of its shortcuts and conveniences. You've learned the basics of editing, and you've also walked through several fundamental file management tasks, including saving, opening, and locating files. Here's where you might want to go next.

■ Now that you know the basics of editing and managing your documents, you may want to learn (or review) the basics of formatting in Chapter 2, "Quick and Effective Formatting Techniques."

■ You'll learn about a wide range of Word productivity tools and shortcuts in Chapter 3, "More Day-to-Day Productivity Tools," including Find/Replace, Go To, page setup, headers and footers, bullets, numbered lists, and borders and shading.

■ You've already seen the importance of heading styles and the value of outlining. To learn more about styles, see Chapter 5, "Styles: The Foundation of Automated Documents." To learn more about outlines, see Chapter 14, "Outlining: The Best Way to Organize a Document."

■ Finally, if you'd like to learn more about Word file management features, such as batch file conversions and document property sheets, see Chapter 28, "Installing and Configuring Word in a Network Environment."

Quick and Effective Formatting Techniques

by Bill Camarda

Millions of Word users know just enough text formatting techniques to get by. Whether you're experienced with Word or not, this chapter will take you far beyond that point. You'll learn quick, efficient ways to format text—techniques you may not have come across before. You'll also discover new ways Word can help you add polish to your documents—without making more work for you in the process! ■

Fast, easy character formatting

Discover shortcuts and tricks for applying fonts, sizes, styles, effects, and other character formatting.

Enhancing your documents with careful character spacing

Word can work in the background to make your documents look like they came from a professional typographer.

Attracting attention with Word's new text animation feature

Las Vegas Lights! Marching Red Ants! Word 97 text animation can visually enhance your electronic documents.

The best ways to use indents and paragraph spacing

Word offers plenty of convenient ways to control indentation and paragraph spacing.

The easiest ways to use tabs—and when to use tables instead

Word's tab feature shines when you need tab leaders or aligned decimal numbers.

Controlling how your documents paginate

Word can help make sure your readers keep reading.

Direct Formatting versus Indirect Formatting

The techniques you'll learn in this chapter are often called *direct* formatting because they involve applying formatting directly to text in your document. Later, you'll learn *indirect* formatting techniques based on styles. In indirect formatting, you create a *style* that includes specific formats. Whenever you want a block of text to use those formats, you apply the style, and Word, in turn, applies the formats.

▶ **See** "What Styles Are and How They Work," **p. 142**

Direct formatting is easier to learn and often quicker to apply. Indirect formatting is more flexible and often more powerful. When should you use each approach? In general:

- Use direct formatting when you're only concerned with formatting a specific block of text, especially short blocks of text that don't comprise whole paragraphs. For example, use direct formatting when you need to italicize the name of a book or magazine. Also rely on direct formatting when you're creating a quick document that won't need to be repeated or built upon later.

- Use indirect formatting when you are applying text formats that you'll need to use again elsewhere in your document or in other documents. Especially rely on indirect formatting in large documents, where styles can help you organize both the formats and the content of your document.

Even if you rightly rely on indirect formatting, you first need to understand the basics of direct formatting. This chapter covers most of those basics; Chapter 3, "More Day-to-Day Productivity Tools," covers the rest.

Understanding Word's Multiple Levels of Formatting

If you've ever wondered why Word formatting behaved in a certain way, it will help to know how Word "thinks" about formatting. Word has three levels of formatting, all of which work together:

- *Font* formatting applies to specific characters. The Format, Font dialog box brings together many of Word's font formatting controls.

- *Paragraph* formatting applies to entire paragraphs. The Format, Paragraph dialog box brings together many of Word's paragraph formatting controls.

- *Section* formatting applies to entire sections of a document. Section formatting controls can be found in the File, Page Setup dialog box and a few other locations.

Most day-to-day text formatting is font and paragraph formatting. This chapter covers font formatting first and then reviews several of the most common paragraph formatting techniques. Section formatting comprises margins, headers and footers, and other elements that are often established once for a document and then left alone.

▶ **See** "A Quick Guide to Page Setup," **p. 92**

Introducing Font Formatting

In Word, you can apply an extraordinarily wide range of formats to specific characters. As already mentioned, Word calls this *font formatting*. It includes the following:

- The choice of font
- Font size
- Font style (for example, bold or italic)
- Underlining
- Font effects
- Font color
- Scaling (font stretching)
- Spacing between groups of letters
- Position of text on a line
- Kerning (spacing of specific pairs of letters)
- Text animation

As already mentioned, you can control any type of font formatting through the Format, Font dialog box. However, when it comes to the formatting you do most, there are usually quicker ways to get the job done.

Quick and Easy Formatting with the Formatting Toolbar

In many cases, the fastest way to apply a format is to use Word's Formatting toolbar (see Figure 2.1).

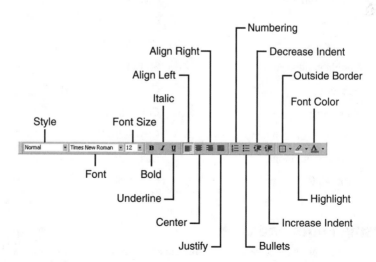

FIG. 2.1
The Formatting toolbar is often the quickest way to apply text formatting.

Part
I

Ch
2

In most cases, you simply select the text you want to format, click the appropriate Formatting toolbar button, and your text is formatted.

 N O T E Both Formatting toolbar buttons and keyboard shortcuts toggle formatting on and off. If you've selected text as bold, clicking the Bold button again eliminates the Bold formatting. ■

Quick and Easy Font Formatting with Keyboard Shortcuts

As usual in Word, there are other options besides the toolbar—and sometimes they're faster. For example, you may find pressing Ctrl+B is a faster way of boldfacing selected text than locating and clicking the Bold button on the Formatting toolbar. There are plenty of keyboard shortcuts for formatting text, including many that don't have Formatting toolbar counterparts. Table 2.1 lists the keyboard shortcuts that apply to font (character) formatting; you'll discover more shortcuts later in this chapter.

Table 2.1 Keyboard Shortcuts for Font Formatting

Task	Keyboard Shortcut
Boldface	Ctrl+B
Italicize	Ctrl+I
Underline	Ctrl+U
Underline words only (not spaces)	Ctrl+Shift+W
Double underline	Ctrl+Shift+D
All caps	Ctrl+Shift+A
Small caps	Ctrl+Shift+K
Toggle capitalization	Shift+F3
Subscript	Ctrl+= (equal sign)
Superscript	Ctrl++ (plus sign)
Format as hidden text	Ctrl+Shift+H
Apply Symbol font	Ctrl+Shift+Q
Clear all font formatting	Ctrl+spacebar

Choosing Fonts and Sizes

 Among Word's most basic formatting capabilities is its ability to work with thousands of Windows-compatible fonts, including TrueType fonts (by default) and Adobe PostScript fonts (if Adobe Type Manager is installed). The easiest way to choose a font is via the Font drop-down box on the Formatting toolbar (see Figure 2.2); the following steps show you how:

1. Select the text you want to format.

2. Click the down arrow next to the Font drop-down box; scroll to and select the font you want.

 You might find the keyboard shortcut to be quicker. Press Ctrl+Shift+F to highlight the font drop-down box. Either type the new font name or scroll to it using the arrow keys. Press Enter. Word applies the font you've selected.

FIG. 2.2

Selecting a font through the Font drop-down box on the Formatting toolbar. Notice the fonts at the top; these are the ones you've used most recently.

The following steps show you how you can specify font size using the Font Size drop-down box on the Formatting toolbar:

1. Select the text you want to format.

2. Click in the Font Size drop-down box (or press Ctrl+Shift+P).

3. Type the size you want and press Enter.

 Sometimes you'll want to increase or decrease text size by only a point or two. Don't bother with the Font Size drop-down box; the keyboard shortcuts are quicker:

Task	Keyboard Shortcut
Enlarge font 1 point	Ctrl+]
Shrink font 1 point	Ctrl+[
Enlarge size 1 increment	Ctrl+Shift+>

continues

continued

Task	Keyboard Shortcut
Decrease size 1 increment	Ctrl+Shift+<

At smaller sizes, the increments Word uses with the Ctrl+Shift+> and Ctrl+Shift+< shortcuts are 1 point, no different from Ctrl+] and Ctrl+[. However, at larger sizes the increments grow. So you can use Ctrl+Shift+> to jump from 36 points to 48 points in a single click.

N O T E   Word actually formats text as large as 1,638 points. Those letters are nearly *two feet high.* If you ever need text larger than 999 points, though, you have to select Format, Font. Font Size box only displays three digits. ▨

Choosing Font Styles, Underlining, Color, and Effects

B

I

U

You've probably noticed that you can apply font styles from the Formatting toolbar by clicking the Bold, Italic, or Underline buttons, or that you can apply them by using the keyboard short-cuts shown earlier in Table 2.1. These and many additional options are available to you in the Font dialog box (see Figure 2.3). To display these options, choose Format, Font and click the Font tab.

FIG. 2.3

The Font tab of the Font dialog box brings together Word's most commonly used Font formatting options.

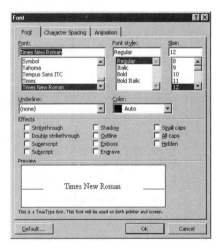

Here, you can conveniently enter all your formats at the same time: font, style, size, underlining, color, and effects. Choose from the corresponding Font, Font Style, and Size scroll boxes.

Selecting Font Underlining   Select the Underline of your choice from the drop-down box. Word 97 provides more choices than ever before, including dotted, thick, dash, dot-dash, dot-dot-dash, and wave underlining. You can see samples of each of these in Figure 2.4. Notice that underlining is a separate control; you can use it with any other font style or text effect.

FIG. 2.4
Word 97 offers many
underlining options.

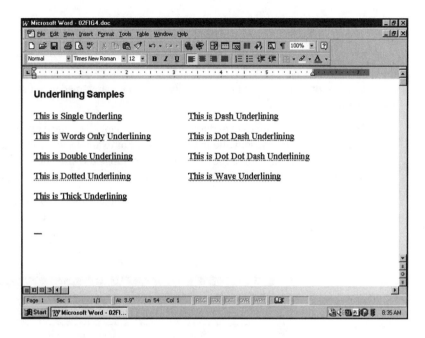

 Any changes you make in the Font dialog box are previewed in the Preview window.

Setting Font Color   In the Color drop-down box, you can select a text color from among 16
font colors—plus Auto, the default setting. Auto is black, unless one of the following situations
occurs:

- You are formatting text against a background shaded to at least 80 percent color, in
  which case Auto reformats the text color to white for readability.
- You have (perhaps inadvertently) changed Windows' overall text color in the Appearance
  tab of the Display section of the Windows 95 or NT 4.0 Control Panel.

N O T E   Word's text color controls might be thought of as *business colors*; they are perfectly
adequate for business uses (or for that matter, most home uses), but not really up to
sophisticated design tasks. For one thing, because Windows 95 and Windows NT don't have precise
color matching systems built in (and Word doesn't provide its own), what you see may not be precisely
what you get when you print.

Setting Text Effects   If you've used Word before, you'll be pleasantly surprised by how
many new text effects Word 97 provides. In addition to the six effects Word 95 provided
(Strikethrough, Superscript, Subscript, Hidden, Small Caps, and All Caps), Word 97 adds the
following:

- Double Strikethrough
- Shadow

- ■ Outline
- ■ Emboss
- ■ Engrave

Be aware that these five additional effects *won't* be maintained if you save a file to Word 6/95 format.

Figure 2.5 shows samples of all ten visible effects. Not all of these effects can be applied together. Sometimes, the limitations are obvious. For example, you cannot apply strikethrough and double strikethrough to the same text. Sometimes the limitations are not so obvious. For example, you cannot apply Shadow or Outline to text you also intend to emboss.

Notice that subscript lowers text by 3 points and reduces its size at the same time; superscript raises text by 3 points and reduces its size. If you want to change the position of subscript or superscript text, select it and use the Position controls on the Character Spacing tab. These are discussed later in this chapter.

FIG. 2.5

Use any of Word's ten font effects to enhance your document.

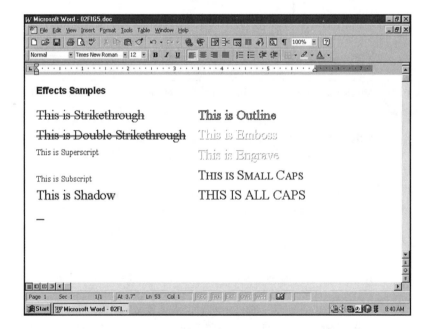

TIP One of the most common effects-related tasks is to *change the case* of selected text to (or from) all caps. You don't have to bother with displaying the Font dialog box to do this: just press Ctrl+Shift+A.

Word recognizes that there are several common ways to capitalize blocks of text. For example, you may want to format text as a sentence, where only the first word is capitalized or as a title, where every Word is capitalized. You can quickly toggle selected text through five types of capitalization by pressing Shift+F3 repeatedly or choose the capitalization you want by selecting Format, Change Case (see Figure 2.6).

FIG. 2.6

The Change Case dialog box lets you format selected text as a sentence, in all lowercase, all upper-case, or as a title. The Toggle Case option lets you instantly switch all capital letters to lowercase, and vice versa.

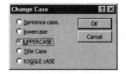

Part

I

Ch

2

Hidden text is most valuable as a way to make temporary notes to yourself. (You don't have to use the Font dialog box to format text as hidden; try the Ctrl+Shift+H keyboard shortcut.) Formatting text as hidden makes it invisible by default, though you can see it by clicking the Show/Hide Paragraph marker.

If you print a document while hidden text is displayed, the hidden text will also print. Also, make sure you "hide" your hidden text before you create tables of contents or indexes. Otherwise, it will lead Word to miscalculate your document's length.

> **CAUTION**
>
> Because hidden text is so easy to view, don't use it as a security precaution. Remember that many people click Show/Hide Paragraph simply to view paragraph marks and tabs, even if they're not looking for your secret, hidden contents. If you really want to secure your document, use passwords and encryption.
>
> ▶ **See** "Word Document Security," **p. 815**

 If you need more sophisticated text effects than those provided here, use WordArt. If you need to create sophisticated text effects for publishing on the Web, use the free add-on Microsoft Draw 97, which includes a version of WordArt that can save Web-compatible GIF files.

▶ **See** "Using WordArt 3.0," **p. 587**

 You've just carefully applied a series of formatting commands in the Font dialog box. Now you'd like to apply them again elsewhere, without returning to the Font dialog box and selecting everything again.

Select the new text and press Ctrl+Y, Word's nifty shortcut for repeating the last editing or formatting command you've made. Ctrl+Y only repeats one command made by toolbar button or keyboard shortcut; however, if you click Ctrl+Y after using a dialog box, it repeats *all* the commands you applied through that dialog box.

Character Spacing: Creating Typographer-Quality Documents

Word includes character spacing controls that were once available only on typesetting systems that cost tens of thousands of dollars—or weren't available at all. You don't have to be a typographer to use them, either. All you need to do is display the Font dialog box and click the Character Spacing tab (see Figure 2.7).

There are two primary reasons to use the controls on this tab:

- They can help you improve the look of your documents, typically in quite subtle ways. Your readers will believe your documents look a cut above the rest—even if they don't know why. Of course, some documents need this refined treatment more than others.

- Some character spacing features can help you control the size of your document, squeezing out one or more pages—which can save you money on production, printing and/or mailing.

FIG. 2.7

The Character Spacing tab controls spacing among characters, kerning between pairs of characters, the height and depth of characters, and their scale.

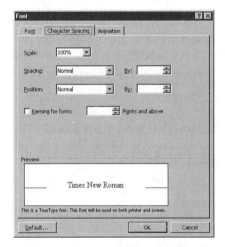

N O T E   These settings are intended for print documents. They aren't supported by HTML or available if you are editing a document using Word's Web page editing tools.

Stretching Your Type with Word 97's Scaling Feature   Scaling, a new feature of Word 97, lets you stretch individual characters either horizontally or vertically. Why scale text? Generally, for design reasons. For instance, you might want to create a drop cap at the beginning of a newsletter article that drops down more than three lines. If the character is a wide one, such as W, it's likely to stretch wider than you might want. You can narrow it by scaling. Be careful to scale all your drop caps for consistency. You can see an example of a scaled drop cap in Figure 2.8.

FIG. 2.8

Sometimes scaling a drop cap can improve its appearance and, not incidentally, make it fit better.

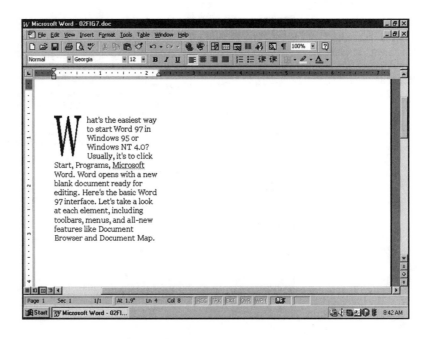

Scaling body text *slightly* can also help you fit more of it on a specific page. This is an issue especially in large directories and catalogs, where narrower text translates directly into fewer pages and lower cost.

Normally, you would use a condensed font such as Arial Narrow for this purpose. However you might not have a condensed font available that meets your needs and fits with the rest of your document's design. Scaling lets you "fake" a condensed font. The results won't thrill a professional typographer who is familiar with the subtleties of quality font design, but for day-to-day business work, scaling does the job.

Figure 2.9 shows the difference in appearance (and size) between standard Times New Roman text and text narrowed to 95% of its normal width.

CAUTION

Don't narrow body text by more than 10%, at most. Beyond that, readability begins to deteriorate significantly.

While the Scale drop-down box includes only eight choices, you can manually enter any value from 1% to 600%.

FIG. 2.9

Standard Times New Roman text, compared with text narrowed to 95% of normal width.

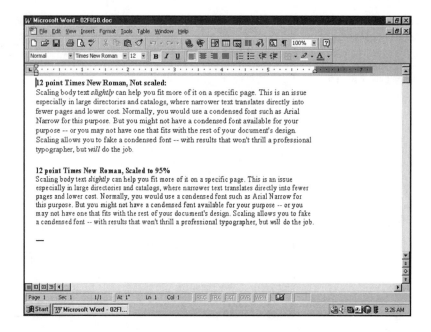

If you set scaling to one of Word's predefined settings, Word automatically shows you an immediate preview. If you enter a custom setting, you can preview what your selected type will look like by pressing tab to move out of the Scale drop-down box.

Controlling Spacing   Spacing is the complement to scaling. Scaling narrows or widens the characters themselves; spacing changes the space *between* characters. Professional designers sometimes call this *tracking*.

Word's default spacing is called Normal; you can tighten or loosen spacing as much as you want. As with scaling, use spacing judiciously. Tightening your spacing just a little can save space and may even make type read faster. That's one reason much advertising copy is spaced a little tighter than normal. On the other hand, tightening type too much will quickly render it illegible.

To control spacing for selected text follow these steps:

1. Choose Format, Font (or press Ctrl+D).
2. Choose the Character Spacing tab.
3. Select Expanded or Condensed in the Spacing drop-down list.
4. In the By scroll box, set the amount by which you want to expand or narrow your spacing. The default is 1 point, and the scroll buttons increase or reduce spacing by tenths of a point. However, you can manually enter spacing values in twentieths of a point if you so desire (for example, 1.05 points).

Kerning: One Secret to Great Looking Text   Kerning is similar to spacing in that it adjusts the space between letters, but spacing controls the space between *all* letters, whereas kerning adjusts the spacing between *special pairs* of letters—and then only if kerning data has been included with your font by its designer.

N O T E   Depending on the quality of a font, there may be as many as 500 *kerning pairs* stored within it—pairs of letters that come with kerning instructions. This is one way expensive fonts can be superior to very cheap ones. ▧

Part

I

Ch

2

You can see why kerning matters in Figure 2.10. In the unkerned word WATCH at the top, the letters W and A are far apart; so are the letters A and T. The effect is subtly distracting; the word looks uneven, not quite natural. Beneath, kerning has been turned on. You can see that the A now slips slightly under the W, and the T is also closer to the A. *It just looks better.* You'll hardly ever see a professionally-produced advertisement that hasn't been carefully kerned.

FIG. 2.10

Notice the difference between the unkerned word at the top and the kerned version beneath it.

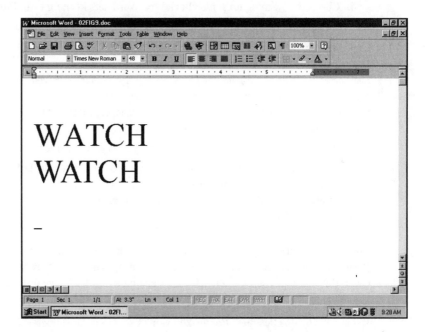

Why not turn kerning on all the time, for every font, size, and kerning pair that supports it? It might slow down your computer, and kerning isn't really necessary for very small text, such as classified advertisements. Here's how to decide when to kern:

- ▧ First, test your computer. If you don't notice a speed difference with kerning turned on, then make it part of your default settings for all text 7 points or higher. You'll learn how to change your font formatting defaults later in this chapter.
- ▧ For day-to-day newsletters, it's usually sufficient to turn kerning on for all headlines but skip the body text. You might set kerning to begin at 12- or 14-point text.

■ For more sophisticated publications, or for high-end customer proposals, kern body text as well. Set kerning to start as low as 7-point text. Especially kern if you are printing on a relatively high-resolution printer, such as a 600 dpi (dots per inch) laser printer.

■ If kerning *does* slow down your computer, consider doing all your editing with kerning turned off; then selecting the entire document and applying kerning to it before you take care of final "design tweaks" such as fixing line and page breaks. If you like, you can record a macro to select and kern your entire document.

To turn on kerning, follow these steps:

1. Select the text you want to kern. If you don't select text, Word starts kerning at the insertion point.

2. Choose Format, Font (or press Ctrl+D).

3. Choose the Character Spacing tab.

4. Check the Kerning for fonts check box. Word sets kerning to 12 Points and Above.

5. If you want, enter a new font size in the Points and Above scroll box.

6. Choose OK.

T I P   Some desktop publishing programs, like Quark XPress, let you automatically kern all text larger than a specific size, and also manually adjust the kerning of individual pairs of letters. Sometimes you can manually improve the look of your headlines by kerning them beyond the settings that come with your font. That's especially true of large headlines—48 points or higher.

You can see in Figure 2.11 how we've improved on the built-in kerning you've already seen.

You can do manual kerning with Word, even though there's no formal setting for it. If you want to tighten or loosen the spacing between two letters, select the first letter, and apply a very small amount of Condensed or Expanded Spacing to it. Word will control spacing down to 1/20th of a point, which should be plenty for virtually any document.

Controlling Position   There's one more feature on the Character Spacing tab to discuss: Position. Look at a line of text, and visualize an imaginary line where the text is "sitting." That's called the *baseline*. The Position setting determines how far above or below the baseline text should appear.

When will you use Position? *Rarely.* You won't use it to create superscript or subscript characters. Using Ctrl++ (plus sign for superscript or Ctrl+= (equal sign) for subscript does a better job. These keyboard shortcuts also shrink the characters the way true subscript and superscripts should appear, and you generally won't use it to create graphics with type. WordArt is much faster.

Occasionally, however, Position will give you control over text that you need and can't easily get any other way. For example, if you want to carefully control the position of just a few letters, and you don't want to mess with inserting WordArt graphics in your text, Position may be just the ticket. Consider the text in Figure 2.12.

▶ **See** "Using WordArt 3.0," **p. 587**

FIG. 2.11

The top example shows automatic kerning. The bottom example shows how manual kerning goes beyond the automatic settings to improve the appearance of type in large font sizes.

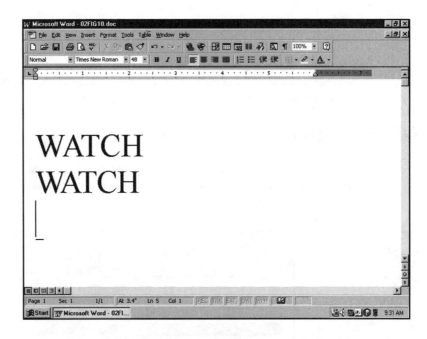

FIG. 2.12

This figure illustrates using Position and Font Size controls together.

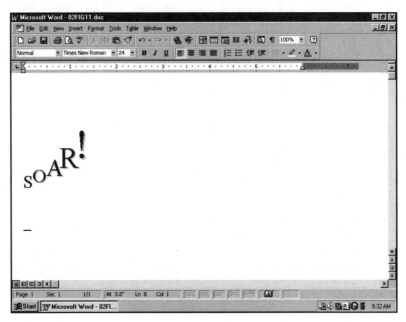

To set the position for selected text, follow these steps:

1. Select the text you want to reposition. (If you don't select text, Word starts repositioning at the insertion point.)

2. Choose Format, Font (or press Ctrl+D).

3. Choose the Character Spacing tab.

4. Choose Raised or Lowered in the Position drop-down box. Word sets the change in position to 3 points. You can scroll to increase or decrease the baseline shift, or type in a position in 1/2-point increments (for example, 2.5 points).

Animating Your Text

Now, let's hop from the subtleties of kerning and baseline shifts to one of the more obvious visual features Word: *text animation*. This new Word 97 feature enables you to apply one of six simple animations to any block of text, calling attention to it when viewed on screen in Word. You can see these animations in Figure 2.13.

FIG. 2.13

Choose from any of Word 97's six new text animations.

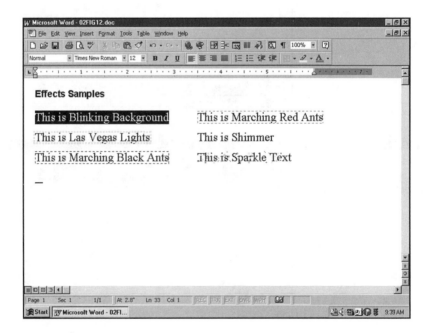

Animations don't print, nor are they supported on standard Web sites. They will, however, show up on Web or intranet pages that are displayed in Word 97 via Internet Explorer 3.0. You might use text animation when you are sharing a document file (or displaying it on a corporate Intranet designed to integrate with Word) and you want to be especially sure your reader looks at a specific block of text.

To animate text, follow these steps:

1. Select the text you want to animate.

2. Choose Format, Font (or press Ctrl+D).

3. Choose the Animation tab.

4. Choose an animation from the Animations scroll box. (The Preview box shows what it will look like.)

> **CAUTION**
>
> Learn from the experience of Web designers who alienated many of their visitors through heavy use of blinking text. Use text animations *very* sparingly.
>
> Use the animations that are least intrusive, such as Marching Black Ants and Sparkle Text, or apply them only to small blocks of text—possibly even single characters, such as Wingding symbols.

Part
I
Ch
2

Setting Default Font Formats

By default, Word formats your text as 12 point Times New Roman. Do you find yourself changing this setting in every new document? It's time to stop reformatting every new document Word opens. It's easy to change your defaults. Follow these steps:

1. Select some text that's formatted as you want your default text to look.
2. Choose Format, Font or press Ctrl+D to display the Font dialog box.
3. Check to see if you want to change any settings. For example, would you like to turn automatic kerning on?
4. Click Default. Word displays a dialog box asking you to confirm the change.
5. Choose Yes.

The new default font formatting will apply in every document you create with the same template you're currently using.

▶ **See** "Understanding the Relationship Between Styles and Templates," **p. 178**

Paragraph Formatting

So far, you've worked only with Font formatting that works at the character level. Next, you'll learn about the formatting that Word can apply to *paragraphs*. In Word, paragraph formatting includes the following:

■ Paragraph alignment
■ Outline levels
■ Indentation
■ Spacing between lines
■ Spacing before and after paragraphs
■ Line and page breaks
■ Tabs

In the next few pages, you'll review all of these (except for Outline levels). First, it's important to understand what Word interprets as a paragraph and how it stores paragraph formatting.

▶ **See** "Applying Outline Levels to Specific Text," **p. 418**

How Word Stores Paragraph Formatting

Word considers a paragraph to be any block of text that ends with a paragraph mark (¶). In fact, Word actually stores the paragraph formatting with the paragraph mark. If you understand this, you can avoid many of the problems that arise in paragraph formatting. There are several implications of Word's storing paragraph formatting with the paragraph mark:

- You can copy paragraph formatting to a new location by copying the paragraph mark (or any part of the paragraph that includes the paragraph mark).

- You may inadvertently copy paragraph formatting you don't want, if you copy the paragraph mark by mistake. If you want to copy a paragraph format to a new location and use the formatting of the surrounding text there, don't copy the paragraph mark.

- If you finish a paragraph and start a new paragraph by pressing Enter, your new paragraph will share the same paragraph formatting (and styles) as the previous one.

- If you delete text that includes a paragraph mark, any remaining text from that paragraph will be reformatted to match the formatting and styles in the *following* paragraph.

Of course, to work with paragraph marks, it helps if you can see them. Click the Show/Hide Paragraph mark on the Standard toolbar, and they all appear.

Some other things appear, too: tab markers, and dots that correspond to spaces between the words in your document. Seeing all this can be helpful, but many people find it distracting. If all you want to see is paragraph marks, follow these steps:

1. Choose Tools, Options.
2. Click the View tab.
3. Check the Paragraph Marks check box in the Nonprinting Characters area.
4. Choose OK.

TIP

Because paragraph marks are so fraught with meaning, you might occasionally want to jump to the next line without entering one. You can use Shift+Enter for this purpose; Word adds a *line break* but not a paragraph mark. (Line breaks are sometimes called *soft returns*.)

Line breaks have many uses. For example, if you have an automatically numbered list, you may want to enter more text underneath a numbered item without having Word automatically enter the next number. If you use a line break instead of a paragraph mark, Word will do this. Then, when you're ready to move on to the next item in your numbered sequence, enter a paragraph mark, and Word will continue automatic numbering as if nothing unusual had happened.

▶ **See** "Using Bullets and Numbered Lists," **p. 108**

Paragraph Alignment

The first aspect of paragraph formatting is paragraph alignment. Word offers four types of paragraph alignment: Align Left, Center, Align Right, and Justify.

Align Left, Word's default setting, starts every line at the left margin, but doesn't reach all the way to the right margin (except on very rare occasions when the word fits precisely without tweaking). When a word comes along that is too long to be squeezed onto the first line, Word jumps it onto the next line, leaving the previous line unfinished. Align Left is sometimes called *flush left* or *ragged right*.

Align Right, of course, works the opposite way; it squeezes all text towards the right margin. Center usually leaves room at both margins when it jumps to the next line. Justify stretches text from the left to right margin edges.

 T I P If you choose to justify text, consider using Word's hyphenation controls (choose <u>T</u>ools, <u>L</u>anguage, <u>H</u>yphenation) to make sure no text is stretched too far to be read easily.

Table 2.2 lists the toolbar buttons and keyboard shortcuts for each alignment option and when each option is most widely used.

Table 2.2 Paragraph Alignment Choices: How and When

Task	Keyboard Shortcut	Toolbar Button	Uses
Align Left	Ctrl+L		Most informal documents
Center	Ctrl+E		Some headings and short copy blocks
Align Right	Ctrl+R		Occasional artistic/design uses
Justify	Ctrl+J		Some traditional books, magazines, and reports

Indenting Text

Word provides total control over the way you indent your paragraphs. You can create the following four kinds of indents:

- *Left indents* (indents that adjust the left edge of every line in a paragraph)
- *Right indents* (indents that adjust the right edge of every line in a paragraph)
- *Hanging indents* (indents that leave the first line alone but move every line beneath it)
- *First line indents* (indents that move only the first line in a paragraph)

You can see examples of all four kinds of indents (left, right, hanging, and first line) in Figure 2.14.

FIG. 2.14

Use left, right, hanging, and first line indents to control the look of your paragraph.

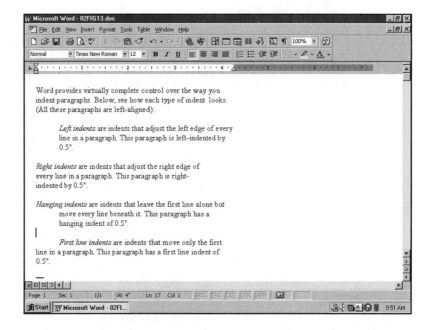

Word also provides four ways to create indents: via the Formatting toolbar, keyboard shortcuts, the Ruler, and the Format, Paragraph toolbar. Each approach has advantages, depending on your work style and what you're trying to accomplish.

Indenting with the Toolbar and Keyboard Shortcuts   The quickest way to indent one paragraph or several paragraphs you've selected is to click the Increase Indent button on the Formatting toolbar—or use the equivalent keyboard shortcut Ctrl+M. This adds a 0.5" left indent to the paragraphs you've selected. If they're already indented, it adds another 0.5". You can reduce or eliminate the indent by clicking the Decrease Indent button or pressing Ctrl+Shift+M.

These toolbar buttons and keyboard shortcuts add a left indent to every line in the paragraph, but you'll often want to create a *hanging indent,* leaving the first line alone but indenting all the lines below it. There's no toolbar button for hanging indents, but there *are* keyboard shortcuts. To create a 0.5" hanging indent, press Ctrl+T. To reduce a hanging indent by 0.5", press Ctrl+Shift+T.

  When you select text and click either the Bullets or Numbering buttons on the Formatting toolbar, Word automatically creates hanging indents along with the bullets or numbers it inserts.

NOTE The size of the indent created by toolbar buttons or keyboard shortcuts is based on Word's default tab settings, which are 0.5" unless you change them. If you change the defaults, you also change any new indents you create afterwards using the toolbar or keyboard shortcuts. ■

Indenting with the Ruler If you're visually oriented, you may want to use Word's Ruler to control indents—much as you might have controlled tabs on a typewriter many years ago. The Ruler is by far the quickest way to create first line indents at the beginning of paragraphs, because there are no toolbar or keyboard shortcuts for this task.

In Word 97, the Ruler typically displays by default. If you don't see it, choose View, Ruler. In Figure 2.15, you can take a closer look at the Ruler and its indent settings.

FIG. 2.15
The Ruler contains separate indent markers for First Line Indent, Hanging Indent, Left Indent, and Right Indent.

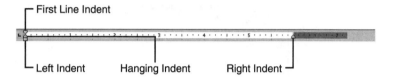

Notice that 0" on Word's horizontal Ruler corresponds to wherever you have the left margin set. (By default, this means it is 1.25" from the left edge of an 8.5" sheet of paper. The right margin is 1.25" from the right edge. Accordingly, there are six inches between margins in a default document.) Indents you create with the Ruler start at the margin and work inward or outward from there.

To create a new indent using the Ruler, first click in the paragraph you want to enter, or select multiple paragraphs. Then drag the indent to where you want it and release the mouse button. Figure 2.16 shows a first line indent being created with the Ruler.

If you want *all* your paragraphs to start with a 0.5" indent automatically, change your Normal style to include a 0.5" First Line Indent.

▶ **See** "Changing Styles," **p. 155**

Creating Precise Indents in the Paragraph Dialog Box You can also create paragraph indents in the Paragraph dialog box. Given that there are so many other easy ways to create indents, when would you bother?

■ When you need a precise indent that you can't reliably set from the Ruler. In the Paragraph dialog box, you can set indents to a precision of 1/100th inch. The Ruler only works to 1/16th of an inch—and then only if your eyes are very good!

■ When you want to set other paragraph formats, such as line spacing, at the same time.

FIG. 2.16

To create a first line indent of 0.5", drag the First Line Indent marker to the 0.5" mark on the Ruler.

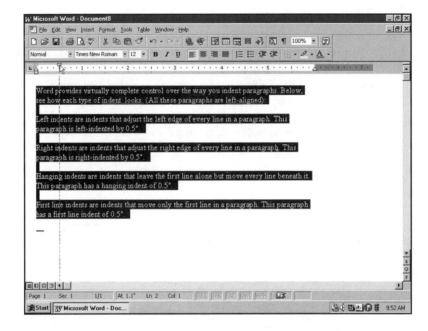

First, choose Format, Paragraph, and click the Indents and Spacing tab (see Figure 2.17). Set any left or right indent from the Left or Right scroll box. If you want to set either a paragraph or hanging indent, choose the Indent you want from the Special drop-down box. Word displays the default indent, 0.5"; if you want to change the setting, enter the new one in the By scroll box.

FIG. 2.17

The Indents and Spacing tab controls paragraph alignment, indentation, and spacing, including line spacing.

 TIP You can also set negative indents, or *outdents*. These can be quite useful. For example, you can use outdents to place headings or icons in the margins of your documents, as shown in Figure 2.18. To set an outdent, enter a negative value (such as -0.5") in the Left or Right scroll box of the Indents and Spacing tab. Or drag one of the Ruler's indent markers into the dark gray area outside your current margin.

FIG. 2.18

Using outdents to display icons associated with specific text.

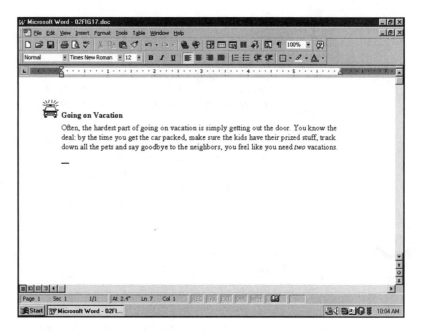

Part

I

Ch

2

ON THE WEB

The icon used in Figure 2.18 comes from Microsoft's new, free Webdings font, available for download at **www.microsoft.com/typography/fontpack/default.htm**.

Setting Paragraph Spacing

As with indents, Word gives you extensive control over paragraph spacing. Using keyboard shortcuts, you can instantly set single-spaced (Ctrl+1), double-spaced (Ctrl+2) and 1.5-line spaced (Ctrl+5) paragraphs. From the Indents and Spacing tab of the Paragraph dialog box, you can specify precise line spacing, to a precision of 1/10th of a point. You can even set exact spacing that Word applies before or after each paragraph.

Now, take a closer look at the precise spacing controls in the Indents and Spacing tab—and when and how you might use them.

Word line spacing can be controlled from the Line spacing scroll box. By default, Word uses single line spacing. This means Word keeps track of the font size you're using and adjusts line spacing so there's just enough room between lines for comfortable reading. In body text, 1/72 inch is added between the characters that reach down furthest from one line (*descenders* like p and q) and those that reach up furthest from the next (*ascenders* like b and k). Of course, the larger the text, the more space Word adds to keep single-spaced lines readable.

You've already learned that Word has keyboard shortcuts for applying 1.5-line and double-spacing between lines. These choices are also available here, along with several others:

- *At Least* spacing sets a minimum space from one line to the next, but allows Word to increase spacing if it encounters larger font sizes or graphics that wouldn't fit in the minimum space.

- *Exactly* spacing tells Word exactly what spacing to use no matter what text or graphics it encounters. If text or a graphic is too large, portions of it may be cut off. You might use Exactly if you're creating a form or other document that must fit on a single page no matter what.

- *Multiple* lets you specify any multiple of Word's single spacing (which, as mentioned above, can vary depending on the font size you are using). For example, to triple-space you would set multiple to 3. You can choose any multiple spacing increment from 0 to 132 lines, in increments of 1/100th of a line. You're unlikely to use settings quite this fine, but Multiple does provide welcome control over document size and appearance.

TIP   If you need to shrink your document by just one page, try Word's Shrink to Fit feature. Click the Print Preview toolbar button; then click the Shrink to Fit toolbar button on the Print Preview toolbar.

▶ **See** "Using Word's Shrink to Fit Feature," **p. 358**

If you include a large text character in a Single-, Double-, or Multiple-spaced line of text, Word accommodates it by increasing line spacing for that line only. If you would prefer that the top of the character be cut off (or nearly cut off) instead of using uneven line spacing, select the paragraph and use the Exactly setting.

TIP   Many people double-space practically everything. If you're one of them, consider adding Word's built-in double-space button to whichever toolbar is most convenient. To add it to the Formatting toolbar, follow these steps:

1. Choose Tools, Customize.
2. Click Commands.
3. In the Categories scroll box, choose Format.
4. In the Commands scroll box, scroll to Double Spacing.

5. Select and drag the Double Spacing icon to the location you choose on the toolbar of your choice. (You might have to move the Customize dialog box out of your way first.)
6. Click Close.

▶ **See** "Customizing Toolbars," **p. 721**

Adding Extra Space Before and After Paragraphs   You've just learned how to set spacing between lines in your document (or within selected paragraphs). You can also add extra space *between* paragraphs, as follows:

1. Choose Format, Paragraph.
2. Choose the Indents and Spacing tab.

3. Enter a new value in the <u>B</u>efore or <u>A</u>fter scroll box. (You'll generally use one or the other, not both.)

4. Click OK.

This is far superior to using the old-fashioned technique of pressing Enter twice at the end of each paragraph. First, you have more precise control. If you only want to add a half-line of space between each paragraph, it's easy to do so. Second, it's easier to change the spacing between paragraphs. If your document is running slightly long, and you decide you want to cut the space after paragraphs from 8 points to 6, select the entire document, display the Indents and Spacing tab, enter the new setting, and press OK.

TIP To add a full line of space before one or more selected paragraphs, use the keyboard shortcut Ctrl+0 (zero).

Setting Tabs

If you ever learned how to use a typewriter, you know what tabs are—stopping points along a horizontal line where you can align text or numbers.

In the early days of word processing, tabs were the state-of-the-art way to create row-and-column tables of information. Now, in Word at least, tables offer a much easier, more powerful way to create these row-and-column matrices.

▶ **See** "Word Tables: They Do It All," **p. 232**

But even now, for some tasks, nothing beats tabs. In particular, there's no better way to

- *Add a dot leader* that connects text at the left margin with text at the right margin, as you might use in a table of contents
- *Align a row of numbers* that contain varying decimal places
- *Center text* over a precise horizontal location on your page

Word tabs are a quantum leap more powerful than those you learned about on that old typewriter. Word 97 provides the following five kinds of tabs:

- *Left Tabs.* After you enter a Left Tab, additional text begins at the tab stop and continues to its right.
- *Right Tabs.* After you enter a Right Tab, additional text begins at the tab stop and continues to its left. The more text you enter, the closer to the left margin the text moves.
- *Center Tabs.* After you enter a Center Tab, additional text moves to the left and right, remaining centered on the location where the tab stop appears.
- *Decimal Tabs.* After you enter a Decimal Tab, rows of numbers that you enter all align on the decimal point, regardless of how many integer and decimal places they contain.
- *Bar Tabs.* With these auspiciously named tabs, you have a quick and easy way to draw a vertical line extending through as many horizontal lines of text as you want.

Figure 2.19 displays samples of all five types of tabs.

FIG. 2.19

Word provides five varieties of tabs—left, center, right, decimal, and bar tabs.

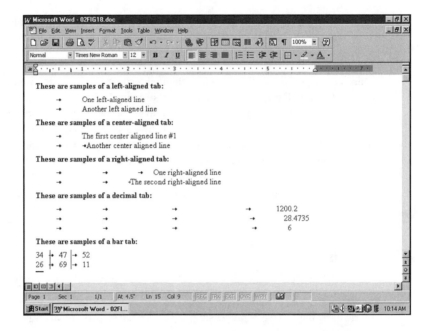

Word places a default tab stop at every 0.5". However, you may need tabs in different locations than where Word places them. If so, Word offers the following two ways to create tabs:

- Using the Ruler, typically the quickest way to get the job done
- Using the Tabs dialog box, which offers more precision and enables you to use advanced features like tab leaders and bar tabs

N O T E Many Word users don't realize that tab settings may vary between paragraphs.

Whether you use the Ruler or Tabs dialog box, the tab stops you create apply to all the paragraphs you have selected. If you don't select a paragraph, they apply to the current paragraph and any paragraphs you add immediately following it by pressing Enter and continuing to type.

To add a tab setting that applies to the entire document, press Ctrl+A to select the entire document, and then add the setting using either the Ruler or the Tabs dialog box. Other tab stops you've created won't be affected. However, it's possible that some tabs you've placed in the document will move to reflect the new tab stops you've added. ■

Creating Tabs with the Ruler

To set a tab with the ruler, follow these steps:

1. Click the tab marker to the left of the ruler. By default, this marker is set to create a left tab. If you do not want a left tab, keep clicking to display the tab you want. The icons change in the following order: first center tab, then right tab, then decimal tab.

2. After you've chosen the right kind of tab, click the Ruler where you want the tab to be set.

T I P To see tabs in your document, click Show/Hide Paragraph. They appear as right-arrow marks.

After you place a tab on the Ruler, you can move it by dragging it to the left or right. In the paragraphs you've selected, any text affected by the tab moves to the left or right as well.

Creating Tabs and Leaders Using the Tabs Dialog Box

You can also set tabs from the Tabs dialog box (see Figure 2.20). To view this dialog box, choose Format, Tabs. Or, if you're already working with paragraph formats, you can click the Tabs button at the bottom of the Paragraph dialog box.

FIG. 2.20

The Tabs dialog box controls tab stops, tab alignment, and leaders.

If you have manually set any tabs that apply to the currently selected paragraph(s), these will appear in the Tab stop position text box. To set a new tab, follow these steps:

1. Enter the location where you want the tab to appear in the Tab stop position text box.

2. In the Alignment area, choose the type of tab you want: Left, Center, Right, Decimal, or Bar.

3. If you want to use a tab leader, select it from the Leader area. You can choose a dot leader, a dash leader, or a solid line leader.

4. Click Set.

5. Click OK.

Changing Default Tab Stops

 As you may recall, Word provides default tab stops every 0.5" and uses these tab stops to determine how far to indent text when you click the Increase Indent/Decrease Indent buttons on the formatting toolbar (or use the equivalent keyboard shortcuts).

You might want to change the default tab stop locations. For example, your document's design might call for indents and tabs at 0.75" increments. To change the default tab stops, follow these steps:

1. Choose Format, Tabs.

2. Enter a new value in the Default tab stops scroll box.

3. Click OK.

Removing Tabs

You may at some point want to remove a tab you have created manually. Use the following steps to clear *all* the tab settings in a specific part of your document (or in the entire document):

1. Select the text or the entire document.
2. Choose Format, Tabs.
3. Choose Clear All.
4. Choose OK.

Use the following two steps to clear a *specific* tab setting:

1. Select all the paragraphs that contain the tab setting that you want to clear.
2. Drag the tab setting beneath the Ruler, so it disappears.

Unfortunately, Word doesn't provide an easy way to know where a tab setting begins and ends in your document. As a result, you may find eliminating tab settings to be a trial-and-error process. Here are a some tips that will help a little:

- If all the text you've selected contains the tab setting, the tab setting appears in solid black on your ruler.
- If some of the text you've selected contains the tab setting, the tab setting appears in gray on your ruler. Dragging the tab setting off the ruler will delete it for those paragraphs you've selected.
- If you've selected a large number of paragraphs that start *before* you applied the tab setting and end *after* the tab setting is no longer present, you won't see the tab setting on your ruler—even though it is still present in some of the paragraphs you've selected.

N O T E   If you remove a tab setting that text in your document depends upon, the text will revert to using Word's default tab settings. ■

Controlling Pagination

For years, typographers and graphic designers have done everything possible to eliminate widows and orphans. This isn't as Dickensian as it sounds. In documents, a widow is the last line of a paragraph that appears by itself at the *top* of a page. An orphan is the first line of a paragraph left to fend for itself at the *bottom* of a page. Left to their own devices, either a widow or orphan can easily be confused with a subhead.

You'll rarely see a widow or an orphan in a Word document, because Word includes a feature called Widow/Orphan control. If Word encounters a paragraph that will be split at the bottom of the page separating one line from all the rest, Word automatically makes sure the entire paragraph prints together. For example, it moves the potentially orphaned line to the top of the next page with the rest of its "family."

Widow/Orphan Control is one of four Pagination settings Word provides in the Line and Page Breaks tab of the Paragraph dialog box (see Figure 2.21). You can use these settings to make sure your page breaks don't unnecessarily interrupt or inconvenience your readers.

FIG. 2.21

The Line and Page Breaks tab controls pagination, and whether line numbers or hyphenation will be applied to selected text.

While Widow/Orphan control is turned on by default, the other three settings are turned off unless you check them. They are as follows:

- *Keep Lines Together.* Whereas Widow/Orphan control prevents page breaks that leave one line by themselves, Keep lines together prevents all page breaks that interrupt paragraphs. When a page break is needed, Word simply jumps the entire paragraph to the next page. Keep lines together can be especially handy in tables, where it prevents a few lines of a table (or, worse, parts of a single table row) from jumping onto the next page by themselves.

- *Keep with Next.* Sometimes, you'll have two paragraphs that must stay together. For example, you might have a figure caption that needs to stay with an accompanying table. Or you might have space on a contract for signatures that needs to be on the same page as other contract clauses.

- *Page Break Before.* This option forces a manual page break before a paragraph. You might use this feature if you expect that a paragraph will create pagination problems and you're not sure Word will handle them properly.

TIP If you have a document that must have one paragraph on each page, use Page break before instead of manual page breaks; it's quicker, easier to keep consistent, and easier to change if necessary.

Like the other paragraph formatting elements you've seen, you can apply Pagination controls to a specific paragraph, paragraphs you select, or you can select the entire document and apply them universally. You can also include Pagination controls in styles, so they can be used automatically throughout your document.

▶ **See** "Using Line Numbering," **p. 101**
▶ **See** "Working with Hyphenation," **p. 135**

Format Painter: The Quick Way to Copy Formats

Few Word direct formatting features are as powerful—or as much *fun*—as Format Painter. Imagine you've worked really hard to format a block of text just the way you want it. Let's say you've formatted it as New Century Schoolbook, 24-point italic, centered, and bordered with a box. Perhaps you've even added an effect, such as embossing.

Now you would like to apply the same formats elsewhere. You *could* create a style—and if you plan to reuse the format repeatedly, you probably *should*, but in this case, you don't care about saving the formatting for posterity; you just want a quick, easy way to apply the formats once or twice more. You can use the Format Painter as follows:

1. Select the text with the formats you want to copy.
2. Click the Format Painter button on the Standard toolbar.
3. Select the text to which you want to apply the formats.

The first time you release the mouse pointer, the formats are applied to the text you've selected. That means some ways of selecting text work with the mouse pointer, and others don't. For example, you *can* drag your mouse pointer across text to select it for format painting. However, if you click in a new location intending to select text with a keyboard shortcut, you're too late; you've already let go of the mouse pointer, and the text you select afterwards won't be reformatted.

TIP If you find this troublesome, use the keyboard shortcuts Ctrl+Shift+C to copy formats and Ctrl+Shift+V to paste them on other selected text.

In the previous example, you applied a set of text formats *once*. What if you want to apply them several times in a row? Double-click the Format Painter button. Then select the blocks of text you want to format paint, one at a time. When you're finished, press Esc or click the Format Painter button again.

Format Painter copies all font formatting, including bold, italic, underlining, effects, character spacing, and animation. If you've copied the formatting from an entire paragraph (including the paragraph mark at the end), it copies all paragraph formatting and paragraph styles as well.

TIP Format Painter and the keyboard shortcut equivalents work *between* documents, too. You can use them to copy formats into another open document without copying text into it.

Troubleshooting Font and Paragraph Formatting

Here are a few potential problems you may run into while using Word's font and paragraph formatting features—and how you can solve them.

TROUBLESHOOTING

A font I expected to see in my font list isn't there. If the font is a PostScript font, check to make sure Windows 95 or NT 4.0 is displaying PostScript fonts. On the taskbar, click Start, Settings, Control Panel. Double-click the Fonts folder. Choose View, Options, TrueType, and make sure the Show only TrueType fonts in the programs on My Computer check box is *cleared*. Then, make sure Adobe Type Manager (ATMCNTRL.EXE) is running *and* that it is turned on.

Word is substituting a font I don't like for one that isn't on my computer. If you open a document that calls for fonts you don't have, Word substitutes other fonts. You can control which fonts are substituted by choosing Tools, Options, Compatibility, and clicking Font Substitution. Word lists the fonts it is currently substituting and lets you choose different ones.

My tabs have gone awry. Did you add or remove tab stops in ways that affected the tabs you placed in your document? Are there still stray tab stops in your document that you thought you deleted?

From Here...

In this chapter, you've learned the basics of Word character and paragraph formatting: quick and easy ways to apply fonts, sizes, text effects, indents, and more. You've also learned ways to use character spacing, tabs, and other features to make your documents stand out from the pack.

- Chapter 3, "More Day-to-Day Productivity Tools," completes your introduction to Microsoft Word by showing you the indispensable tools and techniques you'll use every day, including find and replace, headers and footers, bulleted and numbered lists, and much more.

- Chapter 5, "Styles: The Foundation of Automated Documents," shows you how to use styles to streamline and organize the vast majority of your document formatting tasks.

- Chapter 7, "Automating Your Documents: AutoCorrect, AutoFormat, AutoText, and AutoSummarize," shows how you can eliminate even more routine document formatting by using Word 97's powerful, intelligent AutoFormat feature.

- Finally, Chapter 8, "Tables," shows how you can use Word Tables to create row-and-column tables of information more easily than anyone ever could with tabs.

More Day-to-Day Productivity Tools

by Elaine Marmel

So far, you've learned the basics of Word 97, including basic formatting. In this chapter, we'll cover tools you'll use almost everyday that can vastly improve your productivity in Word. ∎

Find and replace

You can find and replace text, as you would expect, but you can also find and replace formatting, styles, incorrect character case, paragraph marks, and more.

Page setup

Page setup helps you control margins, paper orientation, and the paper tray your printer uses.

Headers and footers

Using headers and footers, you can add a variety of identifying information to your document. You can also establish different headers or footers for different pages or portions of your document.

Bullets and numbered lists

Bulleted and numbered lists help organize information. In Word, you can use the standard bullet characters or numbered lists formats, or you can customize them.

Borders and shading

You can place borders around paragraphs or around entire pages, and you can, of course, customize the border's appearance. Using shading, you can also draw attention to a group of words or a paragraph by applying a color to them.

Using Find, Replace, and Go To

You search for text for various reasons. Sometimes, you need to read what you have written, or you need to start working at a certain location. Other times, you search because you want to change something you have written.

You use Word's Find and Replace commands when you are searching for text or formatting. Typically, you find text because you want to change it or replace it with other text, so you tend to use the Find and Replace commands together.

You use the Go To command when you want to move the insertion point to a location in your document, such as a page number or a bookmark. When do you use the Go To command as opposed to the Find command? Use the Find command when you are focused on searching for text; use the Go To command when you are trying to move the insertion point to a specific location in your document, such as Page 4.

 See "Using Bookmarks," **p. 509**

Basic Find and Replace

 Typically, when you use the Find command, you want to also replace whatever you find with something new. To open the Find and Replace dialog box, click the Select Browse Object button on the vertical scroll bar. Then, click the Find button (see Figure 3.1). In the Find and Replace dialog box, click the <u>M</u>ore button to see the options you can use to control how Word's Find and Replace features operate.

 TIP You can leave the Find and Replace dialog box open while you work. Just click in your document and start working. To reactivate the Find and Replace dialog box, click any gray portion of the dialog box.

TIP If you prefer menus, choose <u>E</u>dit, <u>F</u>ind or press Ctrl+F to open the Find and Replace dialog box to the Find tab. Choose <u>E</u>dit, <u>R</u>eplace or press Ctrl+H to open the dialog box and display the Replace tab.

You type characters in the Fi<u>n</u>d What text box. If you also want to replace what you find, you type characters in the Replace W<u>i</u>th text box. If you click <u>F</u>ind Next, by default, Word searches your entire document for the characters you type in the Fi<u>n</u>d What text box, stopping at each occurrence. If you click Replace, by default, Word searches your entire document for the characters you type in the Fi<u>n</u>d What text box and, if you agree, replaces them with the characters you type in the Replace W<u>i</u>th text box.

For example, suppose Thomas Jefferson wanted to see how the Declaration of Independence would read if he changed rights to privileges throughout the document. In the Find and Replace dialog box, he would have typed **rights** in the Fi<u>n</u>d What box, clicked the Re<u>p</u>lace tab, typed **privileges** in the Replace W<u>i</u>th box, and then clicked the <u>R</u>eplace button.

FIG. 3.1
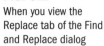
When you view the Replace tab of the Find and Replace dialog box, you can specify both the text you want to find and the text you want to use when replacing.

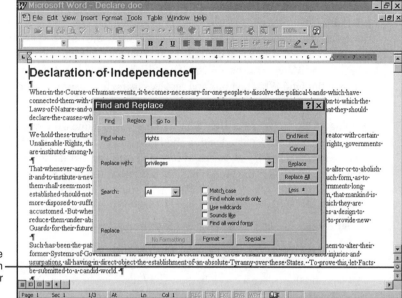

Select Browse Object button on vertical scroll bar

Controlling Direction   Suppose Jefferson only wanted to replace occurrences of "rights" from the insertion point's current location forward in the document. The Search list box lets you control the direction Word searches for the text you specify in the Find What box. You can search the entire document by leaving the setting set at All. Or, you can search forward through the document by choosing Down or backward through the document by choosing Up.

> **N O T E**   When you choose All, Word searches in a circular fashion from the current position of the insertion point forward in your document. When Word reaches the end of your document, it prompts you to begin searching at the top of the document. If you permit the search to continue, Word searches from the top of the document to the current position of the insertion point. ▪

Controlling Case   By default, Word ignores the case you use when specifying words or phrases in the Find What and Replace With text boxes. Instead, Word uses the case it finds in your document. Once again, consider the example where Thomas Jefferson is replacing rights with privileges. Suppose that, in some cases, rights appears within a sentence, while in other cases, sentences begin with Rights. By default, when Word makes the replacement, it capitalizes privileges whenever privileges replaces rights at the beginning of a sentence. Therefore, if you want to replace all occurrences of a word, whether it is upper- or lowercase, and you want Word to match the case it finds in your document, don't worry about the case you type in the Find What and Replace With text boxes.

Part
I

Ch
3

On the other hand, you may have a situation where some occurrences of a word in your document are capitalized and other occurrences are not; further, you may want to replace only the lowercase or only the uppercase version of the word with a new word. In a situation like this one, type the correct case in both the Find What and Replace With text boxes and place a check in the Match Case check box. Then, Word finds only selections that match the case you typed in the Find What text box and replaces using the case you typed in the Replace With text box.

Finding All Occurrences or Only Whole Words   Sometimes, the word for which you are searching could be contained within another word. Consider establish and establishment or when and whenever. If you search with default settings, Word finds every occurrence of the characters you type in the Find What text box. However, to find "establish" without looking at words that contain it, such as "establishment," place a check in the Find Whole Words Only check box.

▶ **See** "Supercharged Find and Replace Techniques," **p. 84**

Working with Wildcards   Remember the wildcard rules from your days in DOS? You can use wild cards to find and replace text. Suppose you type* within the characters of the Find What text box and then place a check in the Use Wildcards check box. You'll tell Word to treat the asterisk as a wild card instead of searching for an asterisk. Use Table 3.1 to help you type a wildcard search. From Table 3.1, you'll note, for example, that including a ? within the characters in the Find What text box tells Word to consider any character in the position of the question mark.

Following are some special notes about wildcard searches:

■ To search for a wildcard character, such as the asterisk (*), type a backslash (\) before the character.

■ Suppose you've got a name that appears several times in your document ordered last name first. You can use the \n wild card to search to rearrange the name so that it appears in first name/last name order. For example, if the name appears as Smith, John, then type **(Smith), (John)** in the Find What text box and **\2 \1** in the Replace with text box. Word finds Smith, John and replaces it with John Smith. Note that placing the comma outside the parentheses in the Find What text box eliminates it when you replace the text (see Figure 3.2).

Table 3.1   Wildcard Characters Used to Search a Word Document

Use This Wild Card	To Find	Examples
?	Any single character	**w?n** finds win, wan, and won.
*	Any string of characters	**l*d** finds learned and limped.
[ ]	One of the specified characters	**s[uo]n** finds sun and son.

Use This Wild Card	To Find	Examples
[-]	Any single character in this range	**[b-d]rown** finds brown, crown and drown. Ranges must be in ascending order.
[!]	Any single character except the characters inside the brackets	**l[!a]st** finds list, lost, and lust, but not last.
[!x-z]	Any single character except characters in the range inside the brackets	**cl[!a-m]ck** finds clock and cluck, but not clack or click.
{n,}	At least *n* occurrences of the previous character or expression	**We{1,}d** finds wed and weed.
@	One or more occurrences of the previous character or expression	**fe@d** finds fed and feed.
{n}	Exactly *n* occurrences of the previous character or expression	**we{2}d** finds weed but not wed.
{n,m}	From *n* to *m* occurrences of the previous character or expression	**10{1,3}** finds 10, 100, and 1000.
<	The beginning of a word	**<(ex)** finds except, exempt, and exercise, but not text.
>	The end of a word	**(al)>** finds exceptional and diagonal, but not albatross or alarm.

Part

I

Ch

3

Finding Words With Spelling Variations   Do you have trouble distinguishing there, their, and they're? How about its and it's? You can review your document for words that sound alike but are spelled differently using Word's Sounds Li<u>k</u>e feature.

▶ **See** "Using Automatic Spelling and Grammar Checking," **p. 124**

 TIP   As an alternative, let Word's Grammar Checker correct mistakes for you.

Type the word for which you want to search, place a check in the Sounds Li<u>k</u>e check box, and click <u>F</u>ind Next.

FIG. 3.2

To reverse text, use the
\n wild card.

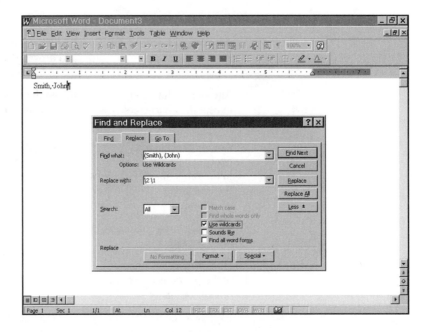

Finding Other Word Forms   Have you ever decided, several pages into a document, that you've chosen a verb and now found one that better describes the action? Changing each occurrence of the verb, in its various incarnations (for example, singular, plural, or adverbial) can be very tedious. Instead, use Word's Find All Word Forms feature.

When you place a check in the Find All Word Forms check box, Word finds all forms of the word you type in the Find What text box. For example, if you type **forbid** in the Find What box, Word finds forbid, forbids, forbidden, and forbidding. If you are replacing a word, be aware that the words you supply in both the Find What text box and the Replace With text box must be the same part of speech—that is, both must be nouns or both must be verbs.

N O T E   The Find All Word Forms feature is not available if you have checked either the Use Wildcards check box or the Sounds Like check box. ■

T I P   If you don't see the Find All Word Forms check box, you may need to run Word Setup, choose Office Tools, and install the Find All Word Forms file.

Supercharged Find and Replace Techniques

Although Find and Replace basics are powerful, there are even more powerful ways you can use Find and Replace.

Cleaning Up Imported Documents   Along comes that time when somebody sends you a document that you must import into Word. In particular, when you import a standard text file into Word, you'll see paragraph marks at the end of every line and word wrapping doesn't function when you force a line break using a paragraph mark.

So, to remove all the excessive paragraph marks, you can use Word's Find and Replace feature to search for a paragraph mark and replace it with nothing. Follow these steps:

N O T E   You won't want to use the Replace All button in this search because then you'll lose paragraph markings, where two paragraph marks appear consecutively.

1. Open the Find and Replace dialog box to the Replace tab (press Ctrl+H).
2. Clear any text you see in either the Find What text box or the Replace With text box, and place the insertion point in the Find What text box.
3. Click the Special button. A pop-up list appears, showing you the special characters for which you can search (see Figure 3.3).

Part
I
Ch
3

FIG. 3.3
You can search for any of the characters on this list and even replace them with any other character on the list.

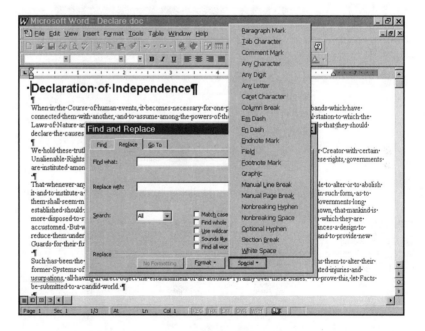

4. Select the special character for which you want to search. Word places a set of characters in the Find What text box that represent the special characters you have chosen. When you search for paragraph marks, you'll see ^p in the Find What box.
5. Click the Find Next button.

Word highlights the first paragraph mark. Because the Replace With box is blank, if you click Replace, Word deletes the paragraph mark, closes up the lines on-screen, and highlights the next paragraph mark. Continue to click Find Next or Replace until the process is completed.

Finding and Replacing Formatting You can search for formatting of various types and replace it with other formatting, if desired. Specifically, you can search for and replace font and paragraph formatting, tab settings, frames, and highlighting.

Place the insertion point in the appropriate text box (Find What or Replace With). If you are searching for text containing formatting, type the text for which you want to search.

TIP If you want to search for all occurrences of some formatting (for example italics), don't type any text in the Find What text box.

Click the Format button. A pop-up list appears, showing the formatting for which you can search (see Figure 3.4).

FIG. 3.4

You can search for font, paragraph, or tab settings.

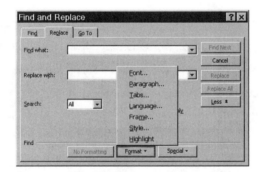

If you choose Font, the Find Font dialog box appears (see Figure 3.5).

FIG. 3.5

Select the font formatting for which you want to search.

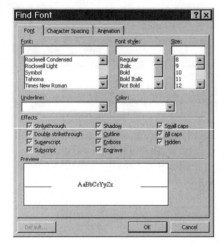

If you choose Paragraph, the Find Paragraph dialog box appears (see Figure 3.6).

FIG. 3.6

Select the paragraph formatting for which you want to search.

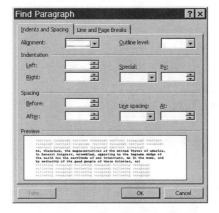

If you choose Tabs, the Find Tabs dialog box appears (see Figure 3.7).

FIG. 3.7

Select the tab settings for which you want to search.

If you choose Frame, the Find Frame dialog box appears (see Figure 3.8).

FIG. 3.8

Select the frame settings for which you want to search.

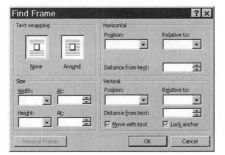

In each of these cases, after you choose OK, Word changes the Find and Replace dialog box to include the formatting you selected. If you choose <u>H</u>ighlight, you won't see a dialog box; Word simply changes the Find and Replace dialog box to include highlighting in either the search or the replacement (see Figure 3.9).

FIG. 3.9

After you select formatting, Word adds the formatting to the appropriate box in the Find and Replace dialog box.

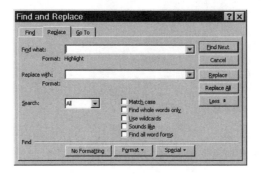

 T I P   To clear formatting from the Find and Replace dialog box, place the insertion point in the Fi<u>n</u>d What text box or the Replace W<u>i</u>th text box, as appropriate, and click the No Forma<u>t</u>ting button.

N O T E   For character formatting (for example, bold, italics, highlight, and so on), you can search for text that does not contain this formatting. For Highlight, select the option twice from the Format menu, and Word changes the Find and Replace dialog box so that you see Not Highlight. For character formatting that you select from the Find Font dialog box, select the opposite of the formatting; that is, select Not Bold or Not Italic, or click any check box twice to remove the check. ■

Finding and Replacing Styles   In Chapter 5, "Styles: The Foundation of Automated Documents," you will learn about using styles to make formatting consistent and easy. When you use styles regularly, you'll find occasions when you want to switch some or all occurrences of one style in your document for another style. Using Find and Replace, you can search for styles and replace them with other styles.

Place the insertion point in the Find What text box (make sure the box contains text only if you want to search for text formatted in a particular style), and click the F<u>o</u>rmat button. A pop-up list appears, showing the formatting for which you can search (refer to Figure 3.4). When you choose <u>S</u>tyle, the Find Style dialog box appears (see Figure 3.10). Select a style and click OK. Your selection appears in the Find and Replace dialog box (see Figure 3.11).

Repeat this process after you place the insertion point in the Replace W<u>i</u>th text box. When you choose <u>S</u>tyle, the Replace Style dialog box appears; it looks just like the Find Style dialog box in Figure 3.5.

FIG. 3.10

From this dialog box, select the style you want to find.

FIG. 3.11

When you click OK, the style you selected appears below the Fi<u>n</u>d What text box.

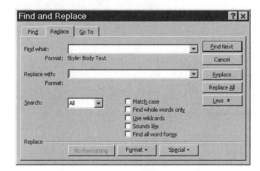

Part

I

Ch

3

  To stop searching for or replacing styles in the Find and Replace dialog box, place the insertion point in the Fi<u>n</u>d What text box or the Replace W<u>i</u>th text box, as appropriate, and click the No Forma<u>tt</u>ing button.

Finding and Replacing Language   *Localized versions* of Word are versions that have been translated into another language. Localized versions are also called International versions. If you have installed Multilanguage Support on your computer (Multilanguage Support is a Windows component that you install the same way you add accessories), you'll be able to edit documents created in other versions' languages without losing information.

You can search for text formatted in various languages or for text formatted with *No Proofing*. For example, mail merged documents are created with portions set to No Proofing, and you can use Find and Replace to change this by searching for No Proofing as a language and replacing it with your default language (for example, English, United States).

Place the insertion point in the Fi<u>n</u>d What text box (make sure the box contains text only if you want to search for text formatted in a particular language), and click the F<u>o</u>rmat button. A popup list appears, showing the formatting for which you can search (refer to Figure 3.4). When you choose <u>L</u>anguage, the Find Language dialog box appears (see Figure 3.12). Select a language and click OK. The selection appears in the Find and Replace dialog box.

FIG. 3.12

Use the Find Language dialog box to find portions of the document formatted in another language or with No Proofing.

 TIP You can clear the language from the Find and Replace dialog box by placing the insertion point in the Find What text box or the Replace With text box, as appropriate, and clicking the No Formatting button.

TROUBLESHOOTING

I set my search to look for a particular phrase that I know appears in my document, but Word can't find it. What am I doing wrong? Several factors could come into play:

- First, make sure you have spelled the text correctly in the Find What text box and you haven't added or left out spaces.

- Make sure you haven't selected any text before you start searching. If you select text, Word searches only the selected text.

- You may be searching in the wrong direction; make sure you see All in the Search list box.

- You may have one or more of the check boxes at the bottom of the Find and Replace dialog box checked when it shouldn't be checked.

- Check to make sure you didn't add formatting of some type to the search. The text may appear without formatting but you may be searching for it with formatting.

- Be sure you didn't accidentally add any special characters, such as a paragraph mark, to the search.

Go To Practically Anything You Like

No matter what you're doing, there are going to be times when you'll want to go someplace in your document. Word makes that convenient for you, because you can go to almost anything.

To use the Go To command, try any one of the following techniques:

- Press F5.
- Open the Find and Replace dialog box and click the Go To tab.
- Press Ctrl+G.

Any of these techniques displays the Go To tab of the Find and Replace dialog box (see Figure 3.13).

FIG. 3.13

Use the Go To dialog box to quickly move around documents.

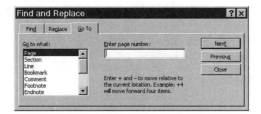

Where Can You Go?   As you scroll through the G<u>o</u> to What list box, you'll see that you can go to the following objects in a Word document:

- Page
- Sectionx
- Line
- Bookmark
- Comment
- Footnote
- Endnote
- Field
- Table
- Graphic
- Equation
- Object
- Heading

Although its usefulness isn't as obvious as some of the other objects, many experienced users go to bookmarks regularly. Try using a bookmark to mark your current place in the document when you suddenly remember something you need to add or edit elsewhere in the document. That way, you can return to the current location to continue to work after making your change. At the current location, create a bookmark that contains no text (you might call it "last") to mark the location of the insertion point before you move to the place where you need to add or edit text. Then, move around your document as necessary. When you're ready to continue where you originally started, "go to" your bookmark by selecting Bookmark from the G<u>o</u> To What list and typing the bookmark's name (if you called it "last", type **last**) in the text box to the right.

▶ **See** "Using Bookmarks," **p. 509**

Searching for Next or Previous Item   Regardless of what you choose to go to, you can go to the next or previous occurrence of that type of object using the navigator buttons that appear on either side of the Select Browse Object button at the bottom of the vertical scroll bar (see Figure 3.14).

Searching for a Specific Numbered Item or Location   Earlier in this chapter, you learned how to use a bookmark to mark your place in a document. When you used the Go To command to return to that location, you went to a named location. The same method works if you want to go to a comment (enter the reviewer's name), a field (enter the field's name), or an object (provide an object type, such as a 1-2-3 worksheet).

Part

I

Ch

3

FIG 3.14

Use these buttons to view the next or previous object.

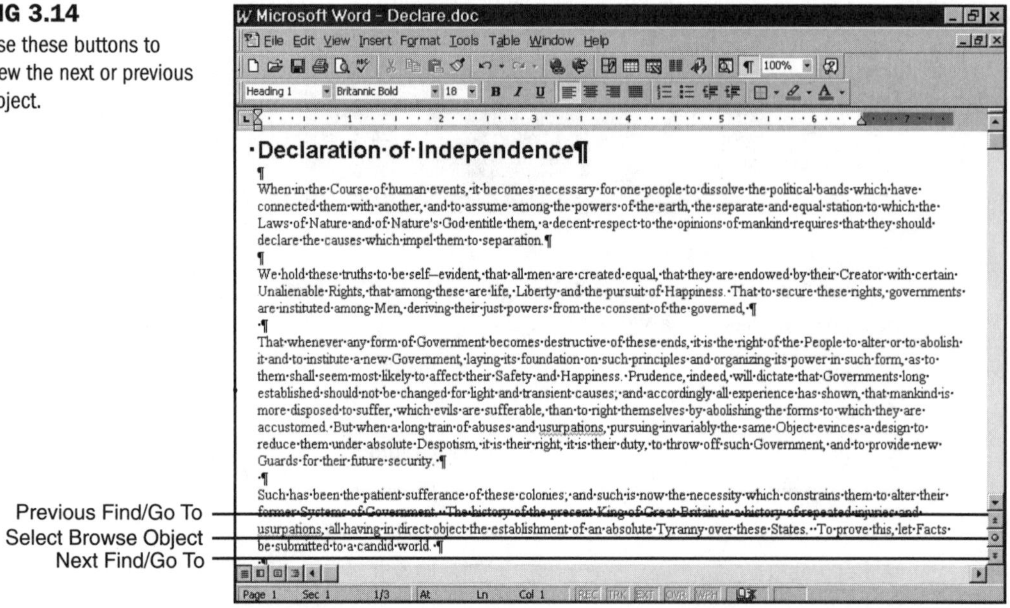

Previous Find/Go To
Select Browse Object
Next Find/Go To

You also can use the Go To tab of the Find and Replace dialog box to move the insertion point to a specific numbered item or location. For example, if you go to page 4, just select Page from the Go To What list box and then type **4** in the text box to the right. You can use numbers for pages, sections, lines, footnotes, endnotes, tables, graphics, equations, or headings. Word numbers these items sequentially as they appear in your document.

A Quick Guide to Page Setup

You accomplish most of your page setup work using the Page Setup dialog box. Often, you'll find that the default settings in the Page Setup dialog box suit your needs, but you will find occasion to change the settings for some or all of your document. From the Page Setup dialog box, you can:

- Change margins (including setting up a document for binding)
- Set the size and orientation of your paper
- Choose the tray from which your printer will print
- Divide your document into sections
- Add line numbers
- Control the vertical alignment of text on the page

Understanding Word's Default Page Setup

Word's Default page settings appear in Table 3.2. In subsequent sections of this chapter, you'll learn how to change these settings, both for new documents or just the current document.

Table 3.2 Default Page Settings	
Feature	**Setting**
Top and Bottom margins	1 inch
Left and Right margins	1.25 inches
Header and Footer margins	.5 inches
Paper Size	Letter (8.5×11 inches)
Paper Orientation	Portrait
Paper Source	Printer-dependent
Section Starts	On a new page
Headers and footers	The same throughout your document
Vertical alignment	Top
Line Numbers	Off

Part

I

Ch

3

Working with Sections

All of the settings in the previous table apply to your entire document, and by default, if you make a change to one of these settings, it will apply to the entire document. But, by using sections, you can apply any setting you establish in the Page Setup dialog box to specific portions of your document.

Why Document Sections Matter   Think of a section as a chapter in a book. If your book were all contained in one document, each chapter would be a section of the document. Sections provide you with a means to establish different settings for different parts of the same document. For example, suppose you need different margin settings for different parts of your document. If the document is divided into sections, you can establish different margin settings for different sections.

As you need to change settings for part of a document, you can let Word automatically create sections for you; you'll see an example of this method later in this chapter when you learn how to change margins. Alternatively, you can create sections yourself and then assign settings to them.

Creating a Section   You can divide a document into sections at any time using the Break dialog box (see Figure 3.15).

FIG. 3.15

Use this dialog box to
start a new section in
your document.

 Notice that you can insert a manual page break from this dialog box. You might find it easier, however, to place the insertion point wherever you want the new page to begin and press Ctrl+Enter.

Word inserts the break immediately before the insertion point. So, move the insertion point to the spot where you want a new section to start and then choose Insert, Break to display the Break dialog box.

Selecting a Type of Section Break   You can create the following different types of section breaks; on-screen, they look similar, but their differences are apparent when you print the document:

- A *Next Page* section break starts the new section at the top of the next page in your document. Both on-screen and when you print, Word starts a new page at the section break.

- A *Continuous* section break starts the new section at the insertion point. On-screen, you see a section break, but when you print, the break is transparent.

- An *Even Page* section break starts the new section on the next even-numbered page. If the section break falls on an even-numbered page, Word leaves the next odd-numbered page blank.

- An *Odd Page* section break starts the new section on the next odd numbered page. Like the Even page section break, if the section break falls on an odd-numbered page, Word leaves the next even-numbered page blank.

You'll see section breaks in your document in Normal and Page Layout views if your settings allow you to display all nonprinting characters (Choose Tools, Options, and, on the View tab in the NonPrinting Characters section, place a check in the All check box). All section breaks have a similar appearance in your document. In Figure 3.16, you see a Next Page section break.

Copying a Section's Formatting   In the same way that paragraph marks store all the formatting for a paragraph, the section break mark that appears after a section stores all the formatting for that section. After you establish formatting for a section, you may want to copy that formatting to another section, and you can do so easily by copying the section break mark. Simply place the insertion point on the section break mark and click the Copy button. Then, move the insertion point to the end of the text you want to format and click the Paste button.

FIG. 3.16
Section breaks appear in your document as double-dotted lines.

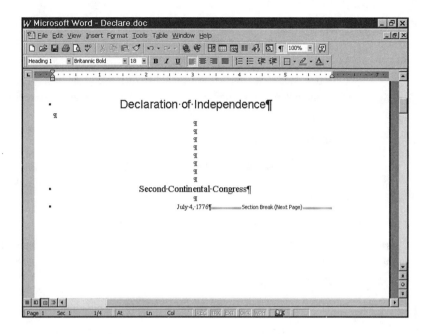

 TIP You can search for section breaks. Open the Find dialog box and, if necessary, click the More button to display the additional Find options. Then, click the Special button and choose Section Break.

Deleting a Section Break You can delete a section break the same way you delete any text; for example, you could place the insertion point on the section break and press the Delete key.

> **CAUTION**
>
> Remember, a section break mark stores all the formatting for the section preceding the break mark. If you delete a section break, the text before the break mark merges with the text after the break mark and assumes the formatting characteristics of the section after the break mark.

 TROUBLESHOOTING

I decided, after typing several pages of text, that I really wanted those pages in their own section. Can I do this? No problem; place the insertion point immediately before the text you want to appear in the section and then choose Insert, Break to display the Break dialog box. Choose the type of section break you want to create, and then choose OK. Then, move the insertion point to the end of the text you want included in the section and insert another section break.

I inserted a Section (Next Page) break when I really wanted a Section (Continuous) break. Can I change the break type? No. If you insert the wrong type of break, you should insert the correct type of break and then delete the incorrect break.

Changing Margins

Margins measure the amount of space that appears on a page between the edge of the page and the text. Margin space surrounds the text of your document. Margin settings initially apply to your entire document, but you can establish different margin settings for different portions of your document. You can change margins using the following two techniques:

- The Ruler
- The Page Setup dialog box

Changing Margins Using the Ruler   Use the Ruler to change margins when you don't need to be precise about your margin settings and when you want to change the margins for your entire document.

To change margins using the Ruler, follow these steps:

1. Open the View menu and make sure you see a check next to Ruler. If you don't, choose Ruler.

2. Choose View, Page Layout.

 TIP You also can change margins using the ruler that appears in Print Preview. Choose File, Print Preview.

3. Slide the mouse pointer into the ruler at the edge where you want to change the margin.

4. When the mouse pointer changes to a two-headed arrow (see Figure 3.17), drag the mouse. Drag a side margin to the left or right; drag a top or bottom margin up or down.

FIG. 3.17
Drag a left margin to the right to make the margin larger and to the left to make the margin smaller.

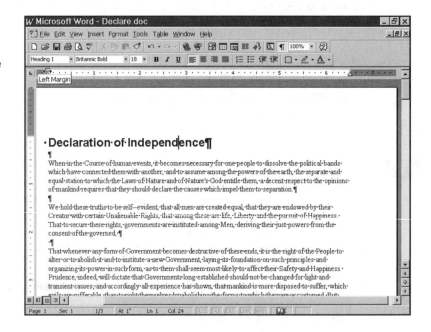

Changing Margins Using Page Setup Dialog Box   You also can use the Page Setup dialog box to change the margins in your document. Use the Page Setup dialog box to change margins when you need precise margin settings or when you only want the change to affect part of your document.

N O T E   The Page Setup dialog box contains an Apply To list box that appears on all tabs of the dialog box. This list box enables you to apply the settings you choose in the Page Setup dialog box to all or part of the document even though you may not have divided the document into sections. If you select text before opening the dialog box, you'll see Whole Document and Selected Text as the choices in the Apply To list box. If you don't select text, you'll see Whole Document and This Point Forward as the choices in the list box. If you choose anything other than Whole Document while making Page Setup choices, Word automatically creates sections in your document. ▨

Place the insertion point at the location where you want the new margins to begin. If you want to change the margins for a certain portion of your document even if you have not divided your document into sections, select the text you want affected by the new margins.

Choose File, Page Setup. The Page Setup dialog box appears (see Figure 3.18). Use the Top, Bottom, Left, and Right boxes to increase or decrease margins. If you selected text and want the settings to apply only to selected text, open the Apply To list box and choose This Section. If you didn't select text and you want the settings to apply to the rest of your document, open the Apply To list box and choose This Point Forward.

FIG. 3.18

Change margins from the Margins tab of the Page Setup dialog box.

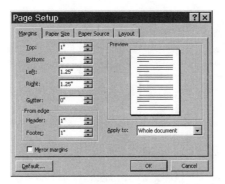

TROUBLESHOOTING

When I dragged to change margins, I ended up indenting the paragraph containing the insertion point. What did I do wrong? You dragged when the mouse pointer shape was not a two-headed arrow. You can control both page margins and paragraph indents from the Ruler, and what you change depends on the mouse pointer shape at the time you drag. Watch for the ToolTips as you move the mouse pointer over the margin.

continues

Part

I

Ch

3

continued

I selected text before I changed margins in the Page Setup dialog box and I chose Selected Text in the Apply To box. Now I've got two markers in my document that say Section Break (Next Page). When I print, the pages break at these markers. I don't want page breaks. I want the text to run continuously with different margins on the same page. What did I do wrong? Nothing. By default, Word inserted Next Page type section breaks. You can insert Continuous section breaks where the Next Page section breaks appear and then delete the Next Page section break.

Preparing Bound Books

When the document you're preparing will eventually be bound, you'll want to make some special page settings. If you plan to print on both the front and back sides of each page, place a check in the Mirror Margins check box (see Figure 3.19). When you check this box, Word automatically sets up your document so that it uses *facing pages*. When you open the book, you'll see two pages: an even numbered page on the left and an odd numbered page on the right.

TIP When you use facing pages, you can position page numbers relative to the inside or outside margin.

In addition, you'll want to set some Gutter space. When you use Mirror Margins and Gutter space, Word leaves extra space on the inside margin of each page for binding (see Figure 3.19).

FIG. 3.19
By using mirrored margins, you set up your document to print with facing pages; using gutter space allows for binding.

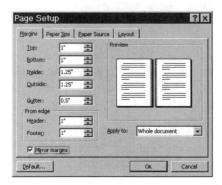

If you plan to bind your document and only print on one side of each page, you'll still want to leave extra space at the left margin for binding. In this case, don't place a check in the Mirror Margins check box, but do set a Gutter size.

Setting Paper Size and Orientation

You set the orientation and size of paper from the Paper Size tab of the Page Setup dialog box (see Figure 3.20). If the Page Setup dialog box isn't open, choose File, Page Setup and click the Paper Size tab.

FIG. 3.20
You set both paper size and page orientation from the Paper Size tab of the Page Setup dialog box.

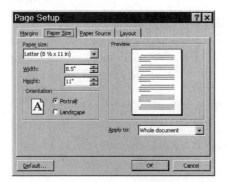

 TIP Don't forget the Apply To list box. You can apply any setting in the Page Setup dialog box to the whole document, a section, or to a selected part of the document.

Portrait versus Landscape To understand the difference between portrait and landscape orientation, consider the text on an $8\frac{1}{2}\times11$-inch page:

- when you choose portrait orientation, the text flows across the $8\frac{1}{2}$-inch side of the page between the left and right margins.
- When you choose landscape orientation, the text flows across the $11\frac{1}{2}$-inch side of the page between the left and right margins.

Available Standard Sizes By default, the following paper sizes are available:

- Letter ($8\frac{1}{2}\times11$ inches)
- Legal ($8\frac{1}{2}\times14$ inches)
- Executive ($7\frac{1}{2}\times10$-inches)
- A4 (210×297 mm)
- A5 (148×210 mm)
- Com-10 Envelope ($4\frac{1}{8}\times9\frac{1}{2}$ inches)
- DL Envelope (110×220 mm)
- C5 Envelope (176×250 mm)
- Monarch Envelope ($3\frac{7}{8}\times7\frac{1}{2}$ inches)

You also can choose Custom Size and set your own paper size.

NOTE As you know, the United States uses $8\frac{1}{2}\times11$ inch paper by default. Most other countries, however, use A4 as the standard paper size. If you need to print a document on $8\frac{1}{2}\times11$ paper that was originally formatted for A4 paper, Word can help you convert the document and still retain most, but not all, of the document's layout. Choose Tools, Options, and then click the Print tab. Place a check in the Allow A4/Letter Paper Resizing check box and choose OK. ■

Choosing Your Paper Source

You also determine the paper tray from which your printer will print using the Page Setup dialog box. If the dialog box isn't already open, choose File, Page Setup and choose the Paper Source tab (see Figure 3.21).

FIG. 3.21

You can select the paper trays your printer will use for the first page and all other pages of your document.

The choices you see in on the Paper Source tab for paper trays depend on the printer you have installed, which is logical because all printers are not created equal. For example, some printers have two paper trays called upper and lower. Other printers have special trays for envelopes. Still other printers may have a multipurpose tray that fills several different roles. The choices you see in Figure 3.21 are for an HP LaserJet 5.

 T I P Don't forget the Apply To list box. You can print part of your document from one paper tray and part from another. This is particularly useful when using letterhead for the first page of a document and second sheets for the subsequent pages. Store the letterhead in one paper tray and second sheets in another and set up your Paper Source accordingly.

Controlling Your Document's Layout

Layout is a broad term that covers a variety of features you can control in your document. Perhaps you need to vertically align your page so that the text is centered from top to bottom. Or, you may want to number the lines of your document so that proof readers can refer to line numbers in their comments. You control these settings on the Layout tab of the Page Setup dialog box.

Setting Vertical Alignment of Text on Page When you're creating a multipage document, such as a legal brief or a report, typically you want the text to align vertically at the top of the page. Suppose, however, that you're creating a short letter or a cover page for a report. You may prefer to align text vertically in the center of the page.

To align text vertically on a page, choose File, Page Setup and click the Layout tab (see Figure 3.22). Open the Vertical Alignment list box and choose Center.

FIG. 3.22
Set vertical page
alignment from the
Layout tab of the Page
Setup dialog box.

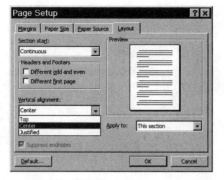

Using Line Numbering Line numbering is a handy feature when you want to give reviewers
something to which they can refer when making comments.

To turn on line numbering, choose File, Page Setup and click the Layout tab. Click the Line
Numbers button and place a check in the Add Line Numbering check box of the Line Numbers
dialog box (see Figure 3.23).

FIG. 3.23
You can number your
document's line
continuously or you can
restart at each page or
section.

Numbers appear in the left margin in Page Layout view, when you print or preview the
document (see Figure 3.24). You can control the initial number and the increments of the
numbering. Use the From Text box to control the space between the numbers and the text.

 To remove line numbering, reopen the Line Numbers dialog box and remove the check from the Add
Line Numbering check box.

Permanently Changing Default Page Setup

Throughout this section, you've seen notes and reminders about the Apply To list box that
indicated that all settings you establish in the Page Setup dialog box could be applied to all or
part of your document. In a similar way, all settings you create in the Page Setup dialog box can
become the default settings for all future documents. Suppose, for example, that you prefer 1
inch instead of 1.25 inch left and right margins for all documents. Instead of changing every
document you create, change the default settings.

Choose File, Page Setup to open the Page Setup dialog box. Then, select the settings you want
to apply to every document, and then click the Default button in the lower-left corner of the
dialog box. Word displays the dialog box you see in Figure 3.25.

Part
I
Ch
3

FIG. 3.24

Line numbering makes reviewers' lives easier.

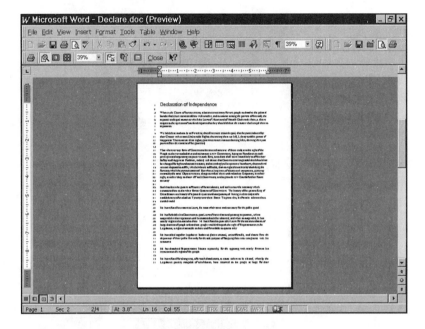

FIG. 3.25

When you choose the Default button in the Page Setup dialog box, Word displays this dialog box.

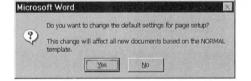

Choose <u>Y</u>es to accept your changes or <u>N</u>o to reject them. Note the following information when changing defaults:

- You are changing defaults for a specific template—the one on which the current document is based.

- When you change defaults, you change them for new documents you create based on the selected template, not for existing documents. If you want to change the settings of existing documents, you must edit each of them individually.

Using Headers and Footers

Headers and footers contain text that repeats on *every* page of your document. By default, the same header and footer appears on each page, but, by using sections, you can set up different headers and footers for different parts of your document.

Working with the Headers and Footers

Headers and footers are visible in either Page Layout view or Print Preview. When you create or edit a header or footer, Word automatically switch you to Page Layout view if necessary.

Creating a Header or Footer   To create a header or footer, choose View, Header and Footer. The insertion point appears in the Header pane on the first page of your document, and you see the Header and Footer toolbar (see Figure 3.26).

FIG. 3.26

While you work with a header or footer, your document appears gray in the background.

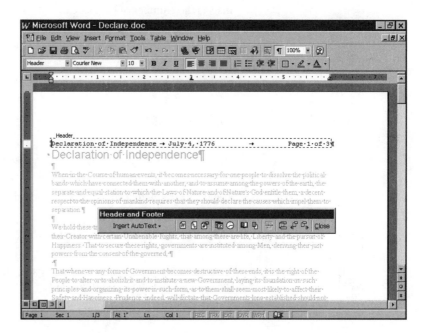

The header or footer pane contains two predefined tabs: a center tab and a right tab. Text you type at the left margin is aligned, of course, with the left margin of the header or footer pane. If you press tab and type, the text you type appears centered between the left and right margins. Similarly, if you press tab again and type, text you type aligns with the right margin. By default, the header and footer you create appear on every page of your document and contain the same information because headers and footers are linked. Later in this chapter, you'll learn how to vary the headers and footers throughout your document.

The buttons on the Header and Footer toolbar help you create headers and footers (see Table 3.3). The six tools at the left edge of the toolbar help you insert commonly used header and footer text. The four tools to the left of the Close button help you navigate between headers and footers in your document. For example, if you are viewing the header pane and you click the Switch Between Header and Footer button, you'll view the footer pane. The Same as Previous, Show Previous, and Show Next buttons become useful when you create different headers and footers for various portions of your document.

Part

I

Ch

3

Table 3.3   Header and Footer Toolbar

Button	Function
Insert AutoText ▾	Pop-up menu provides AutoText entries you can insert.
[#]	Inserts a page number field.
[+]	Inserts the Number of Pages field.
[#]	Opens the Page Number Format dialog box.
[date]	Inserts a date field.
[clock]	Inserts a time field.
[book]	Opens the Page Setup dialog box to the layout tab.
[doc]	Toggles between displaying (in gray) or hiding the text of your document.
[link]	Links and unlinks headers and footers.
[switch]	If the insertion point is in the Header pane, clicking switches to the Footer pane and vice versa.
[prev]	Jumps to the previous section's header or footer.
[next]	Jumps to the next section's header or footer.
Close	Closes the Header/Footer pane.

 TIP After you have created a header or footer, you can edit it by reopening the Header or Footer pane. Either use the menus or double-click a header/footer in Page Layout view.

Shortcuts for Updating Headers and Footers   Much of the text you insert using the Header and Footer toolbar is in the form of fields. Fields are a very powerful feature in Word that you can use to automate your work. In particular, fields store information that can change as you work on your document. For example, if you open the Insert AutoText pop-up menu (see Figure 3.27), you'll see that most of the AutoText entries refer to information that will change as you edit the document. You can easily update field information as conditions in your document change either by issuing a command or by printing your document.

▶ **See** "Automating Your Documents with Field Codes," **p. 695**

FIG. 3.27

Many of the AutoText entries you can place in a header will update automatically as information in your document changes.

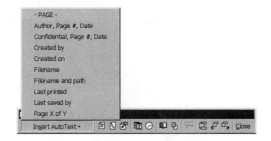

 TIP Word aligns the three-part AutoText entries that are separated by commas using the built-in tab stops. For example, if you choose Author, Page #, and Date, Word displays the author's name at the left edge of the pane, the page number centered in the pane, and the date at the right edge of the pane.

In addition to the AutoText entries, other buttons on the Header and Footer toolbar insert fields. For example, the Date button inserts a date field. If you include this field in your header or footer and reopen your document tomorrow, Word automatically updates the date to the current date when you print the document or update all the fields in your document. Similarly, the Time button inserts a time field that updates whenever you update fields or print your document. If you include the total number of pages in your document by clicking the Insert Number of Pages button, Word updates that number as you add pages to your document.

 TIP You can add the date or time anywhere in the body of your document. Choose Insert, Date and Time. In fact, you can add most of the fields you see on the Header and Footer toolbar to any portion of your document using the Insert, Field command.

Creating Different Headers and Footers in the Same Document

By default, headers and footers that you create are the same on each page of your document. If you create sections in your document, however, you can create a variety of different headers and footers in your document. Specifically, for each section you can create:

- A different header and footer for each section.
- One header and footer for even pages and another header and footer for odd pages.
- One header for the first page and another for subsequent pages.

Initially, when you create a header or footer, it is linked throughout your document; that's how Word knows to use the same header and the same footer on each page of your document. If you divide your document into sections, however, you can create different headers or footers in each section by unlinking the headers and footers for each section.

Creating Different Headers and Footers for Each Section If you divide your document into sections, you can create different headers and footers for each section. In the following steps, you'll learn how to create a different header for Section 2 of a document. To create a different footer, substitute footer for header throughout these steps:

1. Choose View, Header and Footer. When the Header pane appears, you'll see that it also contains a section designation.

2. Use the Show Next button to navigate to the section for which you want a different header. The header pane for the next section appears, and the Same as Previous button on the Header and Footer toolbar becomes available (see Figure 3.28).

FIG. 3.28

When you view the header for any section except the first section, you see the section number in the Header pane.

Section number

Same as Previous button

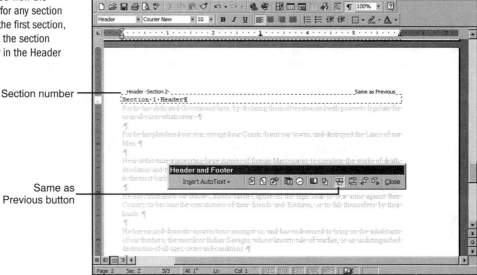

3. Click the Same as Previous button.
4. Change the header text for the second section.
5. Click the Close button.

Check your document in Print Preview. On the pages in Section 1, you'll find one header, but on the pages in Section 2, you'll find a different header.

N O T E If you later decide that you want the same header for both sections, redisplay the Header pane and use the Show Next button to display the header for Section 2. Click the Same as Previous button. Word displays a message asking if you want to delete this header and connect to the header/footer in the previous section. Choose Yes. ■

Creating Separate Headers for Odd and Even Pages To create separate headers or footers for odd and even pages, you use the Page Setup dialog box. Again, we'll give you the steps to create different headers for odd and even pages; substitute footer for header to create different footers. Follow these steps:

1. Choose View, Header and Footer. When the Header pane appears, you'll see that it also contains a section designation.
2. Use the Show Next button to navigate to the section for which you want different headers for odd and even pages. The header pane for the next section appears.
3. Click the Page Setup button. The Page Setup dialog box appears.
4. Place a check in the Different Odd and Even check box (see Figure 3.29).

FIG. 3.29
Using this dialog box, you can set different headers for odd and even pages in a section.

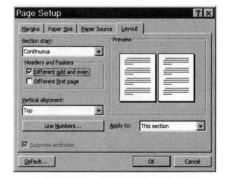

Part
I

Ch
3

5. Choose OK. Word redisplays your document and the Header pane title changes to either Even Page Header - Section X or Odd Page Header - Section X.

Type the text you want to appear in the Even Header pane and then click the Show Next and Show Previous buttons to find the Odd Header pane and complete it.

Creating a Different Header for the First Page You also use the Page Setup dialog box to create a different header or footer for page one. Using a different header for page one is a perfect way to place no header on page one but a header on subsequent pages. You follow the same steps to create a different first page header or footer as you did to create different odd and even page headers and footers. The only difference occurs in Step 4 of the previous example; place a check in the Different First Page check box (see Figure 3.30).

TROUBLESHOOTING

I created a separate first page header but I'm only getting a separate first page header in the first section. I want different first page headers for each section. How do I do that? You must establish a separate first page header for each section. Place the insertion point in each section, open the Page Setup dialog box, and place a check in the Different First Page check box.

I've decided I no longer want a header or a footer in my document. How do I get rid of it? Delete the header and footer text.

FIG. 3.30

In addition to having different odd and even page headers, you also can make the header on the first page of any section different from the other pages.

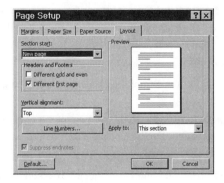

Using Bullets and Numbered Lists

Bullets and numbered lists provide an excellent way to segregate, list, and organize information for a reader. You can control the appearance, or *format*, of a bulleted or numbered list. The bullet or numbering format you used last becomes the default format; that is, the next time you create a bulleted or numbered list, Word uses the same format you used the last time you created a bulleted or numbered list. As you'll learn in this section, you can easily change the default bullet or numbering format by choosing one of seven default bullet formats and or one of seven default numbering formats. You can modify any of these to create your own formats.

Quick and Easy Bullets

 Using the Formatting toolbar, you can quickly create a bulleted list. Place the insertion point in the paragraph to which you want to add bullets and click the Bullets button on the Formatting toolbar. Word inserts a bullet and automatically indents text so that, as word wrap takes over, your text aligns itself correctly. Press Enter to start a new paragraph preceded by a bullet; to stop placing bullets before paragraphs, click the Bullets button when the insertion point appears in the first paragraph you don't want preceded by a bullet. Or, press Enter twice or press Backspace when the insertion point appears at the beginning of a bulleted paragraph.

 You can type an asterisk at the beginning of the paragraph to which you want to add a bullet. Follow the asterisk with a space and type. When you press Enter, Word converts the asterisk to a bullet character and adds a bullet character to the next paragraph.

Choosing One of Word's Standard Bullets

If you don't like the bullet you get when using the Formatting toolbar, you can open the Bullets and Numbering dialog box and select one of the seven standard bullet characters available in Word. Choose Format, Bullets and Numbering or right-click and choose Bullets and Numbering. The Bullets and Numbering dialog box appears (see Figure 3.31).

FIG. 3.31
Select one of these seven standard bullet characters.

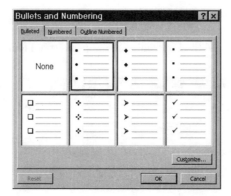

The bullet character you choose becomes the default and appears if you add bullets to a paragraph using the Bullets button on the Formatting toolbar. The bullet character you choose remains the Bullets button default until you choose a different character, even if you close Word and reopen it.

Customizing Your Bullet

Again, using the Bullets and Numbering dialog box, you can customize your bullet by changing the font and character used to produce the bullet. You can also control the way the bullet and text indent.

N O T E If you hit on a bullet format that you particularly like, you may want to make it available all the time. Open the template you use most often and modify the List Bullet style, using your favorite bullet format. All new documents you created based on this template will contain the updated List Bullet style, which you can apply to paragraphs you want preceded by bullets. ■

Changing a Bullet's Font To change the font used to produce a bullet, reopen the Bullets and Numbering dialog box (choose Format, Bullets and Numbering) and select one of the seven standard bullets. Then, click the Customize button (refer to Figure 3.31). The Customize Bulleted List dialog box appears (see Figure 3.32).

FIG. 3.32
Use this dialog box to customize bullets.

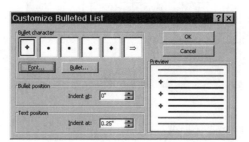

Part
I

Ch
3

The bullet character you select in the Bullets and Numbering dialog box appears selected in the Customize Bulleted List box, but you can, if you want, select one of the other bullet shapes. Then, click the Font button, and the Font dialog box appears (see Figure 3.33).

FIG. 3.33
Select a font for the bullet using this dialog box.

As you select fonts, the Preview box displays the shape of your bullet in the font you selected. When you're satisfied with your selection, click OK to close the Font dialog box; click OK again to close the Customize Bulleted List dialog box, and click OK again to close the Bullets and Numbering dialog box.

Changing a Bullet Character You change the character used for a bullet in a similar way to changing the font set used for a bullet. Open the Bullets and Numbering dialog box, highlight a bullet, and click the Customize button to display the Customize Bulleted List dialog box (refer to Figure 3.32). Click the Bullet button to display the Symbol dialog box (see Figure 3.34).

FIG. 3.34
Select a character for the bullet from the Symbol dialog box.

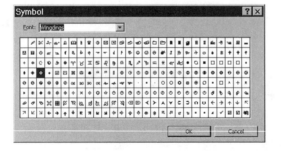

 You can change the font in the Symbol dialog box to see characters available in other fonts. Just open the Font list box and choose the font you want.

In the Symbol dialog box, select a character for the bullet and click OK. Word redisplays the Customize Bulleted List dialog box. Click OK to close the Customize Bulleted List dialog box, and click OK again to close the Bullets and Numbering dialog box.

Controlling Bullet Indentation and Text Position   By default, Word places the bullet character at the left margin and indents text .25" from the bullet character. You can change these settings using the Customize Bulleted List dialog box. Open the Bullets and Numbering dialog box (Format, Bullets and Numbering) and choose a bullet. Then, click Customize. The Customize Bulleted List dialog box appears (see Figure 3.35).

FIG. 3.35
Use the Bullet position and the Text position boxes to control the alignment of bullets and text.

Spinner box arrows

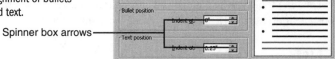

If you use the spinner box arrows to make changes, you can watch the effects of a change in the Preview box. When you finish, choose OK until all dialog boxes close.

Quick and Easy Numbered Lists

Numbered lists work a lot like bulleted lists, so you'll notice many similarities. Using the Formatting toolbar, you can quickly create a numbered list. Place the insertion point in the paragraph to which you want to add a number and click the Numbering button on the Formatting toolbar. Word inserts a number and automatically indents text so that, as word wrap takes over, your text aligns itself correctly. Press Enter to start a new paragraph preceded by a number; to stop numbering paragraphs, click the Numbering button when the insertion point appears in the first paragraph you don't want numbered. Or, press Enter twice or press Backspace when the insertion point appears at the beginning of a numbered paragraph.

As an alternative, you can type the first number in the list followed by a space (use the format you want for the number, for example, 1) or 1.) and begin typing. Each time you press Enter, Word automatically numbers the next paragraph sequentially.

Choosing a Standard Numbered List

If you don't like the appearance of the number you get when using the Formatting toolbar, you can open the Bullets and Numbering dialog box and select one of the seven standard number patterns available in Word. Choose Format, Bullets and Numbering or right-click and choose Bullets and Numbering. The Bullets and Numbering dialog box appears (see Figure 3.36).

Part
I

Ch
3

FIG. 3.36
Select one of these
seven standard
numbering patterns.

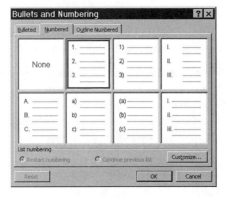

The number pattern you choose becomes the default pattern and Word uses it if you click the Numbering button on the Formatting toolbar. The pattern you choose remains the Numbering button default until you choose a different pattern, even if you close Word and reopen it.

Customizing Numbered Lists

Again, using the Bullets and Numbering dialog box, you can customize your numbered list by changing the font used to produce the number, the style of the list, the starting number, and you can control the way the numbers and text indent and align.

> **N O T E** If you discover a number format that you particularly like, you can make it available all the time. Open the template you use most often and modify the List Number style, using your favorite number format. All new documents you created based on this template will contain the updated List Number style, which you can apply to paragraphs you want preceded by numbers. ■

Changing a Numbered List's Font   To change the font used to produce a number, reopen the Bullets and Numbering dialog box and select one of the seven standard number patterns. Then, click the Customize button (refer to Figure 3.36). The Customize Numbered List dialog box appears (see Figure 3.37).

FIG. 3.37
Use this dialog box to
customize numbers.

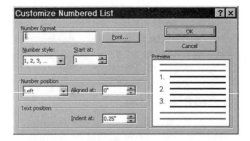

The number character you selected in the Bullets and Numbering dialog box appears selected in the Customize Numbered List box. Click the Font button, and the Font dialog box appears (see Figure 3.38).

As you select fonts, the Preview box displays your number in the font you selected. When you're satisfied with your selection, click OK to close the Font dialog box; click OK again to close the Customize Numbered List dialog box, and click OK again to close the Bullets and Numbering dialog box.

FIG. 3.38
Select a font for the number using this dialog box.

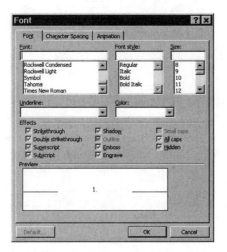

Changing Number Style Using the Number Style boxes in the Customize Numbered List dialog box, you can choose different numbering characters (see Figure 3.39), and you can choose the starting number for your list. Open the Bullets and Numbering dialog box (Format, Bullets and Numbering), click the Numbered tab, and choose a number. Then, click Customize. The Customize Bulleted List dialog box appears. Any changes you make appear in the Preview box.

FIG. 3.39
Choose a Number style and starting number using these controls.
Number Style ——
Starting Number ——

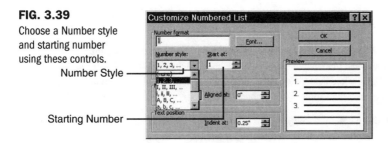

Changing Number Position and Alignment By default, Word places the number at the left margin and indents text .25" from the number. You can change these settings using the Customize Numbered List dialog box. Open the Bullets and Numbering dialog box (Format, Bullets and Numbering), click the Numbered tab, and choose a number format. Then, click Customize. The Customize Bulleted List dialog box appears (see Figure 3.40).

If you use the spinner box arrows to make changes, you can watch the effects of a change in the Preview box. When you finish, choose OK until all dialog boxes close.

FIG. 3.40
Use the Number
position and the Text
position boxes to con-
trol the alignment of
numbers and text.

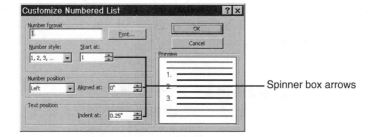

Spinner box arrows

Clearing Bullets and Numbered Lists

Remember, you can stop adding numbers or bullets to paragraphs at any time by pressing
Enter twice, pressing Enter once and then Backspace, or by placing the insertion point in the
paragraph you don't want preceded by a bullet or number and clicking the Bullets or Numbering tool, as appropriate.

TIP You can convert a bulleted list to a numbered list by selecting the bulleted list and clicking the
Numbering button. Use the same technique to convert a numbered list to a bulleted list.

But suppose you've been changing bullet and numbering formats so that, when you open the
Bullets and Numbering dialog box, you don't see the format you want anymore—and you know
it was there when you first started using Word. You can reset your numbering formats to
reinstate Word's defaults. In the Bullets and Numbering dialog box, click the Bulleted or Numbered tab, as appropriate. Then, click a format. If the Reset button is available, you have customized the selected format. Clicking the Reset button gives you the option to restore Word's
original format; you'll see a dialog box asking if you want to restore.

TROUBLESHOOTING

I can't select a bullet or number in my bulleted and numbered lists. What am I doing wrong?
Nothing. Word doesn't let you select the bullet or number character. To change its format, use the
Bullets and Numbering dialog box. To delete the character, place the insertion point in the paragraph
and click the appropriate toolbar button—Bullets or Numbering.

My bullet characters look like clock faces. Why? You're using the Wingdings font set for bullet
characters. Try selecting a different character within the Wingdings font or try using the Symbol font.

How do I add numbers or bullets to paragraphs I've already typed? Select the paragraphs and click
the appropriate button on the Formatting toolbar.

How do I skip numbering a paragraph? Word adds numbers to every selected paragraph or every line
ending with a paragraph mark. To avoid numbering a line, try using a line break (Shift+Enter) instead of
a paragraph break (Enter) to start a new line.

I want to start with 1 and Word wants to continue with the last number it used in the last numbered list. How do I get Word to start numbering over again? Place the insertion point in the first paragraph of the new list, right-click, and choose Bullets and Numbering. In the Bullets and Numbering dialog box, choose the Restart Numbering option button (below the number formats).

How can I insert additional paragraphs between two numbered lists but have the second list start numbering where the first list finished? Place the insertion point in the first paragraph of the new list, right-click, and choose Bullets and Numbering. In the Bullets and Numbering dialog box, choose the Continue Previous List option button (below the number formats).

Using Borders and Shading

Borders and shading add visual interest to your document. In Word you can place a border around a table, any selected text, a word, a paragraph, or a page; similarly, you can add shading to a table, selected text, a word, or a paragraph.

Quick and Easy Borders

Using the Formatting toolbar, you can quickly place a border around any selected text using the Borders button on the Formatting toolbar. This button actually has a list box attached to it; if you click the list box arrow, you'll see the border styles available (see Figure 3.41). After you choose a border style, that style becomes the default for the button; you can simply click the button to apply that border style. To change the style, reopen the list box attached to the button and choose another style. To remove the border, make sure the bordered text is selected; then, click the Borders button list box and select No Border.

FIG. 3.41
You can choose a border style by opening the list box attached to the Borders button.

No Borders

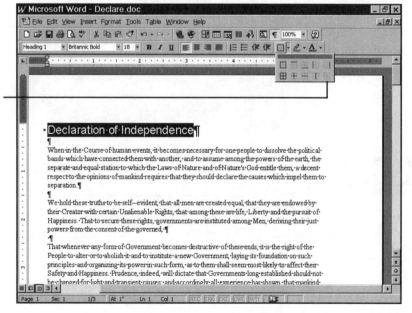

You also can access the Borders button from the Tables and Borders toolbar, which is part of Word 97's new Draw a Table feature. Click the Tables and Borders button to display the toolbar. The Tables and Borders toolbar also contains the Borders button (see Figure 3.42).

FIG. 3.42
To easily apply borders to tables, use the Borders button on the Tables and Borders toolbar.

Customizing Borders

The default border style and effect is quite plain—a thin, solid line. Using the Borders and Shading dialog box, you can add special effects to borders by choosing a border setting such as a shadow or a three-dimensional appearance, and you can change the line style, color, and width of the border.

Choose Format, Borders and Shading to display the Borders and Shading dialog box. From the Borders tab (see Figure 3.43), choose a border setting. Also select a border line style, a border line color, and a border line width. Watch the Preview box to see the effects of your choices.

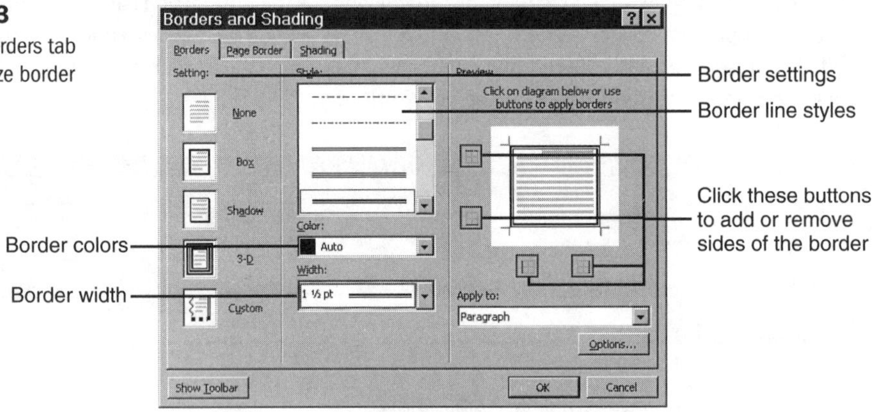

FIG. 3.43
Use the Borders tab to customize border settings.

 TIP The Preview box is interactive; click any of the buttons around it to add or remove that portion of the border.

To remove all custom border settings, choose None on the Borders tab of the Borders and Shading dialog box.

Creating Page Borders

Page borders are very effective for report title pages. You can easily add a border around a page; use the Page Border tab of the Borders and Shading dialog box (choose Format, Borders and Shading, and click the Page Border tab). You have control over the same settings as you had for selected text or paragraph borders (see Figure 3.44).

FIG. 3.44

Add a page border to every page of your document or selected pages.

Click here to add page border art

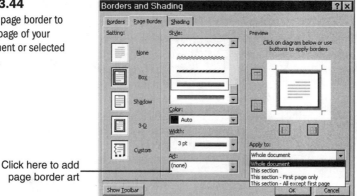

If you want to get fancy, try using page border art (see Figure 3.45). Page border art appear in color on-screen in Print Preview and Page Layout view; when you print, the border art appears in color on a color printer and in shades of gray on a black-and-white printer.

FIG. 3.45

Page Border Art can add a whole new dimension to your page.

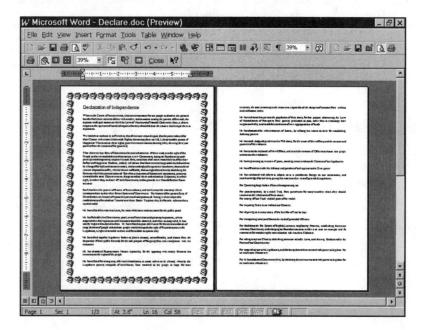

Part
I

Ch
3

To remove a page border, choose <u>N</u>one on the <u>P</u>age Border tab of the Borders and Shading dialog box.

Working with Shading

Borders surround your text; shading covers your text and acts as a background fill. You can add shading to your document from the <u>S</u>hading tab of the Borders and Shading dialog box. And, while you can't tell from Figure 3.46, you can add shading in color or in shades of gray.

FIG. 3.46

If you select text before opening the Borders and Shading dialog box, you'll be able to choose to apply shading to the current paragraph or the selected text.

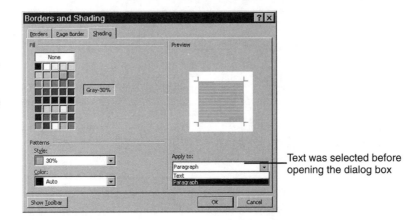

Text was selected before opening the dialog box

 T I P   Exercise care when you choose a shading color, particularly for printed materials. Too much contrast can inhibit the reader's ability to see the text.

In addition to applying a fill color from the palette at the top of the dialog box, you can apply a shading pattern, which consists of a style and color. Shading patterns on text can make your text difficult to read, so add patterns with care.

From Here...

In this chapter, you learned about the more powerful day-to-day productivity tools you'll use in Word: the Find, Replace and Go To commands, page setup commands, headers and footers, bullets and numbered lists, and borders and shading.

■ Chapter 5, "Styles: The Foundation of Automated Documents," provides information on a powerful way to make formatting consistent and easy.

■ Chapter 14, "Outlining: The Best Way to Organize a Document," helps you learn to use Word's outline feature, including working with outline numbers.

- Chapter 18, "Footnotes, Bookmarks, Cross-References, and Hyperlinks," teaches you to use bookmarks, one of Word's more powerful features for storing and reusing information.

- Chapter 25, "Automating Your Documents with Field Codes," shows you how to include information that automatically updates itself, such as dates and page counts.

Building Slicker Documents Faster

CHAPTER 4

Making the Most of Word's Proofing Tools

by Elaine Marmel

Proofing tools can help you improve the quality of your writing, but proofing isn't limited to checking your spelling. This chapter also will cover some topics related to proofing. ■

Word Count

Use this feature to determine the number of words in your document.

Spelling Checker

In addition to using the Spelling Checker to correct spelling mistakes and typographical errors, make the Spelling Checker work for you by using custom dictionaries.

Grammar Checker

The Grammar Checker's new engine should make the Grammar Checker easier to use and more accurate.

Readability Statistics

Learn how to display and understand your document's Readability Statistics.

Thesaurus

The Thesaurus helps you save time when trying to find that special word that's on the tip of your tongue.

Hyphenation

In addition to appearing in combination words such as on-the-job training, hyphenation helps you control the appearance of your document by splitting words.

Counting the Words in Your Document

Sometimes, you need to know how many words are contained in the current document. Using the Word Count feature, you can count more than words, as you can see from the dialog box in Figure 4.1. Choose Tools, Word Count to display this dialog box.

FIG. 4.1

Use this dialog box to count pages, words, paragraphs, lines, and characters in your documents.

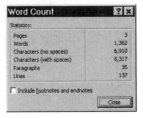

Using Automatic Spelling and Grammar Checking

Check the spelling and grammar in your document as you type. Misspelled or mistyped words appear with a wavy red underline. Questionable grammar appears with a wavy green underline. Choose Tools, Options, Spelling & Grammar to display the dialog box shown in Figure 4.2.

FIG. 4.2

Set spelling and grammar checking options in this dialog box.

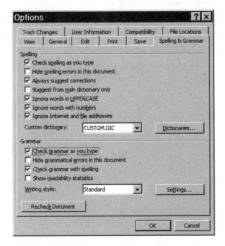

Place a check in the Check Spelling as You Type check box and in the Check Grammar as You Type check box. Also, remove the checks from the Hide Spelling Errors in this Document and Hide Grammatical Errors in this Document check boxes.

 T I P   Automatic Spelling and Grammar Checking may turn themselves off in large documents.

If you see a red or green wavy underlined word or phrase, you can correct the error by right-clicking the word or phrase. A shortcut menu containing suggestions will appear. Occasionally, the shortcut menu will not contain suggestions—for example, if Word suspects that a sentence is actually only a fragment, it offers no suggestions. However, the shortcut menu contains two other helpful commands: one command adds a misspelled word to the dictionary, and the other command opens the Spelling and Grammar dialog box, which you'll learn about in the following sections of this chapter.

 To quickly find the next spelling or grammar problem, double-click the Spelling and Grammar Status icon on the status bar.

Checking Grammar and Spelling in Your Document

Word flags spelling mistakes based on combinations of letters that Word doesn't recognize. The Word 97 dictionary contains more information than previous versions. For example, Microsoft included the names of companies from the Fortune 1000, countries, and U.S. cities with populations of at least 30,000 people. And, the Spelling Checker no longer flags words in uppercase letters, words containing numbers, URLs, UNCs (\\server\sharename), e-mail addresses, registered user names, and organization information.

 UNC stands for *Universal Naming Convention*. In a network environment, a UNC allows you to open a file on a network drive even if you don't have a connection to the network server.

Word lets you check the spelling of your entire document or any part of it, including just a single word. If you don't want to check spelling in your entire document, select the text you want to check. If you want to check only a single word, select that word. Then, press F7 or choose Tools, Spelling and Grammar.

N O T E For spelling and grammar checking purposes, Word behaves the same way it does when you choose the Find and Replace commands. Word starts checking at the location of the insertion point. If you selected text, Word proceeds to the end of a selection and asks if you want to continue checking outside the selection. If you didn't select text and you didn't place the insertion point at the top of the document, Word proceeds to the end of your document and asks if you want to continue checking from the top of the document. ▪

Word displays both spelling and grammar problems in the Spelling and Grammar dialog box (see Figure 4.3); spelling problems appear in red, and grammar problems appear in green.

Choose a suggestion from the list and then choose Change or Change All, or choose Ignore or Ignore All. To add a word to the default custom dictionary, choose Add. To set Spelling and Grammar Checker options, click the Options button. Word displays the dialog box you saw in Figure 4.2. To create an AutoCorrect entry for the flagged error, click the AutoCorrect button. The AutoCorrect dialog box will appear.

Part
II

Ch
4

FIG. 4.3

The Spelling and Grammar dialog box highlights potential problems in your document.

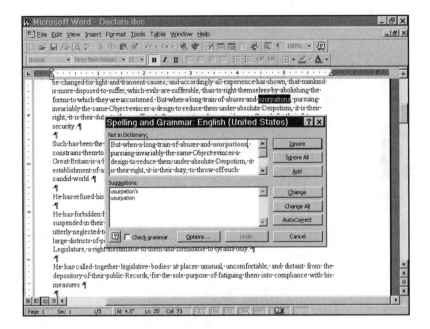

You can add words to any custom dictionary by choosing that custom dictionary, as you'll learn later in this chapter.

After you make a decision about a flagged item, Word searches for the next item. When Word finds no more spelling or grammar problems, you'll see a dialog box telling you that the process is complete.

Custom Dictionaries for Custom Needs

Custom dictionaries let you add power to Word's Spelling Checker. When you run the Spelling Checker, Word compares text in your document with character combinations found in Word's dictionary. Sometimes, however, you use words that are spelled correctly but Word doesn't recognize them. When you choose the Add button in the Spelling and Grammar dialog box, you don't add the characters to Word's dictionary; instead, you add them to a supplemental dictionary, called a *custom dictionary*.

By default, Word supplies you with one custom dictionary (CUSTOM.DIC), and, if you want, you can simply use that one custom dictionary. You also can create other custom dictionaries for special purposes. For example, you can create an exclude custom dictionary. An exclude dictionary contains character combinations that Word would ordinarily recognize as being spelled correctly, but that you want questioned during a spelling check.

Working with Custom Dictionaries

Word lets you use up to 10 custom dictionaries simultaneously. When you create a new dictionary, Word automatically activates it, making it available during any spelling and grammar check. If you decide you no longer want to use a particular custom dictionary, you can deactivate it. Word lists available dictionaries in the Custom Dictionaries dialog box (see Figure 4.4). To display this dialog box, choose Tools, Options, and click the Spelling & Grammar tab. Then, click the Dictionaries button.

FIG. 4.4
The Custom Dictionaries dialog box shows the custom dictionaries being used during a spelling and grammar check.

A custom dictionary is active as long as it appears in the list in this dialog box with a check next to it. To deactivate a dictionary, remove the check that appears next to the dictionary. If you don't want the dictionary to appear in the list, click Remove. The dictionary will no longer appear in the list, but Word will not delete the dictionary from your computer. Use the Add button to make a dictionary appear in the list.

Creating a New Custom Dictionary

You create custom dictionaries by clicking the New button in the Custom Dictionaries dialog box. The Create Custom Dictionary dialog box appears (see Figure 4.5).

FIG. 4.5
This dialog box lets you create a custom dictionary file.

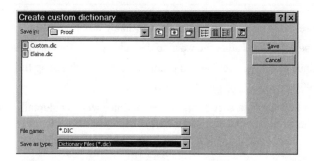

Type the name for your custom dictionary in the File Name box and click Save. At this point, Word displays the new custom dictionary in the Custom Dictionaries dialog box; it's active but empty. You can add words to it while you check spelling, or you can edit the custom dictionary to add words.

Part
II

Ch
4

Choosing a Custom Dictionary While Spell Checking Suppose, during a spelling check, that you find a word that you want to add to a custom dictionary. Follow these steps to select a custom dictionary:

 TIP Word adds new words to the currently selected custom dictionary; you only need to change the custom dictionary if you want to add the word to a different custom dictionary.

1. Make sure the word you want to add appears in the Spelling and Grammar dialog box.
2. Click the Options button. The Spelling and Grammar dialog box appears (see Figure 4.6).
3. Open the Custom Dictionary list box and select a custom dictionary.

FIG. 4.6

Select the custom dictionary to which you want to add a word.

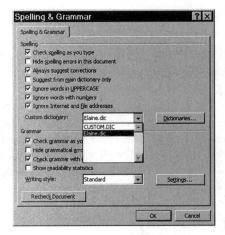

 TIP If the dictionary you want doesn't appear in the list, click the Dictionaries button and add or activate it.

4. Choose OK. The Spelling and Grammar dialog box reappears.
5. Choose Add. Word adds the word to the selected custom dictionary.
6. Continue checking spelling and grammar as usual, changing the custom dictionary as needed.

New Ways to Edit Custom Dictionaries Sometimes, you accidentally add a word to a custom dictionary that you didn't mean to add. Or, perhaps you have a lengthy list of words you want to include in a custom dictionary. You'll find it easy to edit custom dictionaries in Word 97.

1. Choose Tools, Options, and click the Spelling & Grammar tab.
2. Click Dictionaries to display the Custom Dictionaries dialog box (see Figure 4.7).

FIG. 4.7
Choose a dictionary to edit.

3. Select the dictionary you want to edit.

4. Choose Edit. Word displays the contents of the dictionary in a Word document (see Figure 4.8).

FIG. 4.8
Dictionary files look like Word documents.

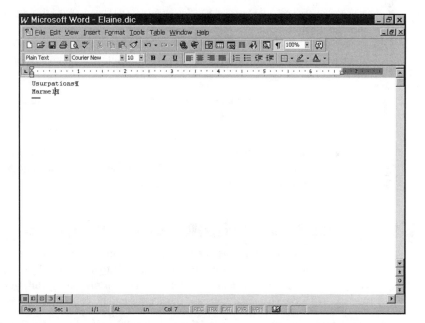

5. To edit or delete an entry, use the same techniques you would use to edit or delete any word in any document. To add a word, type it on a separate line and press Enter.

6. When you finish modifying the custom dictionary entries, click Save or choose File, Save. Then, close the document the same way you close any Word document.

N O T E When you edit a custom dictionary, Word turns off automatic spelling and grammar checking—you may even see a dialog box warning you. After you close the dictionary file, you can turn these features on again by choosing Tools, Options, clicking the Spelling & Grammar tab, and placing checks in the Check Spelling As You Type and Check Grammar As You Type check boxes. ▩

Excluding Words from a Dictionary

Suppose, for example, that you prefer canceled to cancelled—both are correct, but you prefer to use canceled all the time. Include the one you don't want to use (cancelled) in your exclude dictionary so that Word will question it when you check spelling.

N O T E If you don't want to use the Grammar Checker, you can add, to an exclude dictionary, words you commonly mistype that are actually words. For example, if you regularly leave the "a" out of seat, you type **set**. During a regular spelling check, Word will not flag "set" unless you include it in an exclude dictionary. If you include "set" in an exclude dictionary, Word will always flag "set" and you can check its context. ▩

Create an exclude dictionary the same way you would create any custom dictionary, with the following exceptions:

- ▩ Save it in the folder that contains the main dictionary—typically \Program Files\Common Files\Microsoft Shared\Proof or \Windows\Msapps\Proof.
- ▩ When you save the file, use an extension of .EXC and first name that is the same as the main dictionary's name —the U.S. English language main dictionary is called MSSP2_EN.LEX. Users of the U.S. English language main dictionary should name their exclude dictionary MSSP2_EN.EXC.

Using Word's New Grammar Checking Engine

Word flags grammar problems based on a set of grammar rules you can select and modify to suit your needs. You can use the Grammar Checker to automatically check grammar as you type, or, if you prefer, you can hide potential grammar problems while you work. In addition, you can make the Grammar Checker more powerful by controlling the way it works.

The advanced linguistic group at Microsoft developed the Grammar Checker (also known as the Natural Language Grammar Checker). The focus of the advanced linguistic group was to improve the accuracy of proofing tools and make them easier to use. The new Grammar Checker reduces proofreading time by flagging mistakes more accurately and making better suggestions to correct the mistakes.

Checking Grammar

You learned earlier in this chapter that Word flags potential grammar problems as you work by using a green wavy underline. You also learned that you can correct these errors by pressing

F7 to open the Grammar and Spelling dialog box or by right-clicking them and using the short-cut menu that appears.

 TIP To quickly find the next spelling or grammar problem, double-click the Spelling and Grammar Status icon on the status bar.

Word displays the entire sentence containing the questionable grammar in the Spelling and Grammar dialog box and flags the questionable text in green. As you make changes to your document from the Spelling and Grammar dialog box, you can undo the last grammar change you made (see Figure 4.9).

FIG. 4.9
Even if you chose to ignore a grammar problem, you can reevaluate that judgment by clicking the Undo button in the Spelling and Grammar dialog box.

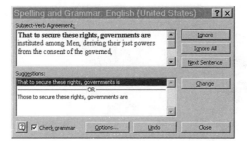

 TIP Undo works only if you open the Spelling and Grammar dialog box by pressing F7.

If you don't understand the problem Word flags, you can click the Help button in the lower-left corner of the dialog box; the Assistant will appear and provide an explanation with examples.

Disabling Grammar Checking

By default, Word checks grammar and spelling at the same time; however, you can disable one or both of the tools. To disable grammar checking, choose Tools, Options, and click the Spelling & Grammar tab. Then, remove the check from the Check Grammar As You Type check box. Alternatively, you can continue checking grammar but simply hide the wavy green underlines by placing a check in the Hide Grammatical Errors In This Document check box. If you hide grammar errors, then you can later check and correct grammatical errors by opening the Spelling and Grammar dialog box.

Strategies for Making Grammar Checking Work More Effectively

To make Word's Grammar Checker work more effectively, you can customize it by selecting a writing style, the rules of grammar you want to use, or you can choose to check grammar for punctuation errors only.

Choosing the Appropriate Writing Style   Word's Grammar Checker applies rules based on one of four predefined writing styles; alternatively, you can define your own writing style. The four predefined writing styles are:

- Casual
- Standard
- Formal
- Technical

TIP   Writing styles are associated with templates, so the template on which you base your document determines the writing style Word uses by default.

To select a writing style, choose Tools, Options, and click the Spelling & Grammar tab. Then, open the Writing Style list box and choose a suitable writing style (see Figure 4.10).

FIG. 4.10

Choose a writing style.

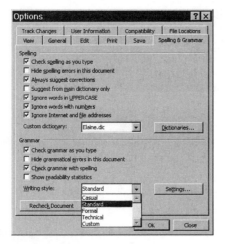

Choosing the Appropriate Rules of Grammar   You may want to create a custom grammar writing style, in which you identify the grammar rules you want Word to use when checking your document—and the grammar rules you want Word to ignore. For example, you may want to create a custom writing style that includes only punctuation rules. To create a custom writing style, follow these steps:

1. Choose Tools, Options, and click the Spelling & Grammar tab.
2. Click the Settings button next to the Writing Style list box. The Grammar Settings dialog box appears (see Figure 4.11).
3. Open the Writing Style list box and choose Custom.

TIP   For an excellent explanation of each of Word's grammar or writing style rules, use Online Help. Choose Help, Contents and Index. Choose the Index tab and type **Grammar Checking**. Under Grammar Checking, choose Options and click Display. From the Topics Found dialog box, choose Grammar and Writing Style Options.

FIG. 4.11
From this dialog box, select the grammar rules you want Word to use.

 T I P To see the grammar rules Word applies for each writing style, select each style and watch the other options in the dialog box.

4. In the Grammar and Style Options list box, remove checks from boxes representing those types of grammar you don't want Word to check.

5. In the Require box, use each list box to determine whether Word should always check, never check, or ignore commas before the last list item, punctuation with quotes, and spaces between sentences.

6. Choose OK to redisplay the Options dialog box.

7. Choose OK to save all your settings.

You can make changes to the other writing styles; if you do, they are saved to the template associated with the document. Should you later decide that you'd like to use Word's defaults, reopen the Grammar Settings dialog box, choose the writing style, and then choose Reset All.

Part
II

Ch
4

Making the Most of Word's Readability Statistics

If you want, you can have Word display statistics about your document that rate its readability. Readability statistics can help you determine if you succeeded in writing to a level suited to your audience.

Displaying Readability Statistics

To display readability statistics, choose Tools, Options, and click the Spelling & Grammar tab. Place a check in the Show Readability Statistics check box, and choose OK. Then, check spelling and grammar in your document by pressing F7 or choosing Tools, Spelling and Grammar. Allow Word to completely check your document; at the end, you'll see a dialog box similar to the one in Figure 4.12.

FIG. 4.12

A sample Readability Statistics dialog box as it appears after checking spelling and grammar in a document.

Interpreting Readability Statistics

As you can see, readability statistics provide you with the same information you get when you use the Word Count command, and you see averages. In the figure, the average paragraph didn't have many words, but the average sentence was fairly long.

At the bottom of the Readability Statistics dialog box, you see readability scores that attempt to measure how easily a reader will understand your document. Each of these scores is based on the average number of syllables per word and the average number of words per sentence.

A percentage for passive sentences appears in this section because text written in the passive voice is more difficult to understand than text written in the active voice.

The Flesch Reading Ease score uses a 100-point scale to rate reading ease. Higher scores imply easier reading; a score between 60-70 would be a good reading-ease score.

The Flesch-Kincaid Grade Level score uses U.S. grade-school levels to rate the understandability of your document. For example, a score of 6 means a sixth grader can understand the document. To ensure understanding without insulting your audience, strive for a score of 7 or 8.

Using the Word Thesaurus

The Thesaurus is another valuable proofing tool that comes with Word. With it, you can easily find synonyms (words with similar meanings) and antonyms (words with opposite meanings); if the original word you look up in the Thesaurus doesn't show you a synonym or antonym you like, you can easily look up synonyms and antonyms for any of the suggested words.

 T I P   If you purchased a set of foreign language proofing tools, the Thesaurus shows you synonyms and antonyms for text formatted in the foreign language. Alki Software also has an expanded Thesaurus available. You'll learn more about Alki Software when you read about foreign language tools later in this chapter.

You use the Thesaurus dialog box to search for synonyms and antonyms; you can quickly open the Thesaurus dialog box by placing the insertion point anywhere in the word for which you want a synonym or antonym and pressing Shift+F7. Alternatively, you can choose Tools, Language, Thesaurus to display the Thesaurus dialog box (see Figure 4.13).

FIG. 4.13
Use this dialog box to find synonyms and antonyms for the selected word.

TIP If you don't see the Thesaurus command, you need to rerun Setup to install the Thesaurus.

After you've opened the Thesaurus dialog box, you can use it to follow a trail of synonyms or to locate antonyms. To follow a trail of synonyms, select the word from the Replace with Synonym list and click the Look Up button. Word looks up the word you selected and displays its synonyms. If you follow a trail of synonyms and decide you don't like any of the choices you see, click the Previous button to return to the original word you looked up. If Antonyms appears in the Meanings list, you can click it to see antonyms for the word you looked up.

Part
II

Ch
4

TIP If you see and choose Related Words in the Meanings list box, Word displays other word forms for the word you looked up.

If you find a word you like, click the Replace button to change the word you looked up in your document to the word you found.

Working with Hyphenation

If you justify text between margins, hyphenating can help you reduce the amount of white space between words. If you justify text at the left margin, hyphenating helps reduce the raggedness of the right margin. Hyphenation can be particularly effective in maintaining even line lengths in narrow columns.

You can let Word hyphenate your document automatically, or you can use manual hyphenation to control where hyphens appear in words. In addition, you can use nonbreaking hyphens or optional hyphens to control where hyphenated words or phrases break.

To use any of these features, make sure you have installed Word's Hyphenation tool—you'll know you didn't install the tool if the Hyphenation command does not appear on the Tools, Language menu.

TIP Wait until you have finished writing and editing to hyphenate your document because adding and deleting text affects the way lines break.

Automatically Hyphenating Words in Your Document

You can let Word automatically hyphenate your document. Follow these steps:

1. Choose Tools, Language, Hyphenation. The Hyphenation dialog box appears (see Figure 4.14).

FIG. 4.14

Use this dialog box
to set and control
hyphenation.

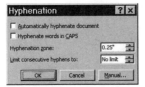

2. Place a check in the Automatically Hyphenate Document check box.

3. (Optional) Place a check in the Hyphenate Words in CAPS check box.

4. Set the Hyphenation Zone—the larger the zone, the fewer hyphens Word will insert, but the more ragged your right margin will appear.

5. Use the Limit Consecutive Hyphens To spinner box to set the number of consecutive lines that Word can hyphenate.

6. Choose OK.

Word will place hyphens throughout your document. If you change your mind and want to remove the hyphenation, repeat these steps and remove the check from the Automatically Hyphenate Document check box.

 To remove hyphenation from a part of your document, select that text, right-click, and choose Paragraph. Choose the Line and Page Breaks tab and place a check in the Don't Hyphenate check box.

Manual Hyphenation: Taking Line-by-Line Control

You can control Word's placement of hyphens by manually hyphenating your document. Re-open the Hyphenation dialog box (choose Tools, Language, Hyphenation) and remove the check from the Automatically Hyphenate Document check box. Then, click the Manual button. Word switches to Page Layout view (if necessary) and displays a dialog box similar to the one in Figure 4.15.

If you like the location within the word that Word has chosen, choose Yes. If you want to move the hyphen, use the left- and right-arrow keys and then choose Yes. If you don't want to hyphenate the word, choose No. If you hyphenate the word, you see an optional hyphen character in the word. If subsequent text moves the word from the end of a line, Word does not insert a hyphen; if, however, the word remains at the end of a line, Word hyphenates the word at the location of the optional hyphen.

FIG. 4.15
Use this dialog box to physically place hyphens.

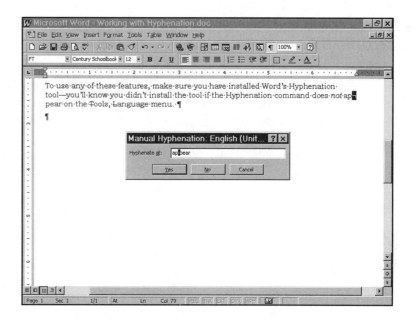

 T I P You can insert an optional hyphen at any time. Place the insertion at the location in the word where you want the optional hyphen to appear and press Ctrl+Hyphen.

In addition to manual hyphenation, you can also use nonbreaking hyphens to prevent a hyphenated word or phrase from breaking at the end of a line. For example, suppose you want all occurrences of "add-in" to appear together on a line, and you don't want Word to split the words so that "add" appears at the end of a line and "in" appears at the beginning of the next line. Use a nonbreaking hyphen between the words—just press Ctrl+Shift+Hyphen to insert the hyphen. Word will always keep the phrase together on a line, forcing a new line if the phrase appears at the end of a line and won't fit.

Using Special Terminology or Foreign Language Proofing Tools

Certain professions have special language requirements because they rely heavily on technical terminology. Custom dictionaries containing special terms, such as business, legal, or medical dictionaries, help you check spelling in documents created for these professions. Foreign language proofing tools enable you to check the spelling of documents created in foreign languages and also provide you with the foreign language's Grammar Checker and Thesaurus.

 T I P You can order *supplementaldictionaries* either for foreign languages or for technical terminology from Alki Software Corporation at 800-669-9673 in the U.S. or 206-286-2600 outside the U.S. Or, visit their Web site at **www.alki.com**.

Part

II

Ch

4

These extra proofing tools work with Word, Excel, PowerPoint, or Access.

When you install foreign language proofing tools, you add dictionary, thesaurus, and grammar checker files to the same folder that contains your original, native-language proofing tools. You also add some .DLL files that enable the proofing tools to work correctly. Installing foreign language proofing tools does not change the default language you use in Word.

Word uses foreign language proofing tools whenever Word encounters text formatted in that language. You don't need to take any special action to use foreign language proofing tools other than to format text in the foreign language. To specify the language of selected text, select the text and choose Tools, Language, Set Language.

 If you are working in a document that contains text in a foreign language and you *don't* own the foreign language's proofing tools, format that text as No Proofing. That way, your default language proofing tools will ignore the selected text, but you can proof the rest of the document.

N O T E When you add Alki's Comprehensive Spelling, nothing changes other than the spell-checking power. That is, you can still press F7 to start checking spelling, and the dialog box you'll see during spell checking is the one you've seen in this chapter. The Comprehensive Spelling package greatly expands the dictionary. It can verify more than 212,000 words that consist of 75,000 technical terms (medical, legal, and business), and 137,000 words come with the standard dictionary. The Comprehensive Spelling package also includes an expanded hyphenation dictionary.

Similarly, the Comprehensive Thesaurus adds power, but the way you work doesn't change. The Thesaurus dialog box looks the same and works the same, but the Comprehensive Thesaurus adds almost 150,000 terms to Word's built-in thesaurus.

TROUBLESHOOTING

Suppose I let Word check my entire document and later add text. When I rerun the Spelling and Grammar Checkers, will Word ask me about all the same words it flagged previously? By default, no, Word will not ask you about the same words it flagged previously. If you want Word to catch previously caught errors, reopen the Spelling and Grammar Options dialog box (either choose Tools, Options and click the Spelling and Grammar tab or click the Options button inside the Spelling and Grammar dialog box) and click the Recheck Document button. Word will ask if you really want to recheck everything you've already checked; choose Yes or No.

My document is written in two languages and I don't have a dictionary for one of the languages. How can I use my proofing tools on the portion of the document written in my native language? You should format the portion for which you don't have a dictionary as No Proofing so that the Spelling and Grammar Checkers will skip that part. Choose Tools, Language, Set Language and then choose No Proofing.

I tried to hyphenate my document and nothing happens. Why? Either no hyphenation is required or you may have formatted your text as No Proofing. Word will not hyphenate any text formatted as No Proofing.

I've disabled Grammar Checking, but when I check spelling, Word is still checking grammar. You may have hidden grammar mistakes rather than disabled grammar checking. Or, you may have disabled Check Grammar As You Type. To completely disable Grammar Checking, choose Tools, Options, and click the Spelling & Grammar tab. Then, remove the checks from the Check Grammar As You Type and the Check Grammar With Spelling check boxes.

From Here...

From here, you can go anywhere you like in this book, because this chapter completes the coverage of Word's proofing tools.

- Chapter 5, "Styles: The Foundation of Automated Documents," provides information about a powerful way to make formatting consistent and easy.

- Chapter 6, "Templates, Wizards, and Add-Ins," explains the difference between templates and styles and provides guidelines for using templates, wizards, and add-ins to organize document production.

- Chapter 7, "Automating Your Documents: AutoCorrect, AutoFormat, AutoText, and AutoSummarize," helps you discover the power of four of Word's slickest automation features.

Part
II

Ch
4

CHAPTER 5

Styles: The Foundation of Automated Documents

by Bill Camarda

Styles are one of Word's most powerful time-savers, for five important reasons.

Styles can *dramatically* reduce the time it takes to format a document—often by 90 percent or more.

Styles can also help you make sure all your documents look consistent, with very little effort on your part.

If you export your Word document to a desktop publishing program, chances are that the program will look for Word styles to help automate *its* work.

If you need to change the way your styled document looks, you only need to change a few styles, not hundreds of manual formats.

If you use styles, you'll find it much easier to take advantage of Word's powerful automation and organization features. For example, Word can automatically build and update a table of contents based on the styles in your document. Without styles, you would have to manually apply a field to every single item you want to include in your table of contents. In addition to tables of contents, Word styles make it easier to use all these features:

- *Web Publishing* (see Chapter 9, "Using Word to Develop Web Content," to learn about saving a styled Word document as an HTML document for easy publishing on the Web).

- *Outlining* (see Chapter 14, "Outlining: The Best Way to Organize a Document," to learn how styles enable you to easily outline and reorganize your document).

- *AutoFormat* (see Chapter 7, "Automating Your Documents: AutoCorrect, AutoFormat, AutoText, and AutoSummarize," to learn how styles enable you to format your document automatically, all at once).

- *AutoSummarize* (see Chapter 7 to learn how styles can help Word build an automatic summary of any document).

- *Outline Numbering* (see Chapter 14 to learn how styles enable you to apply automatic outline numbers to your documents and have Word track them automatically).

- *Tables of Figures* (see Chapter 16, "Tables of Contents and Captions," to learn how styles enable you to build and update figure tables automatically).

- *Master Documents* (see Chapter 15, "Master Documents: Control and Share Even the Largest Documents," to learn how styles enable you to automatically divide a large document into several subdocuments for easy, team-based editing).

Styles really are the foundation of the automated document. Best of all, Word 97 makes it easier than ever to use styles. In fact, you may be able to get the styles you need *without doing anything at all*, by using Word's automatic style definition feature.

Surprisingly, many Word users never bother with styles; they've become comfortable with the easy manual formatting capabilities Word provides. Others use a few styles now and then, but don't take full advantage of Word's style feature. If you fall into either of these categories, this chapter will show you easy ways to dramatically improve your productivity.

 TIP If you simply cannot or do not want to format your document with styles, Word 97 does give you another way to get some of the automation benefits that styles provide. As covered in Chapter 14, you can specify *outline levels* for individual blocks of text, and Word will use those outline levels instead of styles.

However, it's usually more work to create outline levels than styles; outline levels don't work with as many Word features as styles; and you probably need the styles anyway for formatting reasons.

What Styles Are and How They Work

In Word, a style is a series of formats that can automatically be applied to either a paragraph or specific characters. Instead of applying formats one at a time by clicking toolbar buttons, using keyboard shortcuts, or dialog boxes, you choose a style, and Word automatically applies all the formatting for you. If you want or need to change the appearance of your entire document, all you have to do is change the styles.

Word offers two kinds of styles: paragraph styles and character styles.

Understanding Paragraph Styles

Paragraph styles control the formatting of entire paragraphs. Any manual formatting you can add to a font or paragraph can be included in a paragraph style. If you can find it in one of the following dialog boxes, you can add it to a paragraph style by choosing:

- Format, Font (Font, Character Spacing, and Animation tabs)
- Format, Paragraph (Indents and Spacing, Line and Page Breaks tabs)
- Format, Tabs (Tab stops, alignment, and leaders)
- Format, Borders and Shading (Borders and Shading tabs, but *not* Page Borders)
- Tools, Language, Set Language (Specifies the language in which text should be proofed)
- Format, Frame (text wrapping, size, and position). Note that frames have generally been replaced in Word with text boxes, although old frames are still supported. This dialog box only appears when a frame created in Word 6 or Word 95 is selected; you cannot create a new frame in Word 97.
- Format, Bullets and Numbering (Bulleted, Numbered, and Outline Numbered tabs)

Understanding Character Styles

Unlike paragraph styles, *character styles* can be built only from the text formatting options available in the Format, Font dialog box, from borders and shading, and from language formatting.

You'll probably use paragraph styles more often than character styles. Paragraph styles are easier to create, and they can do more. For certain purposes, however, character styles are indispensable. For example, there are times you might have a short block of text that must always be formatted in a specific way, such as a company name. With character styles, it's easier to make sure that this text is always formatted correctly to begin with, and remains formatted correctly as a document evolves.

Part

II

Ch

5

How Paragraph and Character Styles Interact

Character styles are superimposed on paragraph styles. When character and paragraph styles conflict, the font specified in a character style takes precedence. However, if a character style does not specify a formatting attribute and the paragraph style does, the paragraph style will be applied.

For example, imagine you have a paragraph style named Summary that specifies

12-point Times New Roman italic

Now, imagine you superimpose a character style named Smith that specifies

14-point Impact

You'll get 14-point Impact just as your character style requests, but you'll also get italic because your character style hasn't expressed a preference and your paragraph style has. On the other hand, if your paragraph and character styles both specify italic, Word assumes you want to preserve some contrast between the two styles, and format the text as not italic.

How Manual Formatting and Styles Interact

Manual formatting is superimposed on both paragraph and character styles. As in the previous example, however, Word seeks to maintain contrast. So, if you add italic formatting to a paragraph styled to use italic, Word displays nonitalic text.

 To see which formatting elements in a block of text have been created by styles and which have been created by manual formatting, press Shift+F1, and click the What's This mouse pointer on the text that interests you.

To clear all manual formatting and character styles, leaving only paragraph styles, select text and press Ctrl+spacebar.

Displaying Styles with Your Text

Sometimes you might like to view the styles in your document as you work. For example, you may have a set of corporate styles you need to follow. Viewing your styles helps you make sure you're using only the correct ones. Or, you may have styles that look similar to each other. Viewing the style names helps you tell them apart.

Word's Style Area (see Figure 5.1) lets you view style names alongside the text in your document. Style Area works only in Normal View. Follow these steps to display a Style Area:

1. Choose Tools, Options.
2. Click the View tab.
3. Specify a Style Area width greater than 0 inches. (The default setting, 0", means that Word displays no Style Area. That's why you may never have seen one.)

 Try a measurement of 0.75 inches, which is enough to display most style names without reducing the editing area too much.

Once you have a Style Area, you can resize it by following these steps:

1. Place the mouse pointer over the border of the Style Area; the pointer changes to appear as vertical bars.
2. Click and drag the border to where you want it.

FIG. 5.1
Word's Style Area, along the left side of this figure, lets you view your styles and document at the same time.

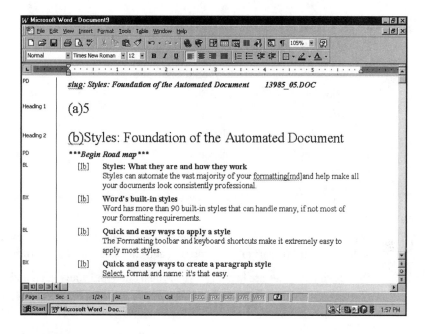

Understanding Word's Default Styles

You're using styles whether you know it or not. Word actually contains more than 90 built-in styles. When you display a new document and begin entering text, Word enters the text using the Normal style, Word's standard style for body copy. (By default, Normal style is 12-point Times New Roman, left-aligned, single-spaced, with an outline level equivalent to body text.) Similarly, whenever you use automated features such as AutoFormat, Tables of Contents, or Indexes, Word is applying built-in styles in many places to ensure overall consistency.

Part
II

Ch
5

Applying an Existing Style

Because Word contains so many built-in styles, the fastest way to add styles to your document is to use the ones that already exist. Here's the easiest way to do so:

1. Select the text you want to style.
2. Right-click the arrow in the Style box on the Formatting toolbar.
3. Choose the style you want from the list that appears.

In Word 97, the Style box doesn't just list the available styles; it shows them formatted, so you can see what they'll look like when you apply them.

Shortcuts for the Most Common Styles

Five of Word's most widely used styles also have quick keyboard shortcuts.

Style	Keyboard Shortcut
Normal	Ctrl+Shift+N
Heading 1	Alt+Ctrl+1
Heading 2	Alt+Ctrl+2
Heading 3	Alt+Ctrl+3
List	Ctrl+Shift+L

Later in this chapter, you'll learn how to associate a keyboard shortcut with any other style you use often.

Sometimes you'll want to apply a different paragraph style to a block of text. You can always do so by selecting any part of the paragraph and choosing a new style from the Style box.

Because many styles are heading styles, you'll often find yourself changing styles in order to change heading level. The most effective way to make these changes is with the tools in Outline view (see Chapter 14). If, however, you're just changing one or two headings, here's another shortcut:

1. Click the Style box or press Ctrl+Shift+S.

2. Use the arrow keys to move up or down to the style you want.

> **TIP**
>
> If you're sure of the style name you want to use, you can simply type it in the Style box. However, if you mistype, Word creates a new style formatted as your text already appears.

To minimize clutter, Word typically displays only four built-in styles in the Style box of a new document: Normal, Heading 1, Heading 2, and Heading 3. All the others included with Word are still available, however. If you want to apply a style that doesn't appear in the Style box, apply it from the Style dialog box (see Figure 5.2) as follows:

1. Choose Format, Style.

2. Select All styles from the List box.

3. Select the style you want from the Styles box.

4. Click Apply.

Applying Multiple Styles at the Same Time

Maybe you'd rather not have your train of thought interrupted by stopping to apply styles as you write. If so, you can write your document the way you normally do and then have Word's AutoFormat feature apply the styles for you, using the built-in styles it recognizes.

You'll learn more about AutoFormat in Chapter 7, but briefly, Word can recognize the following elements and assign styles to them:

FIG. 5.2

The quickest way to choose an existing style is through the Style box on the Formatting toolbar.

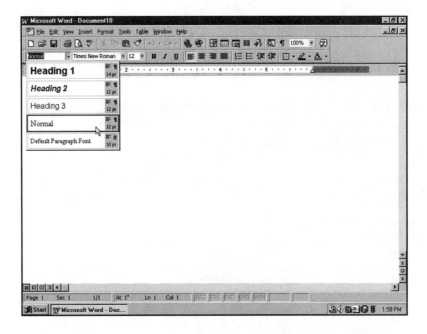

■ *Headings.* If you enter one line of text without a period, ending with a paragraph mark, Word recognizes it as a heading and applies a Heading style. If your headings are not already manually numbered or styled, Word typically uses Heading 1.

If you have already formatted some headings, Word applies the next subordinate heading style beneath your headings. That's useful to know if, for example, only the name of your chapter uses Heading 1 style. Format that one line of copy manually, and Word automatically formats all the other headings it finds as Heading 2. You'll have many fewer to correct manually.

■ *Bulleted and numbered lists.* AutoFormat can recognize some lines of text as belonging to a bulleted or numbered list, and reformat those with built-in list styles. For example, it recognizes lines that begin with an asterisk and a space as parts of a bulleted list.

■ *Body text.* AutoFormat takes the remaining paragraphs that it hasn't reformatted in any other way and formats them using Word's built-in Body Text style. Body Text style is identical to Normal style except that 6 points have been added after each paragraph to compensate for the extra paragraph mark AutoFormat automatically removes.

■ *Letter elements.* Depending on where they appear in a letter, Word can recognize salutations, addresses, and other elements, and apply corresponding built-in styles.

Here's how to use AutoFormat to apply several styles at the same time:

1. Choose Format, AutoFormat.
2. Choose Options.

Part

II

Ch

5

3. On the AutoFormat tab (see Figure 5.3), specify the types of styles you want Word to apply. (These are all in the Apply area of this tab; if you don't want Word to do anything else, clear the other check boxes.)

4. Click OK twice. Word AutoFormats the document.

FIG. 5.3

If you want Word to apply styles automatically but make no other changes to your document, check the boxes in the Apply area of the AutoFormat tab, and clear the boxes in the Replace area.

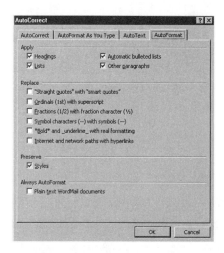

Word isn't perfect. In a long document, you'll want to double-check Word's styles, and you'll probably need to do a little tweaking. However, if your document's structure isn't too out-of-the-ordinary, using AutoFormat can save you a good deal of time.

Creating and Changing Styles

Until now, you've learned how to use the existing styles Word provides. If you do nothing more than use Word's styles, your documents will look consistent; you will spend less time formatting them, and you'll have access to all the power of Word's automation features.

However, considering that Word is—by far—the world's most popular word processor, your documents will have a tendency to look a lot like everyone else's. Moreover, you may encounter situations where there is *no* applicable built-in style. For example, Word doesn't have a built-in style for chapter summaries, or for tips, or for many other elements you'll find in this book.

For these reasons, you should know how to create new styles or change existing ones. Fortunately, Word makes this extremely easy to do.

Quick and Easy Paragraph Styles: Style by Example

The quickest way to create an entirely new style is to use Word's *Style by Example* feature, as follows:

1. Select and format a block of text the way you want it.

2. Click inside the Style drop-down box on the Formatting toolbar (or press Ctrl+Shift+S).

3. Type the new style name in the Style box.

4. Press Enter.

Defining Character Styles

Character styles can't be defined on the Formatting toolbar (although they can be selected from it after they're defined). To define a character style, you'll have to venture into the Style dialog box (see Figure 5.4):

1. Select and format a block of text the way you want it.

2. Select Format, Style.

3. Click New.

4. Enter a style name in the Name box.

5. Choose Character from the Style Type drop-down list.

6. Click OK.

7. Click Apply.

FIG. 5.4
The Style dialog box enables you to create Character styles and gives you extensive control over both Paragraph and Character styles.

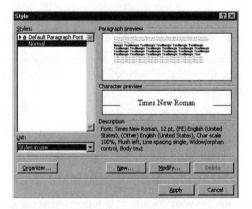

Part
II

Ch
5

Quick and Easy Automatic Style Changes

The same AutoFormat technology that enables you to create all your styles at the same time can also help you *change existing styles* automatically. For example, because Word can recognize a line of type as a heading, it can also recognize when you are formatting a line of type manually to look like a heading. It also can automatically transform your manual formatting into a heading style.

Automatic style definition is part of Word's *AutoFormat as You Type* feature. To use it, follow these steps:

1. Choose Format, AutoFormat.

2. Click Options.

3. Click the AutoFormat As You Type tab.

4. In the Apply As You Type area, specify which elements for which you want Word to automatically create styles: Headings, Borders, Tables, Automatic Bulleted Lists, and/or Automatic Numbered Lists.

5. Check the Define Styles Based on Your Formatting check box at the bottom of the dialog box.

6. Click OK.

7. Click Close.

Controlling Styles via the Format Style Dialog Box

Until now, this chapter has focused primarily on the quickest, easiest ways to create and use styles. However, Word provides some advanced style capabilities that aren't accessible from the Formatting toolbar or a keyboard shortcut. These capabilities can significantly improve your productivity if you spend a few minutes getting to know them.

Word's central control panel for creating and managing styles is the Style dialog box, which you've already seen in Figure 5.4. From here, you can do any of the following:

> Heading 1 ▾

■ *Apply an existing style to selected text.* You would be most likely to use the Style dialog box to apply built-in styles that don't show up in the Style box on the Formatting toolbar. To apply an existing style, select it from the list of Styles, and click Apply.

■ *Review your existing styles and delete any that no longer apply or are redundant.* To delete a style, select it from the list of Styles and click Delete. You can't delete any of the built-in styles in Word's Normal template.

■ *Create a new style.* As you've learned, you must use the Style dialog box to create character styles. However, you would also use the Style dialog box to create paragraph styles when you want to:

- Use advanced features like Based On styles or Following Paragraph styles
- Add your styles to a template
- Automatically update your document to reflect style changes
- Create shortcut keys for a style
- Systematically establish the formatting and attributes for a style
- Modify an existing style's attributes (or formatting)
- Move styles among documents and templates, via the Organizer

Throughout the remainder of this chapter, you'll learn more about creating, modifying, and organizing styles, but first, here's a word about displaying them.

Choosing the Most Convenient Way to List Your Styles

In the Style dialog box, Word can list styles in the following three ways:

■ *Styles in use.* Word lists only the styles you have already assigned to text in your document. You might use this list to make sure all the styles you've used are consistent with your corporate standards.

■ *All styles*. Word lists every style in every currently open template, including the 90+ styles in the Normal template, plus any other styles you've added to it and any styles in any other template to which your document has access.

■ *User-defined styles*. Word lists only the available styles you have created. You might use this list to manage a system of styles you've developed. Style systems are discussed in detail later in this chapter.

Creating a New Style Using the New Style Dialog Box

As you've learned, there are times when you'll want to create a new style using the Style and New Style dialog boxes instead of Style by Example. Earlier in the chapter, you saw how to create a character style this way. Now, you'll take a closer look at several other options available to you.

First, choose Format, Style and click New to display the New Style dialog box. At the top, you see the style Name and Style Type boxes you encountered earlier. Enter the style name you want and choose either Paragraph or Character as your Style type.

Working with Based On Styles

Next, if you want, you can specify the existing style that your new style will be based on. By default, most built-in Word styles are based on the Normal style, and unless you make a change, your new style will also be based on it. Of course, Word uses the formats you specify, but where you do *not* specify a setting, Word makes assumptions based on the Normal style, which includes the following:

■ Font: Times New Roman
■ Size: 10-point
■ Proofing Language: English (United States)
■ Character scale: 100%
■ Alignment: Flush left
■ Line spacing: Single
■ Pagination: Widow/Orphan Control
■ Outline level: Body Text

At times, you might have a different style you would like to use as the basis for your new style—one with formatting that closely resembles the style you are creating.

For example, you might want to base all your headings on your Heading 1 style. That way, if you change the font in Heading 1, all the other headings change automatically. A case study that appears later in this chapter walks through this example in detail.

With the New Style dialog box open, click the Based On box, and choose the style you want to use as the basis for your new style. If you are working with a Paragraph style, you can choose from all the styles available to your current document. If you are working with a Character style, your choices are more limited. They include several styles associated with Web pages,

Part
II

Ch
5

including Emphasis and Strong. These are styles that correspond to the HTML code which Web browsers, such as Microsoft Internet Explorer and Netscape Communicator, use to control the display of text on the Internet and in corporate intranets.

TIP If the Based On style you want to use appears in the Formatting toolbar, the following shows a quicker way to get the same result:

1. Format a block of text using the Based On style.

2. Reformat the text to reflect any changes you want to make.

3. Click in the Style box.

4. Type the new style name and press Enter.

Choosing a Following Paragraph Style

Think about your documents for a moment. In most cases, after you type a heading, you usually type body text. After you type the first element in a list, you usually type *another* list element. Word paragraph styles take advantage of this. When you specify a paragraph style, you can also specify the style that should be used in the *following* paragraph.

By default, the Following Paragraph style is Normal. The following steps show you how to specify a different one:

1. Open the New Style dialog box (see Figure 5.5).

2. Click in the Style for Following Paragraph drop-down box.

3. Choose the style you want to use.

4. When you're finished with the settings on the New Style dialog box, click OK.

FIG. 5.5

The New Style dialog box displays the controls and formatting options you can apply to a new style.

Creating Style Formats from the New Style Dialog Box

You already know that you can quickly establish a style's formats using Style by Example. You might, however, want convenient, centralized access to *every* formatting option associated with a new style, so you can systematically create all your formatting at the same time. Word gives you that access.

With the New Style dialog box open, click the Format button. A list of formatting categories appears (see Figure 5.6). Choose the one you want, and a dialog box appears containing your choices. In most cases, this dialog box is identical to the one you would use elsewhere to create manual formatting. For example, clicking Font displays the Font tabbed dialog box with three tabs: Font, Character Spacing, and Animation.

FIG. 5.6

You can choose a category of formatting to apply by clicking the Format button in the New Style dialog box.

Template or Document? Where to Store Your Styles

By default, Word adds your new style only to your current document. If you've changed a built-in style, that change applies only in your existing document. However, you'll sometimes want to make the style available for many documents. You can do this by adding the style to your existing document template.

It's easy to add a style to a template. From the New Style dialog box, check the Add to Template check box.

It's not quite as easy to decide whether you *should* add a style to your template. Here's what you need to know. Unless you have chosen another template, you are probably working in the Normal template. If you add a new style to the Normal template, you make it available to every document you create. If you change a built-in style, you likewise change it globally, meaning that it is changed for all documents using this particular style. Be careful not to introduce inconsistencies with existing documents that use Word's default styles.

▶ **See** "Understanding the Relationship Between Styles and Templates," **p. 178**

Part

II

Ch

5

CAUTION

Because the styles in your document aren't included in your template unless you check the Add to Template check box, it's possible for different documents using the same template to have varying styles with the same style names.

See the case study later in this chapter for a quick and easy alternative: creating a separate template specifically for your new and revised styles.

Instantly Give All Your Documents a Great New Look

You've just heard the downside of making changes to Word built-in styles. Here's the upside: You can create a unique look for all your documents with little effort. All you have to do is change the Normal style, which underlies all of Word's styles. For example, if you're bored with Times New Roman, you can change the Normal style to a somewhat more interesting face, such as Garamond. That change will cascade through all the styles that are based on Normal.

If you make a change like this, you'll probably have to make a few other changes as well. Some of Word's styles, while based on Normal, also specify their own fonts. For example, Heading 1 uses the Arial font. You'll probably want to change these styles to specify a font that complements the one you've chosen for text.

If you've chosen a serif font for text, generally choose a sans serif font for some or all of your headings. Serif fonts have tiny tails at the ends of each letter to improve readability; sans serif fonts don't. Serif and sans serif fonts complement each other well and often are used in combinations to make book and newspaper designs more attractive. The fonts in this book, for example, include a mix of serif and sans serif fonts.

There's one more thing you should note about choosing fonts for your styles: Different fonts have different widths. Times New Roman is unusually narrow, which simply means that more words fit on a page when you're using it. If you choose a wider font, such as Bookman, you may find you've lengthened a long document by several pages.

Allowing or Preventing Automatic Style Updates

As you've learned, Word can create new styles automatically, by transforming your manual formatting into styles as you type. If you want, Word can also change your styles automatically for you whenever you manually reformat them.

In some circumstances this is a great shortcut, because you can manually reformat one line and your entire document is updated to match. However, it's not always appropriate. Let's say one of your headings refers to the title of a book, which should be formatted in italic. If Word is automatically updating your styles, all the headings using this style will change, even those that shouldn't be italicized.

Word lets you specify which styles qualify for automatic updating. In the New Style dialog box, set your preference by checking or clearing the Automatically Update check box.

Changing Styles

In the past few pages, the primary focus has been on creating new styles. However, you can make changes in existing styles using nearly the same procedures. The following steps show you how to work with an existing style:

1. Choose Format, Style.
2. In the Styles list, choose the style you want to change.
3. Click Modify.

The Modify Style dialog box opens (see Figure 5.7). As you can see, it looks just like the New Style dialog box. However, the existing style you've already chosen is listed in the Name box, and its current settings are also in place.

FIG. 5.7

The Modify Style dialog box looks and works just like the New Style dialog box you've already seen.

As soon as you change a style, Word applies the change throughout your document anywhere you've used the style—or anywhere you've used a style based on it. If you add the changed style to a template, the change takes effect in all new documents based on that template.

However, the changes are *not* automatically made in existing documents. First, you have to save the changes by saving the template. Then, when you open an existing document based on that template, you have to tell Word that you want to update the styles. To update styles, follow these steps:

1. Open a document based on the template that you've changed.
2. Choose Tools, Templates, and Add-Ins. (Make sure the correct template is listed in the Document Template box.)

3. Check the Automatically Update Document Styles check box.

4. Click OK.

Word reformats the document to reflect any style changes you saved in the template.

Creating Keyboard Shortcuts for Your Styles

Earlier, you learned that Word comes with built-in keyboard shortcuts for the three highest-level heading styles, Normal style, and List style. You may discover other styles, new or existing, that you find yourself using quite often. To assign a keyboard shortcut to any style, you want follow these steps:

1. Choose Format, Style.

2. If you are adding a keyboard shortcut to an existing style, click Modify. If you are creating the style, click New instead.

3. Click Shortcut Key. The Customize Keyboard dialog box opens (see Figure 5.8).

4. Press the keyboard shortcut combination you want to use. The combination appears in the Press New Shortcut Key box. If that combination is already in use, the current use is listed beneath the box where the keyboard combination is displayed.

5. If the combination you've chosen is acceptable to you, click Assign. If not, press another keyboard combination, and when you're satisfied, click Assign.

▶ **See** "Customizing New Keyboard Shortcuts," **p. 734**

FIG. 5.8
You can create a convenient keyboard shortcut for any style you expect to use often.

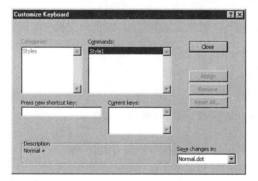

Managing Styles

Before you start accumulating new and changed styles, give a little thought to how you'll manage them. Managing styles involves the following:

■ Deciding which styles should be placed in templates, and organizing those styles in the templates associated with specific kinds of work

■ Naming styles so you and your colleagues understand their purpose

■ Occasionally moving styles or deleting styles you no longer use

You can perform some management tasks in the Style dialog boxes you've already learned about. For other tasks, such as moving styles between templates, you use the Organizer, which is described later in this chapter.

How to Choose Style Names

Spend a few moments thinking about how you'll name your styles. Here are a couple of tips:

- Name your styles based on their function, not their appearance. Don't name a style Arial 48 Bold; what if you decide to change it someday? Rather, name it based on how you'll use it—for example, Front Page Headline.

- Keep your style names as consistent as possible. Let's say you use a set of styles only for projects involving Omega Corp. Consider starting each style name with O. That way, they'll all be listed together—and you'll be less likely to inadvertently use them in projects that don't involve Omega.

Quick and Easy Style Names with Aliases   As you've just seen, there are advantages to creating relatively long style names that clearly explain the purpose of each style. However, what if you *also* like to type your style names in the Style box to select them? It takes too long to type a long name, and if you make a mistake, Word creates a new style, which isn't what you want to happen.

You *can* have it both ways. Use aliases. An alias is an abbreviated style name that Word recognizes in place of the full style name. Follow these steps to create an alias:

1. Display the New Style dialog box.
2. Type the style's full name, add a comma, and then type your alias. For example, to create the style Document Summary and assign the alias DS at the same time, enter:

Document Summary,DS

Both the full name and alias appear in the Style box, but you can select the style by typing only the alias.

> **TIP** You can create aliases for existing styles by adding them in the Name box of the Modify Style dialog box.

Keeping Track of Styles with the Organizer   The Organizer (see Figure 5.9) is Word's control center for copying, deleting, and renaming styles. Follow these steps to display it:

1. Choose Format, Style.
2. Click Organizer. The Organizer opens with the Styles tab displayed.

> **TIP** The procedures you'll learn for working with styles in the Organizer work just as well for working with AutoText entries, Toolbars, and Macro Project Items.

Part
II

Ch
5

FIG. 5.9

You can use the Organizer to move styles between documents or templates.

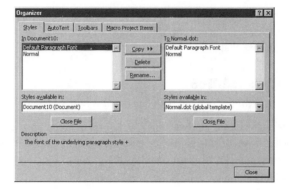

When the Organizer opens, it displays two windows. The left window, named after the document that is currently active, lists all the styles contained in that document. The right window corresponds to the Normal template (NORMAL.DOT).

Copying Styles When you open the Organizer, it is already set to copy styles from the current document to the Normal template. All you need to do is select the style you want to copy, and click Copy (or press Enter). If you're not sure whether you want to copy a style, you can review the style's contents, which are displayed beneath its window.

You can also copy styles in the opposite direction, from the Normal template to the current document. Click a style in the right window. The arrow inside the Copy button switches direction, now facing the Document window.

If you copy a style to a destination that already has a style of the same name, Word displays the dialog box shown in Figure 5.10.

FIG. 5.10

Inside the Organizer, Word warns you when you're preparing to overwrite an existing style.

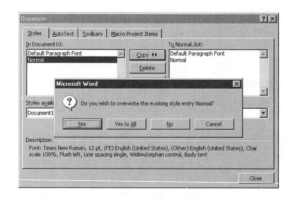

T I P If you'd like to copy a style from one document to another, and the style name isn't already used by the destination document, here's a shortcut. Select some text that's already formatted using the style and copy it. Then simply paste it into the other document.

The style comes along with it and is now listed on the Style box along with all other styles in this document. It'll still be there even after you delete the text associated with the style.

Renaming Styles   Sometimes you may want to rename a style. For example, you might be setting up several styles associated with a specific project and template, and you may want them all to begin with the same letter or word. To rename a style, select it in the Organizer, and click Rename. Then, enter the new name in the Rename dialog box (see Figure 5.11) and click OK.

FIG. 5.11

The Rename dialog box displays the current name, which can be edited or replaced as you want.

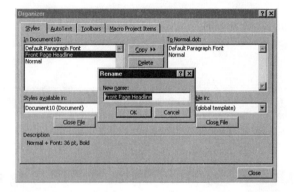

Working with Different Documents and Templates   Until now, you've used the Organizer only to move styles between the current document and the NORMAL.DOT template. However, the Organizer can be used to move styles among any document or template. You simply need to place the appropriate documents or templates in the left and right windows. To move styles among any document, follow these steps:

1. Beneath either the left or right window, click the Close File button. The keyboard shortcut varies depending on the window with which you are working. The window becomes empty, and the button has changed to read Open File.

2. Click the Open File button. Word displays your current list of Document Templates stored in the Templates folder (see Figure 5.12). If you want a template, navigate to it, select the template, and click Open. If you want a document instead, choose Word document in the Files of Type box. Then navigate to the document you want to use and click Open.

3. Repeat the same process in the other window to display the appropriate document or template there.

You can now copy, delete or rename styles just as you've already learned in this chapter.

Part
II

Ch
5

FIG. 5.12

When you click Open File, the Open dialog box opens to Word's list of templates and template subfolders.

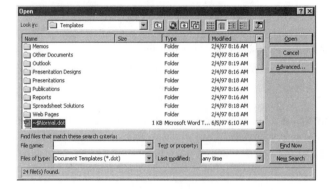

 TIP Because the Organizer's Open File button displays the same Open dialog box you normally use to open files, you have full access to the extensive file search capabilities covered in Chapter 1, "Word: Take the Controls."

 TIP If you're organizing a template with several specific styles, you can create all the styles in a new, blank document, delete the styled text, and save the remaining blank document as a template. Then, use that template whenever you want to access those styles.

Save Time and Money: Use Word Styles in DTP Programs

As you learned at the beginning of this chapter, there is one more benefit to using Word styles. If you export files for use in separate desktop publishing programs, most of these programs can recognize Word styles. Chances are the desktop publisher will want to change the formatting associated with each style, but the styles themselves already exist, eliminating time-consuming "tagging."

If you do your own desktop publishing it's your time you're saving. If someone else does your desktop publishing, however, you may save money. *Make sure to ask.*

All three of the leading word processing programs, Quark XPress 3.3x, Adobe PageMaker 6.5, and Microsoft Publisher 97, offer filters that can import Word 6/95 files. PageMaker and Publisher currently offer filters that directly support Word 97 files. (Publisher's is built-in.)

 ON THE WEB

The PageMaker filter for importing Word 97 files is currently found at

http://www.adobe.com/supportservice/custsupport/LIBRARY/346a.htm

As of this writing, Quark's most recent Word filter, version 3.1, only supports Word 6 or Word 95 files. It won't support the Word 6/95 files created by the original version of Word 97, which are actually RTF (Rich Text Format) files in disguise. The following are several alternatives:

■ Install the Word 97 Service Pack, which allows Word to save "real" Word 6/95 files. If you've purchased Word 97 recently, you may already have the necessary filter.

■ Or, if you've installed Word 97 alongside Word 6 or Word 95, save to Word 6/95 format; then open the file in Word 6 or 95, and save again as a Word 6/95 file that Quark will recognize.

■ If these options aren't available, save your Word 97 files to Macintosh Word 5.1 format. Needless to say, you'll lose any formatting based on features newer than Mac Word 5.1, a program that is well over seven years old.

If your desktop publisher is using the Macintosh Quark XPress 3.0 or 3.1 filter for Word, make sure he or she has installed the Microsoft OLE Extensions as well. These are automatically installed when Word 6 for the Macintosh is installed, but they'll need to be downloaded and installed separately on any system that doesn't have Word 6.

No filter is perfect. Even the best of them don't support all of Word's myriad features. For example, PageMaker 6.5's Word filter doesn't support character styles. Instead, it reformats that text as if you had manually formatted it. However, it does a *very* nice job with paragraph styles.

For all these caveats, though, using Word styles in desktop publishing can still save significant time and money.

Creating a Style System: A Real-World Case Study

In this chapter, you've learned many individual style features and techniques. But the real power of styles is in how they work together. In this final section, you'll walk through a real-world example of creating a *style system*: a set of interlocking styles used for a specific purpose.

Part
II

Ch
5

You might build a style system for your company or organization, or for all work associated with a specific client. In a large company, you might translate your design guidelines into a Word style system, so you can create low-cost brochures, white papers, and other documents without calling upon a professional designer.

For whatever purpose you use them, however, they can enhance both your results and your productivity. Simply put, style systems provide an easy-to-use framework for constructing high-quality, consistent documents.

Step 1: Creating Based On Styles

The first step in creating your style system is to establish the underlying styles on which you want to base your other styles. This example system will use two of these *Based On style*s: one for body copy, and another for headings.

Building on the body copy style, you then create additional styles for bulleted lists and quotations. Building on a style for first-level headings, you can create additional styles for second and third-level headings. Of course, a complete style system would include more styles than this. In the following steps, you'll walk through the process:

1. Open a blank document and manually format a paragraph of body copy (Normal style) the way you want all of your standard body copy to appear. This example uses the Georgia font, formatted at 12 point. Georgia is an attractive new font designed for both screen and print use. Microsoft makes this font available at no cost on its Web site.

2. Add the paragraph formatting you'd like to include. This example, specifies that 8 points of spacing follow each paragraph. This saves space in the finished document compared with adding an entire line of space between paragraphs. It also means that people who use these styles won't have to add a second carriage return after each paragraph. Word adds spacing automatically, and of course, if you ever need to change paragraph spacing later, all you'll need to do is change the style.

3. After you've finished formatting the text, click inside the Style box on the Formatting toolbar and press Enter. The Modify Style dialog box opens. Click the Update the Style to Reflect Recent Changes box, and choose OK. This sets the style for the document.

4. Manually format a first-level heading. Because this example uses Georgia, a serif font, your headings will use a complementary sans-serif font: 24-point Tahoma. This is another Microsoft font that is new, attractive, and free on the Web.

   Word already has a style named Heading 1 which, for this example, is the style name chosen for your first-level headings. By using the existing Heading 1 style instead of creating a new style name like Head1, you'll be able to use Word's heading style-dependent document automation and organization features without having to tell Word to look for any custom styles you've created.

   It's easier to change the existing style to create a new one with the same name, so it is recommended that you format a heading in Word's existing Heading 1 style and then apply the new formatting. Because you've adapted the existing style, any attributes not changed remain as Microsoft created them. For example, the built-in Heading 1 style includes 12 points before and 3 points after each paragraph. In this example, change the before setting to 9 points but leave the after setting alone.

5. To tell Word that it should use your new version of the Heading 1 style instead of its own, click inside the Style box, and press Enter.

Figure 5.13 shows how the new style appears.

Step 2: Building on the Based On Styles

Now that you have two Based On styles, you can easily use them to create new styles. Next, create a Quote style, which will be used whenever you want to insert a quotation in your document. Follow these steps:

1. Select a paragraph formatted as Body.

2. Manually reformat the paragraph as you'd like your quotes to appear. In this example, format the quotes as 10-point italic, with a 0.5-inch left and right indent.

3. Name the style by clicking the Style box, entering **Quote**, and pressing Enter.

FIG. 5.13

In step 1 of creating a style system, you established two styles on which you will base all other styles.

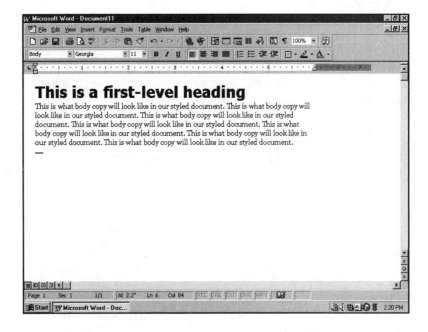

Because the text you started with was already formatted as Body, Word automatically uses Body as the Based On style. As a result, any attributes of the Body style you *haven't* changed, such as the use of the Georgia font, are carried over to the new style automatically.

Next, build a Heading 2 style based on your revised Heading 1 style. First, you need to designate Heading 1 as the basis for our new style. To make this designation, follow these steps:

1. Choose Format, Style.
2. Select Heading 2 from the Styles list. If it doesn't appear in the list, select All Styles in the List box.
3. Click Modify. The Modify Style dialog box opens.
4. In the Based On drop-down box, choose Heading 1.

The Heading 2 style is now based on Heading 1 instead of Normal. Notice something interesting that's also happened. Even though the original Heading 2 style was based on Normal +Arial, Word is smart enough to realize that if you want to base Heading 2 on a different style, you probably want to use the font in the style you've chosen, instead of Arial.

Next, change Heading 2's font size and style. To do so, follow these steps:

1. Click Format, Font to display the Font dialog box.
2. Clear any settings you don't want to include in your new style.
3. Set Font Style to Bold Italic and Size to 20-point. (Of course, you could choose different styles and sizes for your own style system.)
4. Click OK.

Part
II

Ch
5

Heading 2 is now based on Heading 1, but is slightly smaller and formatted as Bold Italic instead of Bold. In this example, follow the same steps to format Heading 3 as Tahoma 16-point Regular. The updated styles, as they should now appear, are shown in Figure 5.14.

FIG. 5.14

In step 2, you've created three more styles: Quote, based on Body; and Heading 2 and Heading 3, each based on Heading 1.

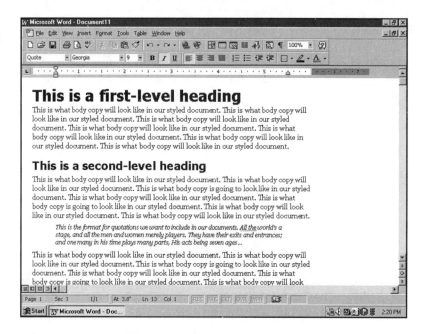

Step 3: Checking Styles for Following Paragraphs

Because you've used Word's built-in Normal and Heading styles as a starting point, you benefit from the intelligence Word has already built into them. For instance, Word assumes that the paragraph after any Heading is likely to be formatted as Normal—that is, formatted as body copy. Similarly, Word expects that the paragraph after a paragraph of Normal text will also be Normal. Most of the time that's true. Typically, you'll type at least a few paragraphs before you need to add a heading or other element.

However, in this example, there's one place you will need to make a change. As of now, the paragraph that follows a Quote will also be a Quote. Because most of the quotations you'll use will only be one paragraph long, followed by Normal body copy, you need to follow these steps:

1. Choose Format, Style.
2. Select Quote in the Styles list.
3. Select Modify.
4. Select Normal in the Style for Following Paragraph box.
5. Click OK.

Step 4: Storing the Style System in Its Own Template

You've created your style system. Now you must store it somewhere. At the moment, it's stored only in your current document, but you have several choices in regard to how you want to store your new style system:

- You can simply leave the styles where they are, in your current document—but then they will only be available while you're working on this document.

- You can add these styles to your existing template. But chances are you've been working in the Normal template, which defines how all of your documents will look (as you'll learn in Chapter 6, "Templates, Wizards, and Add-Ins"). Note that these styles are not likely to be the defaults for *every* document you create. What's more, the other styles in the Normal template aren't all consistent with these new styles.

- You can copy these styles into some other template using the Organizer, as you've already learned. But you might not have a template available for the purpose.

- You can create a *new* template that contains these new styles—a template you can work from whenever you want to use these styles.

For the purposes of this example, the last choice is best; it keeps you organized and it gives you the most flexibility. Now, follow these steps:

1. Select all the text in the document (Ctrl+A) and delete it. You don't need that text any more, now that you've created your styles with it. You don't want that text to show up in all your new documents created with this template.

2. Choose File, Save As.

3. Name the template.

4. Choose Document template in the Save as Type box.

5. Click OK.

That's it; you're finished. How long did that take you? Twenty minutes? A half hour? For your efforts, you now have a complete, self-contained style system that makes any (or all) of your documents look consistent—and significantly reduces the time you will spend formatting your documents.

 TIP Instead of selecting a style from the Style box every time you need to use it, consider creating keyboard shortcuts for the styles you use most.

Follow these steps to establish your own keyboard shortcut for a style you've already created:

1. Choose Format, Style.

2. In the Styles box, select the style you want to work with.

3. Click Modify. The Modify Style dialog box opens.

4. Click Shortcut Key. The Customize Keyboard dialog box opens.

continues

Part

II

Ch

5

continued

5. Press the shortcut key combination you want to use. The combination appears in the Press New Shortcut Key box. If this combination is already in use, its current use will be described beneath the Press New Shortcut Key box.

6. If you want to change your key combination, press another set of keys. If you are satisfied, click Assign.

7. Click Close. Word already provides keyboard shortcuts for the first three levels of headings.

If you use lower-level headings, you might want to assign them Alt+Ctrl+4, Alt+Ctrl+5, and so on.

Troubleshooting Styles

You've already seen a couple of ways in which styles can go awry. For example, you may get unexpected results if you have two styles with the same name: one in your document, and another in your template. You might also forget to tell Word to update the styles in an existing document after you update that document's template. The following troubleshooting tips address some more common problems users encounter in working with styles.

TROUBLESHOOTING

Did a style suddenly change when you weren't expecting it to? Check in Format, Style, New Style to see if Automatically Update is turned on. If it is, Word may have misinterpreted a manual formatting change as an instruction to change the style. Clear the check box.

If that doesn't work, did you change a style that other styles are based on? If so, those styles will change as well, sometimes unexpectedly.

If that doesn't work, is a template that your document depends upon missing? Let's say your document uses a template stored on a network drive. If the server becomes temporarily unavailable, when you open the Word document, Word may use styles with the same name from the Normal template stored on your hard disk.

Does a style look different than you expected? Perhaps you added manual formatting inadvertently, or imported text that already had manual formatting. Press Shift+F1 and click the text to see if there is any unexpected manual formatting. If so, select the text and press ctrl+spacebar to eliminate it.

From Here...

In this chapter, you've learned all you need to know to take full advantage of Word's time-saving style features. Next, you might consider the following chapters.

■ Read Chapter 6, "Templates, Wizards, and Add-Ins," to understand the fundamentals of templates, which are document patterns that can streamline your work even further.

- Discover more uses for AutoFormat and AutoFormat as You Type in Chapter 7, "Automating Your Documents: AutoCorrect, AutoFormat, AutoText, and AutoSummarize."

- Learn how the styles you've created can be used in Word outlines and automatic outline numbering, in Chapter 14, "Outlining: The Best Way to Organize a Document."

- Read Chapter 19, "Word Desktop Publishing," to see if you can use styles to do your own desktop publishing in Word, instead of sending the work out to someone else.

Part
II

Ch
5

CHAPTER 6

Templates, Wizards, and Add-Ins

by Bill Camarda

A template is a pattern for your documents. When you choose a template for your new document, you're telling Word what information—text, formatting, and graphics—you want to appear in that document automatically.

Of course, the more information you can automatically add to your new documents, the less you'll have to add manually. You can use templates to dramatically reduce the number of documents you create from scratch. Depending on your work, you might virtually eliminate them.

That's the first goal of this chapter: systematically slashing the time it takes you to create new documents. That's only half of what templates can do for you. ■

Understanding what templates are, and how they work

Templates enable you to create documents that already include most text and formatting.

Making the most of Word's built-in templates

Word 97 installs more than 20 built-in templates; even more are available if you know where to look.

Create your own templates

You can create a template from scratch or build one from any existing document.

Working with global templates

With global templates, you can give all your documents access to the features of any template.

Managing templates for maximum efficiency

Learn how to build a family of templates.

Using Word wizards

Word wizards walk you step-by-step through the construction of résumés and many other common documents.

Using Word Add-Ins

Third-party add-ins can help you extend Word's power even further.

Using Templates to Build Custom Editing Environments

Templates don't simply place information in new documents. They enable you to create custom editing environments for specific clients, projects, or companies. They store all the tools you and your colleagues need to edit specific documents as efficiently as possible.

That may sound abstract. Let's get more specific. You might build a template designed to streamline document creation for a specific client, project, or company. Your template could include the following:

- *All relevant styles.* As you learned in Chapter 5, "Styles: The Foundation of Automated Documents," you can create a system of styles that make it easy to make specific documents look consistent. You can store this system of styles in a template, making it easy to use when you need it.

- *All relevant boilerplate text (AutoText entries).* For example, your template can include contract clauses, marketing language, product names and descriptions that you often use in connection with a client, project or company. (You'll learn more about AutoText in Chapter 7, "Automating Your Documents: AutoCorrect, AutoFormat, AutoText and AutoSummarize.")

- *Macros that streamline tasks associated with specific documents.* For example, you might include a macro that opens a dialog box where users can define what elements should be included in a proposal. (Chapters 29 through 33 include detailed coverage of Word macros.)

- *New toolbars, menus, or menu items.* These items provide shortcuts for tasks associated with specific documents. For example, if your template helps a user run an electronic mail merge, it might include a toolbar that walks the user through each step of the process. In some cases, the toolbar might borrow buttons from Word's built-in Mail Merge toolbar; in other cases, the buttons might be attached to custom macros. (You'll learn more about customizing Word this way in Chapter 26, "Customizing Word.")

A template like this will be extremely valuable to you, but it can be even more valuable to your colleagues and others who may be working on similar documents. Let's look at a couple of real-world scenarios:

Scenario #1: Creating a Catalog

You're self-employed. You've been hired to create a monthly product catalog. You would like to subcontract much of the keystroking involved, but your typist needs to enter text following very rigid formats. Your template can include dialog boxes and AutoText entries that make these formats easier to follow. These tools will not only improve accuracy, they will reduce the keystroking required—and, potentially, the project's cost.

After the text is entered, it will have to be "massaged" in specific ways. For example, a three-column run-in index will need to be created using Word's Bullet format for indexes. Your template can include a toolbar button that runs a macro which creates just such an index. (You can record this macro; you don't have to know Visual Basic.) As a result, you can work with a typist who is less familiar with Microsoft Word, without worrying that your index will be compiled incorrectly.

Scenario #2: Sending Monthly Reports

You are responsible for sending monthly progress reports to a cross-functional team developing a new product. You create a detailed format for your progress reports, perhaps building on Word's built-in memo or report templates. The report might include Word forms features, such as check boxes or drop-down list boxes.

After you're satisfied, you save the file as a template. Now, you can add macros and toolbar buttons as needed. For example, you can add a macro that converts your progress report to a PowerPoint presentation, or one that e-mails it to a specific list of people.

Not only have you reduced the amount of time it takes to develop your report, you've made it easier to delegate report preparation. If you share your template with others (possibly by storing it in the Workgroup Templates folder your group shares), you've reduced the time it takes everyone to create status reports.

▶ **See** "Using Workgroup Templates," **p. 800**

In the remainder of this chapter, you'll start with the basics, and move on to more sophisticated aspects of working with and managing your templates. Finally, you'll walk through the process of building one of the custom editing environments discussed previously.

Selecting a Template for a New Document

When you create a new document using the File, New dialog box (see Figure 6.1), you're actually choosing a template on which your document will be based. The default Blank Document template that most people use is based on Word's Normal template, an especially important Word template that you'll learn more about shortly.

Using Word's Built-In Template Library

Word comes with nearly 20 associated templates for the documents you're most likely to create: letters, faxes, memos, reports, résumés, and Web pages. Most of these templates actually contain their own directions on how to use them most effectively. For example, the Report templates explain how to insert your own company name, create consistent bulleted lists, and even how to AutoFormat a table consistent with the one already in the document.

Later, you'll learn more about the wizards that also appear in the New dialog box. Wizards walk you step-by-step through the creation of letters, faxes, mailing labels, memos, résumés, Web pages, newsletters, and legal pleadings.

Part
II

Ch
6

FIG. 6.1

The choices in the New dialog box are templates which contain predefined text, formatting, and graphics.

To select a template, display the New dialog box, click the tab containing the template you want, and double-click the template. Figures 6.2, 6.3, 6.4, and 6.5 show examples of documents created with Word's letter, fax, memo, and résumé templates.

FIG. 6.2

A letter created with Word's Contemporary Letter template.

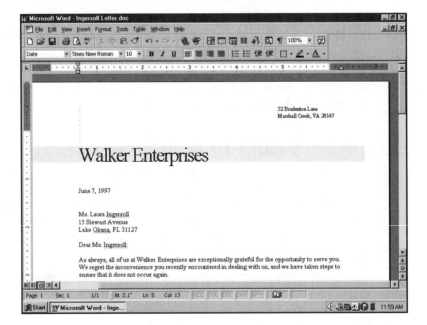

FIG. 6.3
A fax created with
Word's Elegant Fax
template.

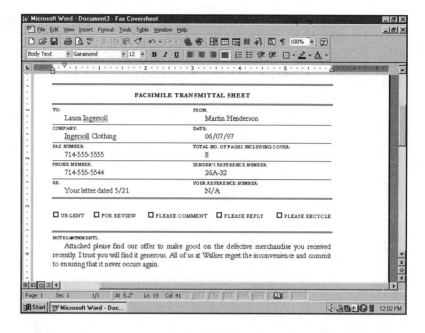

FIG. 6.4
A memo created with
Word's Professional
Memo template.

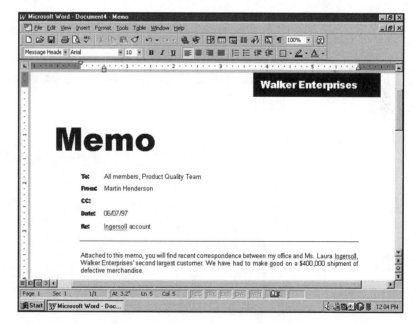

TIP Word 95 came with many templates and wizards that aren't installed in any of the standard Word 97 installations. These include templates for brochures, press releases, newsletters, invoices, purchase orders, time sheets, and theses; and wizards for creating agendas, awards, and calendars. These are extremely useful; two of the best are shown in Figures 6.6 and 6.7.

FIG. 6.5

A résumé created with Word's Contemporary Résumé template.

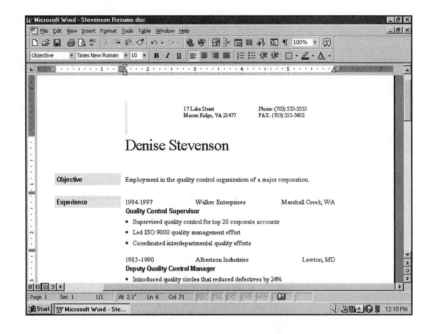

FIG. 6.6

The Word 95 Directory template, available on the Office 97 ValuPack or from an installed copy of Word 95, includes detailed instructions for how to customize it.

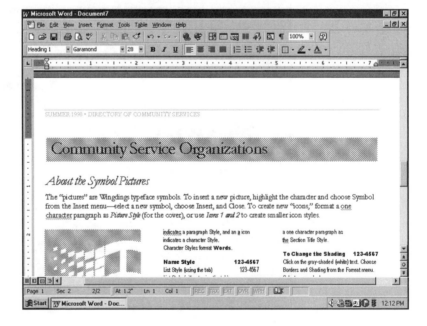

FIG. 6.7

The Word 95 Brochure template, available on the Office 97 ValuPack, also includes detailed built-in instructions.

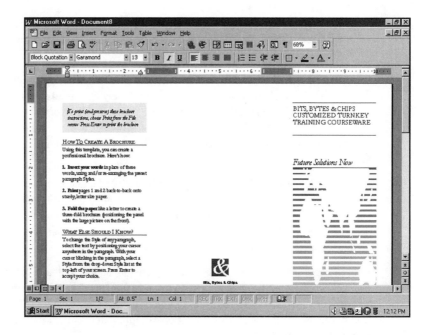

TIP If you installed Word 97 *over* Word 95, Word renames your old template folder Old Office Templates and stores those templates there. If you installed Word 97 elsewhere, you can copy the Word 95 templates into your Word 97 template folder. Each template is converted to Word 97 format the first time you load it. That's why you should *copy* the templates instead of moving them. After conversion, they won't work with Word 95 anymore.

You can also find these templates in the ValuPack folder of the Office 97 CD-ROM. (\ValuPack\Template\Word\). To install them, copy the entire folder into the folder on your hard drive where Word stores its templates.

TIP If you've installed Microsoft Office 97, you can open Word and a document based on a template of your choice, both at the same time. On the taskbar, click Start, New Office Document. Office displays a list of all the templates associated with Word and the other Office programs you may have installed. Double-click any Word template (one with a Microsoft Word icon).

The Normal Template: Crucial to All Documents

No matter which template you choose for a specific document, one template is always open: the Normal template, stored as Normal.dot in Word 97's template folder. While the Normal template doesn't include any text, it does include the following:

■ The 90+ built-in Word styles you learned about in Chapter 5, "Styles: The Foundation of Automated Documents."

■ Word's built-in AutoText entries for letters and other business documents. (See Chapter 7, "Automating Your Documents: AutoCorrect, AutoFormat, AutoText, and AutoSummarize.")

As you work, your new styles, AutoText entries, macros, and many other customizations are stored in the Normal template, unless you deliberately choose to save them elsewhere. Therefore, the longer you work with Word, the more valuable your Normal.dot file is likely to become. This file is so important, it's the first target of macro virus authors. Even if you don't back up your entire Word installation as regularly as you should, at least store a copy of Normal.dot somewhere safe every couple of weeks.

Word looks for Normal.dot whenever it starts up. If Normal.dot is damaged, or renamed, or if Word simply can't find it in the template (or Workgroup template) folder you've specified in Tools, Options, File Locations, it will simply create a new one using Word's default settings. However, the new Normal.dot won't contain any of your styles, AutoText entries, or other customizations.

You can generally use the Organizer to copy custom styles, toolbars, macros, and AutoText entries from the renamed Normal.dot to the new Normal.dot. If, however, your original Normal.dot was virus infected, don't copy macros into the new one. (The Organizer was covered in Chapter 5, "Styles: The Foundation of Automated Documents," and is reviewed again later in this chapter.)

▶ **See** "Preventing and Controlling Word Viruses," **p. 822**

Occasionally in Windows 95, a damaged Normal.dot may cause Word 97 to crash upon startup. You can quickly narrow startup problems to two possible causes: a damaged Normal.dot or a damaged Registry data key. To do so, load Word bypassing these items:

1. On the Windows taskbar, click Start, Run.

2. Enter the following command:

   "C:\Program Files\Microsoft Office\Office\WinWord.exe" /a

   (If your Winword.exe file is in a different location, enter that path within quotation marks instead.)

3. Click OK.

If Word loads properly, you know you either have a damaged Registry key or a damaged Normal.dot. Try the following:

1. In Windows Explorer, rename Normal.dot.

2. Start Word; it will create a new Normal.dot.

If Word now starts reliably, you can copy custom styles, toolbars, macros, and AutoText entries from the renamed Normal.dot to the new Normal.dot using the Organizer, as already mentioned. If Word still does not start reliably, you may have to edit the Registry to delete the defective key, using the Windows 95 Registry Editor (regedit.exe). Editing the Registry is beyond the scope of this book. You can find a detailed discussion of editing the Registry in the *Windows 95 and NT Registry and Customization Handbook*, by Jim Boyce (Que).

Creating a New Template

Now that you've learned what templates are and how to use the ones Word provides, it's time to start creating your own. Word gives you two ways to do so: you can create a template from scratch, or you can save an existing document file as a template. The solution that's best depends on your specific situation. Use the following questions to help you decide which is best for you:

- Do you already have a document that can easily be transformed into a template? For example, if you're creating a template for business proposals, have you made a proposal lately that you're especially pleased with? Would it be easy to edit out the contents that are specific to one client or project, leaving "holes" for you to fill in custom information later? If the answers to these questions are yes, then it makes sense to open that file, make your changes, and save it as a template.

- Are you creating a template for a document where there is no usable model? Then you may want to create it from scratch.

Creating a Template Based on an Existing Document

To create a template based on an existing document, follow these steps:

1. Open the existing document.

2. Edit the document to eliminate the specific references that you won't want to appear in other similar documents.

 T I P Before you delete these references, consider whether they're worth saving as AutoText entries. If you're building your template from a proposal you made to Alpha Corporation, you won't want all your Alpha-related experience to show up in proposals you might make to their fiercest competitor, Omega Corporation, but you would want to have that boilerplate conveniently available as an AutoText entry the next time you make a proposal to Alpha.

3. Add any styles, AutoText entries, macros, toolbars, or keyboard shortcuts you want; or copy existing ones from other templates by using the Organizer.

4. Choose File, Save As.

5. Choose Document Template (*.dot) in the Save As type dialog box. When you do, Word changes the current folder to the one where it saves templates, typically \Program Files\Microsoft Office\Templates (see Figure 6.8).

6. Enter a name for the template in the File Name text box.

 7. If you want to save your template in that folder so it appears in the General tab of the New dialog box, click Save. If you want it to appear in a different tab in the New dialog box, double-click that folder and click Save.

You can also create a new folder by clicking the Create New Folder button and entering a folder name in the New Folder dialog box. Once you create a new folder within the

Part

II

Ch

6

Templates folder, and store at least one template in that folder, the folder appears as a tab within the New dialog box. Any templates you have stored there appear as icons within that tab.

FIG. 6.8
When you tell Word you want to save a template, it switches you to the folder where you currently save all templates.

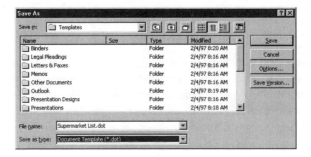

Creating a Template from Scratch

You can also create a new template from scratch, much as you create a new document:

1. Choose File, New.
2. Make sure Blank Document is selected in the General tab.
3. Choose Template from the Create New section in the lower-right corner of the dialog box.
4. Choose OK.

If you follow this procedure to create a template file, you can only save the file as a template, not as a Word document.

Creating a Template Based on an Existing Template

Sometimes you may not have a document that's an adequate model for a template, but Word just might. You can browse the tabs in the New dialog box to find out. Click a template. In the Preview box, Word displays a thumbnail sketch of a sample document based on it.

If you find a template you'd like to work from, click Template to indicate that you want to create a new template instead of a document. Then click OK. A new template opens, containing all the contents of Word's built-in template. Adjust it any way you like, and save it.

Understanding the Relationship Between Styles and Templates

In Chapter 5, "Styles: The Foundation of Automated Documents," you learned how to create a set of consistent styles and store them in a template. The styles available to your current document depend on the templates open at the time. These templates are as follows:

■ The Normal template.

■ Whatever template you based the document upon, if you based it on a template other than Normal.dot.

■ Any other *global templates* that are currently loaded. Global templates will be discussed shortly. By default, no global templates other than Normal are loaded.

What if several templates are open, and each defines the same style differently? This happens often, even if you stay with Word's built-in styles. For example, Heading 1 is 14 point Arial Bold in the Normal template, but 10 point Arial Bold in the Contemporary Letter template. If you open a document based on the Contemporary Letter template, Word uses *its* styles, not those in any other template, global or otherwise.

> **CAUTION**
>
> If you change the styles in your document without storing those changes in a template, the document's revised styles override all the available templates.

Understanding Global Templates

Global templates are templates whose styles and other settings are available to all open documents. As already mentioned, Normal is a global template. However, you can add more global templates, either for your current session or permanently. You might load a global template for the following reasons:

■ You might load a global template temporarily when you want to make sure a set of macros, styles, or AutoText entries are available for use in all documents you plan to create during one session—but not necessarily for all sessions.

■ You often load third-party templates as global templates to make sure their features are available to all your documents without copying the macros into your Normal.dot template. In fact, many third-party templates do not permit you to copy individual macros out of them.

Loading a Global Template for the Current Session

You can add a global template any time during the course of a session. Global templates are controlled in the Templates and Add-Ins dialog box (see Figure 6.9).

To add a global template:

1. Choose Tools, Templates, and Add-Ins.

2. Click Add. In the Add Template dialog box (see Figure 6.10) Word displays a list of the templates currently available in the Templates folder.

3. Browse the list to select the template you want.

4. Click OK.

FIG. 6.9
The Templates and Add-Ins dialog box enables you to add one or more global templates for use in all documents.

FIG. 6.10
The Add Template dialog box works much like the Open dialog box; browse for the template you want, and click OK.

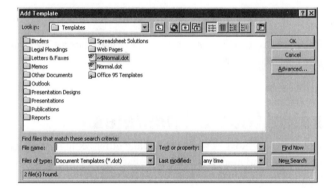

N O T E This menu command has been moved in Word 97. In previous versions of Word, the equivalent to the Tools, Templates and Add-Ins command was File, Templates. ■

 Templates can be stored anywhere on your hard disk, or on a networked hard drive. However, only templates stored in the Office 97 Templates folder or one of its subfolders appear in the New dialog box.

When you return to the Templates and Add-Ins dialog box, the additional template appears in the Global templates and Add-Ins scroll box with a check mark next to it. It remains loaded until you uncheck the box or exit Word. The next time you restart Word, the template will be listed in the Global templates and Add-Ins scroll box, but its check box won't be checked. In other words, it won't be loaded as a global template unless you return to Templates and Add-Ins and check the box.

Loading a Global Template Permanently

Often, you'll want to load the same global template automatically whenever you run Word. The easiest way is to copy the template into Word's Startup folder. In a typical installation of

Microsoft Office 97, this folder is \Program Files\Microsoft Office\Office\Startup. After you do so, if you run Word, the template loads automatically and stays loaded unless you uncheck its check box in Templates and Add-Ins.

N O T E Why wouldn't you load a global template permanently? Conceivably, it might contain confidential information that you wouldn't want others to access routinely. More likely, you're simply trying to save memory by not loading any more templates than necessary. ■

Attaching a New Template to an Existing Document

Every document has one template attached to it (except for documents created by wizards, which have a wizard attached to them, as you'll see later). Typically, the attached template is the one you used to create the document—whether you used Normal, another built-in Word template, or one of your own. However, in some instances, you may want to change the template associated with one or more documents.

For instance, imagine your company, Acme Chocolate, has just been purchased by Intergalactic Candies. Intergalactic has different corporate design standards than Acme. However, it's quite likely that both companies use Word, and it's possible that both companies have Word templates codifying basic document formats such as headings and body text. If so, you may be able to redesign your documents to the Intergalactic standard simply by attaching the Intergalactic template to them.

N O T E Of course, things aren't usually quite this simple. The style names you've used at Acme may not be the same as those used by Intergalactic, or Intergalactic might not have a template containing all of its styles. However, you can still *create* a new template that combines Intergalactic's formatting rules with the style names you've already been using, and achieve the same result. ■

To attach a different template to your document:

1. Choose Tools, Templates and Add-Ins.
2. Click Attach. The Attach Template dialog box opens (see Figure 6.11).
3. Browse to the template you want to attach, and click Open.
4. If you want to update your existing document's styles to reflect those in the new template, check the Automatically Update Document Styles check box.

N O T E Sometimes you'll want to attach a new template but not update the styles. For example, you might be perfectly happy with your document's formatting, but you want access to a set of AutoText entries associated with a different template. In this case, attach the template, but do not check the Automatically Update Document Styles check box. ■

Part
II

Ch
6

FIG. 6.11

Select the template you want to attach, or browse to the folder containing it.

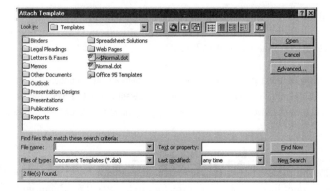

Previewing New Templates with Style Gallery

You might be interested in how your document would look if you used the styles from a different template. (For example, in the preceding example, you might want to know how easy it would be to simply apply Intergalactic's template to your current documents and how much work you would still have to do manually.) To preview what your document would look like by using Word's Style Gallery (see Figure 6.12), follow these steps:

1. Choose Format, Style Gallery.

2. Select a template you would like to preview from the Template scroll box. Word then shows what your document would look like if it were using the styles in that template.

3. If you would like to apply the styles in the new template you've chosen, click OK.

It's important to understand what Style Gallery does—and what it doesn't do. Word does not attach a different template to your document. Rather, it copies styles from that template into your document, where they override any formatting settings from the template that is attached.

FIG. 6.12

The Style Gallery enables you to preview how a document will appear with different style formatting.

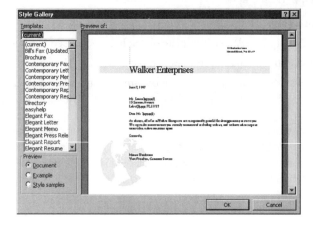

Sometimes you can't tell whether you would like to apply styles from a different template. Possibly, you haven't used styles with the same name in your document yet, so previewing your document with Style Gallery doesn't show you what you need to see. If you are previewing the styles in a built-in Word template, you can ask Style Gallery to show you a sample document that uses all of the styles in that template. With the Style Gallery dialog box displayed, choose Example.

To get an even closer look at the styles that can be imported from another template, click Style samples in the Preview check box. Word displays each style name, formatted as the template specifies (see Figure 6.13).

FIG. 6.13
Previewing style samples from another template.

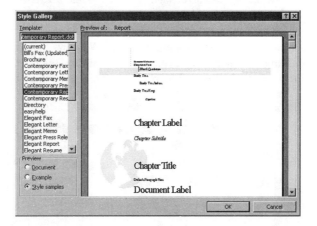

Managing Templates to Minimize Your Work

You now understand the basics of using and creating templates. You're ready to plan a strategy for using templates to minimize your work and improving the efficiency of all your colleagues.

N O T E   Although our example is based on a corporate department or small business, if you work solo you can follow the same steps to streamline the production of your most common documents. ▦

Part
II

Ch
6

Start by giving some thought to the kinds of documents you create most—the ones where templates can give you the most "bang for the buck." Let's say you spend most of your time in Word creating

- ▦ Letters
- ▦ Memos
- ▦ Reports
- ▦ Fax cover sheets

Do you already have Word documents that are formatted essentially the way you want these documents to look in the future? If so, follow these steps:

1. Make sure you've used styles to define the different portions of each document.

2. Delete the elements that are specific to one document, such as the name of a memo's recipient.

3. Save the documents as templates. If you save the templates you expect to use most in the default Templates folder, they will be instantly available when you display the New dialog box.

The tabs of the New dialog box correspond to Windows folders. Assuming you've installed Office 97 in the default location, the templates in the General tab are located in C:\Program Files\Microsoft Office\Templates, and each of the other tabs are subfolders beneath this folder. This means you can reorganize your templates using Windows Explorer or Windows NT Explorer—even adding new subfolders if you need to. You'll see the results immediately in the New dialog box, as shown in Figure 6.14. Note that Word won't display empty template subfolders.

FIG. 6.14

A customized New dialog box displaying templates specific to the Acme Company.

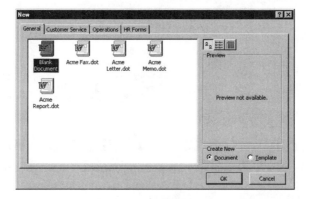

It also means you can move or copy all the templates you use most into the General folder, for quicker access. If you manage Word, you can hide or delete the templates or folders you don't want used. For example, if you've standardized on the Elegant family of templates for letters, faxes, and memos, copy those into the Templates folder, and consider moving the Letters & Faxes and Memos folder elsewhere on your hard drive so they won't appear in the New dialog box at all.

Think for a moment about how you'll name your most commonly used templates. Consider including your company's name (or an abbreviated version) in each of them, to make it obvious that these templates are customized to your company's needs.

If you don't have a model to work from, consider using Word's templates or wizards as the basis for your custom templates (possibly modifying them with new fonts, as discussed in Chapter 5, "Styles: The Foundation of Automated Documents"). After you've adapted them, save them as templates.

Your templates are now model documents that contain all the text and formatting that will be common to all the documents based on them. You've already saved yourself and your colleagues many hours. Your next step is to use the other capabilities of Word templates to build custom editing environments that make you (and your colleagues) even more efficient. To do this, you'll draw upon a variety of Word features that are covered in detail elsewhere in the book:

- Styles (Chapter 5, "Styles: The Foundation of Automated Documents")
- AutoText entries (Chapter 7, "Automating Your Documents: AutoCorrect, AutoFormat, and AutoText, and AutoSummarize")
- Custom toolbars and menu items (Chapter 26, "Customizing Word")
- Recorded macros (Chapter 30, "Recording and Running Visual Basic Macros")

First, take a look at some documents you've already created, and identify blocks of copy that seem to reoccur often. For example, many of your company's status reports might include a table that lists steps to be taken next. You can store a skeleton table as an AutoText entry, and then you can use the Organizer to copy this AutoText entry into your Report template.

▶ **See** "Keeping Track of Styles with the Organizer," **p. 157**

As you think about your documents, you might find elements that should be in them but haven't been added. Now's a good time to create those elements. If you like, you can scour Word's built-in templates and wizards for ideas. An especially good source for business ideas is Word 95's Agenda Wizard (included with the Office 97 ValuPack).

If you're using Office 97, you'll also find that PowerPoint is replete with good ideas you can adapt. To find them, either run PowerPoint's AutoContent Wizard or review the templates in PowerPoint's File, New dialog box.

After you've created these elements, you'll want to let people know about them. The easiest way is to include them on a custom toolbar so they're instantly obvious to anyone creating a document that can use them.

After you've created AutoText entries and copied them into the appropriate templates, you can move on to customizing Word's user interface. As you'll learn in Chapter 26, "Customizing Word," you can include custom menus or toolbars in a template. Then, whenever you or anyone else creates a document based on that template, these custom menus and toolbars will be there to help.

▶ **See** "Customizing Toolbars," **p. 721**

▶ **See** "Customizing Menus," **p. 730**

You might create toolbar buttons that make it easier to insert the AutoText entries you've already provided. Also, think about other Word features you might include to make your toolbar more valuable. For example, your Report toolbar could include a button that inserts an Executive Summary on the first page, using Word 97's AutoSummarize feature.

▶ **See** "Working with AutoSummarize," **p. 225**

Part
II

Ch
6

Both of these examples utilize simple recorded macros that require no Visual Basic experience. If you're prepared to work in Visual Basic, you might include a button that automatically sends your Fax cover sheet and an attachment to a specified list of fax numbers. Suddenly, a task that may have taken a half-hour can be performed in a minute or two. If you've never recorded macros or worked with Visual Basic, perhaps these examples will begin to give you a sense of their power.

Chances are, your letters, memos, faxes, and reports also have a good deal in common. For example, they may all draw upon the same address lists and involve the same colleagues, suppliers, and customers. If so, you might create a menu with commands that apply to all your documents. Then, you can store this menu in a global template that always loads at startup, as mentioned earlier in this chapter.

▶ **See** "Understanding Global Templates," **p. 179**

▶ **See** "Using Workgroup Templates," **p. 800**

 T I P   If your computers are reliably networked, you can store this global template in a central Workgroup Templates folder that everyone can access. Then, when you make changes to this global template, you can store the new one in Workgroup Templates instead of copying it to everyone's computer.

After you're familiar with the Word features involved, you can create the beta version of all these templates in just a few hours, excluding Visual Basic programming. Try it out. If you're working as part of a team, share it with a few of your colleagues. Modify it as necessary. If you've chosen the right documents to automate, your time investment will pay for itself in just a few weeks—or possibly even a few days.

Troubleshooting Templates

You've already encountered a few of the ways templates can misbehave. For example, if you change the template attached to a specific document, the styles in that document won't change unless you instruct Word to change them in the Tools, Templates and Add-Ins dialog box. Here are a few potential template problems that haven't been discussed elsewhere.

- If you ever try to save a regular Word document and find that Word only lets you save it as a template, your computer may be infected by the Concept Virus. For more information about Word viruses.

    ▶ **See** "Preventing and Controlling Word Viruses," **p. 822**

- If you suddenly do not have access to a template you've been using, check to see if it has been moved. Also check to see whether you have lost access to the server where it is stored. If you have exited and restarted Word, also check to see whether the template is a global template that must be reloaded.

- If the Organizer will not let you copy styles, AutoText entries, macros, or toolbars to another template, there are a few possible causes. First, the template may be set as read-only. Second, it may be password-protected. Third, it may be protected for tracked changes, comments, or forms that require a special Word password that allows for revisions, comments, or the use of form fields but nothing else.

▶ **See** "Word Document Security," **p. 815**

Using Word Wizards

Word provides *wizards* that allow you to make a series of choices about how your new document will be constructed. When you finish making the choices, Word constructs the document for you. Then you only need to "fill in the holes" with your specific text and graphics. The entire skeleton is already in place, reflecting your choices. Once you learn how to use them, wizards can save you quite a bit of time.

Wizards Included with Word 97

Word 97 includes wizards for the following types of documents:

- Envelopes
- Fax cover sheets
- Letters
- Mailing labels
- Memos
- Legal pleadings
- Newsletters
- Résumés
- Web pages
  - ▶ **See** "Creating a Page with Word's Web Page Wizard," **p. 259**
  - ▶ **See** "Quick & Easy Newsletters With the Newsletter Wizard," **p. 536**

If you've installed the Office 97 ValuPack or Word 95 Wizards, as discussed earlier in this chapter, you also have wizards for the following documents:

- Agendas
- Awards
- Calendars

 T I P The ValuPack also includes a wizard for creating tables within other Word documents.

Walking Through a Typical Wizard

The best way to get the flavor for how wizards work is to walk through one. Because most wizards look and behave alike, all you need to see is one. Following is a step-by-step look at Word's Résumé Wizard:

Part
II

Ch

6

1. Choose File, New.

2. Click the Other Documents tab.

3. Double-click Résumé Wizard.

The opening window of the Résumé Wizard appears (see Figure 6.15). Along the left side, there's a subway-style map showing the entire process. A green square indicates where you are right now; you can click any other square to "hop" there. Four buttons along the bottom of the window also help you navigate through the wizard. Finally, if you click the Help button, the Office Assistant offers help about this wizard.

FIG. 6.15

A wizard's opening window explains what the wizard does and lists each step required to accomplish the goal.

T I P You don't always have to walk through every step of a wizard. After you've included all the information you want to include, click Finish. Word generates the document based on whatever information you've given it.

Click Next to get started. The wizard asks you to choose from Word's three built-in styles for résumés: Professional, Contemporary, or Elegant (see Figure 6.16). These are the same three style options available in most of Word's templates and wizards, making it easy to build a consistent set of documents. Make a choice, and click Next.

FIG. 6.16

You can choose the overall visual appearance of your Résumé on the Style page.

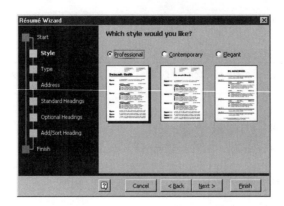

The wizard next asks what type of résumé you want to create (see Figure 6.17). You can choose an Entry-level résumé designed for individuals with little job experience; a Chronological résumé that lists your work experience by date; a Functional résumé that lists types of achievement; or a Professional résumé, which is commonly used in several professions. Make your choice and click Next.

FIG. 6.17
Specify which type of résumé you want, based on your experience and the expectations of your potential employers.

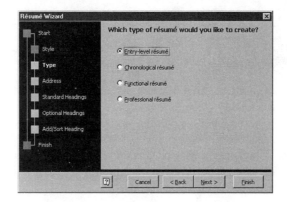

In the Address window (see Figure 6.18), you're asked for the personal information that Word doesn't already know. If you entered your name when you installed Word, that name will already appear in the Name text box. After you enter the personal information once, it appears automatically on this screen whenever you run the Résumé Wizard. When you're finished entering personal information, click Next.

FIG. 6.18
Word may already have your name; if so, enter your address, phone and fax numbers, and e-mail address in the Address window.

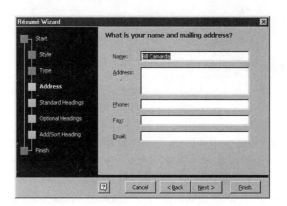

Part
II

Ch
6

In the Standard Headings window (see Figure 6.19), Word displays a list of headings that are commonly included in Résumés. The ones already checked are most commonly included in the type of Résumé you want to create. You can check or clear any of these check boxes. Click Next.

FIG. 6.19

Select from the headings that are most commonly used in résumés.

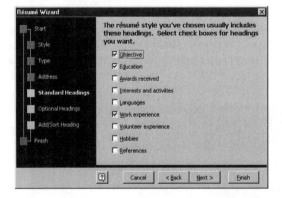

Sometimes you'll have experiences or qualifications that don't fit into typical categories used by résumés. For example, if you're new in the work force, you might want to mention Extracurricular activities or Community activities. If you are a professional engineer, you might have Patents and publications to your credit. You can specify these in the Optional Headings window (see Figure 6.20). When you're done, click Next.

FIG. 6.20

The Optional Headings window gives you a chance to specify more headings to cover additional qualifications or expertise.

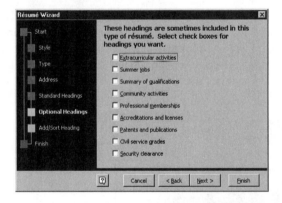

Now, in the Add/Sort Heading window (see Figure 6.21), Word gives you a chance to organize the headings you've chosen or add new ones that weren't included in previous windows. If you want to add a new heading, enter it in the Are There Any Additional Headings... text box, and click Add.

After you've added any new headings, you can make sure your headings are organized the way you want. Select a heading in the These Are Your Résumé Headings text box, and click Move Up or Move Down to move it towards the top or bottom of your résumé. If you decide upon reflection that you don't want a heading—perhaps you don't have enough to include in it, or it's inappropriate for the specific job you're seeking—select it, and click Remove. When you're finished, click Next.

FIG. 6.21

The Add/Sort Heading window gives you a chance to reorganize your headings or add new ones that Word doesn't include.

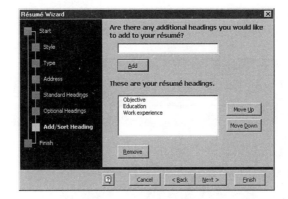

You're now in the final window of the Résumé Wizard (see Figure 6.22). Here's your chance to review your work. You can click any box at the left edge of the window to view its current settings, or click Back repeatedly to move back through the wizard one screen at a time.

FIG. 6.22

The Finish screen gives you a breather—and a chance to check your work.

After you're satisfied, click Finish, and Word creates your document. You can see the results in Figure 6.23. Notice that the Office Assistant appears, offering to walk you through some of the additional tasks involved in completing your résumé.

For example, if you want to send your résumé via fax or e-mail, click Send Résumé To Someone. Word opens your Microsoft e-mail software (Outlook, Exchange, or Internet Mail, depending on which is installed or selected) and attaches a copy of your résumé.

 TIP Of course, it's unlikely you'll be ready to send the résumé just yet, because you haven't filled in your specific qualifications yet. However, you can drag the Office Assistant out of your way until you're ready.

All the text in the résumé that appears within brackets is text you'll need to replace. Simply click inside any set of brackets; Word selects the entire block of text contained there. Start typing, and Word enters your replacement information. When you've added all the information you want to include about yourself, save the file as you normally would.

FIG. 6.23
This figure illustrates the résumé as it appears after the wizard finishes creating it.

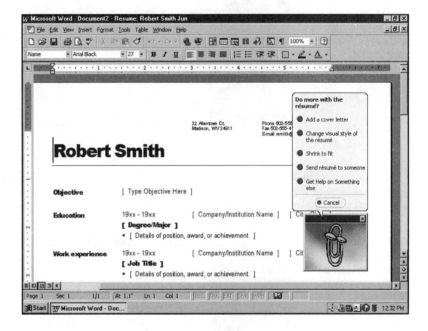

N O T E These clickable areas are actually Macrobutton fields. You can use them whenever you're creating a document where you want others to add information in specific locations. You'll learn more about Macrobutton fields in Chapter 25, "Automating Your Documents with Field Codes." ∎

Because the Résumé Wizard stores the settings you enter in it, it's suddenly much easier to create a customized version of your résumé whenever you apply for a new job. You no longer have to create one-size-fits-all résumés for mass résumé mailings; you can target your résumés to the needs of specific employers.

▶ **See** "AutoText: The Complete Boilerplate Resource," **p. 203**

 If you especially like a document that results from working with a wizard, consider saving it as a template. That way, you'll always have access to a document that's well along the way to completion, without even having to run the wizard.

 The next time you're searching for a job, consider using another Word feature along with the Résumé Wizard. AutoText entries are perfect for saving boilerplate content you can reuse in future personalized résumés and cover letters. For example, if you have language specifically written to highlight your qualifications as an administrative assistant, store that language as an AutoText entry, and reuse it the next time you apply for that position.

Understanding Word Add-Ins

Templates and wizards are powerful, but if you want to customize your Word environment even more, you'll want to know about add-ins. These are separate dynamic link libraries (.DLLs) that extend Word's capabilities, adding new features and custom commands. They're compiled, so they typically run faster than macros can. Like DLLs, they have access to the full capabilities of the Windows operating system. After they're built, they are renamed as .WLLs to indicate that they are Word linked libraries.

If you have installed Word 97's Web development environment, you already have an add-in: HTML.WLL. Many third-party Word add-ins are also available. Some, like Woody's Office Power Pack (WOPR)add several additional capabilities to Word and appeal to a broad range of users. For example, WOPR adds sophisticated envelope creation, file management, and many other features.

ON THE WEB

For more information about WOPR, visit **www.wopr.com**.

Other add-ins offer narrower capabilities designed to be of great value to specific users. For example, the EndNote Plus add-in from Niles & Associates enhances Word with extensive bibliographic reference capabilities. EndNote Plus has been purchased by more than 100,000 academic writers and researchers.

ON THE WEB

For more information about EndNote Plus, visit **www.niles.com**.

After you have an add-in, either follow the instructions that come with it, or install it the same way you install a global template:

1. Choose Tools, Templates and Add-Ins.
2. Click Add.
3. In the Add Templates dialog box, select the add-in you want to load.
4. Click OK.

Like global templates, add-ins normally won't load at startup unless you copy them to Word's startup folder or run a macro that loads them.

From Here...

In this chapter, you've learned how to use templates to slash the time it takes to create new documents and to build custom editing environments that save your colleagues time as well.

Part
II

Ch
6

Now, learn about some of the ways you can use templates to streamline document production even more:

- In Chapter 7, "sAutomating Your Documents: AutoCorrect, AutoFormat, AutoText, and AutoSummarize," you'll take a closer look at one of the most convenient, productive elements you can add to a template: AutoText entries.

- In Chapter 26, "Customizing Word," you'll learn more about creating the toolbars and menus that enable you to build custom editing environments into your templates.

- In Chapter 28, "Installing and Configuring Word in a Network Environment," you'll learn more about Workgroup Templates, and how they can streamline template deployment for an entire department or company.

- Finally, in Chapters 29 through 33, you'll see how recorded macros and Visual Basic can help you extend the power of your Word templates even further.

CHAPTER 7

Automating Your Documents: AutoCorrect, AutoFormat, AutoText, and AutoSummarize

by Bill Camarda

This chapter brings together four of Word's slickest automation features: AutoCorrect, AutoFormat, AutoText, and AutoSummarize. Together, these features can dramatically reduce the time it takes to create a nearly perfect document.

AutoCorrect follows you around as you work, fixing the spelling mistakes you're most likely to make. With AutoText, you can build a library of boilerplate text that virtually eliminates the annoying retyping, which is common in many documents. Then, with just a few keystrokes, you can summon a name, a paragraph, a page—anything you want. (And if a few keystrokes is too many, this chapter will show you how to perform the same magic with no keystrokes at all.)

Working with AutoCorrect

Right now, AutoCorrect is at work fixing nearly 500 common spelling mistakes.

Making AutoCorrect even smarter

You can add entries that make AutoCorrect even more powerful— or tell it what to ignore.

AutoText: The master of boilerplate

AutoText now has dozens of useful built-in entries, but you leverage its real power when you add your own.

Using AutoText to make everyone more productive

AutoText can handle graphics, logos, and signatures, and you can build AutoText libraries that help your whole workgroup get the job done faster.

AutoFormatting: Let Word do the formatting for you

Word's AutoFormat feature can slash the time it takes you to format a document. Word even formats your document in the background as you work.

Working with AutoSummarize

For reports, articles and other highly structured documents, Word 97 can actually generate summaries automatically.

With AutoFormat, you may be able to stop worrying about formatting; you can have Word apply built-in formats and styles for you. With AutoSummarize, remarkably, Word reads a document and builds an executive summary or abstract for you. Given the right documents, AutoFormat and AutoSummarize can deliver surprisingly useful results. In other documents, these two features still betray their nonhuman origins. So this chapter won't just show you how to use them; you'll learn when to use them and how to improve the results you can expect. ■

AutoCorrect: Smarter Than Ever

Are you getting smarter as you get older? You are if you're using Word. With each new version, Word's AutoCorrect feature becomes more powerful. In Word 97, unless you tell it otherwise, Word automatically corrects nearly 500 of the most common spelling mistakes people make. That's not all. Word performs the following tasks:

- Makes sure you start all your sentences with a capital letter
- Corrects words you inadvertently start with two capital letters
- Capitalizes days of the week, such as Tuesday
- Fixes things when you inadvertently press the Caps Lock key
- Replaces character strings like (c) with symbols like ©
- Replace Internet "smileys" like :) with Wingding symbols like ☺

If you're using Word's default settings, this is all happening right now in the background; you haven't had to do a thing. You can take control of Word's AutoCorrect settings and make it back off on certain things, or stop correcting you altogether. Conversely, you can make it even smarter by adding your own entries. To control AutoCorrect, choose Tools, AutoCorrect to display the AutoCorrect tab of the AutoCorrect dialog box (see Figure 7.1).

FIG. 7.1
From the AutoCorrect tab, you control AutoCorrect's overall behavior and specify which text elements it automatically corrects.

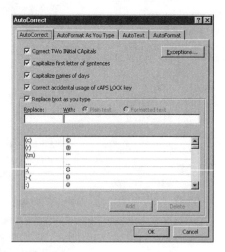

T I P Three more of Word's automation features—AutoCorrect, AutoFormat, and AutoText—can also be controlled from the AutoCorrect dialog box. Rather than accessing this dialog box only when you want to make a single change, consider investing a few minutes in systematically adding entries to AutoCorrect and AutoText, and setting the AutoFormatting controls that make most sense for you.

By default, all of Word's AutoCorrect capabilities are selected. A couple of AutoCorrect options are so innocuous that few people will want to turn them off. Capitalize Names of Days automatically adds a capital letter at the beginning of the seven days of the week: Sunday, Monday, Tuesday, and so on. If you think about it, you'll rarely, if ever, want these words lowercased.

N O T E This feature doesn't change day-of-the-week abbreviations such as Tues. or Thu.; it only affects days of the week that are fully spelled out. ▪

Another option, Correct Accidental Usage of cAPS LOCK Key, is designed for those times when your left pinkie finger inadvertently presses Caps Lock instead of A or Q at the left edge of your keyboard. If this happens part way into a word, Word recognizes you probably didn't mean it. Rather than letting you continue typing until you notice the problem, it turns off Caps Lock and changes the capitalization on all the letters it thinks you reversed. For instance, if you type

   sPORTSMANSHIP

Word will turn off Caps Lock and edit your text to read

   Sportsmanship

N O T E This feature never changes text you capitalized by pressing and holding the Shift key. ▪

The Heart of AutoCorrect: Nearly 500 Built-In Spelling Corrections

When designing Word 97, Microsoft tracked nearly 500 mistakes that writers tend to make most and built these errors into AutoCorrect. These errors fall into the following categories:

- ▪ Spelling errors: Word replaces *acheive* with *achieve*.
- ▪ Common typos: Word replaces *teh* with *the*.
- ▪ Spaces left out between words: Word replaces *saidthat* with *said that*.
- ▪ Errors in usage: Word replaces *should of been* with *should have been* and *their are* with *there are*.
- ▪ Missing or incorrect apostrophes: Word replaces *wouldnt* with *wouldn't* and *you;re* with *you're*.
- ▪ Forgotten accent characters: Word replaces *seance* with *séance*.

Part
II

Ch
7

In addition, Word inserts a wide variety of symbols in place of the fake symbols that many writers use. For example, if you type **(c),** Word will replace it with ©. Word adds a list of Internet/e-mail smileys. For example, Word replaces **:(** with the corresponding symbol from the Wingding font: ☹. The complete list of symbols AutoCorrect replaces is shown in Table 7.1.

Table 7.1 Symbols And Smileys Word Automatically Replaces	
Text You Type...	**Symbol Word Inserts...**
-->	→
:(	☹
:)	☺
:-(	☹
:-)	☺
:-|	😐
:|	😐
<--	←
<==	⬅
<=>	⇔
==>	→

If you're simply not comfortable with Word changing your spelling, you can clear the Replace Text As You Type box, and Word will leave all your potential errors alone. You might, however, simply disagree with some of the replacements Word chooses to make. For example, if you copy text formatted with the Wingding font into an e-mail message, that text may not appear correctly when your recipient gets it. If you are a fiction writer using dialect, you don't want Word to clean up usage like *should of had.* Or, say you work for the CNA insurance company and you want Word to stop changing your company name to "CAN." Follow these steps to remove an AutoCorrect entry:

1. Choose Tools, AutoCorrect.
2. In the list beneath the Replace text box, scroll to the entry you want to remove.
3. Select it. The entry appears in the Replace and With text boxes.
4. Click Delete.

The entry is removed from your AutoCorrect list. However, it remains in the Replace and With text boxes, so if you change your mind, you can click Add to put it back in your list.

TIP If you save a Word file to text-only format, Word reverts the smileys to their original characters. For example, ☺ becomes :) again.

Adding a New AutoCorrect Entry

More often, you'll want to add new AutoCorrect entries that reflect the errors you make most often. To add a new entry, display the AutoCorrect tab by choosing Tools, AutoCorrect, and then type the version you want Word to replace. In the With text box, type the text you want Word to insert. Click Add. The new entry now appears in the AutoCorrect list.

  You can also add AutoCorrect entries while you're spell checking. In fact, that's a great time to do it, because that's when you're systematically reviewing documents and discovering the errors you're most likely to make. Click the Spelling and Grammar button on the Standard toolbar to run Word's spell checker. Word displays your first error in the Spelling and Grammar dialog box. Select the replacement text you want to use; if you want Word to correct this error from now on, click AutoCorrect.

You can also right-click an error within the document; select AutoCorrect from the shortcut menu, and select one of the choices Word provides (see Figure 7.2). Once again, Word automatically corrects the mistake in the future.

▶ **See** "Checking Grammar and Spelling in Your Document," **p. 125**

FIG. 7.2
You can add an AutoCorrect entry from the shortcut menu in any document.

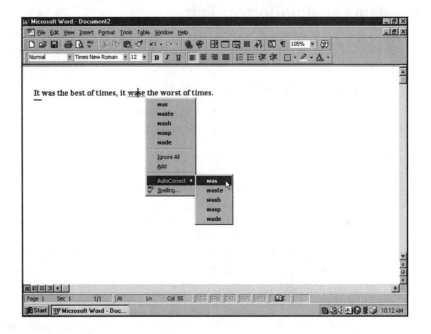

 A word doesn't have to be misspelled for you to ask Word to correct it. For example, if you constantly type **manger** instead of **manager**, you can tell Word to make the change automatically, even though *manger* is a perfectly legitimate word.

Part
II

Ch
7

TIP You may want a list of all the AutoCorrect entries available to you. You can get one by using the AutoCorrect Utility backup and restore macros contained in Macro8.dot—a set of Word 97 macros available in the ValuPack folder with Office 97.

The longer you work with Word, the more entries you're likely to add in the AutoCorrect dialog box. If you get a new computer, can you move those entries with you? Or, can you share these entries with other users? Yes, but the procedure is quite involved. It requires you to create a floppy containing the .ACL file where your entries are stored, copy your NORMAL.DOT file to the floppy and export the registry key associated with your AutoCorrect file, and then copy these files onto your new workstation and reimport the registry key there.

ON THE WEB

If you ever need to do this, you can get detailed instructions from Microsoft Knowledge Base article Q153149, available at the following Web address:

www.microsoft.com/kb/articles/q153/1/49.htm

Changing an AutoCorrect Entry

On occasion, instead of deleting an entry, you might want to change the replacement text Word uses. From within the AutoCorrect tab, follow these steps to change Word default replacement text:

1. In the list beneath the Replace text box, scroll to the entry you want to remove.
2. Select it. The entry appears in the Replace and With text boxes.
3. Enter the new text you want in the With text box.
4. Click Replace.

Using AutoCorrect to Insert Boilerplate Text

Later in this chapter, you'll learn about AutoText, a powerful feature that enables you to manage boilerplate text and insert it into a document with just a few keystrokes. You can also use AutoCorrect this way—not to correct errors, but to insert large blocks of formatted or unformatted text automatically. For example, since the recent securities reform legislation passed Congress, it's common to see a disclaimer such as the one in Figure 7.3. You wouldn't want to type that twice—and your lawyers wouldn't want you to inadvertently miss anything. Follow these steps to have AutoCorrect to insert it automatically:

1. Select the text you want Word to add automatically. (You don't have to copy it.)
2. Choose Tools, AutoCorrect. The text you selected appears as Formatted Text in the With text box. If necessary, the text box expands to two lines to accommodate at least some of the additional text. The text appears with the same boldface, italic, or underline character formatting you applied in the document; this formatting will appear whenever Word inserts the AutoCorrect entry.

FIG. 7.3

A sample block of text you can ask Word to replace automatically with AutoCorrect.

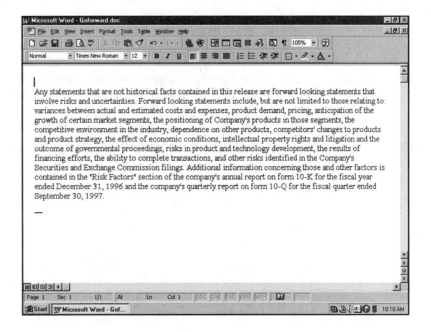

3. In the Replace text box, enter a distinctive sequence of letters that you wouldn't inadvertently use for any other purpose, such as *forwdlkg*.

4. Click Add.

After you've added your AutoCorrect entry, every time you type **forwdlkg** followed by a space, Word will automatically replace that word with the entire block of boilerplate text, shown in Figure 7.3.

You can insert graphics or heavily formatted text with an AutoCorrect entry, as long as you select it before choosing Tools, AutoCorrect. If you create an entry that Word can't display within the AutoCorrect dialog box, such as an image, Word will place an asterisk in its place. When you use the AutoCorrect entry, however, it will work properly.

> **CAUTION**
>
> Word doesn't limit the length of Formatted text you can place in an AutoCorrect entry, but it does limit Plain text entries to 255 characters and cuts off any text that extends beyond that.

Using AutoCorrect to Add Dummy Text

Ever need to quickly add some generic or dummy text, just to get a feel for the formatting of a page? Word has a built-in AutoCorrect entry that'll do it for you. It enters paragraphs full of this classic sentence (carefully designed to use one of each letter in the alphabet): *The quick brown fox jumps over the lazy dog.*

Part
II

Ch
7

To tell Word to insert a paragraph containing this sentence five times over, type **=rand()** and press Enter.

You can actually control how many times the sentence appears and how many paragraphs you get. Type **=rand(p,s)**, where **p** equals the number of paragraphs and **s** equals the number of sentences. This only works when the Replace Text As You Type feature is turned on in the AutoCorrect tab.

AutoCorrecting Initial Caps and Sentence Capitalization

You may have noticed two more options in the AutoCorrect dialog box:

- *Correct TWo INitial CApitals*. If you place two capital letters at the beginning of a word, AutoCorrect makes the second letter lowercase.
- *Capitalize First Letter of Sentences*. If you start a sentence with a lowercase letter, AutoCorrect capitalizes it for you.

Most of the time, these features work as intended, fixing inadvertent mistakes. However, there are times you won't want Word to make these AutoCorrections. For example, what if you include an abbreviation within a sentence, and the abbreviation ends in a period, as follows:

```
Please contact Smith Corp. regarding their overdue invoices.
```

When AutoCorrect was first introduced in Word 6, it would see the period after *Corp.*, see the space after it, and assume wrongly that the word *regarding* started a new sentence. Word 97 (and Word 95) fix this problem by letting you specify *exceptions*—words that AutoCorrect won't fix. In Word 97, AutoCorrect contains a list of 115 common abbreviations. When Word sees one of these abbreviations, it doesn't assume that it has arrived at the end of a sentence, notwithstanding the period in the abbreviation.

If you use specialized abbreviations, such as those common in scientific or technical fields, you might want to add them to your Exceptions list. To do so, follow these steps:

1. Choose Tools, AutoCorrect.
2. Click Exceptions. The AutoCorrect Exceptions dialog box opens.
3. Click the First Letter tab.
4. Enter your new exception in the Don't Capitalize After text box.
5. Click Add.

> **CAUTION**
>
> In the first release of Word 97, AutoCorrect doesn't automatically capitalize the first sentence of a paragraph if it follows a form field or a Web page hyperlink.

Creating Capitalization Exceptions for Product Names, Brand Names, and Acronyms As mentioned earlier, Word also automatically fixes words that start with two capital letters. No standard English words begin with two capital letters, so most of the time you'll want this.

However, you may occasionally come across a product, brand name, or acronym that is capitalized oddly to attract attention. For example, the CompuServe online information service recently renamed itself *CSi*. Word automatically corrects this to *Csi*. You can create an exception for oddly capitalized words as follows:

1. Choose <u>T</u>ools, <u>A</u>utoCorrect.
2. Click <u>E</u>xceptions. The AutoCorrect Exceptions dialog box opens.
3. Click the <u>I</u>Nitial CAps tab.
4. Enter your new exception in the D<u>o</u>n't Correct text box.
5. Click <u>A</u>dd.

Telling Word to Create Exceptions Automatically   Wouldn't it be nice if Word were smart enough not to make the same mistake twice? What if Word saw the fixes you made manually, and added them to its Exceptions list so you wouldn't be bothered again? It can, and it does. In either AutoCorrect Exceptions tab, if you check the A<u>u</u>tomatically Add Words To List check box, Word will watch as you work. If Word corrects a first letter or capitalization, and you immediately backspace to type over the correction (using the left-arrow key), Word adds your correction to the exception list.

> **N O T E**   Word won't add a correction to the exception list unless you use the Backspace key to make the correction. Neither pressing shortcut keys nor using Undo will work. ▪

> **T I P**   There are separate automatic exception controls in each tab of the AutoCorrect Exceptions dialog box, so you can tell Word to automatically add abbreviations to its exceptions list, but not Initial Caps—or vice versa.

AutoText: The Complete Boilerplate Resource

You've already seen how you can use AutoCorrect to enter large blocks of boilerplate text quickly. However, this isn't AutoCorrect's primary function. Another Word feature, AutoText, is designed specifically to help you manage and quickly insert boilerplate text. If you build a library of AutoText entries, you can dramatically reduce the amount of retyping you have to do. At the same time, you can help your colleagues build documents more quickly and more consistently. In other words, whether you're working on your own or in a corporate setting, AutoText offers enormous opportunities to improve productivity.

> **N O T E**   If you're upgrading from Word 2 for Windows, AutoText is the feature you've known as Glossary. ▪

Part

II

Ch

7

AutoText Entries Built Into Word 97

Word 97 comes with dozens of built-in AutoText entries to help you streamline letters and other documents. These are listed in Table 7.2.

Table 7.2 Word 97's Built-In AutoText Entries	
Category (Submenu)	**Options**
Attention Line	Attention:; ATTN:
Closing	Best regards; Best wishes; Cordially; Love; Regards; Respectfully Yours; Respectfully; Sincerely yours; Sincerely; Take care; Thank you; Thanks; Yours truly
Header/Footer	–Page–; Author Page# Date; Created by; Created on; Confidential; Page # Date; Last printed; Last saved by; Filename; Filename and Path; Page X of Y
Mailing Instructions	CERTIFIED MAIL; CONFIDENTIAL; PERSONAL; REGISTERED MAIL; SPECIAL DELIVERY; VIA AIRMAIL; VIA FACSIMILE; VIA OVERNIGHT MAIL
Reference Line	In reply to:; RE:; Reference
Salutation	Dear Mom and Dad; Dear Sir or Madam; Ladies and Gentlemen; To Whom It May Concern
Subject Line	Subject:

Inserting an Existing AutoText Entry

To use one of Word's entries—or any other entry you create—choose Insert, AutoText, and display the cascading menu containing the entry you want to use (see Figure 7.4). Then click the entry, and Word will insert it in your document.

 Some of Word's built-in AutoText entries contain fields that update themselves. For example, if you insert the Author, Page #, Date entry in your header or footer, Word enters three fields: the { AUTHOR } field, which reports the name of the author as it appears in your Properties dialog box; the { PAGE } field, which displays the current page number, and the { DATE } field that displays the current date. You can see sample field results for this AutoText entry in Figure 7.5.

When you display a header or footer, the Header and Footer toolbar appears—including the Insert AutoText button, which lists all of Word's Header and Footer AutoText entries (see Figure 7.6), making them conveniently accessible.

FIG. 7.4
Select an existing
AutoText entry.

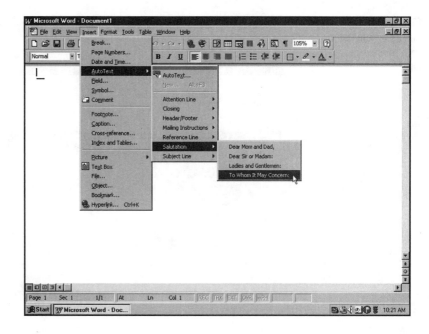

FIG. 7.5
You can get a heading
containing Author,
Page, and Date
information by
choosing it from the list
of AutoText entries.

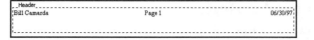

Selecting AutoText entries from menus and toolbars is especially convenient when you are inserting built-in AutoText entries because many of them are relatively long and easy to mistype. However, if you remember the name of your AutoText entry, there's often a faster way to insert it in your document: Type the name of the AutoText entry, and press F3. Word replaces the AutoText entry you typed and inserts the longer text that is associated with the entry.

CAUTION

The AutoText entry must be separate from the text that precedes and follows it in order for Word to recognize it as an AutoText entry when you press F3. However, it can be within parentheses, or immediately before punctuation such as a period, colon, or semicolon.

Part
II

Ch
7

FIG. 7.6
Choose an AutoText
entry for a header or
footer.

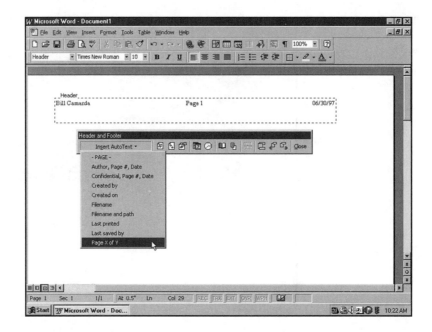

Working with the AutoText Toolbar

If you're planning to work with quite a few AutoText entries at the same time, you may want to display the AutoText toolbar (see Figure 7.7). This toolbar contains three buttons:

■ The AutoText button, which displays the AutoText dialog box, where you can control all aspects of your collection of AutoText entries.

■ A button that displays all your current AutoText entries, or those associated with the style you're currently using.

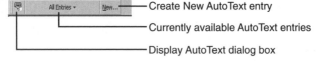

■ A New button appears when you've selected text. Click it to display the Create AutoText entry you've already seen.

FIG. 7.7
If you're working on
many AutoText entries at
the same time, display
the AutoText toolbar.

— Create New AutoText entry

— Currently available AutoText entries

— Display AutoText dialog box

Entering AutoText Entries Even Faster with AutoComplete

Let's say you have an AutoText entry, such as *cancel* that places your company's standard cancellation clause in your document. As you've seen, if you want to use this entry, you can type **cancel**, press F3, and Word inserts the formatted text. But in Word 97, there's an even quicker way. As soon as you type the fourth letter in this (or any) AutoText entry, a ScreenTip appears showing all the text associated with the AutoText entry (or as much as will fit within the ScreenTip). You can see an example in Figure 7.8.

If you are planning to use this AutoText entry, just press Enter and Word inserts the entry at the current insertion point. If you aren't planning to use the AutoText entry—for example, if you're typing another word that just happens to start the same way as an AutoText entry—just ignore the ScreenTip and keep typing.

FIG. 7.8

When you type the fourth letter of an AutoText entry, Word displays the first words of text associated with that entry.

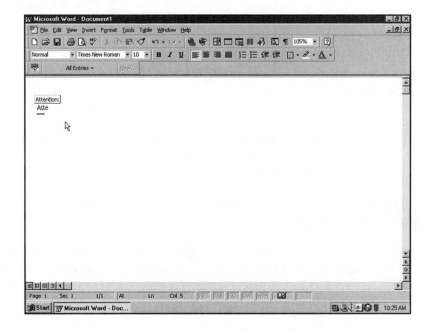

If you have two AutoText entries that start with the same four letters, Word won't display a ScreenTip until you've entered enough text for it to choose the one you're most likely to want.

 TIP AutoComplete doesn't just work with AutoText entries; it also offers to complete months of the year, days of the week, and today's date. Be careful about allowing Word to AutoComplete today's date, however. If you're working past midnight, AutoComplete doesn't always notice that a new day has arrived.

N O T E AutoText ScreenTips have a slight effect on your system's performance. If Word is running slowly, you might try disabling them. To do so, choose Insert, AutoText, AutoText, and then clear the Show AutoComplete Tip for AutoText and Dates check box. ■

Part

II

Ch

7

Creating Your Own AutoText Entry

Word's built-in AutoText entries are very handy, but you won't get the full benefits of AutoText until you start creating your own entries. There are several ways to create your entry. The quickest way is to select the text you want to transform into an AutoText entry, and press Alt+F3. The Create AutoText dialog box opens (see Figure 7.9).

N O T E   You can also display this dialog box by choosing <u>I</u>nsert, <u>A</u>utoText, <u>N</u>ew.

FIG. 7.9
One of the quickest
ways to create an
AutoText entry is to
press Alt+F3 to display
the Create AutoText
dialog box.

Word automatically displays the first word or words in the text you've selected. Edit this text into a brief entry you'll find easy to remember, and choose OK. Now, the entry appears in the AutoText cascaded dialog box with any other entries you may have added.

T I P   If you want your AutoText entry to include paragraph formatting, include in your selection the paragraph mark (¶) at the end of the paragraph containing that formatting.

AutoText entries are stored with whatever character formatting you've applied with them. That saves you the trouble of duplicating complex character formats later. However, paragraph styles aren't saved, so AutoText entries can take on the paragraph style of surrounding text wherever you insert them.

Understanding Where AutoText Entries Are Stored and Displayed

All of Word's built-in AutoText entries are stored in the Normal template. New AutoText entries are stored in the template associated with the document you're working in. In other words, if you are working on a document based on the Normal template, any AutoText entry you create manually is also stored in the Normal template. Then, whenever you are working on a document based on the Normal template, you have access to all the AutoText entries you've stored in the Normal template, with one major exception. If your insertion point is currently within a block of text formatted in a custom style, and if that custom style has AutoText entries associated with it, Word will only display the entries associated with the custom style. You can see this most easily when the AutoText toolbar is displayed. If you are currently working in text formatted in a custom style that has AutoText entries associated with it, that style's name appears in place of All Entries. When you click the button, you'll see only the entries associated with that style.

If you need access to an AutoText entry that isn't displayed, press Shift as you display the list of AutoText entries via either the AutoText toolbar or the Insert, AutoText cascaded menu, or click your insertion point in text formatted with any of Word's standard styles, such as Normal, Body Text, or any built-in Heading style.

Saving an AutoText Entry in a Different Template   At times you might want to store AutoText entries in a different template than Normal. Your AutoText entries might be relevant only when you're creating a specialized kind of document, and you always use the same custom template to create that kind of document. Why clutter up the Normal template with AutoText entries you'll never use in the documents you create with Normal? To create AutoText entries in another template, first create or open a document based on that template; then create the AutoText entry as you normally do.

Controlling the Templates in Which AutoText Entries Are Available   By default, Word makes available AutoText entries in *all* templates that are currently open. For example, if you are working in a file created by a template named SMITH.DOT, you'll have access to all AutoText entries stored in SMITH.DOT, as well as those in NORMAL.DOT—a global template that is always open. If you're using a customized template, you might not want to see the more general AutoText entries you may have associated with NORMAL.DOT.

You can choose any open template and tell Word to display only the AutoText entries associated with that template by following these steps:

1. Choose Insert, AutoText, AutoText. The AutoText tab of the AutoCorrect dialog box opens (see Figure 7.10).

2. In the Look In drop-down list box, choose the template containing the entries you want to see.

3. Click OK.

FIG. 7.10

With the AutoText tab of the AutoCorrect dialog box, you can control which template's AutoText entries are active.

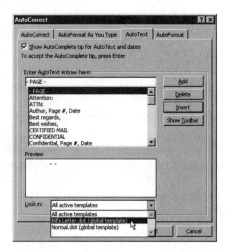

When you return to your editing window, you'll see that AutoText entries associated with other templates are no longer available from the AutoText menu. If you type them in your document and press F3 or use AutoComplete, nothing will happen.

Adding New Categories of AutoText Entries   You might want to add new categories of AutoText entries. That way, when you click Insert, AutoText, your new categories appear along with Word's built-in submenus. For example, imagine you work for the sales department of Acme Corporation; you might like a submenu called Acme Proposals which contains AutoText entries you can include in your sales proposals. Word organizes AutoText entries in submenus, based on the styles with which they are associated. When you want to create a new submenu, you can use this to your advantage.

First, create a new style with the name you want to appear in your custom submenu. To do so, select a paragraph, click the drop-down style box, type the new name, and press Enter. Don't worry much about how your style is formatted. When you select an AutoText entry, it uses the surrounding formatting in your document, not the formatting associated with the style you've just created.

Next, enter the first block of text you want to create an AutoText entry for and format the text using the style you've just created.

Then, create the AutoText entry using whatever method you prefer. Repeat the process for any other text you want to appear in the same submenu; make sure to format the text with your custom style before you create the AutoText entry.

After you've done this, your new AutoText entries will appear in their own submenu whenever you're working in the same template where you created them.

Creative Ways to Use AutoText

You can use AutoText to store virtually anything you can place in a document, not just text. Here are some types of entries that you might want to store as AutoText:

- Your signature and the signature of anyone else for whom you prepare documents
- Your corporate logo
- Photos and drawings
- Complex table formats
- Complex field codes, such as customized cross-references

 TIP   If you are creating a Web page, you can also store AutoText entries that place custom design elements or pieces of HTML code into your document, such as customized bullets and borders.

Using AutoText in the Corporation

If you are responsible for a group of people who use Word, you can organize a series of AutoText entries that your entire team can use to streamline work and improve consistency.

You can then store this set of AutoText entries in a global workgroup template to which everyone has access via the network. Also, you could distribute a new template for installation and use on each individual computer.

> **CAUTION**
>
> If you're distributing a template, don't name it NORMAL.DOT. Installing a template with that name overwrites any custom settings your colleagues have added on their own.

Here's a plan for creating AutoText entries for a workgroup:

1. Give some thought to how you'll name your AutoText entries. Make sure your entry names have an internal logic to them and can be easily remembered by your colleagues. Also try to keep them short so they'll be quicker to enter.

2. Review a selection of representative documents your organization creates to look for language that might be reused. You may want to edit your existing language to improve it before storing it as an AutoText entry. In some cases, you may find entire documents that can be reused and saved as separate templates.

3. Look for other document elements that can be saved as AutoText entries: logos, signatures, formatted tables, and so on.

4. Think about other AutoText entries that would be valuable to have such as proposal language that would assist the entire sales force, boilerplate language such as disclaimers and certifications, and corporate capabilities language, such as the company history, experience and mission statement, and so on. Locate or create the language and save it as an AutoText entry.

5. Consider ways to make the AutoText entries more accessible to inexperienced users. For example, you might create a custom toolbar or menu that contains the AutoText entries your colleagues are likely to use most. Or (as you'll learn shortly), you might embed lists of AutoText options directly into the most common documents you create, using the { AUTOTEXTLIST } field.

6. Give people hard copy listings of all the AutoText entries you're providing them. To do so, print the AutoText entries associated with the template you create. (Printing lists of AutoText entries is covered in the next section.)

   ▶ **See** "Customizing Toolbars," **p. 721**
   ▶ **See** "Using Workgroup Templates," **p. 800**

 TIP If you've been using AutoText, you may already have many of the entries you need. You can move existing entries into new templates through the Organizer. To display the Organizer, choose Tools, Templates and Add-Ins, and then click Organizer. Click the AutoText tab to display all the AutoText entries in your current template (see Figure 7.11). To copy an entry into a different template, select it and click Copy.

While you're in the Organizer, you might find you want to rename some existing AutoText entries. To do so, select the entry you want to rename. Click Rename. Enter the new name in the Rename dialog box. Choose OK and then Close.

Part
II

Ch
7

FIG. 7.11

The AutoText tab of the Organizer enables you to copy AutoText entries from one template to another, as well as to rename or delete entries.

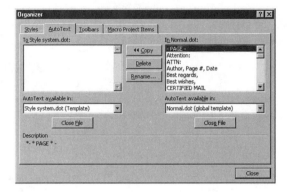

▶ **See** "Keeping Track of Styles with the Organizer," **p. 157**

Printing Lists of AutoText Entries

The more you work with AutoText entries, the more you'll need to keep track of them. You've already seen how you can review your entire list of AutoText entries in the AutoText dialog box, and how you can move entries among templates with the Organizer. You might also want to print a list of entries associated with a specific template. To print the list of entries, follow these steps:

1. Create or open a new document based on the template containing the entries you want to print.
2. Choose File, Print.
3. In the Print What drop-down box, choose AutoText Entries.
4. Choose OK.

Changing an Existing AutoText Entry

You'll occasionally want to change an AutoText entry. To change an entry, follow these steps:

1. Insert the AutoText entry in your document.
2. Edit the AutoText entry to reflect your changes.
3. Select the entire AutoText entry.
4. Choose Insert, AutoText, AutoText to display the AutoText dialog box.
5. Select the name of the AutoText entry you want to change.
6. Click Add. Word will display a dialog box asking whether you want to redefine your AutoText entry (see Figure 7.12).
7. Click Yes.

Changing AutoText entries won't change any text you've previously inserted in a document using those entries. Unless, that is, you use the procedure discussed in the following section.

FIG. 7.12
Word double-checks
that you really want to
change an existing
AutoText entry.

Inserting AutoText Entries That Update Themselves

After you enter text in your document using an AutoText entry, that text looks and behaves no differently than if you had typed it manually. But what if you could enter an AutoText entry that updates itself whenever the AutoText entry is updated? Imagine that your corporate lawyers change the boilerplate disclaimer language you've been using. Wouldn't it be great if your entire workgroup could have access to the new language immediately? It would be nice if you could easily update your existing documents and other documents in progress to reflect the change.

Instead of inserting your AutoText entry using the methods discussed earlier, use an { AUTOTEXT } field as follows:

1. Choose Insert, Field. The Field dialog box opens.
2. Choose AutoText from the Field Names list.
3. Click Options. Word displays a list of all the AutoText entries currently available to you.
4. Select the entry you want to insert.
5. Click Add to Field.
6. Click OK.

If you're displaying field results, your document will look exactly as if you had inserted the AutoText entry the normal way. If, however, you change the text (or other document elements) associated with this AutoText entry, Word can update the field the same way it updates any other fields.

 Remember, you can update all the fields in your document by pressing Ctrl+A and then F9.

Inserting AutoText Options Within Your Document

If you're setting up a document or template for others to work on, you can streamline their work by making it easy for them to choose the right AutoText entries wherever they're appropriate. You do this by inserting an { AUTOTEXTLIST } field at the place in your document wherever a choice needs to be made.

You can see { AUTOTEXTLIST } fields at work in Word's letter templates, which embed multiple options for Salutations and Closings directly in the documents they create. In Figure 7.13, if you right-click the word Sincerely, Word displays a list containing all of Word's built-in choices for letter closings. As you can see in Figure 7.14, if you click the word once, a ScreenTip appears explaining how the { AUTOTEXTLIST } field works.

Part

II

Ch

7

FIG. 7.13

If you right-click the letter closing in a built-in Word letter template, you can choose from all of Word's AutoText entries for letter closings.

FIG. 7.14

You can insert a ScreenTip that includes directions for anyone who single-clicks the { AUTOTEXTLIST } field you entered.

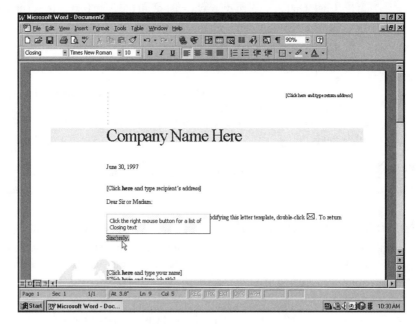

The syntax for an { AUTOTEXTLIST } field is as follows:

```
{ AUTOTEXTLIST "<LiteralText>" \s ["StyleName>"] \t ["<TipText>]]
```

LiteralText is the text you want to appear in the document before the user right-clicks it.

For *LiteralText*, use the text that's most likely to be the right choice. That way, users can often ignore the field.

The \s switch and `StyleName` tell Word to display all the AutoText entries associated with a specific style. You don't have to specify the same style in which the field result is formatted. You can choose any style currently available to the document. If you like, you can ignore the \s switch and format the text using the style containing the AutoText entries you want to show.

The \t switch and `TipText` tell Word what information to display in the ScreenTip when a user hovers his or her mouse pointer over the field. If you don't include a \t switch, Word will still display instructions, similar to those you saw in Figure 7.14.

 Consider the many ways you could use { AUTOTEXTLIST }:

- To choose different text in a proposal based on whether the project schedule is normal or rushed
- To select one of several preformatted tables
- To insert a signature from any one of several people
- To choose the contents of a letter from a set of pre-established AutoText entries

AutoFormatting: The Fastest Way to Format

If you haven't bothered to format your document at all, or if you've received it in ASCII (text-only) format via e-mail, maybe Word can handle the formatting for you. Choose AutoFormat from the Format menu. The AutoFormat dialog box opens (see Figure 7.15).

FIG. 7.15
You can tell AutoFormat to go ahead and reformat anything it pleases, or you can review the results of AutoFormat's handiwork, one change at a time.

To give it a try, click OK, and Word will reformat the entire document for you. Table 7.3 shows many of the changes Word can make.

Part
II

Ch
7

Table 7.3 What AutoFormat Changes

Whenever You Type the Following:	Here's How Word Changes It:
The following sequence: A number; followed by a period, hyphen, closing parenthesis, or > sign; followed by a space or tab; followed by text.	Word begins a numbered list.
The following sequence: An asterisk, one or two hyphens, or any of the following: >, -> --> ; followed by a space or tab; followed by text.	Word begins a bulleted list.
A symbol or inline picture, at least two spaces followed by text or picture.	Word begins a bulleted list, using the symbol as the bullet.
At least three of the following characters in a row above a paragraph: - _ * ~ # .	Word places a border line above the paragraph. (AutoFormat As You Type only.)
Straight quotation marks: "or '.	Word replaces these with curly quotation marks (SmartQuotes).
The following fractions: 1/4, 1/2, or 3/4.	Word replaces these with fraction symbols: $1/4$, $1/2$, or $3/4$.
Ordinal numbers: 1st, 2nd, 3rd, 4th.	Word replaces these with 1st, 2nd, 3rd, 4th.
Hyphens between text (for example, "28 - 56").	Word eliminates space surrounding hyphens; changes hyphen to en dash: 28-56.
Double hyphens surrounded by text.	Word changes hyphens to em dash (—).
Asterisk (*) followed by text and another asterisk.	Word removes asterisks; boldfaces remaining text (or uses other character formatting in Strong character style).
Underline (_) followed by text and another underline.	Word removes underlines; italicizes remaining text (or uses other character formatting in Emphasis character style).
Web address; for example, **www.yahoo.com**.	Word formats Web address as a hyperlink.
Plus sign (+) followed by hyphens, followed by another plus sign.	Word inserts a table, with one column per plus sign.

Whenever You Type the Following:	Here's How Word Changes It:
Formatted list item, followed by one of the following: . : - — ? ! followed by a space or tab; followed by text.	Word applies the same formatting to the lead-in text in the next paragraph. In other words, Word assumes you are continuing a customized list. (AutoFormat As You Type only.)

If your document is a letter (or e-mail), tell Word, and it will do a better job of AutoFormatting. In the AutoFormat dialog box, choose Letter or E-mail instead of General document.

 TIP Try running AutoFormat simply to get an idea of what AutoFormat will do to your document. Next, click Undo, and then (as is discussed in the next section) adjust AutoFormat options so Word doesn't make changes you don't like.

If you want, you can AutoFormat only part of a document; select it before you choose Format, AutoFormat. Don't forget there's a separate set of AutoFormatting controls for tables (choose Table, AutoFormat). The AutoFormat command discussed in this chapter doesn't touch the way your tables are formatted.

To get an idea of what AutoFormat can do, take a look at this before-and-after document makeover. The version in Figure 7.16 contains almost no formatting; Figure 7.17 shows the same document after AutoFormatting was used.

FIG. 7.16

Before: A document that is completely unformatted except for headings that have manually applied boldface.

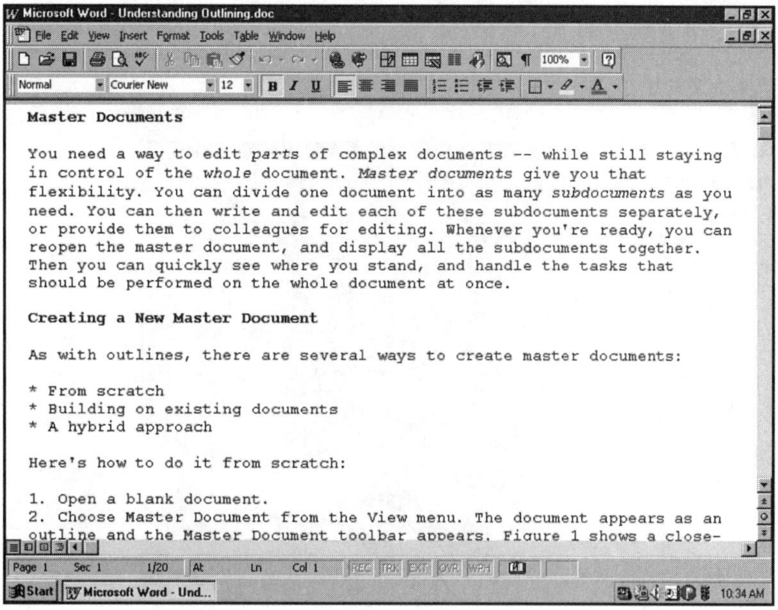

Part

II

Ch

7

FIG. 7.17

After: Word has AutoFormatted the document using default settings.

Extra paragraph marks have been replaced with styles that contain space after paragraphs

Heading styles and outline numbering have been applied

Word missed the first bullet but caught the other two

Word reformatted the numbered list perfectly

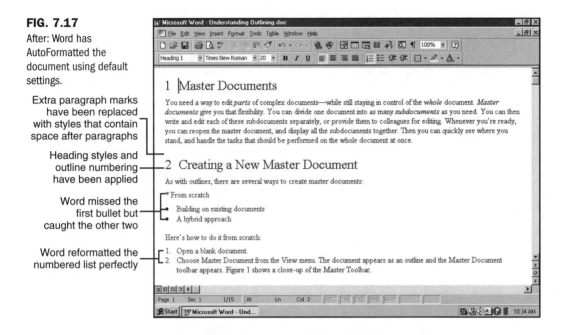

Controlling the Changes AutoFormat Makes

You have a good deal of control over the changes AutoFormat makes. With the AutoFormat dialog box open, click Options. The AutoFormat tab of the AutoCorrect dialog box appears (see Figure 7.18). You can now clear any check boxes corresponding to document elements you want AutoFormat to leave alone.

FIG. 7.18

In the AutoFormat tab, you can control the formatting changes that Word makes when you run AutoFormat.

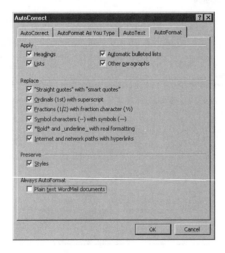

CAUTION

There are two places to control AutoFormatting, and it's very easy to get them confused. The settings in the AutoFormat tab are only applied when you run AutoFormat from the AutoFormat dialog box. The settings in the AutoFormat As You Type tab apply when you are editing a document—except they do not apply when you run AutoFormat from the AutoFormat dialog box. (AutoFormat As You Type will be discussed later in this chapter.) The settings in each tab are similar but not identical. Changes you make to the settings in one tab are not automatically reflected in the other. As a result, it's all too easy to clear a check box in the AutoFormat settings tab and wonder why Word is still making AutoFormat changes automatically as you type—or vice versa. (See the Troubleshooting section at the end of this chapter for more places to look if Word keeps making changes you don't want.)

The document elements Word can change are listed in Table 7.3. Some are fairly self-evident, but others aren't:

- *Headings.* One of the best reasons to use AutoFormatting is to save time in transforming a text-only file into one that can benefit from Word's outlining. Before you try to add heading styles manually, consider clearing every box *except* Headings, and running AutoFormat to see how many headings it can format properly.

- *Other Paragraphs.* Most people who have tried AutoFormat realize that it tries to identify headings and format them using heading styles, but they may not realize that AutoFormat also transforms text formatted as Normal into other formats such as Body Text or Inside Address. If you prefer to keep all text other than headings formatted as Normal, for convenience and simplicity, clear this check box, and Word will not change the styles associated text paragraphs.

- *"Straight Quotes" with "Smart Quotes."* With this box checked, Word replaces straight up-and-down quotation marks and apostrophes with curly ones that look better. SmartQuotes are a little smarter than they used to be. For example, Word 97 and Word 95 realize that SmartQuotes attached to years should look like '98 instead of '98. Word 6 didn't know that. However, if you're exporting your document for use by another program, that program might have trouble displaying SmartQuotes. (In fact, Word itself may have trouble, if you're using a custom font that doesn't contain these specialized characters.) Some people swear by SmartQuotes; others still swear at them.

 TIP

If you're a writer, you might have one client that requires SmartQuotes and another that prohibits them. Sometimes you'll realize part way through working on a document that Word has been adding undesired SmartQuotes. You already know you can turn off SmartQuotes through the AutoFormat As You Type tab of the AutoCorrect dialog box, but what about the ones that are already in your document? Use Find & Replace to get rid of them.

continues

Part

II

Ch

7

continued

One at a time, copy SmartQuote characters into the Find <u>W</u>hat text box of the Edit, Re<u>p</u>lace dialog box; and then type the corresponding traditional quote mark in the Replace <u>W</u>ith text box and choose Replace <u>A</u>ll. You'll have to do it four times: once for the open-quotation mark, once for the close-quotation mark, and once for apostrophes facing each way.

Alternatively, you can enter the symbol numbers in the Find <u>W</u>hat text box:

^145 corresponds to '

^146 corresponds to '

^147 corresponds to "

^148 corresponds to "

You can write a macro that eliminates all SmartQuotes from your document by running Replace <u>A</u>ll four times. You can also write another macro that adds SmartQuotes throughout, by running an AutoFormat with only the SmartQuotes option turned on. Then just run either macro and Word does the work for you.

- *Fractions (1/2) with Fraction Character (½)*. By default, Word replaces 1/2, 1/4, and 3/4 with the better-looking symbol characters. Most fonts don't have symbol characters for other fractions, such as 1/8 or 3/16. If your document uses fractions that can't be reformatted, you may want to clear this check box to keep everything consistent.

- **Bold* and _Underline_ with Real Formatting*. Bold works just the way it's supposed to work. If you type an asterisk followed by text and another asterisk, Word eliminates the asterisks and formats the text as boldface. But the underline feature doesn't do what it's supposed to; it formats text in italic, not underlined. Microsoft says this feature is incorrectly labeled.

N O T E In fact, there's something even more interesting going on here. Word is actually using the built-in character styles Strong and Emphasis. By default, Strong corresponds to boldface and Emphasis corresponds to italic type. If you really want underlining, you can change the Emphasis character style to underlining and this AutoFormat option will gladly give it to you. ▪

- *Internet and Network Paths with Hyperlinks*. This is a welcome feature if you are creating an electronic document; it saves you the trouble of manually adding hyperlinks. It is not so welcome if you are creating a printed document, or if you are providing a disk file for use in another program, such as a desktop publishing program. Word replaces standard text with hyperlink fields which look different (they're blue and underlined) and act differently (they're field codes, which can't be understood by many programs to which you may be exporting your Word file). If this sounds like trouble, clear this check box.

- *Preserve <u>S</u>tyles*. By default, if AutoFormat finds that you've formatted a paragraph with any style other than Normal, it leaves that paragraph alone. If you clear this check box, Word uses its judgment and reformats any paragraph it thinks necessary.

■ *Plain Text WordMail Documents.* If you are on a network, and have selected Word as your e-mail editor through a Microsoft e-mail client, such as Outlook, checking this box tells Word to AutoFormat e-mail documents that arrive as plain ASCII text. Checking this box won't affect any other text-only document, including those you retrieve as ASCII files from other e-mail systems and display in Word via the File, Open dialog box.

AutoFormatting Interactively

You've already learned that you can run AutoFormat, undo the results if you don't like them, and then control the types of AutoFormatting Word applies through the AutoFormat tab of the AutoCorrect dialog box. You can also run AutoFormatting interactively and make decisions one at a time. This gives you finer control over the AutoFormatting changes Word makes. However, because Word stops everywhere it changed an apostrophe into a SmartQuote or replaced spaces with tabs, this can be a very slow process. (There's no way to accept all the formatting changes of a certain type.) Consider using interactive AutoFormatting to correct only the most important errors you believe AutoFormat has made.

Follow these steps to AutoFormat interactively:

1. Choose Format, AutoFormat.
2. Choose AutoFormat and review each change.
3. Click OK.

Word AutoFormats the document and displays the AutoFormat dialog box (see Figure 7.19).

FIG. 7.19

From here, you can accept or reject all changes, review them one at a time, or display the Style Gallery.

The AutoFormat dialog box stays open as you move throughout the document. So before you start reviewing changes in detail, you might want to use the scroll bar and other Word navigation tools to get a rough idea about how close Word has come. If the document looks right on target, click Accept All. If Word's AutoFormatting is far from what you had in mind, click Reject All.

If Word landed somewhere in between, click Review Changes. The Review Changes dialog box opens (see Figure 7.20), and Word displays the text changes it made in your document. Insertions are marked in blue; deletions in red. If you prefer to see the document as it would look if all the changes were accepted, click Hide Marks. If you then want to take a closer look at a specific change, click Show Marks.

Part
II

Ch
7

FIG. 7.20

You can use this dialog box to move through your document to approve or reject individual changes.

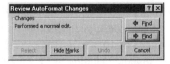

To move toward the beginning of the document, click ← Find. To move toward the end, click → Find. Word selects the first AutoFormatting change it made. When you select a change, Word tells you what it changed—for example, it might say "Adjusted alignment with a tab."

TIP You might find that Word made several of the same changes consecutively. Rather than view each change, position the insertion point after those changes, and then click Find to locate the next change.

Using Style Gallery to Reformat AutoFormatted Text

The AutoFormat dialog box (refer to Figure 7.19) also gives you access to the Style Gallery, where you can quickly reformat your styles to match the styles in a different template. Click Style Gallery to view it. Then, in the Template scroll box, choose a template containing formats you would like to view. If you prefer the formats associated with the template, click OK.

As is always the case when you use Style Gallery (see Figure 7.21), Word doesn't actually change the template associated with the document with which you're working. Rather, it changes the formatting associated with the styles in your current document to make the formatting look like the formatting in the template you chose.

▶ **See** "Previewing New Templates With Style Gallery," **p. 182**

FIG. 7.21

You can quickly change the look of your AutoFormatted document through Style Gallery.

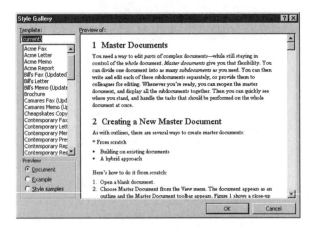

Because all of Word's built-in templates are based on Times New Roman and Arial, most of Word's built-in templates won't radically change the appearance of your document. However, if you've created custom templates that use Word's built-in style names, Style Gallery lets you apply those styles quickly to an AutoFormatted document.

Using AutoFormat As You Type

Word can also AutoFormat as you type, helping to make sure that your document is formatted properly as you work. In many (but not all) cases, the document elements Word reformats on-the-fly are similar to those you've already covered. In other cases, they are different. For example, by default, Word won't convert text that it identifies as headings into Heading styles while you work. Most people find that too distracting. On the other hand, you can ask Word to change headings if you like.

Follow these steps to control Word's on-the-fly AutoFormatting:

1. Choose Format, AutoFormat.
2. Choose Options. The AutoCorrect dialog box appears.
3. Choose the AutoFormat As You Type tab (see Figure 7.22).

FIG. 7.22
The AutoFormat As You Type tab enables you to control formatting changes Word makes while you work.

The following two differences are worth pointing out:

- *Borders.* Unlike regular AutoFormat, Word can transform rows of hyphens or underlines into true bordering.
- *Tables.* Word transforms a row of hyphens and plus signs into a table row, with one column for each plus sign.

Automating Formatting for the Beginning of List Items   When you are creating a list, you may occasionally format the first word or phrase in the list differently than you format the remaining text in each list paragraph. You can see an example of this in Figure 7.23. Word can recognize this specialized formatting and apply it to the new list items it creates each time you press Enter at the end of a list paragraph.

To activate this feature, check the Format Beginning Of List Item Like The One Before It check box in the AutoFormat As You Type tab.

FIG. 7.23

Once you create specialized formatting to begin a list, Word uses that formatting in list items that immediately follow.

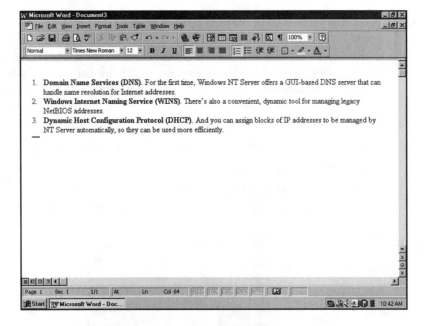

CAUTION

If you're creating a numbered or bulleted list, this feature won't deliver the results you want unless you also check the Automatic Bulleted Lists or Automatic Numbered Lists check boxes.

Using AutoFormat As You Type to Generate Styles Automatically If you can't be bothered with creating styles through the Style box, you can ask Word to watch you work and create the styles based on the manual formatting you apply. To turn this feature on, display the AutoFormat As You Type tab, check the Define Styles Based on Your Formatting check box, and click OK. Make sure the document elements you want to AutoFormat, such as Headings, are also selected, and then click Close.

After you've turned on automated style definition, you can see it at work if you do the following:

1. Open a new document.
2. Type a line of text without placing a period at the end of it. The absence of a period is a cue that you're creating a heading. The line of text must also be at least 20 percent shorter than your current maximum line length, based on the type size and margins you're using.
3. Format the entire paragraph, using any character or paragraph formatting you want.
4. Press Enter to separate the line from those that follow.

Now, if you click your insertion point in the paragraph that you followed, the Style drop-down list box will display the Heading 1 style. Any future paragraphs you format as Heading 1 will use the formatting you just created.

Working with AutoSummarize

Who would have ever thought a computer could summarize your documents for you? Word can. AutoSummarize reviews the entire document, and then scores each sentence based on a variety of factors, such as whether a sentence contains *keywords*—the words that are used most often throughout the document. The sentences that get the highest score are included in your summary.

Because there are subtleties to your document that Word can't understand, the results of running AutoSummarize are mixed—from good to terrible. In general, the more tightly structured your document is, the better chance you'll have of getting useful results. You'll also generally have better luck with documents that cover a few key topics in depth, as opposed to documents that include just a paragraph or two on many disparate topics.

In general, AutoSummarize does a fair-to-good job on the following types of document:

- Reports
- Articles
- Scientific papers
- Theses

AutoSummarize does a poor job on the following document types:

- Fiction
- Most typical correspondence
- How-to instructions (like this book)

Of course, some documents, such as contracts, are just too important to rely on AutoSummarize; there's no alternative to reading every word.

On the other hand, there's no law that restricts you to summarizing only documents you created. Use AutoSummarize as a tool to deal with all kinds of information overload. It's like hiring your computer to skim for you. Run AutoSummarize on any long, well-structured electronic document or Web page, and you'll quickly see whether the document is worth reading in its entirety.

▶ **See** "How Word and Microsoft Internet Explorer Integrate," **p. 287**

 TIP   AutoSummarize works a little bit better if you've installed the Find All Word Forms dictionary. This dictionary installs as part of most Word installations, but not as part of minimal installations, such as those used on notebook computers. If you haven't installed Find All Word Forms, you can rerun Word or Office Setup to add it.

Part
II

Ch
7

If you're creating an executive summary or abstract for a longer document, AutoSummarize rarely delivers perfection, but it often gives you a significant head start. Using the content AutoSummarize creates, you can fill in holes, polish and tighten the text, and make sure your summary reads smoothly—all in significantly less time than it would have taken you to create it from scratch.

To AutoSummarize your document, choose Tools, AutoSummarize. Word immediately builds a summary of your document, and stores it in memory pending your instructions. The AutoSummarize dialog box then opens (see Figure 7.24).

FIG. 7.24

In the AutoSummarize dialog box, you specify where to place your summary and how detailed you want it to be.

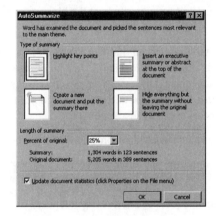

You now have the following four choices:

1. *Highlight Key Points.* Without changing the contents of your document or creating a new document, Word applies yellow highlighting to the sentences it deems most important, as shown in Figure 7.25. The AutoSummarize toolbar appears in your document. Other, unhighlighted paragraphs appear in gray. You can drag the Percent of Original scroll bar to highlight more or less of the document; as you drag it, sentences are highlighted or highlighting is removed.

 Because Word highlights AutoSummarized text in yellow, if you've used yellow highlighting elsewhere in the document, you won't be able to tell the difference. Consider using a different highlight color in documents you plan to AutoSummarize using the Show Highlights Only feature.

2. *Create a New Document and Put the Summary There.* Word creates a new document and places the summary there. This document has no link to the original document, so once the text has been inserted, there's no way to adjust it except for running AutoSummarize again. This option makes sense if you need to provide an executive summary or abstract, but you don't want to change the page numbering or contents of your original document.

FIG. 7.25

Using AutoSummarize to highlight the most important sentences in your document.

Highlight/Show Only Summary

Percent of Original slider

Close button

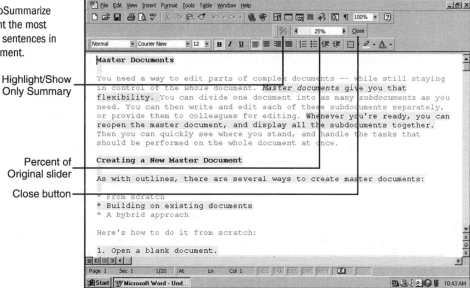

3. *Insert an Executive Summary or Abstract at the Top of the Document.* This copies the AutoSummarized text to the beginning of your document, where it can be edited and saved along with any other document contents. After you've copied the text, you can't adjust the size or contents of the summary except through conventional editing techniques.

 TIP   If you choose either of the previous two options, consider increasing the percentage of sentences Word inserts in your summary because it will be easier to delete sentences from your summary later than to add more. You can change this value with the Percent of Original slider in the AutoSummarize dialog box.

4. *Hide Everything but the Summary Without Leaving the Original Document.* This option makes no changes to the text in your current document; rather, it temporarily hides all the paragraphs that weren't selected to be part of the summary. In other words, your document looks as if it contained only the summary. If you print your document with only the summary showing, only the summary prints. However, when you click Close on the AutoSummarize toolbar, all the hidden text reappears.

You can also control what percentage of your document appears in the summary by entering a value in the Percent Of Original drop-down list box. You can enter any percentage. Or, using the options in the drop-down list box, you can choose a specific number of sentences or words. If you leave Word's default setting alone, Word creates a summary containing 25 percent of the original document. If you're creating an executive summary of a very long document, you may want to shrink it to 10–15 percent, or place a word limit, such as 500 words, to keep things manageable.

Part

II

Ch

7

If you choose either _Highlight Key Points_ or _Hide Everything but the Summary Without Leaving the Original Document,_ you can toggle between these options using the Highlight/Show Only Summary button on the AutoSummarize toolbar. In other words, if you've chosen to hide the parts of your document not included in the summary, you can view them at any time by clicking the Highlight/Show Only Summary button.

Using AutoSummarize to Update File Properties

As you will learn in Chapter 29, "Sharing Files and Managing Word," you can use the Properties dialog box to track information about your document, making it easier to track and search for documents later. As you've seen, among the information that AutoSummarize generates about your document is a list of keywords. Of course, it also includes the summary itself. Because this information is already available, AutoSummarize offers to place it in your Properties dialog box.

▶ **See** "Using Document Properties to Simplify Document Management," **p. 824**

When the Update Document Statistics check box is checked, as it is by default, Word inserts the top five keywords it finds in the Keywords text box in the Summary tab of the Properties dialog box. It also inserts the first few paragraphs of the summary itself in the Comments text box, also in the same tab.

> **CAUTION**
>
> When would you want to clear Update Document Statistics?
>
> If you are already using Keywords or Document Contents information for another purpose, you won't want Word overwriting the information stored there. For example, you might have already specified keywords and used the { KEYWORDS } field to display those keywords in a cover sheet to your document. Unless you clear this check box, when Word displays your summary, it will also replace your keywords with the ones it thinks are most important.

TROUBLESHOOTING

Word keeps making formatting changes I don't want. You've already learned that Word has two separate controls for AutoFormatting in different tabs of the AutoCorrect dialog box (AutoFormat and AutoFormat As You Type). Make sure you've made your changes in AutoFormat As You Type. Also:

- If you tell Word not to replace symbol characters with symbols, and Word keeps inserting symbols, delete the symbol entries in the AutoCorrect tab (accessible through Tools, AutoCorrect).

- If Word is updating a style globally whenever you change it manually in one location, choose Format, Style; select the style; click Modify, and clear the Automatically Update check box.

- If you told Word you don't want it to automatically format headings as you type, and it keeps doing so, clear the Define Styles Based On Your Formatting check box in the AutoFormat As You Type tab of the AutoCorrect dialog box.

Word hangs when I run AutoCorrect. When I click Details, it says `WINWORD caused an invalid page fault in module MSO97.DLL`. You might have a corrupted .ACL file—the file where Word stores your AutoCorrect entries. There are two ways to fix this. On the Microsoft Web site, you can download a special utility, ACLUTIL.EXE, which can fix most corrupted .ACL files. Double-click the file and Word decompresses two files: ACLREAD.TXT which includes the directions you need, and ACLFIX.EXE, the program that actually fixes the files. Or, you can rename the extensions associated with all your .ACL files *except* MSO97.ACL. Word then creates new .ACL files using its default settings.

AutoSummarize isn't summarizing my text. AutoSummarize ignores the following: text formatted in a language other than English; text formatted as "no proofing;" and text that appears inside text boxes, frames, and tables. In short documents, AutoSummarize may not display any sentences at all, unless you increase the Percent of Original setting in the AutoSummarize dialog box.

I saved my AutoSummarized document and now most of it has disappeared. If you run AutoSummarize using the Hide Everything But The Summary option and then save the file while only the summary is visible, Word applies hidden text formatting to all the text not included in the summary. Then, if you reopen the document, you won't see most of your text because it's now formatted as hidden text. To see the missing text, choose Tools, Options, View, and check the Hidden Text check box. To eliminate the hidden text formatting that has made part of your document invisible, press Ctrl+A to select the entire document; choose Format, Font; click the Font tab; and clear the Hidden check box.

From Here...

You've just learned about four of Word's most powerful automation features. Now move on to learn about several more Word features that can save you even more time—and make it even easier to build and manage complex documents:

- With all this talk about AutoFormatting, you might want to refresh your skills with manual formatting. If so, refer to Chapter 2, "Quick and Effective Formatting Techniques."

- Word's Tables feature makes it easier than ever to build organized blocks of information—and you can AutoFormat tables, too. Find out how in Chapter 8, "Tables."

- The Heading styles AutoFormat can enter are even more valuable when you need to organize a long document. Learn how to take full advantage of them in Chapter 14, "Outlining: The Best Way to Organize a Document."

- You can make AutoText entries even more useful to your colleagues if you build them into custom menus and toolbars—as is explained in Chapter 26, "Customizing Word."

Part
II

Ch
7

CHAPTER 8

Tables

by Elaine Marmel

Tables are a powerful feature. You can use them in Word documents to present tabular information, and you can use them to present information while designing Web pages. In this chapter, you learn how to work with tables in Word. ■

Insert a table in a document

You can use the traditional method to insert a table, or you can use Word's new Draw Table feature.

Navigate and edit tables

Learn the tricks of moving around in a table and changing table information.

Automatically format tables

Apply complex formatting to tables easily.

Convert existing information to or from a table format

You can change existing text into a table, and you can convert information in a table to standard text.

Calculate

Typically, you want to add columns of numbers, but you can do more with Word tables.

Sort

You can sort information in tables alphabetically or numerically.

Word Tables: They Do It All

Use tables in Word to present tabular information. Tables are perfectly suited to present parallel column information. Parallel columns display information in each column that is related across the row. For example, you might use a parallel column table to show a term in Column 1 and its definition in Column 2. Or, Column 1 may contain locations, while Columns 2 and 3 contain sales data for those locations for two different years. You can sort the table information in alphabetical or numerical order, based on any column. Using Word tables, you also can add the column containing the sales data without using a separate calculator.

> **N O T E** Don't confuse parallel columns with newspaper columns. In newspaper columns, information flows down one column and into the next column; the information in Column 1 is not necessarily related to the information in Column 2. For example, you might have two different articles appearing on the same page—one in Column 1 and one in Column 2. In Word, to create a newspaper column effect, you use the Columns feature. See Chapter 19, "Word Desktop Publishing." ▪

The information you present in a table might appear in your Word document, or you might use Word tables to help you prepare graphical information you intend to post on the World Wide Web.

> **T I P** Without tables, most people find it difficult to align text and graphics in HTML. HTML authors often use table tags to align text in graphics for the Web pages they create. In Word 97, however, creating these sometimes difficult tables is much easier because you don't have to understand the HTML table syntax to create tables for your Web pages.

Quick and Easy Tables with Word's New Draw Table Feature

The new *Draw Table* feature enables you to draw a table much the way you would draw a picture freehand—but for those of you who are like me and have no noticeable artistic talent, don't worry. While you draw a table, Word makes sure the lines are straight and even. The Draw Table feature works most effectively when you need to create tables that contain uneven columns or rows—similar to the table you see in Figure 8.1.

To draw a table, follow these steps:

1. Click the Tables and Borders button on the Standard toolbar. Word switches to Page Layout view if necessary and displays the Tables and Borders toolbar. The majority of the tools appear gray until after you create a table. (See Table 8.1 for a description of the buttons on the Tables and Borders toolbar.)

> **T I P** The tools you see on the Tables and Borders toolbar work on any table.

2. Move the mouse pointer to the location in the document where you want to draw a table. The shape of the mouse pointer looks like a pencil.

FIG. 8.1
Using the Draw Table feature, you can easily create a table like this one.

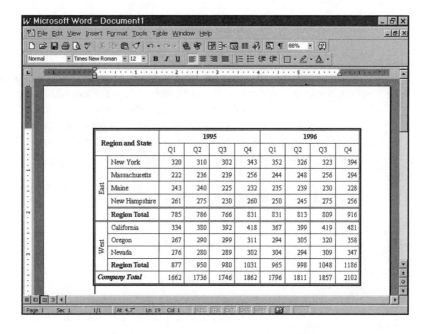

Region and State		1995				1996			
		Q1	Q2	Q3	Q4	Q1	Q2	Q3	Q4
East	New York	320	310	302	343	352	326	323	394
	Massachusetts	222	236	239	256	244	248	256	294
	Maine	243	240	225	232	235	239	230	228
	New Hampshire	261	275	230	260	250	245	275	256
	Region Total	785	786	766	831	831	813	809	916
West	California	334	380	392	418	367	399	419	481
	Oregon	267	290	299	311	294	305	320	358
	Nevada	276	280	289	302	304	294	309	347
	Region Total	877	950	980	1031	965	998	1048	1186
Company Total		1662	1736	1746	1862	1796	1811	1857	2102

3. Drag the mouse pointer down and to the right margin until the outline that you see while dragging appears to be the approximate size you want for the outside boundaries of the table.

4. When you release the mouse button, the insertion point appears inside the table, which looks like a box (see Figure 8.2).

FIG. 8.2
This figure illustrates drawing a table.

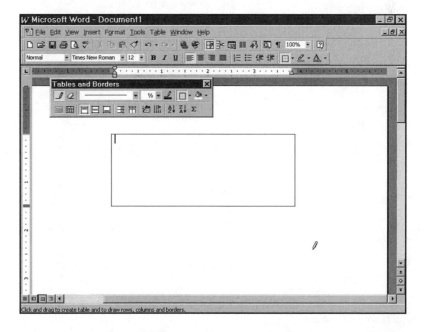

When you first draw a table, it is one large *cell* (the intersection of a row and a column). To create multiple cells that appear in rows and columns, you can draw additional lines inside the original cell, creating multiple cells in the table.

You may find it faster, however, to split the original cell into rows and columns. To create the uneven rows and columns you see in Figure 8.1, you merge cells by erasing row or column borders. You'll learn how to split and merge cells later in this chapter. You'll also learn how to adjust row or column sizes, evenly distribute space across a selected group of cells, and change the direction of text that you type in the cell. Before you get to those editing techniques, however, you learn the other method for inserting a table.

Table 8.1   The Tables and Borders Toolbar

Button	Function
	Draws a table
	Erases borders in a table
	Specifies the style of line used when drawing
½ pt	Specifies the weight of the line used when drawing
	Specifies the color of the line when drawing
	Specifies a border style
	Specifies a cell shading color
	Merges selected cells
	Splits cells
	Aligns text along the top of the cell
	Centers text vertically within a cell
	Aligns text along the bottom of the cell
	Distributes space evenly among selected rows

Button	Function
 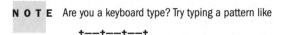	Distributes space evenly among selected columns
	Automatically formats a table
	Changes the direction of text in a cell
	Sorts selected entries in ascending order
	Sorts selected entries in descending order
	Sums the values above or to the left of the cell containing the insertion point

Creating Neat Rows and Columns

If you prefer, you can specify the number of rows and columns at the time you create your table. Place the insertion point in your document where you want the table to appear. Choose Table, Insert Table, and the Insert Table dialog box appears (see Figure 8.3). After you specify the number of rows and columns you want in the table, choose OK. Word inserts the specified table in your document.

FIG. 8.3
Use this dialog box to specify the number of rows and columns you want in the table you're creating.

 Alternatively, click the Table button on the Standard toolbar. When the grid appears, highlight the number of rows and columns you want in your table (see Figure 8.4).

NOTE Are you a keyboard type? Try typing a pattern like

+—+—+—+

and pressing Enter. Word inserts a one-row table. Each cell will be the same width as the number of dashes you typed between plus signs. ■

Editing a Table

Rare is the person who creates the exact table he or she needs on the first attempt. The rest of us mortals edit our tables until they appear the way we want them to appear. You can think of editing a table in two ways: You need to modify the structure of the table, and you need to modify the information in the table.

FIG. 8.4

Use the grid to specify the number of rows and columns you want in the table you're creating.

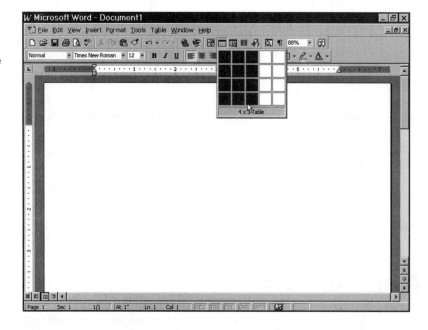

To modify the structure of the table, you can merge and split cells, insert and delete cells, rows, and columns, and change the size of columns and rows. To modify the information in a table, you'll need to know how to navigate in a table and select text. In addition, there are some special techniques you use to cut and paste in a table and to insert tabs in a table cell.

 Many of the buttons on the Tables and Borders toolbar let you perform functions that modify the structure of your table. You can use the Tables and Borders tools on any table, not just on tables you drew.

Selecting Cells, Rows, or Columns

To make changes to a table's structure, you'll need to know how to select in a table. The easiest way to select table elements (a column, row, or cell) is to use the mouse.

To select a column, move the mouse pointer over the top of the column. Click when the shape of the pointer changes to a black arrow pointing downward. To select a row, move the mouse pointer to the left edge of the row. Click when the pointer changes to a white arrow pointing up and to the right.

To select a cell, move the mouse pointer inside the left boundary of the cell. Click when the pointer changes to a white arrow pointing up and to the right. By the way, this white arrow is the same one that you see when selecting a row.

 To select multiple cells but not an entire row, align the mouse pointer correctly to select the first cell but don't click; instead drag across the cell and into the next cell.

Merging and Splitting Cells

As you saw earlier, when you first draw a table, it is one large cell. To create multiple cells that appear in rows and columns, you split the original cell. You may also find that you need to split a cell you created in a table that you didn't draw. The process is the same.

 Click the Split Cells button on the Tables and Borders toolbar, and Word displays the dialog box you see in Figure 8.5. Provide an approximate number of rows and columns for your table—you can add and erase lines from the table later. When you choose OK, Word divides the table evenly into the number of rows and columns you specified, and all cells in the table are selected.

FIG. 8.5

Use this dialog box to split cells in a table.

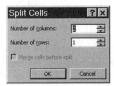

 To create the uneven rows and columns you see in Figure 8.1, you merge cells by erasing row or column borders. Drag across the line you want to erase. As you erase a line, Word selects the line, and when you release the mouse button, Word erases the line (see Figure 8.6).

T I P Create a Header cell for a table by merging all the cells in Row 1 into one cell. Then, apply header formatting to the cell—that is, center information in the cell, use a larger font, and apply appropriate text enhancements, such as bold or italic.

FIG. 8.6

Aptly, the mouse pointer looks like an eraser as you erase lines to merge cells.

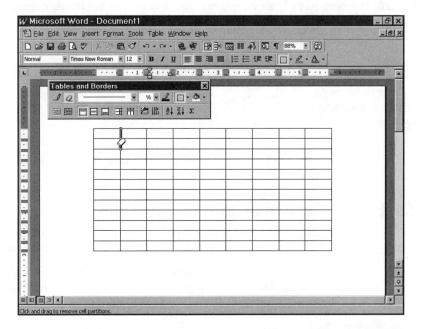

If you prefer to use the menus, you'll find a Merge Cells command and a Split Cells command on the Table menu. To use the Merge Cells command, you must first select the cells you want to merge. You can, but don't need to, select cells before splitting. If you choose the Split Cells command, you'll see the Split Cells dialog box that asks you to specify the number of rows and columns you want to create when you split the cell.

Inserting and Deleting Cells, Columns, and Rows

As mentioned earlier, hardly anybody structures a table correctly the first time. Need to add a row? Delete a column?

To insert a row, place the insertion point in the row you want to appear below the new row. Then, click the Insert Row button or choose Table, Insert Row. Word performs the action. The new row will contain the formatting of the first row you selected—you'll learn about cell formatting later in this chapter.

T I P
You can insert several rows by selecting the number of rows you want to insert before you click the Insert Row button. You can delete several cells by selecting them before you choose Table, Delete Cells.

To delete cells, select the cells (place the insertion point in the single cell you want to delete or select the group of cells you want to delete) and choose Table, Delete Cells. A dialog box will appear, asking you how to adjust the table after deleting the cells (see Figure 8.7). Be aware that you can create a lopsided table by deleting a single cell or fewer cells than contained in the other rows or columns in the table.

T I P
The Insert Rows command and the Delete Cells command, along with other table-related commands, also appear on the Tables shortcut menu. Right-click while the insertion point appears in a table to see the menu.

FIG. 8.7
Choose the adjustment you want to make to the table's structure after you delete a single cell.

To delete a row or column, select the row or column. Then, choose Table, Delete Row or Table, Delete Column.

Controlling Column and Row Dimensions

You might need to make a column narrower or wider, or change the size of a row. Or perhaps you'd simply like to distribute space equally across columns of uneven width.

The quick and easy way to change the size of a row or column is to drag its border or drag the column or row marker in the ruler. The Table Column marker looks like a tiny gray square containing a grid. The Table Row marker is a narrow dark gray rectangle.

If you drag a right column border or marker to the right, you'll make that column wider. Similarly if you drag the border or marker to the left, you'll make the column narrower. If you drag the top border of a row up, you'll make the row taller. If you drag the top border of the row down, you'll make the row shorter. When you drag a row or column border, the shape of the mouse pointer changes to look similar to the mouse pointer shape in Figure 8.8. To see column width or row height measurements on the Ruler, hold down the Alt key as you drag.

FIG. 8.8

When you can drag a row or column border to change its size, the mouse pointer shape changes.

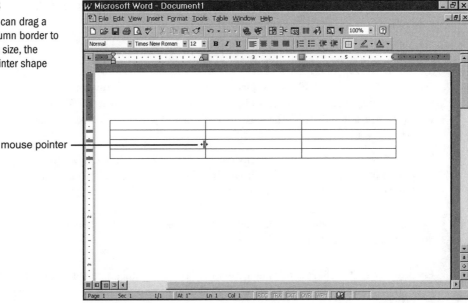

mouse pointer

 TIP If you hold down the Shift key while dragging a column border, you will adjust the width of the selected column, and you will also affect the entire table's size. If you hold down the Ctrl key while dragging, you will redistribute the width of the selected column to all columns to the right.

If you prefer to set row and column dimensions exactly, use the Cell Height and Width dialog box (see Figure 8.9). Choose Table, Cell Height and Width to display this dialog box.

FIG. 8.9

Use the Row and Column tabs to set cell height exactly.

Word's new table commands—Distribute Rows Evenly and Distribute Columns Evenly—are very useful. Using these commands, which appear on both the Tables menu and the Tables and Borders toolbar, you can select multiple rows and make them the same width. These commands also help you select multiple columns and make them the same width. The commands are particularly useful after you have merged cells.

 T I P To automatically adjust a column to accommodate the longest line, use the AutoFit feature. Place the insertion point anywhere in the column you want to adjust. Choose Table, Cell Height and Width, and display the Column tab. Click the AutoFit button.

Typing and Navigating in a Table

When you first create a table, Word places the insertion point in the upper-left corner of the table. To enter information into the table, just type. As you type in a cell, Word wraps text within the cell, automatically adjusting the cell's height to accommodate the information. If you press Enter, you start a new line within the same cell.

You can move the insertion point to any cell by clicking that cell. To move the cell pointer forward to the next cell, press Tab. Press Shift+Tab to move the cell pointer backward one cell. If either cell to which you are moving contains text, Word selects the text.

 T I P If you press Tab while the insertion point appears in the last (lower-right) cell of the table, you'll add a new row to the bottom of the table.

Pressing the Left or Right arrow key moves the insertion point character by character through a cell. When the insertion point reaches the last character in the cell, pressing an arrow key moves the insertion point into the next cell. Pressing the Up or Down arrow key moves the insertion point line by line through the cell. When the insertion point reaches the first or last line of the cell, pressing an arrow key moves the insertion point into the previous or next row.

Press Alt+Home to move the insertion point to the beginning of a row. Press Alt+End to move the insertion point to the end of a row.

Press Alt+Page Up to move the insertion point to the top of a column. Press Alt+Page Down to move the insertion point to the bottom of a column.

Selecting Text versus Cells in a Table

You select text in a cell the same way you select text anywhere in a Word document. But, to truly understand the difference between selecting text in a cell and selecting a cell, you need to display hidden characters so that you can see end-of-cell markers. Press the Show/Hide button on the Standard toolbar. When you display hidden characters, a blank table should look like the one in Figure 8.10.

The funky symbols you see in each cell are the end-of-cell markers, and you may have gotten the impression that they are important—because they are important. Why? If you want to

Part

II

Ch

8

select the text within a cell, make the selection the way you would select text anywhere in Word, but don't include the end of cell marker in your selection. If, however, you want to select the actual cell (and its contents), include the end-of-cell marker in the selection.

TIP As you type in a cell, the end-of-cell marker appears to move, which is logical because it marks the end of the cell.

It is important to understand the distinction between selecting text and selecting an entire cell because you may want to format part of a row or column but not all cells in the row or column by applying, say, shading to those cells. To apply formatting to a cell, you must select the cell marker; otherwise, Word applies the formatting to selected text.

FIG. 8.10

This figure illustrates a table displaying end-of-cell markers.

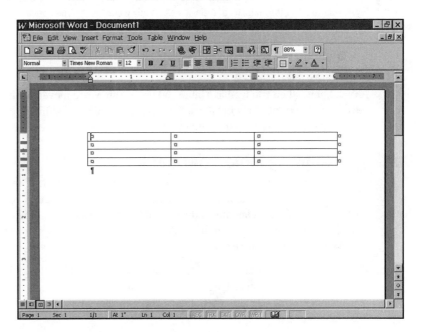

Applying Formatting to Table Cells

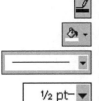

Using the Tables and Borders toolbar, you can easily apply borders or shading to selected cells. Simply select the cells to which you want to apply the formatting, and click the appropriate tool. If you're applying a border, use the Line Style and Line Weight list boxes to set these options. Using the Text Direction tool, you can leave text at its default, which is horizontal in a cell. Or, you can turn text on its side so that you need to tip your head either to the right or to the left to read the text.

Later in this chapter, you'll learn to use Table AutoFormatting, which quickly formats an entire table in a uniform fashion.

Tables and Alignment

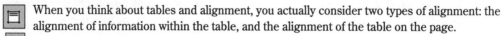

When you think about tables and alignment, you actually consider two types of alignment: the alignment of information within the table, and the alignment of the table on the page.

To align the contents of cells, select the cells and use the appropriate alignment button on the Tables and Borders toolbar.

To align a table on the page, select the entire table, and use the Indent buttons on the Formatting toolbar. To select the entire table, place the insertion point anywhere in the table. Then, choose Table, Select Table or turn off Num Lock and press Alt+5 on the number pad. Remember that changing your page margins will not affect the placement of your table on the page.

> **TIP** If you want to affect the contents of a single cell, simply place the insertion point anywhere in that cell and choose the appropriate alignment button.

Inserting Tabs in Tables

As you know, when you type in a table and press Tab, Word moves the insertion point to the next cell to the right. But what if you find that you need a tab within a cell? Press Ctrl+Tab. Instead of moving the insertion point to the next cell, Word inserts a tab in the current cell.

Cutting or Copying Table Information

To move or copy information from one cell to another, select the text and use standard drag-and-drop methods (drag to move, Ctrl+drag to copy) or use the Cut, Copy, and Paste commands. To replace the contents of the destination cell, select the entire source cell, including its end-of-cell marker. To retain the contents of the destination cell, select text but not the end-of-cell marker in the source cell.

If the text you move or copy contains character formatting, both the text and its formatting will appear in the destination cell; however, you cannot move or copy any cell formatting, even if you include end-of-cell markers. Cell formatting includes borders, shading, text alignment, and text direction.

> **NOTE** In earlier versions of Word, including the end-of-cell marker enabled you to copy cell formatting. In Word 97, you cannot copy cell formatting. ▇

You can also use standard drag-and-drop or Cut, Copy, and Paste commands to move entire rows or columns by selecting entire rows or columns before you move. When you move or copy a row or column, Word automatically overwrites the destination cells with the source information, because the source selection contains end-of-cell markers.

AutoFormatting Tables

As you know, you can use tools on the Tables and Borders toolbar to apply formatting such as shading, borders, text alignment, and text direction to selected table cells. However, using Auto-Formatting, you can apply uniform formatting to an entire table very quickly. Follow these steps:

1. Place the insertion point anywhere in the table you want to format.

2. Click the AutoFormat button on the Tables and Borders toolbar or choose Table, Table AutoFormat. The Table AutoFormat dialog box appears (see Figure 8.11). Watch the Preview box as you make selections in steps 3–5.

FIG. 8.11

Quickly format an entire table using this dialog box.

3. From the Formats drop-down list, choose an appearance for your table.

4. In the Formats to Apply section, place checks in the boxes for the types of enhancements you want Word to apply based on the selected format.

5. In the Apply Special Formats To section, choose the table areas to which you want special formatting applied.

6. Choose OK. Word applies the selected formatting to your table.

 TIP If you don't like what you see after applying automatic formatting, click the Undo button.

Splitting Tables

It happens. You set up your entire table at the top of the page and then realize you need to add text before the table. Or, you decide that you'd really like to split the table into two tables so that you can place some text between the two tables.

To add room at the top of your page for text, click in the first row of the table and choose Table, Split Table. Word adds a paragraph mark above the table and places the insertion point in that paragraph.

To split one table into two tables, click in the row that should become the first row of the second table. Then, choose Table, Split Table. Word divides the table into two tables and places the insertion point in a paragraph that appears between the two new tables.

Controlling Table Page Breaks

Long tables present some unique problems. For example, it would be nice, in a long table that spans several pages, to have a heading that repeats on each page. In some cases, you may not want your table to break across two pages where Word decides to break the table. Instead, you may want to control the placement of the table break.

TIP If you insert a page break in a table (press Ctrl+Enter), Word breaks the table into two tables, with the second table appearing at the top of a new page.

Specifying Recurring Headers

Suppose you have a table that spans several pages or a table that starts on one page and finishes on the next page. It helps your reader if the column headings for the table repeat on each page containing the table. You can easily specify a heading row (or several rows) that will appear at the top of each page created by an automatic page break. The heading row(s) for a table must include the first row of the table. Select the row or rows you want to include in the heading and choose Table, Headings. Word repeats the selected rows at the top of each page containing the table. You can see the repeated row by switching to Page Layout view.

NOTE Table headings appear only after automatic page breaks. If you insert a manual page break in a table (press Ctrl+Enter), no table heading appears on the next page. ■

Preventing Rows from Breaking Across Pages

Suppose you have a table that spans across two pages. Further, suppose that a large amount of text appears in the last cell on page one. Remember that Word extends the height of a cell to accommodate your text. In a situation like this one, it's very possible that the last row on page one will actually extend onto page two. In Figure 8.12, you see an example of this situation. The last row on page one and the first row on page two have been labeled. The large white space in what appears to be the first row on page two actually is part of the last row on page one. You know this because you don't see any end-of-cell markers in the row at the top of page two.

In cases like this one, you might not want Word to split the row. Instead, if a row won't fit entirely on one page, you can tell Word to move the entire row to the next page. Place the insertion point anywhere in the table and choose Table, Cell Height and Width. On the Row tab of the Cell Height and Width dialog box, remove the check from the Allow Row to Break Across

Pages check box. When you choose OK, Word adjusts the table accordingly. In Figure 8.13, Word moved the last row on page one onto page two.

FIG. 8.12
Word allows a row to break across pages.

This line is actually the remainder of the last row on page one

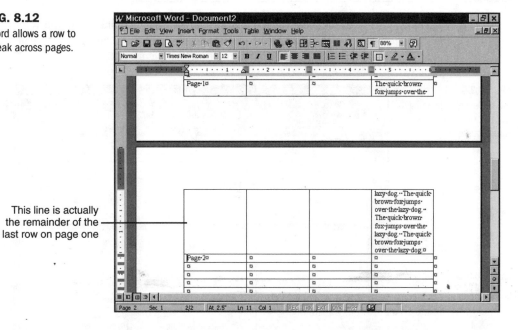

FIG. 8.13
The table after preventing rows from breaking across pages.

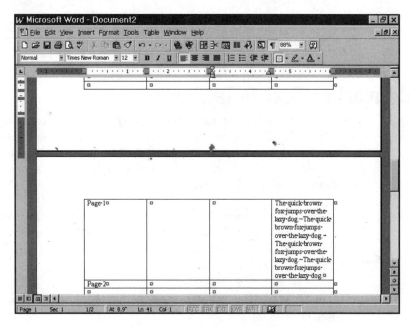

T I P When you change the setting in the Cell Height and Width dialog box, you change it for every row in the table.

The value of this feature becomes even more apparent when you combine it with the Table Headings feature discussed in the last section. Compare the next two figures. The table in Figure 8.14 is much more difficult to follow than the table in Figure 8.15.

FIG. 8.14

The table with a heading row, but rows can break across pages.

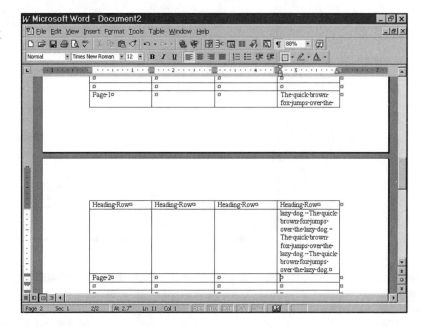

Converting Text to Tables

Suppose you typed some material and subsequently decide that you'd prefer to present the material in a table. Don't retype the information; convert it to a table. You simply need to make sure that the text you want to place in a table contains some common marker, such as a paragraph mark or a tab, that Word can use to distinguish where a new column should begin. To convert text to a table, follow these steps:

N O T E You can convert any text to a table as long as you can identify, for Word, the column separators. Word can easily separate text into columns by breaking columns at paragraph marks, tabs, or commas, but you also can specify any other character.

1. Select the text you want to convert.
2. Choose Tables, Convert Text to Table. The Convert Text to Table dialog box appears (see Figure 8.16).

FIG. 8.15

The table with a heading row, and rows are prevented from breaking across pages.

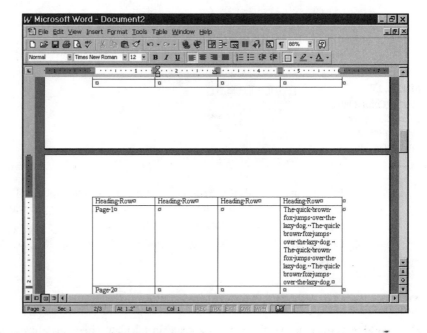

FIG. 8.16

Use this dialog box to describe the table you want to create.

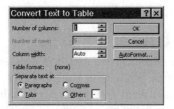

3. In the Separate Text At box, choose one of the following options: Paragraph, Tabs, Commas, or Other. If you choose Other, type the character you want Word to use when separating the selected text into columns.

4. If necessary, change the number of columns you want in your table. Word calculates the number of columns and rows based on the separator you choose.

5. Choose OK. Word converts the selected text into a table.

 TIP If the table doesn't come out as you expected, click Undo, make any necessary modifications to the text, and try these steps again.

Converting Tables to Text

As you might expect, you can convert a table to straight text in paragraphs. To do so, follow these steps:

1. Select the table you want to convert.

2. Choose Tables, Convert Table to Text. The Convert Table to Text dialog box appears (see Figure 8.17).

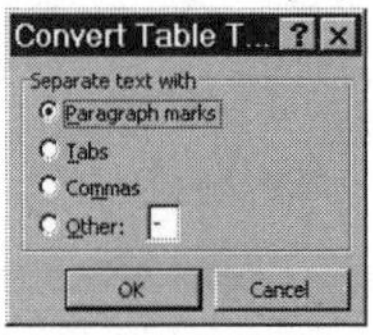

FIG. 8.17
Use the Convert Table to Text dialog box to describe the table you want to create.

3. In the Separate Text At box, choose one of the following options: Paragraph, Tabs, Commas, or Other. If you choose Other, type the character you want Word to use when separating the selected column into text.

4. Choose OK. Word converts the selected table into regular text, breaking at the separator you chose.

Calculating with Tables

Most of the time, people tend to use Excel to calculate. However, you will have occasions to create tables in Word that contain numbers, and you'll need to do the math.

A Quick and Easy Way to Sum Lists of Numbers

Most often, you'll probably want to sum a column of numbers. Whenever you place the insertion point in cell that appears at the bottom of a column of numbers, Word assumes you want to sum that column. Choose Table, Formula. Word displays the Formula dialog box. Choose OK and Word displays the sum of the column in the current cell.

Creating Other Formulas in Word Tables

Although summing is most common, you can create other formulas as well, which are displayed in the Formula dialog box (see Figure 8.18). To create a formula, clear the Formula box and type an equal sign (=) in it, since all formulas in Word begin with an equal sign. Use the Paste Function list box to choose a formula. See Table 8.2 for information about the various functions. Use the Number Format list box to specify the appearance of a number; for example, you can format a number so that it appears as a dollar amount or as a percentage.

FIG. 8.18

Use the Formula dialog box to help you do math in a Word table.

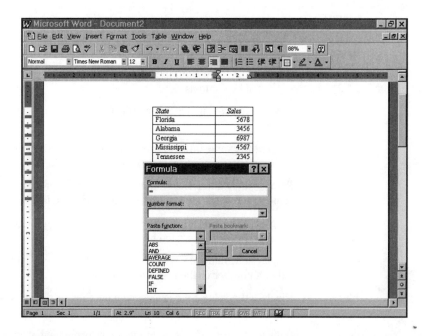

Table 8.2 Functions Available in Tables

Function	Purpose
ABS(x)	Displays the absolute value of a number or formula, regardless of its actual positive or negative value.
AND(x,y)	Used in logical expressions, AND returns the value 1 if both x and y are true, or the value 0 (zero) if either expression is false.
AVERAGE()	Calculates the average of a list of numbers that appear, separated by commas, in the parentheses.
COUNT()	Displays the number of items in a list. The list appears in the parentheses, separated by commas.
DEFINED(x)	Displays 1 if the expression x is valid, or 0 if x cannot be computed.
FALSE	Displays 0 (zero).
IF(x,y,z)	Evaluates x and displays y if x is true, or z if is false. Note that x is a conditional expression, and y and z (usually 1 and 0 (zero)) can be either any numeric value or the words "True" and "False."
INT(x)	Displays the numbers to the left of the decimal place in the value or formula x.
MIN()	Displays the smallest number in the list that appears, in the parentheses, separated by commas.

continues

Table 8.2 Continued

Function	Purpose
MAX()	Displays the largest number in a list. The list appears in the parentheses, separated by commas.
MOD(x,y)	Displays the remainder that results from dividing x by y a whole number of times.
NOT(x)	Returns the value 0 (zero), meaning false, if the x is true, or the value 1, meaning true, if x is false. X is a logical expression.
OR(x,y)	Returns the value 1, meaning true, if either or both x and y are true, or the value 0 (zero), meaning false, if both x and y are false.
PRODUCT()	Displays the result of multiplying a list of values. The list of values appears in the parentheses, separated by commas.
ROUND(x,y)	Displays the value of x rounded to y number of decimal places; x can be either a number or the result of a formula.
SIGN(x)	Displays the value 1 if x is a positive number, or the value –1 if x is a negative number.
SUM()	Returns the sum of a list of numbers or formulas that appear, in the parentheses, separated by commas.
TRUE	Displays 1.

Tracking Cells with the Table Cell Helper Macro

Based on Table 8.2, be aware that the following functions can accept references to table cells as arguments: AVERAGE, COUNT, MAX, MIN, PRODUCT, and SUM. Table cell references are the names by which Word refers to cells. Table cell references in Word are similar to those in Excel: columns have letter names (A, B, C, and so on) and rows have numbers (1, 2, 3, and so on). Because each cell is the intersection of a column and row, refer to the cell by its column letter and row number. The first cell in a table appears in the upper-left corner of the table and is called cell A1. The cell immediately to the right of A1 is cell B1, and the cell immediately below A1 is cell A2.

When you reference cells in a table, you may need to refer to an individual cell or to a group of cells (called a *range* in Excel). To refer to individual single cells, separate the references with commas. To refer to a range of cells, use the first and last cells in the range and separate those two cells with a colon (:).

N O T E   Although you refer to cells in Word the same way you refer to cells in Excel, Word cell references are all absolute references, unlike the references in Excel. That means that the cell references in Word will not automatically change if you add rows or columns to a table. ■

Sometimes, your table is very large, and identifying the location of the insertion point can be tedious. However, Word ships with a special template, Macros8.DOT, that contains some special macros, including the Table Cell Helper macro, which you can use to help you identify the reference for the current table cell.

To use Macros8.DOT, you need to activate it as follows:

1. Choose Tools, Templates and Add-Ins. The Templates and Add-Ins dialog box appears (see Figure 8.19).

FIG. 8.19

Use the Templates and Add-Ins dialog box to activate Macros8.dot.

2. Click Add. In the Add Template dialog box, which functions like the Open dialog box, navigate to the \Program Files\Microsoft Office\Office\Macros folder. Choose Macros8.dot.

3. Choose OK. Macros8.dot appears in the Global Templates and Add-Ins list with a check next to it.

4. Choose OK to close the Templates and Add-Ins dialog box.

This template makes a lot of macros available, including the Table Cell Helper macro. To use the macros, place the insertion point in your table in the cell whose reference you want to identify. Then, choose Tools, Macros, scroll down and select TableCellHelper. When you click Run, Word displays a dialog box similar to the one you see in Figure 8.20. To generate the information you see in the figure, the insertion point was placed in the middle of the number 4567 in the Sales column.

Macros8.dot adds a long list of macros in the Macro dialog box. If you decide you don't want to see these macros when you open the Macros dialog box, you can remove the check in the Templates and Add-Ins dialog box to hide them.

▶ See "Recording Your Macro," **p. 847**

Quick and Easy Sorting

Suppose that you entered information into the table. Then you realized it would be more effective to present the table information alphabetically, or numerically, from largest to smallest. Follow these steps to sort your table information:

1. Place the insertion point anywhere in the table.

FIG. 8.20
The Table Cell Helper macro returns this type of information.

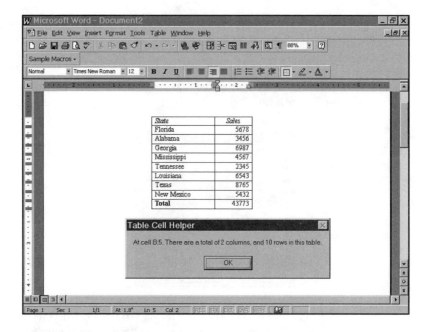

2. Choose Table, Sort. The Sort dialog box appears (see Figure 8.21).

FIG. 8.21
Sort a table alphabetically or numerically.

3. Use the Sort By list boxes to select the primary column by which you want to sort.
4. Use the other two Then By list boxes to identify tie-breakers if Word finds duplicate entries in the primary sort column.
5. Choose OK. Word re-sorts the table information. If you don't like what you get, click Undo and try again.

TIP To sort, you don't even need tables—just paragraphs. Select the paragraphs you want to sort before you start. Then, repeat the steps in this section.

TROUBLESHOOTING

Can I number the rows in my table? Yes. Select the rows and click the Numbering tool on the Formatting toolbar.

I can only see part of the text in a table cell. What did I do wrong? You may have indentations in the cell that you need to adjust, or the row height of the cell may be too small. To change indentations, click the cell and choose Format, Paragraph. On the Indents and Spacing tab, specify new measurements under Indentation. To fix a row height problem, click the cell and choose Table, Cell Height and Width. On the Row tab, set the In the Height of Rows list box to Auto.

From Here...

In this chapter, you learned about Word tables. You learned how to create and edit tables, how to format tables, how to split tables, and control what happens to a table when it spans across pages. You learned that you can sort information and calculate in tables. You also learned that you can convert tables to plain text, or plain text to tables, if you happen to change your mind about the presentation of text you have already typed.

- Chapter 9, "Using Word to Develop Web Content," shows you how to create a Web page in Word and use tables on your Web page to format information.

- Chapter 19, "Word Desktop Publishing," provides information on an alternative way to use a columnar format in a Word document.

Getting the Word Out: The Internet, Intranets, Electronic Files, and Hard Copy

Using Word to Develop Web Content

by Bill Camarda

Even two or three years ago, it would have been difficult to imagine how many documents would have to be created for electronic distribution. Electronic documents have been a reality for years, of course, but it was the World Wide Web that made them an everyday reality for tens of millions of computer users worldwide. A follow-on revolution, the intranet, is becoming the delivery method of choice for an increasingly wide variety of documents within the corporation. Now you can leverage your Word editing skills to easily create documents for intranets and the World Wide Web.

Using Word and Internet Explorer together

Word and Microsoft's free Internet Explorer browser work together to make both authoring and browsing more efficient.

Understanding the Web Page Authoring Environment

Like a chameleon, Word thoroughly adapts its appearance and behavior to the Web page environment.

Getting under the hood: a quick HTML introduction

When you're clicking buttons and choosing menu items, Word's busily writing HTML code. Sometimes you'll want to edit that code directly.

Formatting your Web pages

What you need to know to make your Web pages look great.

Saving Word documents to HTML

It's easy to convert your existing Word documents for use on your Web site.

Using the Web toolbar

Surf the Web—or your hard disk—from the comfort of your own word processor.

TIP Companies are now beginning to extend their intranets to business partners and selected customers. These extended intranets are commonly called *extranets*.

Word 97 introduces a series of powerful new features that enable Word users to build documents for both the World Wide Web and corporate intranets. Word 97 also integrates with the Microsoft Internet Explorer Web browser, so you can connect to the Web directly from Word. In this chapter, you'll learn about these day-to-day features that make Word a practical tool for Web authoring:

- The Word 97 Web Page Authoring Environment
- The Web toolbar and Word 97 integration with Microsoft Explorer

Then, in the following two chapters, you'll learn how to take the individual pages you've created in this chapter and deploy them on a Web site or corporate intranet. ■

Web Page Development: Word's Strengths and Weaknesses

It's important to understand what Word 97 can and cannot do, in order to use the right tool for the job. Word 97's strengths lie in building individual Web pages. As you'll see, you can use Word to insert text and graphics, format your page the way you want it, and create and test hyperlinks to other pages or locations.

N O T E When Word creates a Web page, it is actually inserting HTML code that tells Web browsers how to display the page, what images and other elements to include, and how to handle hyperlinks. Later in this chapter, you'll take a closer look at HTML code and learn some basic techniques for editing HTML code directly. ■

If you're already familiar with Word, working in Word's Web Page Authoring Environment will be a lot more convenient than trying to learn another Web editor. Moreover, as you'll see, you can easily save existing Word documents in the HTML format used to display Web and intranet pages.

If you have the Microsoft Office CD-ROM, you have access to several additional tools for publishing the pages you create. Three of the most impressive are described here:

- The *Web Publishing Wizard* simplifies uploading your files to a Web server.
- The *Personal Web Server* is a complete Web and FTP (File Transfer Protocol) server that is ideal for testing, and for actual deployment of very small intranets.
- *Microsoft Internet Explorer 3.01* is a full-featured Web browser that connects Word to the Web and enables you to see how your pages will look when published.

Although Word is an excellent Web page editor, it does not contain features for tracking, organizing, or updating Web site pages and components, such as graphics. These tracking features become increasingly important as your Web site or intranet grows, and as you make changes to it.

Microsoft's solution for these tasks is Microsoft FrontPage, which comes with extensive Web management and publishing tools, shortcuts for adding advanced interactivity, To Do lists for helping you track outstanding tasks you need to perform, and many other features. In Chapter 10, "Building Your Intranet with Word, Office, and FrontPage," you'll learn how to use or adapt Word-authored Web pages in FrontPage.

Installing Microsoft Internet Explorer

As already mentioned, Word integrates closely with Microsoft's Internet Explorer Web browser. Therefore, you may want to install Internet Explorer on your system before proceeding further. All copies of the Microsoft Office 97 CD-ROM contain a copy of Internet Explorer, in the \Valupack\Iexplore folder. If you choose to install Explorer from the CD-ROM, double-click Msie301.exe, and follow the instructions.

The original release of the Office 97 CD-ROM was accompanied by Internet Explorer 3.01. Since then, this release has been superseded by Internet Explorer 3.02, which fixes a number of security flaws found in 3.01.

More recently, Microsoft has introduced Internet Explorer 4.0, a major upgrade that integrates Web browsing directly into the Windows 95/NT 4.0 desktop. This upgrade adds a variety of features to Internet Explorer and to the Windows desktop, including Active Channels that provide news and entertainment. Once Internet Explorer 4.0 is installed, it becomes the default browser that Word integrates with.

If you want to install Internet Explorer 4.0, you can download and install it at no charge at Microsoft's Web site, **www.microsoft.com/ie/download**. Be aware, however, that the full download is over 20 megabytes.

N O T E Internet Explorer also makes significant changes to the Windows desktop. Most prominently, it changes desktop icons so that they load programs with one click instead of two.

The interface changes that Internet Explorer 4.0 makes will also be part of the Windows 98 upgrade, which is also designed to fully integrate the Windows desktop with the Internet. ▪

Creating a Page with Word's Web Page Wizard

The quickest way to create a Web page from scratch is to use Word's built-in Web Page Wizard. To run it, choose File, New; then click the Web Pages tab, and double-click the Web Page Wizard icon. The first screen of the Web Page Wizard appears (see Figure 9.1).

Here, you can choose from several types of Web pages, including Personal Home Pages, Feedback and Registration forms, a Calendar and a Table of Contents—a page that you might use to list hyperlinks to all the pages on your site. When you make a choice, Word displays the Web page in the background. As you step through the wizard, changes you make are reflected in the background after you move on to the next page.

FIG. 9.1

In the first screen of the
Web Page Wizard, you
choose the type of Web
page you want to create.

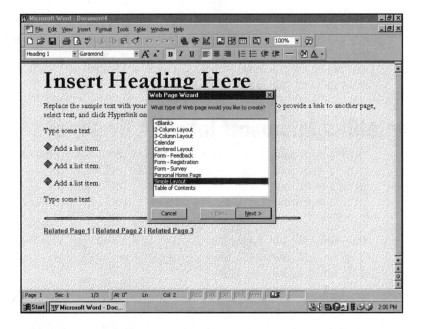

FIG. 9.1

In the first screen of the
Web Page Wizard, you
choose the type of Web
page you want to create.

After you've chosen the type of page you want, click Next. In the second page of the Web Page
Wizard (see Figure 9.2), you're asked which visual style you want to use. If you're planning to
create several pages in your Web site, you'll want to make sure they all use a consistent visual
style. When you make a change, Word changes the background, bullets, and borders used on
the page. When you're satisfied, click Finish.

FIG. 9.2

When you choose a
visual style, Word
changes the background
and bullets it uses on
your Web page to reflect
your choice.

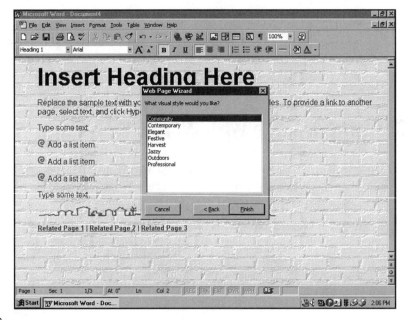

Word now displays a page you can edit and format as if you had created it from scratch. Word displays the page in its new Web Page Authoring Environment, with menus and toolbars that display Word's capabilities as a Web editor.

Creating a Web Page from Scratch

If none of the options in Word's Web Page Wizard do the job, you can create your page from scratch. Start by opening a blank Web page:

1. Choose File, New, or click the New button
2. Choose the Web Pages tab.
3. Double-click Blank Web Page.

NOTE If Word does not give you the option of creating a Web page, chances are you haven't installed the Web Page Authoring Environment. To do so, rerun the Word or Office Setup program, and add the component Web Page Authoring (HTML).

You can now enter and edit text the same way you normally do in Word.

Word's Web Page Authoring Environment: A Closer Look

Whether you create a page from scratch or use Word's Web Page Wizard, Word displays the page in its new Web Page Authoring Environment. In this section, you'll take a closer look at the tools available to you here.

ON THE WEB

Microsoft has recently made available an update to Word 97's Web Authoring Tools which offers the following improvements:

- An improved Web Publishing Wizard which adds a Publish to the Web command to the File menu and allows you to transfer files to the Web directly from within Word.

- A Check Links feature that can check every hyperlink or linked image in a Word HTML document to verify that the links work.

- New templates, styles, and backgrounds, including a new online resume template.

- An improved Conversion Wizard that makes it easier to give all your Web pages a consistent look. This new Wizard allows you to set a common background, navigation bar, or other elements, and apply them to all pages on your site at once—a feature that was previously restricted to Microsoft FrontPage.

- Several additional features, including flexibility in previewing your Web pages on multiple Web browsers, prompts that allow you to repair hyperlinks when you save an HTML page to a different folder, and more.

If you create many Web pages, these tools will be well worth downloading. They're available on the Web at **www.microsoft.com/OfficeFreeStuff/Word/**.

You'll find that many—but not all—of Word's formatting tools are still in place. For example, you can still boldface, italicize, underline, left-align, center, right-align, or indent text. You can still insert tables, and use Format Painter to copy complex formats onto new text. You can still use Find, Replace, Go To, and Spelling and Grammar Checker.

However there are some changes, and the deeper you look, the more you'll find. To start with, the tools available on the Standard and Formatting toolbar are somewhat different when you're editing a Web page. Later, you'll see that the Insert and Format menus have also changed significantly and so have the dialog boxes you can open from them.

Some of these changes correspond to differences between HTML pages and conventional Word documents; others relate to features made available by the Web Page Authoring Environment. In the Standard toolbar, for example, there are three new buttons (see Figure 9.3):

■ *Web Page Preview* opens Microsoft Internet Explorer to preview how your document will look on the Web.

■ *Form Design Mode* displays the Control toolbox, which enables you to insert form elements on your Web page.

■ *Insert Picture* provides a convenient way to insert images in your Web page.

Not surprisingly, a few buttons you're accustomed to seeing have disappeared: Insert Microsoft Excel Worksheet, Columns, and Drawing.

N O T E Columns aren't supported by HTML, although you can create tables that look much as columns would.

Word's built-in Drawing tools can't be used to generate art for Web pages. However, the free, optional add-on Microsoft Draw 97 works just like Word's drawing tools and *does* create Web-compatible files. ■

ON THE WEB

You can download Draw 97 at **www.microsoft.com/officefreestuff/word/dlpages/draw97.htm.**

N O T E Even though you can't insert Microsoft Excel worksheet cells in an HTML page, you can display a Microsoft Excel worksheet on an intranet, or on the Web. You'll learn how in Chapter 10, "Building Your Intranet with Word, Office, and FrontPage." ■

FIG. 9.3
This figure shows the Standard toolbar in the Web Page Authoring Environment.

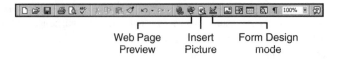

Web Page Preview   Insert Picture   Form Design mode

Similarly, the Formatting toolbar has changed somewhat (see Figure 9.4). It includes four new buttons:

- *Increase Font Size* and *Decrease Font Size* replace the standard font size settings. This is because standard HTML doesn't enable you to specify a type size; that's the responsibility of the browser. You can, however, specify the *relative* size of different blocks of text, so the browser knows which text should be the largest.

- The *Horizontal Line* button enables you to insert a horizontal line that separates two logically distinct sections of text on a Web page. This replaces the Border button; not all of Word's bordering capabilities are supported in HTML.

- The *Background* button enables you to choose a color or texture to appear behind your Web page.

As with the Standard toolbar, you also lose a few options when you're editing a Web page. You've already seen that Word's Border and Font Size buttons are gone; so are Highlight and Justify.

Of course, there's more to formatting a Web page than clicking a few buttons. You'll take a closer look at Word's Web page formatting capabilities shortly, but first briefly consider what Word is really doing while you're working in the Web Page Authoring Environment.

Part III

Ch 9

Decrease Font Size   Horizontal Line

FIG. 9.4
This figure shows new buttons on the Formatting toolbar in the Web Page Authoring Environment.

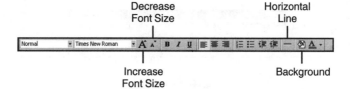

Increase Font Size   Background

A Very Brief Introduction to HTML

Web pages are simply text documents containing HTML codes that specify how they should look and act when opened in a Web browser. HTML is an acronym for Hypertext Markup Language and is a method for tagging elements of a document, so that Web browsers reading these documents can display them appropriately.

Standard HTML documents use tags that, at least in theory, can be recognized by any browser, on any computer—Windows, Macintosh, UNIX, OS/2, or virtually any other recent platform. In theory, then, after you've created an HTML page it can be read anywhere.

That's one of the reasons intranets are becoming so popular. With these intra-company Web sites, firms can provide simple Web browsers to all their employees, regardless of the type of computers they have. Then, those browsers can serve as the portal to all the company's information, from 401K plan updates and employee manuals, to product introductions and standard proposal documents—all stored on the intranet.

N O T E   Startup software costs can be extremely low because Microsoft distributes Internet Explorer free of charge. For companies running Microsoft's Windows NT Server, a powerful Web server is also available free, Microsoft Internet Information Server (IIS). (Other free Web servers, such as Apache for UNIX platforms, are even more widely used.) ■

Word's Web Page Authoring Environment does its best to shield you from the raw HTML code underlying Web pages. However, if you're one of the millions of people who are suddenly being asked to create and edit Web pages for the first time, you'll be more effective if you have at least some idea of what's going on under the hood.

N O T E   Later in this chapter, you'll learn how to edit HTML code directly. You can look at the HTML source code associated with any Web page by choosing <u>V</u>iew, <u>H</u>TML Source in Word's Web Page Authoring Environment. ▨

N O T E   If you really don't care to understand HTML, skip ahead to the section "Creating a Web Page from Scratch." ▨

First, look at a typical Web page as it appears in your Web browser (see Figure 9.5), and then look at the HTML tags that generated the same page (see Figure 9.6). Incidentally, this is the generic page created by the default settings in Word's Web Page Wizard, which you've just learned about.

FIG. 9.5

This figure shows a basic Web page as it appears in your browser.

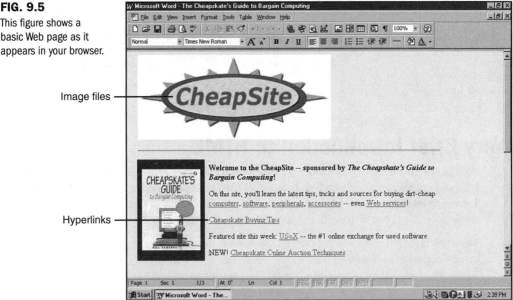

Image files

Hyperlinks

T I P   The <META> tags in the <HEAD> section are read by browsers but not displayed. You can add a <META> tag that helps search engines identify your subject matter and improve indexing. You can enter your own information by choosing File, Properties, More. Insert Keywords and Comments; then choose OK and save the HTML file.

Alternatively you can run <u>T</u>ools, A<u>u</u>toSummarize and Word automatically creates keywords and comments for you. When you save the document, they will appear in your HTML source code.

FIG. 9.6

This figure shows the corresponding HTML tags.

Nearly all Web pages start with a <HTML> tag...

...and a <HEAD> section

This <BODY> tag starts the body of the HTML page

Container tags start with <TAG>, end with </TAG>

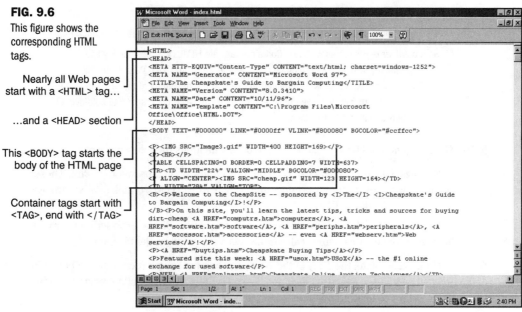

Part
III

Ch
9

HTML Tags and What They Do

HTML tags appear within angled brackets, so a browser can tell them apart from regular document text. Here are some of the things HTML can do:

- Show the function or relative importance of text. (For example, <H1> indicates first-level headings, and <STRONG> indicates text that should be emphasized strongly).
- Specify basic formatting, such as <B> for boldface.
- Insert an element from a separate file, such as <IMG>, which specifies an image to insert (and may specify how large the image should appear).
- Organize or identify the document and its contents, such as <HTML>, which tells a browser that this is an HTML page.
- Indicate links to other Web pages, to other locations within the same page, or to an e-mail program the viewer can use to send feedback (for example, <A HREF>).
- Specify elements of a form, such as <INPUT>.

Structuring an HTML Document

As already mentioned, nearly all HTML documents begin with the <HTML> command, which identifies them as an HTML document. After that, HTML documents contain a section called the *Head*, which includes information needed by both Web browsers and people whose responsibility it is to track and manage Web pages. The Head begins with a <HEAD> tag and ends with a </HEAD> tag.

N O T E There are two kinds of tags:

- *Empty tags* which contain one-time instructions such as <HR> (insert a horizontal rule)

- *Container tags* such as <HEAD>. Container tags are HTML's way of selecting text. For example, if you select and boldface a block of text in Word's Web Page Authoring Environment. Word inserts a container tag, <B>, at the beginning of the text and </B>, at the end. Virtually every Web browser recognizes this as an instruction to boldface all text between the container tags. ■

In HTML code generated by Word, the Head typically includes the following tags:

■ <META> tags, which browsers can read but don't show up in a browser or print. These include how the document was generated, which Word HTML template or wizard was used, and other information

■ A <TITLE> tag, which corresponds to the name to appear on the browser title bar when the page is loaded; this name is almost always different from the file name

After the *Head* is complete, the *Body* of the Web page begins. (You'll recognize the beginning of the Body when you see a tag that includes the word BODY.) This section includes all the tags which display the text, graphics, and hyperlinks in your document.

Next you dissect a couple of the tags on this page to see what they're about. Here's an easy one:

```
<P> Type some text.</P>
```

In this line, <P> indicates the beginning of a paragraph; </P> the end of the paragraph. The browser is asked to display the text in between. The following tag is slightly trickier:

```
<P><IMG SRC="Image7.gif" WIDTH=17 HEIGHT=17> Add a list item.</P>
```

A browser would read this line as follows:

Start a new paragraph. Then, insert an image using the file Image7.gif. (Because there's no path listed, look in the same folder as the Web page.) Display the image at a width of 17 pixels and a height of 17 pixels. After that, insert the text *Add a list item.* Then, end the paragraph.

Now that you know just a little bit about how HTML works, you may not be quite as surprised when Word's Web Page Authoring Environment doesn't do exactly what you expect, and you may have a slightly better idea of how to get the results you really want. In the following pages, you'll learn not only how to use the Web Page Authoring Environment, but also see what Word is doing behind the scenes while you're happily clicking buttons and choosing menu items.

N O T E HTML is becoming increasingly rich, as vendors like Netscape and Microsoft propose extensions to it that provide more capabilities. Unfortunately, Netscape and Microsoft don't often agree on these extensions, so using them can lead to differences in the appearance of your pages on each market-leading browser. ■

For more information about writing and editing HTML code directly, see *Special Edition, Using HTML* by Tom Savola, published by Que.

Applying Font Formatting in Web Pages

You've already seen that you can apply boldface, italics, and underlining to text in a Web page, using toolbar buttons on the Formatting toolbar. You have some other choices for text formatting as well. Choose Format, Font, and a truncated version of the Font dialog box appears (see Figure 9.7).

You'll quickly note that plenty is missing: there are no character spacing controls, and no text animation, for example. HTML browsers don't support custom character spacing, and the animated text you typically see on Web pages is created by Java applets or custom ActiveX controls that Word isn't able to generate.

FIG. 9.7
When you're formatting text for a Web page, you have fewer options than you do elsewhere in Word.

You can choose a font. If you choose a font other than Times New Roman, Word inserts a <FONT FACE> tag indicating which font should be used. However, it's important to remember that your Web page is likely to be read on a wide variety of computers. If you choose a font that isn't universally available, these computers will simply ignore the tag and display the text in a default font. If your Web page layout is heavily dependent on the spacing and appearance of a specific font, you may not like the results.

> **N O T E** The problem is less serious if you are creating pages for an intranet, because you may have more control over the fonts and computing platforms in use throughout your organization. For example, your company may have standardized on Windows computers and Microsoft Word; both Windows and Word come with a set of fonts that the Web page designer may be able to count on being present. ■

You can also specify a font size, but you only have seven choices, corresponding to the seven levels of font size available through HTML. Word's Web Page Authoring Environment can format text in the following sizes: 9, 10, 12, 14, 18, 24, and 36 point. These correspond to the HTML tags <FONT SIZE=1> through <FONT SIZE=7>.

You can choose a color, but you'll want to test the color carefully to make sure the color you pick is accurately displayed on each leading Web browser. Text effects like Shadow and Emboss are not available, but you can still use Strikethrough, Superscript, and Subscript. When you're done, choose OK; Word applies the formatting to the text you selected.

Inserting Bullets in a Web Page

You can format one or more paragraphs with a standard bullet the same way you do elsewhere in Word. Select the paragraphs, and click the Bullets button on the Standard Toolbar. Word inserts typical round bullets.

Behind the scenes, Word places a <UL> (unordered list) tag before the paragraphs in the bulleted list; it also marks each paragraph with the <LI> container tag, indicating that it is an item in the list. Different browsers are free to interpret <UL> and <LI> tags any way they want: with bullets, square dots, or other symbols, depending on the fonts that are available to them.

If you've spent much time on the Web, you've probably noticed that many Web sites make extensive use of *custom bullets*. These tiny graphics make Web pages more attractive, without making the files larger and slower to download. In fact, if you use several identical bullets in a row, the HTML code in your Web page keeps referring to the same image; so you only have to download that image once, no matter how many times your page calls for it.

Word comes with its own library of custom bullets. To use them, choose Format, Bullets and Numbering, and display the Bulleted tab. The Bulleted tab displayed in the Web Page Authoring Environment (see Figure 9.8) does not provide the customization capabilities that exist elsewhere in Word. Instead, it provides a library of bullet images—with access to even more.

FIG. 9.8

In the Bulleted tab, you can choose from a library of custom bullets.

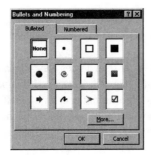

The two square bullets on the right side of the top row are from the Wingdings font. Word doesn't actually tell a Web browser to go looking for Wingdings, however. Rather, it adds an attribute to the <UL> tag, which tells the browser what kind of bullet to go looking for. See the following example:

```
<UL TYPE="SQUARE">
```

This is one of those Netscape extensions to HTML that were once so controversial; now, however, virtually every browser can handle them.

The other eight bullets in the Bulleted tab aren't font characters; they're real images, and if you're not satisfied with any of these, Word has more. Choose More, and the other .GIF bullets stored in the C:\Program Files\Microsoft Office\Clipart\Bullets folder appear in the Insert Picture dialog box (see Figure 9.9).

If you prefer one of these, select it, and choose Insert. Otherwise, choose Cancel; then choose a bullet from the Bulleted tab and click OK. Either way, Word displays the bullet you've chosen in your Web page.

FIG. 9.9

The Insert Picture dialog box shows eight more Web bullets that come with Office 97.

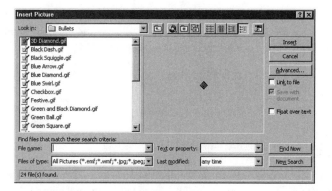

T I P If you have other bullets available to you from Web clip art kits or other sources, copy them to the Bullets folder so they will be easily accessible whenever you want to insert them.

After you've inserted one or more bullets, they behave the same way other Word bullets do. For example, if you press Enter at the end of a bulleted paragraph, a new copy of the same bullet appears at the beginning of the next paragraph.

N O T E If this doesn't work, choose Format, AutoFormat, Options. Display the AutoFormat as You Type tab, and check the Automatic Bulleted Lists check box. ▉

When you save the file, Word copies the bullet from its library of bullets into the same folder as the Web page. It also copies references to the bullet graphic into the HTML source code, as in the following:

```
<P><IMG SRC="Bullet1.gif" WIDTH=13 HEIGHT=13> Text of paragraph. </P>
```

The <IMG> command represents the bullet.

Inserting Numbered Lists in a Web Page

 You can create numbered lists as easily as you can insert bullets; select the paragraphs you want to number, and click the Numbering button on the Formatting toolbar. Word inserts a numbered list. If you then press Enter at the end of a paragraph in the list, Word creates a new numbered list item.

Behind the scenes, Word formats each paragraph as a list item using the <LI> tag and places the <OL> tag above the list, indicating that it is an ordered (numbered) list.

CAUTION

If you have a bulleted list that uses images as bullets, you can't select it and click the Numbering button to convert it to a numbered list. This works elsewhere in Word, but in the Web Page Authoring Environment, Word adds the numbering without deleting the bullets.

To get more control over numbered lists, select the paragraphs you want to number, and choose Format, Bullets and Numbering. Then, display the Numbered tab. Here, you can choose from five numbering schemes recognized in HTML:

- 1., 2., 3…
- I., II., III…
- A., B., C…
- a., b., c…
- i., ii., iii…

In your HTML source code, these are displayed as <OL> attributes. For example, a list formatted using the A., B., C… scheme will be preceded by the following HTML tag:

```
<OL TYPE="A">
```

Controlling Text Colors

 You can always select text and change its color by choosing a new color from the Font Color toolbar button on the Formatting toolbar. To change *default* text colors for the entire document, choose Format, Text Colors.

The Text Colors dialog box opens (see Figure 9.10). In the Body Text Color drop-down box, choose the default color for all body text; in the Hyperlink drop-down box, choose a color for hyperlinks. In the Followed Hyperlink drop-down list box, choose a color for hyperlinks that have already been clicked.

Remember that most Web users have come to expect hyperlinks to be blue and followed hyperlinks to be violet. You might find yourself a little more likely to change the color of body text, especially if a different color, such as teal, dark blue or dark red would complement the page background or texture you've chosen.

> **CAUTION**
>
> If your Web page has a dark background, you'll want to choose a lighter text color for contrast, but don't choose white. Some people turn off backgrounds so their browsers load faster, which would leave them viewing white type on a white screen. They may encounter the same problem while printing. Choose a color that's light enough to provide contrast while dark enough to be visible against a white background.

Using Styles in an HTML Document

You can use styles in an HTML document the same way you use them in Word. For example, you can select and format a block of text, then click in the Style box on the Formatting toolbar, type a style name, and click OK.

After you've created the style, you can format another block of text the same way by selecting the text and choosing the style. Word doesn't actually enter your custom styles in the HTML code, but it does enter all the HTML tags needed to make the text look like the style you defined.

FIG. 9.10
From the Text Colors dialog box, you can change a document's default text colors.

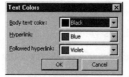

When you work in the Web Page Authoring Environment, Word makes available a special set of styles that correspond to many of the most commonly used HTML tags, as shown in Table 9.1. To apply these tags, all you need to do is choose the style from the Style drop-down box.

Table 9.1   HTML Styles Word Can Insert Automatically

Style Name	What It Does	HTML Tag
Address	Formats selected text, typically an address, as italics	\<ADDRESS>
Blockquote	Indents, italicizes text, typically for quotations	\<BLOCKQUOTE>
CITE	Defines text as a citation	\<CITE>
CODE	Defines text as computer code, for example, a line from a sample program	\<CODE>
Comment	Turns text into a comment that doesn't appear in the Web page	\<COMMENT>
Definition	Formats text in italics; typically used for definitions	\<DD>
Definition List	Formats text for use in a definition list containing both the term and the definition	\<DL>
Definition Term	Formats text as a definition term	\<DT>
Emphasis	Emphasizes text; commonly with italics	\<EM>
H1	Formats as first-level heading	\<H1>
H2	Formats as second-level heading	\<H2>
H3	Formats as third-level heading	\<H3>
H4	Formats as fourth-level heading	\<H4>
H5	Formats as fifth-level heading	\<H5>
H6	Formats as sixth-level heading	\<H6>

continues

Table 9.1 Continued

Style Name	What It Does	HTML Tag
HTML Markup	Formats as hidden text; used to insert HTML code manually	
Keyboard	Formats text in a typewriter-style font	<KBD>
Preformatted	Preformats text using the viewer's current settings	<PRE>
Sample	Formats text as sample output, as from a computer program	<SAMP>
Strong	Strongly emphasizes text; commonly by boldfacing	<STRONG>
Typewriter	Formats text as if typed on a typewriter	<TI>
Variable	Defines text as a text variable	<VAR>

N O T E You can also work with styles by choosing F̲ormat, S̲tyle. This dialog box works exactly as it does elsewhere in Word; for more information, see Chapter 5, "Styles: The Foundation of Automated Documents." ▪

Choosing a Background for a Web Page

 Word makes it easy to add a colored background or texture to a Web page. The quickest way is to click the Background button on the Formatting toolbar and choose a color (see Figure 9.11). Word displays the color in your document and applies a background color attribute in the <BODY> tag in your HTML source code. For instance, if you choose yellow, the attribute BGCOLOR="#ffff99" is inserted; most recent browsers will interpret this properly as yellow.

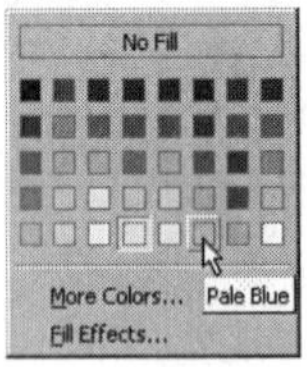

FIG. 9.11
Choosing a colored background from the Formatting toolbar.

If you want a custom color, choose M̲ore Colors from the drop-down box that appears when you click Background. You can either select a built-in color in the Standard tab, or create a custom color in the Custom tab.

▶ **See** "Controlling Colors," **p. 606**

Adding Textures

 So far, you've learned how to add solid colors as backgrounds. Word also provides a set of textures that, used carefully, can make your pages much more attractive. To select one, click the Background button on the Formatting toolbar; then choose Fill Effects. The Texture tab of the Fill Effects dialog box opens (see Figure 9.12).

FIG. 9.12
You can choose a texture from the Textures tab of the Fill Effects dialog box.

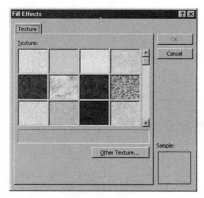

Here, you can scroll among 24 textures. If you like one, click it and choose OK. If you want more textures available, you can access them by choosing Other Texture; the Select Texture dialog box opens (see Figure 9.13). Browse, and select the .GIF or .JPG file you want; then choose OK.

CAUTION

Be aware that coarse-grained textures like Woven Mat or Paper Bag can significantly reduce the on-screen readability of small type.

FIG. 9.13
If you have them, you can find and choose another texture from the Select Texture dialog box.

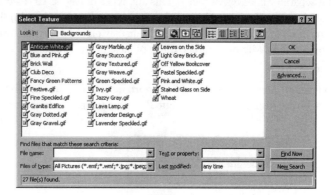

Inserting Horizontal Lines in a Web Page

Because Web pages don't support bordering, the best way to divide blocks of text that are logically separate is with a horizontal line. To insert a default horizontal line, place your insertion point where you want it, and click the Horizontal Line button on the Formatting toolbar. A three-dimensional line appears in your document (see Figure 9.14); Word inserts an <HR> tag in the HTML source code.

FIG. 9.14

This figure shows Word's default horizontal line, corresponding to an <HR> tag.

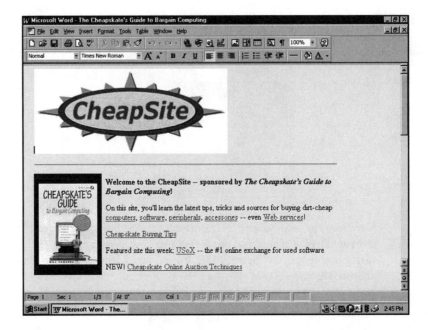

As with bullets, however, your Web page can get a lot more interesting when you insert a custom horizontal line instead of simply adding a default HTML tag. Word offers a library of horizontal separator lines for various moods and types of pages. To select one, choose Insert, Horizontal Line. The Horizontal Line dialog box opens (see Figure 9.15). Pick one and click OK. If none of them satisfy you, click More to display eight additional horizontal lines stored in the C:\Program Files\Microsoft Office\Clipart\Lines folder. You can see a list of these horizontal lines in Figure 9.16).

When you choose a custom horizontal line, Word inserts an <IMG> image tag in your HTML code and copies the corresponding .GIF file into the same folder in which the Web page is contained.

FIG. 9.15

The Horizontal Line dialog box gives you nine more horizontal lines from which to choose.

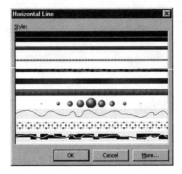

FIG. 9.16
Several additional horizontal lines are available in the Backgrounds folder, via the Insert Picture dialog box.

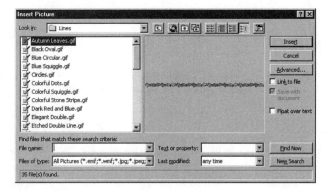

Inserting a Picture

You insert a picture in the Web Page Authoring Environment much the way you do it elsewhere in Word. Choose Insert, Picture; then choose one of the options Word provides in the submenu:

- *Clip Art* opens the Clip Art Gallery; there, you can browse for a picture and insert it.
- *From File* opens the Insert Picture dialog box; again, you can browse for a picture and insert it.
- *From Scanner* opens Microsoft Photo Editor and prepares to scan an image—assuming you have a TWAIN-compliant scanner connected to your PC.
- *Chart* opens Microsoft Graph 97, where you can build a chart and then return to Word; your chart appears on your Web page.

If you've installed the free add-on Microsoft Draw 97, you have another option: New Drawing. All these features behave just as they do elsewhere in Word.

▶ **See** "Working With Other Clip Art," **p. 573**
▶ **See** "Understanding Drawing Objects," **p. 595**
▶ **See** "Understanding Graphs and Charts," **p. 622**

After you insert a picture, you can resize it the same way you would elsewhere in Word; click it and drag one of the corner or side handles. When you save your Web page, the new height and width of the picture are stored in the HTML code.

When you save a Web page containing an imported graphic in a format other than .JPG and .GIF, Word also saves a copy of the graphic in .GIF format. This is a real convenience; you don't have to worry about file formats or conversions.

ON THE WEB

Expert Web page designers know that .GIF has its strengths and weaknesses; in some cases, .JPG is a superior format for saving graphics files. If the fidelity of an image is an issue, you may want to

continues

continued

manually edit it and experiment with different .GIF or .JPG settings, using Microsoft Photo Editor or a third-party program such as Adobe PhotoShop.

If you have many images to convert at the same time, consider a batch conversion program such as Jasc Image Robot, shareware available from Jasc, Inc. (**www.jasc.com**).

ON THE WEB

You have one additional choice for importing pictures: Microsoft Clip Gallery Live, Microsoft's Web site containing links to additional free clip art for Office 97 users, at **www.microsoft.com/clipgallerylive/** (see Figure 9.17). To link to this page, choose Insert, Picture, Clip Art. Then, when the Clip Art Gallery opens, click the Connect to Web for Additional Clips icon at the bottom right-hand corner of the dialog box. Internet Explorer opens, establishes a Web connection, and links to Clip Gallery Live.

FIG. 9.17
Link to Clip Gallery Live,
Microsoft's Web page for
free clip art.

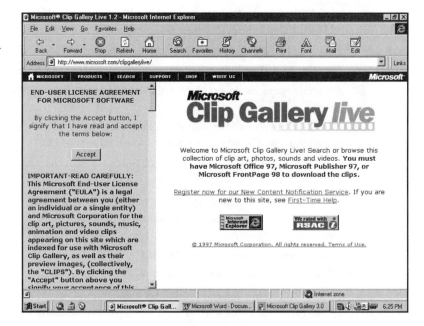

ON THE WEB

Most of the best Web images on Microsoft's site are currently located at **www.microsoft.com/gallery/ files/images/default.htm**. You'll get what you need faster if you go there directly. Note that many of these images are also included in Microsoft Publisher 97.

Controlling a Picture's Behavior Through the Picture Toolbar After you have a drawing in your document, Word makes it easy to control aspects of its behavior. Click the drawing, and the Picture toolbar appears (see Figure 9.18).

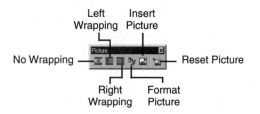

FIG. 9.18

The Picture toolbar enables you to quickly control the behavior of an image.

The three buttons at the left control the way text wraps around a picture. If you choose Insert Picture, the Insert Picture dialog box opens. You can browse to, and select a picture to replace the existing one. Reset Picture eliminates cropping from a picture and restores its original color, brightness, and contrast settings.

Finally, Format Picture enables you to control settings associated with the picture. As you'll see, one option in this dialog box is especially important.

Inserting Text that Displays in Place of a Picture To speed up Web browsing, many people turn off images. What do they see in place of your image? Nothing. That obviously prevents you from communicating your message as clearly, and it's not very polite, either. HTML etiquette and common sense say you should provide text that describes your picture, so even people with text-only browsers will understand what you're trying to communicate. To do so, click the Format Picture toolbar button and choose the Settings tab in the Picture dialog box (see Figure 9.19). Enter your description in the Text box and choose OK.

FIG. 9.19

Here's where you can (and should) insert text to describe the picture you're inserting.

N O T E The description is added to the <IMG> tag in the HTML source code, using the ALT attribute. For example, the following tag would display the words Yankees logo in place of the image, on browsers that don't display graphics:

```
<IMG SRC="Yanklogo.gif" WIDTH=200 HEIGHT=200 ALT="Yankees logo">
```

T I P In Microsoft Internet Explorer, even if you are displaying images, you can read the description as a ScreenTip by hovering your mouse pointer over the image.

T I P   The Position tab of the Picture dialog box provides the same text wrapping controls as the Picture toolbar, and also enables you to control how much distance is maintained between the text and the image.

Inserting Scrolling Text

One of the earliest ways in which Web sites were animated was with "marquee"-style text that scrolled across the screen like a stock ticker. Word's Web Page Authoring Environment enables you to create scrolling text without the complex Java coding or animated GIFs that were required previously.

Choose Insert, Scrolling Text. The Scrolling Text dialog box appears (see Figure 9.20). In the Type the Scrolling Text Here text box, enter the text you want to scroll. Then, control how you want the scrolling text to look and behave.

FIG. 9.20

For intranets and Web sites that only use Internet Explorer, this dialog box gives you an easy way to create scrolling text.

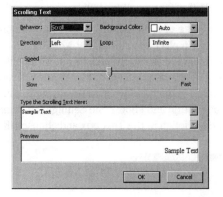

In the Behavior drop-down list box, choose from the following text behaviors:

- Scrolling past the edge of the screen and back again from the other side
- Sliding to the edge of the screen and stopping
- Bouncing back and forth (Alternate) from one end of the screen to the other

In the Direction drop-down list box, choose whether you want the text to scroll Left or Right. In the Background Color drop-down list box, choose a background color. In the Loop drop-down list box, specify how many times you want the text to scroll, slide or alternate; the default setting is Infinite. Finally, in the Speed area, drag the slider to speed up or slow down the scrolling text.

When you click OK, the scrolling text appears in your Web page. You can right-click on the text to display a shortcut menu that lets you Play the scrolling text, Stop it, or change its Properties.

CAUTION

Netscape Navigator and Netscape Communicator don't support the <MARQUEE> HTML tag that Word and Internet Explorer use to display scrolling text. Be cautious about using this feature in any environment where Netscape browsers are in use—which is to say, most Web applications and some intranets.

Embedding Audio

Occasionally, you might want to embed audio in your Web page—perhaps as background music that loops infinitely while people are visiting your site, or perhaps as a brief, personal audio introduction to your site. Be careful with audio; file sizes tend to be large, and compatibility can be an issue. (For example, Netscape's browsers won't play Windows .WAV files without a special plug-in.)

Having said all that, maybe the CEO *insists* on speaking to the troops, and your company has standardized on Microsoft Internet Explorer for Windows. In that case, here's how to add audio to your intranet or Web site. Choose Insert, Background Sound, Properties. The Background Sound dialog box opens (see Figure 9.21).

FIG. 9.21

The Background Sound dialog box enables you to specify a sound and the way it will play.

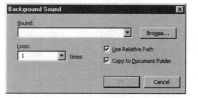

In the Sound drop-down list box, enter the file name of the sound you want. If (as is quite possible) you don't already know the file name, click Browse to display the File Open dialog box. Then browse and select the audio file; choose Open.

 T I P   If you've used a sound clip before, click the down arrow in the Sound drop-down list box; you may be able to select it there instead of browsing for it.

Now, specify how many times you want the sound to play. The default is 1, which means that as soon as someone opens the page, the sound will play once, and then stop. You can set the default to any number from 1 to 5; or specify Infinite, which means the sound will keep replaying as long as the page is open.

N O T E   Word's audio support doesn't give the Web page reader any control. When you insert a sound clip through this dialog box, it simply runs when the page is opened. There's no button to click to run it. For that, you'll need an ActiveX control or Java applet. ■

Note two other settings, both checked by default: Use Relative Path tells Word to include a relative path in the source code, instead of an absolute path with a complete file address that will "break" if you move the file. Copy to Document Folder tells Word to copy the sound clip into the same folder as the Web page. In most cases, you'll want to keep these settings enabled.

N O T E   Later, as your Web page or intranet grows in size, you might want to place all your audio clips in a single folder and edit your HTML code to look in that folder for them. ■

When you're finished, click OK. Now that the sound is in your document, you can check it by choosing Insert, Background Sound, Play.

Embedding Video

All the cautions that apply to audio apply even more to video: It's a bandwidth hog; you can't count on format compatibility, and so on. However, if you want to insert video in your Web page, you can. Click your mouse pointer where you want the video clip to appear. Now, choose Insert, Video. The Video Clip dialog box opens (see Figure 9.22).

FIG. 9.22
The Video Clip dialog box enables you to specify a video clip and how it will play.

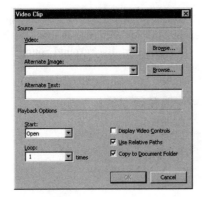

Next to the Video drop-down list box, choose Browse to look for video files in any of these common formats: Windows .AVI, .MOV, .MOVIE, .MPG, .MPEG, .or QT (QuickTime). Because many people who view your Web page won't want (or be able) to watch your video, choose an Alternate Image that displays in place of the video. You can also enter Alternate Text that appears for viewers whose browsers don't display video or images.

By default, your video will play automatically when a user opens your page. You can change this setting in the Start drop-down list box. The Mouse-Over option sets the video to run when users hover their mouse pointer over it; Both sets the video to run when the page opens and when the user points to it.

Use Relative Paths and Copy to Document Folder work the same way as they do in the Background Sound dialog box. There's one more option: Display Video Controls. This places a small TV icon in your editing window (see Figure 9.23). While you're authoring your Web page, you can make changes to the video's behavior by right-clicking this icon and choosing Properties from the shortcut menu. The icon doesn't appear when viewers load your Web page.

FIG. 9.23
If you check Display Video Controls, this TV icon appears in your editing window, giving you easier access to video editing controls.

Working with HTML Tables

Tables are one of the most powerful features of HTML. Not only can you use tables for traditional tabular data, such as financial information, you can also use them to specify the exact position of text or graphics—something that can otherwise be difficult to do in HTML. You can even use tables to simulate multiple-column documents, such as newsletters—again, something HTML doesn't otherwise support. Tables let you create a design grid and a structure that make your content much easier to understand. Figure 9.24 shows an example of how tables can help organize a Web page more effectively.

Part

III

Ch

9

FIG. 9.24

This is a two-column table with a headline at left and hyperlinks at right, set off by color.

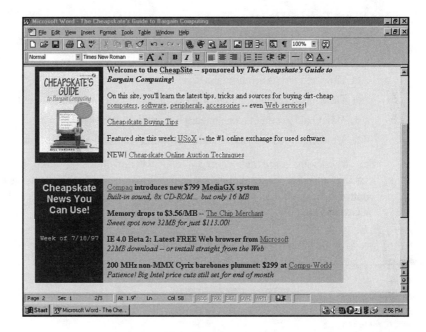

The same table design tools you learned about in Chapter 8, "Tables," work in the Web Page Authoring Environment as well. Make sure to choose Table, Show Gridlines so you can see where to place text or graphics within your table. The gridlines won't show when people view your page through their browsers.

N O T E Tables weren't supported in HTML until recently, and even now they require fairly complex HTML code. For example, the code to specify a table and enter just the first, empty, four-column row looks like this:

```
<TABLE CELLSPACING=0 BORDER=0 CELLPADDING=7 WIDTH=638>
<TR><TD WIDTH="25%" VALIGN="TOP"> </TD>
<TD WIDTH="25%" VALIGN="TOP"> </TD>
<TD WIDTH="25%" VALIGN="TOP"> </TD>
<TD WIDTH="25%" VALIGN="TOP"> </TD>
</TR>
```

continues

continued

Notice that every single cell requires its own line of HTML code! Also notice that cells are measured not in inches, picas, points, or centimeters, but by the percentage of the entire width of the table that each cell takes; in the previous example, each cell has a width equal to 25 percent.

Considering how much complexity is just under the surface, it's quite remarkable how few differences there are between how the Web Page Authoring Environment handles tables compared with the rest of Word. ■

Controlling Table Properties

Now that you've inserted a table on your Web page, you can exercise finer control over how it looks and behaves. For example, you can control the following:

- How text wraps around tables
- How much distance appears between tables and surrounding text
- What background color appears behind the table
- How much extra space is added between columns within the table

Start by clicking in the table you want to format, and choosing Table, Table Properties to display the Table Properties dialog box, shown in Figure 9.25. (The settings in this dialog box control the entire table; to control specific cells, use the Cell Properties dialog box, which will be covered next.)

 T I P   Alternatively, right-click in the table and choose Table Properties from the shortcut menu.

FIG. 9.25
The Table Properties dialog box enables you to control text wrapping, color, and space between columns.

By default, text doesn't wrap around tables; it jumps beneath them. However you can specify that text wrap to the Left or the Right of a table. You can also set a Horizontal Distance and a Vertical Distance that will be left between the border of a table and any text that wraps around it. In the Background drop-down list box, you can choose one of 16 background colors for all cells in your table.

N O T E You have fewer options for table and cell backgrounds than you do for Web page backgrounds, which can make it challenging to choose table backgrounds that coordinate well with page backgrounds. ▣

T I P If your table has several columns in it, you might format them all with the same background color here, and then use Cell Properties to format one column with a different color to make it stand out.

Finally, within the table, Word places 0.15" between each column by default. You can increase or decrease this spacing in the Space Between Columns scroll box.

Controlling Cell Properties

You can also control the behavior of specific cells. To do so, select the cells and choose Table, Cell Properties to display the Cell Properties dialog box (see Figure 9.26). You can control whether the contents of a cell displays at the Top, Middle, or Bottom of a cell. In the Background drop-down list box, you can choose one of 16 colors. Finally, in the Width and Height scroll boxes you can set the width of each cell in inches and the height in points.

FIG. 9.26

The Cell Properties dialog box enables you to set the vertical alignment of text and graphics in a cell, background color, height, and width.

Controlling Table Borders

You can border all the cells in an HTML table—or none of them. In other words, you can't border just selected cells. To control table bordering, choose Table, Borders; the Borders dialog box opens (see Figure 9.27). To add bordering to every cell, specify a width in the Border Width drop-down list box: $3/4$ pt., $1 1/2$ pt., $2 1/4$ pt., 3 pt., $4 1/2$ pt., or 6 pt. Word enters a CELLSPACING attribute from 1 to 6 in the <TABLE> tag that begins the table. Different browsers will handle this attribute differently. Check to make sure you're getting acceptable results on all the browsers you expect your viewers to use.

FIG. 9.27

The Borders dialog box enables you to set borders for all the cells in a table.

Inserting Hyperlinks

The heart of the World Wide Web is hyperlinking—the ability to click text or a graphic and jump to another location which could easily be half a world away. Hyperlinks are covered in detail in Chapter 18, "Footnotes, Bookmarks, Cross-References, and Hyperlinks," but because you'll often use them as you author Web pages, here's a quick overview.

To format text on a Web page as a hyperlink, select it; then right-click to display the shortcut menu, and choose Hyperlink. The Insert Hyperlink dialog box opens (see Figure 9.28).

FIG. 9.28
Use the Insert Hyperlink dialog box to establish a hyperlink in your Web page.

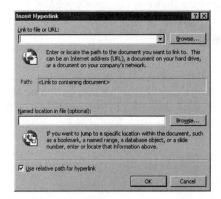

In the Link to File or URL text box, enter the name of the file to which you are linking:

- If you're linking to a page on the World Wide Web, enter its entire address, for example, **http://www.microsoft.com**

- If you're linking to a file elsewhere on your hard disk or network, choose Browse; select the file from the Link to File dialog box, and choose OK.

- If you're linking to another page in the same folder, as is likely if you're creating your own Web or intranet site, enter the file name. The file doesn't have to exist yet.

Click OK; Word reformats the text as a hyperlink. When you save the file, Word places a hypertext reference in the HTML source code, like the following one :

```
<A HREF="smith.htm">Text of hyperlink</A>
```

After the hyperlink is in your Web page, you might want to change the page it links to. To do so, right-click the hyperlink; choose Hyperlink from the shortcut menu, and choose Edit Hyperlink. In the Edit Hyperlink dialog box, enter a new URL, and choose OK.

Creating Your Own HTML Templates

You may invest a significant amount of time creating the formatting for a Web page. Wouldn't it be nice if you could reuse that Web page design on other similar pages throughout your Web site or intranet? You can, by saving your Web pages as templates.

When you have a page you really like, choose File, Save As to save a copy of it under another name. Working from the copy, edit out text you won't want to keep, or better yet, replace it with boilerplate instructions as to what should go in each location, including dummy hyperlinks. If you have a table format you want to keep, select the data and press delete: the data will disappear but the table format will stay in place. Finally, choose File, Save As again, and save the file as a Document Template (using the .DOT extension).

When you create a new file based on this template, all the text, hyperlinks, and table structures you created will already be in place. However, you'll have to add the images themselves. Word makes this easy to do; right-click where you want to insert the picture, and choose Picture from the shortcut menu. Word displays the Insert Picture dialog box, so you can browse to, and select the picture you want.

Part
III

Ch
9

 TIP When you save a template, Word offers to place it in the Templates folder. To store the Web page template with your other Web page templates, browse one level down, to the Web Pages subfolder; then click Save.

▶ **See** "Creating a New Template," **p. 177**

Converting an Existing Word Document to HTML

Sometimes you'll have an existing Word document that you would like to include on your Web site or intranet. It's easy to save a Word document as HTML; just choose File, Save as HTML.

 TIP If you have many documents you want to convert at the same time, use Word's Batch Conversion Wizard, stored in CONVERT8.WIZ (typically found in the C:\Program Files\Microsoft Office\ Office\Macros folder).

▶ **See** "Batch File Conversions," **p. 808**

What happens to a Word document saved as HTML? Quite a bit, depending on what formatting and document elements were contained in the original Word document. Table 9.2 shows you what to expect.

Table 9.2   How Word Features Translate to HTML

Word Feature	What Happens
Animated text	Lost, but text is retained
Bold, italic, underline	Translates properly
Borders around page	Lost
Borders around text	Lost
Columns	Lost; use tables as a substitute

continues

Table 9.2   Continued

Word Feature	What Happens
Comments	Removed, even though there's a corresponding HTML <COMMENTS> tag
Drawing objects	Lost. Use Draw 97 free add-on instead of Word's built-in drawing tools
Drop caps	Lost
Equations and charts	Converted to GIF images
Field codes	Converted to field results; no longer updateable
Fonts	Stored as <FONT FACE> tags that may or may not be recognized by all browsers
Font sizes	Changed to the closest HTML size. HTML displays seven font sizes, from smallest to largest, and depends on the browser to choose exact sizes
Footnotes and endnotes	Lost
Graphics	Converted to .GIF unless already in .JPG format
Headers and footers	Lost
Highlighting	Lost
Margins	Lost
Other text effects	Lost, but text is retained
Page numbering	Lost; every Web page is considered to be one page long
Strikethrough	Translates properly
Styles	Converted to direct formatting wherever possible in HTML
Subscript, superscript	Translates properly
Tabs	Converted to HTML tab character 	 some browsers display as spaces; Consider using tables instead
Tables	Converted, subject to HTML's limitations (for example, can't border individual cells)
Tables of contents and indexes	Converted to text; no longer updateable
Track changes marks	Tracked changes appear; track changes marks are lost (for example document looks as it would if all changes were accepted)

Viewing HTML Source Code

As you've learned, Word's Web Page Authoring Environment adds HTML codes as you create, edit, and format text because it's the best way to do any of the following:

- Troubleshoot a problem that you can't seem to fix without seeing the underlying HTML tags
- Insert an HTML tag that Word 97 doesn't recognize, such as one of the new Dynamic HTML tags recognized by Microsoft Internet Explorer 4.0 or Netscape Communicator
- Insert HTML attributes Word can't insert automatically
- Make wholesale changes to HTML codes using Word's Find & Replace feature

In order to view the HTML code that Word has applied to your Web page, first save the file. Word enters HTML codes for any document elements you've changed. Now, choose View, HTML Source. Your source code appears; you can now edit it any way you want.

N O T E The Formatting toolbar disappears when you view HTML Source because HTML source code is, by definition, text-only. ■

 T I P One tool that remains available while you're working with HTML Source is AutoText. That means you can insert blocks of boilerplate text in source code the same way you can in your document.

Better yet, you can create AutoText entries based on complex HTML coding that you would rather not have to reinsert manually every time you use it.

Entering a Single HTML Tag

Sometimes you'll want to enter a single HTML tag or attribute without going through the trouble of saving the file and viewing all your HTML code. Word makes this easy to do. Enter the text in your Web page—exactly as you want it to appear in HTML source code. Then select it, and choose HTML Markup in the Style drop-down list box on the Formatting toolbar.

The text disappears. In fact, it has been formatted as hidden text and stored as HTML source code, just where you wanted it.

How Word and Microsoft Internet Explorer Integrate

Earlier in this chapter, you learned that Word integrates closely with Microsoft Internet Explorer 3.0, the Web browser included with the Office 97 CD-ROM. You've already seen this integration at work in at least one way: while you're authoring a Web document, you can click Web Page Preview in the Standard toolbar to preview the page's appearance in Internet Explorer. However, the two programs work together more closely than that.

The Web Toolbar

Whether you're currently authoring a Web document or not, you can take advantage of that integration by displaying the Web toolbar. Choose View, Toolbars, Web to display it (see Figure 9.29).

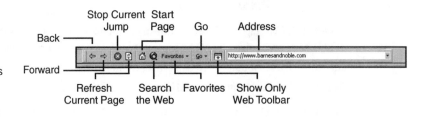

FIG. 9.29

The Web toolbar enables you to access the Web and to move back and forth among Web pages you create.

 TIP

If you only see part of the Web toolbar, drag its left edge to the left edge of the screen, beneath the other toolbars. The entire Web toolbar will appear.

The Web toolbar adds several Internet Explorer toolbar buttons to Word. When you use one of them to browse to a Web page, that page opens in a Microsoft Internet Explorer window. The Favorites button stores the same Web page bookmarks you may have stored in Internet Explorer; the Start button takes you to whatever page you've established as your home page in Internet Explorer.

 TIP

You can go back the other way, too; if you click the Edit button in Internet Explorer, the page is transferred into Word where you can edit its contents.

Note, though, that the contents don't always translate perfectly, and you will usually have to save the file under a new name before you can make changes to it.

After your Internet connection is established, you can use the Web toolbar to switch quickly between local documents and documents on the Web. The Address drop-down list box stores the last 25 documents you've viewed in either Word or Internet Explorer—whether those documents were stored on your hard disk, your network, your intranet, or the World Wide Web. To view any of those documents from within Word, select it from the Address drop-down list box on the Web toolbar (see Figure 9.30).

As you browse local and Web documents in Word, you'll find it convenient to use the browsing buttons on the Web toolbar. You can click the Back and Forward buttons to move among documents you've opened. You can click Stop to halt the loading of a file, or Refresh to reload a fresh copy of it. You also can hide other toolbars that may be in your way by clicking Show Only Web Toolbar.

FIG. 9.30
The Address drop-down list box stores the last 25 documents you've viewed in either Word or Internet Explorer.

Part

III

Ch

9

From Here...

In this chapter, you've learned the basics of creating Web pages with Word, and viewing them in both Word and Internet Explorer. Now that you've learned the basics of creating individual Web pages...

- Walk through the creation of a company intranet in Chapter 10, "Building Your Intranet with Word, Office, and FrontPage," and its deployment in Chapter 11, "Deploying Your Internet or Intranet Site." While you're at it, learn how Word, Office, Microsoft FrontPage, Peer Web Server, and Internet Information Server can all work together.

- Then, learn even more about many of the Word features you can use in conjunction with Word's Web Page Authoring Environment, including hyperlinks (Chapter 18, "Footnotes, Bookmarks, Cross-References, and Hyperlinks") and graphics (Chapter 21, "Drawing in Word").

CHAPTER 10

Building Your Intranet with Word, Office, and FrontPage

by Bill Camarda

In Chapter 9, "Using Word to Develop Web Content," you learned the basics of authoring Web pages in Word 97. In this chapter, you'll go further. You'll learn the basics of intranets—internal Web sites that make it easier to share all kinds of information. You'll learn more advanced Word Web page techniques, such as working with forms, which you'll find especially helpful if you're designing an intranet. Finally, you'll learn how to build on the pages you've created in Word, using Microsoft FrontPage to organize your intranet. Then, in Chapter 11, "Deploying Your Internet or Intranet Site," you'll walk through the final stage of the process by actually testing and deploying the intranet you've designed. ■

Understanding intranets

Companies everywhere are using Web technologies internally to supercharge communications and lower costs.

Planning your intranet

Careful up-front planning will pay off big later, in more efficient management.

Building interactive intranet pages

Word 97's form controls make it much easier to build a highly interactive intranet site.

Introducing Microsoft FrontPage

For truly industrial-strength intranet and Web sites, consider using Microsoft FrontPage.

Creating a Web with FrontPage wizards

Just like Word, FrontPage has wizards that can do much of the work for you.

Importing Word Web pages into FrontPage

You can do all the editing and layouts in Word and import the results into FrontPage.

Understanding Intranets

An *intranet* is a network designed for the private use of an organization but built with the same standards and protocols used by the public Internet. Using an intranet looks and feels like surfing the Web, but instead of visiting multiple public Web sites, you're accessing company information. What kind of information? The kind that previously required enormous numbers of printed manuals and brochures:

- Human resources data such as company employment and benefit policies
- Product information such as spec sheets
- Sales and marketing information such as sample proposals, case studies, and referrals
- Internal directories and contact information
- Forms that would otherwise have to be printed and inventoried

Intranets can be of any size; they can serve an entire company, a division, or even a workgroup. They're especially helpful for cross-functional teams, such as R&D or product development teams, which may need to share the same information even though they are not in the same location. No matter how you utilize your intranet, however, you leverage the same advantages that are familiar to users of the World Wide Web, such as the following:

- Easy, point-and-click navigation to any relevant information, wherever it may be stored
- Lower startup costs than previous solutions and potentially, lower administrative costs as well
- Improved employee productivity through faster access to relevant information

It's no wonder that many observers see intranets growing even more explosively than the World Wide Web has grown.

Planning Your Intranet

There are several ways to approach building an intranet. One approach is to convert all the information you want to publish into HTML files, which are, after all, the language of the Internet. As discussed in the previous chapter, this offers a powerful advantage; virtually anyone, anywhere can read an HTML file through an industry-standard browser.

▶ **See** "A Very Brief Introduction to HTML," **p. 263**

Another approach, which is taking hold among many companies that have standardized on Microsoft Internet Explorer and other Microsoft technologies, is to build a hybrid intranet that incorporates HTML pages wherever it makes sense but also uses the company's existing Microsoft Office documents. Such an intranet can enable users to view documents that still have the rich formatting and information content with which they may have been created. It also lets anyone familiar with a Microsoft Office application contribute content to the intranet. In Chapter 9, you learned how to save Word files to HTML format. Later in this chapter, you'll learn how to use Word files on your intranet in their native format.

Setting Realistic Goals

An important aspect of planning your intranet is to define your goals clearly. You may want to build your intranet in stages, making sure that each stage offers users a clear new benefit. For instance, your intranet goals might look like this:

Stage 1: To make your department's product data, policy manuals, and company directories available on the intranet

Stage 2: To provide interactive forms that allow department employees to request vacation time and benefits changes

Stage 3: To extend the intranet to other departments and locations, and increase its interactivity with more custom scripting and database integration

Identifying Resources and Responsibilities

You may not have to invest much to start an intranet, but the time and resources involved in keeping one up-to-date can be substantial. Before you find yourself saddled with the entire task, make sure resources will be available to support your efforts. In particular:

- Who will be responsible for providing content? When it comes to content, intranets tend to be somewhat different than Web sites designed for external consumption. The information on Web sites is commonly generated (or at least carefully edited) by professional communicators to ensure clarity, accuracy, and legality.

- On many intranets, virtually anyone can contribute. How will you ensure that the contributions will be useful and appropriate? How do you ensure that the people who should make contributions actually will and that information that is updated on paper is also updated on the intranet?

Except in organizations that are unusually open to new technology, you'll have to give some thought to promoting use of your intranet. You may build it, but employees won't necessarily come to your intranet site—even if your content is valuable. Before you start, get answers to questions like these:

- Will management help you encourage the use of the intranet by using it themselves and posting critical information there first?

- Have you encouraged them to do so by demonstrating its value to the company and the money it can save?

- What training will your colleagues need in order to use the intranet? Are they already familiar with Web browsing, for example?

Finally, if custom coding is required (for example, scripting or other programming required to integrate the intranet with your company's database):

- Who will handle the custom coding?

- What role should your company's IT organization play?

Technical Planning Issues

The human issues you've just learned about may be the most important factors in your intranet's success, but they aren't the *only* factors. Technical issues will be nearly as important. For example, the following concerns will impact your intranet's viability:

- What computer will you use as your intranet server? In low-volume and pilot intranets, a fast computer may be able to serve as both a user workstation and an intranet server. As the intranet grows, it will certainly require a server of its own.

- What server software will you use? Microsoft Office 97 and Microsoft FrontPage 97 each come with Personal Web Server (PWS) for Windows 95, a low-volume server that can be used for either Web or intranet sites. PWS, which is covered in more detail in Chapter 11, is a very convenient way to test your site. It may be sufficient to serve the ongoing needs of a workgroup. However, as your intranet grows, you'll most likely need more.

ON THE WEB

You may want to download version 1.0a of Personal Web Server, a slightly updated version available on Microsoft's Web site which fixes some minor bugs. This version can be found at **www.microsoft.com/ ie/download/**.

One solution is Microsoft Internet Information Server (IIS) running on Windows NT Server 4.0, also introduced in Chapter 11. IIS leverages the power and reliability of NT Server, and it's also fully integrated with NT Server, which means it benefits from NT Server's inherent security and other benefits. In fact, it is included with the Windows NT Server package. Even though IIS is free, however, NT Server costs substantially more to implement, in terms of hardware and software licensing costs, than a low-end Windows 95 solution.

- Is your network infrastructure ready to handle the increased traffic an intranet may cause? Will you need to supplement existing Ethernet cards with a LAN switch that delivers more bandwidth? Or swap them out for Fast Ethernet? If your intranet must serve multiple locations, are your wide-area connections sufficient? Will you need to invest additional resources for frame relay or ISDN connections?

- Another performance-related issue is whether your site will utilize large files like audio, video, or even large graphics. Many Web sites limit graphics to a maximum of 50K to minimize download times; some limit entire pages to a maximum of approximately 100K. On a LAN, large graphics and other files can slow down the network for everyone, whether they're using your intranet or not.

- How will you handle security issues? Will you need a firewall to separate your intranet from the public Internet? What file and folder permissions need to be in place to prevent unauthorized users from making changes to content posted on your intranet?

- As discussed earlier, will your intranet be based on "pure HTML," or will you provide access to files in native formats such as Word, Excel, or PowerPoint?

■ What browser will you standardize on? Microsoft provides Internet Explorer at no charge; the primary alternative is Netscape Communicator. Each product has implications that go beyond browsing. For example, Internet Explorer 4.0 provides the Active Desktop, which brings Web-type browsing to Windows itself. It also includes Active Channels that enable a variety of Web broadcasters to deliver information to users.

Similarly, Netscape Communicator is a suite of programs that include software for workgroup collaboration, e-mail, conferencing, Web page composition, and more (including Netscape's own version of channels, called Netcaster). Can you use these features to your advantage? What will be involved in implementing and supporting them? How easy will it be to disable the features you don't want?

 TIP If some people in your organization have standardized on Netscape's browsers, you can still give them access to Word, Excel, and PowerPoint documents via the AXPlugin, a free plug-in for Netscape Navigator and Communicator that lets users of Netscape browsers open these documents in their native formats. This plug-in, NCB5F.EXE, is available on the Office 97 CD-ROM ValuPack in the AXPLUGIN folder.

Part
III
Ch
10

Other Issues to Consider

There are a variety of other issues you should also consider:

Test your site. Leave enough time to accumulate all the content you'll need and fully test your site before launching it publicly. Especially leave time if you're planning forms that require code to be tested on the server.

Carefully think about folder structures and file names. Don't create deeply nested folder structures; they're more difficult to manage, and it's much easier to lose a hyperlink, which might make a large chunk of content completely disappear from your intranet. Reuse graphics files wherever possible to minimize the effort required in updating your site if you want to change the graphics later.

Be aware of corporate design guidelines. Although your intranet is intended for internal consumption, you may have corporate standards for internal communication that you need to follow. If your company already has an external Web site, you can borrow graphics and layouts from there.

Microsoft's 60-Minute Intranet Templates

One quick way to jump start your intranet development is with the Microsoft Office 60-Minute Intranet Kit, currently available for download at Microsoft's Web site, **www.microsoft.com/office/intranet/default.htm**. (Currently, you can also get the 60-Minute Intranet CD-ROM by mail from Microsoft at no charge.)

Microsoft's 60-Minute Intranet site contains four instant intranets, all of which are easy to import and edit in Word or, better yet, Microsoft FrontPage. The sites are optimized to run on Microsoft's Personal Web Server, Internet Information Server, or any Web server running Microsoft's FrontPage Extensions. The four instant sites are as follows:

- A *Research & Development* intranet, designed for beginner intranet developers (see Figure 10.1).

- A *Sales and Marketing* site (see Figure 10.2).

- A *Finance* site that includes working examples of Excel 97 spreadsheets that can retrieve live data from the Internet (see Figure 10.3).

- A *Human Resources* site, designed for more advanced intranet developers. This site includes a live Web database application created with Microsoft Access, Active Server Pages, and 32-bit ODBC drivers (see Figure 10.4).

FIG. 10.1

The Microsoft Research & Development 60-Minute Intranet is designed for beginning intranet developers.

Navigation bar (based on **navbar.htm** file)

Color settings (based on **style.htm** file)

Footer (based on **footer.htm** file)

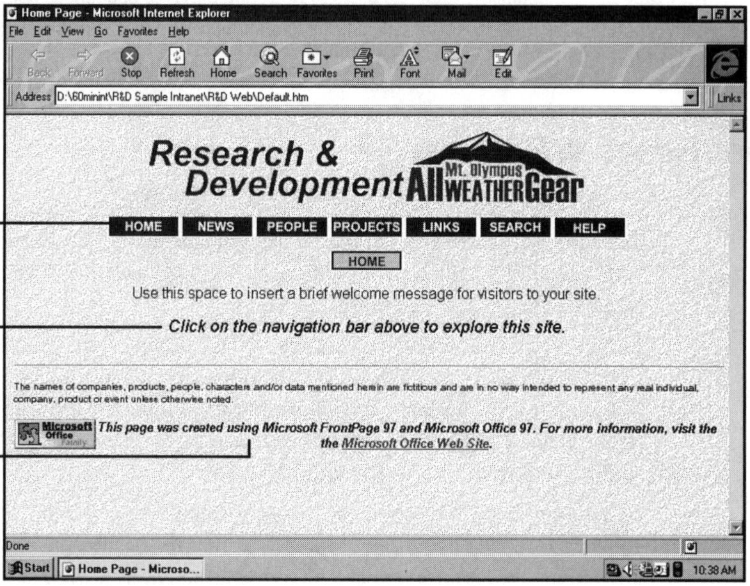

Each prebuilt site includes the following:

- A Home page
- Sample pages covering people involved in a project or department
- A Project page, with links to office documents
- A Links page demonstrating hyperlinks to outside Web sites
- A Search page that contains a Microsoft FrontPage WebBot, which provides basic searching capabilities
- A Help page that provides detailed information about intranets and how to use them

FIG. 10.2

The Microsoft Sales & Marketing 60-Minute Intranet provides many of the basic elements common to many sales force and marketing intranets.

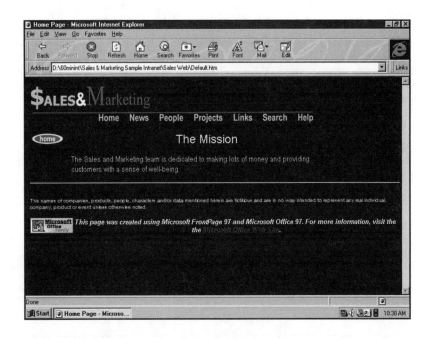

FIG. 10.3

The Microsoft Finance 60-Minute Intranet provides many basic elements common to many finance organization intranets.

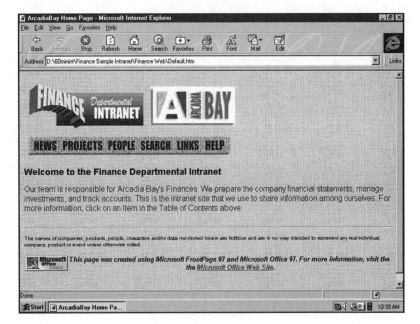

Part
III

Ch
10

FIG. 10.4

The Microsoft Human Resources 60-Minute Intranet provides many basic elements common to many human resources organization intranets.

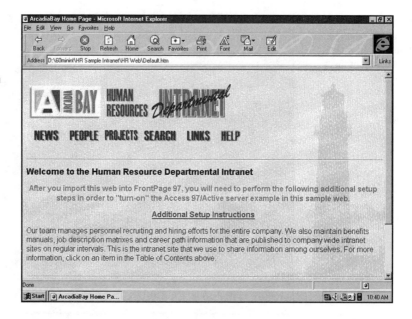

 TIP Even if you don't base your intranet on one of the 60-minute intranets, you may want to use this Help page as a starting point for the help page in your intranet.

Because the internal links in these sites are already in place, it's easy to transform one of them into Stage 1 of your own intranet. Here are some of the steps you might take:

- If the generic site has a fake corporate logo, as the Human Resources intranet does, substitute a .GIF or .JPG file with your own corporate logo. Rename your file with the same name used in the generic intranet. Do the same for any other images you want to change.

- Substitute your own text wherever appropriate. If possible, use the existing structure.

- Save one page as a template so you can use it as the model to create additional pages as you need them.

- Create additional pages and add hyperlinks to them.

CAUTION

It's important to understand the structure of the 60-Minute Intranets. Rather than applying all individual formatting to each page, Microsoft FrontPage places master pages in a separate folder named _private. The Home page, Projects page, and all other pages contain Include WebBots, which go out and find the formatting in these master pages.

The navbar.htm page controls the appearance of the Navigation Bar (refer to Figure 10.1).

The footer.htm page controls the contents and appearance of the footers.

The style.htm page controls the color settings for all the pages in the Web.

The benefit of this is that you only need to change the formatting in a master page to change it globally. However, you need to run the Web on a server that has FrontPage Server Extensions installed or the WebBots will not run properly. You also need to maintain the existing file structure (or, if you change it, do so through FrontPage). Otherwise, your pages won't be able to locate the formatting and images they depend on.

N O T E If you get the 60-Minute Intranet Kit CD-ROM, make sure to review the detailed, step-by-step instructions stored in a Word file named SBS.DOC, in the folder \Intranet Starter Kit\Documents. ▪

Building Interactive Intranet Pages

Chances are, you've seen many Web pages that give you the opportunity to provide feedback. For example, you may be offered the opportunity to reply via e-mail; or you may be able to fill out a form that lets you provide your name and address, or click buttons to make choices. The more interactivity you build into your intranet, the more powerful a communication tool it will become. Word 97 makes it much easier than before to build Web pages that encourage feedback.

Inserting Hyperlinks for E-Mail Replies

The easiest way to solicit user feedback is to create Web pages that invite the reader to reply via e-mail. To do this, you insert a hyperlink as you've already learned how to do, but instead of linking to another Web page or file on your network, you link to the viewer's e-mail software. Follow these steps:

1. Select the text you want to transform into a hyperlink.
2. Choose Insert, Hyperlink to display the Insert Hyperlink dialog box.
3. Instead of entering a Web or file address, choose mailto: from the Link to File or URL drop-down list box. Then, enter the e-mail address. For example:

   ```
   mailto:bjones@smith.net
   ```
4. Choose OK.

Now, when anyone clicks the hyperlink, their e-mail client software opens, with the address you specify already appearing in the text box where the user would normally enter the destination address. Figure 10.5 shows how this looks in Microsoft Outlook.

 T I P You can insert an image as your mailto: hyperlink. The ideal one to use is the animated envelope icon Microsoft Office 97 provides. This 5K file, mail.gif, can be found in the \Program Files\Microsoft Office\Clipart\Animations folder.

FIG. 10.5
Click a mailto: hyperlink,
and your e-mail client
software opens—in this
case, Microsoft Outlook.

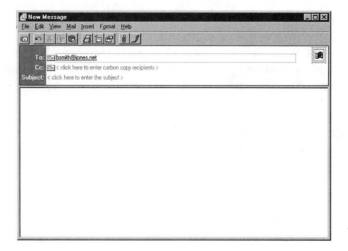

Creating Forms with the Web Page Wizard

Mailto: encourages unstructured feedback. Web forms make feedback easier to provide, help
you define exactly what kind of feedback you want, and can make the feedback easier to work
with after you've received it.

Microsoft Word and Microsoft FrontPage have made creating forms a highly visual process.
You've already learned that Word lets you create a Web page from scratch or generate a generic Web page through the Web Page Wizard. The wizard can also create Web Registration
and Survey forms, along with a Feedback form that allows for more detailed feedback than a
simple mailto: hyperlink. Samples of Web forms created by the wizard are shown in Figures
10.6, 10.7, and 10.8.

N O T E   As you may recall, you can access the Web Page Wizard by choosing File, New, clicking the
Web Pages tab, and double-clicking Web Page Wizard. ▓

Transforming your form into a working element of your Web or intranet site takes more effort
than simply creating the form. You (or a colleague) will need to make sure that your intranet or
Web server knows how to receive the information and what to do with it once it arrives. There
are several ways to approach this.

The traditional approach is to write a Common Gateway Interface (CGI) script, which accepts
the information a browser submits in a form, and then forwards the information to other programs, such as database management systems. This form-handler script may also return a
response, which may vary based on the choices made by the user. Unfortunately, CGI programming has a well-deserved reputation for complexity.

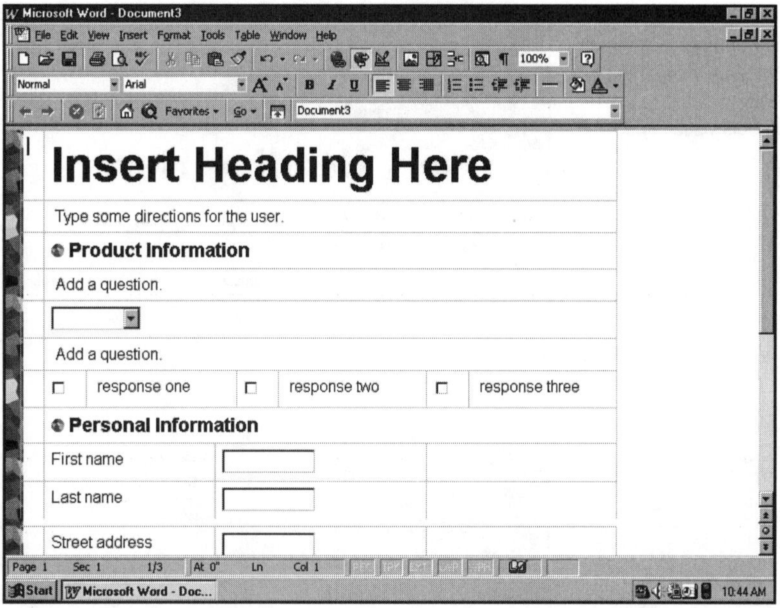

FIG. 10.6
This Web Registration form created by the Web Page Wizard uses the Festive visual style.

FIG. 10.7
This Web Survey form created by the Web Page Wizard uses the Jazzy visual style.

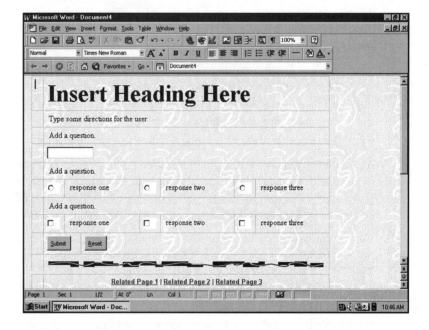

FIG. 10.8

This Web Feedback form created by the Web Page Wizard uses the Outdoors visual style.

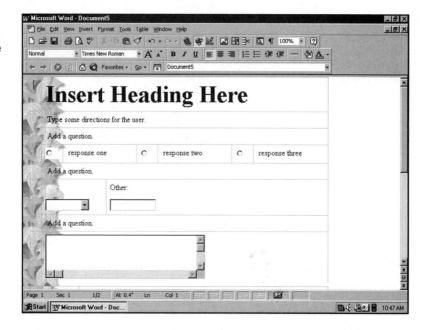

An alternative approach is to use a Microsoft FrontPage WebBot. (You'll learn more about FrontPage later in this chapter.) FrontPage provides automated forms handlers for three common types of forms:

- The *Save Results* WebBot gathers information from a form and copies it to the server in one of several standard formats.

- The *Registration* WebBot can automatically register a user for a service, adding the user's name to an authentication database.

- The *Discussion* WebBot makes it simpler to support participation in online discussions.

All WebBots require your Web or intranet server to have the FrontPage Server Extensions installed. These extensions are available for both Windows and UNIX-based Web servers. However, you'll have to coordinate with your server administrator or ISP to make sure that the extensions are present or that they are considered acceptable for use.

Later in this chapter, in the discussion of Submit Controls, you'll learn about a quick-and-dirty shortcut that enables you to simply e-mail form results to someone instead of worrying about building interfaces with servers and database systems.

Creating Forms from Scratch

It's possible that Word's built-in forms might be all you need or that you can easily adapt them for your needs. It's also possible that you'll need another kind of form altogether—one that will be more efficient to build from scratch. To create a new Web form, begin with these steps:

1. Choose File, New.

2. Choose Web Pages.

3. Double-click Blank Web Page.

4. In the Standard toolbar, click the Form Design Mode button. The Control toolbox appears (see Figure 10.9).

FIG. 10.9

The Control toolbox contains controls you can add to your Web page.

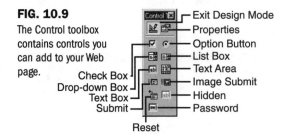

Exit Design Mode
Properties
Option Button
List Box
Text Area
Image Submit
Hidden
Password

Check Box
Drop-down Box
Text Box
Submit
Reset

Part
III

Ch
10

Enter any other (nonform-related) information, formatting, and structures you want to include on the page. For example, if you want a series of buttons to line up one beneath the next, create tables; then you can put each button in a separate row.

Then, when you're ready to place a Button, Text Box, or other interactive control in your form, click your mouse pointer where you want it to go, and click the form control you want. Table 10.1 shows what form controls Word makes available and how to use them. Figure 10.10 shows the most commonly used controls in a finished Web form.

Table 10.1   Available Form Controls

Form Control	What It Does
Check Box	Provides one or more true/false choices, enabling the user to make each choice independently
Option Button	Requires the user to choose only one of a series of options
Drop-Down Box	Enables the user to pick from a list of options you specify
List Box	Similar to a drop-down list, except more options are visible even before the box is selected
Text Box	Enables a user to enter one line of text, such as a name
Text Area	Enables a user to enter as much text as you specify; includes scroll bars to permit longer messages than space is available for on-screen
Submit	Submits the form
Image Submit	Displays an image in the document; when the image is clicked, the form is submitted

continues

Table 10.1 Continued	
Form Control	**What It Does**
Reset	Clears all entries from the form so the user can start over again
Hidden	Creates a Hidden Form control
Password	Enables a user to enter a password; entered text is displayed as asterisks to protect security

FIG. 10.10
A Web form containing several form controls, shown in Internet Explorer 3.0.

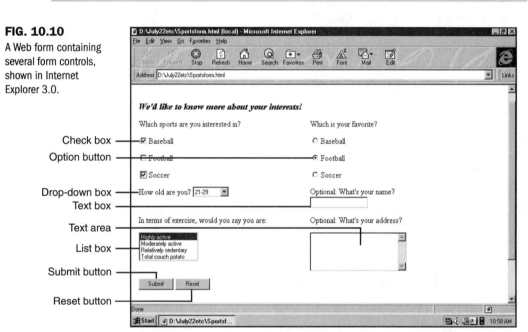

The first time you enter a form control, Word places a Top of Form boundary above it, and a Bottom of Form boundary below it, as shown in Figure 10.11.

Adjusting the Properties of a Form Control

Every form control has its own set of properties. In order for the form control to behave as you want it to, you'll have to set these properties. When you set these properties, some of them appear in your HTML source code, but you're also setting the behavior of a corresponding ActiveX control. Sometimes, working with Form Control properties may require you to understand Visual Basic or ActiveX, but in many cases, knowing what you're trying to accomplish is sufficient to set properties correctly.

To view the properties associated with a control, double-click the control. The Properties window appears (see Figure 10.12).

FIG. 10.11

Word inserts top and bottom boundaries above and below the first form control you place in your document.

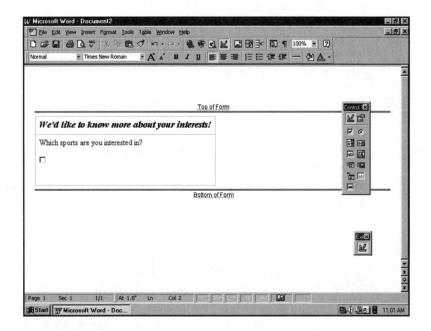

FIG. 10.12

This figure shows the Properties window associated with a drop-down list box.

You can view the control's properties alphabetically, or in categories. If you're new to working with controls, you may find Alphabetic listings easier to work with. In the Alphabetic tab, the left column displays the name of the property. The right column displays its current value or setting.

 Setting Properties for a Drop-Down or List Box   The following list defines the available properties settings for drop-down and list boxes:

- *(Name)*. For all controls, the first property is always the control's name. Word assigns a name automatically. You can leave that name alone, enter a more descriptive name that will make life easier for those who work with the form control later, or write the server-side script to compile the data.

■ *DisplayValues*. In this box, you can enter the choices you want to appear in the drop-down box when a user clicks it. Separate each choice with a semicolon, as shown in the following example:

```
Baseball; Football; Soccer
```

 N O T E All option (round) buttons in a form must have the same name. That's how browsers can make sure a user selects only one option. ■

■ *HTMLName*. In the right box next to HTMLName, enter the field name you want to appear in the HTML source code.

■ *MultiSelect*. By default, a user can choose only one option from a drop-down list box. This corresponds to the setting MultiSelect = False. If you want to enable users to make multiple selections from the same drop-down or list box, click False. A drop-down box appears; select True from the drop-down box that appears.

■ *Selected*. In this box, enter the selection you want to appear in the drop-down box by default. If you leave it blank, the first choice you specified in DisplayValues will appear.

■ *Size*. This controls the depth of the drop-down box as it appears in the browser. By default, drop-down boxes have a depth of 1, meaning that only one choice is visible. If you enter a higher number, the drop-down box becomes a scroll box, allowing a user to choose among multiple visible choices. If you've chosen MultiSelect=True, you'll want to set Size to at least 2, so multiple choices are actually visible.

■ *Values*. The Values property enables you to specify a different value to be transmitted in place of the DisplayValue a user chose. For example, if you've created DisplayValues like the following:

```
Baseball; Football; Soccer
```

For efficiency, you might want to transmit the equivalent field values:

```
1; 2; 3
```

Of course, the destination program that receives this information will need to know what to do with it. However, that's the case even if you send the DisplayValues, and you'll have used limited bandwidth more efficiently.

When you're finished, click the Close button. When you save the file, some aspects of the control appear in the corresponding HTML source code; others are stored only with the ActiveX component associated with the form control.

Setting Properties for a Check Box Now that you've learned how to set the properties for a drop-down box, let's take a look at setting the properties for some of the other controls Word's Web Page Authoring Environment provides. In each case, let's assume you've already opened a Web page, chosen Form Design mode, inserted the control you want, and double-clicked it to display the Properties window.

Table 10.2 describes the properties associated with a check box and how to set them.

Table 10.2 Check Box Properties

Property	How to Set It
Checked	Set to True if you want the check box selected by default.
HTMLName	Enter the internal name you want to use for the ActiveX control.
Value	Enter the data you want sent to the server if the user checks the check box.

 Setting Properties for an Option Button   Table 10.3 describes the properties associated with an option button and how to set them.

Table 10.3 Option Button Properties

Property	How to Set It
Checked	Set to True if you want the option button selected by default. Only one option button in a group can be set to True.
HTMLName	Enter the internal name you want to use for the ActiveX control. All option buttons in the same group must have the same name, but you can create several groups on the same form.
Value	Enter the data you want sent to the server if the user checks the option button.

 Setting Properties for a Text Box   Table 10.4 describes the properties associated with a text box designed to accept one line of text input and how to set them.

Table 10.4 Text Box Properties

Property	How to Set It
HTMLName	Enter the internal name you want to use for the ActiveX control.
MaxLength	Enter the number of characters the user will be allowed to type.
Value	If you want, enter default text that will appear when the user opens the page. If you leave this blank, the field will appear blank.

 Setting Properties for a Text Area   Table 10.5 describes the properties associated with a text area designed to accept multiple lines of text input and how to set them.

Table 10.5 Text Area Properties

Property	How to Set It
Columns	Enter the width of your text area. The width of your entire screen corresponds to roughly 110, but you'll want to experiment to see how this translates in different browsers.
HTMLName	Enter the internal name you want to use for the ActiveX control.
Rows	Enter the number of rows you want to appear in your text area.
Value	If you want, enter default text that will appear when the user opens the page. If you leave this blank, the field will appear blank.
WordWrap	Choose Virtual, Physical, or Off. Some Web browsers recognize Virtual or Physical as a cue to allow text to wrap within the box, so it is all visible even if the user goes past the edge of the box.

 Setting Properties for a Submit Control   A Submit control places a button on the Web page; when the user clicks the button, the form's contents are submitted to the browser. Table 10.6 describes the properties associated with a Submit control and how to set them.

Table 10.6 Submit Control Properties

Property	How to Set It
Action	Enter the URL of the file that processes the form on the server. If you're not the Web or intranet administrator, you'll have to ask the administrator for this information.
Caption	Enter the text that should appear on the Submit button. By default, it's Submit.
Encoding	This property sets the MIME type used to encode the form; the default setting, `application/x-www-form-urlencoded`, can usually be left alone.
HTML Name	Enter the internal name you want to use for the ActiveX control.
Method	Specify POST or GET. POST is usually preferable.

 TIP The quick-and-dirty alternative to worrying about CGI server scripts is to simply deliver the form to an e-mail address and let the recipient deal with the forms manually. You can do so by entering a mailto: address in the Action property as follows:

```
mailto:stewart@Figurenet
```

 Setting Properties for an Image Submit Control   As you may recall, Image Submit controls perform the same function as Submit controls, except they contain custom images such as the 3-D buttons Microsoft Office provides in the \Program Files\Microsoft Office\Clipart\Buttons folder. Image Submit controls have the same properties as Submit Controls, with one addition: the Source control, which you use to specify the name of the image file that should appear when a viewer opens the page.

 Setting Properties for a Reset Control Reset controls clear all the text in a form, so a user can start over again. In addition to specifying an HTMLName for the control, you can specify a Caption—the text that appears on the button. By default, this caption is Reset.

 Setting Properties for a Password Control Password controls enable a user to enter a password privately. Password controls are just like text boxes except that only asterisks display on-screen as a user types his or her password. Table 10.7 describes the properties associated with a Password control.

Table 10.7 Password Control Properties

Property	How to Set It
HTMLName	Enter the internal name you want to use for the ActiveX control.
MaxLength	Enter the number of characters the user will be allowed to type.
Value	If you want, enter default text that will appear when the user opens the page. If you leave this blank, the field will appear blank.

Adjusting the Location of a Form Control

Now that the form control appears in your document, you can select it and drag it to adjust its location, the same way you would if it were a picture. You can also control how text wraps around it. To do so, follow these steps:

1. Right-click the form control.
2. Choose Format Picture from the shortcut menu. The Position tab of the Picture dialog box opens (see Figure 10.13).

FIG. 10.13
In the Picture dialog box, you can set the Position associated with a form control.

3. Specify how you want text to wrap around the form control (None, Left, or Right).

4. In the Vertical scroll box, specify how much vertical (top and bottom) space should appear between the form control and any other text.

5. In the Horizontal scroll box, specify how much horizontal (left and right) space should appear between the form control and any other text.

6. Choose OK.

Integrating with Microsoft FrontPage

In the previous chapter and a half, you've learned how to author Web pages in Word, create hyperlinks, and even create forms that make your intranet a powerful two-way communications medium. Word 97 is quite remarkable, but frankly, you've taken it about as far as it can go. In the remainder of this chapter, you'll get a brief introduction to another Microsoft Office program designed specifically to help you build and manage industrial-strength Web sites: Microsoft FrontPage.

The heart of FrontPage consists of two programs: FrontPage Explorer and FrontPage Editor.

N O T E If you've purchased FrontPage on CD-ROM, you also received a third program, Microsoft Image Composer, which can help you manufacture Web graphics that would be difficult to create using tools such as Microsoft Paint or Microsoft Photo Editor. ■

The following list outlines the most important tasks you can perform using the FrontPage Explorer (see Figure 10.14):

■ Create a new Web or intranet site from scratch, or with a FrontPage Wizard or template

■ Import Web pages you created in Word or anywhere else

■ View the relationships between all the pages in your site

■ Test hyperlinks and fix any that don't work

■ Control who can access your intranet or Web site to add or review content

■ Maintain a to-do list of tasks you still need to perform, such as inserting graphics or customizing the pages created by a FrontPage Wizard

The second program, FrontPage Editor (see Figure 10.15), is where you edit and create individual Web pages. FrontPage resembles Word's Web Page Authoring Environment in some respects, but it's different in others.

As in Word, you can create new pages or save existing files to HTML. In fact, FrontPage Editor uses the same export filters as Word, and handles exports in much the same way. For example, as in Word, images imported in formats other than .JPG or .GIF are automatically resaved to .GIF. FrontPage Editor, however, includes some capabilities that Word doesn't. For example, with FrontPage Editor you can easily insert Java applets or ActiveX controls in your pages. Also, FrontPage Editor and FrontPage Explorer integrate more closely than Word and FrontPage do; for example, you can access the same to-do list from either program.

FIG. 10.14
FrontPage Explorer helps you manage and organize your intranet or Web site, no matter how complex.

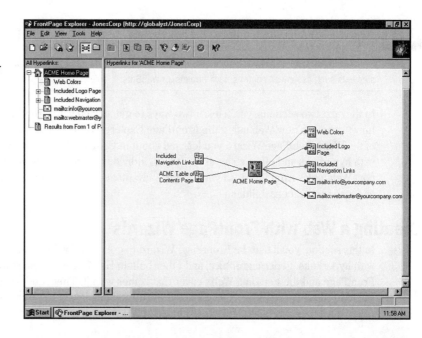

FIG. 10.15
In the Front Page Editor, you can create Web pages from scratch, edit pages you've created in Word, or add features like WebBots and Java applets.

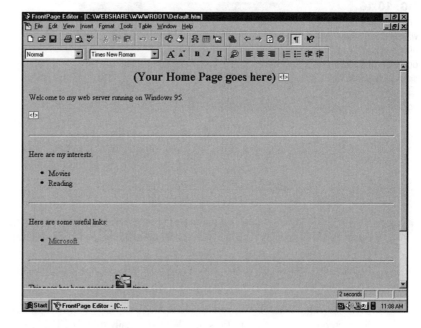

TIP Word offers many editing and graphics tools that aren't present in FrontPage Editor. You might want to create the text (and possibly even the layout) for your pages in Word and then import them into your FrontPage Web. Then, you would use the FrontPage Editor for last-minute touch-ups and to add elements such as ActiveX controls, Java applets, or WebBots.

In the next two sections, you'll learn two ways to get started with FrontPage. First, you'll learn how to create a new Web using the FrontPage Explorer Wizard. This is a supercharged version of the Word Web Page Wizard you learned about in Chapter 9. It creates whole sites, complete with hyperlinks and other structures, not just individual pages. Then, you'll learn how to import Web pages from Word, so you can take advantage of FrontPage's powerful organization and management capabilities.

Creating a Web with FrontPage Wizards

In this section, you'll use the FrontPage Wizard to create a new intranet or Web site, complete with hyperlinks, generic graphics, and other built-in HTML coding. Start by installing FrontPage and the Personal Web Server that comes with it. Then, choose Start, Programs, Microsoft FrontPage. FrontPage Explorer opens and displays the Getting Started with Microsoft FrontPage dialog box (see Figure 10.16).

FIG. 10.16

In the Getting Started with Microsoft FrontPage dialog box, you can open an existing Web or create a new one by clicking From a Wizard or Template.

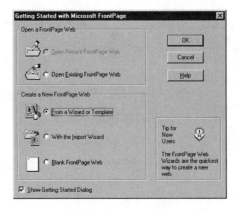

Choose From a Wizard or Template, and choose OK. The New FrontPage Web dialog box opens (see Figure 10.17). Here, you can choose the type of Web you want to create. If you choose to create a Corporate Presence or Discussion Web, FrontPage runs a wizard designed to help you customize the site. If you choose another option, such as a Customer Support Web, FrontPage builds the Web immediately from a template.

In the example that follows, you'll walk through creating a Corporate Presence Web. Many of the elements of a Corporate Presence Web are easily translated to internal intranets. (Other options that lend themselves well to intranets include the Customer Support Web and the Project Web.)

Walking through the Corporate Presence Wizard will take a little time and some thought; the wizard contains many screens. However, when you're done, you'll see that FrontPage has saved you days, if not *weeks*, of effort.

FIG. 10.17
In the New FrontPage
Web dialog box, specify
what kind of Web you
want to create.

Part
III

Ch
10

> **CAUTION**
>
> To create a new Web of any kind on your system, you must first have the Personal Web Server installed and running, or have access to another Web server, such as Microsoft Internet Information Server.

After you've chosen Corporate Presence Wizard in the New FrontPage Web dialog box, choose OK. The Corporate Presence Wizard dialog box opens (see Figure 10.18). Specify a Web Server or file location where your Web will be stored; also give your Web a name. Notice that you can't enter spaces—the space bar is turned off while you're in the Name of New FrontPage Web text box. Choose OK; the Corporate Presence Web Wizard opens.

Click Next to get started choosing the pages you want to include on your site (see Figure 10.19). In addition to the Home page, which is required in all Webs, FrontPage can build five additional pages.

FIG. 10.18
Enter your Web's name
and location in the
Corporate Presence
Wizard dialog box; then
provide a password if
one is requested.

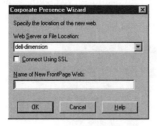

N O T E Notice that you can get help at any time by clicking Help. You can also see how far through the process you are by looking at the bar directly above the Help button. ■

FIG. 10.19

The first screen of the
Corporate Presence Web
Wizard enables you to
choose the main pages
you want to include in
your intranet or Web
site.

FIG. 10.19

The first screen of the
Corporate Presence Web
Wizard enables you to
choose the main pages
you want to include in
your intranet or Web
site.

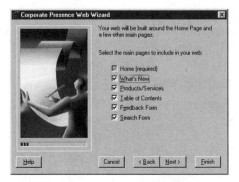

When you're finished choosing the pages you want to include, click Next. FrontPage asks what you want to include on your Home page (see Figure 10.20). When you've made your choices, click Next again to continue. FrontPage now walks through each of the pages you've selected, making suggestions about the content you might include.

FIG. 10.20

Choosing what you want
on your Home page.

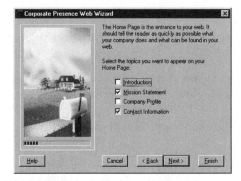

Figure 10.21 shows the options FrontPage provides for a What's New page. Figure 10.22 gives you an opportunity to specify how many products and services you would like to include on your Products/Services Page.

FIG. 10.21

Setting up your What's
New page.

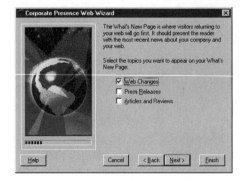

FIG. 10.22

Specifying how many products and services should be included on your site.

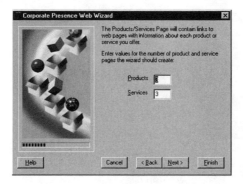

If you tell FrontPage that you want to create a Products/Services page, it will not only create that page, but also a *separate* page for each product or service you want to include. In Figure 10.23, you can specify what kind of information you want on each of those pages. Notice that FrontPage recognizes you may want to say different things about services than you would about products. Make your choices, and click Next.

Part

III

Ch

10

> **CAUTION**
>
> If you select zero products or zero services, FrontPage may generate empty Web pages anyway.

FIG. 10.23

Choosing the content for your Products and Services page.

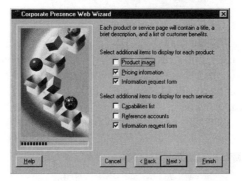

Assuming you chose to create a Feedback Form, you're now asked what information you want to collect from the people who fill out the form (see Figure 10.24). Click Next, and you're asked how you want to store the form's information on your server. You can save it in HTML (Web Page) format. Or you can save it in Tab-Delimited format, which is easy to import into spreadsheets and databases (see Figure 10.25).

FIG. 10.24

In this window, you can decide what to include in a Feedback form.

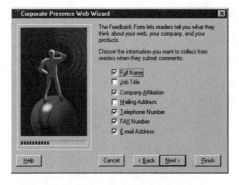

FIG. 10.25

Once you've set the contents of your feedback form, you can choose how to store the information you receive.

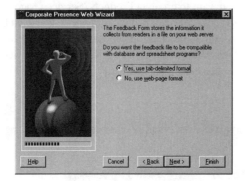

Next, FrontPage addresses the Table of Contents—a page that shows links to all the other pages FrontPage creates (see Figure 10.26). Do you want the table of contents to be kept up-to-date automatically, as you make other changes throughout your site? If you check the Keep Page List Up-to-Date Automatically check box, FrontPage inserts WebBots, which can track changes you make elsewhere in your site and make changes to the table of contents, into your HTML code.

FIG. 10.26

Deciding how FrontPage should manage your table of contents.

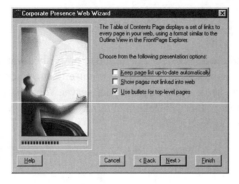

In the next window, you specify the contents of your headers and footers (see Figure 10.27). As you saw earlier in this chapter, FrontPage creates headers and footers once in separate HTML files that will be stored in a _Private folder associated with this Web. After doing so, FrontPage includes references to Include WebBots in all the other pages. Assuming that FrontPage Extensions are installed on the server that runs the Web site, these WebBots track down the latest content in the headers and footers and display every page based on the most up-to-date version of your headers and footers. When you've finished, click Next.

FIG. 10.27
Specifying the elements that should appear in all your headers and footers.

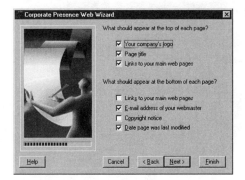

At this point, you're mostly finished with the structure and content of your site. The wizard moves on to style issues. In the following window (see Figure. 10.28), you get to choose one of four overall visual approaches to your site. When you make a choice, it's previewed at the left. The choices you make here are not written in stone; using FrontPage Editor, it's relatively easy to change colors and graphics when you're working in the site.

FIG. 10.28
You can create a site that's Conservative, Flashy, Cool, or Plain, with no graphics at all.

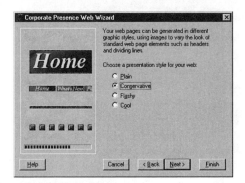

Notice that Plain includes no graphics at all. It's unlikely you'll want to make this choice, unless one of the following conditions is true:

- Network bandwidth is an especially serious issue.
- You're building a site that is likely to be used by many people with text-only browsers.

Part
III

Ch
10

N O T E   Be aware that some individuals use text-only browsers, such as Lynx, in conjunction with software that can read the text of a Web page aloud. ■

Choose a visual style and click Next. Now you can take more control of the colors and patterns that will be used throughout your site (see Figure 10.29). Once again, choices you make are reflected in the preview area at the left.

FIG. 10.29

In this window, you can specify background colors or patterns, as well as text and hyperlink colors.

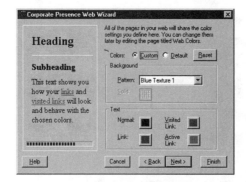

In the following screen, you're asked if you would like to use an animated Under Construction icon on all the pages on your site that aren't finished (see Figure 10.30). These Under Construction logos have become something of a Web cliché; you might want to choose No unless they'll help remind you of work remaining on the pages you visit. Choose Next.

FIG. 10.30

Do you want FrontPage to insert an Under Construction icon on all your pages that aren't finished?

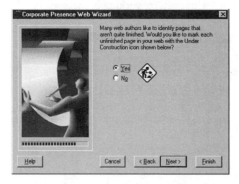

Now, FrontPage asks you for your company's full name, an abbreviated name you may sometimes use, and your company's address (see Figure 10.31). It scatters this information throughout your intranet or Web site wherever appropriate. Click Next; now insert your company's phone, fax, and e-mail addresses (see Figure 10.32). Click Next and you've finally arrived at the end of the wizard. You can pause for a breath, or click Back to move through the wizard and double-check your choices.

FIG. 10.31

In this window, you can enter your company's name and address.

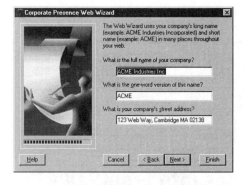

FIG. 10.32

Then provide telephone and electronic contact information.

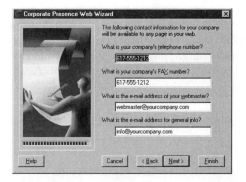

N O T E Many companies have a formal name, and a more casual abbreviated name. For example, your company may officially be named Acme Widgets International, Ltd., and commonly called Acme. The abbreviated name gives you an opportunity to specify how you want your company referred to when it's inappropriate or clumsy to use the full formal name.

When you're confident that all the selections you've made are correct, choose Finish. FrontPage builds the Web and uploads it to the Web server you've chosen. This may take a few minutes; FrontPage has quite a few folders to create and a lot of HTML code to write.

When FrontPage is finished, you'll see a list of tasks for transforming FrontPage's generic Corporate Presence Web into your very own intranet or Web site (see Figure 10.33). If you're ready, you can walk through these tasks one at a time, taking care of them. Click Do Task, and FrontPage takes you to the FrontPage Editor, where you can insert the logos, graphics, or text elements that need to be added. If you prefer to handle these loose ends later, choose Close. You can display the To Do List anytime you want from either FrontPage Explorer or Editor.

FIG. 10.33
The To Do List shows
what you need to do to
personalize your site.

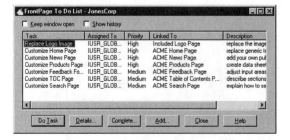

Importing Web Pages into FrontPage

Using a FrontPage Wizard is a great way to start, but what if you've already created some
pages in Word? It's easy to import them into FrontPage. Open FrontPage Explorer, choose
Create a New FrontPage Web With the Import Wizard, and choose OK. The Import Web Wizard dialog box appears; specify where you want the Web stored and what you want to name it.
FrontPage creates the empty Web and displays the first screen of a wizard that helps you import files (see Figure 10.34).

 You can also drag and drop HTML files into FrontPage Webs.

FIG. 10.34
Tell FrontPage where to
look for the files you
want to import.

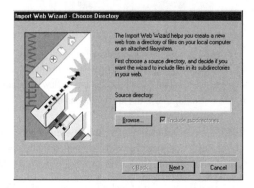

If you don't know the full path and folder name containing the files you want, choose Browse,
and select the folder in the Browse for Folder dialog box. You can choose a location anywhere
on your computer or network and choose OK. After you have selected a folder, choose Next.
The wizard now displays a list of all the files it finds in the folder—including both HTML files
and other documents, such as Word .DOC files and ASCII .TXT files (see Figure 10.35). To
exclude a file, select it, and choose Exclude. When the file list displays all the files you want to
convert, choose Next. Now choose Finish, and Word imports all the files into the Web you've
just created. Any links among files are shown (so are hyperlinks to external Web sites). If the
files don't contain links to each other, however, you'll have to create them with the FrontPage
Editor.

FIG. 10.35

FrontPage Explorer displays all the files you've just imported.

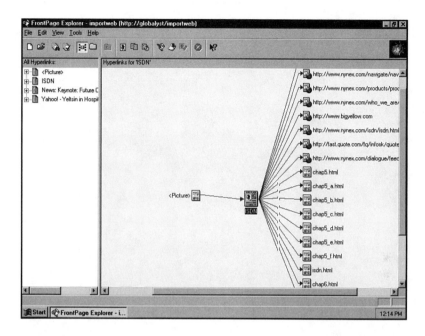

N O T E   The Import Wizard doesn't automatically convert Word files to HTML because it recognizes the possibility that you may want to use native Word formatted files on your intranet. However, you can open the files in FrontPage Editor and resave them as HTML. ■

From Here...

In this chapter, you've learned the basics of using Word and FrontPage to build your own corporate intranet.

■ Now that you've learned how to create Web pages, and you've been introduced to the Microsoft FrontPage site management tool, you're ready to test and deploy your site. Chapter 11, "Deploying Your Internet or Intranet Site," shows you how.

■ Chapter 12, "Printing, Faxing, and E-Mail," tells you all you need to know about using Word to print, fax, and e-mail—and Chapter 13, "Using Mail Merge Effectively," is a comprehensive guide to Word's powerful Mail-Merge capabilities.

■ The more you work with intranet and Web sites, the more you'll want to know about Word and Office's graphics tools—and you can learn all about them in Chapters 20, "Getting Images into Your Documents," and 21, "Drawing in Word."

■ In addition to Web forms, you can build other electronic forms with Word, using the tools you'll learn about in Chapter 24, "Creating Electronic and Printed Forms."

■ Word and FrontPage make heavy use of ActiveX controls, which can be custom designed using Visual Basic. Chapters 30 through 33 introduce you to the basics of Visual Basic. This is information you may be able to leverage later, if you ever want to create your own ActiveX controls, or adapt existing controls to new uses.

CHAPTER 11

Deploying Your Internet or Intranet Site

by Bill Camarda

In Chapter 10, "Building Your Intranet with Word, Office, and FrontPage," you learned more techniques for creating an intranet or Web site containing multiple pages and hyperlinks. This chapter presents a brief overview of testing and deploying your site, so you can make sure it works the way you expect, and users reap the benefits you expect. ■

Planning to test your site

If you don't find the problems with your site, rest assured that your customers, colleagues, or boss will.

Creating a list of Web pages and graphics

If Word is your primary Web management tool, you'll need a little extra help—starting with a list of the files in your Web site.

Testing your hyperlinks

Here's a systematic approach to avoiding broken hyperlinks and annoying error messages.

Setting up your Web server

Microsoft provides free, low-end Web servers for Windows 95 and NT Workstation. Here's how to get them running.

Uploading your site to an Internet Service Provider

Use the Web Publishing Wizard to get files from your computer to your Internet Service Provider's Web server.

Testing your site after you've posted it

Learn how to recognize and fix common Web site errors.

The testing you need to perform falls into three main categories:

- *Appearance*. Will the site look the way you want it to, on all the computers and browsers where you expect it to run?

- *Behavior*. Will the site behave as it should? Do the internal and external hyperlinks work? Do the form handling scripts work? Do the ActiveX components or Java applets work?

- *Performance*. Will the site work as quickly as it should, or will users give up on it because it runs too slowly?

This chapter addresses each of these issues. Hyperlinks can be tested within Word or FrontPage, and this chapter shows you how. Other aspects of your Web site's behavior should be tested on a live Web server. If your files aren't already on a Web server, you'll learn how to get them there.

N O T E If you've created your site with FrontPage, you've already been required to place your files on a Web server. Typically, you'll have used either the Windows 95 Personal Web Server or Windows NT 4.0 Peer Web Services on your own computer, or on the Windows NT Server-based Internet Information Server (IIS) Web server where you actually deploy your site. ■

Creating a Master List of Web Pages

Before you get started, if you're trying to manage even a small intranet or Web site from Word, you may find that you need help keeping track of your files. One place to start is to print or create a list of HTML and/or image files in the folder where you're storing your site. Incredibly, Windows 95 and NT 4.0 provide no easy way to do this. However you *can* do it from MS-DOS:

1. Choose Start, Programs, MS-DOS Prompt. An MS-DOS window opens.

2. Enter a DIR (directory) command followed by a space and the letters >LPT1, which tell DOS to send the information to the printer that is connected to your first parallel port. For example, to print a list of files within the C:\WEBFILES folder, use the command:

   ```
   dir c:\webfiles >lpt1
   ```

T I P If all you want is file names without other information such as file sizes, use the /b switch:
```
dir c:\webfiles /b >lpt1
```
If there are many files in your list, you might consider using the /w switch, which prints just the file names, and lists them in five columns across the page:
```
dir c:\webfiles /w >lpt1
```

3. If the list does not print, or does not print completely, pressing the button on your printer sends the next page. This may be called the form feed button. If you have only one button on your printer's front panel, press that button. If you have no buttons at all, you can send the instruction from your printer software.

Instead of sending the information to your printer, you can collect it in a text file that can you edit and manipulate in Word. By doing so, you can build your own primitive version of FrontPage's To Do List. To create a text file named LIST.TXT with the information in the previous example, use the command:

```
dir c:\webfiles >list.txt
```

If you want your text file to include the contents of subfolders beneath the main folder, use the append (>>) and subfolder switches (/s):

```
dir c:\webfiles >>list.txt /s
```

Testing Hyperlinks

For the user of an intranet or Web site, few things are as frustrating as clicking a hyperlink and discovering that it doesn't work. If you're creating your pages in Word, you'll need to check your links manually. It's not fun, but the next section suggests a few shortcuts to make it less painful. As you'll see, if you're working in FrontPage, your software does most of the checking for you automatically.

Testing Hyperlinks in Word

 In Word, the first step in testing hyperlinks is to make sure that all the pages in your site are in the folders where they belong. Then, you can simply open them one at a time and check each hyperlink individually. When a link works, Word displays the linked document. If the link works, you can return to the original document by clicking the Back button on the Web toolbar. When a link does *not* work, Word may display one of several error messages. You may see the dialog box shown in Figure 11.1, or a message that Word cannot find the server or proxy server needed to connect with the linked file.

FIG. 11.1
This dialog box may appear when you try to follow a broken Word hyperlink.

On a small site, you can simplify matters a great deal by placing all your Web pages in the same folder. Then all your hyperlinks simply need to refer to other documents in the same folder. If you use relative hyperlinks—the kind Word creates by default—you shouldn't have to worry about files getting lost. With relative hyperlinks, if you move the files together, maintaining the existing folder structure, the links will stay intact.

▶ **See** "Using Relative and Absolute Hyperlinks," **p. 527**

Decide in advance whether to store graphics in the same folder, or to create a subfolder where all your graphics will be stored together.

As discussed in Chapter 10, "Building Your Intranet with Word, Office, and FrontPage," the fewer folders you have, the less linking problems you'll suffer.

TROUBLESHOOTING

Why wouldn't a link hyperlink **work?** Here are a few common reasons:

- You're testing an external link across a LAN or on the World Wide Web, and your connection to the LAN or the Web is not working.

- You've moved a link from one folder to another, changing the relationship between the source and destination files.

- You've used absolute rather than relative links.

- You're trying to link to a file with the wrong extension. For example, your link specifies an .HTM file when the destination file actually uses the .HTML extension, or vice versa.

N O T E   Some operating systems truncate the .HTML files Word creates so that the extension only contains the three letters .HTM. Typically, a Web server's administrator must define which extensions can be "served" to visitors, and not all Web servers are configured to recognize .HTM and .HTML files interchangeably. ▪

If you need to change the contents of a hyperlink in order to fix it, right-click the hyperlink, and choose <u>H</u>yperlink, Edit <u>H</u>yperlink from the shortcut menu. Make your change there and choose OK.

▶ **See** "Using Hyperlinks," **p. 521**

Creating a Macro That Helps You Check Hyperlinks

You can save quite a bit of time checking links within Word if you record or write a quick Visual Basic macro that moves you into the next hyperlink and tests whether it actually leads anywhere. You can record this macro as follows:

1. Double-click the REC button on the status bar.

2. In the Macro Name text box, enter **TestHyperlink** (or another name you prefer).

3. Choose <u>K</u>eyboard to assign a keyboard shortcut.

4. In the Keyboard dialog box, enter a keyboard shortcut; Alt+H is typically available.

5. Click Close. The Macro Recorder starts running.

6. Press F5 to display the Go To tab of the Find and Replace dialog box.

7. Choose Field in the G<u>o</u> to What scroll box.

8. Choose Hyperlink in the <u>E</u>nter Field Name drop-down text box.

9. Choose Nex<u>t</u>.

10. Choose Close.

11. Press the right arrow to move into the hyperlink.

12. Press Enter to test the hyperlink.

13. Press the Stop Recording button.

If you're comfortable working in the Visual Basic Editor, you can create the same macro using the following code:

```
Sub TestHyperlink()
' TestHyperlink Macro
Selection.GoTo What:=wdGoToField, Which:=wdGoToNext, Count:=1, Name:= _
        "HYPERLINK"
Selection.MoveRight Unit:=wdCharacter, Count:=1
Selection.Range.Hyperlinks(1).Follow NewWindow:=False, AddHistory:=True
End Sub
```

After you create the macro, you might want to connect it to a toolbar button, so you can click the button to run the macro. For more information about writing macros with Visual Basic for Applications, see Chapters 31 through 34.

▶ **See** "Adding a Command to a Toolbar," **p. 721**

Testing Hyperlinks in Microsoft FrontPage

If you are working in FrontPage, your software can handle most of your hyperlink testing for you automatically. Choose Tools, Verify Hyperlinks to check all the hyperlinks in your intranet or Web site. The Verify Hyperlinks dialog box appears (see Figure 11.2).

Part

III

Ch

11

FIG. 11.2

The Verify Hyperlinks dialog box lists any broken internal hyperlinks, as well as all external hyperlinks— even those that work.

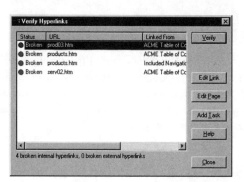

In this dialog box, FrontPage displays any broken hyperlinks it finds within your site. It also displays all the external hyperlinks that appear in your site, broken or otherwise—such as Web pages on the public Internet. Because it may take quite a while to verify all external hyperlinks, FrontPage only attempts to do so when you click Verify. Links that FrontPage hasn't verified appear in yellow; links that are definitely broken appear in red; links that are definitely OK appear in green.

> **CAUTION**
>
> Before you run Verify Hyperlinks, choose <u>V</u>iew, <u>R</u>efresh to make sure FrontPage is displaying the most current information about your site. This is especially useful if many people are providing content. When you refresh your site map, you'll often discover changes you didn't know existed.

If a link is broken, you can fix it immediately by choosing <u>E</u>dit Link. The Edit Link dialog box opens (see Figure 11.3). Here, you can make a change to the hyperlink without having to edit the surrounding page. This is an easy solution if, for example, the owners of a site you've linked with have moved the linked information to another page. Just change the hyperlink and it will work again. You can move through your broken hyperlinks and fix them one at a time. If you know a hyperlink requires more attention, you can choose Add <u>T</u>ask, and the broken link is added to your To Do List.

FIG. 11.3

In the Edit Link dialog box, you can fix a hyperlink without having to open and edit the surrounding page.

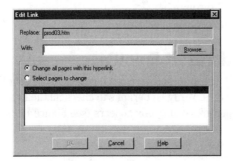

Sometimes, however, you'll also need to change text or formatting surrounding the hyperlink. For example, perhaps a link simply no longer exists, and you need to remove both the link and text references to it. If a whole section of the page referred to the link, you may have to remove tables, graphics, horizontal lines, and other elements. If so, click Edit <u>P</u>age. The FrontPage Editor opens, and you can make your changes.

Getting Your Files onto a Web Server

Although you can test hyperlinks in Word no matter where your files are stored, most of the other testing you'll need to perform requires your files to be on a running Web server. Though this sounds difficult, Microsoft has provided ready solutions. For Windows 95 users, Microsoft makes available the Personal Web Server at no charge on its Web site. Currently, the file to search for is pws10a.exe. This is the same Web server shipped with FrontPage. To install Personal Web Server, download the file, double-click the icon and follow the on-screen directions.

ON THE WEB

Personal Web Server is currently available at **www.microsoft.com/ie/pws/default.htm**.

N O T E You might need your Windows 95 CD-ROM in order to copy some files needed by Personal Web Server. ▮

Personal Web Server (PWS) is an exceptionally low-maintenance program after you have it running the way you want. In fact, if you weren't testing or deploying a Web site on it, you could easily have it running on your computer for months without knowing it was there. However, when you first install it, you should spend a few moments with its administration tools to make sure everything is running the way it should be and that you know how to make changes in the event they're necessary. So, in the rest of this section, you take a "nickel tour" of Personal Web Server management.

After you've installed PWS and rebooted your computer, PWS should appear as an icon in the tray on your Windows 95 taskbar (see Figure 11.4). Double-click the icon to display the Personal Web Server Properties dialog box (see Figure 11.5). The General tab tells you your Web address—or, more likely, the name of your computer as recognized by your LAN.

Part

III

Ch

11

FIG. 11.4

Double-click the Personal Web Server icon to view or change its properties.

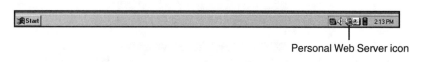

Personal Web Server icon

FIG. 11.5

The Personal Web Server Properties dialog box opens, displaying your Web server's Internet address.

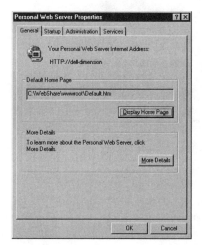

Choose the Startup tab and make sure that Run the Web Server Automatically at Startup is checked (see Figure 11.6). Choose the Services tab (see Figure 11.7) and make sure the HTTP (Hypertext Transfer Protocol) service is running. If you plan to use FTP (File Transfer Protocol), select it in the Service box and choose Start.

FIG. 11.6

In the Startup tab, you can make sure the HTTP (Web) service automatically runs at startup.

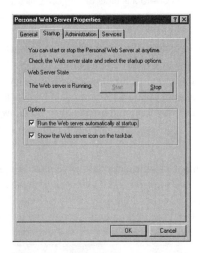

FIG. 11.7

In the Services tab, you can make sure the HTTP or FTP services are running now.

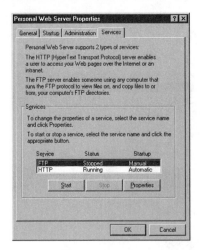

Now choose the Administration tab, and click Administration. Your Internet Explorer browser opens to run the PWS Internet Services Administrator application. You might have to establish your dial-up connection before the Administration application will work. Click WWW Administration to display three *pseudo-tabs,* which are actually separate Web pages containing different settings for your Web server.

■ The *Service* tab (see Figure 11.8) controls time-outs, password authentication, and the theoretical maximum number of connections that can be established at one time. Note that one user can generate many connections at a time. The default setting of 300 connections doesn't mean PWS (Personal Web Server) can handle 300 simultaneous connections; in fact, it won't come anywhere close to that.

■ The *Logging* tab (see Figure 11.9) enables you to create monthly, weekly, or daily logs tracking the activity that occurs on your server. This information might help you determine when it's time to upgrade to a more high-powered server, such as Internet Information Server.

■ The *Directories* tab (see Figure 11.10) enables you to change or delete the default folders where the Web server stores home pages, other documents, and scripts.

FIG. 11.8

In the Service pseudo-tab, you can set the number of connections allowed at once and any required password connections.

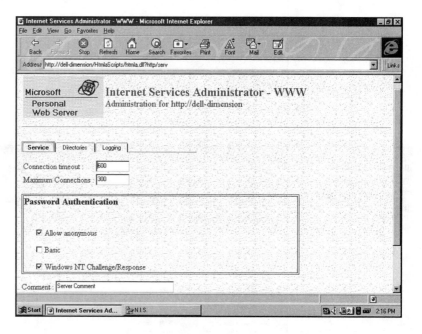

Part

III

Ch

11

In most cases, you can leave the Service and Logging tabs as they are. However, there is one change you may want to make on the Directories tab. You're permitted to change the name of the document that will appear first when a user connects to your site. The current setting is Default.htm. If you've created your Web site with FrontPage, your home page will be called Default.htm automatically, so there's no problem.

If you've created your Web site with Word or another program, however, you might have followed the widespread Web convention of naming your home page index.htm or index.html. In that case, you'll want to change the default page to the one you've created. Otherwise, viewers will see a generic built-in page instead of the home page you have in mind.

FIG. 11.9

In the Logging tab, you can request activity reports and define how often you get them.

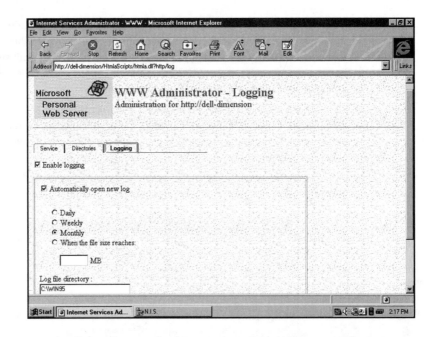

FIG. 11.10

In the Directories tab, you can change where PWS looks for its files and scripts.

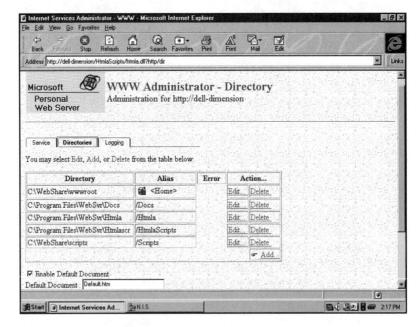

Starting Windows NT Workstation 4.0's Peer Web Services

In Windows NT Workstation 4.0, the approximate equivalent to Personal Web Server is Peer Web Services (also abbreviated PWS). NT's PWS includes a few more capabilities than its Windows 95 counterpart. For example, it can operate as a Gopher server and it provides some performance measurements that Personal Web Server doesn't. It also can benefit from the improved security built into the NT File System (NTFS), assuming it's running on a disk formatted with NTFS.

N O T E   Peer Web Services also has one *disadvantage* compared with Personal Web Server. It is subject to Microsoft's NT Workstation licensing limitations, which restrict one NT Workstation to serving no more than 10 other users at a time. Windows 95 has no such legal restrictions. ■

To get Peer Web Services up and running in Windows NT, follow these steps:

1. Choose Start, Settings, Control Panel.
2. Double-click the Network icon to run the Network applet.
3. Choose the Service tab.
4. Click Add.
5. Choose Microsoft Peer Web Services; then choose OK.
6. Tell NT where to find the Windows NT Workstation 4.0 files it needs. On Intel systems, they're normally in the \i386 folder on your CD-ROM drive.
7. If asked, close any open applications.
8. Choose the services you want to install: WWW, FTP, or Gopher.
9. Specify the directories where you want to store the files associated with each service. If the directories don't exist, Windows NT offers to create them.
10. Choose OK. Windows NT copies the files it needs and starts the corresponding services immediately.
11. Click OK; then click Close to leave the Network applet.

Part

III

Ch

11

N O T E   Under Windows NT, services are programs that start up automatically when you turn on your computer, even if you don't log on. They can be up and running even if the computer appears otherwise inactive. ■

Copying Files to Your Web Server

Assuming you have access to the Web server where you want to test your site—either on your own computer or on the network—you can simply copy your files to the folder where the Web server will look for them. In the case of Personal Web Server, the folder is typically c:\Webshare\Wwwroot unless you've used the Internet Services Administrator to change it. In the case of Internet Information Server, the folder is typically \InetPub\wwwroot on the network drive on which IIS is running.

If you are working with an Internet Service Provider, you'll have to ask to which folder your files have been assigned. Traditionally, you would have to learn FTP protocols (and possibly enter them at a command line) to copy your files to an Internet Service Provider's (ISP) Web server. Microsoft has simplified the process dramatically, via the Web Publishing Wizard, which can be found in the Microsoft Office 97 CD-ROM's Valupack\Webpost folder. To install the Web Publishing Wizard, double-click Webpost.exe and click Yes to accept the license agreement.

ON THE WEB

If you purchased Word as a stand-alone product on floppy disks, you do not have the ValuPack. You can download the Web Publishing Wizard at **www.microsoft.com/windows/software/webpost/**. Microsoft has recently updated the Web Publishing Wizard to include additional capabilities. So even if you already have the Web Publishing Wizard, it might be worth your time to download the new version.

Running the Web Publishing Wizard

After Windows decompresses and installs the Web Publishing Wizard files, you can run the Wizard any time you want. Choose Start, Programs, Accessories, Internet Tools, Web Publishing Wizard. The Web Publishing Wizard opens. Click Next to get started.

In the following window (see Figure 11.11), you can specify a folder or file to upload. If you want to upload a folder, either enter its complete path name or choose Browse Folders to select the folder you want. Notice that the Include Subfolders check box is checked in the Web Publishing Wizard window. Unless you clear it, all folders subordinate to the one you've selected will also be uploaded.

FIG. 11.11
Use this window to choose the folder or file you want to upload.

If you only want to upload one file, first choose your folder, and then click Browse Files to select a single file. After you've selected the folder or file you want to upload, click Next. In the following window (see Figure 11.12) you can choose a server to which you want to upload. There are only two choices on the built-in list: CompuServe's Our World, and SPRYNET's SPRY Society.

FIG. 11.12

Use this window to choose a Web server on which to upload your files.

While these Internet Service Providers are popular, they only have a small share of the market. The odds are that you're not using one of those providers. If not, click New (see Figure 11.13). On the following window, you can enter a name for your Web server. This isn't an official TCP/IP name; it's simply any name you'll recognize when you return to this dialog box. You can now choose your service provider from the slightly longer list at the bottom of the screen.

FIG. 11.13

This figure illustrates how to choose another ISP for uploading your files.

Chances are, you still won't find the right service provider here. If not, choose <Other Internet Provider>. When you're finished, click Next (see Figure 11.14). If you chose <Other Internet Provider>, you can now enter the URL (Uniform Resource Locator) or Internet address your Internet provider has given you. The address might look something like:

www.provider.net/yourname

Notice that you may have to include a subfolder so your files aren't uploaded to the server's root directory. Click Next once more. If you have a dial-up connection to the Internet, the Web Publishing Wizard displays the Connect To dialog box. This is the same dialog box you normally use to establish your connection to this Internet Service Provider.

N O T E Typically, your ISP will not allow you to upload files into a Web server's root directory for security reasons. ▪

FIG. 11.14
This figure shows entering a URL or Internet address for your Web provider.

Click Connect; then follow the log-on procedure you normally follow. After you log on, the Web Publishing Wizard copies the files where you told it to place them. When they're uploaded, in most cases you can access and test them immediately.

N O T E Scripts, ActiveX controls, and Java applets may require more attention on the part of the service provider because most providers have established guidelines for client use of these applications on their servers. ■

Testing Appearance and Behavior

Now that you've uploaded your files to your local Web server or Internet Service Provider, you can begin to test your site more thoroughly. In the following section, you'll walk through a systematic approach to testing your intranet or Web site.

When you first planned and designed your site, you should have given some thought to your target environment, especially which browsers you expect your users to have and how you expect them to connect to your site. Now you should set up one or more test computers using those configurations.

Setting Up Testbeds for an Intranet Site

In a controlled intranet environment, it's easier to test your site because you only need to test a limited number of configurations, and with a little research you can determine what those are. If your company has standardized on a single Web browser, such as Microsoft Internet Explorer or Netscape Navigator 4.0 (part of Netscape Communicator), you may be able to presume that all or most of your users will have access to that browser.

Even in controlled environments, you may need to wrestle with the issue of multiple versions, however. If you're considering an upgrade, you may have to test your site on both Internet Explorer 3.0 and 4.0; or on both Netscape Navigator 3.0 and 4.0.

Prepare your test browsers with any plug-ins, fonts, or other helper software that will be available to the typical user. For example, if you are serving native Word and Excel files to Netscape users, install Microsoft's Netscape AXPlugin that adds ActiveX support to Netscape browsers. You can find this plug-in on the Office 97 CD-ROM, in the Valupack\Axplugin folder.

Setting Up Testbeds for a Public Web Site

In a public Web site, you have a more complex challenge. You will almost certainly have visitors using each recent version of both Internet Explorer and Netscape's browsers. Because each of those browsers operates on multiple platforms, you may have to contend with users running Windows 95, Windows 3.x, Macintosh, UNIX, and OS/2 Warp systems—each with their own minor but occasionally challenging differences. You will encounter users with text-only browsers (either the DOS or UNIX-based Lynx, or another browser configured not to display images).

N O T E You may also encounter small numbers of users running other browsers, such as Mosaic, IBM Internet Connection for OS/2, and a host of others with relatively small market penetration. █

Decide which configurations to test based on the relative prominence of each browser and platform in your audience and your available time and resources. For many public Internet sites, it's reasonable to test on both Netscape and Internet Explorer, Windows 95/NT 4.0 and Macintosh—and leave it at that. If you only have access to a Windows system, at least test both Netscape's and Microsoft's browsers—especially Netscape's, which still owns greater market share.

 T I P If you have limited access to different types of computers and Web browsers, ask your friends, relatives, colleagues, and acquaintances to help you test your site.

To the extent possible, set up your test system(s) to mirror the way your audience will access your site. If you're setting up a LAN-based intranet, place your test system on an Ethernet network. If you also expect telecommuters to access your intranet via 33.6Kbps modems, test that as well. Monitor size, pixels, and color depth also are items you should consider. Images that look exquisite on one monitor may not be comprehensible on another; tables that fit neatly within a browser window on a 17" monitor may stretch beyond the edge of a screen on a 14" monitor.

What to Test

After your equipment and browsers are set up, test the overall appearance of each page. Do the pages look good on each browser? Then, take a closer look at both appearance and performance.

Appearance Issues Use this checklist in reviewing the appearance of your site and making appropriate adjustments in Word or FrontPage:

■ Will viewers see the most important elements of your page immediately? It's not uncommon for Web page designers to discover only in the testing stage that important buttons and other page elements don't show up without scrolling. If viewers can't

Part

III

Ch

11

immediately see what a page provides, and what they can do with it, they're likely to jump elsewhere.

▪ Are the images readable—especially those on navigation bars and other interactive elements of your page? When you click an image map, does it work?

▪ Do extra blank lines appear on some browsers, but not others? You may have to edit out some <P> tags or stray spaces that appear within lines of text.

▪ Does everything fit within the window of your users' "lowest-common-denominator" browser and monitor size? If any graphics are too deep or wide, reduce them in size to 475×340 pixels or less—the height and width a typical 14" monitor can display. Many Web authors find it helpful to design Web sites on 14" monitors to ensure that they build pages that the majority of users can work with.

▪ Is text readable? Be especially careful to check text formatted in the HTML Font Size "1" or "2". (In general, be reluctant to change the default Font Size 3 for body text, except for footnotes, disclaimers, and similar small print.)

▪ If you specified fonts using the <FONT FACE> tag, do they appear correctly—and if the fonts are not available on all target systems, are the substitute fonts acceptable to you? This is especially likely to be a problem if your audience consists of both PC and Macintosh users because the standard fonts on each machine differ greatly.

▪ Do tables appear correctly? Some older browsers don't support the HTML 3.0 standards for creating tables. It's unlikely, but if a significant portion of your audience still uses browsers that have problems with tables, you may have to create separate pages for tables that communicate the information in another way.

▪ Are all your graphics present, or are blank boxes shown in place of some graphics? If you find blank boxes, you'll have to check the <IMG> tags and make sure to place your graphics in the folder they reference.

▪ Does the page look and work properly when graphics are turned off? Are there working <ALT> tags describing every image—especially those designed to be clicked?

▪ Do symbols such as ®, ©, and ™ display properly? Word inserts these using the HTML escape codes &reg, &copy, and &trade. Netscape Navigator does not recognize &trade. Display the page in Word, choose View, HTML Source, and choose Edit, Replace to substitute the HTML escape code &#153, which is recognized by nearly all recent browsers. In general, the numbered escape codes in the following minitable are more likely to be recognized than the ones Word uses.

Symbol	HTML escape code
®	@#174
©	&#153
™	&#169

N O T E There's no code for service marks, but you can use lowercase and superscript to achieve the same effect. ▪

Microsoft Internet Explorer Extensions   You've already encountered a few features that Word and FrontPage casually apply to Web pages without letting you know that they're not universally supported by all Web browsers. For example, Word's Scrolling Text feature inserts a <MARQUEE> tag that no other browser recognizes. If you use this feature in a multiple-platform environment, make sure you've formatted your page so it will look acceptable even if that block of text doesn't scroll.

Some of the HTML support Microsoft provided in Internet Explorer 3.0 has now made it into Netscape Navigator 4.0. For example, Navigator 4.0 recognizes the FONT COLOR attribute, so text colors you set in Word should look OK in the latest version of Navigator, if not previous versions. Be especially careful to check the following:

Part
III

Ch
11

- Background images, especially watermarks
- Background sounds
- Table borders
- Tables with different colors applied to specific rows or columns
- Video clips

In the following figures you can see some of the subtle differences that can show up on the same page when it's displayed on Internet Explorer 3.0 and Netscape Navigator 4.0.

- On Yahoo, the background is gray by default on Internet Explorer (see Figure 11.15); white on Navigator (see Figure 11.16).
- At Surplus Direct, the all-important E-mail Sign-Up button appears where it belongs on Internet Explorer (see Figure 11.17) when displayed at the widely-used 640x480 resolution. However, Netscape 4.0 adds a slightly deeper user interface, so the button doesn't show up without scrolling (see Figure 11.18).
- Finally, at Netscape's own NetGuide page, the hyperlinks at the top of the page use clean, easy-to-read white text on a green background, but on Internet Explorer (see Figure 11.19), the deep blue on green is almost impossible to read (see Figure 11.20).

FIG. 11.15

Yahoo in gray in Internet Explorer 3.0.

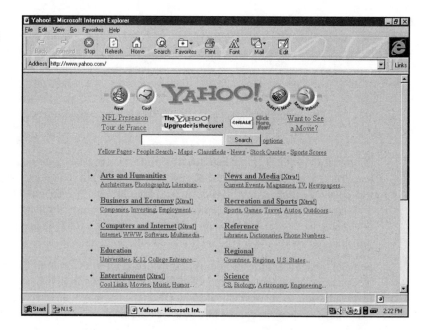

FIG. 11.16

Yahoo in white in Netscape Navigator 4.0.

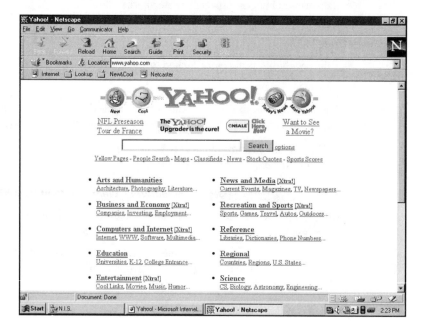

FIG. 11.17
The Surplus Direct
E-mail Sign-Up button
on the opening screen
in Internet Explorer 3.0.

E-mail Sign-Up button

FIG. 11.18
The Surplus Direct
E-mail Sign-Up button
is too low on the
opening screen in
Navigator 4.0.

FIG. 11.19

Clean and readable hyperlinks in Netscape Navigator 4.0.

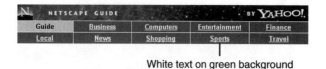

White text on green background

FIG. 11.20

Hyperlinks are barely readable in Internet Explorer 3.0.

Dark blue text on green background

ON THE WEB

You can download a Windows Help file that contains detailed information about all the HTML tags and attributes supported by Word and Internet Explorer. Visit **http://www.microsoft.com/workshop/author/newhtml/** to get this file, named HTMLRef.zip.

Behavior Issues   Use this checklist in reviewing the behavior of your site:

- Are your links still working? In Chapter 10, "Building Your Intranet with Word, Office, and FrontPage," you learned how to test them before uploading files to your Web server. You really should test them again before you launch your site. If links start breaking, check that the file names you used on Windows 95 or NT 4.0 are still intact on your Web server. If you used long file names and moved your files to a UNIX server, they may not be.

ON THE WEB

There are a variety of shareware tools for checking hyperlinks on live Web sites. One of the most powerful is Linkbot 3.5 from Tetranet Software. Linkbot not only flags broken links, it can also list external links that are stale, or that load too slowly. You can download a 30-day trial version of Linkbot at **www.tetranetsoftware.com/linkbot-download.htm**.

- Do your forms appear correctly on each target browser? Can users make choices correctly? Do list boxes show the correct number of choices? This can be a problem on some older browsers.
- Are your forms handling scripts (CGI code or WebBots), receiving data, and forwarding it properly?
- Are your ActiveX controls or Java applets running properly? For users of browsers that do not support ActiveX or Java (or who have disabled that support), have you provided alternate ways to communicate the information you want to get across?

Performance Issues   There's never enough bandwidth. Even on intranets, where you're theoretically operating on at least a 10-megabit network rather than slow dial-up connections, it's easy to overload the network with complex graphics, multimedia, or other elements. If your pages are loading too slowly, there are a few things you can try to make them work more efficiently.

- Double-check that all images have height and width attributes as part of the `<IMG>` tags associated with them. These tags allow a browser to display a page's layout and text contents before all graphics have loaded. If even one button doesn't include height and width attributes, all the graphics will have to be loaded before the text can be displayed. Word does insert height and width attributes by default, but HTML code generated manually or borrowed from elsewhere may not have them.

- Shrink any graphics that you can reduce in size, using a graphics editor such as Microsoft Photo Editor (which comes with Microsoft Office 97 on CD-ROM) or Microsoft Image Composer (which comes with Microsoft FrontPage on CD-ROM).

- Wherever possible, use fewer colors. For example, some images may not suffer too badly if reduced from a palette of 256 colors to only 64. Microsoft Image Composer includes tools to create more compact *custom color palettes*. If you need to change the color palettes associated with many images at the same time, consider a product like Jasc Image Robot (Jasc, Inc.), which provides tools for automating the process.

- For photographs or complex drawn graphics, experiment with storing images as JPG files instead of GIF.

- Consider when black and white or gray-scale images may be appropriate and consistent with your design.

- Wherever possible, reuse the same image on multiple pages; after it's been loaded once, local Web browsers will cache it in memory. It won't have to be downloaded again.

- Limit your use of audio and video. If you use them at all, edit out any parts that aren't absolutely necessary, and save them in the most compact format that delivers acceptable quality (8-bit versus 16-bit, for example).

ON THE WEB

For detailed information about optimizing Web graphics, visit the Bandwidth Conservation Society at **http://www.infohiway.com/faster/** or refer to *Designing Web Graphics*, L. Weinman, New Riders Publishing, 1996.

From Here...

You've now completed three chapters on Web publishing with Word, Office, FrontPage, and Microsoft's other Web publishing tools. Now, move on to the following chapters.

- Deliver your message in other media, via printing, e-mail, and fax in Chapter 12, "Printing, Faxing, and E-Mail."

- "Mass customize" your message using Word's powerful mail merge tools in Chapter 13, "Using Mail Merge Effectively."

Part
III

Ch
11

- Create spectacular page layouts using Word 97's greatly-improved desktop publishing features in Chapter 19, "Word Desktop Publishing," and graphics tools in Chapter 20, "Getting Images into Your Documents," Chapter 21, "Drawing in Word," and Chapter 22, "Using Microsoft Graph."

CHAPTER 12

Printing, Faxing, and E-Mail

by Elaine Marmel

Printing can be just printing, or it can be a more involved process. Printing is just one form of output available in Word. You also can fax a Word document without printing it, and you can attach a Word document to an e-mail message. ■

General printing

You can print your entire document, selected pages, or a draft of your document. You also can print information about your document, such as a list of styles used in the document.

Printing envelopes and labels

Learn the quick and easy way to print a single envelope, a single label, or a page of labels that contain the same information.

Printing and files

If you don't have access to your usual printer, you can print your document to a file that you can later send to your printer when you have access to it.

Print Preview

You can edit your document in Print Preview, changing both text and layout.

Faxing information

Yes, you can print your document and then fax it from a traditional fax machine, or, if your computer contains a fax/modem, you can fax your document directly from Word.

E-Mailing a Word document

You can send a Word document as an attachment in e-mail. This approach can save you lots of time when you need someone else to review a document.

The Basics of Word Printing

Using the Print button is the easiest way to print using Word's defaults. When you click the Print button, Word prints one copy of your entire document to your default printer. If you need to print anything else, display the Print dialog box by choosing File, Print and change settings.

> **N O T E** You can print a Word document without opening Word if you use Windows techniques. One method is to open My Computer and the Printers folder and find the printer to which you want to print. Then, double-click the drive containing the document you want to print and drag the document onto the printer. If you use this method often, you may want to create a shortcut to your printer and place it on your Desktop. ▨

Specifying What to Print

Suppose you don't want to print your entire document, or you want to use a different printer, or you want to print several copies of the document. Choose File, Print to display the Print dialog box (see Figure 12.1) and specify the documents you want to print.

FIG. 12.1
From the Print dialog box, you can specify special printing options.

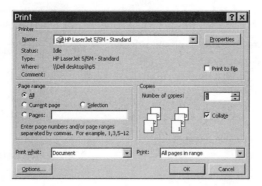

Printing Selected Pages

To print only selected pages of your document, use the Page Range box in the Print dialog box. If you want to print only one specific page, place the insertion point on the page before you open the dialog box. Then, choose Current Page. You can also print selected text by selecting the text you want to print before you open the dialog box. Then, choose Selection in the Page Range box.

If you want to print a certain range of pages, list the range in the Pages text box, separated by a hyphen (-). As you can see from the example in the dialog box, you can supply multiple page ranges using a comma to separate them. In the example, you would be printing pages 1 and 3 and pages 5 through 12.

Printing Multiple Copies

Use the Copies spinner box to specify the number of copies you want to print. Either click the spinner box arrows or type the number of copies you want to print. If you print more than one copy of a document, you can choose to collate the copies. When you collate copies (by placing a check in the Collate check box), Word prints one complete copy of the document before starting to print the next copy. If you choose not to collate, Word prints the number of copies you specify for each page before it starts printing the next page. For example, if you have a five-page document and you print three collated copies, Word prints pages 1–5 and then starts again and prints pages 1–5, and so on. If you choose to print three copies of the same document without collating, Word prints five copies of page 1, then five copies of page 2, and so on.

Printing Other Information

You can print information about your document other than its text. Using the Print What list box, you can print styles, AutoText entries, keyboard shortcuts you assigned while working in this document, the document's comments, or the document's properties. You'll find information about all of these elements in other chapters.

Printing Pages in Reverse Order

To print your document in reverse order, choose File, Print, and in the Print dialog box, choose Options. Word displays the Print options dialog box (see Figure 12.2).

FIG. 12.2
Use this dialog box to set special printing options.

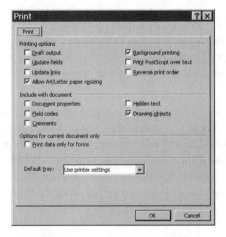

Part
III

Ch
12

> **N O T E** The settings you see in this dialog box are the same as the Print tab of the Options dialog box (choose Tools, Options, and click the Print tab). Any changes you make in this dialog box affect all documents, not just the current document.

Place a check in the Reverse Print Order check box and choose OK twice. Word prints your document from back to front.

Printing a Draft

Printing a draft can save you time if your document contains a large amount of graphics. To print a draft of your document, choose File, Print to display the Print dialog box. Then, choose Options and place a check in the Draft Output check box of the Print options dialog box. When you choose OK twice to print your document, Word prints your document with minimal formatting and no graphics.

N O T E   Some printers don't support this option, so you won't notice any difference. ▨

Printing and Fields

If your document contains fields, you can tell Word to update the fields before you print the document. Choose File, Print to display the Print dialog box. Then, choose Options and place a check in the Update Fields check box of the Print options dialog box. When you print your document, Word updates all fields before printing.

 TIP   The same principle applies to the Update Links check box.

Changing Paper

In Chapter 3, "More Day-to-Day Productivity Tools," you learned that you can choose the size of paper you use in your printer by opening the Page Setup dialog box (choose File, Page Setup) and choosing the Paper Size tab. You also learned that, if your printer is equipped with more than one paper tray, you could change the paper tray from the Paper Source tab of the Page Setup dialog box.

You also can select a different paper tray from the Print options dialog box. Choose File, Print, and, in the Print dialog box, choose Options. In the Print options dialog box (refer to Figure 12.2), open the Default Tray list box and select the tray containing the paper to which you want to print. Remember, though, when you choose a paper tray from the Print options dialog box, you are setting a new default paper tray that remains in effect for *all* documents (not just the current document). When you change the paper tray from the Page Setup dialog box, you affect only the current document.

N O T E   If the paper tray settings are different in the Page Setup dialog box than those settings in the Print options dialog box, the paper source settings in the Page Setup dialog box supersede any paper tray settings in the Print options dialog box. ▨

Printing One Envelope

You use different techniques in Word to print a single envelope or multiple envelopes. In this chapter, we'll cover printing single envelopes; you'll learn how to print multiple envelopes—either to the same addressee or to different addressees—in Chapter 13, "Using Mail Merge Effectively."

To print a single envelope, use the Envelopes and Labels dialog box. Choose Tools, Envelopes and Labels, and choose the Envelopes tab. Word displays the Envelopes and Labels dialog box (see Figure 12.3).

FIG. 12.3

Use this dialog box to print a single envelope.

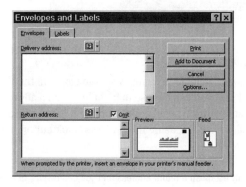

 TIP If you're typing a letter, Word automatically assumes you want the envelope addressed to the envelope recipient. When you open the Envelopes and Labels dialog box, you'll see the recipient's name and address selected.

In the Address text box, type the name and address of the recipient, or click the Address Book button above the box to choose a name and address you have stored in your Personal Address Book (associated with Microsoft Exchange) or in your Outlook Address Book.

 TIP If you have Microsoft Exchange installed, you'll see a Choose Profile dialog box, in which you can specify the correct settings.

After you select a profile, the Select Name dialog box appears (see Figure 12.4).

Open the Show Names From The list box and select an address book. Then highlight an addressee and choose OK. The address recorded in the address book for the individual appears in the Envelopes and Labels dialog box. You can choose Print to print the envelope immediately, or choose Add to Document to add the envelope to the top of your document.

FIG. 12.4

Use this dialog box to
select an address book
and an addressee.

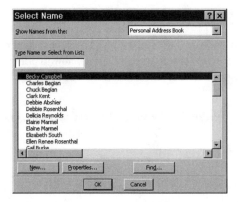

Formatting Your Envelope

You have several options available to format your envelope. In the Envelopes and Labels dialog
box (refer to Figure 12.3), you can choose to include a return address. Remove the check from
the O<u>m</u>it check box and either type an address in the <u>R</u>eturn Address box or select the return
address from your Address Book using the Address Book button that appears above the <u>Re</u>-
turn Address box.

> **N O T E** To permanently establish a return address that you can display or omit whenever you want,
> choose <u>T</u>ools, <u>O</u>ptions and click the User Information tab. Type the return address
> information in the <u>M</u>ailing Address box and choose OK. This default information will appear in the
> Envelopes and Labels dialog box; you can omit it by placing a check in the O<u>m</u>it check box. ■

If you choose the <u>O</u>ptions button, Word displays the Envelope Options tab of the Envelope
Options dialog box (see Figure 12.5).

FIG. 12.5

Use this dialog box to
set options for printing
envelopes.

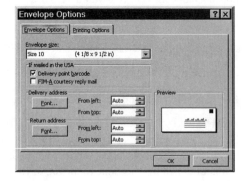

Use the Envelope <u>S</u>ize list box to select one of the predefined envelope sizes; if you choose
Custom, Word displays a dialog box in which you can set the envelope's width and height.

Save money and print a bar code on the envelope by placing a check in the Delivery Point Barcode check box. If your address includes a valid ZIP Code, Word supplies a post office-approved bar code on the envelope.

Select fonts for both the delivery address and the return address by clicking the Font button in the appropriate box and selecting a font. Also, move the location on the envelope of either the delivery address or the return address using the From Left and From Top spinner boxes. Be aware that the Auto setting is actually fairly close to where most people want these addresses to appear.

Envelope Printing Options

Use the Printing Options tab of the Envelope Options dialog box to select a feed method and a paper tray for your envelope. Choose Tools, Envelopes and Labels, and in the Envelopes and Labels dialog box, choose Options. In the Envelope Options dialog box, choose the Printing Options tab (see Figure 12.6).

FIG. 12.6
Select an envelope feed method and paper tray in this dialog box.

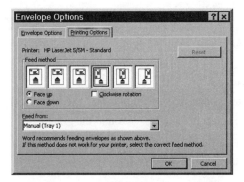

Be aware that Word looks at the printer you have installed and makes recommendations for these settings. Typically, it's a good idea to follow the recommended settings.

Part
III

Ch
12

Adding Graphics to Your Envelope

You can add a graphic to an envelope by creating the envelope in the Envelopes and Labels dialog box and adding the envelope to your document (see Figure 12.7). Then, switch to Page Layout view and, on the envelope, add a graphic by choosing Insert, Picture. Choose the type of graphic you want to add. To position the graphic, drag it. To resize the graphic, drag one of its handles.

Adding a graphic to the return address of an envelope is a little more complex. First, you must either create the graphic or obtain the graphic in a file that you can place somewhere on your computer. Then, you'll use the following steps to create a special AutoText entry (called EnvelopeExtra1) that Word uses on envelopes.

1. Start a new Word document and type the text portion of the return address information. You'll use this to help you correctly place the graphic.
2. Place the insertion point where you want the graphic to appear.

FIG. 12.7

This figure shows a letter to which an envelope was added.

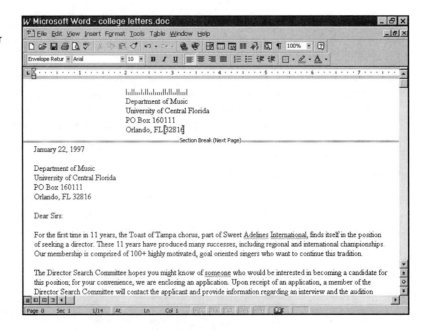

3. Choose Insert, Picture, From File.

4. Navigate to the folder containing the graphic and choose Insert.

5. Click the graphic to select it. Handles surround the graphic.

6. Press Alt+F3 to display the Create AutoText dialog box.

7. Type **EnvelopeExtra1** and choose OK.

Each time you create an envelope, Word inserts the graphic in the return address.

CAUTION

If you choose to omit the return address, Word still prints the graphic.

N O T E   If your graphic also contains the text for your return address, use the previous steps to create the AutoText entry EnvelopeExtra1, but skip Step 1. Then, replace the information for your return address on the User Information tab of the Options dialog box with a single space.

You actually can create two special AutoText entries to use on envelopes: EnvelopeExtra1 and EnvelopeExtra2. If you create these AutoText entries in the Normal template, they will be available to all templates, and therefore, they will appear on all envelopes. If you want to limit their appearance, create the entries in a template other than the Normal template. If you later decide you don't want to include these entries on envelopes at all, delete the AutoText entries.

Printing Labels

Using the Labels tab of the Envelopes and Labels dialog box (see Figure 12.8), you can print a single label or a full page of the same label.

FIG. 12.8
Use this dialog box
to print labels.

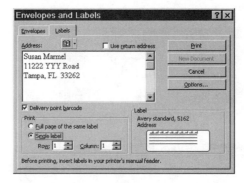

This tab of the Envelopes and Labels dialog box works just like the Envelopes tab in several ways:

- If your document contains an address, Word automatically assumes you want to print labels to that addressee. When you open the Envelopes and Labels dialog box, you'll see the address from your document in the box.

- You can select an addressee from your Address Book using the Address Book button.

- You can type an addressee in the Address box.

- You can print a delivery point bar-code on the label.

 TIP If you want to print a label that contains your return address as it appears on the User Information tab of the Options dialog box, place a check in the Use Return Address check box.

Printing a Page of Labels or One Label

In the Print box at the bottom of the Labels tab, you can choose to print either a Full Page of the Same Label or a Single Label. If you choose to print a single label, you can use the Row and Column spinner boxes to specify where, on the sheet of labels, you want to place the label when you print.

Choosing a Label Type

You select a label type so that Word knows how to set up and print your labels. You can click the picture in the lower-right corner of the Labels tab in the Envelopes and Labels dialog box, or you can choose Options. Word displays the Label Options dialog box (see Figure 12.9).

In the Printer Information box, select the type of printer you are using. If you choose Laser and Ink Jet, check the Tray setting. Use the Label Products list box to select the type of label you are using. You will find predefined settings in Word for most labels you can purchase, which makes your job much easier. After you've chosen a label product, choose a Product Number from the list. The description of that product number appears in the Label Information box, but if you'd like to see a graphic representation, choose the Details button (see Figure 12.10). Word displays the label and its dimensions on-screen, and you'll be able to make changes if necessary.

FIG. 12.9

Specify your printer type, paper tray, and label type in this dialog box.

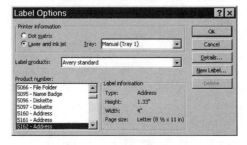

FIG. 12.10

This figure shows a sample of the dialog box that you might see if you choose the Details button.

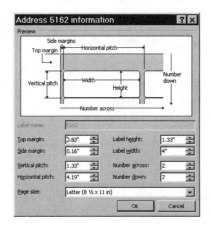

 TIP It is rarely necessary to adjust any of Word's predefined label settings.

Printing Many Files at the Same Time

 Just as you can open more than one file at a time, you can print more than one file at the same time as long as the files are stored in the same folder. Moreover, you don't need to open the files to print them. Click the Open button to display the Open dialog box (see Figure 12.11).

Navigate to the folder containing the documents you want to print and select each document. Click the Commands and Settings button and choose Print. Word prints the selected files.

 TIP To select contiguous files, click the first file, and then Shift+Click the last file. To select noncontiguous files, Ctrl+Click each file.

FIG. 12.11

Use the Open dialog box to print multiple documents.

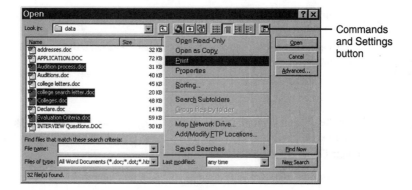

Commands and Settings button

Printing to a File

When would you want to print a document to a file? Suppose your computer is not connected to the printer to which you ultimately want to print. Further suppose that the printer you ultimately want to use is attached to a computer that doesn't contain Word. If you print the document to a file, you can move the file to a computer that is attached the printer you want to use and send the document to the printer using a simple DOS command.

N O T E You must install, on the computer where you will print to a file, the driver for the printer you eventually want to use. ■

To print to a file, follow these steps:

1. Choose File, Print to display the Print dialog box.
2. Make sure the correct printer driver appears in the Name text box.
3. Place a check in the Print to File check box (see Figure 12.12).

FIG. 12.12

Place a check in the Print to File check box to create a printer file.

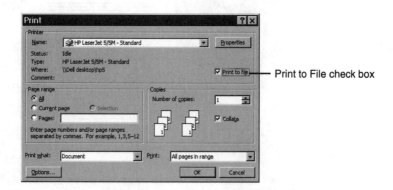

Print to File check box

4. Choose OK. Word displays the Print to File dialog box, which closely resembles the Save As dialog box.

Part
III

Ch
12

5. Supply a name for your printer file; Word automatically assigns an extension of .PRN.

 TIP Use DOS naming conventions—no more than eight characters, and so on, to ensure that the computer receiving this file will be able to read the file name.

6. Choose OK.

To use the file you created, copy it to the computer that is attached to the printer you want to use. If the computer is a DOS-based computer, type the following DOS command at a DOS prompt: **TYPE** *filename* **>PRN**

In this example, filename is the name you assigned in step 5 in the previous list.

Using Print Preview

Print Preview has become much more than just looking at your document before you print it. You also can zoom in and out, view multiple pages at one time, and change margins and other Page Setup features; you even can edit text. Additionally, if you have a document which contains a small amount of text on the last page, you may be able to fit that text onto the previous page using the Shrink to Fit feature.

 To view a document in Print Preview, click the Print Preview button (see Figure 12.13).

FIG. 12.13
This figure shows a document in Print Preview.

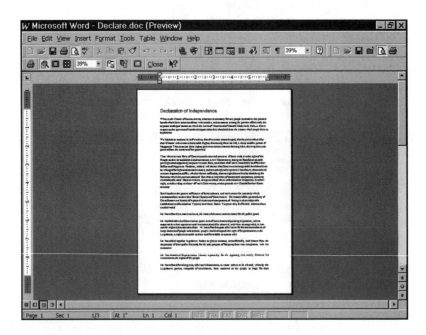

Working in Print Preview

In Print Preview, a document appears the way it will when you print it. But, it is unreadable unless you zoom in and take a closer look. To zoom in, increase the zoom magnification using the Zoom button on the Print Preview toolbar. Decrease the magnification the same way.

 N O T E To quickly zoom to 100% magnification, make sure the Magnifier button is selected and click the page itself. (The mouse pointer will look like a magnifying glass.) To return to your prior magnification, click the page again. ■

You can view more than one page in Print Preview by clicking the Multiple Pages button. When you click this button, Word displays a drop-down graphic; click to select the number of pages you want to view (see Figure 12.14).

FIG. 12.14
Using the Multiple Pages button to view more than one page of a document at a time.

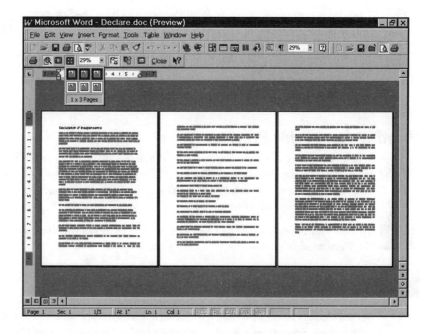

Part

III

Ch

12

 T I P You can quickly return to viewing a single page by clicking the One Page button.

You can edit your document in Print Preview. First, if the Magnifier button is selected, click the page you want to edit. Then, click Magnifier button to cancel its selection and you'll see an insertion point appear on the page. You can start typing and editing. When you finish editing, click the Magnifier button again to enable it.

 N O T E You can change margins while in Print Preview. Use the View Ruler button to make sure that the rulers appear. Then, drag a margin on the ruler—the same way you learned in

continues

continued

Chapter 3, "More Day-to-Day Productivity Tools." By the way, if you want to change margins for only some text, select that text before you drag. ▫

Using Word's Shrink to Fit Feature

If you're working in a fairly small document, and the last page contains a small amount of text, you may be able to use Word's Shrink to Fit feature to condense the document and eliminate the extra page containing the small amount of text.

 T I P This feature works best with small documents like memos or letters.

 To shrink a document, switch to Print Preview and click the Shrink to Fit button. Word reduces proportionately the size of all fonts in the document and attempts to move the text on the last page to the previous page.

N O T E You can undo the effects of shrinking if you click the Undo tool; however, after you save the document, you cannot undo Shrink to Fit. ▫

Printing from Print Preview

 When your document looks the way you want it to look, you can print directly from Print Preview. Just click the Print button. The Print button in Print Preview works just like the Print button on the Standard toolbar; you won't see the Print dialog box because it prints the entire document using default print settings.

 To exit Print Preview, click the Close button or click any of the View buttons at the bottom of the Word window.

 TROUBLESHOOTING

Nothing happens when I try to print a document or envelope. First, make sure that no problem exists with your printer setup in Windows using the Windows Print Troubleshooter. Click the Start button and choose Help. Click the Index tab, and then search for Print Troubleshooting. Click Display, and then follow the instructions in the Windows Print Troubleshooter.

If your Windows printer setup looks correct, check your Word printer settings. Choose File, Print and check the Name text box to make sure that the selected printer matches the printer attached to your computer. Then, make sure that the page range you've selected in the Print dialog box corresponds to the pages you want to print.

Word keeps prompting me to manually feed paper for a letter. You may have the wrong paper tray selected. Choose File, Page Setup, and choose the Paper Source tab. Choose the Default Tray (Auto Select) option for both the First Page and Other Pages.

Text that I print looks different from text on-screen. There are several possibilities:

- Word might be displaying text using draft fonts or printing a draft of your document. Choose Tools, Options, and then click the View tab. Remove the check from the Draft Font check box. This option will be available only if you switch to Normal view before displaying the Options dialog box.

- The font in your document might not be available on the printer you're using or, the font may be available on your printer but no matching screen font exists. Change the font in your document to one that is available on your printer, or change the font to a TrueType font. Available fonts appear in the Font dialog box (choose Format, Font).

- Animated text effects don't print. If text in your document is animated, it will print only with the underlying text formatting.

The Print command on the File menu is gray, indicating that it is not available. First, select a different printer to see whether the command becomes available. If the command is still unavailable, the printer driver may not have been installed properly. Reinstall your printer driver according to the instructions in Microsoft Windows Help. Click the Start button and choose Help. Click the Index tab, and then search for Printer Drivers, Installing.

Text runs off the edge of the page. Make sure that you have selected the correct printer and paper size.

The header or footer is missing or only partially printed. Most printers have a nonprinting area—an area close to the edge of the paper in which text will not print. By making your margins too narrow, you may have placed the text in the nonprinting area of the page. Check your printer manual to see how close to the edge of the paper your printer can print. Then, choose File, Page Setup, and click the Margins tab. In the From Edge box, enter a value that is larger than your printer's minimum margin setting. If Word displays a message stating that a margin is outside the printable area of the page, choose Fix.

I get a blank page at the end of my printed document. You may have created an extra blank page by adding extra paragraph marks (pressing Enter) at the end of your document. Click the Show/Hide button to view nonprinting characters and delete any spare paragraph marks that appear at the end of your document. Then check your document in Print Preview.

If you're printing to a network printer, check the printer for a form feed option. If one exists, turn it off.

I get a Too Many Fonts error message when I print. If you're using TrueType fonts, you may be able to avoid this message by instructing your printer to print TrueType fonts as graphics instead of fonts. Choose File, Print, and then choose Properties. On the Fonts tab, choose Print TrueType as Graphics. If this option doesn't appear, the printer you're using doesn't have this feature and the message from Word is true; you are using more fonts than your printer can handle. Eliminate some fonts from your document and try again.

continues

continued

Even though my envelopes are in a printer tray, Word prompts me to feed envelopes manually.
Switch to another printing tray for Envelopes. Choose Tools, Envelopes and Labels, and click the
Envelopes tab. Choose Options, and choose the Printing Options tab. In the Feed From box, select the
name of the tray you want.

Printing to Fax

You have several different methods available to you to create and send a fax. Word contains a
wizard that will help you create a fax. Word contains four templates you can use as models for
a fax cover sheet. After you create a fax, you can send it the traditional way—print it and place
it in a fax machine—or, if you have a fax/modem, send it via your fax/modem.

A *fax/modem* is an electronic device used to transmit data from one computer to another. A
fax/modem can substitute for a fax machine if the information that you want to send consists of
only the fax cover sheet, or the fax cover sheet and a document stored on your computer. To
use a fax/modem to send a fax, you use software that comes with the fax/modem that helps
you interact with the modem. Typically, the fax/modem comes with such software; two of the
more popular programs are WinFax and QuickLink Fax. As an alternative, you can use the fax
software that comes with Windows 95—Microsoft Fax.

Fax software installs into the Windows environment as a printer. When you finish installing,
check the Windows 95 Printers folder (click the Start button and choose Settings, Printers)
for a new printer listing (see Figure 12.15).

FIG. 12.15
After installing fax
software such as
WinFax, you'll find a new
printer in the Windows
95 Printer folder.

"Why a printer?" you might ask. Well, actually, a printer makes some sense, because both printers and fax/modems are output devices. So, to actually use your fax software in Word, you
print to the fax/modem, as you'll see in just a moment. First, learn how to create a fax cover
sheet in Word.

Using Word Fax Templates

Word provides three different styles of cover sheets. The one you choose is a matter of personal preference. All are artfully designed, and any one of them would represent you well to others. Each of the documents shown in Figures 12.16, 12.17, and 12.18 was created based on templates supplied by Microsoft. Every document that you create in Word is based on a template. Most documents are based on the Normal template, but fax cover sheets are based on one of the three fax templates: Elegant Fax.dot, Contemporary Fax.dot, or Professional Fax.dot.

FIG. 12.16

This figure shows a fax cover sheet in the Elegant style.

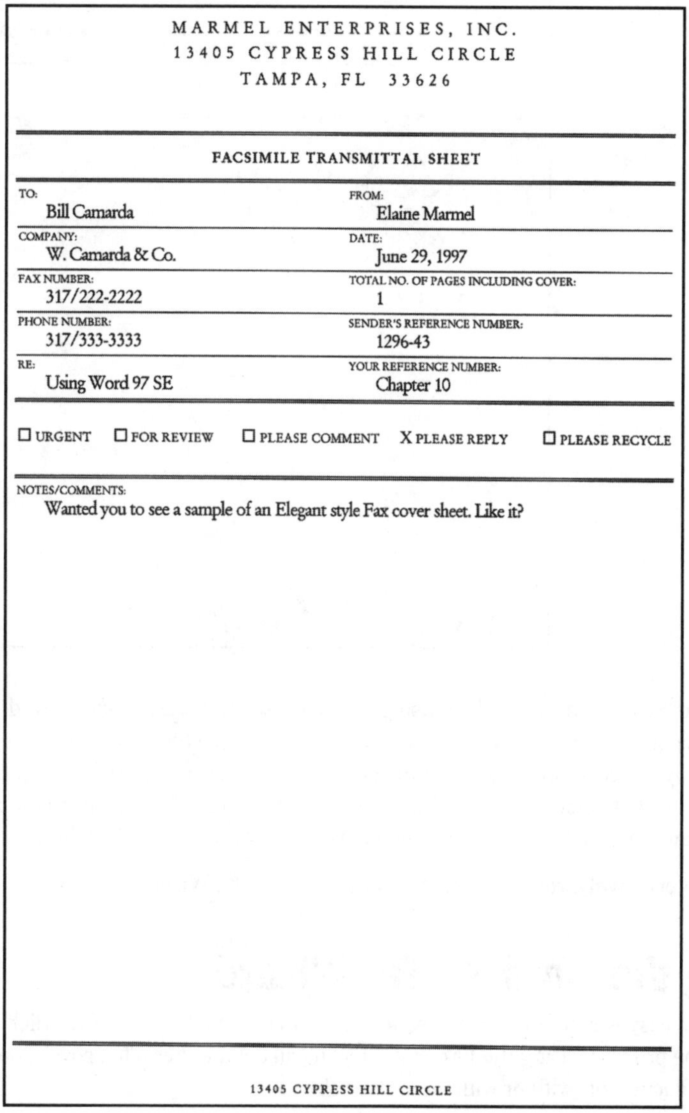

MARMEL ENTERPRISES, INC.
13405 CYPRESS HILL CIRCLE
TAMPA, FL 33626

FACSIMILE TRANSMITTAL SHEET

TO: Bill Camarda	FROM: Elaine Marmel
COMPANY: W. Camarda & Co.	DATE: June 29, 1997
FAX NUMBER: 317/222-2222	TOTAL NO. OF PAGES INCLUDING COVER: 1
PHONE NUMBER: 317/333-3333	SENDER'S REFERENCE NUMBER: 1296-43
RE: Using Word 97 SE	YOUR REFERENCE NUMBER: Chapter 10

☐ URGENT   ☐ FOR REVIEW   ☐ PLEASE COMMENT   X PLEASE REPLY   ☐ PLEASE RECYCLE

NOTES/COMMENTS:
Wanted you to see a sample of an Elegant style Fax cover sheet. Like it?

13405 CYPRESS HILL CIRCLE

Part
III

Ch
12

FIG. 12.17
This figure shows a fax
cover sheet in the
Contemporary style.

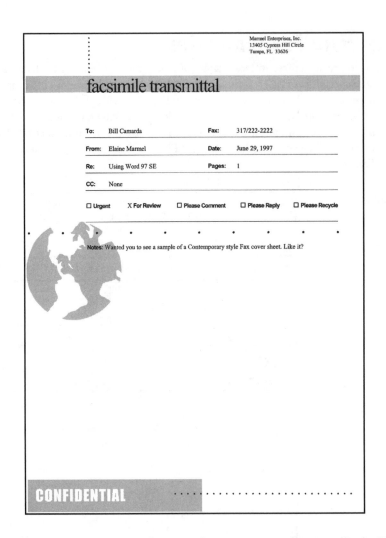

To create a fax cover sheet using one of these templates, start a new document. In the New dialog box, click the Letters & Faxes tab. You'll see the three fax templates; choose one. You may notice several places on the cover sheet that read [Click here and type...]. To move easily between these Click Here blocks, press F11. Word jumps to the next block and selects it. You can then type to replace the instructions with the required information.

Alternatively, you might prefer to use Word's Fax Wizard.

Using the Word 97 Fax Wizard

An easy way to prepare and send a fax is to use the Fax Wizard, which will walk you through the process. Using the Fax Wizard, you can send either a fax cover sheet only or you can send a document (with or without a cover sheet).

FIG. 12.18
This figure shows a fax cover sheet in the Professional style.

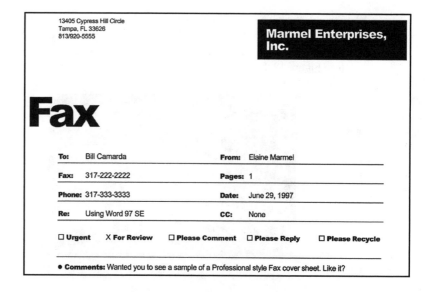

13405 Cypress Hill Circle
Tampa, FL 33626
813/920-5555

Marmel Enterprises, Inc.

Fax

To:	Bill Camarda	**From:**	Elaine Marmel
Fax:	317-222-2222	**Pages:**	1
Phone:	317-333-3333	**Date:**	June 29, 1997
Re:	Using Word 97 SE	**CC:**	None

☐ **Urgent**   X **For Review**   ☐ **Please Comment**   ☐ **Please Reply**   ☐ **Please Recycle**

● **Comments:** Wanted you to see a sample of a Professional style Fax cover sheet. Like it?

N O T E The Fax Wizard will help you create a fax cover sheet. If you also want to send a document, open the document that you want to send. In the steps that follow, you'll notice that the Fax Wizard suggests that you send the open document. Choose that option and continue with the rest of the steps in the section. ▓

To use the Fax Wizard, follow these steps:

1. Choose File, Send To. From the cascading menu that appears, choose Fax Recipient. Word switches to Document 2 and starts the Fax Wizard (see Figure 12.19).

FIG. 12.19
This figure shows the opening screen of the Fax Wizard.

Fax Wizard

- Start
- Document to Fax
- Fax Software
- Recipients
- Cover Sheet
- Sender
- Finish

Fax Wizard

This Wizard helps you create a cover sheet and fax a document to someone.

[?]   Cancel   < Back   Next >   Finish

TIP As with any wizard, you can click any of the choices on the left to go directly to that step, or you can let the wizard walk you through the process from beginning to end.

2. Choose Next. The Fax Wizard asks you what you want to fax. To create a cover sheet, choose Just A Cover Sheet With A Note; to send the open document, choose The Following Document and choose whether to include a cover sheet with the transmission (see Figure 12.20).

FIG. 12.20

Choose whether to include a document with a fax cover sheet or create a cover sheet that contains your message.

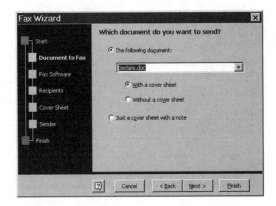

3. Choose Next. On this screen, choose A Different Fax Program Which Is Installed On This System and identify your fax software by selecting the fax printer driver from the list box. If you want to print your fax cover sheet so that you can send it using a fax machine, choose the last option (see Figure 12.21).

FIG. 12.21

Select your fax software using this part of the Fax Wizard.

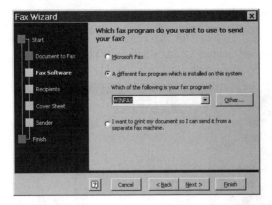

4. Choose Next. Supply the name and fax number for the recipient(s) of the fax (see Figure 12.22). To use an address that you stored in your Microsoft Exchange or Microsoft Outlook address book, click the Address Book button.

5. Choose Next. Choose a style for your fax cover sheet (see Figure 12.23). These are the same styles shown earlier in this chapter, and this box won't appear if you chose not to send a cover sheet in step 2.

6. Choose Next. Supply information about yourself that you want to appear on the fax cover sheet (see Figure 12.24).

FIG. 12.22
Use the Fax Wizard to supply a fax phone number(s) for recipient(s).

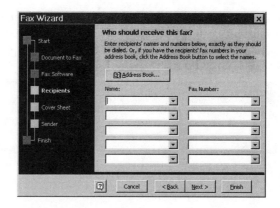

FIG. 12.23
Choose any of the fax cover sheet styles from the choices offered by the wizard.

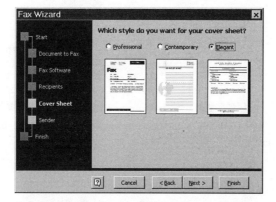

FIG. 12.24
Use the wizard to supply sender information for the fax cover sheet.

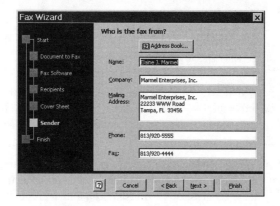

Part
III

Ch
12

TIP If you store your address information in the Options dialog box on the User Information tab, it will appear by default in the Mailing Address text box of the Fax Wizard.

7. Choose <u>N</u>ext. The Fax Wizard displays a final screen that tells you to rerun the Fax Wizard if you don't like the appearance of your cover sheet or if you have trouble faxing.

8. Choose <u>F</u>inish. Your cover sheet appears on-screen (see Figure 12.25).

FIG. 12.25

After you complete the Fax Wizard, your screen will look similar to this one.

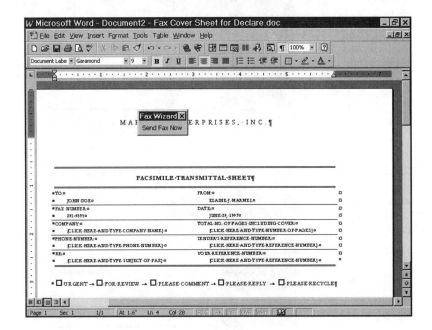

The Office Assistant may appear and explain that you should enter any additional information that you want to appear on the fax cover sheet. As with the Word fax templates, press F11 to move from block to block.

 TIP If you didn't use the Fax Wizard, choose <u>F</u>ile, <u>P</u>rint, change the printer in the <u>N</u>ame text box to the driver installed by your fax software, and click OK.

When you actually send your fax, you'll find that you need to supply, a second time, some of the information you provided to the Fax Wizard. To send your fax, click the Fax Wizard's Send Fax Now button. At this point, your fax software takes control, and you see a dialog box similar to the one in Figure 12.26.

After you choose <u>S</u>end (or OK—whichever appears in the box), Word sends you a message that the Fax Wizard has completed sending the document. Most fax software then displays a status box showing you the progress of the transmission until it is complete.

Using Microsoft Fax

To use Microsoft Fax with Word, you need to first make sure that Microsoft Fax is installed and configured.

FIG. 12.26

You need to supply the minimum information required by your fax software.

To check to see whether Microsoft Fax is already installed, click Start, Programs, Accessories. If you see a folder called Fax, Microsoft Fax is installed and only needs to be configured.

Installing Microsoft Fax

To install Microsoft Fax, follow these steps:

1. Click the Start button and choose Settings, Control Panel.

2. Double-click Add/Remove Programs. When the Add/Remove Programs Properties dialog box appears, click the Windows Setup tab (see Figure 12.27).

3. Place a check in the Microsoft Fax check box, and click the Apply button. One of two things will happen at this point: either Microsoft Fax will be installed, or you will be prompted to insert your Windows 95 setup disk. After you insert the disk and click OK, Microsoft Fax will be installed.

Part

III

Ch

12

FIG. 12.27

Install Windows 95 applets from this tab.

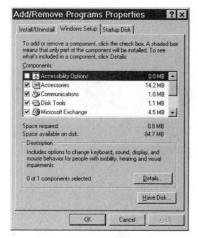

Even if you found Microsoft Fax installed, you may still need to configure it. To configure Microsoft Fax, follow these steps:

1. Click the Start button and choose Settings, Control Panel.

2. Double-click the Mail and Fax icon.

3. Check to see whether Microsoft Fax appears in the list. If it does, highlight it and choose Properties. If it doesn't appear, choose Add.

4. On the User tab, fill in your name and Fax number (see Figure 12.28).

FIG. 12.28

Fill in your name and Fax number. The rest is optional.

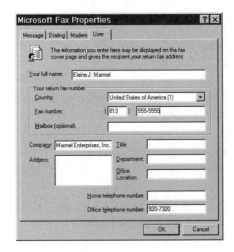

5. On the Message tab, remove the check mark from the Send Cover Page check box (see Figure 12.29).

6. Choose OK twice.

FIG. 12.29

Because you'll be creating your own cover page in Word, you don't want Microsoft Fax to also create a cover page.

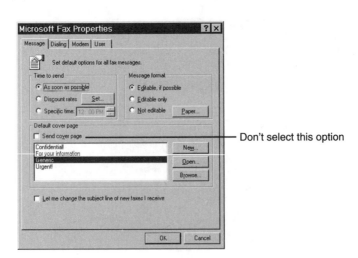

Don't select this option

Most of the process for sending a fax from Word is the same whether you use Microsoft Fax or software supplied with your fax/modem. Here are the differences when you use Microsoft Fax:

■ On the Fax Software dialog box of the Fax Wizard you saw earlier in this chapter (refer to Figure 12.21), choose Microsoft Fax.

■ When you click the Send Fax Now button supplied by the Fax Wizard, you won't see an additional box where you supply information such as the recipient's name and phone number. Microsoft Fax will simply take over and start sending your fax.

■ Microsoft Fax treats each document in Word as a separate fax. Therefore, if you include both a cover sheet and a document when you use the Fax Wizard, Microsoft Fax will place two phone calls when you send your fax.

Word Documents and E-Mail

When you install Word, WordMail is automatically installed. When you send e-mail from inside Word, WordMail delivers the e-mail message to your mail program; from that point, your mail program handles delivering the message.

In Word, you can send a document directly to a recipient, or you can route a document to several recipients in a specified order.

Sending a Document

Suppose that you want to send a memo to a colleague via e-mail instead of printing the memo and sending it via snail mail (a term, probably not particularly appreciated by the U.S. Postal Service, that refers to traditional mail). To e-mail a Word document, follow these steps:

1. Open the document that you want to send.

2. Choose File, Send To. From the subcascading menu, choose Mail Recipient. A WordMail window appears (after a brief delay), and the open document in Word appears as an icon in the message (see Figure 12.30).

NOTE You may be prompted for a Profile depending upon your system configuration. ■

3. Address the mail message as you would address any mail message. Include any additional message text, and format the message the same way you would format any Word document, using fonts, font sizes, character formatting, and so on.

4. Send the message the way that you would send any message in your mail program. The WordMail window closes and your original document reappears. Your mail program takes care of delivering the message.

Part
III

Ch
12

FIG. 12.30
This figure shows a WordMail window containing the opening document.

Routing a Document Through E-Mail

Suppose you have a document that you need to send to several people, and you want each person to review the document and send it on to the next person. Take advantage of Word's Routing Recipient option. Use the steps listed in the last section, but choose, in step 2, Routing Recipient (on the File, Send To menu). If you use this choice, your recipients will find a Next Recipient option on the File, Send To menu when they view your message—and they'll be able to pass the message along simply by choosing this option.

From Here...

In this chapter, you learned about printing, faxing, and sending e-mail in Word.

- Chapter 3, "More Day-to-Day Productivity Tools," provides information Word's Page Setup options that may help you with printing.

- Chapter 10, "Building Your Intranet with Word, Office, and FrontPage," teaches you to build a Web site.

- Chapter 13, "Using Mail Merge Effectively," helps you learn to print multiple envelopes and labels.

- Chapter 23, "Managing Revisions," shows you how to make changes to documents in the online world, letting multiple reviewers revise the same document. Documents can be revised simultaneously by issuing a copy to each reviewer, or sequentially by routing the document through e-mail to the reviewers.

CHAPTER 13

Using Mail Merge Effectively

by Elaine Marmel

Merging is a powerful feature you use to combine information in one Word document with information in another Word document. It is particularly effective when you're sending form letters to a group of people or when you need to create a large number of mailing labels or envelopes addressed to different people, such as a Christmas card list.

You'll see, as you go through this chapter, that merging is more of a step-by-step process than many of the other functions you perform in Word. Starting in the middle of the process could be confusing, so don't be surprised if you find that you want to read this chapter in order. ■

Create a Main document

The Main document of a merge contains the information that won't change as you merge information.

Create a Data Source document

The Data Source document contains the information that will change as you merge information; typically a Data Source document contains name and address information.

Use merge fields

Merge fields allow you to customize a form letter. For example, you can set criteria to include certain information on some letters and different information on other letters.

Merging information

When you merge, you can use all the information in a Data Source document, or only some of the information; in addition, you can sort the merged information.

An Overview of Word's Mail Merge

When you merge information in Word, you use the Mail Merge Helper to combine information contained in two different files. The Mail Merge Helper is similar to a wizard. It prompts you to complete a three-step process:

■ Select or create a Main document

■ Select or create a Data Source document

■ Perform the merge

The Main document contains, primarily, information that doesn't change. If you're creating a form letter, the Main document contains the information that you want repeated in each letter. If you're creating a catalog, the Main document might contain some nonchanging information, such as the word's Item Number.

The Main document also contains *merge fields*. Think of merge fields as titles that represent information, which changes as you merge. Merge fields actually are codes that instruct Word to insert information that changes. On an envelope or a mailing label Main document, typically you'll see only merge fields, and on catalogs, you'll see predominantly merge fields. On form letters, you'll see static information, with merge fields scattered in between the static information.

The Data Source document contains the information that *does* change. For a form letter that you're mailing to a list of people, the Data Source document contains, at a minimum, names and addresses; however, it could also contain other information, depending on the letter that you're sending. For a catalog, the Data Source document contains the item information for each catalog entry. For envelopes and mailing labels, the Data Source document contains predominantly name and address information.

The Data Source document *also* contains merge fields. When you consider the Data Source document, you can think of the merge fields as titles that *identify* each piece of changing information (in the Main document, merge fields *represented* changing information). You can see where this concept is heading; both the Data Source document and the Main document contain a reference to a merge field. A merge field appears on the Main document wherever changing information should appear, and, when you perform a merge, Word uses that merge field to look up, in the Data Source document, the corresponding information and include that information at the appropriate location in the Main document.

There are no set rules about which document you should create first, the Main document or the Data Source document, but there are some schools of thought. This question is similar to, "Which came first, the chicken or the egg?" Because the Data Source document contains the information that will change as you merge, you may have difficulty creating it first because you won't necessarily recognize all the information you need to include in the Data Source document until you have created the Main document. It is recommended that you create a Main document for a merge first, particularly if your Main document will be a form letter.

N O T E When you create a form letter Main document, you might find it easier to first type the letter and substitute placeholders each time you find yourself wanting to use some information that will change from letter to letter. This technique will help you identify the information you need to include in your Data Source document. Later, after you create the Data Source document, you can simply replace the placeholders with the merge fields that represent data stored in the Data Source document. ▪

Creating a Main Document

As you've probably gathered, you can create one of four kinds of Main documents: form letters, envelopes, mailing labels, and catalogs. Main documents contain standardized information—information that won't change after you merge. Main documents also eventually contain merge fields, which are codes that instruct Word to insert information contained the Data Source document.

So what's the difference between the various types of Main documents?

- ▪ When you create a form letter, Word creates a new letter for each set of merge.
- ▪ When you create envelopes, Word creates a new envelope for each set of merge data.
- ▪ When you create labels, Word creates a new label for each set of merge data.
- ▪ When you create a catalog, Word creates *only one* new document that contains all of the merged data. Word repeats any standard text you add to the catalog Main document for each set of data.

N O T E To combine any type of standard text with unique information listed in a separate file, follow the instructions for form letters. You can use this basic process to create legal documents, contracts, and many other types of documents. To print a list of information from a database, such as a parts list or a membership directory, follow the instructions for catalog Main documents. ▪

Creating a Form Letter

To begin building a Main document, follow these steps:

 T I P When you're creating a form letter Main document, you may want to include placeholders in the Main document to help you identify information you'll need to include in your Data Source document later.

1. Choose Tools, Mail Merge. The Mail Merge Helper dialog box appears (see Figure 13.1).
2. Click the Create button to choose a type of Main document to create: Form Letters, Mailing Labels, Envelopes, or Catalog.

Part
III

Ch
13

FIG. 13.1

This figure shows the
Mail Merge Helper.

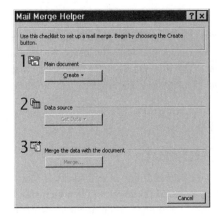

3. Word lets you choose whether you want to create the Main document in the active window or in a new document (see Figure 13.2). If the active window contains a blank document, choose Active Window. Otherwise, choose New Main Document. After you make your choice, Word adds a new button to the Mail Merge Helper: the Edit button.

FIG. 13.2

Use this dialog box to
choose where to create
your Main document.

4. Click Edit and a drop-down list of available Main documents appears.

5. Select Form Letter from the list. Word hides the Mail Merge Helper and displays, instead, a blank document and the Mail Merge toolbar. The buttons that you see on this toolbar will appear available or gray, depending on where you are in the merge process. See Table 13.1 for a list of the buttons on the Mail Merge toolbar and their functions.

6. Type the Main document. Remember that you may want to include placeholders wherever information from the Data Source document will eventually appear. Your letter might look similar to the one in Figure 13.3.

In the figure, you can see placeholders for merge fields; placeholders appear surrounded by square brackets, but you can use any notation you want. You also can see hidden characters such as spaces and paragraph marks; this was deliberate. Notice that the sample Main document includes spacing between placeholders just as if they were regular words and punctuation such as the comma after [City].

N O T E At this point, you can save the Main document; click the Save button and save the document the same way you would save any document. If you need to quit working and want to resume working later, reopen the Main document. To redisplay the Mail Merge Helper, click the Mail Merge Helper button (see Table 13.1). ▨

FIG. 13.3

A sample Main document that includes placeholders for merge fields.

Mail Merge toolbar —

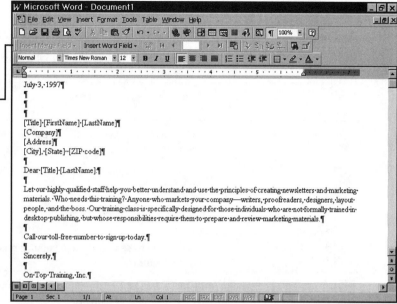

Table 13.1   Mail Merge Buttons

Button	Function
Insert Merge Field ▾	Places a merge field in the Main document
Insert Word Field ▾	Places a Word field in the Main document to customize the document
« » ABC	Enables you to view the Main document while including information from the Data Source document
◄	Enables you to view the Main document while including the first record in the Data Source document
◄	Enables you to view the Main document while including the previous record in the Data Source document
1	Enables you to specify a record in the Data Source document to view in the Main document
►	Enables you to view the Main document while including the next record in the Data Source document
►►	Enables you to view the Main document while including the last record in the Data Source document

Part
III

Ch
13

continues

Table 13.1   Continued

Button	Function
	Opens the Mail Merge Helper dialog box
	Checks the merge for errors
	Performs the merge and places the results in a new document; each merged document makes up a page of the new document
	Performs the merge and prints the resulting merged pages.
	Opens the Merge dialog box
	Enables you to search for a particular record in the Data Source document
	Reopens the Data Form dialog box so you can edit records in the Data Source document

T I P   You can save the Main document and close it (or Word) and return to it at any later time. Just reopen the Main document.

Creating Envelopes, Mailing Labels, or Catalogs

You create an envelope Main document, a mailing label Main document, or a catalog Main document using the same steps you used to create a form letter Main document except that, in Step 2, you choose Envelopes, Mailing Labels, or Catalog. The Main document that appears on-screen will be blank, just like the form letter Main document was blank. You only need to add text to the Main document if you intend to include any unchanging text.

N O T E   You can easily print envelopes or labels to accompany form letters that you create using the Mail Merge Helper. Set up your form letter, create or attach a Data Source document, set your Query Options to filter or sort merged documents, and perform your merge (see later sections in this chapter for help with these tasks). When you have your form letters, reopen the Mail Merge Helper and choose the Main document's Create button. Select either Envelopes or Mailing Labels. Word asks if you want to change the Main document type or if you want to create a new Main document. Choose Change Document Type. Word then asks you to set up the Main document by adding merge fields to it. After you have added merge fields, you can simply merge. Word remembers each of the Query Options you set to filter or sort your merged documents. ■

About Data Sources...

The Data Source document contains merge fields and the information that will change when you merge. When you set up the merge, Word attaches the Data Source document to the Main document; that way, the two documents can share the merge fields. If you create your Data Source document in Word, you'll create a table, and the first line of the table will contain the merge fields. Be aware, however, that you can use a variety of different sources to provide Data Source document information. In fact, you can use any of the following as a Data Source document:

- A Word table
- A Microsoft Outlook Address Book
- A Microsoft Access table or query
- A Microsoft Excel worksheet
- A third-party database

N O T E If you have installed the proper converters, you also can use any of the following file types: ASCII text files, any Word for the Macintosh version 3.0-6.0 file, any Word for DOS 3.0-6.0 file, any Excel version 2.0-8.x file, any WordPerfect version 6.x for Windows or DOS file, or any Lotus 1-2-3 version 2.x-4.x file.

 To attach an existing Data Source document to a mail merge, first make sure you are viewing the Main document. Then, reopen the Mail Merge Helper if it doesn't currently appear on-screen. Choose Get Data and, from the list, choose Open Data Source or Use Address Book (see Figure 13.4).

FIG. 13.4
Select the type of Data Source document you want to attach to your merge.

Part
III

Ch
13

If you choose Open Data Source, you can choose any document type previously listed; if you choose Use Address Book, you'll see the Use Address Book dialog box, from which you can choose an address book to attach to the merge (see Figure 13.5).

FIG. 13.5

Use this dialog box to choose an address book.

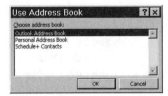

Word 95 shipped with an internal address book called the Personal Address Book, and a tool to access this Personal Address Book appeared on the Standard toolbar. In Word 97, the tool disappeared from the Standard toolbar, but the functionality did not disappear from the program. As you learned in Chapter 12, "Printing, Faxing, and E-Mail," the Personal Address Book is still available for use in the Envelopes and Labels dialog box, and you can merge the names and addresses stored in the Personal Address Book with a form letter or other merge document. Word also lets you use names and addresses stored in address books of other Microsoft products such as Outlook or Schedule+.

Alternatively, you can create a new Data Source document.

 N O T E After you attach a Data Source document to a Main document, you can save both documents and close either or both (you can even close Word) before you finish working. When you're ready to finish setting up the merge, reopen the Main document. The Data Source document should still be attached (redisplay the Mail Merge Helper), but if it isn't, use the Get Data button to open it. ▓

Choosing Categories for the Data Source

If you choose to create your own Data Source document, ask yourself a series of questions to help identify the information you want to store in the Data Source document and how you want to store that information:

1. Do you need to sort your data? For example, you may want to sort mailing labels or envelopes by ZIP Code, particularly if you are preparing a bulk mailing. In this case, be sure to create a separate merge field for the ZIP Code. Do not include the ZIP Code as part of the State merge field.

2. Do some records contain more information than others? For example, are some addresses two lines long while others are only one line long? In these cases, create the Data Source document to accommodate the longest record. You can leave merge fields blank in a Data Source document, and blank merge fields will not necessarily create blank lines in the merge document.

3. Do you need to use similar information in different ways? For example, you may use the recipient's entire name and title in the inside address (for example, Ms. Mary Smith), but, later in the letter, address her directly (for example, Ms. Smith). If you need to use the same information in more than one way, break the information up into separate merge fields; for example, create merge fields for Title, First Name, and Last Name.

4. Do you plan to use the Data Source document with more than one Main document? You might want to use a name and address Data Source document for a form letter and to produce corresponding mailing labels or envelopes. You can selectively choose which fields will be merged into the Main document; therefore, set up a single Data Source document that includes all the information you think you will need for all uses of that Data Source document.

Creating a new Data Source document is usually easiest when you use the Mail Merge Helper. Follow these steps to set up the merge fields that Word will include in the Data Source document:

1. If the Mail Merge Helper dialog box doesn't appear on-screen, display it.

2. Choose Get Data.

3. Choose Create Data Source. The Create Data Source dialog box appears (see Figure 13.6), displaying all merge fields that will, by default, appear in the Data Source document in the Field Names in Header Row list box. Notice that merge fields appear to be titles that represent a type of data.

FIG. 13.6

Use this dialog box to select the merge fields you want to include in your Data Source document.

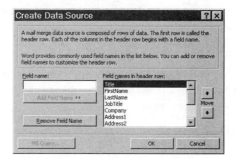

4. To remove a merge field, highlight it in the Field Names in Header Row list box and choose the Remove Field Name button. Notice that any field you remove then becomes available for adding (see the next step).

 TIP The *Header Row* will contain the merge field names. When you create a Data Source document using the Mail Merge Helper, the header row appears as the first row of a Word table.

5. To add a merge field, type it in the Field Name text box and choose the Add Field Name button.

6. To reorder the merge fields in the Data Source document, highlight the merge field you want to move in the Field Names in Header Row list and click a Move arrow repeatedly to move a merge field up or down in the list.

 TIP Reordering merge fields is completely optional. Word inserts the merge field data wherever you specify in the Main document, regardless of the order in which the data appears in the Data Source document.

Part
III

Ch

13

7. Choose OK when you finish defining the merge fields you want to include in the Data Source document.

Word displays the Save As dialog box so that you can save the structure of your Data Source document. Supply a name in the File Name text box and choose Save. Word then presents a dialog box like the one you see Figure 13.7, from which you can decide to edit the Main document or the Data Source document.

FIG. 13.7

Choose whether to edit the Main document or the Data Source document.

Microsoft Word

The data source you just created contains no data records. You can add new records to your data source by choosing the Edit Data Source button, or add merge fields to your main document by choosing the Edit Main Document button.

Edit Data Source   Edit Main Document

Creating a Separate Header Source

Suppose that you are using a Data Source document from some external source, and this Data Source document's first row contains data instead of merge field names. Or, suppose that you use many different Data Source documents that all contain similar information. In cases like these, you may want to create a separate *Header Source* document that you use *along with* a Data Source document. A *Header Source* document is a document that contains *only* the header row (the merge field names) for a Data Source document. If you create a separate Header Source document, you can use it with many different Data Source documents. Of course, you would *not* include a header row in any of the Data Source documents, because the Header Source document will provide the header row.

Keep the following issues in mind when you use a Header Source document along with a Data Source document:

- The number of merge field names in the Header Source document must be equal to the number of data fields in the Data Source document.

- Merge field names in the Header Source document must appear in the same order as the corresponding information in the Data Source document.

- Merge field names in the Header Source document must match the merge field names you have included in the Main document.

To use a Header Source and a Data Source document, make only one change to the procedure of assigning a Data Source document in the Mail Merge Helper dialog box; when you click the Get Data button, first choose Header Options to select a Header Source document. Word shows you a dialog box that lets you either create or open a Header Source document. If you choose Create, you'll see a dialog box that looks and operates like the Create Data Source dialog box (refer to Figure 13.6). If you choose Open, you'll see a dialog box that looks and operates like the Open dialog box and you can navigate to the folder that contains the Header Source document.

After you have attached a Header Source document in the Mail Merge Helper dialog box, choose the Get Data button again, and this time, choose either Create Data Source or Open Data Source. In this way, you'll attach both a Header Source document and a Data Source document to the Main document.

Creating Records in the Data Source

At this point, you have defined the names of the types of changing information you intend to include in the document, but you have not yet provided the actual information. You need to add information to the Data Source document and the easiest way to do that is to use the Data Form dialog box (see Figure 13.8).

 N O T E If you chose Edit Data Source in Figure 13.7, you'll be viewing the Data Form dialog box. If you had to close up shop and you're now coming back and want to add information to the Data Source document, first open the Main document. Then, click the Edit Data Source button. ▪

FIG. 13.8
Use the Data Form dialog box to quickly and easily add information to the Data Source document.

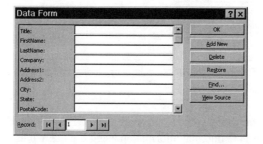

Type the requested information into each text box, pressing Tab to move from text box to text box. If you don't have information for each line, skip that line, but don't include any blank spaces in that line. Don't include punctuation such as a comma after the city because that qualifies as Main document information. That is, you can type it once on the Main document; if you don't type it there, you'll need to type it on *every* entry in the Data Form dialog box, and that's unnecessary extra work.

As you finish an entry (all information about one entry is called a *record*, and each individual piece of information, such as the Title or the Address2, is called a *field*), choose the Add New button to start a new entry. Or, if you have finished entering information, click OK.

 T I P Remember that you can reopen this dialog box at any time to add records by clicking the Edit Data Source button.

Finding Information in Records

 Suppose you made a mistake and want to change a record. Reopen the Edit Data Source dialog box. You can view each record in the Data Source document using the buttons at the bottom of the dialog box (see Figure 13.9).

Part
III

Ch
13

FIG. 13.9

Use these buttons to browse through records in the Data Source document.

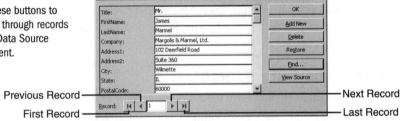

Previous Record ——— 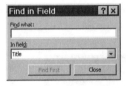 ——— Next Record

First Record ——— Last Record

Alternatively, use the Find button (refer to Figure 13.9) to display the Find in Field dialog box (see Figure 13.10).

FIG. 13.10

Select the field for which you want to search and type the information it should contain.

 T I P You can Open the Find in Field dialog box directly by clicking the Find Record button on the Merge toolbar.

Type the information for which you want to search in the Find What text box, and select the field Word should search to find that information using the In Field list box. Then, choose Find First. After you find the record for which you are searching, you can change the record by simply replacing or adding information to the appropriate field. You can ignore the changes by choosing Restore, or you can delete an entire record by choosing Delete.

T I P You can copy information from one field to another field (even on different records) by using the standard Windows keyboard shortcuts for Copy (Ctrl+C) and Paste (Ctrl+V).

Working Directly with the Data Source

As mentioned earlier in this chapter, when you create a Data Source document in Word, the information in the Data Source document is stored as a Word table, and the first row of the table—also known as the *header record*—contains the merge field names.

If your Data Source document becomes large, you may prefer to simply work in the table instead of using the Data Form dialog box. To see the table, click the View Source button in the Data Form dialog box (refer to Figure 13.9). The Data Source document will appear on-screen (see Figure 13.11).

FIG. 13.11

This figure shows a Data Source document created in Word.

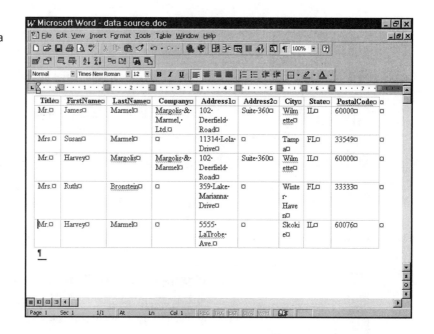

Notice that each row of the table contains all information for one entry (record), and each column of the table contains the information for one field. You edit the Data Source document the same way you would edit any Word table, and you may also notice a special Data Source Document toolbar that contains buttons to help you make changes. See Table 13.2 for a description of these buttons.

 TIP You don't need to worry about the width of the columns. When you use the Data Source document to merge, Word ignores the column widths and inserts the data in the space allotted on the Main document.

Table 13.2 Data Source Document Toolbar

Button	Function
	Displays the Data Form dialog box.
	Displays the Manage Fields dialog box.
	Adds a new row at the bottom of the table for a new record.

continues

Part

III

Ch

13

Table 13.2   Continued

Button	Function
	Deletes the row containing the insertion point.
	Sorts records in the database in alphabetical order (A–Z) based on the field containing the insertion point.
	Sorts records in the database in reverse alphabetical order (Z–A) based on the field containing the insertion point.
	Opens the Database dialog box so that you can replace the information in the Data Source document with information contained in a different Data Source document.
	Updates the information in the database if you inserted the information as fields.
	Displays the Find in Field dialog box discussed earlier in this chapter.
	Redisplays the Main document.

A few of these buttons bear special mention. For example, you can't simply change the name of a merge field in the header record using traditional editing techniques. To change the name of a merge field, click the Manage Fields button. Word will display the Manage Fields dialog box (see Figure 13.12).

FIG. 13.12

Use this dialog box to add, delete, or rename merge fields.

To switch to a different Data Source document, click the Insert Database button to display the Database dialog box (see Figure 13.13).

 After you select a new Data Source document, the other buttons in this dialog box become available. In particular, the meaning of the Update Fields button becomes clearer if you click the Insert Data button in the Database dialog box. Word displays the Insert Data dialog box (see Figure 13.14). Notice the Insert Data As Field check box. Using this box, you can include information in a Data Source document that is not static, but changes as needed, such as a date field. If you choose to include information in the form of a field code, you can select the column containing the field code and click the Update Fields button to refresh the information in the Data Source document.

FIG. 13.13

When you click the
Insert Database button,
you see this dialog box.

FIG. 13.14

Use this dialog box to
insert all or specified
records from the new
Data Source document.

Using Merge Fields

So far, you've read that merge fields appear in both your Main document and your Data Source document. You've seen the merge fields in the Data Source document; they were the titles that appeared in the Data Form dialog box (refer to Figure 13.8), and they also comprised the header row when you viewed the Data Source document in the form of a Word table.

Now, you need to learn how to add merge fields to the Main document so that, when you perform a merge, Word will know where to place merged information.

Inserting Merge Fields

You add merge fields to your Main document wherever you want Word to insert information that changes. To insert a merge field, follow these steps:

1. View the Main document. If you've been viewing the Data Source document, click the Mail Merge Main Document button. If necessary, reopen the Main document.
2. Place the insertion point at the location where you want a merge field to appear.

TIP If you created a form letter and used placeholders, select the first placeholder.

3. Click the Insert Merge Field button. Word displays the merge fields available to your Main document (see Figure 13.15).
4. Click the merge field you want to insert. Word places the merge field in your document at the location of the insertion point.

TIP If you selected a placeholder, Word replaces the placeholder with the merge field.

Part
III

Ch
13

FIG. 13.15

Use this list to insert merge fields.

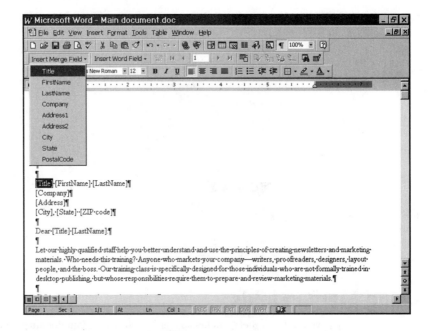

5. Repeat these steps for each merge field you need to place in your document.

6. Save the Main document.

At this point, you could simply perform your merge—particularly if you don't want to customize your merged documents. So, if you're ready to merge, skip to "Preparing to Merge" on p. 392 in this chapter.

Customizing Merged Documents with Word Fields

Sometimes, form letters are form letters; each recipient should see the exact same thing. Sometimes, form letters need to vary slightly. Word Fields give you the opportunity to make your form letters change. Sometimes, you'll want different text to appear, depending on the recipient. Other times, you may want to skip certain recipients altogether without deleting them from the Data Source document. Word Fields provide many ways in which you can customize a merge. To insert any Word Field, place the insertion point in the Main document where you want the field to appear, click the Insert Word Field button (see Figure 13.16), and choose a Word Field.

Word Fields do not apply to form letters only; you can use them on any type of Main document.

FIG. 13.16

This figure shows the available Word Fields.

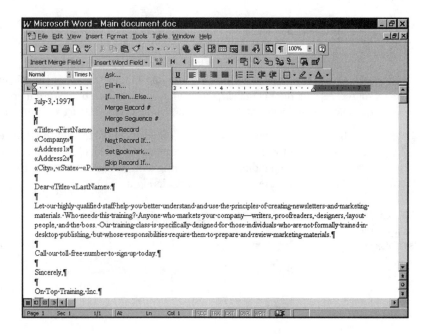

Using the Fill-In Field The Fill-In field displays a prompt so that, during a merge, you can add personal notes to clients or add other information that is not suitable to store in a data source. The Fill-In prompt appears when you start a merge; unless you instruct Word otherwise, the Fill-In prompt appears each time Word merges a new Data Source document record with the Main document; that way, you can enter unique information for each resulting form letter or other merged document. Insert a Fill-In field in the main document where you want to print your response to the prompt.

To create your Fill-In field, choose Fill-In from the Insert Word Field list; you'll see the dialog box shown in Figure 13.17.

FIG. 13.17

Use the Fill-In dialog box to create the Fill-In field.

In the Prompt text box, type the words you want to appear on-screen to prompt you. In the Defaults Fill-In Text text box, type the text you want Word to supply if you don't type anything in the Fill-In text box when it appears. If you place a check in the Ask Once check box, Word asks you for fill-in information only when merging the first data record, but Word prints your response on *all* merged data records.

Part
III

Ch
13

When you start the merge process, Word displays a Fill-In dialog box that prompts you using the information you supplied when you created the Fill-In field.

Using the Ask Field   The Ask field also displays a prompt during the merge so that you can add personal notes to clients or add other information that is not suitable to store in a data source. As with the Fill-In field, the prompt appears each time Word merges a new Data Source document record with the Main document unless you instruct Word otherwise.

So, what's the difference between an Ask field and a Fill-In field? An Ask field uses a bookmark name to represent your response. To create an Ask field, place the insertion point where you want to be prompted for information during a merge and choose Ask from the Insert Word Field list. You'll see the dialog box shown in Figure 13.18.

FIG. 13.18

This figure shows the Ask dialog box.

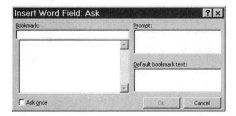

In the Bookmark text box, type the name for the bookmark you want to create in this dialog box; the name can be up to 40 characters long but cannot include spaces. In the Prompt text box, type the text you want Word to display when it prompts you for the bookmark. In the Default Bookmark Text text box, type the information you want Word to include in the Main document when you type nothing in the Ask dialog box that appears when you start the merge process. Remember that the Ask dialog box contains the information you supply when you create the Ask field using the dialog box in Figure 13.17.

If you place a check in the Ask Once check box, Word displays the Ask dialog box only when merging the data for the first record; however, Word prints your response on *all* merged documents.

T I P   The information you supply when you include an Ask field can be used in other fields; for example, if you supply a number as the response to an Ask field, you can later use that number as a basis of comparison in an If...Then...Else field.

Using the If...Then...Else Field   When you click the Insert Word Field button and choose If...Then...Else, Word displays the dialog box you see in Figure 13.19.

The Word Field If...Then...Else is a conditional statement that requires Word to compare some information. That is, Word checks to see if certain conditions exist; if they do, Word performs one set of actions, but if they don't, Word performs a different set of actions. Use If statements to provide Word with one of two alternative actions to perform, depending on a condition you specify.

FIG. 13.19

Use this dialog box to insert an If...Then...Else field into a merge document.

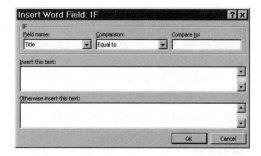

Suppose, for example, that some of your form letters go to recipients in Tampa, while others go to recipients in Orlando. If you're asking your recipient to make an appointment, you may need to provide different phone numbers for Tampa and Orlando residents to call. In this case, you could use an If...Then...Else statement to tell Word which phone number to include if the city is Tampa and which phone number to include if the city is Orlando.

In the Field Name list box, choose the merge field you want Word to use when making the comparison. In the Comparison list box, choose the comparison operator. In the Compare To text box, type the text you want Word to search for in the selected field. In the Insert This Text text box, type the text you want Word to insert if the comparison is true. In the Otherwise Insert This Text text box, type the text you want Word to insert if the comparison is false.

Using the Merge Record # and Merge Sequence # Fields The distinction between the Merge Record # field and the Merge Sequence # field is difficult to understand. When you choose either Merge Record # or Merge Sequence # from the Insert Word Field list, Word inserts a field into the Main document; these two fields are similar in that, after merging, both provide a number on the Main document. The issue at hand is the distinction between the numbers each field provides.

The Merge Sequence # field always starts with 1 and sequentially numbers each successfully merged document. So, if you include a Merge Sequence # field on your Main document and merge five documents, the first contains a 1, the second a 2, and so on.

The Merge Record # field also returns a number, but the number it returns is based on the first record selected from your Data Source document. As you'll learn later in this chapter, you can select to merge only certain records when you perform a merge, and you can sort those records. Suppose, for example, that your Data Source document contained 25 records, but you specifically chose to merge only records 5-10 (ignore sort order for now, to make this easier to understand). If you include a Merge Sequence # and a Merge Record # field on the Main document, the first merged document displays the number 1 for the Merge Sequence # but 5 for the Merge Record #. Similarly, the second merged document displays the number 2 for the Merge Sequence # and 6 for the Merge Record #.

Part

III

Ch

13

Using the Next Record and Next Record If Fields   When you choose Next Record from the Word Field list box, you instruct Word to merge the next data record into the current document, instead of starting a new merged document. The Next Record field produces no printed result. Word automatically uses this field when you set up Mailing Label, Envelope, and Catalog Main documents by using the Mail Merge Helper. The Next Record field is useful to print a specific number of data records in one resulting merge document.

Insert a Next Record field *after* the first set of merge fields in the Main document; otherwise, Word skips merging the first data record. Reinsert the set of merge fields and the Next Record field in the Main document only the number of times it takes to fill one page or to print the number of data records you want.

The Next Record If field is closely related to the Next Record field; when you choose the Next Record If command from the Insert Word Field list, you'll see the dialog box shown in Figure 13.20.

FIG. 13.20

This figure shows the dialog box that appears if you choose Next Record If.

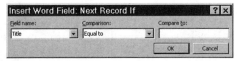

Notice that this dialog box is very similar to the If…Then…Else dialog box. You select the Field Name you want Word to compare, the Comparison operator, and the Compare To text. If the comparison is true, Word merges the next data record into the current document.

Merge fields that follow the Next Record If field in the main document are replaced by values from the next data record rather than the current data record. If the comparison is false, Word merges the next data record into a new merge document.

TIP   Don't use the Next Record If field in the current version of Word. You can select data records more easily by clicking the Query Options button in the Mail Merge Helper dialog box, as you'll learn later in this chapter.

Using the Set Bookmark Field   This Word Field lets you define information and represent it by a specific bookmark name. You can include the bookmark in another field, such as If. When you choose this field from the Word Field list, you'll see the dialog box shown in Figure 13.21.

FIG. 13.21

This figure shows the Insert Word Field: Set dialog box, in which you define bookmarks.

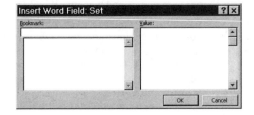

In the Bookmark text box, type the name you want to give to the bookmark. In the Value text box, type the text you want the bookmark to represent. To print the information, you must insert a Ref or Bookmark field in the document or include the bookmark in an Ask or If...Then...Else field.

Using the Skip Record If Field The Skip Record If field works just like the Next Record If field, except it lets you skip the current record if the comparison is true. If you choose Skip Record If from the Insert Word Field list box, you'll see the dialog box shown in Figure 13.22.

FIG. 13.22
This figure shows the dialog box that appears if you choose Skip Record If.

TIP Don't use the Skip Record If field in the current version of Word because you can select data records more easily using the Query Options dialog box available through the Mail Merge Helper. Also, don't use the Skip Records If field with the Next Record field.

Including Other Types of Fields

The Mail Merge Helper toolbar supplies most of the fields you'll need when you're creating a merge, but there are a few, less common fields that you can use in a merge. You can see these fields if you choose Insert, Field and highlight Mail Merge in the Categories list (see Figure 13.23).

FIG. 13.23
The Mail Merge fields available through the Fields dialog box.

You'll notice that some of the fields that appear in the Field Names list seem familiar and they are the same as the fields we just discussed in the previous section. For example, the Next Record Word Field performs exactly the same function as the Next field you see in the Field dialog box.

You will notice, however, some additional fields in the Field dialog box that didn't appear in the Word Field list. Specifically, you'll see these fields:

- Compare
- Database
- MergeField

When you use the Compare field, Word looks at two values and displays the result 1 if the comparison is true or 0 (zero) if the comparison is false.

The Database field helps you insert the results of a query to an external database in a Word table. The Database field contains all the information needed to connect to a database and perform a Structured Query Language (SQL) query. You update the field to query the database again. The Insert Database button (discussed earlier in this chapter when you viewed the Data Source document) inserts a Database field.

The MergeField field is a field you use automatically when you use the Mail Merge Helper. It is the field that tells Word to display merge fields inside the symbols you see in Figure 13.24.

FIG. 13.24

The MergeField field causes merge fields to display inside these symbols in a Main document.

MergeField field symbols

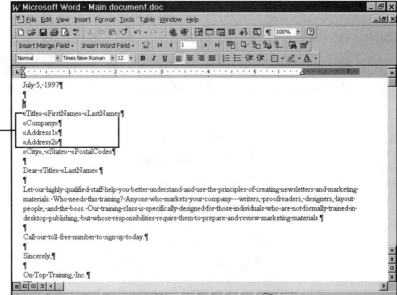

Preparing to Merge

After you set up a Main document and Data Source document, and place merge fields in the Main document, you are ready to merge the Main document with the Data Source document.

As you learned earlier in this chapter, you can select records to merge instead of merging all records that exist in the Data Source document.

Also, as a part of the merge process, you can choose whether to merge to your printer or to a new document, which will include page breaks for each merged record. You also can send the merge documents via e-mail or fax.

Choosing the Records to Merge

You might think that you have to create a merged document for each record that appears in the Data Source document, but you don't. You can specify records to merge, or you can set up filtering criteria to select records that match your criteria.

 For example, suppose you know that you want to merge the 5th through the 10th records from the Data Source document. Click the Mail Merge button to display the dialog box shown in Figure 13.25.

FIG. 13.25

Select specific records to merge using this dialog box.

In the Records to be Merged text box, type record numbers into the text boxes.

If you need to set filtering criteria, click the Query Options button to display the dialog box you see in Figure 13.26.

FIG. 13.26

Use the Filter Records tab to specify criteria for Word to use when selecting records to merge.

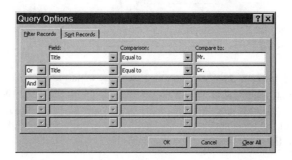

Select a Field, a Comparison operator, and type Compare To text. For example, to send letters only to men, select the Title field, the Equals (=) comparison operator, and type **Mr.** in the Compare To text box.

Part
III

Ch
13

To include men and doctors, add a second line to the Filter criteria that is set up the same way, only type Dr. instead of Mr. In the Compare To text box. You'll notice an additional list box at the beginning of the second line, and it contains only two choices: Or and And. These are logical operators, so use them carefully. For example, to send letters to men *and* doctors, set the logical operator to Or (not And). In our example, setting the logical operator to Or tells Word to look for and include in the merge any record that contains either Mr. or Dr. in the Title field. Further, in our example, setting the logical operator to And would mean that the Title field must contain *both* Mr. *and* Dr.—a condition that would never be met.

Sorting Merged Records

You may also decide that you want to produce your merged documents in a specific order. For example, to meet bulk mailing standards for the U.S. Postal Service, you must bundle letters going to the same ZIP Code; if you produce your merged documents in ZIP Code order, you'll save yourself some effort.

 To set a sort order for your merge, use the Sort Records tab of the Query Options dialog box. Click the Mail Merge button and, in the Merge dialog box, click the Query Options button. When the Query Options dialog box appears, choose the Sort Records tab (see Figure 13.27).

FIG. 13.27
Set the sort order for a merge in this dialog box.

Open the Sort By list box and choose a merge field by which to sort. Also select Ascending or Descending. If you want to set a tie-breaker sort field, set up the Then By list box the same way you set up the Sort By list box. Word uses the tie-breaker sort field if it finds two or more records that meet the first criteria you specify. So, for example, you might sort your letters first by ZIP Code and then alphabetically by last name.

 T I P   Optionally, you can set more then one "tie-breaker" sort field.

Previewing Your Mail Merge

 Before you actually merge, you can preview your merge document on-screen by clicking the View Merged Data button on the Mail Merge toolbar in the Main document. When you click this button, Word replaces the merge fields in the Main document with the first record in the Data Source document that meets your Query Options criteria (see Figure 13.28).

FIG. 13.28

You can preview merged documents before actually merging.

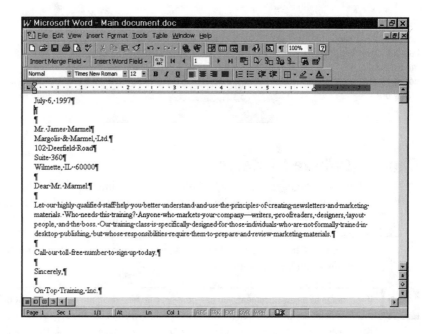

 Use the buttons immediately to the right of the View Merged Data button to change the record you are previewing. Previewing a merge is particularly effective if you have a large merge to perform; previewing can save you significant time if you notice an error that you can quickly correct before merging.

TIP Click the View Merged Data button again to resume viewing merge fields.

Handling Blank Lines

When you learned about creating a Data Source document, it was suggested that you set up the Data Source document to accommodate the longest record you may have. So, in a Data Source document that contains names and addresses, some records may be three lines long, some may be four lines long, and some may be five lines long. Naturally, when you merge, you don't want Word to leave blank lines where you didn't provide information in the Data Source document.

 To control the way Word handles blank lines, use the Merge dialog box. Click the Mail Merge button on the Mail Merge toolbar in the Main document. The Merge dialog box appears (see Figure 13.29).

In the When Merging Records box, choose one of the option buttons to determine whether Word will print or suppress blank lines Word encounters in the Data Source document.

Part

III

Ch

13

FIG. 13.29
Control the way Word handles blank lines in the Data Source document using this dialog box.

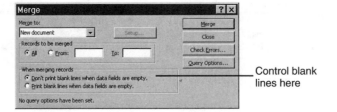

Control blank lines here

Choosing Where to Merge

When you merge, you can merge directly to your printer or you can have Word stored all merged information in a new document. If you merge to a new document, Word inserts page breaks after merging each record from the Data Source document. From the Mail Merge toolbar in the Main document, choose the Merge to Printer button or the Merge to New Document button. Choosing either button makes the merge take place immediately using any special criteria you have already set up.

TIP If you merge to a new document, you can print specific records in the new document by placing the insertion point anywhere on that page, choosing File, Print, and use the Pages box to select the merged documents you want to print. See Chapter 12, "Printing, Faxing, and E-Mail," for more information.

Special Considerations for Broadcast E-Mail or Fax

If your computer contains a MAPI-compatible e-mail or fax program, you can use the Mail Merge Helper to create broadcast e-mail or broadcast faxes.

NOTE MAPI stands for Messaging Application Programming Interface and it's a standard used in the computer industry for e-mail and fax programs. Microsoft Schedule+, Microsoft Fax, Microsoft Outlook, and Microsoft Exchange Server conform to the MAPI standard. ■

To successfully merge to either e-mail addresses or fax numbers, you must include them as merge fields in the Data Source document. You do *not* need to include these merge fields on your Main document.

To merge to either e-mail or broadcast fax, follow these steps:

1. Open the Query Options dialog box (see Figure 13.30) and, on the Filter tab, set up a filter criteria that uses the e-mail addresses or the fax numbers in the Field box and, in the Comparison list box, choose Is Not Blank.

TIP To open the Query Options dialog box, click the Mail Merge button. Then, click the Query Options button and choose the Filter Records tab.

FIG. 13.30

Set up a filter criterion statement that specifies that the field containing the e-mail address or the fax number is not blank.

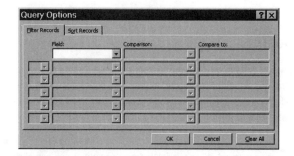

2. Choose OK to redisplay the Merge dialog box.

3. Open the Merge To list box and choose either Electronic Mail or Electronic Fax (see Figure 13.31).

FIG. 13.31

To distribute merged documents via e-mail or broadcast fax, select the appropriate location in the Merge dialog box.

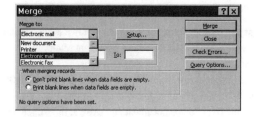

4. Click the Setup button. The Merge to Setup dialog box appears (see Figure 13.32).

FIG. 13.32

Use this dialog box to identify the field containing the electronic address and to specify a subject line for the broadcast.

T I P For e-mail documents, place a check in the Send Document as an Attachment check box to preserve its formatting; otherwise, Word inserts the text into an e-mail message.

5. Choose OK to redisplay the Merge dialog box.

6. Choose Merge.

Part

III

Ch

13

TROUBLESHOOTING

Merge fields are printing instead of information from the Data Source document. Why, and how can I fix this problem? Your Print options are set to print field codes instead of field results. Choose Tools, Options, and click the Print tab. Then, remove the check from the Field Codes check box in the Include with Document section.

Also, be sure that you don't click the Print button on the Standard toolbar unless you have first merged your information to a new document. While viewing the new document, you can click the Print button on the Standard toolbar.

 I don't want to use a Main document as a Mail Merge Main document anymore, but Word keeps prompting me to locate a data source. Can I convert a Main document to a non-Mail Merge document? Yes. In the Main document, open the Mail Merge Helper. Choose the Create button, and then choose Restore to Normal Word Document.

I keep getting a message saying that my Data Source document is a Main document. Why? How do I fix it? In your case, you were viewing the Data Source document when you reopened the Mail Merge Helper, so your Data Source document was accidentally chosen as the Main document. Your problem is solved in the same way the previous problem was solved. Switch to the Data Source document and follow the procedure described previously to convert the Data Source document to a Normal Word document. Save the Data Source document and close it. Then, open the document you want to use as a Main document, use the Mail Merge Helper to create the Main document, and then attach the Data Source document using the Get Data button in the Mail Merge Helper dialog box.

How can I make the formatting for merged information appear differently when it is merged? Merged information takes on the formatting of the merge field in the Main document; any formatting you apply in the Data Source document will be ignored. Format your merge fields in the Main document to make merged data appear the way you want.

I bought a new printer, so I've changed the size of the envelopes and labels I use. How do I fix my Envelope and Mailing Labels Main documents? You can adjust an Envelope Main document, but you cannot adjust a Mailing Labels Main document. To solve the problem for the Mailing Labels Main document, create a new Mailing Labels Main document.

To adjust the envelope for your Envelope Main document, choose Tools, Envelopes and Labels, and choose the Options button to set up the new envelope. When you do your merge, Word uses the new envelope settings.

I've created mail merges in prior versions of Word. Can I use them? Do I need to do anything special? You automatically can use Main documents you created in Word 95 (Word 7.0). If the Main documents are attached to Data Source documents, you also can use Main documents created in Word 6 for Windows and Word 2 for Windows. If the Main documents contain a DATA field that identifies the Data Source document, you also can use Main documents created in Word 1 for Windows. Last, if the Main documents contain a DATA instruction that identifies the Data Source document, you can use Main documents from Word for the Macintosh or Word for MS-DOS.

From Here...

In this chapter, you learned how to prepare Mail Merge documents, which combine information contained in two different documents: a Main document and a Data Source document.

- Chapter 5, "Styles: The Foundation of Automated Documents," provides information on a powerful way to make formatting consistent and easy.

- Chapter 7, "Automating Your Documents: AutoCorrect, AutoFormat, AutoText, and AutoSummarize," shows you additional ways to automate your work in Word.

- Chapter 18, "Footnotes, Bookmarks, Cross-References, and Hyperlinks," teaches you to use one of Word's more powerful features for storing and reusing information, and bookmarks can be used when merging.

- Chapter 25, "Automating Your Documents with Field Codes," shows you how-to information that automatically updates itself, such as dates and page counts. Understanding field codes may help you better understand some of the more advanced merging techniques.

Part

III

Ch

13

The Big Document: Powerful Tools and Strategies

CHAPTER 14

Outlining: The Best Way to Organize a Document

by Bill Camarda

After you understand just a few basic concepts, you'll find Word's outlining feature remarkably easy to use and extraordinarily powerful. Outlining gives you a quick and convenient way to organize (and reorganize) any document. The larger your documents, the more valuable you will find the organizing capabilities that outlining provides. With outlining, it's easy to view your document at a very high level, and then drill down to any specific element that needs attention. You can see the forest *and* the trees.

Outlining works with the heading styles you already have—or, if you haven't applied heading styles, Word can do it for you automatically, while you work on your outline. As you've already learned, once your heading styles are in place, you can use them to automate many Word features. In this chapter, you'll discover one of the best of those automated features: Word's simple, quick Outline Numbering feature. You'll learn how Word can instantly number all your headings and subheads—and *keep* them numbered properly, come what may. ■

Creating a new outline

You can create a new outline in Outline view, or you can just use Heading styles and let Word do it for you.

Using the Outlining toolbar

Get to know the Outlining toolbar—and Word's quick keyboard shortcuts for outlining, too.

Adding, promoting, and demoting headings

Word streamlines outline-building by making it easy to change the relative importance of headings.

Moving paragraphs within an outline

Outline view is the best place to move large chunks of a document around.

Controlling how you view your outline

You can view your outline at the highest level, or zoom in to examine specific sections.

Using Word's automatic outline numbering

Never manually keep track of heading numbers again; Word can do it for you—automatically.

Creating a New Outline

An outline is embedded in every document you create, but unless you deliberately look for it, you might never realize that because Word treats an outline as just another way to view a document. This means you don't have to actively *create* an outline to *get* one. It also means that when you *do* want a polished outline, you can simply refine the one that's already built into your document.

 There are two ways to create an outline. The first is to work from scratch. Open a new blank document, and click the Outline View button to display it in Outline view (see Figure 14.1).

FIG. 14.1
When you display a blank document in Outline view, an "outlined" minus sign appears.

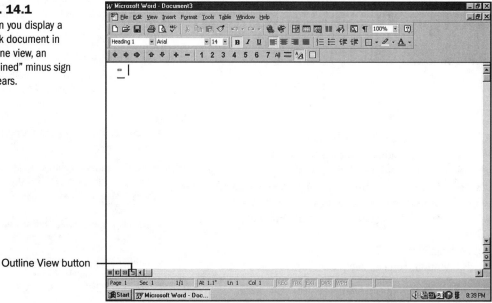

Outline View button

You can create an outline from scratch if you're starting a major new project, such as a book or manual, and you don't yet have any text. Working from scratch is convenient because you don't have to worry about moving existing blocks of text or reorganizing material that should have been handled differently from the outset. You can organize the document the best way right from the beginning. If you're leading a team of writers, you can divide your outline into sections and delegate each part.

 TIP   With Word's closely-related Master Documents feature, you can divide the document into subdocuments, assign each subdocument to a different writer, and then edit and manage all the subdocuments *together*, as if they were still part of one longer document.

▶ **See** "Creating a New Master Document," **p. 433**

TIP Use Outline view in connection with Word 97's Track Changes and Versions tools to streamline the process of getting your outline approved.

The second way to create an outline is to do nothing at all. Work as you normally do, and apply heading styles as part of the formatting you would ordinarily be doing. Then, whenever you're ready, switch to Outline view; Word displays your existing document as an outline. Figure 14.2 shows a typical document displayed as an outline.

FIG. 14.2
Whenever you're ready, click the Outline View button to display your document as an outline.

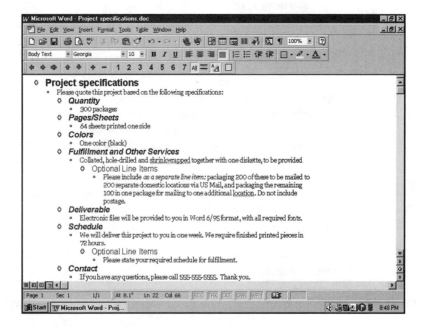

 TIP If you want the organizational benefits of outlining but you don't like the appearance of Word's Heading styles, you can change them:

Format a paragraph using one of Word's built-in Heading styles.

1. Manually reformat the paragraph.

2. Click the Style drop-down list box on the Formatting toolbar.

3. Press Enter. The Modify Style dialog box opens.

4. Make sure the Update the Style to Reflect Recent Changes button is selected, and click OK.

Your style changes will be reflected in all views, including Outline view. Repeat the process for each heading you intend to use.

▶ **See** "Applying an Existing Style," **p. 145**

Part
IV

Ch
14

Soon, you'll learn techniques for polishing your outline to make sure your document is actually structured the way you want. First, however, there are three things you'll notice about Outline view right away:

- *Each paragraph has a symbol to its left.* These symbols tell you what you need to know about the paragraph's relationship to surrounding text:

  - *A plus sign (+)* tells you there is text subordinate to the paragraph. This may be lower-level headings, paragraphs formatted in styles that Word does not recognize as a heading or outline level, or both.

  - *A minus sign (-)* tells you there is no text subordinate to the paragraph. In other words, the paragraph has a heading style or outline level, but no subheads or body text are beneath it.

  - *A small square* tells you the paragraph is body text.

- *Paragraph formatting such as indents and line spacing disappears.* In fact, Word grays out the Format, Paragraph menu command, so you can't use it to add new paragraph formatting. In its place, Word displays its own outline indenting to make it obvious which paragraphs are most important (for example, which appear at the highest level of your outline) and which are subordinate.

 TIP You can, however, use keyboard shortcuts for indenting. (The indents won't be visible until you switch out of Normal view.) You can also right-click to access a shortcut menu that includes some formatting controls (see Figure 14.3).

- The Outlining toolbar appears. This toolbar contains all the tools you'll need to edit and manage your outline.

FIG. 14.3

Right-click anywhere in Outline view to see a shortcut menu that provides indentation, font formatting, and bullets and numbering options.

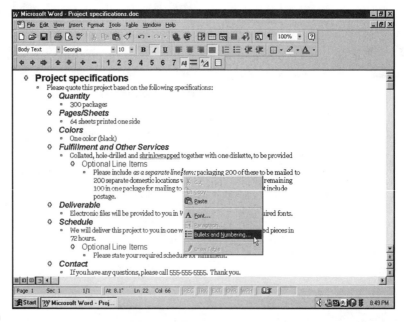

TIP You can switch back and forth between views at any time. You might use Outline view whenever you're organizing your document, Normal view when you're editing content, and Page Layout view whenever you're primarily concerned about graphics and the appearance of your pages.

If you're working in Normal view and you decide to change a heading level, you might want to switch into Outline view right then and there so you can quickly change all the subordinate headings at the same time.

Using the Outlining Toolbar

Take a closer look at the Outlining toolbar (see Figure 14.4) which includes Word's tools for organizing and managing your outline. These buttons fall into the following three categories:

- Tools for increasing or decreasing the relative importance of paragraphs (Promote, Demote, and Demote to Body Text)
- Tools for moving paragraphs up or down in the document (Move Up, Move Down)
- Tools for controlling which paragraphs display and how they look (Expand, Collapse, Show Heading 1 through 7, Show All Headings, Show First Line Only, and Show Formatting)

 N O T E Clicking the Master Document View button at the right edge of the Outlining toolbar displays Word's Master Document controls. ▪

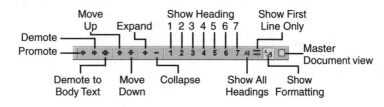

FIG. 14.4
The Outlining toolbar appears only when you are working in Outline view; you can't display it anywhere else.

By now, you won't be surprised to hear that nearly all of these buttons have a keyboard shortcut equivalent, as listed in Table 14.1.

TIP The Promote, Demote, Demote to Body Text, Move Up, and Move Down keyboard shortcuts work in every view, not just Outline view. There's no quicker way to change heading styles or move paragraphs!

Part
IV

Ch
14

Table 14.1   Keyboard and Toolbar Shortcuts for Working in Outline View

Task	Keyboard Shortcut	Toolbar Button
Promote paragraph	Alt+Shift+left arrow	⬅
Demote paragraph	Alt+Shift+right arrow	➡
Demote to body text	Ctrl+Shift+N	➡
Move selected paragraph(s) up	Alt+Shift+up arrow	⬆
Move selected paragraph(s) down	Alt+Shift+down arrow	⬇
Expand text beneath heading	Alt+Shift+plus sign	➕
Collapse text beneath heading	Alt+Shift+minus sign	➖
Expand/collapse all text or headings	Alt+Shift+A	All
Toggle character formatting	/ (on numeric keypad)	ᴬ𝐀
Toggle to display only first line of body text	Alt+Shift+L	=
Show only Level 1 headings/text	Alt+Shift+1	1
Show all Levels through	Alt+Shift+[# from 1 to 7]	1 7

It's helpful to understand what the Outlining toolbar buttons and symbols don't do, so you won't make the common mistakes that trip up many first-time outliners:

■ The right arrow button does not insert a tab, even though it looks as if it might. It does indent text much like a tab does. *Remember: the right arrow key demotes a paragraph by one heading or outline level.*

■ The numbered buttons do not specify heading or outline levels. *They simply control how many levels you can see at the same time.*

- The plus and minus buttons do not increase or decrease the importance of selected text. *Rather, they hide or display all the subordinate text and headings beneath the paragraph you've chosen.*

   Similarly, the plus and minus symbols next to each paragraph say nothing about the heading level associated with the paragraph. *All they tell you is whether the paragraph has text subordinate to it.* It's common to have two headings next to each other, both formatted in the same style, but one adorned with a plus sign and the other a minus sign.

Adding New Subheadings

Now that you've taken a tour of Word's outlining tools, it's time to start using them. If you open a blank document and switch to Outline view, Word displays a minus sign to the left of your text. This indicates that, for the moment at least, no text is subordinate to the line in which you are working.

If you start typing the first line of an outline, Word formats your text as a first-level heading, using the Heading 1 style. If you finish your paragraph and press enter to start a new one, Word creates a new paragraph, also with the Heading 1 style. You can see this in Figure 14.5.

FIG. 14.5

If you press Enter after creating a first-level heading in Outline view, Word starts another first-level heading.

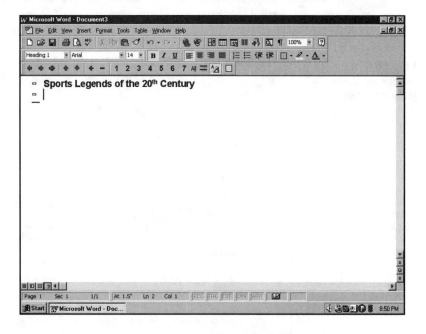

N O T E In this respect, Word behaves differently in Outline view than in other views. Elsewhere in Word, if you press Enter to create a new paragraph after a heading, Word assumes you want to create Normal text—text formatted with the Normal style. (That's what Word's built-in Heading style settings tell it to do.) However, people rarely create text in Outline view, so Word assumes instead that you're creating another heading like the one you've just finished. ■

Part

IV

Ch

14

Promoting and Demoting Headings

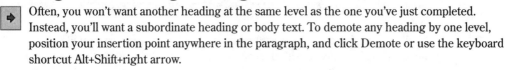

Often, you won't want another heading at the same level as the one you've just completed. Instead, you'll want a subordinate heading or body text. To demote any heading by one level, position your insertion point anywhere in the paragraph, and click Demote or use the keyboard shortcut Alt+Shift+right arrow.

When you demote a heading, Word indents it, and also changes the heading style. For example, if you demote a first-level heading, Word changes the style associated with it to Heading 2. If the heading contains text, you'll also see the character formatting change to reflect the new style.

Of course, you can promote subordinate headings as well; click the Promote button or Alt+Shift+Left Arrow. Again, Word changes the style and formatting as well as the indentation.

Dragging Headings with the Mouse

You can also drag a heading to a new level. Click the outline symbol next to it; your mouse pointer changes to crosshairs and Word selects the heading and its subordinate contents. Then drag the mouse to the right. The mouse pointer changes to horizontal double-arrows, and you'll see a gray vertical line that moves as you jump from one heading level to the next (see Figure 14.6). When you've arrived at the heading level you want, release the mouse pointer.

FIG. 14.6
You can drag a paragraph left or right to a new heading level.

Vertical line indicates level where selected text is being moved

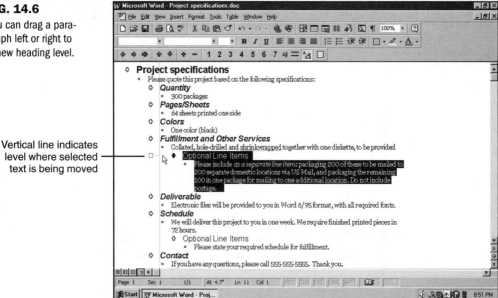

TIP If you want to move a heading by several levels, it's often quicker to change the style instead. For example, to move a heading from second to sixth level, choose Heading 6 in the Style drop-down list box.

Demoting Text to Body Text

To demote any heading to body text, click Demote to Body Text or press Ctrl+Shift+N. Word reformats that text in the Normal style, and displays the small square Body Text symbol next to it. When you finish a paragraph of body text, you can start a new one by pressing Enter; another Body Text symbol appears to the left of the new paragraph.

 TIP You probably won't want to edit your whole document in Outline view, but you might have some ideas you'd like to jot down while you're organizing a new document in Outline view. Click Demote to Body Text in a new paragraph and start typing.

N O T E Some people format all body text using Word's Body Text style instead of the Normal style. In fact, Word often makes this change automatically when you run AutoFormat. Unfortunately, Normal and Body Text are two different styles. In particular, Body Text adds 6 points of space after each paragraph, and Normal does not. As a result, you may inadvertently introduce small formatting inconsistencies into your document if you use Demote to Body Text.

Demote to Body Text doesn't demote to the Body Text *style*. It does, however, demote to the Body Text *outline level*. You'll learn about the distinction later in this chapter.

If any of this bothers you, spend five minutes recording a quick macro that replaces the Normal style with the Body Text style throughout your document.

Promoting or Demoting Several Headings at the Same Time

If you select one heading and promote or demote it, nothing changes elsewhere in your document. That might be just fine with you. However, when you promote or demote a heading, you'll often want all your subordinate headings to be carried along with it.

Word makes this easy to do. Instead of selecting the paragraph, click the outline symbol next to it. This selects both the current paragraph and all the paragraphs subordinate to it. In Figure 14.7, you can see a first-level heading that has been selected along with the second and third-level headings and body text beneath it.

Figure 14.8 shows what happens after you click Demote. The first-level head is now a second-level head; the second-level head is now a third-level head, and so on. Text formatted in non-heading styles does not change, however. To transform body text into a heading, you have to select it and promote it.

 TIP You can select and promote several consecutive paragraphs of body text at the same time, as long as your selection doesn't contain any headings.

Part
IV

Ch
14

FIG. 14.7

Clicking the outline symbol next to a paragraph selects the paragraph and all the subordinate headings and body text beneath it.

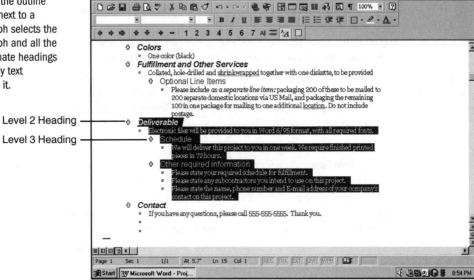

Level 2 Heading

Level 3 Heading

FIG. 14.8

After you click Demote, all the selected heading levels are demoted, but text formatted with other styles does not change.

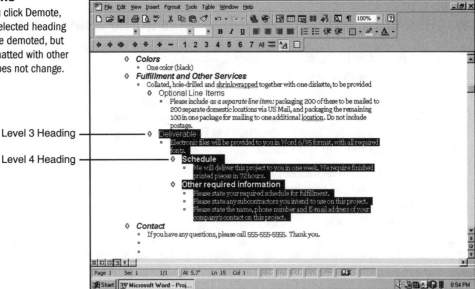

Level 3 Heading

Level 4 Heading

Moving Paragraphs Within an Outline

As you organize your outline, you might find a heading or a block of text that you would like to move toward the front or rear of the document. Word's Cut and Paste tools work within Outline view. However, if you are simply moving a heading or text by one (or a few) paragraphs, there's a quicker alternative.

 Place your insertion point in the paragraph you want to move, and click the Move Up or Move Down button on the Outlining toolbar. The entire paragraph moves. If you want to move more than one paragraph, select them before clicking Move Up or Move Down.

If you're moving text further than a paragraph or two, there's a quicker solution: drag and drop it. Click the Outline symbol next to a paragraph. Your mouse pointer changes to a crosshair. Drag the mouse up or down. The pointer changes to a vertical double-arrow, and a gray vertical line appears, moving as you jump from one paragraph to the next (see Figure 14.9). When you've arrived at the location you want, release the mouse pointer.

FIG. 14.9

Dragging text up or down in a document.

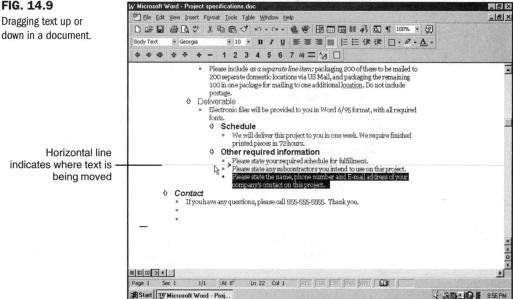

Horizontal line indicates where text is being moved

TIP The technique you've just learned works if you're moving just one paragraph (and its subordinate contents). However, what if you want to move *several* consecutive paragraphs that all share the same heading level?

1. Select all the paragraphs.
2. Press Alt and click the Outline symbol next to the first paragraph.
3. Drag the paragraphs to their new location.

Part
IV

Ch
14

Controlling Your Outline View

You've already heard that Word's outlines allow you to "view the forest and the trees." In fact, you can control the exact level of detail you view at any time. It's as if you could not only view the forest or the trees, but also specific leaves, branches, trunks, individual trees, or groups of trees as well.

Displaying Only Selected Heading Levels

Imagine you're reviewing a complex document with several levels of headings. You might want to start by looking at the document at a very high level—viewing only first-level headings. Click the Show Heading 1 on the Outlining toolbar, and Word hides all paragraphs except those formatted as first-level headings (see Figure 14.10). The gray underlining beneath some of these headings tells you there is subordinate text you aren't seeing.

FIG. 14.10

A document showing only first-level headings.

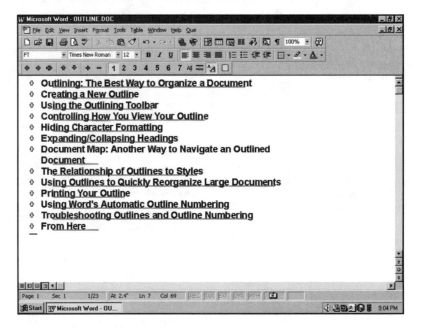

After you're satisfied with the high-level organization of the document, you can drill deeper; click the Show Heading 2 button to view both first-level and second-level headings, click 3 to view the first three levels of heading, and so on.

TIP

Displaying only one or two levels of headings can make it much easier to find a distant location in a large document. After you find it, you can click its heading and start editing there—in Outline view or any other view you choose.

TIP

Word supports nine outline levels, but the Outlining toolbar doesn't contain Show Heading 8 or Show Heading 9 buttons. To display eighth-level headings, press Alt+Shift+*. To display ninth level headings, press Alt+Shift+(.

Alternatively, you can click Show All Headings twice. The first click displays all headings and body text, including Heading 8 and Heading 9. The second click hides the body text but leaves all nine heading levels visible.

Displaying the Entire Document, Including Body Text

 At some point, you may want to view the entire document, including body text. Click the Show All Headings button, and the entire document appears, appropriately indented and marked with outlining symbols.

Displaying Only the First Line of Body Text

Sometimes headings aren't enough to tell you the gist of a paragraph—but displaying entire paragraphs takes up so much space that you can lose track of the document's structure and context. Click the Show First Line Only button, and Word displays the first line of text in every paragraph in the document (see Figure 14.11). Ellipses (...) indicate where body text has been cut off.

FIG. 14.11
Show First Line Only shows the first line of every paragraph, giving you a better idea of the paragraph's contents.

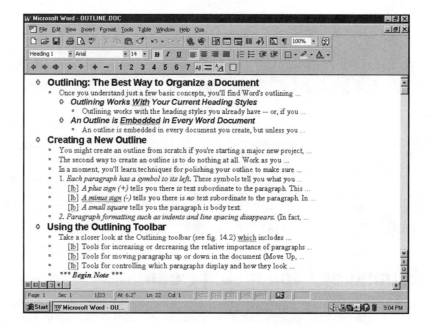

N O T E Show First Line Only displays the first lines of paragraphs only if they would otherwise have been displayed in full. For example, if you have clicked Show Heading 3 to show only the first three levels of headings, Show First Line Only won't display any body text. ■

Hiding Character Formatting

You've already learned that Word hides paragraph formatting while you're working in Outline view. However, it displays font (character) formatting. If your headings are especially large, or if they are formatted in display typefaces, you might find that character formatting makes working with your outline difficult.

Part
IV

Ch
14

To display only unformatted text, indented to reflect the relationships between paragraphs, click the Show/Hide Formatting button on the Outlining toolbar. You can see the results in Figure 14.12.

FIG. 14.12

Word can display all outline headings and body text as unformatted text.

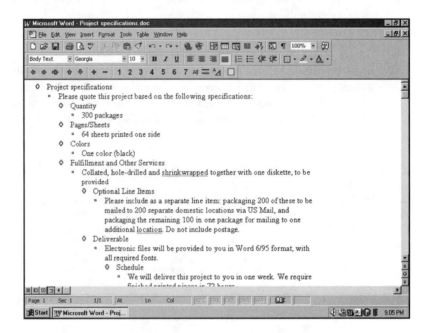

TIP If Word displays unformatted text that is too small to read, use the Zoom control on the Standard toolbar to enlarge it.

Expanding/Collapsing Headings

Sometimes you'll want to focus on a specific section of your document and review it in much greater detail than the rest. You can double-click the Outline symbol next to any paragraph, and Word will display all the headings and body text subordinate to it. Double-click again and Word will hide the subordinate contents.

You can also use the Expand and Collapse toolbar buttons to precisely control the detail at which you view a section of a document. Let's say all headings and body text are currently displayed. Click the paragraph that you would like to view at a higher level (for example, the paragraph that contains subordinate text you would like to hide). Then choose from the following options:

■ Click Collapse to hide all body text. Only headings remain visible.

■ Click Collapse again to hide the lowest heading level subordinate to the paragraph with which you are working.

■ Keep clicking Collapse to hide heading levels until you've reached the level you want.

TIP If you have a Microsoft IntelliMouse, you can expand or collapse selected paragraphs using the wheel between the two mouse buttons as follows:

1. Click the Outline symbol you want to expand or collapse.
2. Press and hold Shift. Roll the wheel forward to expand the selected text one level at a time; roll it back to collapse it one level at a time.
3. When you're at the level you want, release the wheel.

Navigating an Outline Document with Document Map

Word 97 introduces a new feature, Document Map (see Figure 14.13), which makes it easier to navigate through complex outlined documents. Document Map compiles all your headings (and text you've assigned outline levels to) in a separate window.

 To see the Document Map, click the Document Map icon on the Standard toolbar, or choose View, Document Map. After Document Map opens, you can click any entry and move to the corresponding location in your document.

FIG. 14.13
Document Map compiles all your headings and outline levels in a separate window to the left of your document.

Document Map button —

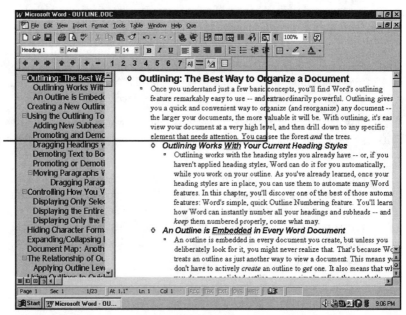

 NOTE Document Map works in all five Word document views, but if you switch to Outline view while it's open, Document Map closes. Word assumes you're already looking at an outline, so you don't need it. You can easily reopen it by clicking the Document Map button again.

When you switch out of Outline view to any view in which you opened the Document Map, the map is again displayed. You do not have to reopen it unless you closed it before switching to Outline view. ■

TIP You can also use Word 97's new Browse feature to move quickly from one heading to the next. To set Word up to browse headings, follow these steps:

1. Click the Select Browse Object button beneath the vertical scroll bar.

2. With the Browse options displayed, choose Browse by Heading. The Previous Heading/Next Heading double-arrow buttons turn blue.

3. Click Previous Heading to find the previous heading, or click Next Heading to find the next one.

Applying Outline Levels to Specific Text

Throughout this chapter, you've seen that when you change the level of a heading in Outline view, Word also reformats it using the appropriate Heading style. Fourth-level paragraphs are automatically formatted in Heading 4 style, and so on. Any heading levels you apply anywhere in Word automatically correspond to outline levels in Outline view.

In previous versions of Word, heading styles were the only way to define outline levels. Heading 1 was a first-level heading by definition; Heading 2 a second-level heading, and so on. But there were some problems with this approach.

For example, what happens if you want to organize the levels of your document using different style names than the Heading names Word provides? By default, Outline view displays any style name other than Heading 1–9 at the level of body text. What if you have titles, subtitles, or other elements that should appear at a higher level in your outline?

Or what if you have blocks of body text that you would like to be included in the first level of your outline? This text is important, but it's still body text; you don't want to format it using the Heading 1 style.

Previous versions of Word couldn't solve these problems without complicated workarounds. Word 97's Outline Levels change all that. Now you can format any paragraph for any of nine levels of importance (or format it as Body text, which is the least important of all). Then, when you work in Outline view, those paragraphs are displayed based on their Outline level, not their style. Follow these steps to format a paragraph with an Outline level:

1. Select the paragraph or paragraphs.

2. Choose Format, Paragraph.

3. In the Outline level drop-down list box, choose the outline level you want: Level 1 through 9 or Body text.

4. Choose OK.

N O T E   The existence of outline levels doesn't change the way Heading styles behave. Heading 1
still corresponds to a first-level heading, Heading 2 to a second-level heading, and so on.
Word does not let you change the outline levels associated with these built-in Heading styles. ▦

 T I P   You might find you always want text formatted in the Title style to be treated as a first-level outline
element. In that case, modify the Title style to include Outline Level 1 as one of its attributes.

Using Outlines to Quickly Reorganize Large Documents

Now that you understand Word's tools for changing heading levels, moving paragraphs within
an outline, and viewing outlines the way you want, let's put all these techniques together to see
how outlining can be used to quickly improve the organization of a long document.

Start by making sure that all your document's headings have appropriate heading styles. Unless your document is exceptionally complex, you probably don't want to use more than three
or four heading levels. If you have chapter or document subtitles that need to be treated as
first-level headings, consider formatting them with style names such as Chapter Name or Title,
and then modifying those styles to include a Level 1 outline level.

T I P   If you've included no heading styles in your document at all, see if AutoFormat can add them for you.
You can always click Undo if AutoFormat doesn't add headings where you want them, or if it makes
other changes you don't want.

▶ **See** "AutoFormatting: The Fastest Way to Format," **p. 215**

 Now that your heading styles are in place, switch to Outline view. Click the Show Heading 2
button to show first- and second-level headings. Now review your document to see if the high-
level structure is what it should be. Do all your major points flow logically?

You may find that you want to move all the text associated with one high-level heading to another location in your document. Collapse the document; then click the high-level heading and
drag it to the new location you want. You've moved all the text subordinate to it at the same
time.

After you're satisfied with the high-level organization of your document, expand your view of
the document to review headings at a deeper level. With all your headings displayed, review
your headings to make sure they're descriptive of the contents that follow. If not, double-click
the Outline symbol to display the contents beneath a heading, skim the body text, and write a
new heading.

Do all the headings fit where they ought to? Are some third- or fourth-level headings important
enough to be assigned higher-level heading numbers? Should some high-level headings be
downsized in importance? Are all your second-level headings associated with first-level headings, and so on?

Part

IV

Ch

14

If you have time, display only your headings and read your document from top to bottom. (If you have a Microsoft IntelliMouse, use the wheel to scroll through the document.) Now that you've made your changes, would the logical structure of your document make sense to someone who was reading only the headings? (That's just what many of your readers will do; they're as rushed as you are.) Will someone who reads only headings understand the most important points you're trying to make?

Finally, switch out of Outline view and edit your body text to make sure all the internal references reflect the way you've restructured things. For example, if you refer to something that has already been covered, but you've moved that coverage to another place in the document, you'll have some revising to do.

 TIP At a time like this, you'll be glad you used Word's cross-reference tools, which can automatically update page references. Word cross-references can even automatically change a page reference that says

> **See page 46 below**

to one that says

> See 18 above

▶ **See** "Working with Cross-References," **p. 511**

Printing Your Outline

Occasionally, you might want a printed copy of your outline. For example, you might need approval for an outline before proceeding to draft your entire document. Follow these steps to print an outline:

1. Display your document in Outline view.

2. Display the elements of your outline that you want to print. For example, specify how many levels of headings you want, and whether you want to collapse or expand any parts of your document.

 3. Click the Print button on the Standard toolbar.

 TIP Word doesn't provide an easy way of copying only outline headings into a new document. Here's the workaround. First, save your file under a new name. Then, find all text formatted using the Body Text or Normal style, and replace it with nothing at all, as follows:

1. Press Ctrl+H or choose Edit, Replace to display the Find and Replace dialog box.

2. Enter ^? in the Find What text box.

3. Click More to make sure all the Find and Replace options are available.

4. Click Format, Style.

5. In the Find Style dialog box, choose whichever style you are using for body text (typically Normal or Body Text), and choose OK.

6. Make sure the Replace With text box is empty, and click Replace All.

If you use more than one style for body text formatting, repeat the process for the others. The end result will be a document with only headings.

Using Word's Automatic Outline Numbering

Have you ever had to number the headings in a document—and then change the numbering every time you add or move one of them? In this section, you'll learn how to let Word insert and manage all your heading and outline numbering for you.

Word includes seven built-in outline numbering schemes that can handle many of the documents you're likely to create. To use one of them, first select the paragraphs you want to number. If you want to add numbering throughout the document, press Ctrl+A to select the entire document. Next, choose Format, Bullets and Numbering, and click the Outline Numbered tab (see Figure 14.14).

FIG. 14.14
The Outline Numbered tab gives you seven standard choices to select from; or click Customize to create your own.

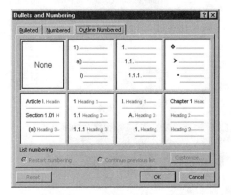

> **CAUTION**
>
> If you only want to number headings, not paragraphs of body text, be sure to use one of the numbering schemes in the bottom row of the Outline Numbered tab. The schemes in the top row number both headings and body text.

Choose the scheme you want. If you want your numbering to restart at 1 (or A) after each subheading, click the Restart Numbering button. If you prefer that the numbering continue where it left off, click Continue Previous List. Then click OK. Figure 14.15 shows outline numbering applied to a sample document.

Part
IV

Ch
14

Creating Customized Outline Numbering

If you're in a position to decide how your outline numbering will appear, try to use one of Word's defaults; you'll save yourself some trouble. However, your document may require a numbering scheme that isn't one of Word's default settings. That's where Word's extensive Outline Numbering customization capabilities come in handy.

FIG. 14.15
Outline numbering based on the second numbering scheme in the bottom row of the Outline Numbered tab.

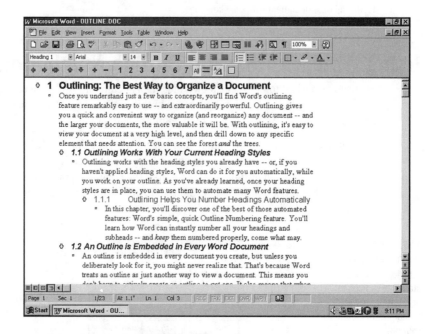

FIG. 14.16
In the Customize Outline Numbered List dialog box, you can change and preview virtually any aspect of a numbered list.

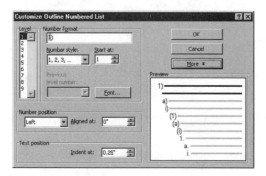

To customize outline numbering, choose Format, Bullets and Numbering, Outline Numbered. Then, in the Outline Numbered tab, select the numbering scheme closest to the one you want, and click Customize. The Customize Outline Numbered List dialog box opens (see Figure 14.16). In the Preview box, you can see how the entire outline numbering scheme behaves; any changes you make are shown there immediately.

Choosing the Outline Level You Want to Customize   You can customize each of Word's nine levels of outline numbering separately. Choose the level you want from the Level drop-down list box at the top left. Word displays the current settings for the level you've selected. These settings will vary not just based on outline level, but also based on the scheme you chose to start from.

TIP It's easy to forget which level you're working in. While you're customizing your outline numbering, glance at the Level drop-down list box every now and then to make sure you're customizing what you *think* you're customizing. Or if you prefer, check in the Preview box; the currently-selected level is displayed in black while others are displayed in light gray.

Choosing Text to Accompany Your Lettering or Numbering In the Number Format text box, you can specify any text or symbols you want to appear before or after the number or letter Word inserts next to your heading or paragraph. You do this by editing the text *surrounding* the grayed out number or letter. For instance, in the example shown in Figure 14.16, Word adds a closed parentheses mark. You might want to place an open parentheses mark *before* the number as well, so Word inserts numbers like (1) instead of 1).

Choosing a Pattern for Your Numbering or Lettering You can't use the Number Format text box to control the automatic lettering or numbering that Word adds to your document. Rather, you select the lettering or numbering pattern you want Word to choose from the Number Style scroll box. Word 97's lettering and numbering schemes include the following:

- 1, 2, 3…
- I, II, III…
- i, ii, iii…
- A, B, C…
- a, b, c…
- 1st, 2nd, 3rd…
- One, Two, Three…
- First, Second, Third…
- 01, 02, 03…

Word also includes several bullet styles from which you can choose, or you can select a different character to be used as a bullet.

NOTE If you choose New Bullet, the Symbol dialog box opens, enabling you to choose the bullet you want to appear.

 TIP You can also choose to use no lettering or numbering at all. If you choose (none) in the Number Style scroll box, Word only inserts the text you enter in the Number Format text box. Imagine you're writing the feature description of a product, and you want to add a word like **NEW!** before every second-level heading in your document. You could use this feature to do so.

Part
IV

Ch
14

Choosing a Number or Letter from Which to Start By default, Word assumes you want your numbering to start at 1 and your lettering to start at A, but you might not. For example, if you're contributing the fourth chapter of a book, you might want your first-level heading to start with the number 4. In the Start At scroll box located to the right of Number Style, choose the number you want to appear next to the first heading of the current level.

Including a Previous Outline Level with Your Numbering   It's common to see documents that include the following multilevel numbering:

> 1.A
>
> II.A

You can instruct Word to insert numbering like this. To do so, first establish any other settings for your numbering. Then, in the Previous Level Number drop-down list box (located beneath Number Style), choose the level of outline numbering you want to appear next to your lower-level headings or paragraphs. For example, if your first-level headings are numbered (1), (2), (3), and you want your second-level headings to be numbered (1A), (1B), (1C), and so on, select Level 1 in the Previous Level Number box.

Notice that Word doesn't add the surrounding text you included in the Number Format text box for the previous heading level; just the letter or number itself. Otherwise, you could easily wind up with ((1)A) or something equally unattractive.

N O T E   Because there is no level prior to Level 1, the Previous Level Number drop-down list box is grayed out when you're customizing Level 1 headings. ▦

Customizing Font Formatting   You can spice up your outline numbers with almost any character formatting you like. Choose Format, Bullets and Numbering, Outline Numbered, Customize. Then, in the Customize Outline Numbered List dialog box, click Font. The Font dialog box opens. You can choose any character formatting, spacing, or animation.

N O T E   Every font formatting option you normally have is available for numbered headings with two exceptions: you cannot use the Outline or Small Caps text effects. ▦

Customizing the Position and Alignment of Outline Numbers   Some of Word's built-in schemes left-align all outline numbers, regardless of levels. Other schemes indent outline numbers; the deeper the outline level, the greater the indent. You might want to change these built-in settings. For example, you might like everything about a scheme *except* the way it indents paragraphs.

Outline numbering alignment is controlled from the Number Position drop-down list box in the Customize Outline Numbered List dialog box. You can choose to left-align, center, or right-align outline numbers. You can also specify where the outline numbering is aligned *against*. The Aligned At scroll box specifies how far from the left margin the alignment point will be. For example, if you choose Centered as the Number position, and you choose 1" as the Aligned At location, your outline number will be centered over a point 1" from the left margin.

N O T E   The Alignment setting doesn't control whether the entire line is left-aligned, centered, or right-aligned. It only controls how the outline numbering within the line is aligned.

Remember, you'll have to change the Number position separately for each outline level you expect to use. ▦

T I P To see the effect of these changes in your document, switch to Normal or Page Layout view; changes are not accurately reflected in Outline view.

Customizing the Position and Alignment of Text Near Outline Numbers   You can also control the distance between the end of Word's automatic outline number and the start of the paragraph's text. To do so, enter a setting in the <u>I</u>ndent At scroll box, in the Text position area of the Customize Outline Numbered List dialog box.

The <u>I</u>ndent At setting is measured from the left margin. If the <u>I</u>ndent At setting is very small, it may have no effect on the first line of a paragraph, because the outline number itself already extends beyond the indent. (Word won't overlap an outline number on top of paragraph text.) Indent At behaves like a hanging indent. In Figure 14.17, you can see first-level headings that are left-aligned at 0.25" with text indented at 1.5".

FIG. 14.17
The first-level headings in this sample are left-aligned at 0.25" with text indented at 1.5".

0.25" left-alignment ———
1.5" indent ———

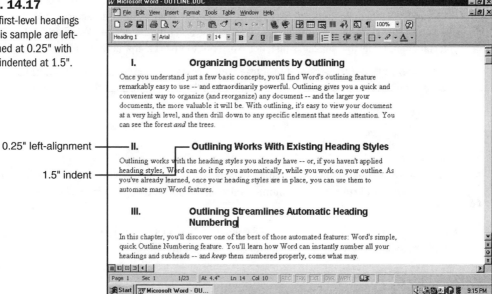

Advanced Outline Numbering Options

Some outline numbering customizations are rarely used, but when they're needed, they're needed very badly. You can control these by clicking <u>M</u>ore in the Customized Outline Numbered List dialog box. More options appear (see Figure 14.18).

Linking an Outline Level to a Style   The Lin<u>k</u> Level to Style drop-down list box in the Customize Numbered List dialog box enables you to attach any style to an outline numbering level. That way, whenever you enter or format a paragraph using that style, Word automatically includes numbering, just as it includes all the other formatting associated with the style.

Part
IV

Ch
14

FIG. 14.18
You can control more advanced aspects of outline numbering from the "expanded" version of the Customize Outline Numbered List dialog box.

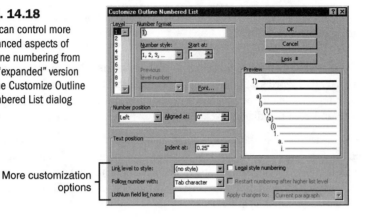

More customization options

Choosing a Spacer Character   The Follow Number With drop-down list box in the Customize Numbered List dialog box enables you to choose the noneditable character that Word places between your outline number and your paragraph text. By default, Word uses a tab, but you can change this to a space, or instruct Word not to insert a character at all.

Placing Two Outline Numbers on the Same Line   In some documents, notably contracts, you may be required to include two outline numbers on the same line, as in the following example:

> Article I.
>> Section 1.01   (i)
>>   (ii)

Word lets you do this, although it's a little involved. You use the ListNum Field List Name drop-down list box, an advanced outline number customization feature. You also have to use the ListNum field.

First, set up your headings as you normally would. Then, place your insertion point where you want the first extra heading to appear, and do the following:

1. Choose Insert, Field.
2. Select ListNum from the Field Names box.
3. Enter a name in quotation marks and click OK. Word can use this list name to recognize which fields you want to include in a specific sequence. For example, all fields named

   ```
   {LISTNUM Sequence1}
   ```

   will be included in the same sequence, while all fields named

   ```
   {LISTNUM Sequence2)
   ```

   will be included in a different sequence.
4. Select the entire field, and copy it to every other location where you want a heading just like it.

If you view the field results, you'll see that you've now added a basic heading, such as

a)

Follow these steps to attach all the headings in the same sequence to a level in your outline numbering scheme, so they will look exactly as you want them to:

1. Choose Format, Bullets and Numbering, Outline Numbered.
2. Extra headings are most commonly used with the Section and Article scheme (the scheme on the bottom row at the left). Select this scheme and click Customize.
3. Click More to display the advanced options.
4. Make sure you're working at the level you want and that the Number Format settings are the way want them.
5. In the ListNum Field List Name drop-down list box, enter the same word you used in your ListNum field. In our example, that would be Sequence1.
6. Click OK.

You now have normal outline numbering as well as an extra outline number that uses the Number format of the level *immediately beneath* the first outline number. In other words, if the outline number you applied through Format, Bullets and Numbering is formatted as Level 1, the outline number you applied through Insert, Field will be Level 2.

▶ **See** "What Fields Can Do for You and Your Organization," **p. 696**

Applying Legal Style Numbering   Some legal documents must utilize Arabic numbering (1, 2, 3…) throughout. For example, even though Word's numbering scheme for legal documents may specify that Articles use Roman numerals in some levels (for example, Article I, II, and so on), this may not be appropriate for your document. You *could* change every level's Number style to Roman numerals individually. However, Word 97 provides a shortcut; you can simply check Legal Style Numbering in the Customize Outline Numbered List dialog box, and Word will do it for you.

Incrementing List Numbers in a Specific Level   By default, Word restarts numbering whenever a list level follows a higher list level. You can see this behavior in Figure 14.19.

However, if you clear the Restart Numbering After Higher List Level check box near the bottom of the expanded Customize Outline Numbered List dialog box, Word will continue to increment the numbers from where they left off (see Figure 14.20).

Specifying Where Your Changes Should Apply   By default, if you make changes anywhere in the Customize Outline Numbered List dialog box, they apply globally to the entire document as soon as you click OK to exit. However, you might have a portion of a document that you want to treat differently. You have two additional options, available through the Apply Changes To drop-down list box.

Choosing This Point Forward tells Word to apply your changes to the rest of your document, starting at the insertion point.

Part IV
Ch 14

FIG. 14.19

By default, Word restarts numbering whenever a lower list level follows a higher list level.

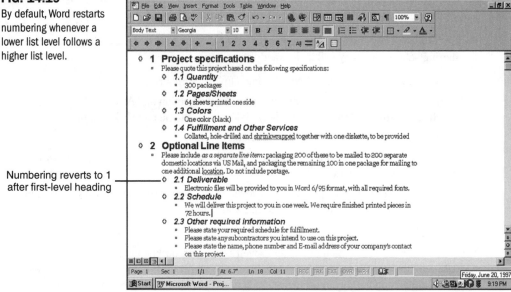

Numbering reverts to 1 after first-level heading

FIG. 14.20

Clearing the Restart Numbering After Higher List Level check box instructs Word to keep incrementing lower-level headings instead of restarting them at 1.

Numbering continues to increment from 1.4 to 2.5

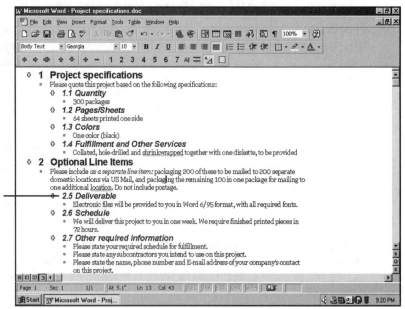

Choosing Selected Text tells Word to apply your changes only to paragraphs that are currently selected (or to the current paragraph, if no text is selected).

TROUBLESHOOTING

I used Zoom to change magnification in Outline view, and now my text is garbled. This is a well-known bug in Word 97. To solve the problem, switch to Normal view and switch back to Outline view. The magnification you want will still be there, and the display should behave properly.

I collapsed my outline in order to print it, but when I display and print it from Print Preview, I see (and print) all the text I thought I hid. This is another known Word 97 bug; until Microsoft fixes it, print from Outline view.

Word 97 crashes when I click Alt and drag a heading to promote or demote all the subordinate text. This is yet another bug; use the Promote or Demote toolbar buttons on the Outlining toolbar instead.

When I use Outline Numbering to number headings, I number body text paragraphs also—and that's not what I want. Word 6 and Word 95 didn't do that. Outline Numbering has been redesigned to number body text paragraphs as well as headings by default. However, if (in the Outline Numbered tab of the Bullets and Numbering dialog box) you choose a numbering scheme that includes the word Headings, Word will only number headings.

From Here...

Now that you've learned how to work with Word's powerful outlining features, you can learn more about how to leverage outlining to streamline your long documents, create PowerPoint presentations more quickly, and make your documents look better.

- Refer back to Chapter 5, "Styles: The Foundation of Automated Documents," for a closer look at the heading styles that Word automatically applies when you promote or demote headings in Outline view.

- In Chapter 15, "Master Documents: Control and Share Even the Largest Documents," you'll learn how to use outlining techniques to control multiple documents at the same time through a Master Document.

- See Chapter 27, "Integrating with Microsoft Office," to learn how you can transform your Word outline into a PowerPoint presentation with just a few clicks.

Part
IV

Ch
14

Master Documents: Control and Share Even the Largest Documents

by Bill Camarda

So you're in charge of a five-hundred-page manual that includes chapters created by multiple authors, or maybe you're locked away in your attic, pounding away at the Great American Novel. Either way, you're responsible for a complex document—and you've got your hands full.

You need a way to edit *parts* of that document—while still staying in control of the *whole* document. *Master documents* give you that flexibility. With master documents, you can divide one document into as many *subdocuments* as you need. You can then write and edit each of these subdocuments separately, or provide them to colleagues for editing.

Whenever you're ready, you can re-open the master document and display all the subdocuments together. Then you can quickly see where you stand, using Word's navigation tools to move around the entire document. You can also handle all the tasks that generally should be performed on the entire document at the same time, such as:

- Ensuring consistent formatting throughout
- Spell checking and ensuring consistent spelling of specialized terms
- Building an index and table of contents
- Reorganizing the document, moving large blocks of text among chapters
- Printing

N O T E Microsoft says you can create 255 subdocuments in the same master document, though most users report performance and reliability problems when trying to use anywhere near that many. ■

How Master Documents Help You Maintain Consistency

The master document helps you maintain consistency among subdocuments in several ways. For example, no matter what formatting is attached to styles in your subdocuments, when those subdocuments are displayed as part of a master document, they all use the formatting associated with styles in the master document's template. So if you stay with a basic set of headings and other styles, you're virtually assured of consistent formatting.

In addition, when you display subdocuments as part of a master document, all cross-references, footnotes, outline numbers, and page numbers are automatically updated to reflect the new location of the subdocument within the larger document.

If you've learned how to use outlines, you're halfway toward understanding master documents, too. Master documents closely resemble outlines, and you control them using Word's outlining tools. The primary difference is that you're outlining material that comes from several documents instead of one.

▶ **See** "Creating a New Outline," **p. 404**

In fact, except for the fact that they contain other documents, master documents behave very much like regular Word documents. You can format them, save them, and print them just like you would any other document.

There's one more benefit to using master documents. Because Word 97 usually works faster when editing smaller documents, creating subdocuments from a large main document can significantly enhance performance.

CAUTION

While master documents are generally reliable, Word users in the past have found them to be a bit less reliable than the rest of Word. Word 97 improves the reliability of master documents, but they are still not perfect. On most systems, with most documents, you won't have trouble. But check the Troubleshooting section for a few lingering software bugs that might conceivably cause you grief if you aren't aware of them.

Creating a New Master Document

As with outlines, there are two ways to create master documents:

- You can do it from scratch, by outlining your document and then dividing it into subdocuments.

- You can make existing documents part of your master document.

Whenever possible, you're better off creating your master documents from scratch. It's quick, easy, and you have total control over all the subdocuments you create.

If you start from scratch, it's also much easier to maintain consistency throughout the editing process. Here's why:

- You usually don't have to worry about users working from different templates. All your subdocuments automatically share the same template—so they share the same styles, AutoText entries, and macros.

- You don't have to worry about tracking the locations of your subdocuments. You can just place them all in the same folder on your local hard disk or shared network drive, and tell people to leave them there.

- You usually don't have to worry about people inadvertently editing the wrong version of the file. There *is* only one: the subdocument you created.

However, you may not always have the luxury of starting from scratch. You may be asked to build upon existing text—updating it, including new topics, broadening coverage with new chapters. So Word makes it very easy to incorporate existing documents in your master document.

You might find yourself taking a hybrid approach: outlining the entire master document from scratch; then inserting existing documents where they exist, and reorganizing the master document to reflect the contents you already have.

Finally, remember that a master document can contain anything a regular document can, while containing subdocuments at the same time. So you might choose to create and edit some of your text in your master document—and use subdocuments only for the chapters others are responsible for.

Creating a Master Document and Subdocuments

In this section, you'll learn how to create a master document from scratch, by building an outline and dividing your document into subdocuments.

N O T E   A master document is simply a document that contains subdocuments, so adding subdocuments to any document transforms it into a master document. ▪

Start by opening a blank document and choosing Master Document from the View menu. Word switches you into Master Document view, which looks just like Outline view and contains all the tools on the Outlining Toolbar. You'll notice one addition you don't see in Outline view: the Master Document toolbar.

Working with the Master Document Toolbar

Figure 15.1 shows a close-up of the Master Document toolbar. It contains tools for inserting, removing, and managing subdocuments that are the components of a master document. Each tool is explained in Table 15.1.

FIG. 15.1
The Master Document toolbar includes Word's tools for managing subdocuments and master documents.

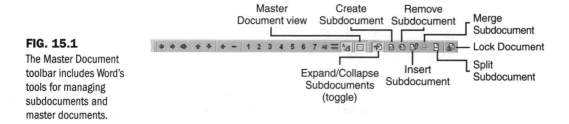

Table 15.1   Master Document Toolbar Buttons

Button	Name	What It Does
	Expand/Collapse Subdocuments	Toggles between showing all the contents of a master document and showing hyperlinks in place of subdocuments
	Create Subdocument	Create a new subdocument from selected text; or create multiple subdocuments from text selections that incorporate several headings of the same level
	Remove Subdocument	Eliminate a subdocument and place its text in the master document
	Insert Subdocument	Insert an existing document as a subdocument in the current master document
	Merge Subdocument	Combine two or more subdocuments into one
	Split Subdocument	Divide one subdocument into two, at the insertion point
	Lock Document	Toggle between locking and unlocking a subdocument

N O T E   In Word 97, the Master Document Toolbar buttons appear grayed out if all your
subdocuments are collapsed, or they are expanded but locked. ▪

Creating Subdocuments

The first steps in creating a master document are to create and organize your outline as you
normally would, using Word's outlining tools.

After you have the outline the way you want it, you can divide it into subdocuments. If you set
up your document properly, Word can organize your entire document into subdocuments with
one click. Of course, it's also easy to set up individual subdocuments manually, if you prefer.

  T I P   If your outline needs to be approved, get the approvals you need before you divide it into
subdocuments.

Creating Multiple Subdocuments at the Same Time

The quickest and most intuitive way to set up subdocuments is to create an outline where
every first-level heading—for example, every paragraph formatted with the Heading 1 style—
corresponds to a new subdocument. For example, if you're writing a book or manual, you
might format chapter titles with the Heading 1 style, so each subdocument you create corresponds to a separate chapter. Of course, these subdocuments will contain all the headings and
body text subordinate to the Heading 1 paragraph with which they start.

N O T E   It's equally important *not* to use Heading 1 style for any block of text you *don't* want to be
set apart in its own subdocument. ▪

Follow these steps if you want to create a subdocument for every Heading 1 style in your
document:

  1. Click Collapse Subdocuments to display only first-level headings.

2. Press Ctrl+A to select the entire document.

  3. Click the Create Subdocument button on the Master Document toolbar.

Word divides the entire document into subdocuments automatically.

  T I P   You can collapse subdocuments by clicking Ctrl+\. This is the only master document tool with a
corresponding keyboard shortcut.

Creating Multiple Subdocuments from Lower-Level Headings

While you're most likely to use Heading 1 styles as the dividing lines between your
subdocuments, you are not limited to this option. You can just as easily use subdocuments to
share smaller chunks of your document for editing by colleagues. You don't have to select the
entire document; you can select any group of headings, as long as

- Your selection includes more than one heading of the same level.
- The first heading in your selection is styled with the heading level you want to use as your dividing line between subdocuments

When might you divide a document based on lower-level headings? Imagine you're making a sales proposal that covers a wide range of products, each of which will be covered in only a page. You can create subdocuments for second-or-third-level headings corresponding to each product.

 TIP   After you've created these small, modular subdocuments, you can insert them in future documents as well. As your products are updated, have your product managers revise and re-save their subdocuments. You can then include these subdocuments in future proposals and be assured that you're including the most current information about each product.

You might even record macros that automatically insert each subdocument, and attach these macros to a special toolbar, so your salespeople can insert current information about any specific product with a single click.

Creating a Single Subdocument

 You don't have to create multiple subdocuments at the same time. You can create a subdocument from *any* block of text that includes at least one heading. To do so, select the text you want to incorporate in a subdocument. After the text is selected, click Create Subdocument.

 TIP   Usually, the quickest way to select text for inclusion in a subdocument is to click the outline symbol next to the highest-level heading you want to use. Word will select all text subordinate to that heading.

Taking a Closer Look at Subdocuments

Within the master document, Word marks the subdocuments you create in two ways (see Figure 15.2). First, text in a subdocument is surrounded by a thin, gray border. Second, a subdocument icon appears to the top left of the first heading in the subdocument.

In Master Document view, you can select the entire subdocument by clicking this subdocument icon. You can open the subdocument in its own editing window by double-clicking the subdocument icon. Later in this chapter, you'll learn more about organizing, formatting and editing subdocuments.

When Word creates subdocuments, it separates them by adding continuous section breaks, which are section breaks that start the next section on the same page. In Master Document view, these section breaks resemble the outline symbols for body text, which you learned about in Chapter 14, "Outlining: The Best Way to Organize a Document." Unlike paragraphs of body text, however, they don't add empty space in your document that would cause you problems when you print.

FIG. 15.2
Text that has been selected as a subdocument is bordered with a gray rectangle; a subdocument icon also appears to its top left.

Marker for section break ─

Subdocument icon ─

Subdocument border ─

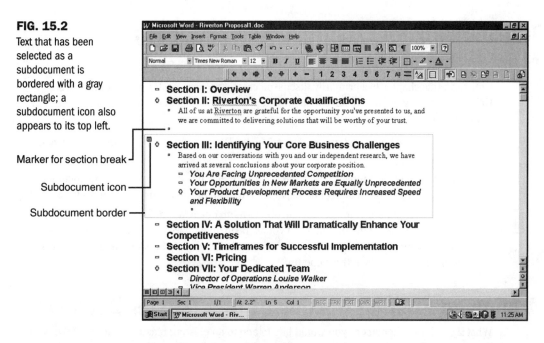

These section breaks make it convenient to add text that you may want to appear between subdocuments. If you click the Show/Hide Paragraph button on the Standard Toolbar, or if you switch to Normal View (see Figure 15.3), you'll see the section break markers. You can delete them without damaging your subdocuments, but in general you'll want to leave them alone.

FIG. 15.3
Word separates subdocuments with section break markers.

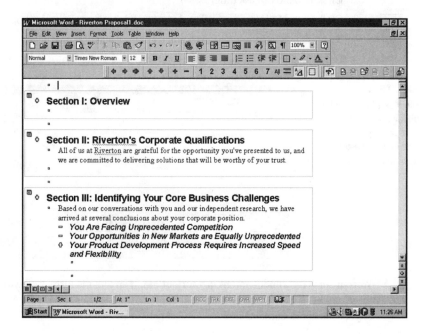

Transforming an Existing Document into a Master Document

Until now, this chapter has primarily discussed creating a new master document from scratch. However, what if you already have a document you want to turn into a master document? Follow these steps:

1. Open the document and choose View, Master Document to display it in Master Document view.

2. Use Word's outline tools to organize the document. If possible, arrange the document so that each first-level heading corresponds to one of the subdocuments you want to create.

3. Create your subdocuments. You can create them one at a time by selecting text and clicking Create Subdocument. Or if you've been able to organize your document by first-level headings, select the entire document and click Create Subdocument to create all your subdocuments at the same time.

Adding an Existing Document to a Master Document

What if you have a document you would like to add to an existing master document? (Or what if you would like to add your document to a conventional document, thereby turning it into a master document?) Do the following:

1. Open the master document.

2. Click Expand Subdocuments.

3. Click Insert Subdocument. The Insert Subdocument dialog box opens (see Figure 15.4).

4. Browse to select the document you want to insert.

5. Click Open.

FIG. 15.4

The Insert Subdocument dialog box enables you to make any document part of your master document.

Word inserts the subdocument in your outline. If any text is formatted with styles that have the same names as those in your master document, those styles will be displayed to match the rest of your master document.

Saving a Master Document

You save a master document the same way you save any other Word file: by clicking the Save button, pressing Ctrl+S, or choosing File, Save.

 When you save a master document that contains new subdocuments, Word creates new files for each subdocument, and stores them in the same folder as the master document. Word automatically names your subdocuments, using the first letters or phrase at the beginning of each subdocument. If the names of more than one subdocument would be identical, or if another identical file name already exists in the same folder, Word adds a number to distinguish them, for example

```
Chapter1.doc
Chapter2.doc
Chapter3.doc
```

N O T E   The file names Word automatically creates can be very long, but they stop when Word encounters a character (such as a period or colon) that cannot be included in a Windows 95/NT file name. ■

CAUTION

Double-check the file names Word chooses to make sure they're appropriate. If you save a subdocument named Section 1 to a folder that already has a file named Section1, Word renames your file Section2. Then it'll name your Section 2 subdocument Section3.

If Word ever chooses a subdocument name that you don't like, open the subdocument from within the master document, choose File, Save As, and rename it. The master document will now contain the renamed file.

To avoid this problem, consider setting up a separate folder for your master document and subdocuments.

After you create and save a subdocument, Word stores its contents in the subdocument—*not* in the master document. This has two important implications: First, as you'll see shortly, it means you (or a colleague) can edit a subdocument without opening the master document. You simply open the document as you normally would. Assuming nobody else is using the file, nothing tells you you're working on a subdocument instead of a normal document. Second, it means that if you delete a subdocument—or move it without informing the master document—it will disappear from the master document.

CAUTION

If you save a master document to HTML format, the subdocuments won't be included in the new HTML file. Rather, the master document and each subdocument will be saved to separate, disconnected HTML files.

Because the following outlined process eliminates the master document/subdocument relationships you've painstakingly built, you may want to make a copy of your master document first and remove the subdocuments from the copy instead of the original.

To include all your subdocuments in an HTML file, follow these steps:

1. Open the master document and view it in Master Document view.

2. Click a subdocument.

3. Click Remove Subdocument to move the contents of the subdocument back into the master document.

4. Repeat the process with each additional subdocument.

5. Choose File, Save as HTML to save the file in HTML format.

> **CAUTION**
>
> If you save an existing master document to a new location, such as a remote server or FTP site, Word *should* save all the subdocuments in the same location. However, it doesn't always do so. Sometimes the subdocuments are simply saved in their current location. If this occurs, you'll have to save the subdocuments to the new location individually, by opening them one at a time from within the master document, choosing File, Save As, specifying the new location, and clicking OK.

Opening a Master Document

After you create, save, and close a master document, its appearance will change the next time you open it. Instead of seeing headings that correspond to the top-level headings of each subdocument, you'll see hyperlinks that show the name and location of each subdocument in your master document (see Figure 15.5).

FIG. 15.5

When you reopen a master document, you see hyperlinks to each subdocument contained in it.

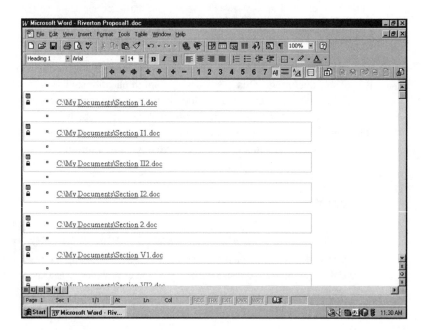

T I P Previous versions of Word did not display hyperlinks as placeholders for subdocuments. Rather, they displayed the first line of each subdocument, formatted with whatever style it contained (often Heading 1).

Some Word users prefer seeing formatted headings instead of hyperlinks. Follow these steps to view them:

1. Click Expand Subdocuments to view all the contents of your Master Document and its subdocuments.

2. Click Show Heading 1 on the Outlining toolbar to collapse the Master Document to first-level headings only.

Editing a Subdocument from Within the Master Document

To open a subdocument for editing, click the hyperlink. The subdocument now appears in its own window. Section breaks appear at the end of the document, as discussed earlier.

N O T E As with other Word hyperlinks, the hyperlinks in a master document change color from blue to magenta after you've clicked them once. However, whenever you close the master document, they all revert to blue the next time you open it. Moreover, if you edit and save a subdocument, its hyperlink also reverts to blue.

 ▶ **See** "Using Hyperlinks," **p. 521** ▣

Often, you may prefer to edit a subdocument with the rest of the master document's contents visible. For example, you may want to move text from one subdocument to another, or create references to text in another subdocument. To view the contents of the entire master document, click Expand Subdocuments. Now you can use Word's outlining tools to focus in on the specific areas of text you want to edit.

No matter how you open a subdocument, you're not limited to viewing and editing it in Master Document or Outline view. Select whatever view makes the most sense for the editing you need to do.

TROUBLESHOOTING

 All my subdocuments suddenly disappeared! Did you click the Show All Headings button to display all heading levels while only hyperlinks were displayed? Word thinks you want to see only headings and body text, and there aren't any—only hyperlinks. First, click Expand Subdocuments, and then click All.

Editing Subdocuments Outside the Master Document

 As you've learned, you don't have to open a master document in order to edit one of its subdocuments. You can open the subdocument directly, by using the Open dialog box or by double-clicking on its icon in Windows Explorer. If you're using master documents to manage a document with several authors, this is typically how your colleagues will open the subdocuments you delegate to them.

Here's a general rule of thumb: open subdocuments separately when you intend to make changes that affect only the subdocument. For example, it's fine to open the subdocument separately if you plan to

- Edit text within the subdocument
- Create footnotes to appear at the bottom of the page or at the end of the subdocument
- Create temporary headers or footers that you only want to print from within the subdocument
- Check spelling *within* the subdocument
- Print only the subdocument

 T I P

For example, you might add a subdocument footer that includes the words PRELIMINARY DRAFT. This footer would print whenever you opened the subdocument on its own. However, the official footer you establish for final documents will appear instead whenever the subdocument is printed from the master document.

On the other hand, if you plan to make organizational, formatting, or editing changes that affect the entire document, open the subdocument from within the master document.

CAUTION

Never rename or move a subdocument that you've opened outside the master document. Word has no way of tracking the change. The next time you open the master document, the renamed or moved subdocument will be missing.

To rename or move a subdocument, open it from within the master document; display the Save As dialog box; enter the new name or location, and click OK.

Style Behavior in Master Documents and Subdocuments

If you open a subdocument from within a master document, the subdocument uses all the styles stored in the master document's template. If you open it separately and make style changes or apply a different template, your subdocument reflects those style changes as long as you're editing it outside the master document. However, if you save it, open the master document, and reopen the subdocument, you'll find that the master document's styles now take precedence wherever they conflict. If you insert an existing document into a master document, and the existing document is based on a different template, once again the master document's template takes precedence.

Reorganizing a Master Document

 All the outlining skills you learned in Chapter 14, "Outlining: The Best Way to Organize a Document," come in especially handy when you need to reorganize a master document. Display your document in Master Document view, and click Expand Subdocuments to view all the contents of your subdocuments. Now you can use Word's outlining toolbar and keyboard shortcuts to rearrange any elements of your master document.

Part

IV

Ch

15

Moving an Entire Subdocument

You might decide that you want to move an entire subdocument to a different location in your master document. First, click the subdocument symbol to select the entire subdocument (see Figure 15.6).

FIG. 15.6
You can select an entire subdocument by clicking its subdocument icon.

Subdocument icon ——

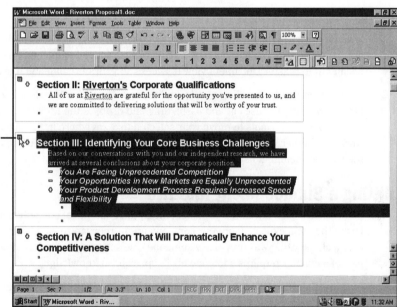

Now you can perform any of the following actions:

- *Move the subdocument intact to another location in your document.* Drag the subdocument into the empty space between two other subdocuments. (By default, when you create subdocuments, Word leaves one paragraph of body text between them, just for this purpose.)

 - *Move an entire subdocument into another subdocument, by using the Move Up or Move Down buttons.* You get the same result as you would by merging subdocuments: you now have one subdocument containing both chunks of text.

N O T E   If you use Move Up/Move Down to move a subdocument into another subdocument and then move it back out, the text will be placed in the master document. *It will no longer be a separate subdocument.* You'll have to click Create Subdocument to make it a subdocument again—or click the Undo button until you revert back to where you were when you started. ▣

■ *Use drag and drop to move an entire subdocument into another subdocument.* This behaves differently than Move Up or Move Down. Now the subdocument where you've dropped the file contains its own subdocument. You're likely to use this feature only in exceptionally complex documents, where you may delegate a large section to someone who will in turn delegate smaller portions to others.

As you move subdocuments or elements within them, a gray line appears, showing where your selected text will land if you release the mouse button.

Moving Parts of Subdocuments

When it comes to moving or reorganizing individual headings and subordinate text, there's no difference between master documents and conventional documents. First, display your master document in Master Document view to access all your outlining and master document tools.

Now, you can click a heading to select all the text subordinate to it—or select just one paragraph. You can then use cut and paste, drag and drop, or the Move Up/Move Down buttons and keyboard shortcuts to move your selected text anywhere in the master document. It all works—whether your destination is in the same subdocument, a different subdocument, or in the master document itself.

Splitting a Subdocument into Two

Sometimes as you develop a large document, the contents of one subdocument may grow larger than you expected, or your company might reorganize, and two people may have to take over a chapter that was previously someone else's responsibility. You might also discover that part of a chapter requires someone else's specialized knowledge.

In short, there are many reasons you might decide that one subdocument needs to be split into two. Follow these steps to split a subdocument:

1. Display the contents of the subdocument from within the master document.
2. Click to position the insertion point where you want to split the subdocument.

3. Click Split Subdocument.

Combining Multiple Subdocuments

Alternatively, you might find that you need one person to handle multiple subdocuments. In that case, you can combine two or more subdocuments into one as follows:

1. Open the document and display it in Master Document view.

2. Click Expand Subdocuments.

3. Make sure the subdocuments are adjacent; use Word's outlining tools to move them if necessary.

4. Click the subdocument icon next to the first subdocument you want to combine.

5. Press Shift and click the subdocument icon next to the last subdocument you want to combine. You have now selected the first and last subdocuments, and any subdocuments in between.

6. Click Merge Subdocument.

You can't combine subdocuments if they're marked with a padlock icon. Locking and unlocking subdocuments is discussed later in this chapter.

When you merge subdocuments, all the information in the merged subdocuments is stored in the file that previously contained only the first subdocument.

> **CAUTION**
>
> The other subdocuments you merged into the first subdocument no longer appear as separate subdocuments within your master document. *However, they still exist as separate files on your hard disk.* Be careful that nobody edits these "stranded" files, mistakenly believing they are working on the current version of the document. Consider deleting old files that are no longer part of your master document.

Removing a Subdocument

Sometimes you want to keep the information contained in a subdocument, but you no longer want to store it in a separate subdocument. Possibly your colleague has finished with it, and you would like to move it back into the master document, so you'll have one less subdocument to manage. Follow these steps to eliminate the subdocument while moving its contents to the master document:

1. Click the subdocument icon to select the entire subdocument.

2. Click the Remove Subdocument button.

TIP Of course, if you want to eliminate the text from your document entirely, you can do that, too. Just click the subdocument icon and press Delete.

TIP You can eliminate all subdocuments at the same time by pressing Ctrl+A to select the entire document, and then clicking Remove Subdocument.

Creating a Table of Contents, Index, or Cross-References for a Master Document

From within your master document, you can create tables of contents and indexes that reflect the contents of all your subdocuments. Follow these steps:

1. Open the master document and display it in Master Document view.

2. Click Expand Subdocuments to make the contents of all subdocuments visible.

3. Position your insertion point where you want to create your table of contents, index, or cross-reference.

4. Follow Word's procedures for inserting an index, table of contents, or cross-reference.

> **CAUTION**
>
> If you open a subdocument using File, Open instead of opening it from within the master document, any table of contents, index, or cross-reference you create won't reflect the contents of the master document.
>
> ▶ **See** "Quick and Easy Tables of Contents," **p. 454**
>
> ▶ **See** "Creating a New Index Entry," **p. 478**
>
> ▶ **See** "Working with Cross-References," **p. 511**

Printing Master Documents and Subdocuments

You print master documents and subdocuments the same way you print any other documents. You can click the Print button on the Standard toolbar to get one complete copy of whatever document you're working in, or you can choose File, Print to display the Print dialog box and select printing options.

In general, what you see is what you print:

■ If you click Expand Subdocuments and then print a master document in Normal view, Word prints the entire master document, including all subdocuments. All styles, headers/footers, and page numbering will be defined by the master document, not by individual subdocuments.

■ If you print a master document with hyperlinks showing, the hyperlinks prints instead of the document text.

■ If you print a master document from Outline view, Word prints whatever headings and body text are currently displayed; for example, if you collapse part of the master document or display only the first line of body text paragraphs, only the elements that appear on-screen print.

■ If you double-click a subdocument icon in a master document and display a subdocument in its own window, clicking Print prints only the subdocument—using the master document's styles and template.

■ If you open a subdocument without first opening the master document, the subdocument prints as if it were an independent document—using its own styles and template.

Working with Others on the Same Master Document

You've learned that master documents can simplify collaboration. You can delegate parts of your document for others to edit while working on other elements yourself; then when you're ready, you can review and edit the document as a whole.

By default, Word gives you complete access to any subdocument you are the author of (assuming that subdocument is stored in a folder you have rights to access). Word gives you more limited access to subdocuments you did not author.

N O T E You may be wondering how Word knows who the author is. It looks in the Author field of the File, Properties dialog box. How does the name of the author get there in the first place? It comes from the information you gave Word when you installed it—or changes you've made since, in the User Information tab of the Tools, Options dialog box.

If you want to make sure that your colleagues have first dibs on accessing the documents they're responsible for writing, you can enter their names in the Properties dialog box of each individual subdocument. Of course, you might then have to wait for them to finish working before you can edit their submissions. ■

If you did not author a subdocument, you may find that it is locked when you try to open it. You can tell that a subdocument is locked when a small padlock icon appears beneath the subdocument icon (see Figure 15.7).

FIG. 15.7
The padlock icon appears whenever a subdocument is locked.

Padlock icon ——

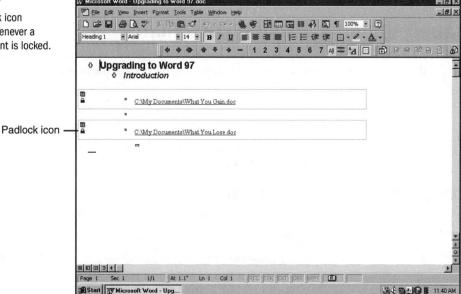

When you first open a master document, displaying subdocuments as hyperlinks, all subdocuments are locked, no matter who authored them. If you click Expand Subdocuments, the Lock icons disappear, except in the following cases:

- *If someone else is already working on their subdocument,* Word displays a message offering to create a copy on which you can work. (If you create a copy, the word Copy appears in the title bar of the document you create.) Alternatively, you can wait until the first user has finished, and then open the original subdocument.

- *When the subdocument's author saves it as Read-Only Recommended,* using the check box in the Save Options dialog box. When you try to open a Read-Only Recommended file, Word displays a dialog box asking, in effect, whether you want to respect this preference. You can click No, and edit the document.

- *When the subdocument's author has established a Password to Modify,* also using options in the Save Options dialog box. You can read this subdocument, but you can't edit it without knowing the password.

- *When the subdocument is stored in a shared folder to which you have only Read-Only rights.* Again, you can read the file—but you can't edit it unless you convince your network administrator to upgrade your rights. The words Read Only appear in the title bar of a read-only document.

If a subdocument is locked, you can attempt to unlock it as follows:

1. Open the master document and display it in Master Document View.
2. Click Expand Subdocuments. (Until you expand your subdocuments, they're *all* locked.)
3. If the subdocument you want to edit is still locked, click anywhere in it.
 4. Click the Lock Document button on the Master Document Toolbar.

Troubleshooting Master Documents

As you've learned, master documents still have a few rough edges. Unfortunately, that means this troubleshooting section is one of the longest in the book. If the information here doesn't help you, then

- Make sure your copy of Word 97 reflects Microsoft's summer '97 bug fixes. If not, install the bug fix upgrade, available on Microsoft's Web site (**http://www.microsoft.com**).

- Search the Microsoft Knowledge Base, also on Microsoft's Web site, for recent articles about Word 97 master document problems.

Fixing Corrupt Master Documents

On rare occasions, while working in a Master document, you may receive this message:

```
This document may be corrupt.
```

Here's one scenario that occasionally leads to corrupt master documents: using Word 97, you open a Word 95 master document that contains bullets or numbering, and you make changes to it. Word fails to track the changes properly and reports the master document as corrupt. There are other ways a master document may be corrupted as well.

Don't panic. Even in the worst case, you can nearly always select all the contents of your master document (including the contents of subdocuments) and copy them to a new document. You may have to copy the contents of subdocuments individually, or you can create a new master document that incorporates the existing subdocuments, which are rarely if ever damaged.

In response to problems with corrupt master documents, Microsoft has released a special utility, mdocutl.exe, available on the Microsoft Web site. Double-click mdocutl.exe to extract the template mdocutl.dot, which contains macros that can repair many damaged master documents.

If Word Won't Save Your Master Document

Word's capacity for managing subdocuments varies with the number of files and programs you have open, how much memory your computer has, and other factors specific to your system. It is possible to run out of resources while you're trying to save a master document. If Word won't save a master document:

- First, cancel the save; close any other open programs and files, and try again.
- If this doesn't work, convert some subdocuments into text in the master document by selecting them and clicking Remove Subdocuments. Then try saving again.

If you find that your system can't support the master document you're trying to create, you have some alternatives. One is to use Word's Insert File feature, which is covered next. A fallback position is to use Office 97 Binders, which enable you to group many documents together for printing or distribution but don't offer the editing and management capabilities of Word master documents.

▶ See "Using Binders to Combine Multiple Documents," p. 771

Inserting Files Instead of Using Master Documents

Occasionally you may want to combine several Word files, and you don't care if they maintain a "double life" as independent subdocuments (or you simply don't *want* them to). In this case, you may want to use Word's Insert File feature instead of master documents. Follow these steps to use Insert File:

1. Click where you want to insert a file.
2. Choose Insert, File. The Insert File dialog box appears (see Figure 15.8).
3. Browse to the file (or files) you want to insert, and select them.
4. Click OK.

N O T E If you're inserting a file that isn't a Word 97 file—for example, a file from an older version of Word or a competitive word processor—Word attempts to convert it first. If the file can be converted, Word inserts it. If not, Word displays an error message. ▬

FIG. 15.8

The Insert File dialog box looks much like the Open dialog box, with these differences: you can only select one file at a time, and you can select a Range of Cells in an Excel worksheet.

Insert File actually inserts an INCLUDETEXT field in your document that includes a reference to the document you inserted. As with master documents, you can reflect the latest information in the source document, though the process is slightly less automatic. You have to select the field and press F9 to update it, just as you would with any other Word field.

▶ **See** "What Fields Can Do For You and Your Organization," **p. 696**

Insert File also lets you build tables of contents, indexes, and cross-references that take into account the text from another document. There is one major difference, however, that limits the usefulness of Insert File: You can't click the field to open and edit the file you've inserted.

 However, you can edit the text you've inserted. After you do, you can press Ctrl+Shift+F7 to update the source document so it reflects your edits.

 In one respect, Insert File is more powerful than Master Documents. You can insert as many files as your hardware can handle, whereas you're limited to 255 subdocuments in a master document, no matter how powerful a computer you have.

Using Insert File to Insert Part of a Document

You can also use Insert File to insert part of any document into your current document. For example, you might want to quote a portion of a current price list. Inserting part of a document is a two-step process.

First, open the *source document* that contains the text you want to insert, and do the following:

1. Select the text you want to insert.
2. Choose Insert, Bookmark.
3. In the Bookmark Name text box, enter the name of a bookmark that will be associated with this text. (Keep it short so you'll remember it.)
4. Save and close the document.

Next, open the *destination document* where you want to insert the text, and do the following:

1. Place your insertion point where you want to insert the text.

2. Choose Insert, File.

3. Select the document containing the source text.

4. In the Range text box, enter the name of the bookmark you've just inserted in the source document.

5. Click OK.

The source document's current text will appear in the destination document. Afterwards, you can update the destination document to reflect any changes in the source document by selecting the field and pressing F9.

CAUTION

You won't be able to update the text if the source document is moved, or if it is edited to eliminate the bookmark.

▶ **See** "Using Bookmarks," **p. 509**

From Here...

Now that you've learned how master documents enable you to create tables of contents, indexes, and cross-references that span multiple documents, learn more about these features in the next three chapters of this book:

- Tables of Contents are covered in Chapter 16, "Tables of Contents and Captions"; Indexes in Chapter 17, "Indexes;" and cross-references in Chapter 18, "Footnotes, Bookmarks, Cross-References, and Hyperlinks."

- You've briefly seen hyperlinks at work. However, you've only scratched the surface of what they can do. See Chapter 18, "Footnotes, Bookmarks, Cross-References, and Hyperlinks," to take a closer look at this powerful new feature.

- You've learned that master documents can be a powerful tool for helping teams work together. In Chapter 23, "Managing Revisions," you can learn about Word's equally powerful workgroup tools for tracking revisions and managing multiple document versions.

- Finally, if you need to brush up on the outlining skills you need to use master documents effectively, skip back to Chapter 14, "Outlining: The Best Way to Organize a Document."

CHAPTER 16

Tables of Contents and Captions

by Bill Camarda

If you've ever had to prepare a table of contents manually, you'll appreciate how thoroughly Word automates the process. It's the same story for tables of figures, illustrations, equations, and even legal citations. Word can do in moments what used to take hours.

In this chapter, you'll learn the quickest ways to compile tables in your documents. You'll also learn a few tricks for getting your tables to look exactly the way you want them to, when Word won't do the job as automatically as you might like.

You'll also learn about a Word feature that's as remarkable as it is underused—*captioning*. Did you know Word can insert all your captions for you *automatically*, and keep them numbered accurately with no effort on your part? If you create documents that include captions, this is your chance to save a lot of time! ■

Quick and easy tables of contents

If you've used heading styles, you can have a table of contents in a matter of seconds.

Formatting your table of contents

Word offers several built-in table of contents formats or lets you create your own.

Creating table of contents entries that don't use styles

You can include anything in your table of contents, not just headings.

Including chapter numbers in your table of contents

It doesn't have to be as complicated as Word makes it out to be!

Building tables of figures

You can collect anything you want into a table of figures.

Using Word's Caption feature

Why manually insert and track captions when Word can automate as much of the process as you like?

Marking and compiling legal citations

Attention: lawyers, paralegals, and law students! Here's how to mark legal citations and compile them into a winning Table of Authorities.

Quick and Easy Tables of Contents

Sometimes you need a table of contents but you don't especially care what it looks like. If you've used heading styles in your document, you can have your table of contents less than 60 seconds from now. Follow these steps to create a default table of contents:

1. Click where you want your table of contents to appear.

2. Choose Insert, Index and Tables.

3. Click the Table of Contents tab (see Figure 16.1).

4. Click OK.

FIG. 16.1

From here, you can control all aspects of your table of contents' appearance—or simply click OK to get a default table of contents.

Word inserts a table of contents based on the first three heading levels in your document, using the built-in table of contents styles in your current template, with a dotted-line tab leader and right-aligned page numbers. If you've already inserted specially formatted page numbers in your document, such as page numbers that include chapter numbers, those will appear in your table of contents.

In short, you now have Word's default table of contents (see Figure 16.2). If that isn't enough for you, the rest of this section shows how to change Word's default settings to get the exact table of contents you have in mind.

 T I P The page numbers in Word tables of contents behave just like hyperlinks. Click one, and you hop straight to the text in the document corresponding to the table of contents entry.

When Word inserts a table of contents in your document, it's actually inserting a TOC field with the specific instructions you've given Word about how to build the table of contents. Later, you'll learn a little more about this field, so you can manually control some aspects of your tables of contents that can't easily be controlled through the Table of Contents tab of the Index and Tables dialog box.

FIG. 16.2
A sample table of contents built with Word's default styles and settings.

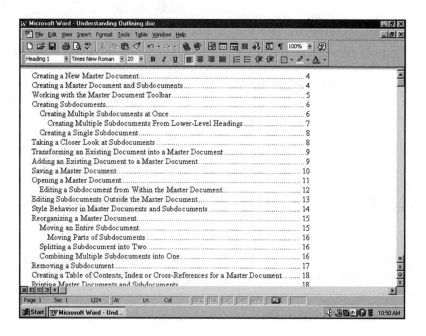

TIP Before you compile your table of contents, there are a few steps you can take to make sure you get an accurate one:

1. Double-check to make sure you've used heading styles for all the headings you want Word to include in your table of contents. As you'll see, you can include other styles and text in a table of contents, but it's usually simplest to use headings.
2. Make sure you've properly set margins and other section formatting that can affect page count.
3. Make sure hidden text is actually hidden—and make sure your document is displaying field results instead of the fields themselves.

Formatting Your Table of Contents

Sometimes the default table of contents format Word applies isn't appropriate for your document. If so, you have two choices:

- ■ Try out one of the six additional table of contents formats Word provides.
- ■ Adapt Word's built-in table of contents styles to your specific needs.

Choosing One of Word's Built-In Formats

Word offers six built-in table of contents formats: Classic, Distinctive, Fancy, Modern, Formal, and Simple. One of these might do the job if you don't have sophisticated requirements or a set of graphic standards with which to comply. (In truth, none of Word's built-in formats are especially Classic, Distinctive, Fancy, Modern, or Formal, though Simple *is* reasonably simple.)

To try out a built-in format, first choose Insert, Inde<u>x</u> and Tables, Table of <u>C</u>ontents. Next, choose the format in the Forma<u>t</u>s scroll box. In the Preview box, Word shows a generic table of contents that uses this format. If you like what you see, click OK, and Word will build a table of contents that follows the format you've chosen.

Building Your Own Table of Contents Format

Because it's quite possible that Word's built-in formats and TOC styles won't do the job for you, Word's Index and Tables dialog box includes a <u>M</u>odify option, which connects you to Word's Style dialog boxes where you can change these styles.

▶ **See** "Creating and Changing Styles," **p. 148**

There's a quicker way to change your TOC styles than digging your way through Word's nested Style dialog boxes. Follow these steps to change your TOC styles:

1. Choose <u>I</u>nsert, In<u>d</u>ex and Tables.
2. Choose the Table of <u>C</u>ontents tab.
3. Click OK to insert a table of contents in your document. Don't worry about changing any formatting settings.
4. After the table of contents is inserted, select the first TOC 1 entry Word has inserted. Be careful not to select the entire table of contents.

 T I P   Sometimes, Word won't let you select the first line of a field result without selecting the entire field (for example, the entire table of contents). Here's the workaround; click *after* the first character in the first line, and press Enter. Now, you can select the *second* line, reformat it, and then edit it to place the first character back where it belongs.

5. Reformat the TOC 1 entry the way you want it to look.
6. Repeat steps 2–3 for each additional TOC style in your table of contents.

If you've used Word's default settings, you'll only have to do it twice more, for TOC 2 and TOC 3. As you change each style, Word immediately updates all the TOC entries that use the same style to reflect the new formatting.

> **CAUTION**
>
> After you have the TOC styles you want, don't choose another Forma<u>t</u> in the Tables of Contents tabbed dialog box. If you do, Word won't just reformat your table of contents; it will reformat your custom styles with the built-in formats you just chose.

Creating Tables of Contents Without Page Numbers

Occasionally, you might want to compile tables of contents without page numbers. For instance, many people insert tables of contents without page numbers as a way of generating a quick document outline.

To tell Word not to include page numbers in a table of contents, display the Table of Contents tab, clear the Show page numbers box, and choose OK.

> **TIP**
>
> In Word 97, Document Map serves much the same purpose without requiring you to insert extraneous text.

Changing the Alignment of Page Numbers

Word includes page numbers in all of its built-in table of contents formats. In most cases, those page numbers are right-aligned, as shown earlier in Figure 16.2. However, you can tell Word to place the page numbers next to the table of contents entries instead of right-aligning them.

To tell Word not to right-align page numbers in a table of contents, display the Table of Contents tab, clear the Right Align Page Numbers check box, and choose OK.

Changing the Tab Leader Used in a Table of Contents

If you create a table of contents based on the TOC styles in the Normal template (for example, if you use the From template format in the Table of Contents tabbed dialog box), Word inserts a *tab leader* on each line. By default, Word uses a series of dots that runs from the end of the table of contents text entry to the page number.

You can change the tab leader, or eliminate it altogether. Display the Table of Contents tab, and choose the leader you want in the Tab leader drop-down list box. Word offers dotted and solid underlines—or you can choose (none) to show no leader.

Choosing the Number of Levels in Your Table of Contents

By default, Word builds tables of contents from the first three heading levels. In other words, it collects all text formatted with the Heading 1, Heading 2, and Heading 3 styles, and incorporates that text in the table of contents.

Of course, this means your table of contents won't include Heading 4 through Heading 9 text. This may be a problem, especially if you've used Heading 1 only as a chapter heading. In that case, your table of contents has only two levels to cover everything important that's going on within your chapters.

You can tell Word to place from one to nine levels in a Word table of contents. Display the Table of Contents tab of the Index and Tables dialog box; then enter a number from 1 to 9 in the Show Levels scroll box.

Changing the Styles That Appear in Your Table of Contents

Sometimes you'll want to compile tables of contents based on styles *other* than Heading 1 through Heading 9. Word enables you to pick any styles you want and choose the order in which they'll be placed in your table of contents. Display the Table of Contents tab, and click Options. The Table of Contents Options dialog box opens (see Figure 16.3).

FIG. 16.3

The Table of Contents Options dialog box lets you specify what styles and table entry fields Word will compile into your table of contents.

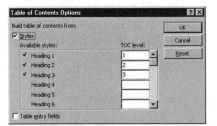

Check marks appear next to all styles that are already in your table of contents. If you want to remove a style, delete the number in its corresponding TOC Level box. To add any style that's already in your document, click its TOC Level text box and enter a number from 1 to 9 there. More than one style can share the same level.

When you're finished, click OK to return to the Index and Tables dialog box. If your other settings are the way you want them, click OK again to compile your table of contents.

N O T E If you decide to revert to Word's default styles (Headings 1 through 3), click the Reset button in the Table of Contents Options dialog box. ■

When You Can't Use Styles: Table of Contents Entry Fields

On rare occasions, you might want your table of contents to include entries that aren't associated with styles at all. For example, you might want the first sentence of each chapter to appear in your table of contents, but you might prefer not to create a separate style for the paragraphs where these sentences may be found. Here are a few other times you might prefer to create at least some of your table of contents entries without using styles:

■ When you'd like to include an entry that paraphrases text in your document instead of repeating it precisely

■ When you'd like to include only one entry formatted with a given style, not all of them

■ When you'd like to suppress page numbering for selected table of contents entries, but not for all of them

You can instruct Word to include any text in a table of contents by using Table Entry fields. It's a two-step process; first you insert the fields in your document, and then you instruct Word to use them in building the table of contents by checking the Table Entry Fields check box in the Table of Contents dialog box.

▶ **See** "Inserting a Field," **p. 697**

Step 1: Inserting TC Fields   *TC fields* are markers that Word can use in compiling a table of contents. They flag locations that Word should compile as part of a table of contents, and specify the text that should appear in the table of contents. You can insert TC fields anywhere in your document.

¶ You can insert TC fields through the Insert, Field dialog box. You can also enter them directly into your document by pressing Ctrl+F9 to display field brackets and entering the syntax between the brackets. However, if you work within field brackets, make sure to toggle the Show/ Hide Paragraph Formatting button, because TC fields are immediately formatted as hidden text that won't otherwise be visible for editing.

Using Insert, Field is a little easier, especially if you're not accustomed to working directly with fields. But working with field brackets is quicker—especially if you're inserting multiple TC fields in your document.

TC fields use the following syntax:

```
{ TC "Words you want to appear in table of contents" [Switches] }
```

In other words, immediately after the field name TC, enter the text you want Word to place in your table of contents, *within quotation marks*. Then follow it with one or more of these switches:

Switch	What It Does
\l Level	Specifies which level of your table of contents to use. If no switch is included, Word assumes Level 1. Example: { TC "Continental League" \l 3 } tells Word to insert a third-level entry consisting of the words Continental League and formatted using the TOC 3 style.
\n	Tells Word not to include a page number for this entry. Example: { TC "Bonus Coverage" \n } tells Word to include the words Bonus Coverage in the table of contents, but not to include the page number the field appears on.
\f Type	Specifies the list of figures in which to include this entry. If you want the entry included in your table of contents (as opposed to a table of figures, such as a table of illustrations), you can ignore this switch. Example: { TC "Mona Lisa" \f m } tells Word to include a table of contents entry named Mona Lisa whenever a table of contents is compiled from all the TC fields that use the \f m switch.

Here are a couple of examples:

Example Field	What It Does
{TC "Martha's Vineyard" \l 2 }	Inserts a second-level table of contents entry Martha's Vineyard (including page numbers).
{ TC "Smith" \l 1 \n}	Inserts a first-level entry *Smith*, with no page number.

TIP After you have the TC syntax correct, you can copy TC fields wherever you need them, changing only the elements that need to change, such as the text that Word will place in the table of contents.

Step 2: Telling Word to Use Your TC Fields   After you've entered TC fields wherever you need them, choose Insert, Index and Tables to reopen the Table of Contents tab. Click Options to view the Table of Contents Options dialog box. Next, check the Table Entry Fields check box.

If you want your table of contents to be built only from TC fields, clear the Styles check box. Click OK to return to the Table of Contents tab; click OK again to compile the table of contents.

Updating a Table of Contents

Even though you usually wait as long as possible before creating a table of contents, chances are your table of contents entries will change after you create them. Perhaps edits or margin changes have affected your page numbering. Possibly new headings have been added to your document, or you've had to reorganize existing headings. Or maybe you've used Word's outlining tools to change heading levels. Follow these steps to update your table of contents to reflect changes like these:

1. Click anywhere in the table of contents.

2. Press F9.

3. Choose whether you want to update only page numbers or the entire table (see Figure 16.4).

4. If you update the entire table, you'll lose any manual formatting or editing you've done within it. However, you may have no choice if you've added or reorganized headings; these changes won't be reflected if you update only page numbers.

▶ **See** "Working with Cross-References," **p. 511**

FIG. 16.4

Word asks whether you want to update page numbers or the entire table.

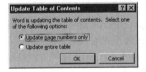

 TIP What if you've done extensive formatting and editing in your table of contents? It seems a shame to lose all that work for just one or two new headings. You don't have to. You can patch your table of contents to reflect the new headings. Click where the new heading should appear in your table of contents, and type it in manually. Even better, use Word's Cross-Reference feature *twice*—first to insert the heading text, and then again to insert the page reference. You may also have to manually apply the heading style that corresponds to the heading level you want, and polish up the formatting to make sure it matches its surroundings.

As a result you'll have a cross-reference field that will update just like the rest of the table of contents will. Everything will work fine—unless you forget and tell Word to update the entire table instead of just page numbers. (That's what Undo is for!)

Adding a Second Table of Contents to Your Document

You might want to add a second table of contents to your document. What kind of documents have two tables of contents? It's increasingly common for how-to books to have a very high-level, "at a glance" table of contents, as well as a more detailed, conventional table of contents that goes several levels deep into the document. Also, you might want to insert separate tables of contents for each major section of a book, as well as an overall table of contents in the front. Whatever your reason, adding a second table of contents is easy to do.

After you insert your first table of contents, do the following:

1. Position your insertion point where you want your second table of contents to appear.
2. Choose Insert, Index and Tables, and display the Table of Contents tab.
3. Create the settings you want to use for the second table of contents; chances are, they will be different from those you used for the first table of contents.
4. Click OK.
5. Word asks if you want to replace your existing table of contents. Click No.

Creating a Table of Contents for Part of a Document

The procedure you've just learned works fine most of the time. For example, it's perfect for including a second high-level table of contents that only includes one or two heading levels. But what if you want to insert a table of contents for only *part* of a document? Use a TOC field.

As you learned earlier, when Word inserts a table of contents, it's actually inserting a TOC field with switches that correspond to the choices you made in the Table of Contents dialog box. However, there are a few things you can do with the TOC field directly that you can't do through a dialog box, and compiling a table of contents for only part of a document is one of them.

Step one is to create a bookmark that covers the part of the document for which you want to create a table of contents:

1. Select the text for which you want to build a table of contents.
2. Choose Insert, Bookmark.
3. In the Bookmark Name text box, enter the name of a bookmark that will be associated with this text.
4. Click Add.

Now that you have a bookmark, create your field code. Include the \b switch and the bookmark name. Here's a bare-bones example:

```
{ TOC \b Jones }
```

 The TOC field has many switches. Follow these steps to get the exact partial table of contents you want without learning them all:

1. Create and insert your table of contents the conventional way, by making choices in the Table of Contents tab of the Index and Tables dialog box.

2. Click anywhere in the table of contents you just inserted.

3. Press Shift+F9 to display the field code Word entered.

4. Click inside the field code, next to the right bracket.

5. Type \b followed by the name of the bookmark.

6. Select the entire field.

7. Press F9 to update the field.

 If you're sure that nothing will change in your table of contents except page numbers, there's an easier way to get a partial table of contents. Insert a table of contents the way you normally would, and just edit out the entries you don't need.

After you've done this, remember to update only page numbers, not the entire table.

TROUBLESHOOTING

Some of my page numbers have been replaced by the words `Error! Bookmark not defined`. Chances are you deleted the corresponding heading from your document and then updated the table of contents using the Update Page Numbers Only option. You have three options:

- Restore the heading in your document.

- Delete the offending line from your table of contents manually.

- Update the table of contents, and when Word displays the dialog box asking whether you want to update the entire table, choose the Update Entire Table option (thereby also removing any manual formatting or editing you may have added).

Some of the body text in my document has found its way into my table of contents. That can happen if body text is formatted with a custom style, and if that style contains an outline level other than Body Text. If possible, change the style to include an outline level of Body text. If this is not possible, you can delete the text from your table of contents manually (all though it will reappear if you update it using the Update entire table option).

The page numbering in my table of contents still isn't right. If you've tried the tips at the beginning of this section and the numbering is still wrong, click anywhere in your table of contents and press F9 to update the table.

Introducing Tables of Figures and Captions

Often, you'll want other tables in your document besides a table of contents. For example, you may want a table that compiles all the figures in your document, or all the equations, or for that matter, all the Word tables. You can build tables like these in much the same way you've just learned how to build tables of contents.

However, Word contains a few extra tricks that might make your life even easier. For example, it can automatically insert captions for you—and then build your table of figures from the captions it has inserted. In the next sections, you'll review Word's powerful captioning features. After you understand captioning, you'll learn how to compile your captions into tables of figures—or any tables you like.

Inserting Captions: An Overview

You can't have a table of figures if you don't have any figure captions to compile into your table. So your first step is to get some figure captions into your document and let Word know that they're figures. There are three ways to do that.

You can insert your figure captions manually, using a style that you won't use for anything except captions. You may not be surprised to learn that Word has a built-in style, *Caption*, that's exquisitely suited for this purpose. You also can use Word's Caption feature. Or, best of all, you can tell Word to automatically insert a caption whenever it sees you inserting something that ought to be captioned.

Using Word's Caption Feature

If you're ready for some help with your captions, choose Insert, Caption to display the Caption dialog box, as shown in Figure 16.5. Word displays its default caption, *Figure 1*, in the Caption text box. If you want to add a description of the figure, you can type it after the figure number, click OK, and Word inserts the entire caption at your insertion point.

TIP If you insert new captions or move existing ones, Word automatically renumbers all the captions for you whenever you display the document in Print Preview, print the document, or update your fields. To see the new numbering right away, click Ctrl+A to select the entire document, and press F9 to update all your fields.

Creating Captions for Other Document Elements

What if you aren't creating captions for figures? If you're creating captions for equations or tables instead, choose Equation or Table in the Label drop-down list box. If you're creating another element, such as a photo or map, you can create a special label by clicking New Label. The New Label dialog box opens (see Figure 16.6). Type your label and choose OK.

FIG. 16.5

The Caption dialog box enables you to enter specific caption information while Word handles boilerplate text and automatic caption numbering.

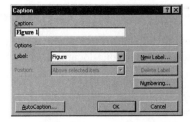

The new label will now appear in the Caption text box, and it will be added to the list of available Labels for future use. If you decide you no longer need it at some point, click Delete Label to eliminate it.

FIG. 16.6

If you're creating captions for something other than a Figure, Table, or Equation, enter your custom label in the New Label dialog box.

Changing the Sequence Word Uses to Number Captions

By default, Word numbers captions with Arabic numbers (1, 2, 3…). However, you can change this. In the Caption dialog box, click Numbering; the Caption Numbering dialog box opens (see Figure 16.7). In the Format drop-down list box, choose a new sequence, such as capital letters or lowercase Roman numerals. Click OK.

FIG. 16.7

The Caption Numbering dialog box enables you to change the sequence Word uses to number captions, or to add a chapter number to your caption numbers.

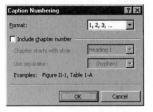

Adding Chapter Numbers to Your Captions

Often, you'll want your captions to include chapter numbers as well as sequence numbers, much like the captions in this book. You should know that Word's "official" approach to inserting chapter numbers is surprisingly complex, and it makes sense only if you have multiple chapters in your document. If you are editing a document that contains only one or a few chapters (even if it's part of a larger book), skip ahead right now for some easier ways to accomplish this!

Word connects chapter numbering in captions with the Outline Numbering feature. That means you have to insert outline numbers in your document before you can get chapter numbers in your captions. If you don't, you're likely to encounter the bewildering message box shown in Figure 16.8.

▶ **See** "Using Word's Automatic Outline Numbering," **p. 421**

FIG. 16.8

Word doesn't want to insert chapter numbers in your captions because you haven't inserted outline numbers throughout your document.

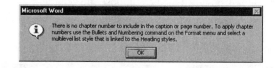

Part **IV**

Ch **16**

By connecting captions to chapter numbers, Word can use { STYLEREF } fields that look for the most recent example of a style, and borrow the text they need from there. This way, Word knows when a caption should read Figure 1.1 and when it should read Figure 2.1.

This is a hassle, especially if you weren't intending to use outline numbering, but go along with it—for now.

Step 1: Set Up Your Document for Outline Numbering   Start by using Word's outlining tools to make sure you've used heading styles throughout your document. This won't work if you simply use outline levels; you have to use the heading styles Heading 1, Heading 2, Heading 3, and so on. Set aside one heading level—typically Heading 1—specifically for your chapter numbers. In fact, don't include any other text in those headings. Figure 16.9 shows how your first-level headings should look in Outline view.

Step 2: Insert Your Outline Numbering   Next, insert your outline numbering, as follows:

1. Select the entire document (or at least all sections where you'll be adding captions).
2. Choose Format, Bullets and Numbering.
3. Choose the Outline Numbered tab.
4. Select a heading numbering scheme from the bottom row of four options. (If you choose from the top row, Word numbers all your paragraphs, not just headings—and your figure numbers won't match your chapter numbers.)
5. Click Customize to make any changes to your outline numbering scheme, or just click OK to insert the outline numbers.

Step 3: Insert Your Captions   Now that you have outline numbers in your document, follow these steps to insert your captions:

1. Place your insertion point where you want your first caption.
2. Choose Insert, Caption.
3. In the Caption dialog box, add any information you want to your caption. If necessary, add a new label.

4. Click <u>N</u>umbering. The Caption Numbering dialog box opens.

5. Check the Include <u>C</u>hapter Number check box.

6. Choose Heading 1 in the Cha<u>p</u>ter Starts With Style drop-down list box. (This example assumes that chapter numbers are formatted with Heading 1 style—and, as already discussed, they are the only text formatted with that style.)

7. In the Use Se<u>p</u>arator drop-down list box, choose the separator character you want from the following selection: a hyphen, period, colon, em dash, and en dash.

8. Click OK twice.

FIG. 16.9

Make sure you use Heading 1 only for chapter numbers and you include nothing but chapter numbers in your "Heading 1"s.

Style box ─┐

First-level headings ─┘

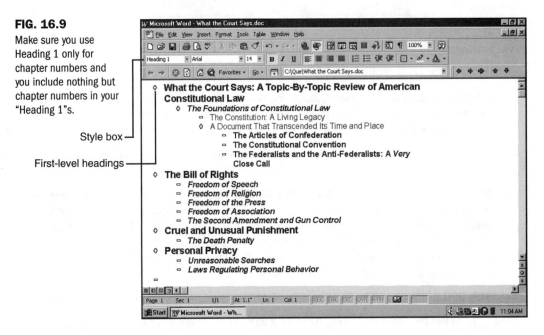

The caption appears in your document, containing the number of the current chapter. Underneath the hood, here's what's happened. Word has inserted a { STYLEREF } field that searches toward the beginning of the document for the first Heading 1 style. When a Heading 1 style is found, the text formatted in that style is displayed as the field result.

TIP

If you've gone through all this, and then decide you don't want outline numbers after all, here's a possible solution. When the document is absolutely finished, select it all (Ctrl+A). Then follow these steps:

1. Press Ctrl+Shift+F9 to unlink all the fields in your document, so none of them will update ever again. (This affects all fields, including the fields that track caption numbering within the chapter—so be careful!)

2. With the entire document selected, choose <u>I</u>nsert, Bullets and <u>N</u>umbering, O<u>u</u>tline Numbered. The Outline Numbered tab appears.

3. Choose None and click OK. The outline numbers disappear, but the captions stay the way they were.

Easier Ways to Add Chapter Numbers

Boy, *that* was hard work. Isn't there an easier way? You'd better believe it.

You really don't have to include outline numbering to get chapter numbers in your captions.

Adding Chapter Numbers to Captions in One-Chapter Documents   Consider the easiest case: a document containing only one chapter. Maybe you've been asked to write Chapter 12 of a book. You're not working from within someone else's master document (or, if you are, they aren't requiring you to use Word's outline numbering approach to captions).

Follow these steps to insert chapter numbers:

1. Use Word's Insert, Caption feature to insert captions without chapter numbers.

2. Choose Edit, Replace and then use Word's Find and Replace feature to search for all references to the word figure that are styled using the Caption style, and replace them with figure followed by your chapter number and whatever separator character you want to use. You can search for a style by clicking the Format button in the Replace tab, clicking Style, and choosing the style you want to search for.

   ▶ **See** "Finding and Replacing Styles," **p. 88**

Creating Custom Caption Numbering for All Your Documents   You can go a step further and create a chapter numbering solution you can reuse in all your documents, no matter how many chapters they contain—without ever using outline numbering unless you want to. Follow these steps:

1. Select the chapter number anywhere in your document and format it with a *character* style through the Format, Style dialog box. For this example, name the character style **Chapnum**.

   ▶ **See** "Understanding Character Styles," **p. 143**

2. Use Insert, Caption to insert a caption that doesn't contain a chapter number.

3. If you like, reformat the caption to your tastes, and update the caption style to reflect your changes. (After you reformat the caption, click in the Style drop-down box, press Enter, and click OK in the Modify Style dialog box that appears.)

4. Click where you want the chapter number to appear within your caption.

5. Press Ctrl+F9 to insert field brackets.

6. Type the following within the field brackets:

   ```
   styleref chapnum
   ```

7. Press F9 to update the field. It should now display the chapter number to which you applied the character style.

8. Create an AutoText entry based on your caption. To do so, select the caption; choose Insert, AutoText, AutoText; type a entry name such as *fig*, and click OK.

Now, whenever you start a new document you want to contain automatically numbered captions, do the following:

1. Type the chapter number and mark it as a bookmark named *chapnum*.

2. Wherever you want to insert a caption, type the AutoText entry and press F3 to turn it into a complete caption

Automating Captions

You can take Word's captioning feature one giant step further. Word can automatically add captions any time you add specific graphics or other elements to your document. To use Word's AutoCaption feature, choose Insert, Caption to display the Caption dialog box. Then, click AutoCaption. The AutoCaption dialog box opens (see Figure 16.10).

FIG. 16.10

From the AutoCaption dialog box, you can choose which document elements will be captioned automatically, which label to use, and where those captions should appear.

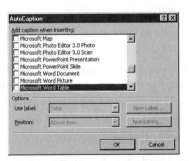

In the Add Caption When Inserting scroll box, you see a list of document elements. This list will vary depending on the software you've installed on your computer; it includes (among other things) files from all the programs you own that are OLE (Object Linking and Embedding) servers.

Check the box next to every item you would like Word to caption. Then, specify the label you want to use (or create a new label, if you wish). In the Position drop-down list box, choose whether you want your caption to automatically appear below or above the item you insert. If you want to change automatic caption numbering, click Numbering and make your changes in the Caption Numbering dialog box you learned about earlier.

When you're finished, click OK in the AutoCaption dialog box. Word will begin adding captions automatically whenever you insert a document element you've told it to seek.

Building Tables of Figures

Now that you've learned about captions, it's time to discuss ways you can compile those captions into tables of figures. First, choose Insert, Index and Tables, and click the Table of Figures tab (see Figure 16.11).

FIG 16.11

The Table of Figures tab offers many of the same options as the Table of Contents tab.

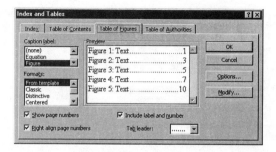

The Table of Figures tab looks quite similar to the Table of Contents dialog box you learned about earlier in this chapter. For example, you can choose whether page numbers should appear in your table, and if so, whether they should be right-aligned or appear next to the caption text. If you right-align your figure listings, you can choose a tab leader. You can also choose from five formats: Classic, Distinctive, Centered, Formal, and Simple. You can see the effects of any change you make in the Preview box.

N O T E   While these formats complement the Table of Contents formats with the same names, they're not identical. As with Tables of Contents, you can see what a format will look like in the Preview box.

When you choose a Table of Figures format and choose OK, Word inserts the table in your document. Word applies its built-in Table of Figures style, after changing the style to reflect the format you chose.

There are some differences, however. Each table of figures Word compiles is based on one set of captions in your document. In other words, if you've created some captions using the Table label, and others using the Figure label, each set will have to be compiled separately into its own table of figures—but then, that's what you probably want. In the Caption Label drop-down list box, choose the type of captions you want to compile.

If you want to include the label and number themselves, check the Include Label and Number check box; otherwise, clear it. If you're now satisfied with your table, click OK and Word will insert it in your document. Figure 16.12 shows a default table of figures using the built-in styles in the Normal template.

Building Tables of Figures from a Different Style

Until now, you've learned how to build tables of figures by telling Word to collect the contents of every figure formatted with the Caption style. Because Word automatically uses the Caption style for all the captions it creates, you're in good shape as long as you use Word's automatic captioning feature. But what if you would like to compile a table from text formatted in a different style?

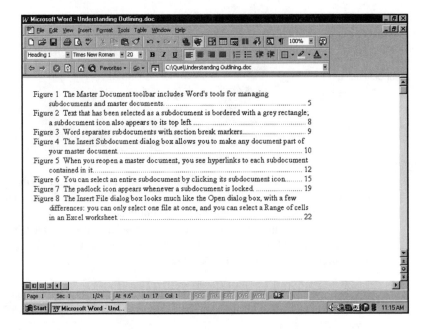

Choose Insert, Index and Tables, then choose the Table of Figures tab displayed, and click Options. The Table of Figures Options dialog box opens (see Figure 16.13).

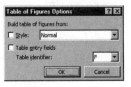

To choose another style, check the Style check box, and select the style from the drop-down box next to it. Click OK to return to the Table of Figures tab, and click OK again to insert the table in your document.

Building Tables from Figures with Different Styles

Occasionally, you might want to create a table of figures based on document elements that don't share a common style. For example, you might want a table of figures that contains all the quotations in your document. Because those quotations appear within paragraphs of various types scattered throughout your document, you can't compile them into a single figure table based on one style.

Earlier in this chapter, you learned about TC fields, which Word can use to build tables of contents without using styles. TC fields come to your rescue again now. As you've learned, there are several procedures for inserting fields. Either refer back to the earlier discussion, or follow this procedure:

1. Choose Insert, Field.
2. Choose TC from the Field Names scroll box.
3. In the Description text box, enter the text you want to appear for this reference when the table of figures is compiled. Be sure to place the text within quotation marks.
4. After the close quotation mark, enter \f followed by the letter of the alphabet you intend to use for all entries in this table of figures.
5. Click OK.

Part
IV

Ch
16

Continuing with the quotation example discussed in the "Building Tables from Figures with Different Styles" section, imagine your document has a quotation by Washington. You might enter the TC field:

```
{ TC "Washington" \f q }
```

Then, later, you come across a quotation by Jefferson you'd like to flag:

```
{ TC "Jefferson" \f q }
```

Because they both use the \f q switch, you can compile them together by following these steps:

1. Choose Insert, Index and Tables, Table of Figures to display the Table of Figures tab.
2. Click Options to display the Table of Figures Options dialog box.
3. Check the Table Entry Fields check box.
4. Choose Q (or whatever letter you've inserted after \f in your TC fields) in the Table Identifier drop-down list box.
5. Click OK twice.

As shown in Figure 16.14, Word builds a table of figures which contains the names of all the people you've quoted, and the page numbers where the quotes may be found.

Marking Citations

If you're responsible for preparing legal documents, you know that special techniques are required to insert and track *citations*, which are references to cases, statutes, or other legal documents. Word streamlines both marking citations and collecting them into tables of citations.

Enter your citations throughout your document, as you normally would. In the first reference to a citation, enter the long (full) version, which typically includes case numbers, dates, and other essential information. In later references, enter the short version, which typically includes only the name of the case.

FIG. 16.14

Word built this table of notable quotables from a series of TC fields that all used the \f q switch.

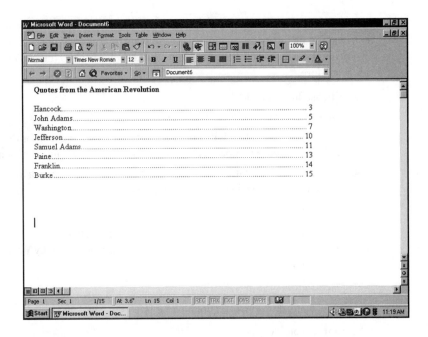

Then, when you're ready to start marking citations, select the first long citation in your document, and press Alt+Shift+I to open the Mark Citation dialog box (see Figure 16.15).

FIG. 16.15

You can insert and manage citations in a legal document through the Mark Citation dialog box.

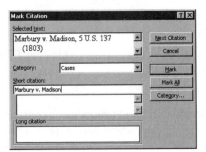

Your citation appears in the Selected Text box. Edit and format it so it looks the way you want it to appear in your table of authorities. Your citation also appears in the Short Citation text box. Edit the Short citation so it matches the short citations you've placed in your document. Typically, this means deleting everything except the case name.

Because some tables of authorities are organized by category (for example, cases in one table, statutes in another), choose a Category from the drop-down list box. Word includes seven built-in categories: Cases, Statutes, Other Authorities, Rules, Treatises, Regulations, and Constitutional Provisions. If you need to create a table of authorities for a different category, you can create the category yourself. Word provides nine generic categories, numbered 8 through 16, which you can rename any way you like. Follow these steps to create a custom category:

1. In the Mark Citation dialog box, select one of the numbered categories.
2. Click Category. The Edit Category dialog box opens (see Figure 16.16).
3. Enter the new name in the Replace With text box.
4. Click Replace.
5. Click OK. You return to the Mark Citation dialog box with your new category already selected.

FIG. 16.16

You can add up to nine custom categories of citations using the Edit Category dialog box.

You've now prepared your citation for marking. If you want to mark only the long citation you've already selected, click Mark. If you want Word to search your entire document and mark all references to the same citation, long and short, click Mark All.

Now that you've marked all references to the first citation, you can move on to the next. Word searches your document for the next block of text it thinks might be part of a citation. For example, Word flags the abbreviation *v.* and the phrase *In re*, both commonly used in case names. Word also flags the symbol § that often appears in statute citations.

If Word has flagged a citation you would like to mark, click the document, and select the entire citation. Then click the Mark Citation dialog box; the citation you selected appears in both the Selected Text and Short Citation text boxes. You can then edit and mark it following the steps you've already learned.

N O T E When you mark a citation, Word inserts a TA (Table of Authorities) field in your document. This field stores the information that will be compiled when you create your table of authorities. For long citations, the TA field will look like this:

`{ TA \l "Marbury v. Madison, 5 U.S. 137 (1803)" \s "Marbury v. Madison" \c 1 }`

As you can see, the TA field for a long citation includes both the detailed text of the long citation and the abbreviated version Word uses to search for short citations. The Mark Citation dialog box doesn't let you edit a long citation after you've marked it, but if you need to, you can edit the field directly.

For short citations, the TA field looks like this:

`{ TA \s "Marbury v. Madison" }`

Word inserts TA field codes formatted as hidden text. If you press Alt+F9 to toggle field codes and you still don't see your TA field codes, click the Show/Hide Paragraph button on the Standard toolbar to display them.

Adding More Citations Later

Let's say you've already marked the citations in your document, and you return to add new citations—either long citations, or additional references to short citations you've already marked elsewhere. To mark them, just press Alt+Shift+I to open the Mark Citation dialog box, and click Next Citation; Word searches for the first citation it hasn't already marked. If Word doesn't find one of your new citations, select it and then press Alt+Shift+I; the citation will be displayed in the Mark Citation dialog box when it opens.

Compiling Tables of Authorities from Citations

After you've created your citations, you can compile them into tables of authorities. Choose Insert, Index and Tables, and click the Table of Authorities tab (see Figure 16.17).

FIG. 16.17

The Table of Authorities tab of the Index and Tables dialog box gives you extensive control over how your tables of authorities compile.

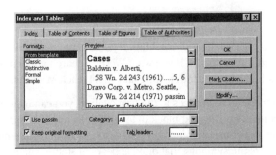

If you've used tables of contents or figures, this dialog box will seem familiar. By default, Word builds your table of authorities from styles in your current template. Or you can choose from one of four formats: Classic, Distinctive, Formal, and Simple. You can also specify the tab leader to use—or no tab leader at all. A default table of authorities is shown in Figure 16.18.

> **CAUTION**
>
> Word's built-in Tables of Citations formats meet the requirements of most courts and jurisdictions, but it never hurts to compare your table of authorities with similar documents the court has accepted, or conceivably to double-check with the court clerk if you're not sure.

 TIP You can also click Modify on the Table of Authorities tab to change the TOA Heading style Word uses to build tables of authorities—but as discussed in the table of contents section of this chapter, it's faster to reformat and update the styles in your document.

By default, Word includes every citation in your table of authorities. If you want a separate table for one category of citation, choose it from the Category drop-down box located on the Tables of Authorities tab.

FIG. 16.18
A default table of authorities using the built-in styles in Word's Normal template.

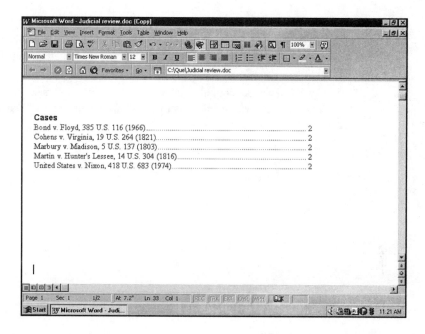

It's common practice, when listing citations that appear repeatedly in a legal document, to substitute the word *passim* for the multiple page references. By default, Word substitutes passim whenever you have at least five references to the same citation. To display the actual page numbers instead, clear the Use Passim check box on the Tables of Authorities tab.

Many citations contain complex character formatting, especially boldface, italic, and underlining. By default, Word carries that formatting into your table of authorities. However, you can tell Word not to do so by clearing the Keep Original Formatting check box on the Tables of Authorities tab.

From Here...

You'll find that many of the techniques in this chapter, including the steps required to insert tables and fields, will be useful elsewhere in Word. In particular:

- Now that you've learned how to build tables of contents, figures, and authorities, Chapter 17, "Indexes," shows you how to use the same techniques to compile indexes.
- The easiest tables of contents are built with heading styles. If you need a refresher on using heading styles, refer to coverage of style in Chapter 5, "Styles: The Foundation of Automated Documents," or the outlining discussion in Chapter 14, "Outlining: The Best Way to Organize a Document."

- Throughout this chapter, you've been inserting fields such as TC, TOC, STYLEREF, SEQ, TA, and TOA fields, to name a few. To get a better idea of what those fields are doing and how they work, check out Chapter 25, "Automating Your Documents with Field Codes."

- Finally, if you want to compile a table of contents that covers several documents, refer back to detailed coverage of master documents in Chapter 15, "Master Documents: Control and Share Even the Largest Documents."

CHAPTER 17

Indexes

by Bill Camarda

If you ever create documents that need to be indexed, Word's powerful, built-in indexing features can do two valuable things for you: They can *automate* the aspects of indexing that a computer is smart enough to do more or less on its own. For some documents, that means Word can automate nearly 100 percent of the work. They can *streamline* the more subtle aspects of indexing for which there's still no substitute for human judgment.

In this chapter, you'll learn how (and when) to use Word for each purpose. ■

Marking index entries

Word can build your indexes for you, if you tell it what to include.

Automatically marking many entries at the same time

You can automatically mark all references to specific text, or you can go further and AutoMark the entire document.

Creating subentries

You can create multilevel indexes that match the sophistication of your document.

Compiling your index

Use the Index and Tables dialog box to control aspects of your indexes' appearance and behavior.

Creating custom indexes

You can create custom indexes that include only some entries, or some letters of the alphabet.

Using { XE } and { INDEX } field codes for more control

If you can't control it from the Index and Tables dialog box, chances are you *can* control it directly, by editing field codes.

Creating dictionary-style headings for your index pages

Help readers get answers from your index ASAP—by providing headers that tell them where they are.

How Word Indexes Work

Building an index with Word is a three-step process. First, you mark your index entries—either one-by-one, or a batch at a time. Next, you tell Word which types of entries to include in your index and how to format the index. Then there's the easy part—actually compiling the index.

> **N O T E** In general, compiling your index should be one of the last things you do with your document. Indexing last reduces the number of times you'll have to rebuild your index. It also tends to increase the quality of your index because you have access to the entire document while you're making decisions about how individual entries should be handled. ■

Creating a New Index Entry

The quickest way to mark an index entry is to select it, and press Alt+Shift+X. The Mark Index Entry dialog box opens (see Figure 17.1). The text you've selected appears in the Main Entry text box. In some cases, that text will serve perfectly well as your index entry. In many other cases, you'll want to edit the entry. For example, you may want to make any of the following revisions:

- Switch last and first names, so your main entry reads *Austen, Jane* instead of *Jane Austen*.

- Spell out and explain abbreviations, using the most familiar version first, so references to PCI boards appear as *PCI (Peripheral Component Interconnect)*.

- Change word forms for consistency or simplicity, so your entry reads *law* instead of *legalities*.

- Standardize and simplify usage, so your main entry reads *Singers* instead of *Vocalists*.

FIG. 17.1
You can control all elements of your index entries through the Mark Index Entry dialog box.

If you're satisfied with your entry, click <u>M</u>ark. Word inserts an { XE } field code in your document that contains the text of your entry. Because the field code is hidden text, you won't see it unless you display it by clicking the Show/Hide Paragraph button on the Standard toolbar.

After you mark the index entry, the dialog box remains open, so you can create another entry elsewhere in the document. Click the document; select the text you want to index; then click <u>M</u>ark again in the Mark Index Entry dialog box. The text you've selected now appears in the

Main Entry text box. You can move throughout the document this way, using Word's navigation tools, creating entries as you go. When you're finished, click Close and the Mark Index Entry dialog box closes.

 TIP If you plan to create an index entry that doesn't use any of the words in the surrounding text, don't select any text before pressing Alt+Shift+X. Then you won't have to delete any.

 TIP You can apply boldface, italic, or underlining to any index text you enter in the Mark Index Entry dialog box. Simply select and format all or part of the text. This enables you to create index entries for book titles that require italic. It also helps you call attention to special aspects of an entry, as in the following example:

```
Dickens, Charles, quoted, 307
```

If you plan to create a lot of index entries, it'll be worth your time to create a toolbar button that displays the Mark Index Entry dialog box. To create a toolbar button, follow these steps:

1. Choose Tools, Customize.
2. Click the Commands tab.
3. In the Categories scroll box, click Insert.
4. In the Commands scroll box, select Mark Index Entry and drag it out of the dialog box to any toolbar. A new toolbar button appears, containing the words Mark Index Entry.

 TIP If the toolbar button is too wide for you, right-click it; click the Name command, and edit the name. (You might shorten it to XE, the name of the field code it will insert.)

▶ **See** "Customizing Toolbars," **p. 721**

5. When you're finished, close the Customize dialog box.

Marking Multiple Entries at Once

If you want, you can tell Word to mark *all* references to specific text. Follow these steps:

1. Select the text you want to index. Unlike marking single entries, you can mark multiple entries only if you select text before you open the Mark Index Entry dialog box.
2. Press Alt+Shift+X; the Mark Index Entry dialog box opens.
3. Edit the Index Main Entry box to reflect the exact entry you want. Word marks all locations in your document where it finds the text *you originally selected*, not the edited version in the Mark Entry box.
4. Choose Mark All.

Later in this chapter, you'll learn how to use Word's AutoMark feature to mark many different entries at the same time.

CAUTION

In order for you to see the index entries you're placing in your document, Word displays Hidden Text after you enter your first index entry. When you're finished marking index entries, you'll need to re-hide this hidden text manually, by clicking the Show/Hide Paragraph button on the Standard toolbar. Make sure to hide your index entries before you compile a table of contents, or your page numbering is likely to be incorrect.

Formatting Page Numbers as Bold or Italic

Many indexers like to call attention to some entries by boldfacing or italicizing the page numbers. For example, it's common to italicize page numbers associated with entries that refer to photos rather than body text. To add formatting to a page number, check the Bold or Italic check box in the Mark Index Entry dialog box.

Creating Subentries

Often, it's not enough to create an index entry. You'll also want a subentry that gives your readers a better sense of what they'll find. Subentries are typically used when you expect to make several references to an item in your index, and each reference covers significantly different points, as in the following index excerpts:

```
Brinkley, J.R.
      goat gland prostate surgery, 24
      medical license suspended, 32
      XER radio station, 27
Bryan, William Jennings
      Cross of Gold speech, 106
Spokesman for Florida real estate, 127
      Scopes trial prosecuting attorney, 148
```

To create an index entry that contains a subentry, either select text to be indexed or click where you want the index entry to be placed; then click Alt+Shift+X to display the Mark Index Entry dialog box again. Enter your main entry. Be careful to be consistent about how you create main entries you expect to use more than once. Then, enter text in the Subentry text box as well, and click Mark.

Creating Multilevel Subentries

In some respects, building an index isn't much different from creating an outline; it's conceivable you'll want more than two levels of outline entries. Occasionally, you'll find an index entry fits most naturally as a subentry to another subentry. Here's an example:

```
Procter & Gamble
      Peanut Butter, 47
      Soap, 113-122
            Camay® brand, 116
            Ivory® brand, 113-117
                  Recent repackaging, 114
            Oil of Olay® brand, 118
```

Follow these steps to create a multilevel subentry:

1. Press Alt+Shift+X to display the Mark Index Entry dialog box.
2. Enter the main entry you want to appear in your index.
3. In the Subentry text box, enter each level of subentry, separated by a colon. Don't leave space between levels. For example,

   ```
   Soap:Ivory® brand:Recent repackaging
   ```

Word supports up to seven levels of index entry, though it's unlikely you'll ever want to use more than three or four.

N O T E In the example shown previously, the Proctor & Gamble index entry has no page number. If you create a subentry attached to a main entry, but you never create any index entries based on the main entry alone, Word displays the main entry with no page number.

Inserting Text Instead of a Page Number

By default, Word includes a page number along with each index entry: the page number where it finds the { XE } field when it compiles the index. This is how Word behaves when the Current Page button is selected in the Mark Index Entry dialog box. Sometimes, however, you won't want a page reference. Instead, you'll want to refer people to a different index entry, as in the following examples:

```
Farming, See Agriculture

Second-strike capability, See also Retaliatory strike
```

To create a cross-reference in your index, set up the rest of the entry as you normally would; then click the Cross-Reference button and enter the cross-reference text you want to include, next to the word *See*.

N O T E You don't have to use the word *See*, which Word provides as a suggestion. You can edit or replace it if you prefer a different way of referring to other index entries.

These cross-references have nothing to do with the automated cross-references you can place throughout your document via the Insert, Cross-Reference dialog box.

Controlling Index Entry Page Numbers

Sometimes you'll want to create an index entry for a discussion that stretches across two or more pages. Word makes this easy: first you create a bookmark corresponding to the block of text you want to index; then you specify the bookmark as part of the index entry.

Follow these steps to create the bookmark:

1. Select the text for which you want to create the entry.

2. Choose Insert, Bookmark.

3. Enter a name for the bookmark.

4. Click Add.

Now, build the index entry using the bookmark:

1. Click Alt+Shift+X to display the Mark Index Entry dialog box.

2. Enter the main entry and/or subentry text you want.

3. Click the Page Range button.

4. Choose the bookmark from the Bookmark drop-down list.

5. Click Mark.

Compiling Your Index

Now that you've learned how to create index entries, move on to compiling them. To prepare your index for compilation, place your insertion point where you want the index (typically at the end of the document). Then, choose Insert, Index and Tables, and click the Index tab (see Figure 17.2).

FIG. 17.2
You can control nearly all aspects of compiling an index through the Index tab of the Index and Tables dialog box.

If you've read the coverage of tables of contents in Chapter 16, "Tables of Contents and Captions," you'll see some familiar elements in this dialog box. For instance, as with tables of contents, Word's default format for indexes is From Template, which simply means it uses the Index styles built into any template you're using.

Word also provides several more formats: Classic, Fancy, Modern, Bulleted, Formal, and Simple. If you've chosen one of these formats for your table of contents, you'll probably want to choose the same format for your index. When you change a format (or make most other changes), Word shows what you can expect in the Preview box.

The Normal template contains nine index levels, all formatted as 12-point Times New Roman, with each level indented 0.14 inches more than the level before it. If you want to change these formats manually, follow these steps:

1. Insert an index in your document.

2. Reformat text based on the Index 1 heading manually.

3. Click the Style drop-down list box and press Enter.

4. In the Modify Style dialog box, choose Update the Style To Reflect Recent Changes and click OK.

5. Repeat steps 2–4 for each index style you want to modify.

After you've finished making changes throughout this tab, click OK, and Word inserts an index in your document. Notice that the index appears in a section of its own—if for no other reason than it is usually a different number of columns than the surrounding text. You can see a default Word index in Figure 17.3.

FIG. 17.3
An index is built using all of Word's default settings.

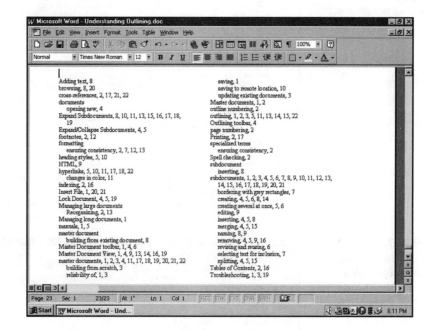

Part
IV

Ch
17

 Because the index is contained in its own section, you can create a separate header or footer for it, or customize its page numbering.

 Unlike the From Template format, four of Word's alternate index formats—Classic, Fancy, Modern, and Bulleted—also add headings for each letter of the alphabet. A sample index formatted with the Bulleted format is shown in Figure 17.4. If you would like these headings but you want to maintain the default From Template style for everything else, use the Classic format.

Creating Run-In Indexes

If you're short on space, you may want to create a run-in index, such as the one shown in Figure 17.5. Often, using the Run-In option can shorten your index by as much as 30 to 40 percent.

The more subentries you use, the more space you'll save. To create a run-in index, click the Run-In button in the Index tab.

FIG. 17.4

In this index built with Word's Bulleted format, each letter that contains an index entry has its own heading. Word skips letters without index entries.

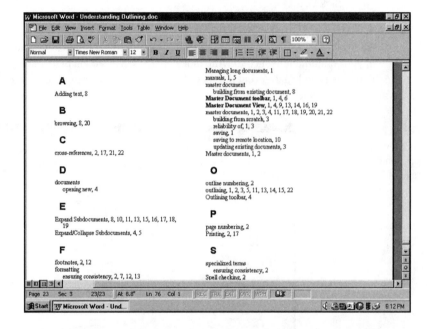

FIG 17.5

Using the Run-In option can substantially reduce the number of pages required for your index.

Typical run-in index entry

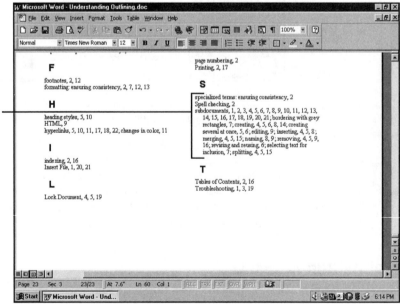

Creating Alphabetic Headings for Accented Letters

You may need to index a document written (entirely, or in part) in a language that uses accented letters such as À, Ë, or Ñ (for example, French, Spanish, or German). If you are also using a format that will include headings for each letter of the alphabet, to respect your international readers, you'll want Word to create separate alphabetic headings for these accented letters. If so, check the Headings for Accented Letters check box in the Index tab.

Right-Aligning Page Numbers in an Index

Except for Word's Formal index style, all of Word's built-in index styles place the page number right next to the end of the index entry text. If you prefer to right-align the page numbers, (see Figure 17.6), check the Right Align Page Numbers check box in the Index tab.

FIG. 17.6
This index uses right-aligned page numbers with a dot leader.

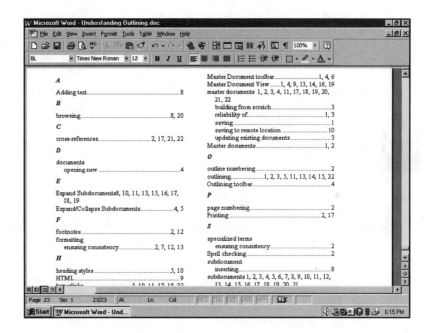

Part **IV**

Ch **17**

If you choose to right-align page numbers, Word also lets you select a Tab Leader that Word will use between the entry text and the page numbers.

Controlling the Number of Columns in an Index

By default, Word creates two-column indexes. Most books use two-column indexes, and in most cases, so should you. However, you may occasionally want to change this setting, especially if

- You're using a relatively wide page size
- You're using relatively small type for your index entries

Word will build indexes of up to four columns. Enter the number of columns you want in the Columns list box of the Index tab.

Adding Chapter Numbering to Your Index

If your document has multiple chapters, each renumbered from page 1, you'll probably want an index that includes chapter numbers with each listing, as in the following example:

```
Van Diemen's Land (Tasmania), 4-2, 12-18, 14-29
```

Word automatically includes chapter numbering in your document *if* you have used Word's page numbering feature (Insert, Page Numbers) to insert these numbers in your header or footer.

CAUTION

In order to use Word's page numbering feature, you have to first use Outline Numbering. This issue is discussed at length in Chapter 16, "Tables of Contents and Captions."

Updating an Index   What if you make changes in your document after you create your index (as is nearly inevitable)? You can update your index by clicking anywhere in it and pressing F9.

TIP   Often it's easier to select the entire document (Ctrl+A) and press F9. You also get the added benefit of updating all your other fields at the same time.

You'll obviously update your index any time you make significant changes in your document. However, you'll also want to systematically walk through your index after you create it for the first time to fix the entries that aren't quite right and then update it to fix the problems you found. For example, you should look for the following:

- Are there redundant entries that use slightly different variations on a word, or are there duplicate entries for a word in capitalized and lowercase form?
- Are there better ways of organizing high-level concepts?
- Are any entries misspelled?

The best way to review an index is to open a second window on your file and set up Word so you can view the index in one window while you view the document in another. To do so, follow these steps:

1. Open the document containing the index. (It should be the only document you have open.)

2. If your { XE } index entry fields are not visible, click the Show/Hide Paragraph button on the Standard toolbar to make them visible.

3. Switch to Normal view if you aren't already there.

4. Choose Tools, Options, View, and check the Wrap to Window check box if it isn't already checked. This ensures that you can see all your text no matter how narrow your windows are.

5. Choose New Window from the Window menu.

6. Choose Arrange All from the Window menu. You now have two half-sized windows, splitting the screen horizontally. Both windows display the same document.

7. Drag each window's borders so the two documents appear as shown in Figure 17.7.

8. In the left window, scroll to the top of the index.

9. In the right window, scroll to the top of the document.

FIG. 17.7
Set up to review an index alongside the document being indexed.

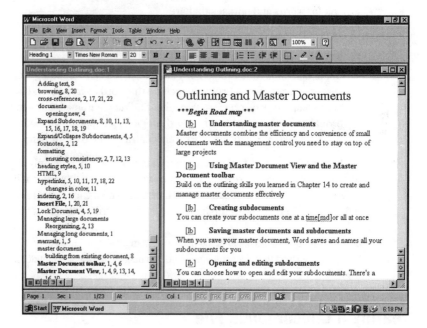

Now you can move through the index one item at a time; whenever you find an item that needs changing, click in the window that displays the document, navigate to the { XE } field code that caused the problem, and edit it. When you're done, click in the index (or select the entire document) and press F9 to update the index.

Automating Indexing with Concordance Files and AutoMarking

Earlier, you learned how to mark all the references to specific text in a document at the same time by selecting the text, pressing Alt+Shift+X to display the Mark Index Entry dialog box, and clicking Mark All. You can go much further than this, telling Word to automatically mark (AutoMark) all references to *many* different words and phrases at the same time.

To do so, you first create a special file called a *concordance file*. Then you tell Word to use that concordance file to identify text for AutoMarking and to specify what each automated index entry will say. In a moment, you'll walk through AutoMarking a document, but first, you should decide if AutoMarking is the best alternative.

Is AutoMarking Worth Your Time?

To decide whether it will really save time to build and use a concordance file, scroll through your document looking for elements that lend themselves to automatic indexing. Names of any kind are excellent candidates, including people's names, product names, and brand names. Also, look for words and phrases that are

- Typically used in a context that you'll want to index.
- Used consistently throughout your document.
- Important enough to index. For example, if you were building a concordance file for this paragraph, you would probably include the word *concordance*. It's relevant, specific, and your computer won't have any trouble finding it automatically. On the other hand, you probably wouldn't include the word *computer*; it appears virtually everywhere in the book, and when it appears, it's rarely central to the topic at hand.

Don't be surprised if you find that a concordance file will handle only a quarter or a third of the index entries you need to create. If it can do even that much, however, it'll still save you quite a bit of time in indexing a large document. Best of all, it'll take care of the mind-numbing, rote aspects of indexing, leaving you with the more interesting entries—the ones that require judgment.

N O T E The concordance indexes you build with Word aren't true concordances, which are generally understood to incorporate every word in a document. However, that doesn't make them any less useful.

Creating a Concordance File

To create a concordance file, click New on the Standard toolbar to display a new blank document. Then insert a two-column table. There are several ways to do so; the easiest is to click the Insert Table button, drag across the matrix to create a two-column table, and release the mouse button (see Figure 17.8).

Now start adding entries. In the left column, type words or phrases for which you want to search. In the right column, type the entry the way you want it to appear in your index. If you don't enter anything in the right column, Word creates an entry using the text in the left column. Because indexing is case-sensitive, make sure your left column includes all variations of words that might appear both capitalized and lowercase. However, make sure you standardize on either lowercase or uppercase for the right column, so Word won't generate duplicate entries you don't want. Also make sure you capture all forms of a word, such as *explode*, *exploding*, and *explosion*.

Some people find it easier to set up the editing window so the concordance file appears at the left and the document to be indexed appears at the right. You learned how to do this in the discussion of updating indexes, earlier in this chapter. If both documents are visible, it's easy (and more accurate) to copy entries from one to the other.

When you've finished adding entries, save and close the file.

FIG. 17.8

This two-column table is ready to be used as a concordance file.

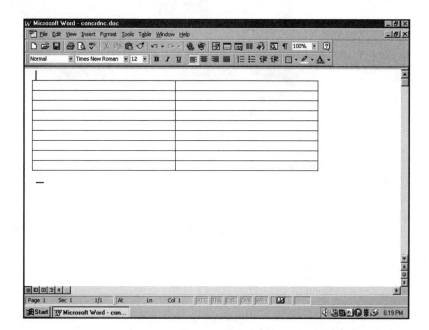

CAUTION

AutoMark can't find words that contain hyphens, even if they're in your concordance file.

If you have a few important index entries that contain hyphens and recur often throughout your document, you can run Find and Replace to temporarily replace the hyphens in those words or phrases with a different character. Then run AutoMarking. Once the index entries have been created, run Find and Replace again to place the original hyphens back where they belong.

Using the Concordance File for AutoMarking

Open the document you want to index, if it isn't already open. Choose Insert, Index and Tables, and display the Index tab. Next, click AutoMark. Word displays the Open Index AutoMark File dialog box (see Figure 17.9). Browse and select the concordance file you just created. Click Open. Word inserts index entries wherever you've told it to.

Placing More Than One Index in a Document

Occasionally, you might want to include more than one index in your document. For example, you might want a separate index for all quotes, or one that compiles all troubleshooting tips.

FIG. 17.9

Choose the concordance file you've just created, and click Open.

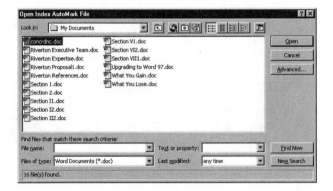

Word enables you to create up to 25 different indexes in the same document. To do so, first create a bookmark that covers all the text you want to incorporate in one of your indexes:

1. Select the whole area of your document for which you want to create a separate index.
2. Choose Insert, Bookmark.
3. Enter a name for the bookmark. In this example, use Index2 (though you can use any name you want).
4. Click Add.

Now, position your insertion point where you want to create your index, and follow these steps:

1. Press Ctrl+F9 to display a set of field brackets.
2. Within the field brackets, enter the following text:

   ```
   INDEX \b Index2
   ```

   This field tells Word to create an index covering only the block of text corresponding to the bookmark named Index2.
3. Press Ctrl+A to select the entire document.
4. Press F9 to update all the fields, including the { INDEX } field you just entered.

N O T E In this example and some that follow, other switches you might need have been excluded for simplicity. The best way to edit the { INDEX } field code is to first use the Index tab of the Index and Tables dialog box to create as many settings as possible, and then display the field code to add the settings you can't make elsewhere. ■

Indexing Only Selected Letters of the Alphabet

If your index is especially large, you may want to split it into two or more indexes to improve Word's performance. You might, for example, create one index that covers letters A through M and another for N through Z.

> **TIP** Even if Word is performing perfectly well, you might occasionally want to compile an index based on only part of the alphabet for review purposes. Large indexes require careful review; you might ask one reviewer to handle letters A through M and another reviewer to handle N through Z.

To create an index covering only some letters of the alphabet, create all your index entries as you normally do; then insert the index into your document the way you normally do. Right-click anywhere in the index, and choose Toggle field codes to display the field code instead of the field result. Add the following to your { INDEX } field code:

```
\p n--z
```

Notice the double hyphens. In this example, you've told Word to compile the index from N to Z. Of course, you can substitute any letters you like.

Compiling an Index with Only the Entries You Select

Word indexes typically contain all the index entries you've selected. However, you can create custom indexes that only contain the items you specify. For example, you might be forwarding a large document to a reviewer with expertise about one specific topic. If you create a custom index, you can call attention to the pages that contain information you want reviewed. That'll save the reviewer time. It might also discourage the reviewer from slowing you down with gratuitous comments about other areas of the document.

Assuming you've already indexed the document, click Show/Hide Paragraph to display hidden text, including the contents of your { XE } index entry fields. Now, in each entry you want to appear in your specialized index, add the \f switch, a space, and any letter of the alphabet except *i*. Word interprets *i* as a direction to include an entry in the default index. Use the same letter in every entry you want to compile together. So, for example, you might have an index entry that reads:

```
{ XE "Cobb, Ty" \f r }
```

Sound like a lot of work? Here's how to streamline it. With all the field codes visible, use Word's Edit, Replace dialog box to add the \f r switch to all identical fields at once.

In the previous example, you might include the following in the Find What box:

XE "Cobb, Ty"

and add the following in the Replace With box:

XE "Cobb, Ty" \f r

Then click Replace All, and Word will fix them all at the same time. You can use this technique any time you need to make a global change in many fields at the same time.

After you've finished customizing your index entries, create and insert your index the way you normally do. Click anywhere inside the index and press Shift+F9 to view the { INDEX } field code. Click inside the field code and add the same switch at the end—for example,

```
{ INDEX \f r }
```

Using { INDEX } Field Codes to Control Other Index Formatting

You've already seen how manually editing an { INDEX } field code can allow you to create partial indexes based on letters of the alphabet or specific index entries. Occasionally, you may have to use other { INDEX } field switches to generate index formatting you can't get any other way.

Creating Separator Characters

The \d switch sets the separator character that Word places between chapter numbers and page numbers in index entries. By default, Word uses a hyphen, as in the following example:

```
League for Industrial Democracy, 3-8, 5-6
```

However, it's not uncommon to use colons or other characters:

```
Jagger, Mick, 4:6, 9:12
```

You can separate chapter numbers from page numbers with any character. You can even use several characters (up to five). Within your { INDEX } field, add the \d switch and a space. Then add quotation marks containing the characters you want to use, as in the following example:

```
{ INDEX \d ":" }
```

Creating Separator Characters for Page Ranges

Just as you can create separator characters that go between chapter numbers and page numbers, you can also create separator characters that go between the numbers in ranges of pages. By default, Word uses an en dash, as in the following example:

```
Wilder, Thornton, 62-68, 104-113
```

Use the \g switch to change the separator. The syntax is exactly the same as for the \d switch. For example, to use a colon as a separator, enter the following:

```
{ INDEX \g ":" }
```

Controlling the Appearance of Alphabetical Headings

Earlier, you saw that Word can insert headings before the index listings associated with each letter of the alphabet. You can use the \h switch to control the appearance of these headings. You're most likely to use this switch in two ways: to insert a blank line between letters instead of a heading, or to lowercase the letters in your headings for design reasons.

To insert a blank line, edit your existing { INDEX } field code to include the following:

```
\h " "
```

To lowercase your headings, edit the \h switch in your existing { INDEX } field code to include the following:

```
\*lower
```

For example, if your current field code reads as follows:

```
{ INDEX \h "A" \c "2" }
```

then edit it to read

```
{ INDEX \h "A" \*lower \c "2" }
```

Creating Dictionary Style Headings for Your Index Pages

How often have you seen an index like the one shown in Figure 17.10? It's exceptionally easy to reference, because the heading at the top of the page tells you where you are in the index. It's easy to do the same thing in Word, if you know how. You can use the { STYLEREF } field, which locates the first or last paragraph on a page that is formatted with a particular style and displays the contents of that paragraph anywhere you insert the field.

In the following procedure, you follow the steps to insert { STYLEREF } fields that show which letters are covered on each page of your index:

1. Click anywhere inside your index.
2. Choose View, Header and Footer to display the header of your index section.
3. If the words Same as Previous appear at the top of the header box, click the Same as Previous button to detach this header from previous headers in your document.
4. Insert the following:

```
{ STYLEREF "Index Heading" }-{ STYLEREF "Index Heading" \l }
```

   Make sure to insert the { STYLEREF } fields inside field brackets. You can press Ctrl+F9 in your document to display field brackets, and enter the text between those field brackets. Also notice the \l switch in the second field, which tells Word to look for the *last* reference on the page instead of the first.

5. Press Ctrl+A to select the entire document.
6. Press F9 to update all your fields.

TIP You can use this technique in practically any document. For example, if you substitute the style Heading 1 for Index Heading in the previous procedure, Word tracks the top-level headings throughout your document and always includes the current heading in your header or footer. You can see how this works by looking at the heading of any right-hand page in this book.

Of course { STYLEREF } is also perfect for directories and similar documents.

Within an index, you can sometimes use the same technique to display specific index entries instead of alphabetic letters in your header or footer. Substitute the words Index 1 for Index Heading in your fields. There is a problem, however: Word inserts the complete index entries, including page numbers or run-in text that you may not want to appear in your headings.

FIG. 17.10
This index contains
dictionary style
headings.

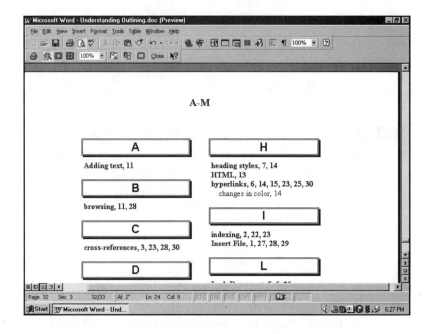

TROUBLESHOOTING

I'm having trouble getting the right chapter numbering in indexes built around master documents.
Sometimes, indexes in master documents won't show paragraph numbers when they're supposed to, or
they will refer to Chapter 0 instead of the correct numbers. Do the following:

1. In each subdocument, use Outline Numbering to number the headings.

2. In each subdocument, use Insert, Page Numbers to add page numbering.

3. In the master document, select the entire document and use Outline Numbering to number all
   the headings again.

The page numbering in my index is wrong. Make sure to hide the hidden text in your document
before building the index. Also, build the index after you create tables of contents and other document
elements that affect page numbering.

**I split my index into multiple adjacent indexes, but Word added a space between each index. How
can I get rid of that space?** You can't. It's a bug. However, you can avoid the problem in the first place.
Leave space between your { INDEX } fields as you create the indexes. If Word already finds space there,
it won't add space of its own. After you've inserted the indexes, manually delete the space you had
placed there.

▶ **See** "Using Word's Automatic Outline Numbering," **p. 421**

From Here...

In this chapter, you've learned about Word's powerful tools for creating index entries, building indexes, and updating them automatically. Now that you've learned about indexes, discover several more tools Word provides to simplify long documents.

- Building an index that covers an entire book, or multiple smaller documents? Refer back to the coverage of master documents in Chapter 15, "Master Documents: Control and Share Even the Largest Documents."

- In Chapter 18, "Footnotes, Bookmarks, Cross-References, and Hyperlinks," you'll learn about footnotes, bookmarks, cross-references, and Word 97's exciting new Hyperlinks feature.

- You've spent a lot of time with field codes in this chapter. Interested in learning some field code formatting tricks that will give you even more control over indexes, tables of contents, and the other document elements you've been learning about? Jump to Chapter 25, "Automating Your Document with Field Codes."

Part
IV

Ch
17

Footnotes, Bookmarks, Cross-References, and Hyperlinks

by Bill Camarda

In the last four chapters, you learned about many of Word's tools for managing and constructing large documents. In this chapter, you'll learn about four easy-to-use tools that can help you and your readers find and reference text anywhere in your document—and beyond.

You'll learn how Word's footnotes/endnotes feature can automate the numbering and compilation of your footnotes; how you can place bookmarks in your document that make it easier to find information and include it in Word indexes; how Word can keep track of your cross-references, keeping page numbers accurate as you edit your document, and finally, how Word 97's new hyperlink feature can help you build electronic connections from your document to the rest of the world. ■

Inserting footnotes and endnotes

Word makes it easy to insert footnotes and endnotes—and it keeps track of footnote/endnote numbering, so you don't have to track it yourself.

Controlling footnote numbering, location, and appearance

You can quickly customize Word to follow any specific rules for footnotes and endnotes.

Using bookmarks

Bookmarks make it easy for you to find material in a long document—and they also make it possible for Word to automate a wide variety of tasks.

Inserting cross-references

Word makes it easy to insert and update cross-references to headings, bookmarks, footnotes, figures, and many other document elements.

Inserting hyperlinks

Now you can create live connections to any document on your computer, your network, your intranet, or the Internet.

Using Footnotes and Endnotes

Footnotes and endnotes are notes that provide more information about specific text in your document. In Word, footnotes appear at the bottom of your current page. Notes compiled at the end of a document—or at the end of a section—are called *endnotes*. Both footnotes and endnotes are equally easy to insert—and easy to work with after you've added them. If you want, you can use both footnotes and endnotes in the same document.

Inserting Footnotes and Endnotes

To insert a standard footnote, place your insertion point where you want the footnote to appear, and press Alt+Ctrl+F. Word inserts a reference mark containing a number. If this is the first footnote in your document, the number is 1; if you have already inserted footnotes, Word uses the next number after your last footnote.

In Normal view, Word also displays the Footnote pane (see Figure 18.1), where you can type your footnote. In Page Layout view, there is no separate Footnote pane (see Figure 18.2). You simply edit the footnote wherever it's located on the page—typically beneath a footnote separator line that stretches about one-third of the way across the page.

If you prefer to create an endnote, press Alt+Ctrl+E. Word inserts an endnote in your document and (in Normal view) opens the Endnote pane (see Figure 18.3), where you can type your endnote. By default, Word uses the sequence i, ii, iii, and so on for endnotes. Later, you'll learn how to change this sequence if you want.

FIG. 18.1

When you press Alt+Ctrl+F to enter a footnote, Word places a footnote reference mark at your insertion point, and opens the Footnote pane for editing.

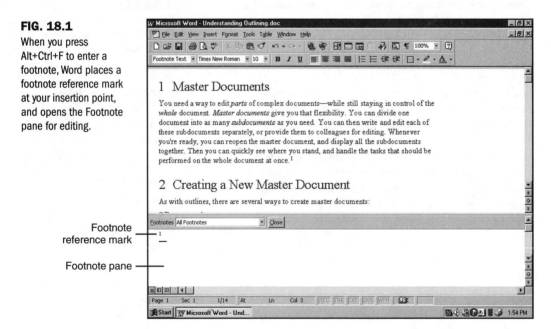

Footnote reference mark

Footnote pane

FIG. 18.2
In Page Layout view, the footnote appears in its location on the page; you can edit it there in the same way that you edit other text in your document.

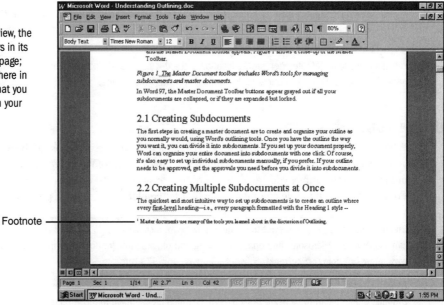

Footnote ————

FIG. 18.3
The Endnote pane works just like the Footnote pane, except the notes you create are compiled as endnotes.

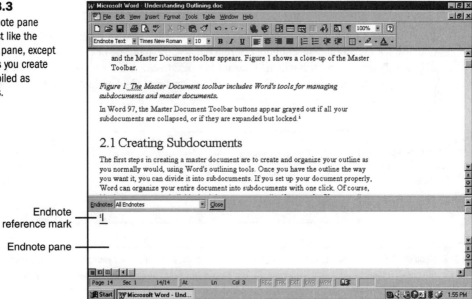

Endnote
reference mark ————

Endnote pane ————

If you're creating endnotes, work in Normal view. If you create an endnote in Page Layout view, Word moves you to the list of endnotes at the end of the document or section. You can edit the endnote there, but you won't be able to see the document text to which it relates.

You can move to a footnote or endnote's location in the document and close the Footnote/Endnote pane at the same time. Just double-click the reference mark in the pane.

Editing Footnotes

Within the Footnote or Endnote pane, you can edit or format text in most of the ways with which you're accustomed. You can even add images or tables. A few of Word's features are off-limits, but not many. For example, you can't use Word 97's drawing tools, or insert comments or captions. (You can't create multiple columns either, but multicolumn tables are a possible work-around.)

On rare occasions, you might want to create a drawing for inclusion in a footnote or endnote. If so, you can use Draw 97, Microsoft's free optional drawing add-on, available for download from the Web at **www.microsoft.com/officefreestuff/word/dlpages/draw97.htm**

After you install Draw 97, open a new file, and create a new drawing by choosing Insert, Picture, New Drawing. Create the drawing using Draw 97's tools, which are identical to those built into Word 97. Then choose File, Save as HTML. This saves your blank document along with a .GIF formatted image file you can copy or paste into a footnote or endnote.

If you are working in your document and you want to edit the text associated with a note, double-click the footnote or endnote reference mark; the footnote or endnote pane opens, displaying the footnote with which you want to work. In Normal view, you can also view the footnote pane by choosing View, Footnotes. If you prefer to view endnotes, you can choose All Endnotes from the Footnotes drop-down box (see Figure 18.4).

FIG. 18.4

Use the Footnotes drop-down box to switch from viewing footnotes to viewing endnotes.

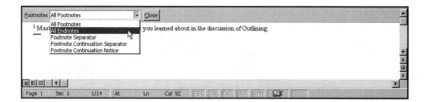

If you don't need to edit the text of a note, but you would like to see it, hover your mouse pointer over the note's reference mark in your document. The mouse pointer changes shape to resemble a piece of note paper; then a ScreenTip appears displaying the contents of the note (see Figure 18.5).

If you're working in a document with many footnotes or endnotes, you might want to view more than those that appear in the footnote or endnote pane. Follow these steps to adjust the size of the active pane:

FIG. 18.5

Hover your mouse pointer over a note reference mark, and Word displays the note's contents in a ScreenTip.

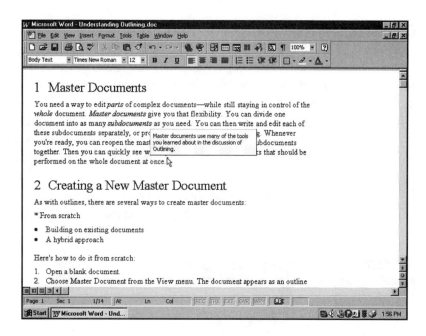

1. Place your insertion point on the top border of the pane; the pointer changes to double vertical arrows (see Figure 18.6).

2. Click and drag the border up or down to resize it.

3. Release the pointer.

FIG. 18.6

This figure illustrates resizing a Footnote pane.

Resize pointer ———

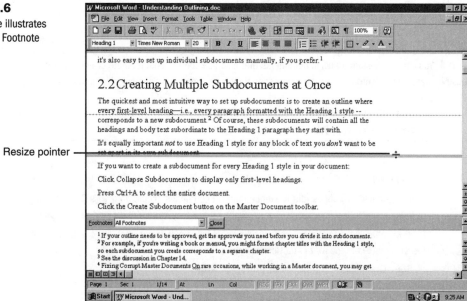

Customizing Your Footnotes and Endnotes

Word gives you total control over the appearance, sequence, and location of footnotes and endnotes. In the next few pages, you'll learn how to change each of Word's default settings, beginning with the change you're likely to make most often: customizing the character Word uses as its footnote or endnote reference mark.

Inserting a Custom Mark In documents where you only have a few footnotes or endnotes, you may want to use a *custom mark*—a special character that appears in place of the number or letter Word would normally use as its reference mark. Follow these steps to create a custom mark:

1. Place your insertion point where you want the footnote or endnote.
2. Choose Insert, Footnote. The Footnote and Endnote dialog box appears (see Figure 18.7).

FIG. 18.7

You can create a custom mark in the Footnote and Endnote dialog box.

3. Choose Footnote or Endnote to specify what kind of note you're creating.
4. Click in the Custom Mark text box and enter the character(s) you want to use in your reference mark. (You can insert up to ten characters in a reference mark.)
5. Click OK.

TIP You can use custom marks in documents that also use conventional footnote or endnote reference marks. When Word numbers the conventional reference marks, it skips any custom marks in your document.

You can't edit a reference mark directly; you must create a custom mark (or change Word's automatic numbering sequence, as you'll learn about shortly).

CAUTION

Don't use the © symbol as your reference mark. In certain instances, Word 97's Grammar Checker will mistakenly delete footnotes using this reference mark if they appear at the end of a sentence.

Word will change the text (c) to a copyright symbol by default. If you want, you can prevent this by removing the © symbol from the list of AutoCorrect entries.

▶ **See** "Changing an AutoCorrect Entry," **p. 200**

Inserting Symbols in Your Custom Mark   You might want to use a symbol as your footnote reference mark, such as † or ‡. If so, follow steps 1–3 from the previous section; then click the Symbol button in the Footnote and Endnote dialog box. The Symbol dialog box appears (see Figure 18.8). Choose the symbol you want to use and click OK. The symbol you chose now appears in the Custom mark box. Click OK to finish creating the footnote or endnote.

FIG. 18.8
Choose a symbol from the Symbol dialog box. To choose from a different character set, select another symbol font (such as Wingdings) from the Font drop-down box.

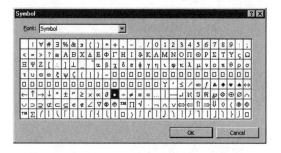

If you're running Word 97 with Windows 95, and the Symbol dialog box shows only squares in all fonts except normal text, you may have a video driver problem. Contact your video card manufacturer to see if a new driver is available. If not, one work-around is to use the standard or Super VGA driver provided with Windows 95. According to Microsoft, the problem arises with the following video chipsets and video cards:

Alliance Semiconductor V4.1.19

Cirrus Logic 7548 1.32a PCI v.4.0

Diamond Stealth 3D 2000 series v4.02.020

IBM Think Pad 760C, 365ED

S3 Trio

Trident CXI/TGUI 9440

Trident TGUI9400

Viper VLB

WindPortrait Cirrus Logic Driver 4.0

Controlling Footnote Numbering and Location

As you've seen, Word automatically numbers footnotes using the sequence 1, 2, 3.... Word also assumes that you want your footnotes to number consecutively throughout your document, beginning with the number 1. Finally, Word assumes you want your footnotes to appear at the bottom of each page. You can change each of these default settings.

To control footnote numbering and location, choose Insert, Footnote, and click Options. The Note Options dialog box opens. To control footnotes, choose All Footnotes if it isn't already chosen (see Figure 18.9). To control endnotes, choose All Endnotes (see Figure 18.10). As you can see, both tabs are quite similar.

FIG. 18.9

You can control footnote numbering and location through the All Footnotes tab of the Note Options dialog box.

FIG. 18.10

If you want to control endnotes, choose the All Endnotes tab instead.

NOTE Any changes you make in the Note Options dialog box affect all your footnotes or endnotes—both the ones you will insert and the ones you've already inserted. ▨

Controlling Where Footnotes or Endnotes Appear   In the Place At drop-down box within the Note Options dialog box, you can control where your footnotes or endnotes appear: at the bottom of each page, or beneath text.

If you're working with Footnotes, your choices are Bottom of Page, the default setting; or Beneath Text. If you choose Beneath Text, your footnotes will be placed directly underneath the last line of text on each page. This means the location of footnotes can vary, depending on how far down the page your document text extends.

If you're working with Endnotes, your choices are End of Document, the default setting; or End of Section. If you choose End of Section, all the endnotes in each section will be compiled after the last line of that section.

▶ **See** "Why Document Sections Matter," **p. 93**

Controlling the Numbering Sequence   In the Number Format drop-down box in the Note Options dialog box, you can choose the sequence Word uses to number your footnotes or endnotes. Your choices are the same whether you're working with footnotes or endnotes. They are

1, 2, 3…

a, b, c…

A, B, C…

i, ii, iii…

I, II, III...

*, †, ‡, §...

The last option inserts a series of the most commonly used footnote symbols. After you go past four footnotes or endnotes, Word "doubles-up" the characters. The reference mark associated with footnote #5 is **; footnote #6 is ††, and so on.

Controlling the Starting Number of Footnotes or Endnotes   Word assumes that you want your footnotes to begin numbering with 1 and your endnotes to begin numbering (or, perhaps, *lettering*) with "i"). You might, however, be creating a chapter of a book that already contains footnotes or endnotes. You know that several notes appear before yours. To start with a different number (or letter), select it in the Start At spin box.

N O T E   The letters or numbers in the Start At spin box change, based on the Number format you've chosen. If you enter a different in the Start At spin box, and later change the Number format, your starting number automatically changes to the corresponding number or letter in the new sequence. ▪

Restarting Numbering for Each Section or Page   By default, Word numbers footnotes or endnotes continuously throughout the document. However, you might want your notes to begin numbering again with 1 (or whatever starting number you've chosen) at the beginning of each new document section. If so, click the Restart Each Section button on the All Footnotes or All Endnotes tab.

If you're working with footnotes, you have an additional option: to restart footnote numbering with each new page. To choose this option, click the Restart Each Page button.

Converting from Footnotes to Endnotes (and Vice Versa)   Occasionally, you might start out creating footnotes and later decide that you want endnotes instead. Or perhaps you start out with endnotes and discover that your client or publisher prefers footnotes. You can convert between footnotes and endnotes whenever you want; you can even swap endnotes and footnotes at the same time. Follow these steps to convert all your footnotes or endnotes the same time:

1. Choose Insert, Footnote.
2. Choose Options.
3. Choose Convert. The Convert Notes dialog box opens (see Figure 18.11).
4. Select one of the available options.
5. Click OK.

Follow these steps if you need to convert only one footnote to an endnote (or vice versa):

1. Double-click the reference mark to display it in the footnote or endnote pane.
2. Right-click the footnote text to display the Note Shortcut menu (see Figure 18.12).
3. Choose Convert to Endnote (or Convert to Footnote).

FIG. 18.11

You can convert all footnotes to endnotes, all endnotes to footnotes, or swap footnotes *and* endnotes at the same time.

FIG. 18.12

The Note Shortcut menu appears whenever you right-click a footnote or endnote text in a footnote or endnote editing pane.

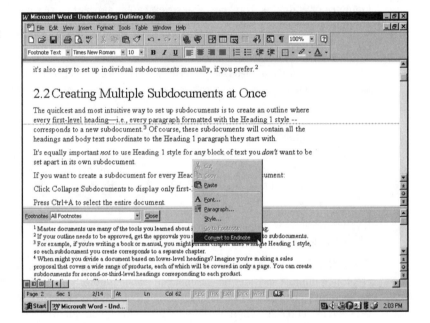

Working with Footnotes

You've already learned that you can edit any footnote or endnote in the footnote or endnote pane. Now, let's take a closer look at working with footnotes and endnotes—both in your document and in the footnote or endnote pane.

The reference mark in your document and the text of your footnote or endnote are connected. Whenever the reference mark moves in your document, the footnote/endnote text moves with it. This means you can

- Duplicate a footnote by selecting, copying, and pasting the reference mark.
- Move a footnote by cutting and pasting (or dragging and dropping) the reference mark.
- Delete a footnote by deleting the reference mark.

Of course, you don't have to cut, copy, paste, or delete only the reference mark; chances are you'll also be editing related surrounding text at the same time. The reference mark moves with the surrounding text. Whenever you move, copy, or delete a reference mark, Word automatically updates the numbering of all the footnotes or endnotes in your document.

> **CAUTION**
>
> If you delete text that includes a reference mark, you delete the accompanying footnote or endnote as well.

Navigating Among Footnotes and Endnotes

You've already learned that you can double-click any footnote or endnote reference mark to display the footnote or endnote pane. Whenever you click inside a footnote or endnote in the pane, Word also displays the corresponding location in the main document.

You can move among notes in the main document without opening the footnote or endnote pane. Follow these steps if you want to move to a specific footnote:

1. Press F5 to display the Go To tab of the Find and Replace dialog box.
2. Choose Footnote in the Go to What scroll box.
3. Enter the footnote number.
4. Click Go To.

Follow these steps to move from one footnote or endnote to the next:

1. Click the Browser button.
2. Click Browse by Footnote or Browse by Endnote.
3. Click the blue double-arrow key *below* the Browser to move to the *next* footnote or endnote. Click the blue double-arrow key *above* the Browser to move to the *previous* footnote or endnote.

Reformatting Footnotes

Word builds footnotes using two built-in styles: Footnote Text for the contents of the footnote and Footnote Reference for the reference mark (as it appears in both the document and the footnote pane). For endnotes, Word uses Endnote Text and Endnote Reference. This means footnotes and endnotes in the same document can look different.

Follow these steps to change the appearance of either footnotes or endnotes by changing their associated styles:

1. Select footnote or endnote text, or a footnote or endnote reference mark that you want to change.
2. Reformat the footnote or endnote text or reference mark to appear the way you want all similar text or reference marks to look.
3. Click anywhere inside the Style drop-down box on the Formatting toolbar.
4. Press Enter. Word displays a dialog box that asks whether you want to change the style or revert selected text to the style that already exists.

5. Choose Update Style to Reflect Recent Changes.

6. Press OK.

▶ **See** "Quick and Easy Paragraph Styles: Style by Example," **p. 148**

Controlling Footnote Separators and Notices

By default, Word separates footnotes from the text of your document by inserting a line roughly one-third the width of a standard page margin. This is called the footnote or endnote *separator*. If a footnote is so long that it must jump to the next page, Word separates it from the text on that page as well, using a footnote or endnote *continuation separator*. By default, this is a line that extends across the entire width of the page. You can see examples of both in Figure 18.13.

FIG. 18.13

Word uses separators to divide footnotes and endnotes from other text in the document.

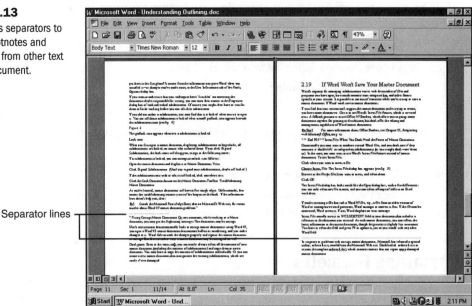

Separator lines —

You can change the appearance of either the separator or the continuation separator. You can also edit them to include text. To do so, follow these steps:

1. Display the Footnote or Endnote pane by double-clicking any footnote or endnote reference mark in Normal view.

2. From the Footnotes or Endnotes drop-down box, select the element you want to edit. The current setting appears; typically either a short or long line.

3. Edit the element to include the text, underlining, or formatting you want.

4. Click Close.

TIP If you want, you can also add text that tells users a note is jumping to the next page. With the Footnote pane open, choose Footnote Continuation Notice. (Or with the Endnote pane open, choose Endnote Continuation Notice.) Then enter and format the text you want. Click Close.

By default, there is no Footnote or Endnote Continuation Notice.

 ## TROUBLESHOOTING

My endnotes won't print on a separate page. By default, Word places endnotes on the same page as the last text in the document. If you want them on a separate page, you'll have to add a manual page break (Ctrl+Enter).

My footers are printing right on top of my footnote text. This may happen if *both* the footer and footnote text exceed five lines *and* a section break appears on the same page. If you can't remove the section break, add some blank lines above the footnote text in the footnote pane.

I tried to delete a footnote, but the reference mark still appears in the document. You may have deleted the footnote text in the footnote pane, but you also must delete the footnote reference mark in the document.

Using Bookmarks

Part
IV

Ch
18

Chances are, when you put down a book, you use a bookmark to keep track of where you were. It's much the same when you're creating a long complex document; you'll often want a quick way to move to a certain block of text in your document. Word's other navigation tools won't do the trick, because you won't always know the page number or heading where your specific block of text is located. For this purpose, Word provides bookmarks.

Bookmarks are even more valuable than they appear. Word itself uses bookmarks to track blocks of text it needs to know about. Bookmarks allow Word to

- Compile index entries that span multiple pages (see Chapter 17, "Indexes").
- Build formulas that include references to numbers elsewhere in a document (see Chapter 8, "Tables").
- Create custom properties that reflect the changing contents of a document (see Chapter 28, "Installing and Configuring Word in a Network Environment").
- Manage internal cross-references (discussed later in this chapter).
- Ask users for input and then display that input throughout the document (discussed later in this chapter).
- Build hyperlinks that connect to specific locations in external documents (discussed later in this chapter).

Here's the nicest part: bookmarks are *exceptionally* easy to use.

Inserting Bookmarks

Follow these steps to insert a bookmark:

1. Select the text you want to associate with a bookmark.

2. Choose Insert, Bookmark. The Bookmark dialog box opens (see Figure 18.14).

3. Enter a bookmark name. Bookmark names must begin with a letter, and can't include spaces or most punctuation—though they can include underscore characters (_).

4. Click Add.

FIG. 18.14

You can Add, Delete, or Go To bookmarks from the Bookmark dialog box.

Viewing Bookmarks in Your Document

You might, at some point, want to view the borders of the bookmarks in your document. (For example, you might be editing text that you suspect is near the boundary of a bookmark. You might want to know whether the text you add or delete is part of the bookmark.) To view the bookmarks in your document, choose Tools, Options, View, check the Bookmarks check box, and click OK. Text you've bookmarked is now displayed within dark gray nonprinting brackets (see Figure 18.15).

Finding Bookmarks

There are two ways to find a bookmark after you've created it.

- You can display the Bookmark dialog box, select a bookmark, and click Go To.

- Or you can press F5 to display the Go To dialog box; choose Bookmark in the Go to What scroll box; select a bookmark name from the Enter Bookmark Name text box; and click Go To.

In both cases, when you go to a bookmark, Word selects all the text contained in the bookmark.

Moving from One Bookmark to the Next

Surprisingly, there's no Browser option for moving among bookmarks. However, you can browse from the Bookmark dialog box. Choose Insert Bookmark to display the Bookmark dialog box; then sort your bookmarks by Location. One at a time, click each bookmark in the list and click Go To. The Bookmark dialog box remains open as you work (although you might want to drag it out of your way). When you're finished, click Close.

FIG. 18.15
Dark gray brackets mark the boundaries of bookmarks within your document.

Nonprinting
bookmark brackets

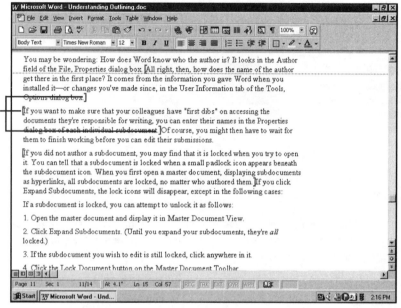

Deleting Bookmarks

Perhaps you created a bookmark temporarily, to track specific text while you were focusing on one element of your document. Now you'd like to delete the bookmark so it no longer clutters up your bookmark list. Follow these steps to delete a bookmark:

1. Choose Insert, Bookmark.
2. Select the bookmark.
3. Click Delete.
4. Click Close.

NOTE If you delete all the text associated with a bookmark, the bookmark will be deleted automatically. ▪

Working with Cross-References

Cross-references are exceptionally useful, because they make it very easy for readers to find related material elsewhere in a long document. However, most writers avoid them because they've been extremely difficult to manage and update. Every time you edit your document and change its page numbering, who'll go through the entire document and fix every cross-reference? Word will. Word 97 automates cross-references, giving you more flexibility and convenience than ever before. If there's something Word won't handle by itself, chances are you can still make it happen with a field code.

▶ **See** "Fields You May Already Be Using," **p. 626**

You insert nearly all your references through the Cross-Reference dialog box. To display it, choose Insert, Cross-Reference (see Figure 18.16).

FIG. 18.16

The Cross-Reference dialog box can insert virtually all your cross-references.

The Cross-Reference dialog box enables you to create cross-references to nine different elements of your document, and customize the contents of any of them. More specifically, you can create cross-references to

- Headings you've formatted using one of Word's built-in Heading styles
- Numbered items (paragraphs or headings) you've numbered using Word's Outline Numbering feature
- Bookmarks you've created anywhere in your document
- Footnotes or endnotes
- Equations, Figures, and Tables that you've created captions for, using Word's Caption feature

To understand cross-referencing, it helps to first understand the steps involved in creating *any* cross-reference, and then take a closer look at the cross-references you're most likely to create: headings, bookmarks, footnotes, and figures.

Creating a Cross-Reference

Whenever you create a cross-reference from the Cross-Reference dialog box, you follow these steps:

1. Choose a Reference Type—the kind of document element you want to cross-reference. Reference types include headings, numbered items, bookmarks, footnotes, and so on.

2. Choose the specific element you want to reference. For example, if you've chosen Footnote as your reference type, you now choose the specific footnote you want to use.

3. Decide which aspect of the document element you want to reference. For example, if you're referencing a footnote, do you want your reference to include the footnote number, the page number the footnote appears on, or something else? The options available to you depend on the reference type you've chosen.

4. Make one or two more decisions about your footnote. Should it appear as a hyperlink that readers can click and jump to? Should it include the word "above" or "below"? You'll learn more about these options later.

5. Click Insert to place the cross-reference in your document.

In the next section, you take a closer look at some of the cross-references you'll use most.

Cross-Referencing a Heading or Bookmark

Headings are natural reference points within a document. They stand out due to size and formatting, so they're easy for your reader to find. Moreover, they define important topics in your document that are often worth referencing.

Sometimes, though, you'll want to cross-reference a block of text that doesn't correspond neatly to a document heading. For example, you might want to refer to an anecdote that was covered elsewhere in a different context; the anecdote may not have been important enough to warrant its own heading. To cross-reference a block of text, first select it and use Insert, Bookmark to create a bookmark. Creating bookmarks is covered in more detail earlier in this chapter.

After you've created a bookmark (if necessary), follow these steps to cross-reference either a heading or bookmark:

1. Place your insertion point where you want the cross-reference to appear.

2. Choose Insert, Cross-Reference.

3. Choose Heading or Bookmark as the Reference type. All the headings in your document appear in the For Which Heading scroll box.

4. Select the heading you want.

5. In the Insert Reference To drop-down box, choose the aspect of the heading you want to reference. The following options are available:

   - If you choose Heading Text or Bookmark Text, Word inserts the entire text of the heading or bookmark.

   - If you choose Page Number, Word inserts the page number on which the heading appears.

   - If you choose Heading Number, Word inserts the heading number that appears in your document, if you've already inserted heading numbers with Word's Outline Numbering feature.

   - If you choose Heading Number (No Context), Word inserts an abbreviated heading number, if you're in the same section as the text you're referencing. For

Part

IV

Ch

18

example, if you're in section 6.F, and you insert a cross-reference to heading 6.C, Word inserts the reference C instead of 6.C. You might use (No Context) if you think it would be redundant to include the section number. This setting has no effect if you cross-reference a document element elsewhere in your document. For example, if you're in section 6.F and you insert a cross-reference to heading 3.L, Word inserts 3.L no matter what—never just L.

- If you choose Heading Number (Full Context), Word inserts a full heading number, even if you're in the same section as the heading you're referencing.

- If you choose Above/Below, Word inserts the word above or below in your cross-reference, depending on whether the referenced text appears earlier or later in the document. If you move the cross-reference or the reference text, Word automatically switches above to below, or vice versa.

6. Clear the Insert as Hyperlink check box if you do not want the cross-reference to appear as a hyperlink.

7. Click Insert. The cross-reference appears in your document.

TIP

To really help readers find their way to your cross-reference, consider using two cross-references near each other: one that references the heading text, and another that references the page number. You can see how this works in the following example:

For more information, see The Retreat at Dunkirk, page 146.

If you create a complex cross-reference that you expect to reuse several times in the document (for example, you expect to reference the same text in the same way), select it and create an AutoText entry. Then insert the AutoText entry wherever you need the cross-reference.

▶ **See** "AutoText: The Complete Boilerplate Resource," **p. 203**

Cross-Referencing a Footnote or Endnote

You might at times wish to cross-reference a footnote or endnote. To do so, follow these steps:

1. Place your insertion point where you want the cross-reference to appear.

2. Choose Insert, Cross-Reference.

3. Choose Footnote or Endnote as the Reference type. All the headings in your document appear in the For Which Footnote (or For which Endnote) scroll box.

4. Select the footnote or endnote you want.

5. In the Insert Reference To drop-down box, choose the aspect of the footnote or endnote you want to reference. The following options are available:

- If you choose Footnote Number (or Endnote Number), Word inserts the number of the footnote or endnote.

- If you choose Page Number, Word inserts the page number where the footnote began.

- If you choose Above/Below, Word inserts the word above or below in your cross-reference, depending on where the referenced text appears.

- If you choose Footnote Number (Formatted) or Endnote Number (Formatted), Word inserts the number formatted as if it were another footnote (or endnote) in your document. This allows you to create multiple footnotes that refer to the same footnote text and share the same footnote number, as is often required by scientific journals.

6. Clear the Insert as Hyperlink check box if you do not want the cross-reference to appear as a hyperlink.

7. If, in Step 5, you chose an element other than Above/Below, you can still ask Word to include the word above or below in your cross-reference by checking the Include Above/Below check box.

8. Click Insert. The cross-reference appears in your document.

Cross-Referencing a Figure (or Other Caption)

If you've just placed a figure in your document, it's likely you'll want to cross-reference that figure in text somewhere nearby. If you've created the figure using Word's caption or AutoCaption feature, you can easily insert the cross-reference using the Cross-Reference dialog box as well. To cross-reference a figure, table, or equation you've already captioned, follow these steps:

1. Place your insertion point where you want the cross-reference to appear.

2. Choose Insert, Cross-Reference.

3. Choose Figure, Table, or Equation as the Reference type. All the corresponding elements in your document appear in the For Which scroll box.

4. Select the figure, table, or equation.

5. In the Insert Reference To drop-down list box, choose the aspect of the figure, table, or equation you want to reference. The following options are available:

- If you choose Entire Caption, Word inserts the entire text of the caption, including its label and figure number.

- If you choose Only Label or Number, Word inserts the label and figure number, for example, Figure 1.1.

- If you choose Only Caption Text, Word inserts the text of the caption, excluding label and figure number.

- If you choose Page Number, Word inserts the number of the page where the figure, equation, or table appeared.

- If you choose Above/Below, Word inserts only the word above or below, depending on the figure's location relative to the cross-reference.

6. Clear the Insert as Hyperlink check box if you do not want the cross-reference to appear as a hyperlink.

Part
IV

Ch
18

7. If, in Step 5, you chose Page Number, you can ask Word to include the word above or below in your cross-reference by checking the Include Above/Below check box.

8. Click Insert. The cross-reference appears in your document.

 TIP Figure cross-references make splendid AutoText entries because they're usually all identical within a chapter or document. Create an AutoText entry named *fig* that includes the cross-reference you inserted, and any surrounding text you habitually use, for example, use

(see Figure 14-A)

Then you can enter a figure reference anywhere you like, by just typing **fig** and pressing F3.

How Word Cross-References Work

When you insert a cross-reference, you're actually inserting a field. In most cases, Word inserts a { REF } field, with the following exceptions:

■ If you create a cross-reference to a page number, Word inserts a { PAGEREF } field.

■ If you create a cross-reference to a footnote or endnote, Word creates a { NOTEREF } field.

You can see some examples of these fields in Figure 18.17.

FIG. 18.17
This figure illustrates cross-references showing results, and toggled to show the underlying field codes.

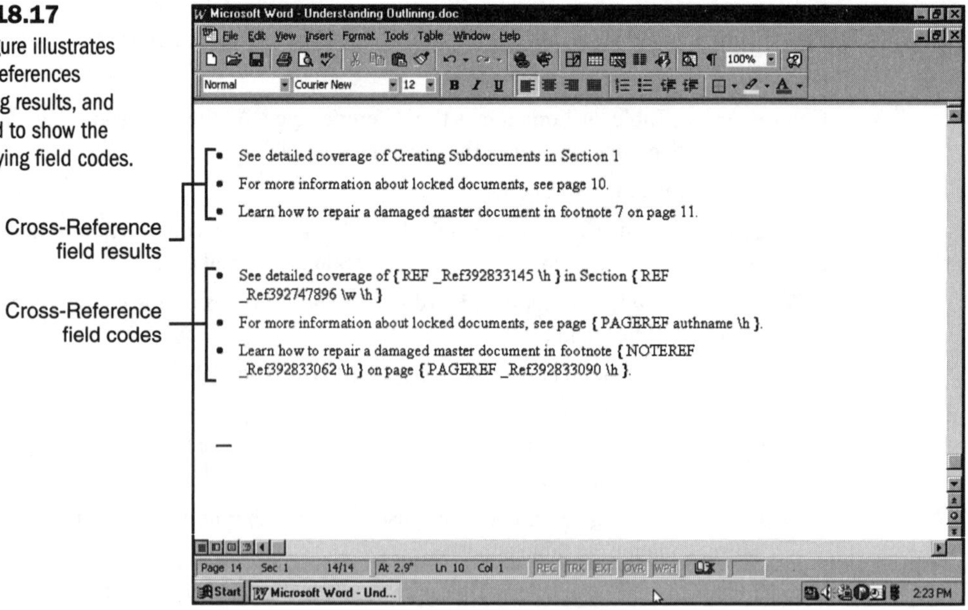

Cross-Reference field results

Cross-Reference field codes

N O T E   Word also places a hidden bookmark at the location containing the material you're cross-referencing. That's why, if you toggle a cross-reference to view the underlying field code, you'll see something like:

> { REF _Ref392747853 \h }

The long string of letters and numbers is the name of the hidden bookmark for which the { REF } field looks. ■

Why do you care that cross-references are really fields in disguise? There are three reasons:

- You can update a cross-reference just as you would update any other field: by selecting it and pressing F9.

- There are a few tricks you can use to format cross-references—tricks that aren't available through the Cross-Reference dialog box. For example, you've seen that you can insert a reference to a heading number such as Section 4.8.2.2. You might want your reference to exclude the word Section, even though it appears in the automated heading numbering you placed in your document. You can arrange this by editing the field to include the \t switch. Or you can use one of the standard formatting switches available to most fields, such as * Upper, which formats the cross-reference in ALL CAPS.

- If a cross-reference isn't working right, you can occasionally troubleshoot it by viewing the field's contents. For example, if you get the message ERROR! Bookmark not defined. you can press Shift+F9 to toggle the field code and see which bookmark it's looking for.

Formatting Cross-References as Hyperlinks

As you've seen, Word 97 inserts cross-references into your document as hyperlinks, which means that if you click a cross-reference, Word jumps to the spot in the document you cross-referenced. Note that Word doesn't format hyperlinked cross-references any differently than the surrounding text; they are not blue and underlined, as are other hyperlinks. In fact, the only difference between a hyperlinked cross-reference and one that isn't is the presence of an \h switch in the field code.

You can add hyperlinking to a cross-reference by adding the \h switch, or remove it by deleting the \h switch.

With this note in mind, there's little reason not to format cross-references as hyperlinks. Even if you're creating a document for print, leaving Insert as hyperlink checked makes it easier for *you* to move to the text you're referencing, making sure your references are accurate and read as they should.

Using the { ASK } Field to Create References that Reflect User Input

Imagine the following scenario: you have a standard boilerplate letter, as shown in Figure 18.18. As you can see, this letter offers a discount to a specific customer. What if you want to offer an extra-large discount to a specific customer? You can set the letter up to request input from whomever is preparing the letter. Word stores that information as if it were a bookmark, and then inserts it anywhere your cross-reference looks for that bookmark.

FIG. 18.18

A sample letter that can be customized to specify the size of a customer discount.

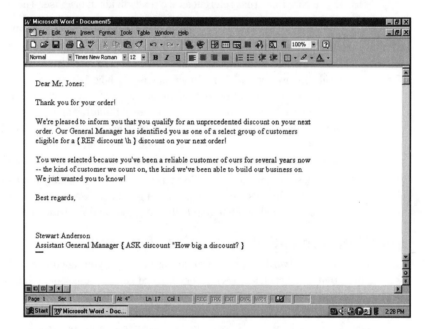

Here's how to set it up:

1. Press Ctrl+F9 to display field brackets.

2. Enter an { ASK } field that requests input and stores it in a bookmark. In the following example, the bookmark is named *discount*; the text in quotes is what appears in the dialog box that requests input from the user:

   ```
   { ASK discount "How big a discount?" }
   ```

3. Select the field and press F9 to update it. Figure 18.19 shows the dialog box that appears.

4. Enter sample input in the dialog box, and press OK. (You must do this because the { ASK } field doesn't create the bookmark until you've provided input.)

FIG. 18.19

Word displays a dialog box containing the text you placed between quotes in the { ASK } field.

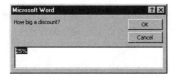

Now that you've created the { ASK } field and provided it with sample input, you can create your cross-reference:

1. Choose Insert, Cross-Reference.
2. Follow the steps described earlier to create a reference to a bookmark. Use the bookmark name you specified in the { ASK } field.
3. Click Insert to place the cross-reference in your document.
4. Repeat Steps 1-3 to insert another identical cross-reference anywhere you want the same information to appear.

You're done—except for one thing. You can't always rely on other users to press F9 and display the dialog box you've created for them. However, you can do it for them by recording a simple macro that consists of just two commands:

■ Press Ctrl+A to select the entire document.
■ Press F9 to update all fields.

If you plan to reuse the same letter over and over again, name the macro AutoOpen. It will run—and display the dialog box—every time you open the document.

If you plan to save the letter as a template and create new letters based on it, name the macro AutoNew, and store it with the new template. It will run every time you create a new document based on that template.

▶ **See** "Creating Macros that Run Automatically," **p. 853**

Part

IV

Ch

18

Using Fields to Create "Smart" Cross-References

You might not want to decide each customer's discount individually. What if you could set up a cross-reference that would automatically know what discount each customer was eligible for, based on some *other* piece of information you provide, such as the size of the order they placed? You can, though it'll take a little doing.

In our example, let's assume that customers who place orders larger than $10,000 are eligible for a discount of 10 percent on their next orders. Customers with smaller orders aren't eligible yet, but they *will* be if they reach the $10,000 threshold—and you'd like to encourage them to do so.

First, create an { ASK } field, as you've already learned how to do. This { ASK } field asks a user to specify the dollar value of a customer's orders to date. After the user responds, the information is stored in a bookmark named dollarvalue:

```
{ ASK dollarvalue "Value of customer's orders to date?" }
```

TIP As discussed earlier, you can write a quick and easy macro that updates fields automatically when you open this document, so the dialog box requesting user input appears automatically.

Now that you've captured the value of a customer's order in a bookmark, you can use the { IF } field to show Word what decisions you want it to make—and what text you want it to place in your letter as a result. A generic { IF } field uses the following syntax:

```
{ IF test "DoIfTrue" "ElseDoThis" }
```

At the heart of an { IF } field is a *test*. You specify a condition, and Word sees if that condition has been met. For example, the test might include a formula that asks: "Has the customer ordered at least $10,000 worth of merchandise?"

To create a formula like this, first create a bookmark for the location in your document that contains the value you want to test. Often, you'll want to bookmark a table cell. In the following example, you've created a bookmark named dollarvalue and used it in a formula that will serve as the test:

```
IF dollarvalue >=10000
```

Next, the { IF } field specifies the text you want Word to insert if the condition has been met. In this example, you'll use the following text, surrounded by quotation marks:

```
"You've just qualified for a 10% discount on your next order! Thanks for being
such a great customer!"
```

Finally, the { IF } field specifies the text you want Word to insert if the condition has *not* been met. Again, this text should appear in quotation marks.

```
"Qualify for a 10% discount when you place $10,000 in orders! You're well on your way!"
```

Now build the { IF } field by putting all three components together: the test, the text that should appear if the test comes back "true," and the text that should appear otherwise:

```
{ IF dollarvalue >=10000 "You've just qualified for a 10% discount on your next
order! Thanks for being such a great customer!" "Qualify for a 10% discount when
you place $10,000 in orders! You're well on your way!" }
```

After Word knows the size of the order, it also knows what text to add to the letter.

You might want to place the same text in several locations throughout your document, or perhaps on an accompanying envelope stored as page 0 of the same file. That's the easy part. Select the entire field (or field result) and mark it as a bookmark. In this example, the bookmark is named discount. Then insert a cross-reference to the bookmark anywhere you want the text to appear.

Troubleshooting Cross-References

You've already seen that you can troubleshoot some cross-references by selecting them and pressing Shift+F9 to view the underlying field. Of course, if you see the bracketed field instead of the cross-reference text, you can also click inside it and press Shift+F9 to see the result you want.

◆

TROUBLESHOOTING

I want to cross-reference a heading, but it doesn't appear in the list of headings. Did you format it with one of Word's built-in heading styles (for example, Heading 1 through Heading 9)? If not, do so. If you can't (or don't want to), select it as a bookmark and cross-reference it the same way you would cross-reference any other bookmark.

Cross-References in my master document are returning error messages. Make sure the subdocuments your cross-references refer to haven't been removed from the document. Make sure they are available and open.

Using Hyperlinks

Hyperlinks are blocks of underlined text, typically blue, that you can click to jump to another location. You can use hyperlinks to jump to

- Other locations in a Word file
- Other Word files on your computer or local area network (LAN)
- Specific locations in Excel worksheets on your computer or LAN
- HTML pages on an intranet or the Internet
- Other Internet/intranet sites, including Gopher, Telnet, newsgroup, and FTP sites

In short, at their best, hyperlinks can give you one-click access to the entire world.

N O T E For more information about how Word 97 integrates with the World Wide Web, see Chapters 9–11. ■

You've already seen hyperlinks at work twice in this book. In Chapter 15, "Master Documents: Control and Share Even the Largest Documents," you saw that Word formats the subdocuments in a master document as hyperlinks, and earlier in this chapter, you saw that Word formats cross-references as hyperlinks by default.

Inserting Hyperlinks Automatically

The easiest way to insert hyperlinks is to let Word do it for you, using AutoFormat As You Type. To do so, follow these steps:

1. Choose Format, AutoFormat.
2. Choose Options.
3. Choose AutoFormat As You Type.
4. Check the Internet and Network Paths with Hyperlinks check box.
5. Click OK.

From now on, Word will automatically convert any text it recognizes as an Internet or e-mail address, or any text it recognizes as a location on a network, as a hyperlink.

If Word creates a hyperlink you don't want, move your insertion point into it using the arrow keys (don't click it) and press Ctrl+Shift+F9 to unlink the field, turning it back into normal text.

CAUTION

If you often make reference to Web pages or e-mail addresses in documents that are designed solely for print, *don't* use this AutoFormatting feature: Word reformats all this information with blue underlining.

▶ **See** "Using AutoFormat As You Type," **p. 223**

Inserting Hyperlinks Manually

Word can't automatically create all your hyperlinks, and as you've just seen, you may not *want* it to create them. Moreover, you'll often want to control the text that appears in your hyperlink as well as the destination to which the hyperlink jumps. It's quite likely you'll want the text of your hyperlink to consist of something other than a file name.

You can control the text and links associated with a hyperlink through the Insert Hyperlink dialog box. To do so, follow these steps:

1. Type the text you want to appear as a hyperlink.
2. Select the text.
3. Press Ctrl+K, or choose Insert, Hyperlink. The Hyperlink dialog box opens (see Figure 18.20).
4. In the Link to File or URL text box, enter the path to the document with which you're linking:
   - If you're creating a link to a Web site, just enter the Web address, such as **www.microsoft.com**.
   - If you're creating a link to a location on your computer or LAN, you can enter the address directly, or click Browse to display the Link to File dialog box (see Figure 18.21), select the file there, and click OK.
5. Click OK in the Insert Hyperlink dialog box. Word inserts the hyperlink in your document.

 T I P   If you don't select text before inserting a hyperlink, Word creates a hyperlink including the complete file name, path, or Internet address.

FIG. 18.20
In the Insert Hyperlink dialog box, you can insert the Web address, network address, or path of the document to which you are linking.

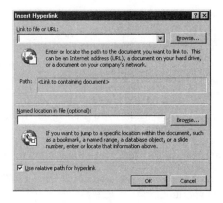

FIG. 18.21
You can browse to any local network or FTP location through the Link to File dialog box.

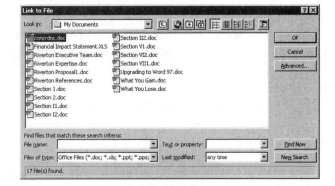

Hyperlinking to an Internet FTP Site

Long before the World Wide Web became famous, the Internet hosted hundreds (now thousands) of FTP (File Transfer Protocol) sites, where individuals could connect and download files. Nowadays, FTP sites are widely used by computer companies as a convenient way to make available updates, drivers, and other useful files. Most FTP sites are named just like Web sites, except that **www** is replaced with **ftp**. For example, Microsoft's FTP site is

ftp.microsoft.com

Unfortunately, knowing the name of an FTP site is rarely enough to create a useful link; you need to know the complete location name for the file with which you're linking. For example, Microsoft's current list of Knowledge Base articles about Microsoft Word is located at:

ftp.microsoft.com/deskapps/word/kb/index.txt

There are three ways to create a hyperlink to a specific location at an FTP site:

■ You can type the FTP address into the Link to File or URL text box manually—assuming you know it.

■ You can use a Web browser such as Microsoft Internet Explorer or Netscape Communicator to browse to the specific file you want; then copy the file address into the Link to File or URL box of the Insert Hyperlink dialog box (if using Internet Explorer). Internet Explorer's Edit, Copy command doesn't work within the Address text box, but you can select the address and press Ctrl+C, or right-click in the Address text box and choose Copy from the shortcut menu.

■ You can establish a Web connection while Word is open, and then Browse to the file you want from the Link to File dialog box.

To create a hyperlink by browsing to an FTP file from within Word, follow these steps:

1. Place your insertion point where you want to create the hyperlink; or select the text you want to transform into a hyperlink.

2. Open your Internet connection as you normally do—typically by running your browser, or by connecting through Windows 95/NT Dial-Up Networking.

3. With Word open, choose Insert, Hyperlink.

4. Choose Browse (next to the Link to File or URL text box). The Link to File dialog box opens.

5. In the Look In drop-down box, choose Add/Modify FTP Locations. The Add/Modify FTP Locations dialog box opens (see Figure 18.22).

6. Enter the site name you want to add, and click OK. The site name appears in the Link to File dialog box.

N O T E   This dialog box also includes a location for inserting a User name and a Password. Public Internet sites customarily allow access to Anonymous users without a secure password. However, if you are connecting to an FTP site on a corporate intranet, you'll probably have to insert a "real" user name and password here. ■

7. Choose the site name and click Open. After a few moments, the folder structure of the FTP site appears.

8. Browse to the specific file for which you're looking. You may have to browse through several levels of folders; you may also have to change Files of Type to specify All Files or Internet Files.

9. Select the file with which you want to link.

10. Click OK. You're returned to the Insert Hyperlink dialog box.

11. Click OK again.

FIG. 18.22
You can add an FTP site—and establish a password if necessary—through the Add/Modify FTP Locations dialog box.

Hyperlinking to a Specific Location in a File

Until now, you've created hyperlinks only to complete documents or Web pages. However, if you're linking to another Word document, or to an Excel worksheet, you can create links to a specific location within the file. In Word, you link to bookmarks. In Excel, you link to named ranges, which consist of one or more cells to which you have already assigned a name.

Hyperlinking to a Word Bookmark

Follow these steps to create a hyperlink to a bookmark in another Word document:

1. Select the text you want to reformat as a hyperlink.
2. Choose Insert, Hyperlink.
3. From the Link to File or URL text box, Browse to the file containing the bookmark.
4. Select the file and click OK.
5. To the right of the Named Location in File text box, click Browse. The Bookmark dialog box opens (refer to Figure 18.14).
6. Choose the bookmark you want.
7. Click OK twice.

Hyperlinking to an Excel Named Range

To create a hyperlink to an Excel named range, first name the range of cells as follows:

1. Open Excel and display the file in which you want to create the named range.
2. Select the cell or cells you want to name.
3. Click in the Name drop-down box at the left end of the formula bar (beneath Excel's Formatting toolbar, as shown in Figure 18.23.)

FIG. 18.23

Creating a named range in Excel for use in a Word hyperlink.

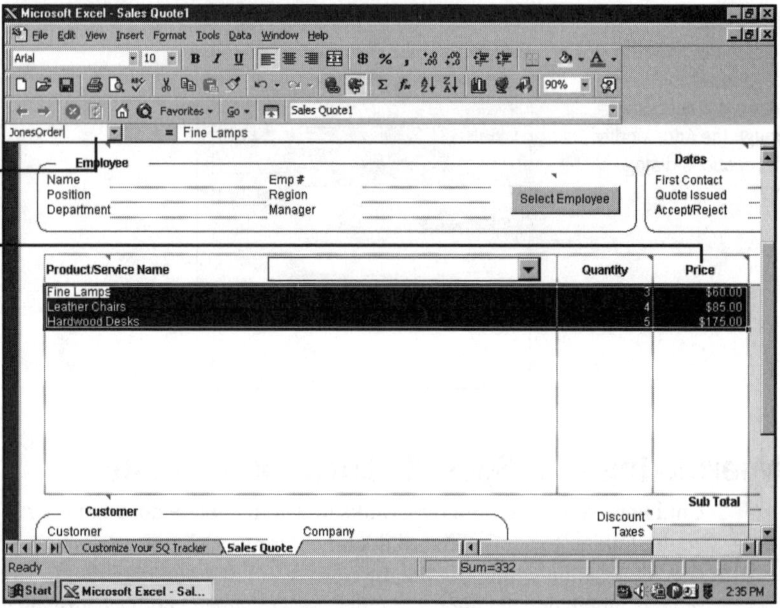

Name drop-down box —

Named range —

4. Enter the name you want to use.

5. Press Enter.

6. Save and close the file.

Now that the named range exists, follow these steps to create a hyperlink that connects to the named range:

1. Select the text you want to reformat as a hyperlink.

2. Choose Insert, Hyperlink.

3. From the Link to File or URL text box, Browse to the file containing the bookmark.

4. Select the file and click OK.

5. In the Named Location in File text box, enter the named range you want to use. (You can also use actual cell names, such as A1:C19.)

6. Click OK.

When you click a hyperlink to an named range in an Excel document, Excel opens with that range of cells selected.

Hyperlinking to a Slide in a PowerPoint Presentation

You can follow the same steps to create a hyperlink to a slide in a PowerPoint presentation. In Step 5, enter the number of the slide you want to use, instead of a named range.

When you click a link to a PowerPoint slide, Word opens the PowerPoint slide viewer (not the main PowerPoint application). From there, you can view any slide in the same presentation.

Creating a Hyperlink Within a Document

Most hyperlinks connect with other documents, but there's no reason you can't use hyperlinks to create links within a document as well. You've already learned one way to do it; insert a cross-reference as a hyperlink. However, if you want to create a hyperlink that's *formatted* as a hyperlink, follow these steps:

1. Select text at the location to which you want to link.
2. Click the insertion pointer where you want to create the hyperlink.
3. Choose Paste as <u>H</u>yperlink from the <u>E</u>dit menu.

 TIP If you're creating a hyperlink that's near the text you're linking to, you might find easier to use drag and drop:

1. Select the text you want to move.
2. Right-click the selected text and drag it to the location where you want the hyperlink.
3. Release the mouse pointer. The Drag-and-Drop Shortcut menu appears.
4. Choose Create <u>H</u>yperlink Here.

Using Relative and Absolute Hyperlinks

You'll sometimes find that you want to move a file to which you've created a hyperlink. Imagine you're building an intranet; the day will come when you want to copy all the linked files to a network drive or a Web server. Word's hyperlink feature takes this into account by establishing *relative links* that are based on the relative location of the file compared with the linking document. As long as you move the files together, maintaining the folder structure that already exists, the links will stay intact.

The alternative to a relative link is an absolute link, where the complete path name associated with a file is specified. If the path name ever changes, the link is broken. In general, you'll use relative links, but on occasion you can create an absolute link to a file that you know will never move.

You can see the difference between relative links and absolute links in Table 18.1. Note that relative and absolute links appear the same for networked locations.

Table 18.1   Differences Between Relative And Absolute Links

Relationship Between Files	Relative Link	Absolute link
Both documents in same folder	file.doc	c:\folder\file.doc
Destination document in higher level folder	..\file.doc	c:\file.doc

continues

Part

IV

Ch

18

Table 18.1   Continued

Relationship Between Files	Relative Link	Absolute Link
Destination document in folder stored on another computer	\\otherpc\d\file.doc	\\otherpc\d\file.doc
Destination file stored on the World Wide Web	www.yoursite.com/file.htm	www.yoursite.com/file.htm

Working with Hyperlinks

As you've learned, by default hyperlinks appear in your document as blue, underlined text. If your hyperlink contains text or a graphic instead of the file address it links with, you can still see where the hyperlink goes by hovering your mouse pointer over it. A ScreenTip appears, including the complete hyperlink address (see Figure 18.24).

FIG. 18.24

If you hover your mouse pointer over a hyperlink, Word displays a ScreenTip showing the file address to which the hyperlink connects.

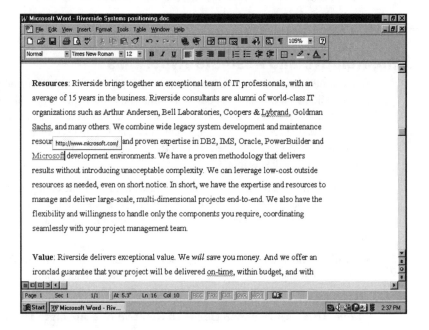

When you click a hyperlink, Word attempts to jump to the site. If the site is on the Internet, and you're not currently connected, Word displays the Dial-Up Networking screen you usually use to gain access. Follow whatever steps you normally use (including, perhaps, identifying yourself with a user name and password).

TIP If you click a hyperlink containing a file that Word doesn't know how to open, such as an Adobe Acrobat .PDF file, Word may display Internet Explorer and download the file. You then will be given a choice between saving the file to disk and attempting to open it using an Internet Explorer/Netscape Navigator plug-in.

After you click a hyperlink, it changes color from blue to magenta for the duration of your current editing session.

Because these colors are widely understood among Web users, you'll rarely want to change them. However, if you have a special design reason to change them, you can. Hyperlink formatting is set in two built-in Word styles: Hyperlink for hyperlinks that haven't been clicked yet, and FollowedHyperlink for those that have. Change these styles and you change the appearance of your hyperlinks.

It can be tricky to reformat hyperlinks in your document, because clicking them displays the linked document or location. Therefore, instead of using Style by Example, you might find it quicker and easier to use the Format, Style dialog box to change your hyperlink styles.

These changes only affect hyperlinks within Word documents; the color of text in a Web browser is set through HTML code or by the browser itself.

▶ **See** "Creating and Changing Styles," **p. 148**

By now you won't be surprised to hear that hyperlinks—like cross-references, indexes, tables of contents, and so many other Word features—are actually fields in disguise. Typically, the { HYPERLINK } field contains only the word HYPERLINK, plus the complete file address in quotation marks. However, there are a few field options you can add to slightly modify the hyperlink's behavior.

You can add \h to keep the link from being added to the history list when you click it. You can add \l followed by a bookmark, you tell Word to jump to the bookmarked location (in the current or another document). As you'll see shortly, it's usually easier to accomplish this through the Edit Hyperlink dialog box.

If you add \m you specify that the link is an HTML 2.0 image map; and if you add \n the hyperlink opens in a new window by default.

Part
IV

Ch
18

Working with the Hyperlink Shortcut Menu

If you right-click a hyperlink, a shortcut menu appears (see Figure 18.25), giving you several choices for working with the hyperlink. You can see the choices if you point to Hyperlink on the Hyperlink shortcut menu.

■ *Open* displays the hyperlinked document in Microsoft Internet Explorer, opening Internet Explorer if necessary. This command only works with hyperlinks to Web pages, not to other documents on your computer.

FIG. 18.25
The Hyperlink shortcut menu gives you several options for working with a hyperlink.

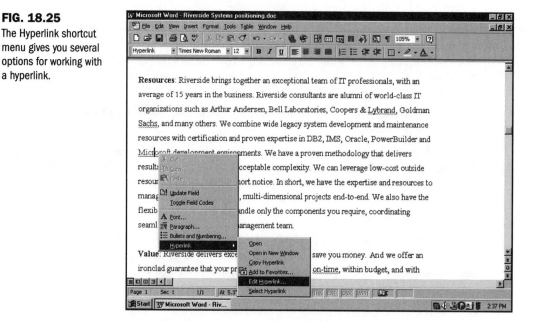

■ *Open in New Window* also opens the hyperlinked document in Internet Explorer, but opens a new copy of Internet Explorer if one is already open. Again, this command only works with hyperlinks to Web pages, not to other local documents.

N O T E In Word 97 Service Release 1, if you clicking Open or Open in New Window on a hyperlink connected to another document, the Web toolbar will open, and the document's path will appear in the Address drop-down box there. If you select the address, the document will open. ■

■ *Copy Hyperlink* lets you copy the hyperlink to another location in the current document, or any other Microsoft Office 97 document.

■ *Add to Favorites* places a shortcut to the hyperlinked file in the Favorites folder—the same folder the Internet Explorer Web browser already uses to keep track of the Web pages you've marked as Favorites.

■ *Edit Hyperlink* displays the Edit Hyperlink dialog box (see Figure 18.26) where you can change the link with which the hyperlink connects.

■ *Select Hyperlink* is an easy way to select an entire hyperlink without actually opening that file or moving to that location.

FIG. 18.26
From the Edit Hyperlink box, you can change the document, bookmark, or named range of an existing hyperlink.

TROUBLESHOOTING

I clicked a hyperlink, but I got an error message. If the hyperlink is an Internet location, are you connected to the Internet? If the hyperlink is on a network, is the network server running properly and do you have access to it? If the hyperlink is on your own computer, did you create an absolute link and then move the linked file?

I'm having trouble with punctuation characters in hyperlinks. If you create a hyperlink to a file that contains the symbol #, Word truncates the file name and generates an error message. You'll have to change the file name to eliminate the # character. In addition, Word sometimes has trouble with hyperlinks that include colons, semicolons, closing parentheses, and exclamation points. If you have problems, you may have to edit your hyperlink to eliminate these characters. You can also try adding a space between the text of the hyperlink and the punctuation character.

My computer slows down (or I start running out of memory) when I hyperlink between Word and Internet Explorer, Excel, or PowerPoint. When you click a hyperlink to another type of Office document or to a Web page, another application opens alongside Word; in some cases, multiple instances of an application may open. If you begin to run out of memory, close all programs and reopen them; this should release the memory used by the programs so your computer can run more quickly.

From Here...

In this chapter, you've taken a close look at four of Word's most powerful features for navigating long documents and streamlining document production: bookmarks, footnotes, cross-references, and hyperlinks.

- Hyperlinks are just one of Word 97's capabilities for building Web pages. Refer to Chapters 9, "Using Word to Develop Web Content," 10, "Building Your Intranet with Word, Office, and FrontPage," and 11, "Deploying Your Internet or Intranet Site" for a detailed look at creating Web content with Word.

- You'll often create footnotes, endnotes, and cross-references that span several documents in a single master document. For a close look at how master documents work, refer to Chapter 15, "Master Documents: Control and Share Even the Largest Documents."

- In the next section, starting with Chapter 19, "Word Desktop Publishing," you'll learn desktop publishing and graphics techniques for making sure your documents pack a visual punch.

- Long documents are rarely the work of one person writing alone. If you write as part of a team, see Chapter 23, "Managing Revisions," for detailed coverage of managing a collaborative revisions process.

The Visual Word: Making It Look Even Better

Word Desktop Publishing

by Joe Lowery

By now it's pretty clear that Word 97 has a tremendous amount of power under the hood when it comes to manipulating language. What some people don't realize is that Word has very strong visual capabilities as well. If you need to spice up your reports, dash off a flyer, or crank out a newsletter—Word can handle it. In this chapter, you'll begin to explore how the desktop publishing side of Word 97 can make your work really stand out. ■

Using the Newsletter Wizard

You can make a professional-looking document with the Newsletter Wizard.

Creating documents with multiple columns

You can make your publication's text much easier to read with the control Word gives you over columns.

Making graphics from text

Drop-caps and special symbols can easily be inserted in Word to create graphic effects with text.

Working with text boxes

Text boxes enable you to place your text anywhere on the page. Word 97 has added a linking text box feature to let your articles flow from page to page.

Building a newsletter case study

Here's an example that puts it all together and discusses how best to approach your own newsletter layout.

Beyond Word 97

If you find that you need more desktop publishing capabilities than what Word can offer, you can carry over many of your Word skills to Microsoft Publisher.

Planning Your Document

If you're working with a one-page document, such as an announcement or mailer, consider quickly sketching out your preliminary layout, especially if you're using any kind of graphic like logos, clip art, or photographs. Getting your ideas on paper, even roughly, can give you a better idea of what size your images should be, how large you can make your headings, and how much room you'll have for your basic text.

When you are putting together a larger publication, like a newsletter or quarterly report, it's best to gather all your materials before you begin designing the document. One of the biggest problems you'll have as a layout artist is getting the text to fit within a specific number of pages. Whether you have too much text or too little, it is much easier to make it fit when you have all the pieces. If you must lay out a document without all the elements in hand, use rectangles and text boxes the approximate size as placeholders. This gives you a truer picture of how your text is fitting.

TIP

If you want to see how text will flow around a picture or an AutoShape, but don't have the text yet, you can use Word's built-in random text generator. Place your insertion point where you want the text to start, type **=Rand()** and press Enter. Word inserts three paragraphs of repeating phrases.

One final word about planning your document: moderation. When you're choosing fonts, font sizes, and styles for your publication, select the smallest number of options that can do the job. Two fonts and three different font sizes are adequate for a great number of publications. An advertisement or other document with too many changes in fonts and/or font sizes is difficult to read and detracts from your message. Just because you can change fonts every letter doesn't mean you have to.

Quick and Easy Newsletters with the Newsletter Wizard

Word includes a handy template for creating newsletters. The Newsletter Wizard includes most of the standard newsletter features: columns, graphics, wrapping text, headlines, and repeating elements such as headers and footers. In addition to providing a tool that can make your document shine even if you have no layout talent, the Newsletter Wizard also offers a nice tutorial on useful techniques.

To create a publication using the Newsletter Wizard, follow these steps:

1. Choose File, New.

2. From the New dialog box, click the Publications tab.

3. Double-click the Newsletter Wizard icon. In the Create New section, make sure that Document rather than Template is selected.

   You can customize several parts of your newsletter. Click the Next button to begin.

4. On the screen that appears, first select any of the available newsletter styles. Then, select whether your publication is to be in color or black and white. Click Next.

5. On the screen that appears, you can type in a title for your newsletter as well as a date, volume, and issue number. Click the Next button when you are through.

6. On the screen that appears, select whether your newsletter should leave room for a mailing label or not. Click Next to proceed.

7. As with all wizards, you can click the back arrow keys to change your choices. Click Finish when you are ready for Word 97 to create your newsletter.

TIP The Newsletter Wizard automatically creates five pages instead of the four you would expect for an average newsletter. Use the extra page as a work area to temporarily store articles or pictures. Delete the page when you are finished.

A Wizard-created newsletter is shown in Figure 19.1. Each of the different elements, such as main headlines, subheads, body text, and bylines, are set in a particular style, so it's easy to quickly modify the overall look of the newsletter. See Chapter 5, "Styles: The Foundation of Automated Documents" for more on Styles.

FIG. 19.1

The Newsletter Wizard can easily create a publication with a professional appearance.

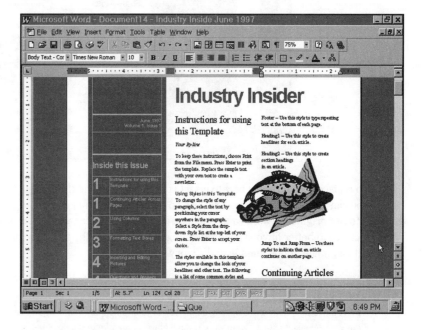

To customize the newsletter, you replace the placeholder text with your own. Here's one method you can use if you already have your articles created:

1. After you've built your newsletter with the Newsletter Wizard, open the document with your replacement text.

2. Highlight and copy the text for your first article.

3. Choose <u>W</u>indow, and then your Wizard-created letter document to switch to it.

4. Highlight the placeholder text for the first article. Click the Paste button on the toolbar.

5. Repeat the process to replace additional articles and text.

Figure 19.2 shows how our case study newsletter looks after the placeholder text has been replaced by my newsletter text. The next step is to change the pictures so that they're meaningful to you and your audience.

FIG. 19.2

A wizard-created newsletter with text replaced.

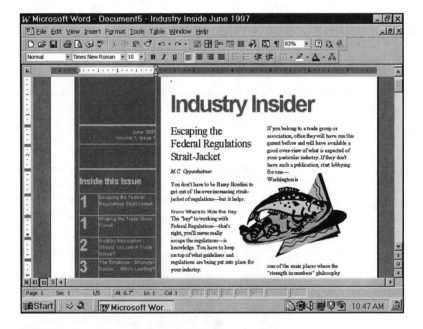

To replace a graphic, it's best to insert your image first and then delete the placeholder image. You can choose from pictures in the Clip Art Gallery, scanned-in photographs you might have, or other original artwork saved on disk. In the next chapter, you'll learn how to resize and crop pictures to better fit your publication. Figure 19.3 shows the first page of our newsletter, now with an image more suitable to the story.

CAUTION

Don't make the mistake of selecting all the text in your newsletter with the <u>E</u>dit, Select A<u>l</u>l command. Unless every text element is in its own text box, you'll erase your entire template. If this should happen accidentally, click the Undo button from the toolbar.

FIG. 19.3
Completed wizard-created newsletter with new graphics and text.

Setting Up Multiple Columns

You may not realize it, but you're already using columns. Regular text layout, as in a letter or report, is in one column. Word 97 has the capacity to produce multiple columns. Multiple columns are used to break up large blocks of text and make them more readable. Although multiple columns are not suitable for most correspondence, they are perfect for newsletters and brochures. You can even use multiple columns within certain reports to offset a particular section of your document. Columns can affect the entire document, one section of a document, or just selected text.

Word uses what are referred to as *newspaper columns*. Text in newspaper columns flows from the bottom of one column to the top of the next. If Columns are turned on for more than one page, text from the bottom of the last column on a page continues at the top of the first column of the next page. For an extra bit of layout definition, Word can automatically draw a vertical line between each column.

There are two main column controls. The first is the Column button on the Standard toolbar. When you click the Column button, a drop-down box offers you an initial choice of one to four columns; you can click and drag to the right to get up to six columns. The Column button quickly produces columns of equal width in the full document, one section (if you are using section breaks) or the selected text. Use this control when you don't need any of the special features of columns such as unequal size or lines drawn in-between.

TIP You must be Page Layout view to see side-by-side columns. You can get there by choosing View, Page Layout.

Part
V

Ch
19

Follow these steps to quickly see how columns work:

1. Select a paragraph or more of text.

2. Click the Column button on the Standard toolbar.

3. Choose two or more columns.

4. Release the mouse button.

TIP The Column button is great for making quick headings that span your columns. Select the text that you want to spread across your columns and click the Column button. Choose 1 Column and you'll get a result like that shown in Figure 19.4.

FIG. 19.4
You can make any text span your columns by using the Column button.

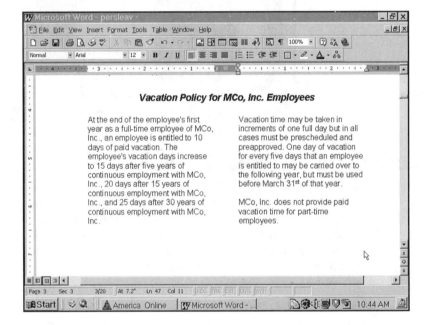

The second way to access column controls, through the Format menu, is covered in the next section.

Using the Format Columns Dialog Box to Control Formatting

To gain complete control over your columns, you have to choose Format, Columns to open the Columns dialog box as shown in Figure 19.5. With this dialog box you can add as many columns as you have room for, customize the size of the columns and the spacing between them, and add vertical lines between each column.

In the Presets section of the Column dialog box, you can choose between one, two, or three equally divided columns or columns with two different unequal widths. The width of your columns depends on your left and right margins; the wider the margins, the narrower the columns will be. If you choose one of the unequal width presets, Left or Right, the "named" column is set to a little less than one-half the width of the other column. For example, on a page with one inch left and right margins, selecting the Left preset makes the left column 1.83" and the right column 4.17" with a .5" space in-between; selecting the Right preset switches the widths of the columns.

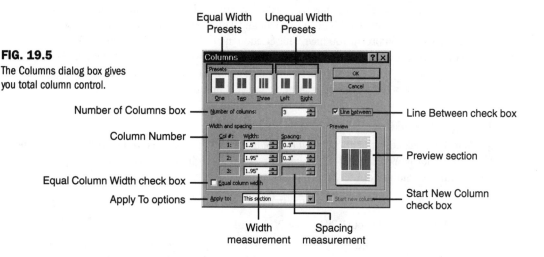

FIG. 19.5
The Columns dialog box gives you total column control.

Equal Width Presets — Unequal Width Presets

Number of Columns box

Column Number

Equal Column Width check box

Apply To options

Line Between check box

Preview section

Start New Column check box

Width measurement — Spacing measurement

Columns of unequal width—your first column being narrower than your others, for example—are used to add more visual variety to a large format publication, such as a newsletter. There are no hard and fast rules for sizing your columns other than to be sure that your text can still be read. If a large number of the lines in your column end in hyphenated or broken words, your column is too narrow.

To manually create columns of unequal width, follow these steps:

1. Select the document, section, or text that you want to convert to columns.

2. Choose Format, Columns.

3. To create two or three columns, click the corresponding Preset buttons.

4. To create more than three columns, type a value in the Number of Columns text box or use the incrementer arrows.

5. In the Width and Spacing section, remove the check in the Equal Column Width box by clicking the box. The Width text boxes for columns other than Column 1 become active.

6. Type a new value in a Width text box for a particular column or use its incrementer arrows.

   If you use the incrementer arrows, you can see how the other columns shrink or grow according to your choices. The Preview section gives you a general idea of how your columns will appear.

7. Click OK when you have completed your selection.

Part
V

Ch
19

The gutter between your columns is controlled by the Spacing measurement. Generally, it's a good idea to keep your spacing between .25 and .5 inches. You can use a larger measurement if you decide to use the Line Between option to place vertical line separating each column. Turn on the Line Between by clicking in the check box next to the option.

The Apply To section of the Columns dialog box controls which portions of your document are converted to columns. If you haven't selected any text prior to opening the Column dialog box, your choices are between Whole Document and This Point Forward. (If you've inserted a continuous section break, you have This Section instead of Whole Document.) This Point Forward creates the columns from the insertion point to the end of the document. When This Point Forward is selected, the Start New Column box becomes active. When checked, Start New Column has the same effect as inserting a column break.

Changing Column Widths with the Ruler

To make quick adjustments when you want to eyeball the changes, you can click and drag new column widths. You can also click and drag the left or right margins for each column, thus affecting the gutter between the columns.

When you want to adjust your column margins by hand, follow these steps:

1. If your Ruler is not visible, select View, Ruler.
2. To change the width of a column and keep the spacing between columns constant, click the center Column Marker (see Figure 19.6) and drag the mouse to a new location when you see a vertical dashed line. Release the mouse button.
3. To adjust the spacing between columns, click either the left or right Column Marker (or the left or right column margin, if your insertion point is in that column) and drag it to a new location when you see the vertical dashed line. Release the mouse button when you are finished.
4. Repeat steps 2 and/or 3 for every column adjustment.

 After you've moved your columns to a new place, use the Undo/Redo buttons to toggle between two different widths for your columns. It's a quick way to compare two choices.

Starting a New Column with Column Break

Normally, the text in your columns flows down to the bottom of a page and then continues at the top of the next column. However, there are times when you want to start a new column at a particular place in your text, at a specific paragraph or with a new heading, for example. A column breaks works just like a page break—in fact, you've probably seen the command if you've ever inserted a page break because it's in the same dialog box.

To start a new column with a column break, follow these steps:

1. Place your insertion point in front of the text where you want to start the next column.
2. Select Insert, Break.

Column   Center Column   Left column   Right column
Marker   Marker   margin   margin

FIG. 19.6

Adjusting column
widths on the Ruler is
very quick.

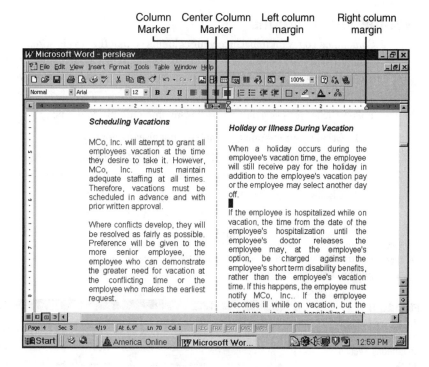

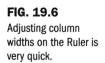

3. In the Break dialog box (see Figure 19.7), click the <u>C</u>olumn Break option in the Insert section.

4. Click OK to close the Break dialog box.

FIG. 19.7

Column breaks help
you control the flow
of text.

 If you're having trouble seeing where to insert column breaks, you can see—and edit—the whole page at the same time by clicking the arrow next to the Zoom control and selecting Whole Page.

You remove column breaks just as you would a page break. The easiest way to see the break is to switch to Normal view by choosing <u>V</u>iew, <u>N</u>ormal. Then select the Column Break line. Press Delete to remove it.

 If you don't want to switch to Normal view to delete the column break, place your insertion point in front of the line that starts the new column. Press Backspace to remove the column break.

Evening Your Columns

Sometimes you want to balance your columns so that the text is spread evenly over all of your columns. This choice can be made for aesthetic ("It just looks better") or practical ("I couldn't follow the article") reasons. Word has an easy way for you to even out your columns no matter where they end.

Follow these steps to balance text flowing into multiple columns:

1. Create your columns, if you have not already done so.
2. If necessary, switch to Page Layout view by choosing View, Page Layout.
3. At the end of the text that you want to balance, click to place the insertion point.
4. Choose Insert, Break.
5. From the Break dialog box, select a Continuous Section Break.
6. Click OK to close the dialog box.

Figure 19.8 shows a before-and-after view of text that has been balanced using the Continuous Section Break.

FIG. 19.8

The text on the right was balanced with a Continuous Section Break.

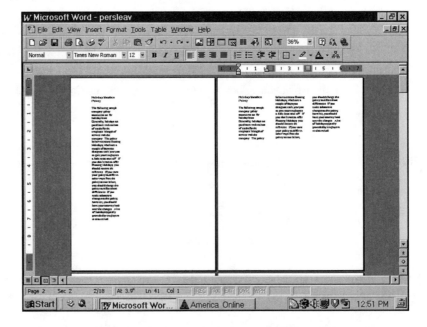

CAUTION

Depending on how your document is formatted, you may find that you need to separate the text that follows your balanced columns. One technique for doing this is to select the first blank line after your balanced columns, in the first column, and then click the Column button on the toolbar. Select 1 Column. This makes the blank line span all the other columns and forces a separation.

Using Drop Caps

Word can easily create large initial capitals, more commonly known as *drop caps*, that give your documents a distinct, magazine style appearance. Drop caps work extremely well in newsletters, particularly those formatted with columns.

Drop caps are so named because usually it is the first letter or word of a paragraph, formatted in all capitals, and "dropped" into the paragraph so that the first 2 or 3 lines are pushed to one side. Figure 19.9 shows an example of a drop cap as well as the Drop Cap dialog box.

FIG. 19.9

A drop cap adds visual spice to a page.

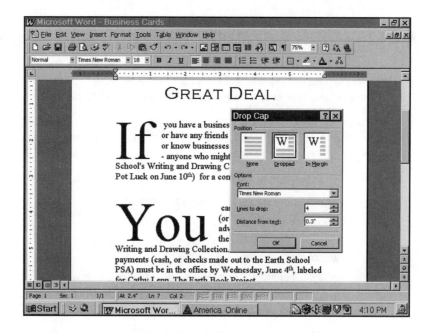

Part
V

Ch
19

Follow these steps to add a drop cap to any paragraph:

1. Highlight the letter(s) or word(s) you want to convert to a drop cap.
2. Choose Format, Drop Cap.
3. From the Drop Cap dialog box, first select the position you want your drop cap to appear in. Click either Dropped or In Margin.
4. Next, you can select a different font for the drop cap by clicking the arrow next to the Font text box.
5. To change the size of the drop cap, type a new value in the Lines To Drop text box or use the incrementer arrows.
6. To alter the amount of space between the drop cap and the surrounding text, type a new value in the Distance from text box or use the incrementer arrows.
7. Click OK to see the result.

Word makes your drop cap by putting your selected text into a special frame. To alter your options and get a different look, click the frame with the drop cap and select that Format, Drop Cap again. To remove a drop cap, click the frame, select that Format, Drop Cap and choose None.

T I P   A classic designer trick is to pick a font for the drop cap that's from a different typeface than the one used for the body of the paragraph. For example, if your paragraph is in a sans-serif font like Times New Roman, use a serif font like Arial for your drop cap.

Working with Special Characters and Symbols

If you do any sort of international work, you need to be able to include foreign language characters in your documents. Word can handle a wide range of international characters, as well as special characters, such as copyright © and trademark ™ symbols.

The primary tool for accessing the special characters is the Symbol dialog box. In addition to selecting symbols and other characters one at a time, the Symbol dialog box also lets you setup a variety of shortcuts for often used characters.

The basic steps for inserting a special character or symbol are as follows:

1. Place your insertion point where you want the special character to appear.
2. Choose Insert, Symbol.
3. From the Symbol dialog box, as shown in Figure 19.10, click a character box to see the symbol more clearly.
4. To select a character or special symbol from a different font, click the arrow next to the Font text box and choose a font from the drop-down list.
5. Press the Insert button to put the character in your text.
6. Press the Close button to clear the dialog box from the screen.

FIG. 19.10

Special characters magnify when selected.

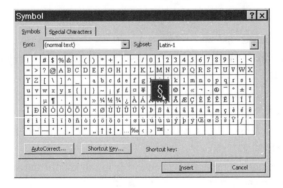

TIP If you need to add a series of special characters (for example, when you're typing a foreign language address or phrase), you can keep the Symbol dialog box open. Simply click in your main document to continue typing until you need your next special character.

You can automatically produce certain symbols such as a copyright © or trademark ™ symbol with Microsoft's new AutoCorrect feature.

TIP To stop AutoCorrect from converting what you type into a symbol on a case-by-case basis, press Backspace after the symbol appears.

Using Text Boxes

The text box is a completely free-floating object, independent of your regular document. The position and size of text boxes is completely user-definable, so you decide where to put the text box and how big it should be. You don't have to worry about precisely placing your text box the first time—you can always adjust the size and position later. Text boxes are used to display quotes pulled from an article or any other specially positioned text.

Follow these steps to insert a text box into your document:

1. In your document, go to where you want to place your text box.
2. Choose Insert, Text Box. Your pointer becomes a small crosshair.
3. Click where you want the upper-left corner of your text box to appear and drag out a rectangle.
4. Release the mouse button when your text box is the right size and shape.

When the text box appears, it will look like the one in Figure 19.11. When selected, the text box has a special diagonal line border with eight sizing handles around it. Inside, a new insertion point blinks. The text box also has its own ruler settings, which enable you to set tabs independently from the rest of the document. You can deselect the text box by clicking anywhere outside of it.

Part
V

Ch
19

TIP You can use the default size if you have no idea how large you want your text box to be initially. Choose Insert, Text Box; when you see the pointer become a small crosshair, just click once. The default text box appears.

TIP Text boxes can be a little tricky to get rid of. The key is, after you've selected it, click the border of the text box again. The border changes from a diagonal to a dot pattern. Press Delete.

FIG. 19.11

The special diagonal line border easily identifies a text box.

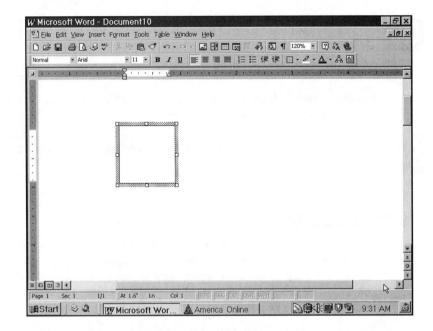

Normally, when you type any new text into your document, its position is dependent upon the margins, and the amount of text and paragraph marks that go before it. Text boxes permit you to place text anywhere on the page, regardless of what else might be there. In Word 97, the capabilities of text boxes have been significantly improved. Some of the new features of text boxes are included in the following list:

- Linking from one text box to another to permit text to flow through the document
- Creating a watermark image that is visible beneath the regular text
- Enhanced formatting properties, including control over 3-D effects, shadows, border styles and colors, fills, and backgrounds
- More text wrapping options
- Text boxes can be rotated and flipped
- The orientation of the text can be adjusted to achieve various effects
- Text boxes can be layered, aligned, and grouped with each other or with other drawing objects

N O T E   In Word 97, text boxes are used in many of the ways that frames were used in previous versions of Word. However, you still need to use a frame instead of a text box if you need to position text or graphics that include any of the following: a note reference mark, a comment mark, or certain fields, including AUTONUM, AUTONUMLGL, AUTONUMOUT—used for numbering lists and paragraphs in legal documents and outlines—TC (Table of Contents Entry), TOC (Table of Contents), RD (Referenced Document), XE (Index Entry), TA (Table of Authorities Entry), and TOA (Table of Authority) fields. You can convert a text box to a frame by selecting your text box, choosing Format, Text Box from the menu, and clicking the Text Box tab. Click the Convert to Frame button. ▣

Formatting a Text Box

Chances are, you'll need to format your text box to get exactly the look you want. The default text box has a thin (.75 point) black line surrounding a white-filled interior and the wrapping is set so that text flows across the top and bottom of the box.

The Format Text Box dialog box (see Figure 19.12) has five different main sections: Colors and Lines, Size, Position, Wrapping, and Text Box. The Picture tab is only active when you are inserting a picture.

FIG. 19.12
The Format Text Box dialog box gives you a lot of options.

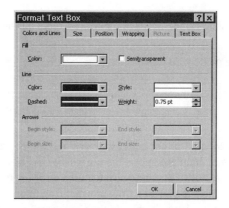

There are two ways to open the Format Text Box dialog box:

- ▣ Select your text box. From the menu, choose Format, Text Box.
- ▣ Select your text box. Right-click the border of the text box to open the Quick Menu. Choose Format, Text Box.

Working with Text Box Colors and Borders

Until fairly recently, there wasn't much point to using color in your documents. You could change the shading of a table's header row to make it stand out a bit more, but everything was in gray because that's all office printers could handle. That's all changed with the advent of low-cost color inkjet printers, not to mention Word's Web publishing capabilities. Now, you can (almost) justify using the hot-pink background with a half-inch thick deep purple border for your semi-annual sales report. Word text boxes give you full color control in addition to the gray shading that the boss still wants.

As mentioned previously, you can independently control the border color and the *fill* or background color of your text boxes. A fill is a solid color; Word can also use color blends called gradients (covered later in this chapter). If you choose the No Fill option, your text box is transparent—a technique used to lay text over a picture. Similarly, you can choose the No Line option to turn off your text box's border entirely. To alter your text box's fill or border color, follow these steps:

1. Select your text box.
2. Choose Format, Text Box.
3. From the Format Text Box dialog box, click the Colors and Lines tab, if necessary.
4. To select a new background color, in the Fill section, click the arrow next to the Color drop-down list box.
5. Choose a new color from the standard color options. To see additional choices, click the More Colors button.
6. To select a new border color, in the Line section, click the arrow next to the Color drop-down list box.
7. Click any of the 40 available colors or click the More Colors button for additional selections.
8. Click OK when you've made your choices.

 TIP Clicking the Semitransparent check box in the Fill section gives you a lighter shade of your chosen color that allows anything behind it (text or graphic) to show through. Lighter tones work better than the darker colors.

When you click the More Colors button for either Line or Fill color, you get a dialog box with two tabs: Standard and Custom. Standard shows the normal SVGA 256-color palette arranged in a color hexagon (see Figure 19.13). Standard also features a 16-step grayscale blend between black and white. The Custom tab lets you pick from any of the additional colors available if your Color Palette is set to 16-bit color or higher. In the Custom tab, you can also specify a color by its Red-Green-Blue values or its Hue-Saturation-Luminance numbers.

FIG. 19.13
Additional color options are found under the More Colors button.

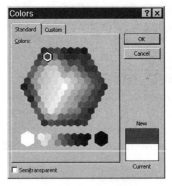

In addition to changing the color and pattern of a border, you can also control the line's appearance, style, and weight. This is how you make a dashed line to indicate a cut-out coupon or a caption box for a legal pleading. All the controls are found in the Format Text Box dialog box.

Word offers 36 different patterns for text box borders. From the Format Text Box dialog box, in the Line section, click the arrow next to the Color drop-down list box. Choose Patterned Lines to select a pattern other than solid. You can also change the Foreground and Background color of the pattern.

Follow these steps to alter the look of a text box border:

1. Select your text box.

2. Choose Format, Text Box.

3. From the Format Text Box dialog box, click the Colors and Lines tab, if necessary.

4. In the Line section, click the arrows next to these options:

   - *Dashed.* Offers eight different appearances ranging from a solid line (the default) to dash-and-dot combinations.

   - *Style.* Gives you nine preset single line widths (¾ point is the default) and four multiple line options.

   - *Weight.* Enables you to type in a new value, in points, or use the incrementer arrows to change the thickness of the line. The default is .75 points.

5. Click OK after you've made your selections.

Selecting a Fill Effect

Solid fills are just the bare bones of what is possible with text boxes backgrounds. Word fill effects include the following:

- *Gradients* are blends between user-selectable or preset colors in a variety of set patterns.

- *Textures* are multicolor designs based on images, such as marble, wood, or denim.

- *Patterns* are repeating designs created from two user-selectable colors.

- *Pictures* allow a text box to have an image as a background.

Follow these steps to select a fill effect:

1. Choose Format, Text Box to open the Format Text Box dialog box.

2. In the Fill section of the Colors and Lines tab, click the arrow next to the Color drop-down list box.

3. Select Fill Effects.

4. Click OK on the Fill Effect dialog box after you have made your selections.

Using Word's Built-In Gradients

If you really need to emphasize some text, Word has a collection of very snazzy text box backgrounds, known as gradients. A gradient is a blend that uses two shades of one color, two different colors, or a range of preset colors. You can pick the single or two colors to use in a gradient; Microsoft includes 24 different preset gradients to choose from in Word.

Gradients are terrific for certificates, special awards, or "plaques" such as the one in Figure 19.14. Some of the preset gradients can even be used thematically, like Early Sunset, or Rainbow, when coupled with the appropriate text.

To access the gradient controls, follow the steps for Fill Effects and then click the Gradient tab. When you first bring up the Gradient dialog box, no specific color is selected and the examples shown in the preview section are rendered in grayscale. Click one of the following options to enable additional choices:

FIG. 19.14

Gradients allow subtle blending of two or more colors.

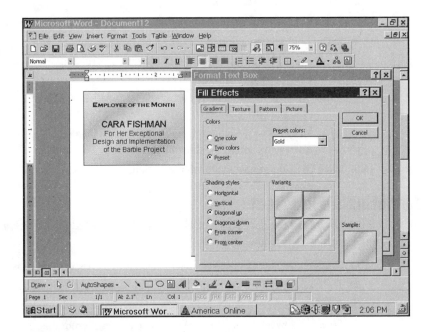

■ *One Color.* Opens up a selector for choosing the color to blend from dark to light shades. A slider enables you to vary how dark or how light the shades will be.

■ *Two Color.* Gives you Color 1 and Color 2 selectors for designing a custom blend. Click the respective arrow to open the Color dialog box.

■ *Preset.* Displays the option list for the professionally designed multicolor gradients. Click the arrow to see the drop-down list.

Controlling Shading Styles

The gradient color choices covered in the previous section are used in combination with the shading styles found on the bottom portion of the Gradient tab.

There are six different shading styles that can be selected. All styles have four different options to choose from except for the last one, From Center, which only has two. The six shading styles are as follows:

Horizontal

Vertical

Diagonal Up

Diagonal Down

From Corner

From Center

> **CAUTION**
>
> If you use one of the Gradient Presets and you don't have a color printer—or if the document is going to be photocopied—be sure you can still read the text. Some of the brighter color combinations don't have enough contrast to make text readable when reduced to grayscale.

Adding Textures

Textures are another alternative to filling your text boxes with solid colors or gradients. *Textures* are small pictures that are tiled or repeated as much as necessary to fill out a given text box. A texture can be as subtle as parchment or as broad as a fish fossil—complete with fish! You can even use your own images as a texture.

What distinguishes textures from the other fill effects is that textures can be made from any graphic file, including photographs that have been digitized for use on your computer. A photographic background can give a text box a very realistic look. The various marble and wood textures work well in year-end reports and corporate newsletters.

Part
V

Ch
19

To include a Texture fill in a text box, follow these steps:

1. Select your text box and open the Fill Effect dialog box by choosing Format, Text Box and clicking the arrow next to the Color drop-down list box in the Fill section of the Colors and Lines tab and then clicking Fill Effects.
2. Click the Texture tab.
3. From the Texture tab (see Figure 19.15), click one of the 32 samples in the scrolling list.
4. If you want to use a file of your own as a texture, click the Other Texture button and open the appropriate file.
5. Click OK on the Fill Effects dialog box when you have finished making your selection.

FIG. 19.15

Some of the 32 preset textures available.

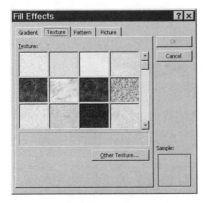

Adding Patterns

Patterns are two-color repeating designs. Word uses the same 36 patterns for filling a text box as it uses for making a patterned line. The process is identical to choosing a 2-color gradient. Click the Pattern tab of the Fill Effects dialog box. Click one of the available patterns. If you want something other than the black-and-white defaults, you can choose different foreground and background colors. Click OK when you've made your choices.

A word of warning about using a Pattern Fill Effect. Unless you're using very large fonts, you'll probably find that the background fill overwhelms the text rendering it unreadable. The other thing to look out for is the high contrast default colors. You might like the results more if you choose two colors closer in tone.

Adding a Picture as a Fill Effect

The final Fill Effect option is Picture. Like the Texture effect, this puts any graphic, including photographs, into the background of a text box. There are, however, two differences between Texture and Picture. First, the Picture effect does not tile to fill out the size of the text box like the Texture effect does. Second, the Picture effect stretches the image to fit the text box. After it is filled with a Picture, resizing the text box also resizes the graphic.

One powerful use for the Picture effect is in the development of catalogs. Not only will a smaller text box produce a thumbnail of a larger image, but because it is a text box, important information such as a stock control code or price could easily be overlaid. Figure 19.16 shows a typical use of a Picture Fill Effect.

FIG. 19.16
A Picture Fill Effect provides an effective background for text.

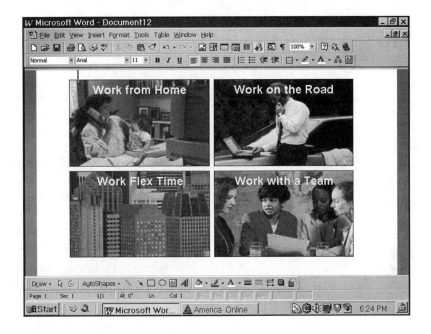

Follow these steps to add a Picture as a Fill Effect:

1. Select your text box and open the Fill Effect dialog box by choosing Format, Text Box and clicking the arrow next to the Color drop-down list box in the Fill section of the Colors and Lines tab and then clicking Fill Effects.

2. Click the Picture tab.

3. Click the Select Picture button.

4. From the Open Picture dialog box, select the picture you want to use as a text box background.

5. The Picture area shows the original file. The Sample area shows the file, stretched to fit a square text box. Note that this does not mean this is how the picture will look in your text box, if your text box is the same aspect ratio as the picture.

6. Click OK to close the Fill Effects dialog box.

Precisely Controlling Text Box Size and Position

How many times have you looked at a document produced in-house and thought, "Something was off, but I can't figure out what it is?" Even a relatively untrained eye notices tiny discrepancies when objects on a page are not perfectly aligned or when one box is just slightly larger than another. When precise measurements are essential, Word can size and place objects to within $1/100$ of an inch.

Word has added some new facilities to align objects with each other and relative to the page, but you can still use the numeric positioning capabilities when dealing with text boxes on

Part
V

Ch
19

different pages. Repeating elements in exactly the same position, page after page—especially in something like a newsletter or business report—greatly enhances the professional appearance of your documents. This applies to the size of text boxes as well.

▶ **See** "Aligning and Distributing Drawing Elements," **p. 617**

To use numeric measurements for text box position and size, follow these steps:

1. Select your text box.

2. Choose F_ormat, Text B_ox.

3. To alter the size or shape of the Text Box, click the Size tab in the Format Text Box dialog box. Then you have the following options:

    - In the Size section, type new percentages in the Height and Weight boxes or use the incrementer arrows.

    - In the Scale section, type new percentages in the Height and Weight boxes or use the incrementer arrows.

    - Select the Lock Aspect Ratio to maintain height and width relative to each other.

4. To alter the placement of the text box, click the Position tab in the Format Text Box dialog box.

5. Select the anchor from where the text box is positioned by clicking the arrow next to the From box for both the Horizontal and Vertical directions and selecting one of the options.

6. In the Horizontal and Vertical, type new values or use the incrementer arrows to alter the position of the text box.

7. If you want to make sure that the text box stays with the paragraph it is anchored to, select the Move Object with Text check box.

8. If you want to make sure that the text box stays on the same page as the paragraph it is anchored to, select the Lock Anchor check box.

9. Click OK in the Format Text Box dialog box when you have completed your choices.

TIP The Format Text Box is also great for checking the exact size and position measurements when you want to duplicate them for another text box, in the same document or another.

Wrapping Text Around a Text Box

I'm sure you've seen magazine articles where a quote from the article is put in a box, in larger type, and the rest of the article flows around the box. If you've ever wondered how they did that, this section is for you. Those effects are known as pull quotes (because they are pulled from the article) and Word handles them with its text box wrapping features.

You get to the Wrapping options by selecting your text box and choosing F_ormat, Text B_ox. Then click the Wrapping tab. You make your choices from this dialog box as shown in Figure 19.17. Take the three sections one step at a time: first, select the Wrapping Style; then select what you want to Wrap to (from the available choices) and finally change the Distance from the text. Table 19.1 identifies each option and describes what it does.

FIG. 19.17
Wrapping text around a text box is often used in newsletters and special reports.

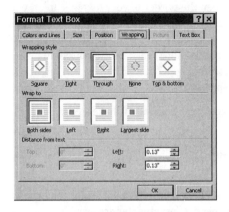

Table 19.1   Text Wrapping Options

Symbol	Name	Description
	Square	Wraps text on all four sides of box.
	Tight	Wraps to image inside of box.
	Through	Also wraps to image inside of box, through any open spaces.
	None	Turns off wrapping.
	Top & Bottom	Wraps text above and below text box.
	Both sides	Text wraps on either side of the box.
	Left	Text only wraps on the left side of the box.
	Right	Text only wraps on the right side of the box.
	Largest side	Text only wraps on the side of the box with the most room.

Part
V

Ch
19

The Tight and Through options work only with pictures or AutoShapes. To enable the Wrap To options, you must have selected either the Square, Tight, or Through wrapping style.

▶ **See** "AutoShapes," **p. 599**

Setting Internal Text Box Margins

Just as you can set the distance between your text box and the text that flows around it, you can also set the distance between the border of your text box and the text inside. The default is to have a .1-inch left and right margin and a .05-inch top and bottom margin. This works well in most circumstances, but there are times where you need to take control of the margins. You could, for instance, need just a little more space on the bottom to make the last line fit correctly. Or, if you use a very heavy border, like 8 point or higher, you might want to emphasize your text with a little extra white space around it.

To alter the internal margins of a text box, follow these steps:

1. Select your text box.
2. Choose Format, Text Box.
3. Click the Text Box tab.
4. In the Internal Margin section, type in new values for the Left, Right, Top, or Bottom margin, or use their respective incrementer arrows.
5. Click OK.

Linking Text Boxes

The ability to link text boxes is a new feature implemented by Word and previously found only on dedicated desktop publishing applications like Microsoft Publisher or Adobe PageMaker. With linked text boxes you can start an article on page 1 of your newsletter and continue it on page 3, or run an ongoing sidebar in an annual report that connects from one page to the next. When text is deleted or added in one linked text box, the text is adjusted in all the other linked boxes.

 TIP   If you're working a lot with linked text boxes, it's best to turn on the Text Box toolbar. On it are controls for making, breaking, and following text box links. To enable the toolbar make or select a text box, choose View, Toolbar, and then choose Text Box from the submenu.

Follow these steps to link one text box to another:

1. Make a minimum of two text boxes.
2. Select the first text box.

3. Click the Create Text Box Link from the Text Box toolbar. The pointer changes to an upright pitcher.
4. Click the second text box. When you are over a text box available for linking, the upright pitcher changes into a pouring pitcher.

You can now create another text box and link it to the second box by following the previous steps 2 through 4. You can either create and link all your text boxes ahead of time—when you are designing your newsletter—or add your boxes and link them as needed. Figure 19.18 shows one text box linking to a second and preparing to link to a third.

FIG. 19.18
You can link text boxes on the same page as well as on different pages.

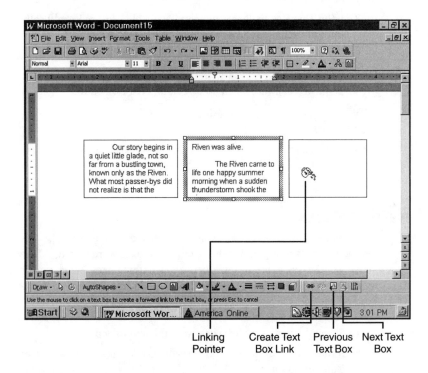

Linking Pointer   Create Text Box Link   Previous Text Box   Next Text Box

You can have multiple articles running through separate links. From a practical point of view, you don't want to do this with every item in your newsletter; it makes the articles too hard to follow.

> **CAUTION**
>
> Linked text boxes are limited to staying within one document; you can't link one text box in one document to another in a separate file. Nor can you link text boxes between subdocuments when you're using a Master Document structure.

Following a Link

After your text boxes are linked, you can follow the links forward or backward. When you have finished editing a story or article, it's a good idea to follow your text through all the linked boxes to make sure it formats the way you want it. Linked text boxes are very susceptible to widows (the last line at the bottom of a text box by itself) and orphans (the first line at the top of a text box by itself).

Part
V

Ch
19

To follow a series of linked text boxes, follow these steps:

1. Select the first text box.

2. If the Text Box toolbar is not already visible, choose View, Toolbar and then Text Box from the submenu.

3. Click the Next Text Box button on the Text Box toolbar. Word jumps to the next linked text box.

4. To move backward, click the Previous Text Box button.

> **CAUTION**
>
> Keep an eye on your last text box to make sure that all the text is visible. Word doesn't provide any signals to indicate whether or not there is any text hidden and remaining to be flowed.

Breaking a Link

Occasionally, you need to break a link between text boxes—maybe you need to reflow some text and start over or perhaps the wrong text boxes were linked. Whatever the reason, you'll find it very simple to break a link between two text boxes. When you do break a link, the text remains in the first box, ready to be linked again, and the second text box is cleared.

To break a link between text boxes, follow these steps:

1. Select the text box where you want the text to end.

2. If the Text Box toolbar is not already visible, choose View, Toolbar and then Text Box from the submenu.

3. Click the Break Forward Link button on the Text Box toolbar.

> **CAUTION**
>
> Keep in mind that if you break a link between two text boxes (say, Text Box A and Text Box B) all the links connecting after the second text box (Text Box B) are also lost.

Building Your Own Newsletter: A Case Study

When you lay out a newsletter, it's best to work from the background to the foreground. First, put in the elements that repeat. Repeating elements include those that repeat in every issue like your logo and masthead and those that repeat on every page, such as headers and footers. Don't forget to layout any repeating graphics like borders or rules.

It's best to create the total number of pages needed right at the start. After opening a new blank document, insert page breaks to create the new pages. Then, if your newsletter uses facing pages, you can switch to a Two Page view of your document so that you can make sure that articles and columns are lining up correctly.

If you are using facing pages, you'll probably want to use different headers and footers, so that the even numbered left-hand page appears opposite of the odd numbered right-hand page. To set this up, choose File, Page Setup and click the Layout tab. In the Headers and Footers section, enable the Different Odd and Even check box. Because most first pages differ from the other pages—the logo figures prominently as well any table of contents or special features—check off Different First Page also.

At this point, it's good to also lay out any elements that are not flexible, like your masthead or From the CEO column. Figure 19.19 shows stage one of our newsletter in a two page view with the repeating elements—the main logo and headers and footers—in place.

FIG. 19.19

Page One and Two of a newsletter with main logo and other repeating elements in place.

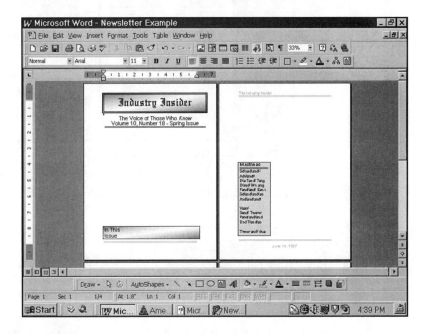

> **TIP**
>
> When you're happy with your basic layout, save it as a template. Then, when you begin to lay out the next issue, you'll have the initial work completed and you'll ensure a continued style.

Next lay out your basic column structure. Keep it to two or three columns—more than that and the page becomes too cluttered. Whether each column is the same size or varied is a matter of taste. Unequal columns are less conservative, but generally accepted, if the difference between the size of the columns is not too drastic. Don't worry about placing your graphics at first; Word can easily flow text around inserted graphics at any point.

For anything longer than a paragraph or two, it's best to write your articles in Word separately and insert the files later. This allows many people to contribute articles while one person controls the final layout. If possible, make sure that all articles use the same styles to format their document. That way, you can achieve a uniform look and easily modify all headings, by-lines, and regular paragraphs at one time. Figure 19.20 shows the text flowed into a 3-column layout, with lines automatically drawn between.

FIG. 19.20

Stage two of creating a newsletter flows in the text.

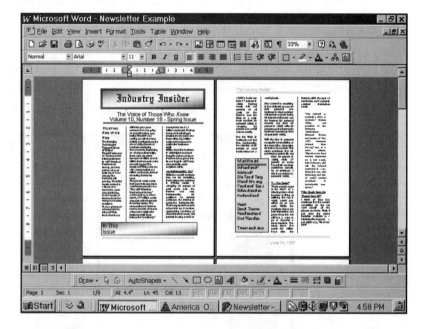

CAUTION

If you flow your text into your newsletter and your text boxes containing logo, masthead, and other elements disappear, click Undo and check the wrapping options for your text boxes. To keep the text boxes from moving, the best Wrapping Style setting for text boxes is Square—that way, the text flows all around the box.

Now it's time to bring on the graphics! If you're using drop caps, apply them first; they'll have a major effect on the look and the flow of text as the graphics are dropped in. Next, create text boxes for any pull quotes you might want to use; a good technique is to have the quotes partially span two columns with the wrapping style set so that text flows on either side. Finally, insert your pictures and clip art. Here, once again, careful selection and moderation is the key. Use only enough images to enhance your message. You'll learn how to work with inserted clip art in the next chapter—but you'll find a lot of similarities to working with text boxes, especially when it comes to the wrapping options. Figure 19.21 shows the completed newsletter with all the drop-caps, pull-quotes, and clip art in place.

If Word Isn't Enough: Microsoft Publisher

Word 97 has taken major strides to enhance its desktop publishing capabilities—but it's still not a desktop publishing program. Microsoft Publisher 97 is an easy-to-learn program with all the bells and whistles necessary to output a wide range of publications. Publisher comes with a variety of templates and wizards to make producing everything from a newsletter to a business form a snap.

FIG. 19.21
The finished newsletter with graphic elements in place.

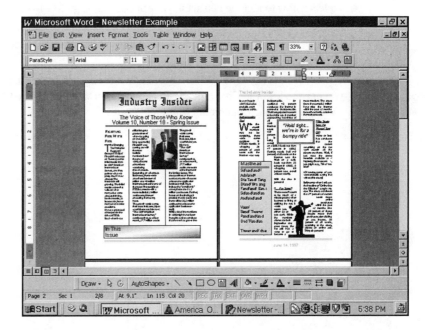

Publisher is based entirely on concepts similar to those we just learned with linking text boxes. All text goes into what are called Text Frames and, similarly, all graphics go into Picture Frames. The learning curve is fairly flat when going from Word to Publisher and there is significant integration between the two programs. In addition to importing Word files, Publisher enables you to set Word as your primary editor so you can do all your extensive editing work in a familiar environment while you layout your publication in Publisher.

From Here...

In this chapter, you began to explore Word's visual side, first planning your document and then taking advantage of Word's Newsletter Wizard. Next, you learned how to work with columns, drop caps, and symbols. Then you explored text boxes and all their capabilities. Finally, you examined how a newsletter might be built from scratch. Here's where you might want to go next.

■ If the idea of saving and re-using your basic newsletter and other publications is appealing, Chapter 6, "Templates, Wizards, and Add-ins," has the basics and more on storing and using templates.

■ To review AutoCorrect so that you can automatically insert symbols, you might refresh your memory with a glance at Chapter 7, "Automating Your Documents: AutoCorrect, AutoFormat, AutoText, and AutoSummarize."

■ To learn how to include clip art in your publications, go to Chapter 20, "Getting Images into Your Documents."

■ If you're interesting in producing your own graphics, be sure to look over Chapter 21, "Drawing in Word."

■ When you're ready to create forms and other business-related documents, you'll find all you need to know in Chapters 24, "Creating Electronic and Printed Forms," and 25, "Automating Your Documents with Field Codes."

Getting Images into Your Documents

by Joe Lowery

In the last chapter, you began to explore the visual power of Word and saw how text could become an effective graphic in and of itself through the use of columns, text boxes, and other tools. Next you'll see how separate graphic files—photographs, logos, and drawings—can be combined with your text to create effective, attractive documents that greatly enhance your communications. ■

Maximizing the Clip Gallery

Here, you'll learn not only how to add pictures from the Clip Gallery to your documents, but also how to take advantage of Microsoft's ever-growing online collection.

Managing additional clip art

The more you work with clip art, the more made-to-order clip art you'll gather. This section shows you how to keep track of it all—and keep it accessible at all times.

Customizing clip art

Very seldom is clip art perfect as is. In this section, you'll learn how to resize, crop, and recolor artwork to suit your needs.

Working with graphic file sizes

Embedded graphics can make a document too large for efficient backup or transfer; here is a technique to reduce your file size.

Supercharging your text with WordArt 3.0

Increasingly, you need to make your text stand out. Microsoft's WordArt is the perfect tool to make your text into a high-power graphic.

Correcting common graphic difficulties

What could go wrong with putting in a few pictures? You guessed it, plenty. Here are some solutions to common problems.

Microsoft Office 97 Clip Gallery

The term "clip art" comes from the time when newspapers used to cut—or clip—drawings and other images from their original source and paste them on separate pages of these enormous scrapbooks. Microsoft's Clip Gallery brings this practice into the computer age—and with the new Clip Gallery Live feature, into the Age of the Internet as well.

Choosing the right image is important; select an image that conveys both the message of your publication and its tone. An image's *aspect ratio,* or how the height relates to the width, is more important than the image's overall size; you can always resize your graphics, but you can't make a tall, skinny picture fit in a short, wide space without seriously distorting the image. Later in this chapter, you'll learn how to resize and crop images, but first you'll learn how to select the graphic best suited to your document.

Using the Clip Gallery

The term clip art is used when referring to illustrations, drawings, cartoons, photographs, and logos. As you can see by Figure 20.1, you select your graphics by looking at small pictures known as *thumbnails*. You can also limit your search to a specific category. In addition, Microsoft includes a keyword search to quickly find all the images with a common theme across categories.

FIG. 20.1

The Clip Gallery offers over 5,000 images on the CD-ROM—and thousands more online.

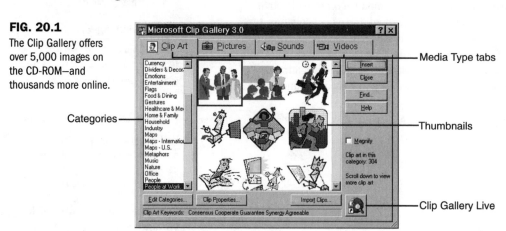

The Clip Gallery is basically a database of images. Keep in mind that the Clip Gallery only shows you thumbnails of images included in the Gallery itself; it isn't a general image manager and can't show you thumbnails of other pictures you might have on your hard drive or on the network. You can, however, import images and add them to the Clip Gallery; you'll learn how later in this chapter.

Microsoft considers graphics produced with a drawing program such as Microsoft Draw or Adobe Illustrator to be Clip Art; photographs are categorized as Pictures. Images in the Clip Art category typically use fewer colors than images in the Pictures tab and are often *vector-based* graphics as opposed to *bitmapped* graphics. Vector-based graphics can be resized with much better results, whereas bitmapped graphics can show their individual pixels when expanded beyond their original size. Furthermore, if you want your text to flow tightly around a graphic, it's better to use an image from the Clip Art category than a Picture.

 Clip Gallery 3.0 extends the definition of clip art beyond drawings and photographs to include two additional media types: sounds and video. These are designed to be used in producing pages for the World Wide Web or for an internal Web known as an intranet.

To add a graphic from the Clip Gallery to your document, follow these steps:

1. Place your insertion point where you want the image to appear.
2. Choose Insert, Picture, Clip Art.
3. Click the Clip Art tab for drawings and illustrations or the Picture tab for Photographs.
4. Scroll through the images until you find a suitable graphic.
5. Double-click the thumbnail to insert the full-sized graphic.

   The Clip Gallery closes and the image appears in your document.

 Click Magnify to get a better view of your image. Don't be put off by the graininess of the picture—the thumbnails used in the Clip Gallery are produced at a much lower resolution to keep their file size small. This is particularly noticeable in the photographs found in the Picture tab.

Searching for Images by Category   With more than 5,000 images available in the Clip Gallery, there'd better be a way to find what you need—and fast. All the images represented in the Gallery are indexed under one or more categories. There are more than 40 categories to choose from, including Business, Dividers & Decorations, People at Work, Special Occasions, and Symbols.

To see what's included in a category, you simply click the category name found in the scrolling list on the left side of the Clip Gallery dialog box. Thumbnails for each of the images are shown in the main preview pane, while a count of the images is displayed on the right.

If you find a number of images that you use frequently, you can modify their properties so that they all appear in the same group. This gives you quick and easy access to a wide variety of images that you most commonly use. You can even group them in their own new category.

To adjust a Clip Art image's category, follow these steps:

1. Select an image from the Clip Gallery dialog box.
2. Click the Clip Properties button.
3. From the Clip Properties dialog box shown in Figure 20.2, click any unchecked categories to add them; click checked categories to deselect them.
4. If you want to add a category not in the list, click the New Category button. Enter the new category name and press Enter.
5. Click OK on each of the dialog boxes to accept your changes.

Part
V

Ch
20

FIG. 20.2

Modifying a graphic's categories enables you to create custom group images.

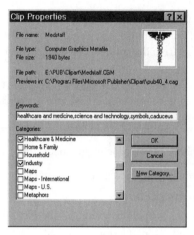

Some previews for images that come with the Clip Gallery are locked and you have to modify their properties before you can change—or even look at—their categories. From the Clip Properties dialog box, note the Previews In: path and file name. Open Windows Explorer and right-click to select the file. Choose Properties and click the General tab. Deselect the Read-Only box. Close the Properties dialog box. Close and reopen the Clip Gallery dialog box. The Clip Properties for your picture are now unlocked.

Searching for Images by Keyword   How do you find an image when there isn't a category for it yet? Imagine you're doing a program for the next presidential debate and you want to drop in some appropriate symbols. Now imagine the debate is tonight. Searching through all 5,000+ images is out of the question and there isn't a category for elections, politics, or debates. How can you find what you need? Keywords. All the graphics in the Clip Gallery have one or more keywords associated with them and a search by a keyword shows you thumbnails of all the associated pictures.

There are other search capabilities that you can use if you know the file name or the file type. These can be used in conjunction with the keyword search. Searches are performed on a tab-by-tab basis. To see both the Clip Art and the Pictures associated with a keyword, you must click each tab and then perform the search.

Follow these steps to find a group of pictures using the keyword technique:

1. Choose Insert, Picture, Clip Art to open the Clip Gallery dialog box.

2. Click the Find button.

3. From the Find Clip dialog box, shown in Figure 20.3, you have the following options:

   - Keywords enables you to search for an image by an associated term.
   - File Name Containing is used if you know some or all of the image's file name.
   - Clip Type enables you to limit your search to a specific file type. This is important if you are building a Web page that can only use GIF or JPEG files.

FIG. 20.3

Keyword searches can help you find related images.

4. Click the Find Now button to begin the search.

   Results of your search are displayed in the Main Preview pane. A temporary category, Results of Last Find, is created.

5. To search again, click the Find button to repeat the process. In the Find Clip dialog box, a list of past searches can be found by clicking the arrow next to the Keywords or File Name Containing list box. The Clip Type box displays a list of available options.

6. Double-click a thumbnail to select a found image.

N O T E The keyword search capabilities are fairly limited. You can input only one keyword at a time—so you can't use logical modifiers like AND or OR, or a list of words separated by commas. ▪

 As with the categories, you can modify a clip's keywords. Select the thumbnail and click Clip Properties. Enter your changes in the Keywords box. Keywords can either be separated by comma or a single space.

Available Resources

A Clip Gallery with more than 5,000 images sounds pretty impressive—until you go looking for the one that's not there. With clip art, it's not having the most images that counts, it's having the right image. Luckily, Microsoft has gathered hundreds of additional images and put them online where you can get them quickly. Perhaps even more fortuitously, the online collection is indexed and searchable so that you have a much better chance of finding the image you need.

There are, of course, images available other than those found in Microsoft's library and you'll see later how to import an image into the Clip Gallery. However, the online resource, known as Clip Gallery Live, has the added advantage of integrating automatically into your Clip Gallery, ready to preview with categories and keywords assigned. Just like the CD-ROM version, you can search for the clip art you need visually, by media type (Clip Art, Picture, Sound, or Video), by category, and by keyword.

Part
V
Ch
20

CAUTION

You need two things to access Clip Gallery Live: an Internet connection, and Microsoft Clip Gallery 3.0. Although you can import clips into the earlier version of the Clip Gallery, it's not as well integrated as what is described here. Microsoft recommends that you use either Internet Explorer or Netscape Navigator for your browser and that you set your screen resolution to 800×600 and at least 256 colors.

Using Clip Gallery Live You can easily get to the online resource, Clip Gallery Live—there's a direct link from the Clip Gallery dialog box to the Web site. If you choose to connect by going to the Web address (**http://www.microsoft.com/clipgallerylive/**) via your browser, it's recommended that you have the Clip Gallery open.

 The Clip Gallery Live button is located in the lower-right corner of the Clip Gallery dialog box. Click it once and, if necessary, your browser launches and you're taken right to the Web site. There is a end-user license agreement on the left side of the screen that you must accept before going any further.

This particular Web site currently uses *frames* which means that the Web page is divided into sections. As you can see in Figure 20.4, the search utility is on the left pane and the results are shown in the right pane. Generally with frames, one pane remains relatively static while the other changes.

FIG. 20.4
The Clip Gallery Live Web site features a searchable database of images.

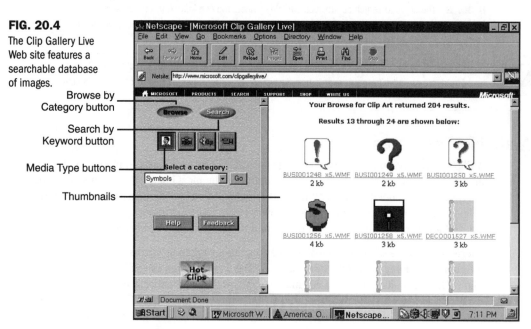

To locate and use images from the Clip Gallery Live Web site, follow these steps:

1. Open Clip Gallery 3.0 by choosing Insert, Picture, Clip Art.

2. Click the Clip Gallery Live button.

3. After the Web site loads completely, click the Accept button in the left pane of the frame to agree to the terms of the license agreement.

4. To search by category, click the Browse button and then select a subject from the Select a Category box. Click the Go button to start the search. The results are displayed in the right pane of the frame.

5. To search by keyword, click the Search button and enter one or more keywords in the Keyword text box. Click the Find button to start the search. The results are displayed in the right pane of the frame.

6. After you have located a clip that you want to include in your collection, click the name under the image.

   The file downloads and is automatically included in your Clip Gallery collection. In addition to its assigned categories, the imported clip goes into a new category, Down-loaded Clips.

7. When you have finished downloading images, you can go offline, if you want. Click the Close button of the Clip Gallery dialog box to remove it from the screen.

Two featured buttons merit the "cool" badge of honor: Hot Clips and Feedback/Notification. Click the Hot Clips button and you get the latest clips available for the selected media type; the Hot Clips are updated regularly and download just like all the others. Click the Feedback button and not only do you get to tell Microsoft what you think of the site and make suggestions for additional images, you can also sign up for a notification service that e-mails you whenever any new images in your chosen categories are available. You have to fill out a brief survey first, but the service is well worth the time.

Other Online Resources   If you can't find the image you need on the CD-ROM or at Microsoft's official site, don't despair; there are literally thousands of sites dedicated to graphics and clip art on the World Wide Web. With Clip Gallery Live, it's a one-step process—click the image and it downloads and integrates into your Clip Gallery. With other online images, the same procedure takes two steps: Step one downloads, and step two imports. You'll learn how to bring any files into the Clip Gallery in the next section, "Adding Your Images to the Clip Gallery." The current section covers locating and downloading clip art from any site on the Web to your hard drive.

Looking for the right image on the Web might seem like trying to find needle in a haystack, but luckily there are some excellent "needle finders" available. If you're online, you've probably come across numerous *search engines*. A search engine is a Web site dedicated to helping you locate your topic in the ever-growing mountain of Web pages. Lycos, Yahoo!, InfoSeek, Excite, and AltaVista are some of the more popular search engines.

Part
V

Ch

20

Most search engines work in a fashion similar to the Clip Gallery keyword search; type a word or phrase into the search text box and press the Search (or Go!, Find It!, and so on) button. In a few moments, your search results are returned as a list of Web linked addresses. If you see something promising, click the link and check it out.

Searching with only the keyword has a major drawback though when you're looking for clip art; you'll also get tons (and I do mean tons) of unrelated links through which you have to sift. A number of the search engines have special ways for you limit your search to only graphics. The following list outlines how some of the search engines work:

- AltaVista (**www.altavista.com**) lets you limit the keyword search to a graphic right in the Search text box. For example, if you type "image:mars" in the Search text box, you'll get a list of available NASA photographs. Because many search engines use the AltaVista core program, this technique works on other sites as well.

- HotBot (**www.hotbot.com**) includes a Media Type panel where you can check off graphics, video, audio, or whatever type of clip you're seeking. You can even have it hunt for specific file extensions such as .gif, or .jpg.

- Image Surfer (**isurf.yahoo.com**) is Yahoo!'s dedicated graphics search engine. You can do a keyword search or browse the categories (Arts, Entertainment, People, and so on). and subcategories. Click a link and you'll get a screen similar to the one in Figure 20.5.

- Lycos (**www.lycos.com**) has a special Pictures and Sound category that searches their multimedia database for clip art, photographs, and more.

FIG. 20.5
Yahoo!'s Image Surfer shows you thumbnails of images you can download.

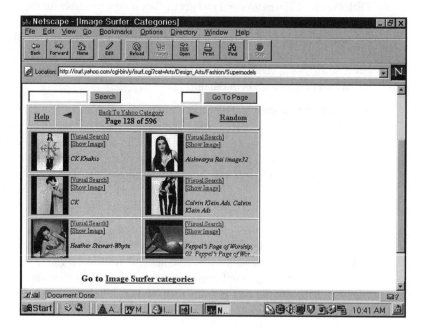

After you've located your image, how do you bring it onto your system? If you're getting your images from a clip art collection, chances are they will have files specifically designed for downloading, often the files are compressed into a ZIP format. With most, you click the file name and the download process begins; your browser opens a Save As dialog box to enable you to save the file to a special location or with a different name. After the download starts, another dialog box opens and displays the progress of transfer.

You can also download any graphic you see on the Web. Move your mouse pointer over an image and right-click. You'll get a Quick Menu where one of the options is Save Image As… (or Save Picture As…). This menu choice opens a regular Save As dialog box; all you have to do is pick the folder, name the file, and click Save; the image downloads onto your hard drive. From there, you can insert the image into your Word document as it is or include it in your Clip Gallery; the next section describes both techniques.

N O T E Be sure you read the copyright information associated with each collection. Many, but not all, images are free to use privately. Most ask to be contacted by you if you're using their art work for a profit-making venture. ▪

Working with Other Clip Art

As noted previously, you're not limited to the images that come with Clip Gallery. You can incorporate any images available on your system into Word. Moreover, you can import any image that you might use frequently into the Clip Gallery in order to have it right at your fingertips whenever you need it.

There are two types of graphic files: vector and bitmap. A *vector-based graphic* is composed of points and lines that are described in space, for example, "a perfect circle with a diameter of one inch, filled with a bright yellow color and outlined with a 1-point wide black solid line." Complex vector-based drawings are composed of layers and layers of such images. Because the graphic is described rather than exactly plotted (like the bitmapped image), it is said to be scalable which means that it can be resized without losing quality. Vector-based graphics reproduce to the highest resolution of the display device. Although you might see a few "jaggies" on a perfect circle on your monitor with the naked eye, when reproduced on a 2,400-dpi or higher printer, you'll have to get out the magnifying glass. Typical file types, and their extensions, for vector-based images are Windows Metafiles (.wmf), Computer Graphics Metafiles (.cgm), Corel Draw (.cdr), and Encapsulated Postscript (.eps). The Clip Gallery categorizes all vector-based images under the Clip Art tab.

Bitmap images, on the other hand, are display-resolution dependent. When you resize or zoom in on a bitmapped image, you get each pixel magnified and the overall picture blurred, if not unrecognizable. The effect is similar to a tile mosaic where each tile is one color—if you stand too close, you can't see the whole picture. However, bitmapped images can contain millions

Part
V

Ch
20

more colors than vector-based images and the smooth shading of color can fool the eye into perceiving additional resolution. Bitmap images are typically used for photographs and background images. The main file types are bitmap (.bmp), Graphics Interchange Format (.gif), and Joint Photographic Experts Group (.jpeg or jpg). One final word about those last two formats: GIF (pronounced with a hard "g") and JPG ("j-peg") are the two most commonly used formats on the Web, so if you capture a graphic, it's likely to be in one of these two bitmap formats.

Adding Your Images to the Clip Gallery

If you use your own images repeatedly, it's a good idea to add them to the Clip Gallery. The Clip Gallery keeps your visual files accessible in one place—and, if you use a number of files, you can easily group them in their own category to make them easy to choose from and find.

The Clip Gallery creates a thumbnail for your clip art and places your image into its main divisions, Clip Art or Pictures, depending on the file type (as determined by the file name extension). You can assign keywords to describe the image, decide which categories apply, and even create new categories if none of the existing ones are appropriate.

N O T E Word can import and convert 17 different graphic file types. If you're unsure if Word 97 works with your graphics files, you can find out using the Help system. Choose Help, Contents and Index, and select the Index tab. In the first box, type **graphics file formats** and display the listed entry. On this help screen you'll a list of convertible file types and their restrictions. Some file types require a specific graphics filter, which can be installed during setup. ■

Follow these steps to import any graphic file into your Clip Gallery:

1. Open Clip Gallery 3.0 by choosing Insert, Picture, Clip Art.
2. Click the Import Clips button.
3. Select your file from Add Clip Art to the Clip Gallery dialog box. The Clip Properties dialog box opens.
4. Type any desired keywords in the Keywords text box.
5. Check the appropriate boxes in the List of Categories check box.
6. If you want to create a category specifically for your imported images, click the New Category button.
7. Click OK when you're finished with the Clip Properties dialog box. Click Close to remove the Clip Gallery dialog box.

Inserting Your Own Pictures

If you only occasionally use graphics in your documents, you can insert your own pictures without going through the Clip Gallery. When an image is included in your document, it is placed in a floating frame for quick positioning with all the adjustable parameters—fill colors, borders, resizing, placement, wrapping, and cropping—available for other Clip Art.

T I P You can also bring pictures into Word 97 directly from your scanner if you have installed the Microsoft Photo Editor software. Choose Insert, Picture, From Scanner. The Photo Editor opens and begins to acquire the image from your TWAIN-compatible scanner. Make any alterations necessary and, when you're finished, close the Photo Editor to bring the picture into your Word document.

Follow these simple steps to insert a picture into your Word document:

1. Place your insertion point where you want the image to appear.
2. Choose Insert, Picture, From File.
3. The Insert Picture dialog box opens as shown in Figure 20.6
4. Locate and highlight your file.
5. Select the image specific options on the right side of the dialog box:
   - *Link to File*, when checked, maintains a connection between the graphic as a source file and your document as a destination file that is automatically updated whenever you open your Word document or when you edit your graphic while the Word document is open.
   - *Save with Document* includes the graphic file with your document when Word save the file. See the section, "Minimizing Graphics File Size," found later in this chapter for more information on this feature.
   - *Float over Text* enables you to move the graphic independently by clicking and dragging it. When the box is deselected, the graphic is anchored to its place in the text and can be moved by cutting and pasting.

FIG. 20.6
Inserted pictures can be screened by enabling the Preview mode.

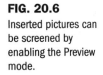

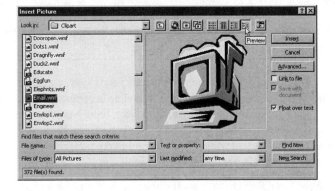

6. Click OK to insert the picture.

 T I P An alternative to using the Clip Gallery is to keep your images in their own folder (or folders, if you have a variety of them) and use the Preview mode while searching for the right picture to include. Choose Insert, Picture, From File to open the Insert Picture dialog box. Click the Preview View button (it's the second from the right on the dialog box toolbar) and as each file is highlighted, a thumbnail appears on the right of the Insert Picture dialog box.

Editing Clip Art to Serve Your Needs

At the very least, you'll probably need to reposition and perhaps resize your clip art to integrate it into your document. However, you can do so much more; clip art can be cropped, brightened, recolored, and even redrawn. You can adjust how your graphics work with the other page elements. Does text wrap around the rectangular frame or follow the curves of the image? How much room do you want between your text and graphics? Should your image stay with a specific paragraph or on a specific page? Can the text appear behind the picture or the picture behind the text? You'll find answers to all these questions and more in the section that follows.

TIP If you'd prefer to use a specific paint program to create or edit your images from within Word, you can include the graphic as an object. Choose Insert, Object to begin. If you're creating a graphic, stay on the New tab and double-click the object type. To insert an existing picture, click the Create from File tab and browse for your image. After the object is inserted in Word, you can double-click it at any time to edit using the source program.

Positioning

When inserting clip art from the Clip Gallery—your own file, or direct from a scanner—the first instruction is always to place your insertion point where you would like the picture to appear, approximately. Your positioning is approximate at this point because the initial position varies depending on whether you choose to float the picture over the text. How do you know which option to choose? Naturally, it depends on what effect you are trying to achieve.

TIP Remember, if you're inserting a picture not in the Clip Gallery, the Float Over Text option is turned on as the default. Deselect it by clicking its check box. To change the float status of a Clip Gallery image (or any other), choose Format, Picture, and click the Position tab. The Float Over Text option is on the lower half of the Format Picture dialog box.

When the Float Over Text check box is selected, your image appears above the paragraph in which your insertion point is located, even if the line is composed of only a single paragraph mark. From there, it's a simple matter to move your mouse pointer over the graphic and, when the moving pointer (a four-headed arrow) appears, click and drag your image to a new position. You float an image over text when the placement of the picture is more important than the text it is next to, as with many newsletter photographs.

Turn the Float Over Text check box off when it's important for an image to appear directly above, below, or next to a specific paragraph. When the Float Over Text check box is cleared, an inserted image appears exactly where the insertion point is placed, even if it is in the middle of a line. This option also enables you to position your image using the alignment buttons in the toolbar; it's an easy way to center your image horizontally on the page.

TIP If you're using Word 97 to build Web pages and want to use inline images, turn off the Float Over Text option for your graphics. When Word saves your document as an HTML page, it does this anyway; if your images are floating, you could get unwanted results.

If your image is floating, precisely place your image by choosing Format, Picture, and then clicking the Position tab. Picture positioning works exactly the same way as text box positioning. You can set the horizontal position relative to the page, margin, or column; and you can set the vertical position relative to the page, margin, or paragraph. The last option (setting the vertical position of the image relative to a paragraph) is only available if the Move Object with Anchor option is selected.

Resizing Clip Art

There are no clues in the Clip Gallery to indicate how large or how small a piece of clip art is going to be when it is inserted. Quite often clip art, even an image that you have created, has to be resized to blend properly with your text. While resizing is generally a very straightforward process, it can also be very frustrating. You can easily stretch an image out of shape by changing the width more than the height or vice versa. With clip art, the ratio between the height and the width is very important. Some images, such as photographs, look wrong if they are resized even slightly out of proportion. Luckily, there are tools and shortcuts to ensure that your image is resized proportionally.

When an image is selected, eight sizing handles appear around its surrounding frame. The different handles have different effects:

- *The corner handles* permit you to resize your image in both directions at the same time. If the aspect ratio is locked (the default), the clip art resizes proportionately.
- *The middle handles* enable you to resize the object only vertically (using just the top and bottom handles) or only horizontally (using the handles on the side).

To unlock the aspect ratio of any selected clip art, choose Format, Picture, and click the Size tab. Clear the Lock Aspect Ratio check box. After this is cleared, you can temporarily resize your image proportionately by holding down the Shift key while you click and drag the corner sizing handles. Be sure to release the mouse button before the Shift key or else your clip art snaps back to its nonproportionate size.

TIP The Ctrl key, if pressed while resizing, forces the object to resize from the center. This works with any sizing handle.

The Size tab of the Format Picture dialog box has two ways for you to resize your object precisely. As shown in Figure 20.7, you can alter the height or width measurements directly by changing the values in the Size and Rotate section, or you can resize your clip art relative to the original by changing the values in the Scale section. If the Lock Aspect Ratio check box is

Part V

Ch 20

selected, altering just the height adjusts the width and vice versa. This works in both the Size and Rotate and the Scale sections. The Rotation text box only becomes active when the selected object was created in Word, such as a drawing object. For more information about drawing objects, see Chapter 21, "Drawing in Word."

FIG. 20.7
The Size tab of the Format Picture dialog box facilitates precise resizing.

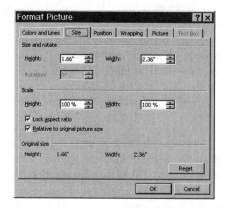

Cropping Clip Art

With clip art, to crop means "to cut away." Clip art is cropped to eliminate extraneous elements in an image, to focus the reader's attention on a particular part of the picture, or to make the graphic fit on the page. In the nonelectronic world, you crop a photo with a pair of scissors or a razor blade. Word 97 uses a cropping tool with a distinct electronic edge; when you crop a picture in Word, you hide part of the image rather than cut it away and you can reveal any hidden portions later.

 To use the cropping tool, you have to turn on the Picture toolbar. Do this by choosing View, Toolbars, and selecting Picture from the submenu. When a graphic is selected, the Cropping tool becomes active. Select the Cropping tool, and click and drag any sizing handle on the image frame. The handles and keyboard modifiers (the Shift and Ctrl keys) have the same effect with cropping as with resizing. Figure 20.8 shows a picture before and after it was cropped.

To reveal a cropped section of a picture, reverse the process. Select the clip art. Click the Cropping tool from the Picture toolbar. Click a sizing handle and drag away from the picture to "uncrop" the image.

 Just as you can precisely resize an image using the Format Picture dialog box, you can crop an image "by the numbers." Select your image and then choose Format, Picture to open the dialog box. Click the Picture tab. In the Crop from section, change the values in the Left, Right, Top, or Bottom boxes. Unless you're working with a series of pictures with similar characteristics, achieving your desired result with this technique is much more difficult than clicking and dragging with the Cropping tool.

FIG. 20.8
Cropping clip art can hide unwanted sections of a picture.

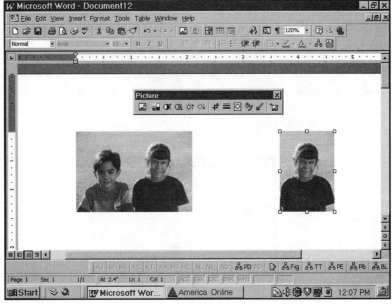

Recoloring Whole Images

Almost all the available clip art today is produced in color. Word 97 enables you to convert any image from full color to a grayscale or to a straight black and white. You can also adjust the brightness and the contrast of an image to de-emphasize it or make it stand out even more. Finally, Word includes a default watermark setting that converts your picture to one that works well behind text.

All of the color controls are located in the Format Picture dialog box. Follow these steps to recolor your clip art:

1. Select your clip art and choose Format, Picture.
2. Click the Picture tab.
3. In the Image Control section, choose one the following options from the Color drop-down list box:

    - *Automatic* uses the same colors as your original clip art. Use it to reset the colors, if necessary.
    - *Grayscale* converts colors to their gray equivalent, preserving relative contrast and brightness.
    - *Black & White* changes multicolored images to two colors. It is useful for creating high contrast line art.
    - *Watermark* sets the Brightness to 85% and the Contrast to 15%. This generally allows text to be readable when placed over the picture while still permitting the picture to be visible.

Part
V

Ch
20

4. Adjust the Brightness or Contrast by clicking and dragging their respective Slider controls.

5. Click OK to see the results.

TIP Figure 20.9 shows the effect of converting a colored graphic by using the Watermark setting. You'll learn more about the different techniques for placing images behind text in the next chapter, but briefly here's how it's done: Right-click your clip art. From the Quick Menu, choose O_rder, and then Send Be_hind Text in the submenu.

FIG. 20.9

When you convert a graphic to a Watermark, the text and picture can both be seen.

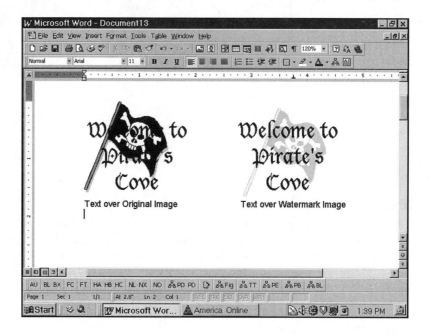

For more information about combining images and text, see Chapter 21, "Drawing in Word."

Wrapping Text Around Your Clip Art

The ability to wrap text around graphics is an essential design alternative when developing newsletters, annual reports, and other publications. Word 97 includes a wide variety of text wrapping options similar to the ones covered in the previous chapter on text boxes. You can also force the text to follow the shape of the actual image and not just the surrounding frame. Moreover, you can adjust exactly how text flows around any clip art—including photographs. For more information about text wrapping, see Chapter 19, "Word Desktop Publishing."

While you can access some of the wrapping options through the Picture toolbar, all the possibilities are found on the Wrap tab of the Format Picture dialog box. As with text boxes, you can force text to wrap above and below the graphic, on either or both sides of a picture, or turn off the wrapping to have the text flow through the image. The additional graphics-only options are as follows:

- *Tight* wraps text so that it follows the shape of the image and not just the bounding box.
- *Through* is basically the same as Tight, but it also allows text to flow into any open parts of the picture.

You can change the flow outlines created by both of the previous options for more precise wrapping control. You alter these wrap points to make your text more readable or to create special effects. As Figure 20.10 shows, you can even make the text flow over a normally rectangular object, such as a photograph. Follow these steps to change the way text wraps around an irregular object:

FIG. 20.10

You can control where the text goes by editing the wrap points.

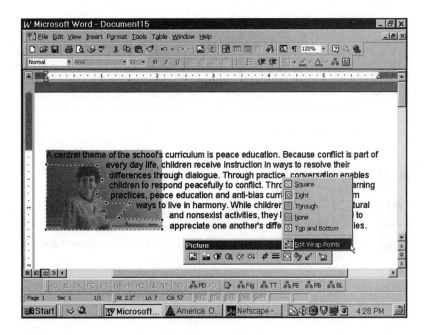

1. Select your clip art.
2. From the Picture toolbar, click the Text Wrapping button.
3. From the menu, click the Edit Wrap Points button.

   A dotted outline appears around the object, with as many square control points needed to define the shape.
4. To change the outline shape, place your pointer over one of the control points. Click and drag the point to a new location and release the mouse button.

You can add new control points by placing your pointer over any portion of the dotted outline and clicking and dragging out a new point.

You can also delete existing points by pressing Ctrl and clicking a control point.

Part
V

Ch
20

You can set the amount of space you want between your text and your graphic. Select your picture and then choose Format, Picture. Click the Wrapping tab and look at the Distance from Text section. Depending on which wrapping option you have enabled, you can independently change the values for the To̱p, Botto̱m, Le̱ft, and Ri̱ght areas around the graphic.

Reshaping Your Clip Art

Any extensive clip art alterations are probably best handled by a dedicated graphics program like Microsoft Draw, Adobe Illustrator, or Adobe PhotoShop. However, that is not to say that you do not have a fair amount of editing power available to you within Word 97. For quick specific tasks, like moving the points of a vector-based drawing, Word works just fine.

As noted earlier in this chapter, vector-based graphics such as those found in the Clip Gallery's Clip Art section are composed of layers of shapes grouped together. Word lets you ungroup the shapes and individually color or reshape any or all of them. The process is the same as the one used for editing wrap points as described previously. However, it does involve accessing another toolbar, the Drawing toolbar.

Follow these steps to change the shape of any vector-based clip art:

1. Select your clip art.
2. If not already active, choose View, Toolbars, Drawing.

 3. Click the Draw button on the left side of the Drawing toolbar.

 4. To work on one part of the image, select the Ungroup button and click the part you want to change.

 5. Click the Draw button again, and select the E̱dit Points button. The outline of the shape displays all the available control points.

   To move a control point, click and drag it.

   To add a new control point, click the outline and click and drag a new point.

   To delete a control point, press Ctrl and click the point you want to remove.

6. Click anywhere away from the object to hide the control points.

 After you've ungrouped a graphic to alter a piece of it, the image needs to be regrouped before you attempt to move or resize it. If you do not regroup it, only the selected part is affected. You can regroup a graphic by selecting any part of the group and clicking the Regroup button found under the Draw button on the Drawing toolbar.

Figure 20.11 shows a sample advertisement where the same clip art was duplicated five times. One image was selected, ungrouped, and a portion of the picture was reshaped as described previously.

FIG. 20.11
Clip art can be re-shaped by editing the control points.

N O T E   Note that you can only change the shape of a vector-based graphic. To extensively alter any part of a bitmapped image, such as a photograph, you need to use a graphics program like Microsoft Photo Editor or Adobe PhotoShop. ■

Minimizing Graphics File Size

How big can a text file with graphics be? The answer is "very." When Word inserts a picture, the default is to embed the image as an object, combining its file size with that of your text. Some images, especially large, high-resolution photographs produced by scanners, can be over a megabyte by themselves. You can imagine how large a file a catalog with 50–70 separate images could be.

How do you keep the file size down? The simplest way is to keep the graphics and the text separate, but linked. Whenever you insert a picture, you have the option to just link the picture to the text. In addition to the link, you can independently decide whether or not to save the picture with the file. Keeping the graphics linked to the text assures that any updates made to the image separately are reflected in the copy in the text file; sometimes this is desirable and sometimes it is not.

If you're working with a lot of graphics and you want to minimize the size of your files, follow this procedure for every image you insert:

1. Choose Insert, Picture, From File.
2. Select the Link to File check box.
3. Clear the Save with Document check box.

TIP Clip art inserted via the Clip Gallery is always embedded in the text; there is no way to just link it. If you know where your graphic files are located on your hard drive, you can use the Insert Picture procedure described previously. You can find where an individual file is located in the Clip Gallery by clicking the Clip Properties button and looking at the path name.

Using WordArt 3.0

Clip art that combines text and graphics falls into a special category. Many logos include the name of a company or a special phrase and it's obviously impossible to find ordinary clip art that matches your company's name or trademarked tag line. Word 97 has integrated a wonderful program for creating fancy text objects: WordArt. With WordArt your text has added dimension, color, and style. Best of all, your WordArt creation is completely customizable—even to the point of changing the wording.

WordArt can also be used to generate key words to highlight a particular section of a document, such as "Sale!" or the ever-popular "New." Fancy text objects like WordArt are best used sparingly. While you can produce an entire (small) paragraph with WordArt, it would probably be difficult to read and the impact is diluted with overuse; transform only your key words into WordArt to achieve the maximum impact.

CAUTION

Keep in mind that WordArt objects are really drawing objects. WordArt objects cannot be checked for spelling or used by any other text function such as Find and Replace.

Although there are a lot of WordArt options, the initial creation is very straightforward. Follow these steps to make a basic WordArt object:

1. Click the Drawing button in the toolbar to view the Drawing toolbar.

2. Click the WordArt button on the Drawing toolbar. (You can also use the menus; choose Insert, Picture, WordArt.) The WordArt Gallery is displayed as seen in Figure 20.12.

3. Double-click any of the 30 preset designs. The Edit WordArt Text dialog box opens.

4. Type in your text to replace the "Your Text Here" phrase.

5. If desired, change the font or font size by selecting from the Font and Font Size boxes, respectively.

6. Your text can be made bold or italic by clicking the Bold or Italic button.

7. Click OK. WordArt creates your object with sizing handles around it and opens the WordArt toolbar.

8. Click anywhere outside of the WordArt object to return to the regular document.

FIG. 20.12
The WordArt Gallery offers 30 customizable preset designs.

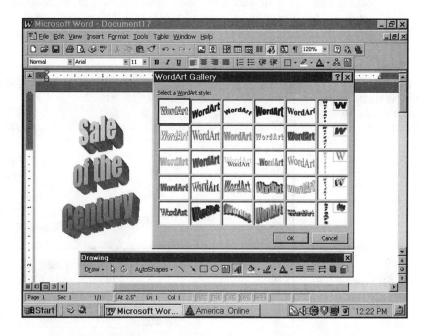

After your WordArt object is created, you can change the text by double-clicking it. This opens the Edit WordArt Text dialog box described previously.

 T I P If you select a word or phrase prior to starting the WordArt process, your text automatically appears in the Edit WordArt Text dialog box.

Modifying Your WordArt Shape

After you've created your basic WordArt shape, it's easy to modify. You can either try different preset effects through the WordArt Gallery or combine a preset with one of 40 different shapes. Your new shape can then be stretched, resized, and rotated. Experimentation with the

Part
V

Ch
20

various shapes is the best way to understand what generates the best look for your particular WordArt object. Often, trying to achieve one effect will lead you to a completely unexpected, but wonderful, result.

 Click your WordArt creation to open the WordArt toolbar. If it doesn't open, choose View, Toolbars, WordArt. Click the WordArt Gallery button to see your choices for a different preset. Double-click any image to see how your text looks with that formatting.

The WordArt Gallery presets combine a particular shape, color fill, shadow, alignment, and other options. You can use the presets as a jumping off place and then modify any of the options to your own preferences. I've often found that I like the coloring and shadowing of a preset option, but my text is not as readable as it should be given the preset shape. In this case, I change the shape to something simpler and keep all the other options. Figure 20.13 is a before-and-after picture that shows just such a circumstance.

FIG. 20.13
You can modify just the shape with the WordArt Shape button.

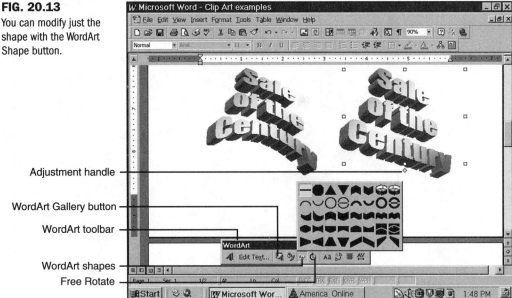

To change just the shape of your WordArt object, follow these steps:

1. Select your WordArt object.
2. Click the WordArt Shape button.
3. Select one of the 40 available shapes (refer to Figure 20.13).

As you might expect, you can move and resize your WordArt object just as you would any other clip art. To move your object, click and drag it when the four-headed pointer appears. Click and drag the sizing handles to change its height and width. The keyboard modifiers work as they do with text boxes and clip art; Shift maintains the current aspect ratio; and Ctrl causes the object to resize from the center.

There are two additional controls unavailable to other clip art that work with WordArt: Adjustment and Free Rotation. Most, but not all, WordArt shapes have an additional handle when selected. Unlike the open square sizing handles, this additional Adjustment handle is a yellow diamond and it controls the intensity of the shape. How this handle affects the shape when it is clicked and dragged depends entirely on the form of the shape. In a shape with a curved bottom, the adjustment handle alters the degree of the curve; in a shape that fades on the right, the adjustment handle moves the vanishing point.

 The second additional control, Free Rotation, is available with other drawing objects, including ovals, rectangles, and AutoShapes. Free rotation is a very valuable WordArt tool, because even a slight adjustment can make your object more readable. When you click the Free Rotation button on the WordArt toolbar, the handles change to green dots and the pointer takes on a circular arrow look. Click and drag any of the rotation handles and the object rotates on its center. As you move the object, you see only a dotted line indicating the top and bottom of the WordArt object. Release the mouse button to see the results. For more information about ovals, rectangles and other drawing objects, see Chapter 21, "Drawing in Word."

The two keyboard modifiers (Shift and Ctrl) are also used here, but with different purposes:

■ *The Shift key* constrains the free rotation to increments of 15 degrees.

■ *The Ctrl key* causes the object to rotate using the rotation handle diagonally opposite from the one selected as its center.

> **CAUTION**
>
> The WordArt Free Rotation mode is a toggle; it stays on until you click the button again. If you turn on Free Rotation, click outside the object and then click the WordArt object again; you'll find the Free Rotation mode still in effect.

Formatting WordArt Objects with Special Effects

You can change the way WordArt objects look with three major tools. To do so, follow these steps:

■ *The Format WordArt dialog box* has Colors and Lines, Size, Position, and Wrapping options, all of which function as they did with text boxes and clip art.

■ *The WordArt toolbar* includes numerous alignment and character spacing possibilities as well as specialty letter height and vertical text tools.

■ *The Drawing toolbar* controls the fill, line, shadow, and 3-D effects.

For more information about text wrapping, see Chapter 19, "Word Desktop Publishing." For more information about 3-D objects, see Chapter 21, "Drawing in Word."

Using The Same Letter Height Tool   One unique formatting option on the WordArt toolbar is the Same Letter Height tool. This tool, also a toggle like the Free Rotation button, could be described as the inverse of the Small Caps formatting option. Small Caps turns all the lower-case letters into uppercase letters but keeps them the same size as before. Conversely, the Same Letter Height tool makes lowercase letters the same height as the uppercase ones but keeps them the same case as before. Figure 20.14 shows a phrase before and after the Same Letter Height tool is applied.

FIG. 20.14

The WordArt object on the bottom has the Same Letter Height activated.

 TIP   The Same Letter Height tool, like all the WordArt toolbar formatting options, affects the entire WordArt object and can't be selectively applied to one word or a part of a phrase. To achieve that result, you need to create two (or more) WordArt objects, apply the Same Letter Height formatting to one, and then click all the objects by using Select Objects from the Drawing toolbar. Finally, click the Draw button and then Group button.

 Creating Vertical Text   There are five different presets that use vertical text in the WordArt Gallery. If you're interested in an effect that stacks the letters on top of one another, try these first—they're all located in the last column on the right of the WordArt Gallery dialog box. If none of those options are exactly what you are looking for, you can also convert any other WordArt shape into stacked text by using the Vertical Text tool from the WordArt toolbar.

To use the Vertical Text tool, first create and select your WordArt object. Click the Vertical Text button; your text stacks one letter on top of another. If necessary, adjust the width or height of the WordArt object by clicking and dragging the sizing handles. Often you can improve the look of your vertical text with one of the alignment and spacing options covered later in this chapter.

TIP You can create columns of text by placing a paragraph mark at the end of each word or phrase you want in a separate column in the Edit WordArt Text dialog box prior to using the Vertical Text button.

Adjusting WordArt Alignment and Spacing   Because a WordArt object is fundamentally a drawing object, the alignment and spacing options go far beyond the normal left, center, and right justify. A WordArt object adds letter, word, and stretch justify capabilities.

All of the alignment options can be found by clicking the Alignment button on the WordArt toolbar. Table 20.1 gives an overview of all the alignment possibilities and examples. Note that a "paragraph" can consist of a single word, as long as it is followed by a paragraph mark inserted by the Enter key.

Table 20.1 WordArt Alignment Options

Button	Name	Description
	Left Align	Paragraphs are aligned to the left edge of bounding box.
	Center	Paragraphs are centered in bounding box.
	Right Align	Paragraphs are aligned to the right edge of bounding box.
	Word Justify	Paragraphs are justified to the edges of the bounding box by stretching the spaces between words. If there is only one word on a line, the letters are spaced out equally.
Letter Justify	Letter Justify	Paragraphs are justified to the edges of the bounding box by spacing the letters and the spaces between words equally. Single word lines are treated the same as with Word Justify.
Stretch Justify	Stretch Justify	Paragraphs are justified to the edges of the bounding box by stretching the letters and the spaces between words equally.

Part
V

Ch

20

Character spacing works differently with WordArt objects than with regular text. With text, you specify that the character spaces are expanded or condensed by a certain number of points. WordArt spacing is percentage based: Normal spacing is 100 percent; condensed or tighter spacing is less, and expanded or looser spacing is more. Also changing the spacing of regular text moves the letters closer or farther apart; WordArt spacing alters the spacing by narrowing or widening the characters themselves.

 To alter a WordArt object's spacing, click the Spacing button. WordArt provides five preset values (Very Tight, Tight, Normal, Loose, and Very Loose) as well as a Custom box. You can also fit characters such as "A" and "V" more tightly together by enabling the Kern Character Pairs. Figure 20.15 contrasts the two preset extremes, Very Tight and Very Loose, against a Normal setting.

FIG. 20.15

WordArt spacing alters the shape of the letters rather than the size of the spaces.

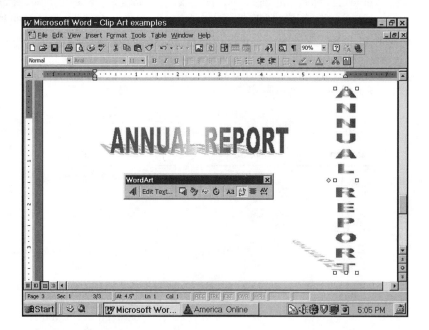

N O T E   The Troubleshooting section covers some of the most common problems encountered with clip art. If you don't find your specific problem here, try asking the Office Assistant. Choose Help, Microsoft Word Help to access the Office Assistant. In the Search text box type **clip art trouble**. You'll get 10 different topics, all related to the difficulties of working with clip art.

TROUBLESHOOTING

Previously I placed my clip art images in a file. When I reopened the file to make some final edits, the images were gone. How can I get them back? Most Word users work in Normal view. Graphics are viewable in only Page Layout or Print Preview. Choose View, Page Layout to edit your clip art.

I received a file that I am told is full of graphics, but all I see is text. What happened? Check your options—the Picture Placeholders options might be enabled. When enabled, Picture Placeholders show all graphics as an empty box; this is intended to speed up the display for graphic intensive documents. Choose Tools, Options and click the View tab. If the Picture Placeholders box is checked, click to clear it. While you're on the Option dialog box View tab, double-check the Drawings check box. If this is not selected, you won't see any of the drawing objects—including text boxes. To see all your graphics, check the Drawings box and clear the Picture Placeholders box.

N O T E   If you're creating a catalog-like publication and inserting a number of images on separate pages, one after the other, I can almost guarantee you'll run into this problem. Unfortunately, because floating is the default condition, you have to do this for *every* image you insert. If you're doing a publication with many images, sooner or later, you'll probably forget and get your images stacking up on top of one another. See the following troubleshooting section. ■

I've added all these images to my document, but they don't stay on the page I put them on. What should I do? The default for inserting a picture is to have it float over the text. If you are trying to keep each image on its own individual page, you have to clear the Float Over Text check box before clicking OK, unless each image is so large that more than one can't fit on a page. To alter the float status of an image already in your document, you have to access the Format Picture dialog box. Choose Format, Picture and click the Position tab. Clear the Float Over Text check box, and click OK.

I spent hours converting my company logo into a perfect watermark. When I typed my first page, it looked great, but when I got to the second page, the watermark disappeared. Where'd it go? In order for a watermark to appear on every page (or any other logo, for that matter), the graphic must be in a header or footer. This may seem to stretch the definition of a header or footer if it extends the full length of the page, but it works.

Be sure to turn the text wrapping off for any watermark image in the header or footer; otherwise, the header pushes the regular text beneath it. To turn off the wrapping option, select your watermark and choose Format, Picture. Click the Wrapping tab and select None.

When I tried to import a graphic, Word gave me a message indicating that it doesn't recognize the file type. What do I do now? Make sure that you have installed the necessary graphics filter. The easiest way to do this is to choose Insert, Picture, From File to open the Insert Picture dialog box. Next check the list of filters in the Files of Type box. If the filter you need is not listed, run Setup again, and install the filters you need.

If the file you need is not one of those supplied by Microsoft, but you can still open it with another graphic program, you have two choices. First, after opening the file in a drawing program, select the graphic, copy it, and paste it into your Word document. The graphic becomes a Windows metafile (.wmf). Your other option is to open the file in another graphics program, and then save it in a format that can be imported into Word.

From Here...

In this chapter, you began to explore how clip art is integrated into your Word 97 document, starting with Microsoft's Clip Gallery. You also saw how you could import your own pictures and include them in the Clip Gallery. Next, you examined the Word editing options available for clip art. Then, WordArt—the blending of graphics and text—was explored. Finally, several problems and solutions were covered in the troubleshooting section. Here's where you might want to go next...

- To review how to work with headers and footers for repeating logos and watermarks, see Chapter 3, "More Day-to-Day Productivity Tools."

- You can automatically include graphics using the AutoText features explained in Chapter 7, "Automating Your Documents: AutoCorrect, AutoFormat, AutoText, and AutoSummarize."

- If you want to turn your newfound graphic capabilities to the Web, go to Chapter 9, "Using Word to Develop Web Content," for a better understanding of using Word to produce HTML documents.

- If you're interest in positioning ordinary text like you can with WordArt, see the section on text boxes in Chapter 19, "Word Desktop Publishing."

- To learn how to use the in-house drawing tools of Word 97, continue on to Chapter 21, "Drawing in Word."

Drawing in Word

by Joe Lowery

So far in this section on the visual Word, we've delved into desktop publishing and explored the realm of clip art. Next, we open up our artist's toolbox and see how the enhanced Word drawing utilities enable you to create customized, professional-looking graphics to enhance your text and images. ■

Tour the Drawing toolbar

The Drawing toolbar has been revamped to give you quick and easy access to a whole new set of improved functions.

Begin with the basics

The basic drawing tools—lines, arrows, rectangles, and ovals—give you the power to highlight your text without overpowering it.

Creating professional graphics

If you ever spent way too many hours trying to make a simple announcement, craft a flowchart, or annotate a document with callouts, you'll really appreciate the new AutoShape capabilities.

Control fill and line options

The enhanced Fill and Line Color properties available to text boxes can also be applied to any of the shapes you create—and even to the page of your document.

Make your graphics jump off the page

Microsoft has enhanced the Shadow tool and integrated a 3-D utility—here's how it all works.

Edit drawing objects

As you create more and more complex drawings within Word, you'll need the corresponding power to make adjustments.

The Drawing Toolbar

Word 97 has significantly beefed up its artistic prowess. The new Drawing toolbar encompasses over 100 commonly used shapes, a library of sophisticated gradients and pattern fills, and newly added shadow and 3-D effects. Not only do you have much more creative drawing power now in Word, but your editing capabilities have also gone through the roof. Drawing objects in Word can be nudged, aligned, distributed, grouped, ungrouped, rotated, flipped, moved in front, moved in back, and moved behind text—just to name a few possibilities. The Drawing toolbar has put more of your most commonly accessed formatting functions, such as line thickness and style, right up front.

 This section takes you on a quick, guided tour of the Drawing toolbar. You open up the toolbar by clicking the Drawing button on the Standard toolbar. Figure 21.1 shows the toolbar and Table 21.1 gives you an overview of all the various buttons and their functions.

FIG. 21.1

The Drawing toolbar centralizes all the drawing object creation.

Table 21.1 Drawing Toolbar Features

Button	Name	Description
 Draw ▾	Draw	Contains editing controls for manipulating drawing objects.
 ▨	Select Objects	Allows the selection of one or more drawing objects.
 ▨	Free Rotate	Enables click-and-drag rotation of any drawing object.
 AutoShapes ▾	AutoShapes	Contains the library of automatic shapes, including lines, basic shapes, flowchart elements, stars and banners, and callouts.
 ▨	Line	Enables you to click and drag a line.
 ▨	Arrow	Enables you to click and drag an arrow.
 ▨	Rectangle	Enables you to click and drag a rectangle.
 ▨	Oval	Enables you to click and drag an oval.
 ▨	Text Box	Enables you to click and drag out a text box.

Button	Name	Description
	WordArt	Starts the creation of a fancy text object.
	Fill Color	Controls the color, pattern, or effect inside a drawing object.
	Line Color	Controls the color, pattern, or effect of a drawing object's border.
	Text Color	Controls the color of selected text.
	Line Style	Enables quick formatting for a line's thickness and style.
	Dash Style	Enables quick formatting for a line's appearance.
	Arrow Style	Enables quick selection from a variety of arrowhead styles.
	Shadow	Controls shadow appearance for any drawing object.
	3-D	Controls the 3-D appearance for any drawing object.

▶ **See** "Using Text Boxes," **p. 547**

Understanding Drawing Objects

The key word in the phrase "drawing objects" is probably the last one you'd pick: "objects." Every drawing object created is an individual unit; this is both a blessing and a curse. You can modify each element separately to create some quite complex illustrations; however, if you have more than a handful of drawing objects, they can be difficult to manage. But don't despair—there are techniques to make the most of the good and to minimize the bad aspects of drawing objects.

A drawing object is more technically referred to as a *vector-based graphic*. As you saw in Chapter 20, "Getting Images into Your Documents," a vector-based graphic is one that is described, as opposed to bitmapped. A described object can be resized or magnified with far greater success than one that is based on discrete pixels (like a photograph). Another distinction between vector-based and bitmapped graphics is that a bitmapped image is one big object while vector-based images can be made up of many separate objects layered on top of one another and grouped together.

Layering is an important concept when dealing with drawing objects. Most of the time your text and graphics sit side-by-side, on the same level. Word 97 has added the ability to stack graphics behind—or in front of—text. This layering facility greatly expands the repertoire of

Part
V

Ch
21

"what's possible," not only when combining graphics and text, but also when it comes to creating more complex images by overlaying different graphic objects.

Each single drawing object element (with the exception of lines and arrows) has an inside and a border. The inside is either unfilled (and thus transparent) or filled. The filling, until Word 97, was either a solid color or a two-color pattern. Now Word can also fill objects with gradients—a blend of colors—or textures, typically illustrations or pictures of real-life surfaces like marble, wood grain, or stone. Microsoft has also added a semi-transparent capability that's very useful for displaying text behind a colored object.

The border is independent of the inside fill. Most often the border is a simple black line that delineates the drawing object better. However, the line can become a design element in and of itself—a dashed line surrounding a coupon, for example. In addition to taking on a color other than black, a line can be a pattern for a more unique look.

To get a sense of how complex drawing objects are created, take a look at Figure 21.2. On one side is a fairly standard No Smoking sign; to the right of that image are the individual drawing objects—all four of them—that it took to make the finished sign.

FIG. 21.2

What appears to be a single drawing object is actually composed of many separate drawing objects.

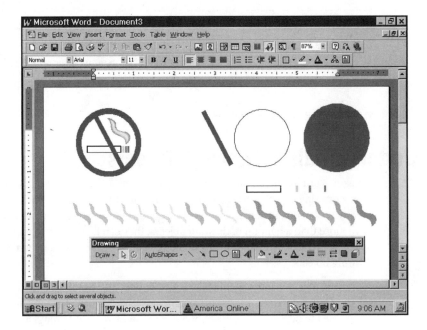

Basic Shapes

Most of the time, you'll probably use a drawing object to highlight some existing text or point out a portion of a graphic. The basic drawing objects are easy to create and perfectly suited to these tasks. Draw a line to separate two sections of a document. Point out an important statistic with an arrow. Throw a semitransparent rectangle over a couple of paragraphs to distinguish them. Set off a heading with an oval around it.

Because these basic shapes are so commonly used, they each have their own button on the drawing toolbar. They all operate identically; to place a basic shape in your document, follow these steps:

1. Click the shape button—line, arrow, rectangle, or oval. Your pointer changes into a small cross-hair.
2. Click the beginning point of your object.
3. Drag out the shape.
4. Release the mouse button.

The initial default settings of the drawing toolbar create a solid black line, .75 points thick. The rectangle and oval are not filled with any color or pattern. The object is set to wrap text on the top and bottom, the Move Anchor with Text option is enabled.

 You can create new defaults for drawing objects at any time. Format an object the way you want the default objects to appear. Select the object, and click the Draw button on the Drawing toolbar. Choose Set AutoShape Defaults. Any object you now make will have the same formatting as your original object. To return to the initial default set, you have to repeat the process with an object formatted as it was originally.

Lines and Arrows

Although these are not hard and fast rules, straight lines are generally used to separate one part of a document from another, and arrows are generally used to point to something. Of course, both can be used as a general design element to break up large blocks of text and make your document more visually appealing.

As noted previously, to create a line or arrow you click the appropriate button on the Drawing toolbar and then click and drag to the desired length. It's fairly easy to draw a straight horizontal line or arrow; by default, the line snaps to an invisible grid spaced every $\frac{1}{10}$ of an inch. (You can turn off the snap feature by clicking Draw on the Drawing toolbar and choosing Grid; then clear the check box next to Snap to Grid.)

 Here's a way to add a horizontal line to your document without using the Drawing toolbar. On a blank line, type three hyphens (–) and press Enter. A thin, black line expands across your page, from the left to the right margin. This technique also works with the underscore character to produce a thicker line and the equal sign character to make a double line. If you make this line by accident, immediately press Backspace to change the line back into the three characters.

There are two keyboard modifiers for drawing lines and arrows:

■ *The Shift key* constrains the line you are drawing to draw at 15-degree angles from its starting point

Part
V

Ch
21

■ *The Ctrl key* lengthens the line in opposite directions from the first end point as you drag. This gives the effect of expanding from the center.

Although the default wrapping style is Top & Bottom, which normally causes text to stop above an object and restart below it, wrapping has no effect on a horizontal line or arrow. You can draw a thick 12-point arrow right through the middle of a paragraph, as long as it is horizontal.

After you've drawn your line, you can change it's formatting quickly with several buttons on the Drawing toolbar.

■ *Line Color* opens the standard color menu and gives you options for additional colors or for patterned lines.

■ *Line Style* offers nine different preset widths for single lines and four different multiple line sizes.

■ *Dash Style* displays seven different dash and dot configurations in addition to the standard solid line.

The default arrow has one arrowhead and no ending element. When creating a default arrow, your first click is the end point and the arrowhead is drawn where you release the mouse button. All of the line formatting options listed previously work with arrows as well.

There is a special formatting button for Arrows on the Drawing toolbar called Arrow Style. On the menu, there are 11 preset arrow shapes with varying widths and arrowheads. In addition, you can select the <u>M</u>ore Arrows option to bring up the Format AutoShape dialog box with the arrow choices enabled. As shown in Figure 20.3, you can choose from different beginning and ending styles and sizes.

FIG. 21.3

You can combine line and arrow formatting to create a wide variety of arrows.

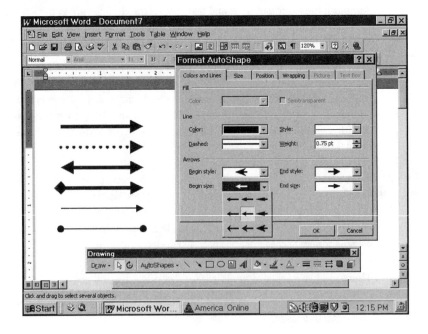

Rectangles and Ovals

If you just want to put a box around a paragraph, you're better off selecting the text and then clicking the Outside Border button on the Formatting toolbar than using a rectangle or an oval. Use rectangles or ovals when you want to create a free-floating object that is easy to position. The other elements that distinguishes rectangles and ovals are the fill capabilities—especially now that Word 97 can fill with all manner of multicolor gradients, textures, and even your own pictures.

▶ **See** "Using Borders and Shading," **p. 115**

Quite often, you don't want to create a rectangle or an oval; you want a square or a circle. To create these, use the Shift keyboard modifier. Click either the Rectangle or Oval button on the Drawing toolbar. Your pointer changes into a small cross-hair. Press Shift while you click and drag out your shape and the object is constrained to either a square or a circle. Make sure to release the mouse button before you let Shift go, or else your shape will revert to a rectangle or an oval. You can combine the Shift key modifier with Ctrl to make your object draw from the center.

T I P You're not limited to putting text in text boxes. Any drawing object—with the exception of lines and free-form drawings—can hold text. Right-click your object and choose Add Text. The drawing object is framed and a insertion point appears in the object. Type in your text, and then click outside the object when you are finished.

Follow these steps to create the basic shape with special fill and text:

1. Click the Rectangle or Oval button from the Drawing toolbar.
2. Click and drag out the approximate size and shape of your object.
3. Right-click the object and choose Add Text from the Quick menu.
4. Type your text into the object. Apply any desired formatting.
5. If your text is too large or too small for the object, resize using any of the handles around the object's frame.
6. On the Drawing toolbar, click the arrow next to the Fill Color button. Select Fill Effects.
7. From the Fill Effect dialog box, choose from one of the four available categories: Gradient, Texture, Pattern, or Picture. Click OK after you select your sample. The example in Figure 21.4 uses a wood-like Texture.
8. Move your object into place by clicking and dragging it.

AutoShapes

Word 97 comes equipped with a set of ready-made shapes you can include in your documents. These *AutoShapes* can be resized, rotated, flipped, colored, and combined with each other (or your basic ovals and rectangles) to make more intricate shapes. Many AutoShapes have an adjustment handle you can use to change the most prominent feature of a shape—for example,

Part
V

Ch
21

you can enlarge or shrink the point of an arrow. You get to these preset shapes by clicking the AutoShapes button on the Drawing toolbar (see Figure 21.5) and choosing from one of the subcategories: Lines, Basic Shapes, Block Arrows, Flowchart, Stars and Banners, and Callouts.

FIG. 21.4

You can insert text into almost any drawing object.

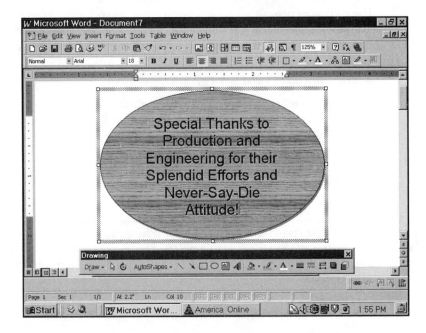

FIG. 21.5

AutoShapes contain over 100 predefined graphic shapes.

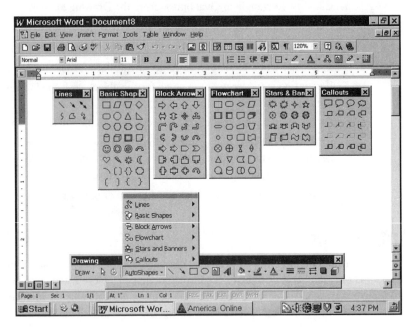

To use any of the AutoShapes at a predetermined size—and more importantly, proportion—after selecting your AutoShape, click once anywhere in the document. If you want to drag out your own size, use the technique described in the previous discussion about Rectangles and Ovals.

You can resize any AutoShape by clicking and dragging the sizing handles (the small open boxes). The adjustment handle appears as the yellow diamond and is also manipulated by clicking and dragging. The keyboard modifiers correspond to those used for resizing clip art. To preserve the aspect ratio (height to width) press Shift while you drag from a corner sizing handle. Pressing Ctrl while resizing causes the AutoShape to expand or contract from its center.

If you find that you're having to access a particular AutoShape menu repeatedly, you can "tear off" the menu and put it anywhere on your screen for immediate access. Click AutoShapes from the Drawing toolbar. Select one of the categories such as Lines or Callouts. Highlight the bar on the top of the submenu and that submenu becomes an independent toolbar that you can reposition. Click the Close button to remove it from the screen.

Freehand Drawing

While Word gives you a large number of preset shapes to choose from, sooner or later you'll probably need a graphic that can't be found among the AutoShapes. In that event, the Drawing toolbar gives you access to three freehand drawing tools. You can choose from a tool that creates curves, one that uses a combination of straight lines and freehand drawing, and one that relies entirely on freehand drawing.

The freehand drawing tools are all located under the Lines submenu of the AutoShapes button. Lines also contains a basic Line tool, a regular Arrow tool, and a Two-Headed arrow tool along the top row of the submenu. You create any of these shapes by clicking and dragging.

The Curve Tool   You use the Curve tool to achieve a smooth turning line or shape. After selecting the Curve tool, click where you want your shape to start and move the mouse—a line follows your movement. Click again where you want the next curve; continue clicking and moving the mouse to build your shape. If you want to an open shape (such as a curving line) press Esc or double-click where you want the shape to stop. To close a shape, click your starting point.

Freehand drawings can use the Fill and Line options just like any other drawing object. You can even fill a shape that isn't closed. The only limitation is that you can't add text to a freehand shape.

The Freeform Tool   The Freeform tool enables you to create an object made of straight lines and freehand drawing. After selecting the Freeform button from the Lines submenu, you can freehand draw by clicking, holding down the mouse button, and moving the mouse; when you release the mouse button, a line expands from your last point to your current pointer location. Click again to make a straight line. As with the Curve tool, you can press Esc to make an open shape or click the starting point to create a closed shape. Figure 21.6 shows the outline of a state created using the Freeform tool.

FIG. 21.6
The Freeform tool lets
you make a shape from
both straight and
freehand lines.

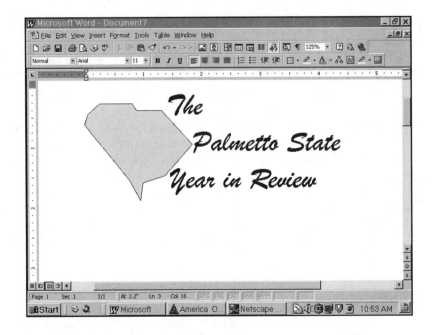

 TIP You've just about finished your freehand drawing masterpiece and you clicked a point or line down in the wrong place. Do you have to start over? No, all you have to do is press Backspace and your last point is erased, just like a mistyped character. In fact, you can keep pressing Backspace to delete all your points one-by-one.

 The Scribble Tool   The final freehand tool is known appropriately as the Scribble button. This is a complete freehand drawing mode, used by clicking and dragging. To create an open shape, just release the mouse button. To create a closed shape, release the mouse button over your starting point. It is very difficult to create any graphic with this tool that doesn't look like a scribble because the mouse does not make a terrific input device for complete freehand drawing.

The Building Blocks of Shapes

Basic shapes like rectangles, ovals, and lines are often all you need. However, what really makes Word 97 drawing objects stand out are its collection of AutoShapes. Under the AutoShapes button you'll find a library of ready-made shapes that can be inserted into your document with a click. Moreover, these preset designs can be customized and combined to make very distinct, professional-looking graphics with a minimum of effort.

There are three general purpose categories of AutoShapes: Basic Shapes, Block Arrows, and Stars and Banners. Each operates in the same manner. Click the shape you want from the AutoShape menu. Click in your document to place the graphic. Click and drag the sizing handles to adjust the shape. Most, but not all, of the AutoShapes come with one or more yellow diamond adjustment handles. Click and drag these to see the effect—it varies with the shape.

Basic Shapes   In addition to containing the primary shapes (rectangles, triangles, and ovals) the Basic Shapes menu is a bit of a catch-all for drawing objects that couldn't be categorized otherwise. Here you'll find a collection of crosses, cylinders, beveled frames, lightening bolts, suns, moons, rainbows, and the ubiquitous smiley face (whose adjustment handle can literally turn a frown upside-down). Basic Shapes also holds a very useful assortment of parenthesis, brackets, and curly braces, appropriate for equations and other math-related signs.

Block Arrows   There are 28 different types of Block Arrows ranging from simple directional (right, left, up, and down) arrows to more elaborate two-headed callout arrows. The callout arrows are particularly useful now that you can add text to them without having to overlay a text box; simply right-click your callout arrow and select the Add Text option.

Changing the direction of a Block Arrow is no problem. Select your Block Arrow and click the Draw button. Choose Rotate or Flip and then either Flip Horizontal or Flip Vertical for a 180 degree turn. Choose Rotate Right or Rotate Left to move your object 90 degrees. Of course, you can choose Free Rotate for any degree of movement.

Stars and Banners   Anyone in an office who has shown the slightest aptitude for desktop publishing knows that she is the one everyone else goes to when a special announcement needs to be rushed out the door. Now, instead of doing the work yourself, you can just tell them all about the Stars and Banners option under the AutoShape menu. Unless you just want to keep this quick and easy method to yourself—and let everyone else think you're this incredible artist.

 TIP   To get a more subtle effect using one of the explosion AutoShapes from the Stars and Banners category, try filling it with a gradient and turning off the outline. As you can see in Figure 21.7, the shape of the object contains the gradient, but turning off the outline allows it to blend better with the page.

The Stars and Banners category contains a couple of explosions (good for announcing new products and sales events), six different stars with varying numbers of points (that's what the blue numbers in the center of the stars indicate), and eight types of banners. If you're creating a long banner, a good technique is to insert the banner into the document with a single click to create the correct aspect ratio and then to widen it by clicking and dragging either of the horizontal sizing handles. The adjustment handles on the banners allow a wide range of looks by varying the size or placement of the decorative scroll.

Creating Organizational Charts and Flowcharts

There are 28 very specific symbols under the Flowchart category of the AutoShape collection. In addition to depicting computing, processing, and programming schemes, the Flowchart symbols can also be used to create organizational (org) charts. The concepts and the techniques are the same; the only major difference is that technical flowcharts tend to use the symbols in their original proportions and org chart symbols can be resized to fit name or title as well as demonstrate hierarchy.

Part
V

Ch
21

FIG. 21.7
You can get different
effects by turning off
the outline of a
filled AutoShape.

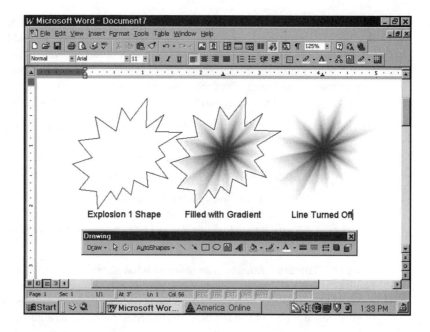

You use the Flowchart symbols like any other AutoShape element: click the symbol and click where you would like it to appear. Of course with any sort of chart, you must have connecting lines—the Line tool is perfect for this. The big trick is to get your lines to meet perfectly on your shapes. Luckily, there's a small solution to the big trick; you can snap one object (a line) to another (a flowchart element). Click the Draw button on the Drawing toolbar and choose Grid. From the Grid dialog box, select the Snap to Shapes check box. Click OK. Now connecting a line between shapes is literally a snap. The org chart shown in Figure 21.8 was created using this technique and objects from the Flowchart collection.

Using Callouts

In a increasingly collaborative work environment, you may be called upon to share ideas and comments with colleagues who are often in another office, if not another country. Word has a sophisticated method for tracking comments and revisions within the text of a document, but what if you need to refer to something visually like part of a logo? AutoShape features a category of drawing objects perfectly suited for this circumstance called Callouts.

▶ **See** "Working with Track Changes," **p. 656**

A callout can be described as a pointing text box. The *pointing* is usually handled by a line (that connects the box and its subject) called a leader. You've seen examples of callouts throughout this book to illustrate specific screen elements. Some of Word 97's callouts are more imaginative than a simple box-and-leader combination and look like the word or thought balloons used in cartoons; some callouts make the box invisible, leaving only a leader connecting comment and subject. In all, there are 20 different types of callouts.

FIG. 21.8

An organizational chart uses elements from the AutoShapes Flowchart menu.

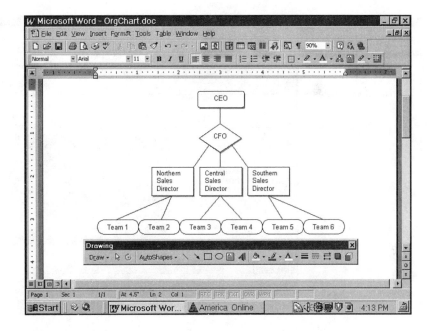

The process for using a callout is a bit different from what you have seen so far with other AutoShapes. Follow these steps to insert a callout into your document:

1. From the Drawing toolbar, click the AutoShapes button.

2. Choose Callouts, and then select the particular callout you want to insert. The pointer changes into a small cross-hair.

3. Click the subject of your callout first, and then hold down the mouse button while you drag to where you want the callout box to appear. Release the mouse button. An insertion pointer flashes within the callout box.

4. Type your text and apply any formatting.

5. If necessary, resize the callout box by clicking and dragging any of the sizing handles.

6. You can adjust the placement of the leader by clicking the yellow diamond adjustment handle at the end of the line as seen in Figure 21.9. Some callouts have multiple adjustment handles to manipulate the angles of the leader.

7. Click anywhere outside of the callout box to return to the regular document.

TIP Callout leaders have their own formatting dialog box. To access it, right-click the callout and choose Format AutoShape from the Quick menu. Go to the Text Box tab where you can manually adjust the size of the callout text box, if necessary. Click the Format Callout button at the bottom of the dialog box. Select the options you want from the Format Callout dialog box and click OK when you're done. Note that these options are not available for callouts that use non-line leaders like the thought or word balloons.

Part
V

Ch
21

FIG. 21.9
Callouts can be used to
label parts of an image.

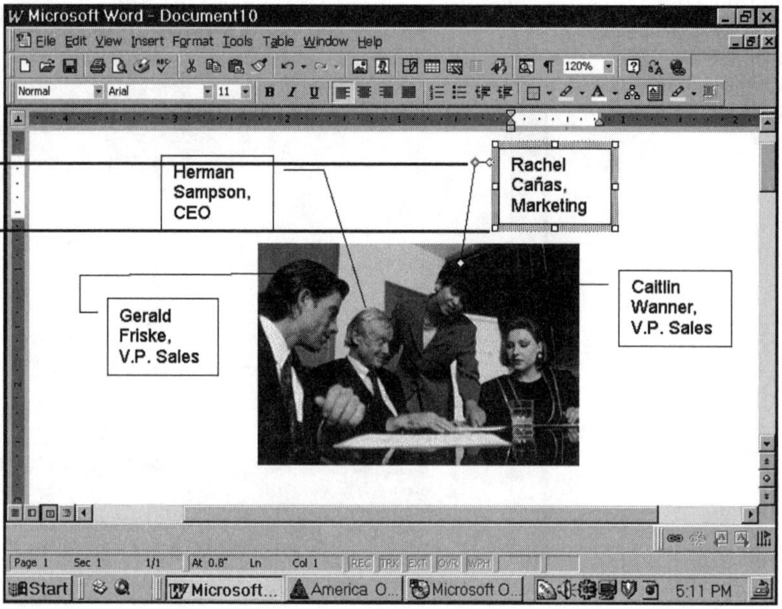

Adjustment handles ———

Sizing handles ———

Controlling Colors

Without color, all the drawing objects you create are merely outlines. Word lets you choose
from a full range of colors—including shades of grays—to fill your objects, change your borders, and modify your text. In addition, you can fill your shapes with multicolor gradient
blends, preset textures, and even user-selectable pictures. The same color dialog boxes used
for text boxes are used for fills, and (with some restrictions) lines and text. After you learn how
to use one, you know how to use them all.

▶ **See** "Working with Text Box Colors and Borders," **p. 549**

CAUTION

If you're working with a printer that can only reproduce grayscale, like most laser printers, be careful of using
colors that don't have enough contrast to reproduce well. The color you choose may work well on the screen
but be either unreadable or indistinguishable when printed. It's a good idea to always print a test copy when
working with color.

Changing Fill and Line Color

Keep in mind that drawing objects (with the exception of lines and arrows) have not one, but
two parts that can be colored. Although the interior fill color is the most obvious, you can also
independently control the border color. The only difference between the two is that with lines
you don't have access to some of fill's niftier multicolor possibilities like gradients and textures.

The easiest way to change a fill or line color is by clicking the correct button on the Drawing tool. Both the Fill Color and Line Color buttons have option arrows that open a similar Color menu with 40 color swatches and extended options. Click any of the on-screen colors to change either the fill or line color of your selected drawing object. Clicking the No Fill or No Line options makes those respective choices transparent.

You get the same dialog box whether you choose More Fill Colors or More Line Colors. The Colors dialog box has two tabs, Standard and Custom. The Standard tab displays a default 256 color palette in a hexagon shape (as seen in Chapter 19 in Figure 19.13) as well as a 16-step grayscale blend between black and white.

▶ **See** "Working with Text Box Colors and Borders," **p. 549**

If your Color Palette is set to 16- or 32-bit color (also called High Color or True Color), you can use the Custom tab shown in Figure 21.10. Click anywhere in the Hue area on the left to choose a basic color, then select its intensity by clicking the Luminance strip on the right. The Red-Green-Blue and Hue-Saturation-Luminance values change as you select different colors.

FIG. 21.10

You can choose from 16 million colors through the Custom tab of the Colors dialog box.

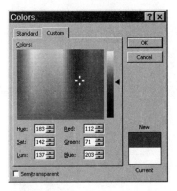

 T I P Here's a technique for matching colors between two drawing objects: Select the object whose color you want to match and bring up the Colors dialog box by clicking either the Fill Color or Line Color button. Click the Custom tab and note either the Red-Green-Blue or the Hue-Saturation-Luminance set of numbers. Close the dialog box and select your new object. Open the Colors dialog box, go to the Custom tab and type in the values for the other object.

Lines can change their patterns as well as their color. The available patterns are a collection of two-color designs shown in Figure 21.11. You can vary your background and foreground colors from the default black and white, although be sure to pick highly contrasting colors if you do. You might not see a very noticeable difference in the border unless you increase the thickness of the line from the default .75 point. Do this by selecting one of the options found under the Line Style button on the Drawing toolbar.

Changing Text Font Color

 As color printers become more prevalent, changing the color of your text will probably be as normal as making it bold or underlined: it's already as easy. Highlight your text and click the

Font Color button found both in the Formatting and the Drawing toolbar. The line under the A symbol reflects the current color. Click the down arrow next to the button to see the 16 available options, as shown in Figure 21.12.

FIG. 21.11
Over 48 preset patterns are available for your object border in the Line Pattern dialog box.

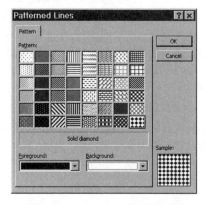

FIG. 21.12
The 16 color choices against a white and a black background.

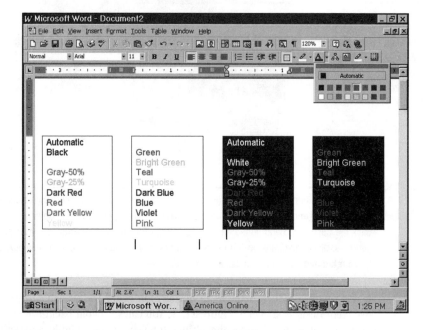

The default is the Automatic choice, which is located at the top of the drop-down option box. This allows your text to change from black to white if the background shading is made too dark. Unfortunately, Word doesn't switch the color unless the shading is 80% (where 100% is black) or higher. If you use medium to dark backgrounds, you might want to make the change manually.

Backgrounds and Textures

Not only can you use the same wide range of fill effects for drawing objects that you saw in text boxes (including gradients, textures, and pictures), but you can also fill the background of your entire document. In truth, this technique is really only useful for creating Web pages—in fact, you can't even see the background unless you're in Online Layout view.

To select a new background for your document, follow these steps:

1. Choose Format, Background.
2. Select a standard color from the Color menu by clicking one of the color swatches.
3. To see additional color choices, click More Colors to open the Color dialog box.
4. To access gradients, textures, patterns, or choose a picture for a background, click Fill Effects.

   If necessary, the document view switches to Online Layout view. To change to another view, choose View and then Normal, Page Layout, Outline, or Master Document.

   ▶ **See** "Selecting a Fill Effect," **p. 551**

Adding Depth to Your Graphics

Word 97 includes two new, effective tools to make your graphics appear to leap off the page. Any drawing object—including lines, freeform drawings, or clip art—can now cast a shadow, in almost any direction and any color. Shadows go a long way toward appearing to separate a graphic from it's background of the page. The second depth-defying tool allows all drawing objects (with the exception of clip art) to extend into the 3rd dimension; it's appropriately called 3-D. Both tools are available through the Drawing toolbar.

> **CAUTION**
>
> Shadowing and 3-D are mutually exclusive. Although both menus remain active for drawing objects, you can't apply both effects at the same time. For example, if you have turned on the 3-D effect for a freeform object and apply a shadow effect, the shadow replaces the 3-D.

Shadowing

Shadows are perhaps the single best technique for making anything two-dimensional appear three-dimensional. Word 97 has greatly enhanced the number of styles and controls to enable you to find exactly the right shadow for your object. Generally speaking, the best shadow is one that doesn't attract attention to itself but makes your object stand out better.

 The shadow for any drawing object you create using AutoShapes or the basic shapes of rectangle, oval, or line work as you would expect. You might get unexpected results when applying shadows to clip art. Photographs and some clip art can only display a rectangular shadow while with some vector-based artwork the actual shape is "shadowed." Experimentation is your best guide.

To apply a shadow to a drawing object, follow these steps:

1. Select the object you want to shadow.
2. Click the Shadow button on the Drawing toolbar.
3. Choose from one of the 20 preset shadows displayed in Figure 21.13.
4. You can adjust the shadow's position and color by selecting Shadow Settings. Make your selections from the Shadow Settings toolbar.

FIG. 21.13

The same drawing object shown with four different shadow settings.

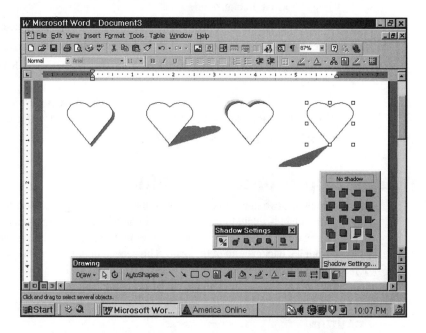

The Shadow Settings toolbar enables you to turn the shadow on or off; nudge the shadow up, down, left, and right; or pick a new color for the shadow. The shadow color settings contain a special Semitransparent Shadow option that allows text to be seen through the shadow. In many cases when combining text and an object's shadow, it's probably a better idea to move the object behind the text via the Order command (covered later in this chapter).

 TIP Two of the shadow styles create an embossed or engraved look by eliminating the outline of the object. If you choose either of these (Shadow Styles 17 and 18) and then pick another shadow style, you must re-apply the border. To do this, click the Line Style button from the Drawing toolbar and select one of the presets. (The default is $^3/_4$ pt.)

3-D

Word 97's new 3-D tool gives you the power to take a two-dimensional drawing object, give it apparent depth by extending the edges, and rotate it to any angle. This technique of expanding the edges is called extruding. You can control both the depth of the extrusion and the direction. What makes the extrusion look three dimensional is the use of a computer-generated light source that creates an illusion of light and shadow; Word 97 even gives you control over the direction and intensity of the light. Finally, you can choose from four different surface types: Wireframe, Matte, Plastic, or Metal.

 The 3-D tool works much like the Shadow tool. Select a drawing object and click the 3-D button from the Drawing toolbar. Choose any of the 20 preset 3-D effects. Figure 21.14 shows what four standard 3-D styles look like when applied to the same object. After you have applied a basic 3-D style, you can adjust the settings to an amazing degree by selecting the 3-D Settings option from the 3-D menu. Table 21.2 outlines the options available to you.

FIG. 21.14
Any drawing object can be extended into the third dimension with the 3-D tool.

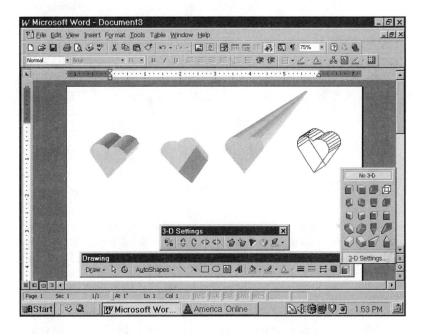

Table 21.2 3-D Settings

Button	Name	Description	Options
	3-D On/Off	Enables or disables the 3-D effect.	Toggles between on and off.
	Tilt Down	Each mouse click moves the object down five degrees.	Shift moves the object in 45 degree increments; Ctrl moves the object in one degree increments.
	Tilt Up	Each mouse click moves the object up 5 degrees.	Shift moves the object in 45 degree increments; Ctrl moves the object in one degree increments.

Part
V
Ch
21

continues

Table 21.2 Continued

Button	Name	Description	Options
	Tilt Left	Each mouse click moves the object five degrees to the left.	Shift moves the object in 45 increments; Ctrl moves the object in one degree increments.
	Tilt Right	Each mouse click moves the object five degrees to the right.	Shift moves the object in 45 degree increments; Ctrl moves the object in 1 degree increments.
	Depth	Controls the size of the extrusion.	There are six preset values (including Infinity) and a Custom option.
	Direction	Controls the direction of the extrusion.	There are nine preset values, and Parallel or Perspective options.
	Lighting	Controls the direction and intensity of the light.	There are eight preset directions and three preset intensities.
	Surface	Controls the reflectiveness of the extruded surface.	Surface types include: Wire Frame, Matte, Plastic, and Metal.
	3-D Color	Controls the color of the extrusion.	Uses the Colors dialog box.

The depth of your 3-D object is expressed in point size—the preset values include 0 pt. (no extrusion), 36 pt., 72 pt., and so on. Think of the depth as how thick your object appears; a depth of 72 pt. makes your object an inch thick. (There are 72 points in an inch.) In addition to the Custom option, which lets you enter your own depth value, there is an Infinity alternative. Selecting Infinity causes your object to extrude to its *vanishing point*—a term used in perspective drawing to indicate the place where all lines meet.

Perspective also comes into play when selecting the direction of your 3-D object. You can choose between Parallel and Perspective style for any direction. Perspective uses the vanishing point when drawing the extrusion whereas Parallel continues all edges in their original direction. In general, Perspective gives a more three-dimensional appearance.

 TIP There are limitations to the 3-D effects. You can use them only on drawing objects such as lines, rectangles, ovals, and AutoShapes and, to a limited degree, text boxes. Although you have access to the full range of 3-D options with text boxes, only the frame around the text is affected, not the text itself. Consequently, only the effects in which the face of the drawing object does not tilt (such as 3-D Style 1) work well.

Fine-Tuning Your Creations

When it comes time to edit your drawing objects, Word has a robust set of tools to help. Your main toolbox is opened by clicking the Draw button on the Drawing toolbar. Here you'll find commands to move your object from front to back, nudge it just a little, align it with other objects, flip it this way or that, rotate it by hand, and alter its very appearance. These options work together with the dialog box you can access by right-clicking the object and choosing Format AutoShape (or choosing Format, AutoShape from the main menu).

Like any other element in Word, before you can edit your drawing object you have to select it. By now, you're probably very familiar with selecting one object—move the pointer over the object and when it changes into the four-headed move arrow, click. To select a number of objects press Shift while you click the various objects; this can become tedious if there are many and impossible in some situations when one object is covering another. Instead use the white arrow button on the Drawing toolbar; this is the Select Objects button. After you choose the Select Objects button, you can easily click any single object as before, but its real value becomes apparent when you have to select multiple objects. Click outside of the objects and drag out a marquee to fully surround any objects. Release the mouse button and they are all selected. Now any changes you make either via the Drawing toolbar or the Format dialog box effect all the objects. You exit this mode by clicking the Select Objects button again.

Working with Layers

Each drawing object you create is placed in an individual layer. By default, your text layer is on the bottom. Every time you add another object, it is drawn in the layer on top of the previous object. The stacking order becomes noticeable when objects overlap each other—the object last drawn is on top and obscures a portion of any objects that were drawn earlier.

You can move objects to a different position in a stack. This is referred to as changing the stacking or *Z-order*. (In describing coordinates on paper, X refers to horizontal, Y, the vertical, and Z, the depth.) For example, you can move objects up or down within a stack one layer at a time, or you can move them to the top or bottom of a stack in one move. Naturally, this means that you don't have to draw the bottom object first—you can always move it later. Because text is on its own layer, Word has two special commands for moving an object behind, or in front of text.

TIP One way to find an object on a page is by using the Tab key. Click your top object. Press Shift+Tab to select the object below the current one; press Tab by itself to select the object above the current one. Continue pressing the keys until your object is highlighted.

To change the Z-order of any object, click the Draw button and choose Order. The Order submenu appears where you can choose from the following options:

- Bring an object all the way to the front.
- Send an object all the way to the back.

Part
V

Ch
21

■ Bring an object forward one layer.

■ Send an object backwards one layer.

■ Bring an object in front of the text.

■ Send an object behind the text.

Figure 21.15 shows one example of how you can achieve different effects just by shifting the order of the elements.

FIG. 21.15

Changing the order of drawing objects radically changes the appearance of your overall image.

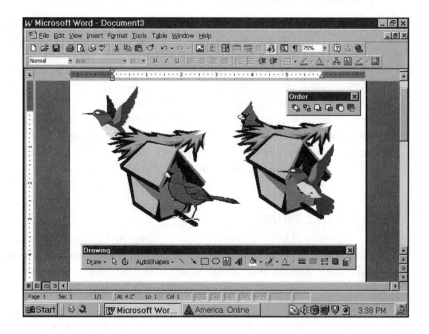

 If you place an object behind text, but it won't stay there, check your Wrapping options. The Wrapping must be set to None for text to completely flow over a drawing object.

Rotating Illustrations

You saw how the Free Rotate could be used with Word Art to turn an object around in Chapter 20. There's a Free Rotate button on the Drawing toolbar as well that works in the same manner. Click it and green circular rotation handles appear on the selected object; click and drag this to any new position. When working with AutoShapes, you often want to have the object face in the other direction and Free Rotation won't do the job. Under the Draw button, you can choose the Rotate or Flip option.

▶ **See** "Modifying Your WordArt Shape," **p. 585**

Aside from Free Rotate, there are four possibilities under Rotate or Flip:

- *Rotate Left* turns the object 90 degrees in a counter clockwise direction.
- *Rotate Right* turns the object 90 degrees in a clockwise direction.
- *Flip Horizontal* turns the object 180 degrees horizontally.
- *Flip Vertical* turns the object 180 degrees vertically.

 You can't flip or rotate pictures or clip art by using these tools—only drawing objects. Moreover, if you are using a fill effect, like a gradient or texture, the fill does not flip or rotate with your object. To achieve these effects, it's best to use an outside graphics program and insert your altered image.

Using the Grid to Line Up Objects

There's an invisible grid that helps you align your objects in Word 97. The grid allows for quick and easy alignment by clicking and dragging your objects with the mouse. By default, the Snap to Grid feature is turned on and the grid is set at increments of 1/10th of an inch, both horizontally and vertically. Naturally, you can adjust the increments to whatever you want; it's accurate to $\frac{1}{100}$ of an inch. You can even set where on the page your grid is to start.

To access the Grid control, click the Draw button on the Drawing toolbar. Choose Grid to open the Grid dialog box. You can input new values for both the Horizontal and Vertical spacing by either typing in the values directly or using the spinner arrows. As you would suspect, the Horizontal spacing controls the grid lines going across the page and the Vertical spacing controls the grid lines going down the page. Generally, you can leave the Horizontal Origin and the Vertical Origin both at 0; that indicates that the grid is to start in the upper-left corner of the document.

The two Snap options can either be used independently or together. If you have Snap to Grid checked, object movements lock to the nearest grid point. If you have Snap to Shapes checked, your object automatically aligns with the (invisible) rectangular frame around an AutoShape. If both are checked, Snap to Objects overrides Snap to Grid.

 You can temporarily turn off the Snap to Grid option by pressing Alt while moving your drawing object.

Nudging an Object

If you've ever tried to use your mouse to position an object just right there, you'll appreciate this next feature. While the mouse is great for quickly moving an object around a page, it isn't the world's best when it comes to precise placement. You can move your object in increments as small as one pixel at a time using the Nudge option found under the Draw button of the Drawing toolbar. You can nudge an object in any direction—left, right, up, or down—by selecting this command. The amount the object moves depends on your Grid options; if you have either Snap to Grid or Snap to Objects selected, a nudge moves your object one grid measurement. If neither of the Snap options are enabled, your object moves one pixel in the chosen direction.

Part
V

Ch

21

TIP   You can also nudge any selected object by pressing any of the arrow keys. Using this technique, your
object always moves one pixel at a time in the chosen direction, regardless of whether the Snap
options are enabled in the Grid dialog box.

Grouping and Ungrouping Objects

As you begin to work more and more with objects, you'll find yourself having to deal with more than one—sometimes many more than one—at a time. If you're building an org chart, for example, you might need to move half of the elements' boxes over an inch to make room for a new division. Or your boss says he'd like to see all the VP's in red and salespeople in blue. Rather than try to adjust them all one by one, it's far more efficient to group your objects and then make your changes.

To group two or more objects, follow these steps:

1. Select your drawing objects either by using the Shift key extended selection method or clicking the Select Objects button on the Drawing toolbar and dragging a rectangle around all of the target objects.

2. Click the D**r**aw button on the Drawing toolbar.

3. Choose **G**roup. The individual sets of sizing handles around each object are replaced by one set of sizing handles around the entire newly formed group.

When you group objects, you combine them so you can work with them as though they were a single object. You can flip, rotate, and resize or scale all objects in a group as a single unit. You can also change the attributes of all objects in a group at one time; for example, you can change the fill color or add a shadow to all objects in the group as shown in Figure 21.16. You can also create groups within groups to help you build complex drawings.

You can ungroup a group of objects at any time; simply select your group and then choose D**r**aw, **U**ngroup from the Drawing toolbar. Some attributes cannot be altered when an object is part of a group—an object's point's cannot be edited, for example. To work around that constraint: Group a collection of objects, move or resize them as one, ungroup them to make a minor change to one of the objects, and then regroup them. Regrouping is just as easy; select any one of the objects that was previously grouped, and then choose D**r**aw, Regr**o**up from the Drawing toolbar.

TIP   If you move to another document or change views after ungrouping a collection of objects, you'll need
to select each object and regroup them again. The easiest way to do this is to click the Select Objects
button on the Drawing toolbar and drag out a marquee around all of the objects. Then choose D**r**aw,
Group.

You can also ungroup clip art (assuming it's a vector-based drawing that Word 97 can import) and alter one or more parts of it to customize the graphics. Grouping is also helpful when using the powerful alignment and distribution tools covered in the next section.

FIG. 21.16
A group of disparate objects can be made to share common characteristics, such as the shadow shown here, by using the Group command.

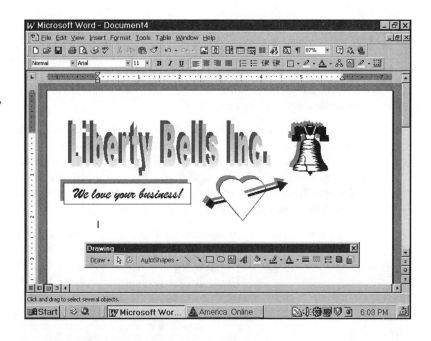

Aligning and Distributing Drawing Elements

In addition to precisely positioning an object on the page, Word also offers relative positioning. A drawing object can be aligned relative to another object or to the page itself. This means that two or more objects can be lined up along any of their edges or centers. They can also be centered on the page or aligned along the edge of the page. Furthermore, you can have Word evenly space your objects across (or down) the page. All in all, there's a tremendous amount of power packed under the Align or Distribute commands, accessed by clicking the D̲raw button on the Drawing toolbar.

To align objects, follow these steps:

1. Select the objects you want to align. You can do this by either clicking the Select Objects button on the Drawing tool and dragging a marquee around the objects you want to select or by pressing Shift while you click each object.
2. Click D̲raw, A̲lign or Distribute on the Drawing toolbar.
3. From the Align or Distribute submenu, select one of the following:
   - *Align Left* lines on objects along the left edge of the object furthest left.
   - *Align Center* lines on objects along the vertical center of the selected objects.
   - *Align Right* lines on objects along the right edge of the object furthest right.
   - *Align Top* lines on objects along the top edge of the highest object.
   - *Align Middle* lines on objects along the horizontal center of the selected objects.
   - *Align Bottom* lines on objects along the bottom edge of the lowest object.

Part
V

Ch
21

You'll often need to center a drawing object on the page. To do this in Word 97, click Draw, Align or Distribute on the Drawing toolbar and then click Relative to Page. After this feature has been enabled, all align or distribute commands use the page as a super object that controls the positioning. This means that if you have Relative to Page checked and choose Align Center, your selected object(s) is centered horizontally on the page; Align Middle moves your objects to the vertical center of the page.

You might not think you need the Distribute commands until you use them once—but after you understand what they can do, you'll use them all the time. When objects are distributed, they are arranged evenly with an equal amount of space between them, either horizontally or vertically. If you select three objects, click Align or Distribute and choose Distribute Horizontally, Word spaces the objects out evenly, using the outside objects as boundaries. If Relative to Page is enabled, Word uses the margins as its boundary.

You often use the Align commands and the Distribute commands one after another. Figure 21.17 shows a typical three-step process. First, you create the objects, roughing out the placement. Next, you choose Align Top to line up the objects. Finally, after checking Relative to Page, you select Distribute Horizontally to arrange the objects across the page.

FIG. 21.17
The Align and Distribute tools are used together to achieve an even, balanced look.

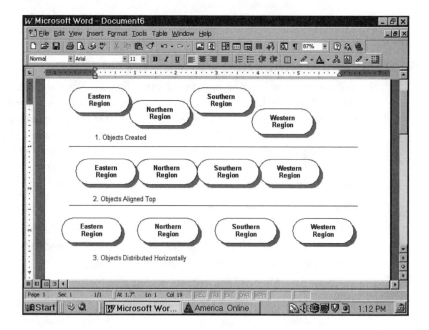

TROUBLESHOOTING

My drawings look great on-screen, but when I print them they don't show up at all. What could be wrong? First, make sure you're not printing in Draft mode. Choose Tools, Options, click the Print tab, and then clear the Draft Output check box. Next, be certain the Drawing Objects option, which prints graphics, is selected. From the Print tab of the Option dialog box, select the Drawing Objects check box, if it is not already checked.

Finally, some printers have settings that override the Word 97 options. Check your printer settings by choosing File, Print and then clicking the Properties button on the Print dialog box.

How do I center some, but not all, objects on the page? It takes a while to get used to the new Align or Distribute commands, especially when you're trying to center some object on the page, but not others. A common mistake is to mistakenly leave the Relative to Page option on the Align or Distribute menu checked. Because you have to click the Draw button each time you change one of these options, it's easy to forget. If you're doing a lot of work with aligning or distributing, you can separate the menus by clicking and dragging the bar across the top of the Align or Distribute submenu. Drag it to a convenient place on your screen, and then you have one-click access to all the commands, including Relative to Page.

How do I get my text to fit correctly within the drawing object? Drawing objects do not resize automatically; to make text fit, you have to either reduce the size of the text or enlarge the drawing object by clicking and dragging the sizing handles. To adjust text placement, you have to use all the formatting options at your disposal to get the effect you want—the alignment buttons, paragraph marks, tabs, nonbreaking spaces (Ctrl+Shift+Space), and so on—to move the text where you want it.

From Here...

In this chapter you learned how to use the Drawing toolbar to create basic shapes, Word 97 AutoShapes, and other drawing objects. You learned to customize them with the fill, line, shadow, and 3-D options. Then you looked at how to edit and arrange your drawing objects by grouping, aligning, distributing, nudging, or switching their stacking order. Next you might want to look over the following chapters:

- If you're interested in using your new found graphic skills to make Web pages, be sure to look at Chapters 9–11.
- The Drawing toolbar includes buttons for both Text Boxes and WordArt. To learn more about using text boxes, see Chapter 19, "Word Desktop Publishing;" for WordArt, check out Chapter 20, "Getting Images into Your Documents."
- Sometimes you need to create graphics that relate to your data. To see how to use Microsoft Graph 97, go on to Chapter 22, "Using Microsoft Graph."

Part
V

Ch
21

Using Microsoft Graph

by Joe Lowery

To round out our exploration of the visual side of Word 97, this chapter examines the chart-producing capabilities of Microsoft Graph 97. Charts and graphs fall in a special category of images, one that brings together the worlds of information and graphics. ■

Starting out with Graph 97

Here's an overview to charts in general and a guide to get you up and running quickly with Graph 97 in particular, including everything you need to know to produce a chart from an existing table.

Customizing your charts

You need the information in this section on formatting your charts to make the most out of Graph 97.

Using the Datasheet

Graph 97's Datasheet is your connection to a chart after it has been inserted into your document. In most cases, the Datasheet is where you make any data revisions—this section shows you how to get around the Datasheet with the greatest of ease.

Linking to outside files

Office 97 includes an underlying mechanism for sharing information across documents and even programs. In this section, you'll see how to tie the charts produced by Graph 97 to data elsewhere in the document or even in another file.

Solving chart problems

Graph 97 is part graphics program, part spreadsheet, and part Word component. Here's a section devoted to troubleshooting all your cross-over problems.

Understanding Graphs and Charts

A chart is a visual representation of your information. A chart or graph enables you to see both individual and related data so that developing trends can be quickly spotted. In addition to spicing up a report with graphics, charts can consolidate facts to make the big picture more easily grasped.

To help you include dynamic graphs in your documents, Word 97 has integrated a utility called *Microsoft Graph 97*. Graph 97 is invoked whenever you create a chart based on selected data. The data can be on the same page, in the same document or in another file altogether. After you have created a Graph 97 object, you can access all of its specialized charting features by editing the object.

There are many different types of charts you can create with Graph 97: bar, column, and pie charts are among the most common. All charts, however, have one thing in common: a data source. Whether you start with existing data from a table in your Word document, import a chart built in Excel or open a new Graph 97 chart, you'll always find that your chart is connected to data somewhere. You have the option of either maintaining a link from your data to your chart so that the chart is automatically updated or breaking the link after the chart is set-up.

The ideal chart clarifies your data and drives home the point that you're trying to make. To this end, there is a lot of formatting power that can be applied to your graph. There's no element in a chart that you can't significantly alter. You can also use most of the graphic tools covered in the previous three chapters, including text boxes, WordArt, callouts, and fill effects. In fact, Word 97 integrates the graph function so completely, it considers it to be just another type of picture.

In this chapter, you'll learn a number of ways to create a chart using Graph 97. Let's start with the simplest approach—building a chart based on an existing table.

Making a Basic Chart from a Table

A table is an excellent tool for displaying your facts and figures. All your information is neatly organized and easy to follow. A table is also the perfect foundation for building a chart. Many charts use the same form of correlated information that comes from combining rows and columns where you can easily see how many widgets sold in the first and second quarters of the year. The headings for the rows and columns become the data labels necessary for identifying the different elements of the chart.

When Graph 97 creates a chart from your table, it also opens a small window that contains your data in a form called a *Datasheet*. The Datasheet is in a typical spreadsheet format with the columns labeled alphabetically (A, B, C, and so on.) and the rows numerically (1,2,3, and so on.). The Datasheet reserves the first row and the first column for the headings that translate into data labels. The rows and columns become a *data series*.

The Datasheet is necessary if you want to make any changes to the chart's data. You can link your table to the chart if you want (you'll see how later in this chapter), but an unlinked chart is the default.

Follow these steps to create a chart from a table:

1. Select the information in your table you want to chart. Be sure to include in your selection at least one header row or column.

2. Choose Insert, Picture, Chart.

   Word inserts a 3-D column chart based on your data, below your table, in a floating frame as seen in Figure 22.1. Graph 97 toolbars and menus temporarily replace those of Word 97. The Datasheet window opens.

3. To return to your regular document, click anywhere outside of the chart frame.

Graph 97 menus   Graph 97 toolbars

FIG. 22.1

Graph 97 can quickly convert your table data into a moveable, resizable chart.

Original table

Datasheet

Default
format chart

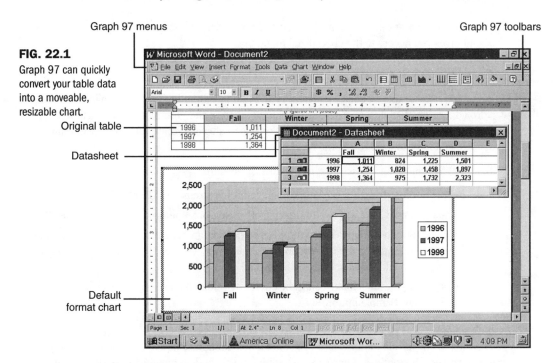

Quickly Changing a Chart

The chart that Graph 97 creates by default is a 3-D column chart using standard colors against a gray background with gridlines and a legend. While the default configuration may be precisely what is needed for some data, it is the barest tip of the iceberg when it comes to what Graph 97 can do. For openers, you can choose between 18 different chart types, most with 5 to 8 different variations or sub-types. From there you can modify every feature of the chart—titles, legends, grids, data series, size, placement, and wrapping—and you can use Word 97's enhanced fill and color capabilities as well to include gradients, textures, and patterns in your charts.

To make any changes in your chart, you must double-click the object first. This invokes Graph 97 and gives you access to the specialized menus.

Changing the Chart Type

 When you're in Graph 97, click the Chart Type button's option arrow in the toolbar. You'll see a drop-down list of 18 different graphs. Highlight any one and your chart changes to that type. This toolbar shortcut gives you the quickest access to altering your chart, but if you want more options, you have to go through the menus.

To see all the charts and their sub-types, follow these steps:

1. From your main document, double-click your chart to invoke Graph 97.
2. Choose Chart, Chart Type. The Chart Type dialog box opens as shown in Figure 22.2.
3. From the Standard Types tab of the Chart type dialog box, click any of the Chart types in the left column to see the corresponding Chart Sub-Types on the right. Use the scroll button to see additional selections. Select the desired sub-type.
4. To see how your data looks using the currently selected chart type, click the Press and Hold to View Sample button.
5. Click OK when you have completed your selection.

The Custom Types tab of the Chart Type dialog box contains a listing of standard chart types that have been customized. There are 20 built-in presets and, at opening, one user-defined preset. You'll see later in this chapter how to create your own custom chart type.

 If you're not particularly fond of 3-D column charts—the 3-D effect can distort your data and 3-D graphs don't reproduce well on low-end printers—you can switch the Graph 97 default chart to any available. Choose Chart, Chart Type to open the Chart Type dialog box. From the Standard Types tab, select the Chart type and sub-type you want as your new default. Click the Set as Default button. Click OK to close the dialog box. Now every time you highlight a table in Word 97 and choose Insert, Picture, Chart Graph 97 uses your new default.

FIG. 22.2
You can choose from a full range of graphs and their sub-types from the Chart Type dialog box.

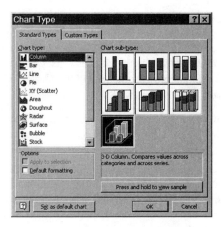

Part
V

Ch
22

Updating Your Data

After you've created your chart, the Datasheet is your main conduit for altering the data figures. As noted previously, you can also link your chart to your in-document table using a process described later in this chapter. In the Datasheet window, click the value you want to update. As in spreadsheet programs like Microsoft Excel, a single click of a cell—the box formed by the intersection of column and row—selects it, just like you had double-clicked a word in the regular document. Type in your new number and the old number is replaced. You can move from cell to cell by pressing Tab, Enter, or any of the arrows. After you enter a new value, the chart updates when you confirm your entry by moving out of the cell.

 If you're working with a two-dimensional chart type, you can actually use the mouse to click and drag the data marker on the chart itself and the corresponding Datasheet cell will change. When you're editing your chart in Graph 97, click the data series and then click the data marker you want to change (don't double-click as that opens the Format Object dialog box). Click and drag the data marker to a new place. When you release the mouse button, the Datasheet updates to display the value representing your changed graph point. Please note that this technique only works with two-dimensional chart types.

> **CAUTION**
>
> As of this writing, there is a bug in Graph 97 that causes the program to crash under Windows 95 when switching to another open document. To avoid the crash, always click outside of your chart to exit Graph 97 before moving to a different document. The bug is not evident under Windows NT 4.0.

Setting Chart Options

Now that you've got the basic chart in the document, it's time to start customizing. This section shows you how to add a new title, change the data labels, select gridlines, insert a legend, and include a data table. All of these elements become part of the chart, and should you resize or move the chart, they are resized or moved as well.

Once you're in Graph 97, all of these features described here are found by choosing Chart, Chart Options and opening the Chart Options dialog box. You can also right-click the chart and choose Chart Options from the Quick menu.

 You might have noticed by now that Graph 97 has its own help system. When you're editing your chart, click the Office Assistant button on the toolbar or choose Help, Contents and Index.

Inserting a New Title

When it comes time to title your chart, you can approach it one of two ways. First, you can type in a title on the line above your inserted chart and work with the title normally, applying your formatting via the Format toolbar or Format, Font menu. This has the advantage of a flat learning curve because you're probably already familiar with these basic techniques. Depending on the document's pagination, one possible disadvantage is that the chart and the title could end up on separate pages. (Enable the Lock Anchor option on the Positioning tab of the Format Object dialog box to avoid this.)

The second approach is to insert the title as part of the chart. The major difference between the two approaches is one of style. With the new gradient and texture fills, you can really make a chart distinctive on a page—it's up to you how you want the title to integrate with the chart and your chart with the overall document.

In addition to an overall chart title, you can add labels for the various available axes. To insert a title or axes label, follow these steps:

1. Double-click your chart to edit it.
2. Choose Chart, Chart Options. The Chart Options dialog box opens as seen in Figure 22.3.
3. If necessary, click the Titles tab.
4. Enter your title text into the Chart Titles box. Press Tab to move to the next available axis title box. The preview on the right side of the Chart Options dialog box updates to display your newly input title, in a default format.
5. If desired, enter new labels for the X, Y, or Z axes. Depending on the type of chart you are using, not all axes will be available.
6. Click OK when you are finished.

FIG. 22.3

Add your chart titles through the Chart Options dialog box.

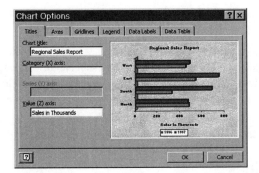

Part

V

Ch

22

The title and axis labels are inserted in the chart in text boxes. To edit your text, click the box twice; be sure not to double-click. Double-clicking opens the Format Title dialog box so you can change the format (color, font, size) of any of these items. To reposition your titles, click the title once to highlight the box and then click and drag the borders of the box. Note that unlike with other text boxes, the pointer does not change shape.

> **CAUTION**
>
> Any text in a chart automatically resizes when the overall chart is resized. This can lead to undesirable results. To turn off the automatic resizing, open the Format dialog box for the text and, on the Font tab, clear the Auto Scale check box.

Changing the Data Labels

The data labels that appear on the chart are linked to the headings of the columns and rows seen in the Datasheet. If, for example, you change "2nd Quarter" to "Q2" in a header cell on the Datasheet and press Enter to accept the edit, the label on your chart is updated. To edit a label on the Datasheet without erasing it, double-click its cell.

If you want to enable or disable the axes labels altogether, use the Format Options dialog box. On the Axes tab you'll find check boxes for the Category (X) axis as well as the Series (Y), and Value (Z) axes, if they are used by the particular chart type. The default option sets the Category axis to Automatic, which displays the X-axis as time-scale only if the cells are date-formatted, otherwise they are displayed as categories. There are also options to specify either Category or Time-scale display.

To change the formatting of the data labels, double-click the label you want to change. This opens the Format Axis dialog box. Here, you'll find tabs for formatting these areas:

- *Patterns* enables you to change the markings that accompany each data label known as tick marks. You have control over tick marks at both major and minor levels.

- *Scale* permits you to set a range of values for a numeric label. You can set maximums, minimums, and intervals.

- *Font* is the standard font dialog box tab where you can change the font name, size, style, and color.

- *Number* enables you to set how the label, if numeric or date-related, is to be formatted. There are 12 major categories (with numerous subcategories), ranging from General for text to Custom for user-defined entries. If the Linked to Source check box is checked on this tab, the Number format on the Datasheet values overrides any selection made here.

- *Alignment* lets you choose between horizontal, vertical, or angled text. You can choose between preset increments of 15 degrees or input your own custom angle.

Inserting New Gridlines

Gridlines can make your chart more readable—or more obscure. Graph 97 gives you complete control over the gridlines along each axis and enables you to easily turn them on or off as well as format them however you like. To enable or disable a gridline, click its corresponding button in the Graph 97 toolbar. The Value Axis Gridline button controls the major horizontal lines; the Category Axis Gridline button controls the major vertical lines. Some chart types, such as pie chart deactivate this buttons as they are not applicable.

You can also turn on the gridlines—with a lot more flexibility— through the Chart Options dialog box. Click the Gridlines tab as shown in Figure 22.4. Here you'll find not only access to each of the axes major gridlines, but also check boxes enabling the minor gridlines as well. If you enable all the gridlines, the chart becomes very dense with lines and difficult to read; it's best to use as few gridlines as possible.

FIG. 22.4
You can control both major and minor gridlines through the Gridlines tab of the Chart Options dialog box.

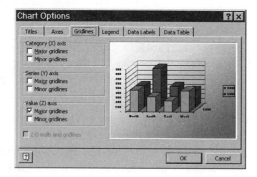

Inserting a Legend

Legends are used to explain the color or pattern conventions used in the chart. The legend can be placed automatically on any side of the chart desired or it can be moved into a specific location. You can turn the chart's legend on or off by clicking the Legend button on the Graph 97 toolbar (or with the Show Legend check box on the Legend tab of the Chart Options dialog box).

Double-clicking the legend opens the Format Legend dialog box. As you would expect, you can specify the various Font and Pattern characteristics. One nice effect added to Graph 97 is the Shadow check box on the Pattern tab; when enabled, the shadow sets-off the legend from the rest of the chart. You can also control the positioning of the legend in the chart. The Placement tab enables you to choose between bottom, corner, top, right, or left options. In addition to altering where the legend appears, it also changes whether the legend items are stacked on top of one another or positioned side-by-side.

Adding a Data Table

 If you insert a chart based on a data table somewhere in your document, you could find your chart overshadowing your table. Sometimes it's better to keep both the table and chart together. By clicking the Data Table button on the Graph 97 toolbar, your figures are included in a table on the bottom of your chart. As you can see in Figure 22.5, the data table looks just like the Datasheet without the numeric and alphabetic column and row headings.

FIG. 22.5
This figure shows a data table displaying figures right on the chart.

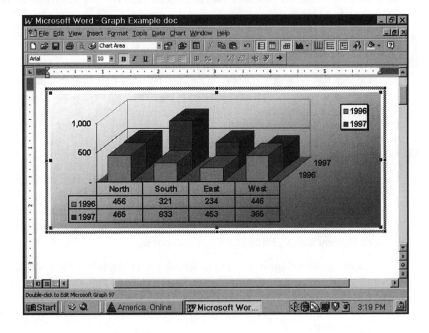

You can format your data table by double-clicking it. In addition to the usual Font and Pattern options, you can select which set of gridlines to include: horizontal, vertical, or outline.

Formatting Chart Elements

With a chart, sometimes the hardest thing about formatting an element is selecting it. It takes a little practice to know when to click and when to double-click. As a general rule of thumb, each time you click you select a smaller portion of the chart. The first click selects the chart itself and another click could select one data series, while one more click could select a particular data marker. After your object is selected you could either double-click it to bring up the appropriate Format dialog box or click the Format button on the toolbar.

> **CAUTION**
>
> If you're like many users, you get a lot of mileage out of the Undo button, especially when it comes to trying out formatting changes. Graph 97 has an Undo button, but unlike Word 97, it's only one level deep. This means that it only undoes your last action and if you click it again, it redoes it.

There's another way to select chart elements: by name. Next to the Format button is a Chart Object text box that shows the currently selected element. Click the Chart Objects arrow and you can scroll down the list of chart parts you can format. Did you know, for instance, that you could independently format the walls and the floor of a 3-D bar chart? You can also click and drag one of the corners after they're selected, and rotate a wireframe representation of your chart in 3-D in real-time.

 When trying to select a specific chart element, it helps to have their names appear. Graph 97 can display the name of a chart item in a tip when you rest the pointer over the item, but you must have the Show Names check box selected in the Chart tab under Tools, Options. If you're looking at a data marker, you'll get both the column and the row label. The Chart tab also has an option that enables you to see the value of the data.

Working with Patterns

Graph 97 gives you access to the major improvements Word 97 implemented with its fill options. You can now fill any of your chart elements, including individual data series, using the advanced color and fill effects available to other drawing objects. In addition to an easy-to-use color picker, you can also give your charts textures, pattern, and gradient fills: You can even fill an element with a picture of your own choosing.

To give a chart element a different fill color or effect, follow these steps:

1. Select the chart object you want to format.
2. Click the Format button on the Graph 97 toolbar. The appropriate Format dialog box opens.
3. If necessary, click the Patterns tab.
4. To choose a standard color, click one of the color swatches in the Color section. For additional color options, click the More Colors button.
5. To choose one of the enhanced effects (gradients, textures, patterns, or picture), click Fill Effects. Choose the appropriate tab and fill effect.
6. Click OK when you have made your choices.

▶ **See** "Selecting a Fill Effect," **p. 551**

Figure 22.6 shows a chart that uses patterns, with each data series having its own separate texture fills (with the shadowing turned on). The inner plot area uses a picture background and the chart area is filled with a marble texture, as is the legend area. Naturally, when you start adding textures like these to the background, you have to beef up the fonts for your axes by making them bold or a larger point size or else the information would get overwhelmed. No matter how involved you make your various elements, never forget your goal—to present your data as effectively as possible.

FIG. 22.6
Adding textures and fill effects to a chart can give it a great deal of depth.

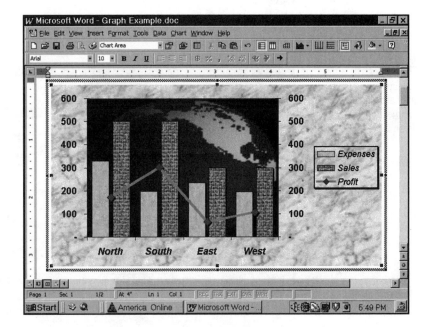

Adding Callouts with Graph's Drawing Tools

As you learned in the last chapter, callouts are used to highlight a portion of some text or graphic in your document. It's not too much of a stretch to realize that you could use the same feature to comment on your Graph 97 produced charts and make them part of the chart itself. The tools and the techniques are the same, all you have to do is apply them both to your charting elements.

You'll remember that callouts, as well as the other drawing objects, can be accessed through the Drawing toolbar. Here are the steps needed to put a callout in your Graph 97 chart as shown in Figure 22.7

1. Click the Drawing button on the standard Graph 97 toolbar to open the Drawing toolbar.
2. Click the AutoShapes button on the Drawing toolbar.
3. Select Callouts and then choose a callout to insert. The pointer changes into a small crosshair.

4. Click your callout's subject first and then, holding down the mouse button, drag to your callout location. Release the mouse button. An insertion pointer flashes in the callout box.

5. Input your text and apply any formatting desired.

6. If necessary, you can resize the callout box by clicking and dragging any of the sizing handles.

7. You can also adjust the placement of the leader by clicking the yellow diamond adjustment handle(s).

8. Click anywhere outside of the callout box to return to the chart.

▶ **See** "Using Callouts," **p. 604**

FIG. 22.7

Callouts let you emphasize and comment on your Graph 97 chart.

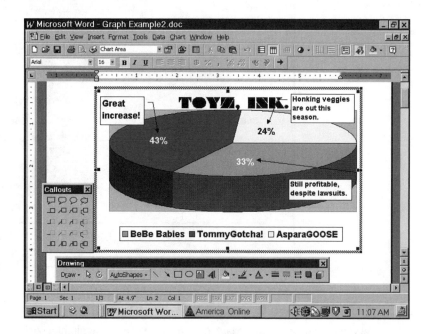

CAUTION

You have different degrees of flexibility when it comes to formatting callouts in Graph 97 and in Word 97. There is no Format Callout option available for formatting the callout leader in Graph 97 as there is in Word, although you do have enhanced vertical alignment options for the text.

Creating Your Own Custom Chart Type

You may remember that when you go to Chart Types there are two tabs: Standard Types and Custom Types. The custom chart types are similar to a template or a style in Word. You can build a library of chart types that you use over and over and quickly change the look of your chart. Each custom chart type is based on a standard chart type and contains additional formatting and options, such as a legend, gridlines, data labels, a secondary axis, colors, patterns, fills, and placement choices for various chart items.

Graph 97 comes with a variety of built-in custom chart types. To see these, choose Chart, Chart Type from the Graph 97 menu. Click the Custom Types tab. You can either use these Microsoft supplied custom charts or you can build your own: You can even build your own using these as a basic design. You can switch between the supplied and user-created by clicking either the User-Defined or the Built-In radio buttons in the Choose From section.

How to Create a Custom Chart

You create a custom chart by first creating an example. Format a chart however you want it, complete with specific fills, typefaces, chart options, and colors. After you have built the chart the way you want it, follow these steps:

1. Choose Chart, Chart Types.
2. When the Chart Types dialog box opens, click the Custom Types tab.
3. Click the User-Defined radio button in the Select From section.
4. Click the Add button.
5. Type the name for this new chart type in the Name text box. If you like, you can also type a brief description in the Description text box. This section could include when the chart was previously used, what it is to be used for, who created it, and so on.
6. Click OK on both the Add dialog box and then the Chart Types dialog box.

In addition to adding your name and description, Graph 97 also includes a small thumbnail of your chart in the Preview section. Depending on the aspect ratio of your chart, the thumbnail may not be truly representative, like the one in Figure 22.8. However, if selected, the chart maintains the height-to-width proportions of the original.

How Custom Chart Types Can Support Your Corporate Design Standards

If you're working in a large office you might have a set of custom chart types that you want to standardize. How do you copy a custom chart type from one computer to another in a network environment? Simple, you open a document with the desired chart in it on your system and follow the procedure outlined previously. You don't even have to have the file saved on your desktop system, you just have to be able to access it. Graph 97 doesn't save the actual charts when you include a new user-defined custom chart type; it saves the description and the thumbnail.

FIG. 22.8
You can add a custom chart type for any graph you have developed.

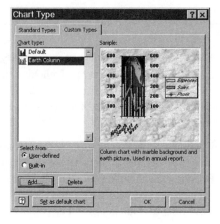

 If you're a network administrator and you want your users to work from a common set of charts, the User-Defined custom chart types are saved in the file Grusrgal.gra generally found in the Office directory of Microsoft Office.

Creating a Chart from Scratch

You don't have to have an existing table in your document to create a chart. In fact, there are times when you want the focus to remain on the big picture and not the details, so you don't want your figures accessible in a table. In cases like these, you can insert a new chart into your object. Graph 97 creates a default chart using a set of mock data that you can easily modify.

To insert a chart without a table, place your insertion point where you want the chart to appear. Then choose Insert, Picture, Chart. As shown in Figure 22.9, the default chart uses dummy figures to create a two-series 3-D column chart.

FIG. 22.9
When you create a chart from scratch, Graph 97 supplies the temporary data which you must modify.

		A	B	C	D	E
		1st Qtr	2nd Qtr	3rd Qtr	4th Qtr	
1	East	20.4	27.4	90	20.4	
2	West	30.6	38.6	34.6	31.6	
3	North	45.9	46.9	45	43.9	

Document3 - Datasheet

Working in the Datasheet Window

As with a chart created from your own table, you modify the data by editing the figures found in the Datasheet window. The generic data includes three data series (East, West, and North) tracked over four quarters. You can either blank out the entire sheet and start fresh or replace the figures and labels one at a time.

If you've ever worked in a spreadsheet, you'll be comfortable working in the Datasheet. Here's are some brief pointers on Datasheet editing:

- To clear any section of the Datasheet, select an area by clicking and dragging over it and then pressing Delete.

- You can quickly select the entire sheet by clicking the unmarked button in the upper-left corner of the columns and rows.

- To overwrite any existing data, just click the cell and input your new value or label.

- To edit any existing data without retyping it, double-click in the cell. Alternatively, you can select the cell and press the F2 key.

- After entering any new values or labels, you must confirm them by pressing Enter, Tab, or any arrow and moving out of the present cell.

- Graph 97 reserves the use of the first column and row for data series labels (with the exception of data for an xy (scatter) or bubble chart, where the first row or column contains values). It also freezes these cells, so that they are still visible no matter how far you scroll in the window.

- If your label or data is too many characters to fit in the width of the column, you can adjust the column by clicking and dragging the line on the right between the column headings. When your pointer is positioned correctly, it changes into a double-headed arrow. When a column is too narrow to properly display a value, Graph shows a series of hash marks (for example, "#####") until the column is widened.

- You can exclude a data series from the chart without erasing it by double-clicking the corresponding row or column heading. The row or column turns a light gray to indicate that it is inactive. To activate it again, double-click it.

Moving Data in the Datasheet

Datasheet figures can be cut and pasted like most other elements in Word. Remember that to highlight a cell on the Datasheet, all you have to do is click it once. From there, Cut, Copy, and Paste work as expected. You can also drag and drop your cells to replace one value with another. To drag and drop a cell, position your pointer on the black border around a selected cell, then click and drag your cell to a new location. Release the mouse button. If the new location has a value already in it, Graph 97 asks for confirmation to replace it.

> **CAUTION**
>
> If you find that the Drag-and-Drop feature is not working for you, it may have been disabled. From the Graph 97 menus, choose Tools, Options, and click the Datasheet Options tab. Make sure the Cell Drag-and-Drop check box is checked.

Formatting Data in the Datasheet

Because so much of the information in your chart is linked to the cells in your Datasheet, it's important to understand how to format those cells. Graph 97 has a number of shortcuts in it's Formatting toolbar for the most common choices as well as fuller options available through the menus.

You can change the format of any numeric values to those commonly used by clicking any of the following buttons in Graph 97 Formatting toolbar:

- *Currency Style* adds a leading currency symbol. In the US, this means that the figure 1234 is shown as $1,234.00.

- *Percent Style* displays the value times 100, followed by a percent sign. To depict 50 percent the value would need to be .5.

- *Comma Style* adds a thousands separator, a decimal separator, and decimals to two places. If applied to the value 1234 the number displays 1,234.00.

- *Increase Decimals* is used with the previous styles. Each time you click this button, the decimal increases by one.

- *Decrease Decimals* is used with the previous styles. Each time you click this button, the decimals decrease by one.

Figure 22.10 shows a Datasheet with values formatted using the Currency, Percent, and Comma styles.

FIG. 22.10
You can quickly access common number formats through the Graph 97 Formatting toolbar.

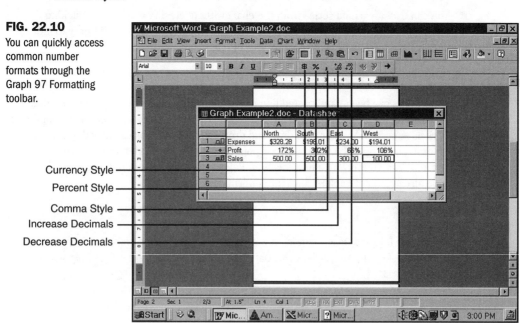

Currency Style
Percent Style
Comma Style
Increase Decimals
Decrease Decimals

For more complex number formatting, choose Format, Number. This opens the Format Number dialog box where you can choose from a dozen format categories including Number, Currency, Accounting, Date, Time, and Scientific. In each category there are numerous subcategories detailing different options involving negative numbers and other choices. There is also a Custom Category where you can construct your own formatting option by entering your choice in the Type text box.

Using Trendlines and Error Bars

Spotting trends is a major use of charts and data. Graph 97 uses formulas developed through the study of regression analysis to create trendlines. Trendlines extend the actual data forward to predict a possible course. You can also test your trend analysis by extending the data backwards and comparing it against actual figures.

Trendlines can be used in a variety of chart types: unstacked area, bar, column, line, stock, xy (scatter), and bubble charts. However, you cannot add trendlines to a 3-D, stacked, radar, pie, or doughnut chart type data. If you have trendlines in place and you convert your chart to one that does not support trendlines, the trendlines disappear.

It's very easy to add a trendline to your chart. Choose Chart, Add Trendlines from the main Graph 97 menu. (If Add Trendlines is not active then your chart type doesn't support this option.) The Add Trendlines dialog box opens as shown in Figure 22.11. On the Type tab, there are six different Trend/Regression types to choose from: Linear, Logarithmic, Polynomial, Power, Exponential, and Moving Average. You can find detailed explanations of each formula by choosing Help, Contents and Index, clicking the Index tab, and typing **Equations, Chart Trendlines**.

FIG. 22.11

Choose a trend analysis from six different types.

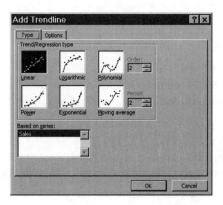

After you've chosen a formula type for your trendline, click the Option tab of the Add Trendline dialog box. Here, you can give your trendline a custom name and set the number of periods your trendline will forecast both forward and backward. After you have set these options, your chart will have a trendline similar to the one in Figure 22.12. You can change the color, style, and weight of the trendline (as well as resetting any of the previously chosen options) by selecting the line and clicking the Format button on the Graph 97 toolbar.

FIG. 22.12

Trendlines predict future developments based on current data.

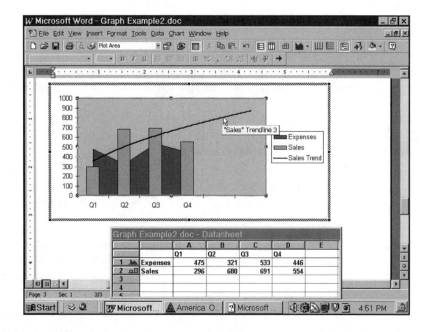

If you've ever heard how a poll is accurate (for example, plus or minus 3 percent), you've already been exposed to error bars. Error bars are the visual equivalent to that plus or minus 3 percent, relative to each data marker in a series. The error bars display as small T-shaped lines, upright to show error in the positive range and inverted to show error in the negative range. Error bars can be added to data series in area, bar, column, line, xy (scatter), and bubble charts.

To add error bars to your chart, follow these steps:

1. Select the data series to which you want to add error bars.

2. Choose Format, Data Series.

3. In the Format Data Series dialog box, click the Y Error Bar tab shown in Figure 22.13. (If you are working with a xy (scatter) and bubble charts, your dialog box will also have a X Error Bar tab.)

4. In the Display section, choose between these options: Both, Plus, Minus, or None.

5. In the Error Amount section, choose between Fixed Value, Percentage, Standard Deviation(s), or Standard Error. You can enter values for all but Standard Error.

6. Click OK when you've completed your choices.

FIG. 22.13
Error bars depict the potential error amounts relative to each data marker.

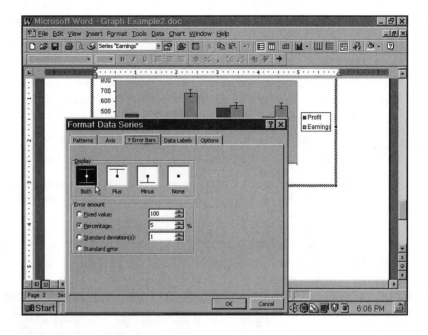

Revising Charts Automatically

Previously, you saw how a chart created from a table was no longer connected to that table. In this section, you'll see how to maintain the link between your table and graph, whether the table is in the same document as your graph or another.

Much of the data necessary for charts is formulated in spreadsheet programs like Excel. You can create charts in Word based on Excel data and keep them linked to boot! You'll see how later in this section.

Establishing a Link Between Word and Graph

If you find yourself updating a report on a weekly or monthly basis, you could waste a lot of time building and rebuilding the necessary charts. In most systematized reports, the data is what changes, not the style or type of chart. In fact, it's usually preferred that the overall format of the chart stay the same from report to report in order for focus to remain on the changing information. Graph 97 has an easy way for you to link your in-document table to your chart, so that all you have to change is information in the table.

Follow these steps to create a chart linked to a table:

1. Select the area of the table you want to use as the basis for your chart.
2. Click the Copy button on the Standard toolbar.

3. Choose Insert, Picture, Chart. Graph 97 creates a default chart from your data.

4. If not already active, click the Datasheet.

5. Choose Edit, Paste Link.

6. A dialog box asks for confirmation to replace the figures in the Datasheet. Click OK to confirm. Graph 97 redraws the screen with your linked data.

7. Format your chart however you like.

8. Click outside the chart area to return to the regular document.

9. Any changes now made to the table are reflected in the newly linked chart.

Not only can you change the data figures of your chart, you can also change the column or row headings. The chart is updated as soon as you confirm your entry by pressing Tab or otherwise moving from the cell. As you can see from Figure 22.14, you can even add a data series through a linked table. You add a row just as you normally would with a table, by pressing Tab when your insertion point is in the final cell of the last row. Graph 97 creates a new entry in the chart's legend and fills in the information as it is entered.

FIG. 22.14
After a table is linked to a chart, all the data input can be handled in the regular document.

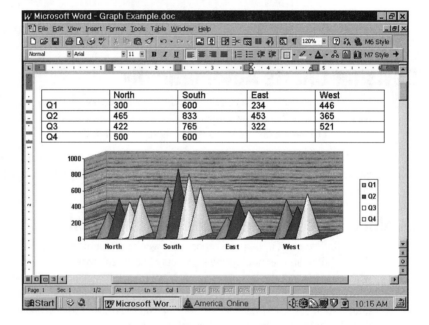

 What if you decide you don't want the link any more? You can break the link at any time by entering Graph 97 and selecting your chart. Then, choose Edit, Links. From the Link dialog box, click the Break Link button.

Establishing a Link with Microsoft Excel

The process for linking a chart with Excel (or any other compatible program) is basically the same as the one described previously for linking a table and chart in the same document. You select and copy the information in Excel, switch to Word and insert a chart, if one is not already in the document. Then, after selecting the Datasheet in Graph 97, you choose Edit, Paste Link.

However, because you are working with two separate files now, the updating is not instantaneous unless both are open and you are in Graph 97 mode. After you have changed, saved, and closed your Excel file, you can update your chart by opening your Word document and double-clicking the chart to invoke Graph 97. The same holds true if your source data is in another Word document or a file created by another program such as Lotus 1-2-3.

TIP If you don't want to link your data to an external file, you can also just import it. Open Graph 97 by double-clicking your chart. Choose Edit, Import File and select the file from the dialog box. You can then choose to import either the entire sheet or a selected data range.

TROUBLESHOOTING

How do I know which type of graph to use? The Graph 97 help system has a really good overview of how the different charts are best used. To see it, first choose Help, Contents and Index. Then from the Contents tab, click Changing the Type of a Chart, and then double-click Examples of Chart Types. From the help screen, choose the chart type you want more information on, and click.

Can I get a hard copy of my Datasheet? If you've created your chart from scratch and want a print out of your Datasheet, you have to perform a few extra steps; Graph 97 doesn't let you print the Datasheet directly. Your first option is to include a data table in your chart. Click the Data Table button on the Graph 97 toolbar to do this. (For more information, see "Adding A Data Table" earlier in this chapter.)

Your second option for printing your Datasheet is to move the information to where it can be printed. First, select the contents of the Datasheet, then exit from Graph 97 by clicking outside of the chart area. Next paste the copied information from the Clipboard into your current Word document or into a new one. Your information comes in as plain text, but you'll probably want it presented in a table format. Select the text in your document and choose Table, Convert Text to Table. In the conversion dialog box, make sure that Tabs are selected in the Separate Text At section. Click OK.

When I resize my chart, everything else resizes. Can I just resize the chart by itself? Resizing your chart can cause you some grief, primarily because most of the elements automatically resize right along with the rest of the chart. This can make certain labels too big or make them seem to disappear altogether. To inhibit this proportional scaling for all labels, double-click the chart area (the blank area between the chart and the plotted data). From the Format Chart Area dialog box click the Font tab. Clear the Auto Scale check box by clicking it again.

continues

continued

My labels disappeared when I resized my chart. What do I do? If you find that when your chart is reduced the text disappears, the font size is probably too small to display properly when aligned horizontally. You can either enlarge the chart by clicking and dragging the sizing handles or double-click the axis. Then from the Alignment tab of the Format Axis dialog box, switch to a vertical or angled text.

Can I resize a 3-D chart? Temporarily switch your 3-D chart to 2-D by using the Chart Type button on the Graph 97 toolbar and selecting a 2-D option from the drop-down choices. Resize your chart and then switch back to 3-D.

From Here...

In this chapter, you learned the basics of converting your Word information into charts with Graph 97. You saw how to customize your chart, build a graph from scratch and link to an outside document. Next you might want to look over the following chapters:

- ▥ Investigate the enhanced fill capabilities covered in the section on text boxes in Chapter 19, "Word Desktop Publishing."

- ▥ Review how to use the various drawing objects, including callouts and other AutoShapes as seen in Chapter 21, "Drawing in Word."

- ▥ Learn more about working with other Office products, such as Excel, and Word in Chapter 27, "Integrating with Microsoft Office."

The Corporate Word

CHAPTER 23

Managing Revisions

by Bill Camarda

In this chapter, you'll learn how to make the most of Word's reviewing tools—from the Highlighter, the electronic equivalent to the classic yellow marker you used in school, all the way to sophisticated revision tracking, commenting, and document comparison tools designed for business workgroups. ∎

Working with Comments

With Comments, you can add important suggestions and observations without changing a document's text or pagination.

Working with Track Changes

Word 97's Track Changes feature makes it easy to insert proposed revisions and almost as easy to review and resolve them.

Using Compare Documents

You can see all the differences between one draft and another with Word's Compare Documents feature.

Using Merge Documents

Combine everyone's changes into a single review document that's easy to use.

Storing multiple document versions in the same file

Versioning enables you to keep an audit trail containing every draft of a document—all in the same file.

An Overview of Word's Team Writing Tools

Nowadays, few documents of any size are written entirely by one individual. In the corporate setting, most documents must be shepherded through a hierarchy; increasingly they must also be reviewed by cross-functional teams. Even freelance writers, of course, face the sharp red pencils of editors—often, more than one.

Word can't do much to make the substantive aspects of the review process easier. But it can work absolute wonders for the logistics of document review. If your review needs are especially simple, Word's Highlighting tool might be enough—just as it might have been enough for you in high school. For more complex reviews, Word offers the following tools:

■ A *Comments* tool that enables reviewers to annotate your document with suggestions and recommendations without actually changing the text of the printed draft

■ A *Track Changes* tool that helps you keep track of all the changes made by multiple reviewers, and then evaluate, incorporate, or reject them one at a time—or all at once

■ A *Lock Documents* feature that enables you to prevent changes to your document except for annotations or tracked changes

■ A *Reviewing toolbar* that brings all of Word's reviewing tools together in one convenient location

■ A *Versioning* feature that enables you to maintain multiple versions of a document in a single file

■ Close integration with *Microsoft Outlook* to help you send file attachments to reviewers and track their progress

The Reviewing Toolbar

In previous versions of Word, reviewing tools were scattered throughout Word, making it more complex than necessary to make your way through the review process. Word 97 adds the Reviewing toolbar, which brings most of those tools together in one convenient location. If you're planning to review a document, start by choosing View, Toolbars, Reviewing to display the Reviewing toolbar (see Figure 23.1).

FIG. 23.1

The Reviewing toolbar brings together Word's Comments, Track Changes, Highlighter, Versioning, and E-mail tools in one place.

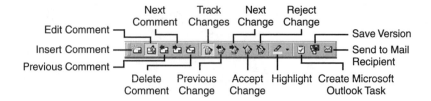

Using the Highlighter

Word's simplest reviewing tool is the Highlighter, which works just the same as the highlighting pen you may have used in high school. For the most informal reviews, the Highlighter may be all you need.

N O T E For more complex reviews, you'll want to use *Track Changes*, which make it easier to track, accept, and reject changes made by multiple reviewers. The advantage of using Comments is that they make it easier to understand why someone is calling attention to a specific block of text. ■

To highlight one block of text, select it and click the Highlight icon on either the Formatting or Reviewing toolbar. By default, your text is highlighted in see-through yellow. Figure 23.2 shows highlighted text in a document.

Part
VI

Ch
23

FIG. 23.2
Highlighted text.

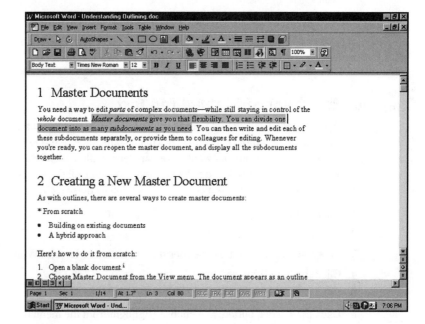

If you plan to highlight several blocks of text, click the Highlight button before you select any text. Then, select the first block of text; Word highlights it. Select another block of text; Word highlights that one, too. Word keeps highlighting text you select until you press Esc or click the Highlight button again.

If you prefer to use a color other than yellow, click the down arrow next to the Highlight button, and a choice of 15 colors appears (see Figure 23.3). Select the color you want to use. This becomes the default color for all highlighting you do until you change it again.

T I P Consider standardizing each member of your workgroup on a different highlighting color, and assigning them the same color for the changes they make using Word's Track Changes feature. Or, consider standardizing colors for each type of change that must be made; for example, use blue for text that may have to be removed later, green for text that needs a technical review, and so on.

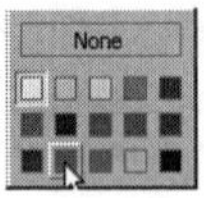

FIG. 23.3
Changing the default
highlight color.

You may find that some highlight colors which are acceptable for online reading are too dark when you
print them. Even if the highlighted text is readable, you may not want highlighting to appear in your
printed draft. Here's how to hide the highlighting on-screen and in your printed copy:

1. Choose Tools, Options.

2. Choose the View tab.

3. Clear the Highlight check box.

4. Click OK.

Changing the Color of Highlighted Text

What if you've added yellow highlighting throughout your document and then decide your
highlights should be a different color? Or what if someone else has reviewed the document
using yellow highlights and you would like to reserve yellow highlighting for yourself—let
them use blue? You can use Word's Replace tool to change all the text highlighting in your
document to a different highlight color. To do so, follow these steps:

1. Change the highlight color to the one you want.

2. Choose Edit, Replace.

3. Make sure there's no text in either the Find What or Replace With text boxes.

4. Click the Find What text box.

5. Click No Formatting.

6. Click the Format button, and choose Highlight from the menu that appears.

7. Click the Replace With text box.

8. Repeat steps 5 and 6.

9. Choose Replace All. Word replaces all the existing highlights in your document with new
   highlights in the color you've just specified.

Removing Highlighting from Your Document

It's been nice, but now your highlighting has outlived its usefulness, and you'd like to get rid of
it. Follow these steps to remove highlighting:

1. Press Ctrl+A to select your entire document.

2. Click the down arrow next to the Highlight button, and choose None.

Working with Comments

It's a classic problem; how do you make (or invite) comments in a document without introducing text changes that have to be undone later? The solution is Word's *Comments* tool (formerly called *annotations*). With Comments, you have a way of annotating your document that won't get in your way while you're editing and formatting your document. Then, when you're ready, your inserted comments will be easy to view, print, and resolve. Follow these steps to insert a comment:

Part

VI

Ch

23

1. Either click where you want your comment to appear, or select the text in the document that relates to the comment you want to make.

2. Press Alt+Ctrl+M, or click the Insert Comment button on the Reviewing toolbar. (You can also choose Insert, Comment.)

A pale yellow comment mark appears in your document, containing your initials (as stored in the Tools, Options, User Information tab). If you selected a block of text for comment, the entire block of text now appears in pale yellow.

The dotted line beneath the comment mark is your cue that comments are hidden text; they only appear when your document is set to show hidden text. To hide Comment marks, click the Show/Hide ¶ button on the Standard toolbar.

 You can also use Comments to create notes to yourself about facts that need checking, additional text that needs to be added, and other unfinished business.

The Comment mark also contains a number. Each time another comment is added to the document, the number increases. This helps reviewers keep track of individual comments.

When you insert a comment into a document, the Comments pane opens (see Figure 23.4). This pane works much like the Footnote and Endnote panes you saw in Chapter 18, "Footnotes, Bookmarks, Cross-References, and Hyperlinks." You can type your comment next to the Comment mark in the Comment pane. If you want, you can leave the Comments pane open as you navigate through the document, inserting comments wherever necessary.

Occasionally, you may want to make the same comment in several places. (For example, the writer whose draft you're reviewing may have made the same error repeatedly.) Insert the comment and edit the text in the Comment pane. Then copy the Comment mark and paste it wherever you want the comment to appear.

 If you turn on Track Changes before you start making comments, your comments will also be tracked as changes, making it easier for the document's author to resolve both comments and proposed revisions at the same time. In particular, you'll make it possible for the author to combine your comments with the tracked changes and comments made by others, using the Merge Documents feature. (You'll learn more about tracking changes and merging documents later in this chapter.)

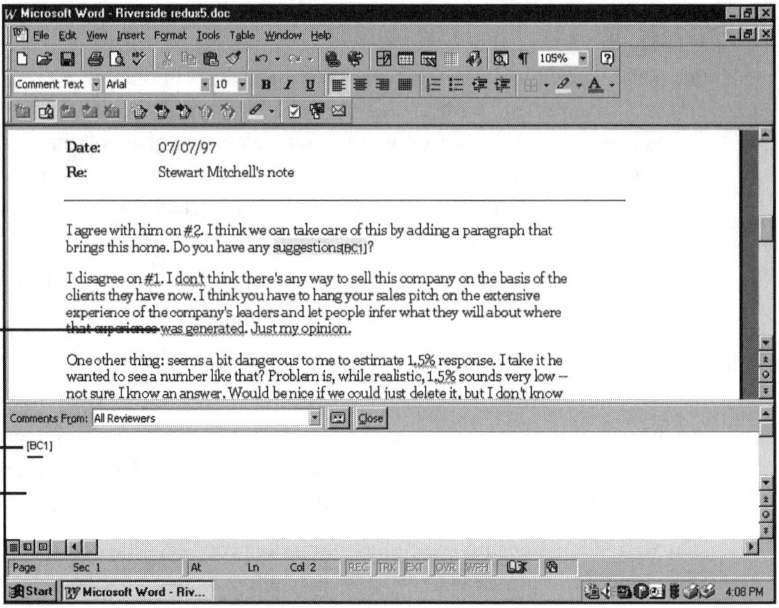
Microsoft Word - Riverside redux5.doc
File Edit View Insert Format Tools Table Window Help
Comment Text
Arial
10
Date: 07/07/97
Re: Stewart Mitchell's note
I agree with him on #2. I think we can take care of this by adding a paragraph that brings this home. Do you have any suggestions[BC1]?
I disagree on #1. I don't think there's any way to sell this company on the basis of the clients they have now. I think you have to hang your sales pitch on the extensive experience of the company's leaders and let people infer what they will about where that experience was generated. Just my opinion.
One other thing: seems a bit dangerous to me to estimate 1.5% response. I take it he wanted to see a number like that? Problem is, while realistic, 1.5% sounds very low -- not sure I know an answer. Would be nice if we could just delete it, but I don't know
Comments From: All Reviewers
Close
[BC1]
Page Sec 1 At Ln Col 2
Start
Microsoft Word - Riv...
4:08 PM
Highlighted comment
Comments mark
Comments pane

FIG. 23.4
You can type your comments in the Comments pane.

Inserting Comments from Multiple Reviewers

Several people can use Word's comments feature to annotate the same file. Word automatically places each reviewer's initials in their comment marks if their initials appear in the User Information tab. To check that your initials appear there, choose Tools, Options, and click the User Information tab.

TIP If you're using someone else's computer to make comments on a document, change the User Information and your initials will appear in future comment marks. This won't change comment marks that already appear in your document. Remember, however, to change the User Information back when you're finished.

Inserting Voice Comments

Occasionally, you might want to insert a brief audio comment in a file. For example, there may be a point you find it hard to explain in writing, but easy to explain verbally. Or you may have a digitized quote you would like to include. If you have a microphone and a sound card, Word makes it easy to add an audio comment.

1. Choose Insert, Comment (or click the Insert Comment button on the Reviewing toolbar). The Comments pane opens.
2. Click the Cassette Tape icon at the top of the Comment pane. The Windows 95 or Windows NT Sound Recorder applet opens (see Figure 23.5).

3. Click the Record button, and speak.

4. When you finish speaking, click Stop.

5. Choose Exit & Return from the File menu.

FIG. 23.5

The Windows 95 (or Windows NT) Sound Recorder opens whenever you want to insert an audio comment.

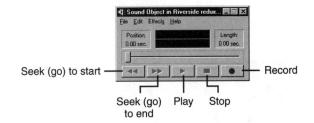

Seek (go) to start — Record

Seek (go) to end   Play   Stop

Part
VI
Ch
23

 TIP While Sound Recorder is open, you can edit your sound file. For example, you can choose Edit, Insert File to insert another audio file into the comment. Or you can play your recorded file to the point where you made your most important point, and choose Edit, Delete Before Current Position to edit out everything that came before it.

 TIP You can include text along with an audio comment. Just enter it alongside the Speaker icon in the Comments pane.

Audio comments appear in your document as small Speaker icons (see Figure 23.6). To listen to an audio comment, double-click the icon. To edit the comment, right-click icon; the shortcut menu appears. Choose Wave Sound Object, Edit, and the Sound Recorder applet opens.

FIG. 23.6

The Speaker icon signifies an audio comment; double-click the speaker to hear it.

CAUTION

Make your audio comments brief. Audio can quickly balloon the size of your files, reducing performance and straining your network if you share files with colleagues, and of course, your reviewer will need a sound card and speakers to hear your audio comments.

Locking Documents for Comment

As you've learned, one of the main benefits of Word's Comments feature is that it prevents reviewers from cluttering up a document with text that will simply have to be deleted later. You can go beyond inviting reviewers to use Word's Comments feature. Follow these steps to set up your document so they can do nothing but make Comments:

1. Choose Tools, Protect Document. The Protect Document dialog box opens (see Figure 23.7).

2. Choose Comments.

3. If you want, enter a password that readers will have to know in order to do anything beyond inserting comments.

4. Click OK.

FIG. 23.7

In the Protect Document dialog box, you can protect a document from any changes except for comments (or tracked changes, or forms).

If you choose to enter a password, you'll be asked to enter it again in the Confirm Password dialog box (see Figure 23.8). Do so, and click OK.

FIG. 23.8

If you choose a password, you'll be asked to confirm it. Remember that Word passwords are case-sensitive.

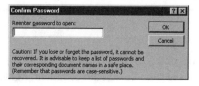

 N O T E If you do not use a password, when a reviewer opens the document he or she will still be restricted to making Comments only. However, choosing Tools, Unprotect Document unlocks the document for any kind of editing. ■

 TIP If you forget your password, you can press Ctrl+A to select the entire document, Ctrl+C to copy it, and Ctrl+V to paste it into another file.

Viewing and Editing Comments

So you've sent your document around for review, and you now have more comments than you know what to do with. Word makes it easier than ever to read, edit, and delete your comments. You can review all your comments systematically in the Comments pane, or review them more informally in the editing window.

TIP Before you start, consider saving a version of your file that contains all the comments as inserted by your reviewers. That way, you'll have a complete record of your document as it appeared before you decided what to do about each comment.

To save a version, choose File, Versions, and click Save Now. (You'll learn more about versioning later in this chapter.)

Reviewing Comments in the Comments Pane

To review comments in the Comments pane, choose View, Comments to display the Comments pane. By default, Word displays all the comments made by all your reviewers. In some instances, you might want to review all the comments made by a single reviewer, or walk through the document one reviewer at a time. To view only the comments made by one reviewer, select the reviewer's name from the Comments From drop-down list box, as shown in Figure 23.9.

FIG. 23.9
Choosing whose comments to view.

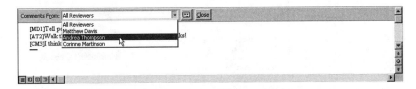

Whenever you click a comment within the Comment pane, Word displays the corresponding text in your document, making it easy to see what a reviewer is reacting to. If a reviewer has suggested language you would like to use in your document, you can select it and copy it into your document. More likely, you might want to edit a comment before incorporating it. Nearly all of Word's editing tools are available in the Comments pane.

When you finish working in the Comments pane, click Close or press Alt+Shift+C to close it.

 If your document contains many comments, you might want to enlarge the Comments pane by dragging its top border higher in the editing window.

Reviewing Comments in the Document Window

Occasionally, you'll notice the presence of a comment, and you may be curious about it, but you may not want to bother opening the Comments pane. (Maybe you're busy doing something else, and you don't want to get too involved in reviewing comments just now—but you suspect you shouldn't wait to find out what your reviewer has said about this block of text.) To view the contents of a comment, hover the mouse pointer anywhere in the comment. The comment's highlighting turns a deeper shade of yellow, and a ScreenTip appears, showing the full name of the reviewer and the contents of the comment.

 You can use Edit, Find to locate specific text in a comment. In fact, Find searches Comments, even if the Comments pane is closed and the comment marks are hidden in your document.

Using the Comment Shortcut Menu

Right-click anywhere in the comment, and a shortcut menu appears (see Figure 23.10). To edit the comment, choose Edit Comment; the Comments pane appears. To delete the comment, choose Delete Comment.

FIG. 23.10

You can edit or delete any comment using the Comments shortcut menu.

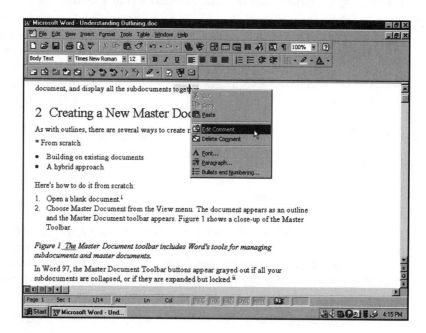

 TIP If the Reviewing toolbar is visible, you can also use the Edit Comment or Delete Comment buttons.

CAUTION

If you delete document text that includes a comment, the comment is deleted as well.

Moving from One Comment to the Next

You've already seen that you can click a comment in the Comments pane to move to it in the document. There's a more systematic way to review comments, however. Choose View, Toolbars, Reviewing to display the Reviewing toolbar. Then, move from one comment to the next, using the Previous Comment and Next Comment buttons. Each time you click the button, Word displays the next or previous comment along with the ScreenTip detailing the reviewer's name and what he or she had to say.

 TIP You can also move among comments by using Word 97's Browser. Click the Browser (Select Browse Object) button beneath the vertical scroll bar, and then choose Browse by Comment. Once you select

Browse by Comment, you can use the up-double-arrow and down-double-arrow buttons to move to the Previous Comment or the Next Comment.

If you'd like to walk through the document, resolving comments by a specific reviewer, you can do so with the Go To tab of the Find and Replace dialog box as follows:

1. Press F5 to display the Go To tab (see Figure 23.11).
2. Choose Comment in the Go to What scroll box.
3. Choose the reviewer's name in the Enter Reviewer's Name box.
4. Click Next to move to the reviewer's next comment (or click Previous to move to the preceding comment).
5. When you're finished, click Close.

Part
VI

Ch
23

FIG. 23.11

Moving among Comments in the Go To tab of the Find and Replace dialog box.

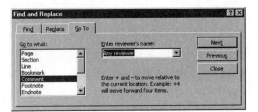

 T I P You don't have to enter a reviewer's name in the Enter Reviewer's Name box. If you want to view a specific comment, enter the comment number. If you want to jump ahead (or back) a specific number of comments, enter a positive or negative number with the corresponding plus or minus sign. For example, enter +3 to jump ahead three comments or –2 to jump back two comments.

Printing Comments

Comment marks and comment highlighting do not normally appear in your printed document. If you want Comment marks to appear in a printed document, follow these steps:

1. Choose Tools, Options.
2. Choose the Print tab.
3. Check the Comments check box in the Include with document area.
4. Click OK.

While the comment marks appear wherever you placed them, the comments themselves appear at the end of the document. If you want, you can run a separate print job that prints only the comments. To do so:

1. Choose File, Print.
2. In the Print What drop-down box, choose Comments.
3. Click OK.

TIP The first time you print comments, Word inserts page numbers in the Comments pane to indicate which comments appeared on each page. Those page numbers stay in your Comments pane unless you delete them manually.

If you find it valuable to have page numbering appear in the Comments pane, you can print a set of comments (or if you don't want to waste paper, just one page of comments) in order to get them.

Working with Track Changes

Comments are invaluable when you or your reviewers want to make observations about the text in a document. But when it comes to line-by-line editing changes, Word offers a better tool: Track Changes (called Revision Marks in earlier versions of Word).

With Track Changes turned on, you edit a document normally, and Word keeps track of all the text you add and delete. Then, you (or your colleague) can walk through the changes, deciding which to accept, which to reject, and which to modify.

The quickest way to start tracking changes is to double-click the TRK button in the status bar, or press Ctrl+Shift+E. If the Reviewing toolbar is open, you can also click the Track Changes button. (When Track Changes is on, you can use any of these methods to turn it off.)

No matter which procedures you use to turn Track Changes on, Word will start tracking changes in your document as follows:

■ *New text you add* will appear in red, with underlining. (Word may select a different color if you aren't the first person to review the document.)

■ *Existing text you delete* will remain visible, but be formatted in red with strikethrough applied. You can see an example in Figure 23.12.

■ *New text you add and then delete* won't appear in the document at all.

■ *Wherever an editing change is made,* a vertical line will appear in the document's outer margin (Word uses the right margin, unless you've chosen Different Odd and Even Pages in the Layout tab of the File, Page Setup dialog box.) This makes it easier to find and focus on changes, especially in printed documents.

Tracking Revisions in the Background

If you're making extensive, line-by-line revisions, you may quickly find all these marks distracting. If so, you can hide them. Choose Tools, Track Changes, Highlight Changes. The Highlight Changes dialog box appears (see Figure 23.13). Clear the Highlight Changes on Screen check box, and click OK. Assuming the Track changes While Editing check box is checked, Word continues to mark all the changes in your document, but you won't see the change marks unless you check this check box again.

FIG. 23.12
With Track Changes turned on, new text is underlined, and deletions are marked with strikethrough character formatting.

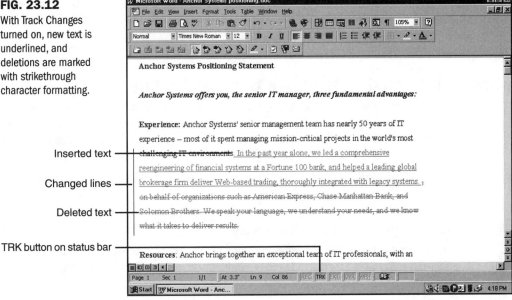

Inserted text

Changed lines

Deleted text

TRK button on status bar

N O T E When you clear the Highlight Changes on Screen check box, your document looks like it would if every change you made was accepted. ■

FIG. 23.13
From the Highlight Changes dialog box, you can control whether changes are visible, and whether they print.

CAUTION

If you're creating a document for a Web page, resolve all your tracked changes before you save it to HTML format. If you use File, Save as HTML to save a file with text you've marked for deletion with Track Changes, that text appears in your HTML page with no record that you intended to delete it.

Choosing Whether to Print Revisions

By default, Word reflects Tracked Changes when you print your document. If the Highlight Changes on Screen box has been checked and the changes are visible on-screen, the change marks will be visible in the printed document. If you've hidden the changes, you won't see the change marks; the document will print as though the changes had been accepted.

If you want to see the change marks while you work, but you don't want to see them in your printed document, clear the Highlight Changes in Printed Document check box in the Highlight Changes dialog box. The printed document will still reflect the changes, but the change marks won't be visible.

Options for Controlling the Track Changes Feature

As you've learned, Word marks the first reviewer's insertions as red underlined text, the first reviewer's deletions as red strikethrough, and adds change bars on the outside border of your page wherever a revision has been made. These are default settings; you can change them if you want. For example, you have the following options:

- If your document already contains extensive underlining, you might want to distinguish change marks with double-underlining.

- If you don't want Word to automatically assign new colors to each reviewer, you can specify the color a reviewer will always use.

- If you want to see reviewer's additions, but you're not very interested in what a reviewer has deleted, you can format deletions as hidden text instead of strikethrough.

- If you want to see where a reviewer has changed formatting, you can specify a color and mark for formatting changes.

- If you print interim drafts for distribution in three-hole binders, you can specify that change lines always appear on the right margin, making them easier to see.

You can control all these aspects of Track Changes through the Track Changes dialog box (see Figure 23.14). Follow these steps to view it:

1. Choose Tools, Track Changes, Highlight Changes.

2. Choose Options.

 TIP You can view the same settings by choosing Tools, Options, Track Changes.

FIG. 23.14
You can control the colors used in the review process through the Track Changes tab of the Options dialog box.

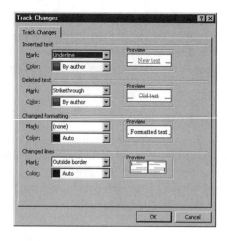

Specifying How Insertions and Deletions Are Marked

To change the mark that Word applies to text inserted while Track Changes is turned on, choose a new Mark in the Inserted Text area. In addition to the default underline, your choices are bold, italic, and double-underline.

To change the mark associated with deletions, choose a new Mark in the Deleted text area. In addition to the default strikethrough, you can choose hidden text, or you can tell Word to insert a ^ or # placeholder symbol in place of the text you deleted. This shows that text has been deleted, but doesn't clutter up the screen with hard-to-follow strikethrough marks. This technique is widely used in legal documents.

When you change a mark—or any other setting in this dialog box—Word displays a preview to the right of the area in which you're working.

N O T E The new settings that you establish in the Track Changes tab apply to both the changes you've already made and those you make in the future. In other words, if you change the settings and then open another document that already contains change marks, those will reflect the new settings. ▪

Specifying How Word Assigns Colors to Reviewers

By default, Word assigns colors to reviewers automatically. When a reviewer turns on Track Changes, Word looks in the User Information tab to see who the reviewer is. If the reviewer has already made changes, Word assigns the same color the reviewer has used before. If not, Word assigns the next available color. If Word runs out of colors, two reviewers have to share a color.

This system usually works well. However, you might want to permanently assign colors to individual members of your team, so you can tell at a glance who made each revision—especially if you're looking at a document printed on a color printer. Follow these steps to choose a specific color for all changes you track on your computer:

1. Choose Tools, Options, Track Changes to display the Track Changes tab.
2. In the Color drop-down box (in the Inserted Text area), choose a color.
3. In the Color drop-down box (in the Deleted Text area), choose a color—typically the same color you just chose for inserted text.
4. Click OK.

N O T E This procedure establishes the color that will be used to mark all changes made on the same computer. If someone else sits down to make changes on your computer, their changes will be marked in your color. ▪

 T I P Because the 15 color choices in Track Changes are the same as those available for Highlighting, you can assign reviewers the same color for both purposes.

Specifying How Formatting Changes Are Marked

Prior to Word 97, if you made a formatting change with Track Changes (Revision Marks) turned on, Word didn't bother to track that change. Now, Word does track formatting changes. When you make a formatting change, Word inserts a vertical line in the outer margin, just as it would if you made a text change. However, by default, Word does not apply a change mark to indicate where the formatting change was made. The rationale is simple: change marks appear as formatting. Users might find it hard to tell which formatting has been applied by the reviewer and which is part of the change mark itself.

Unfortunately, the result can be even more confusing. If you review a document that contains tracked formatting changes, the vertical lines will tell you that changes have been made, but you'll have no way to tell what those changes were. If this proves troublesome, you can specify a change mark and a color for Word to use whenever it tracks a formatting change. Choose Tools, Options, Track Changes to display the Track Changes tab. Then, with the Track Changes tab open, follow these steps:

1. Select a Mark in the drop-down list box in the Changed Formatting area (bold, italic, underline, or double underline).
2. Select a Color in the Changed Formatting area.
3. Click OK.

Specifying the Appearance of Changed Lines

As you've learned, Word inserts a black vertical line at the outside border of any line that contains a tracked change. This is called a *changed line*. To control changed lines, open the Track Changes tab, as described in the previous section. Then follow these steps:

1. Select a Mark in the Changed Lines area (Outside border, Left border, Right border, or None).
2. Select a Color in the Changed Lines area.
3. Click OK.

Protecting a Document for Tracked Changes

Earlier in this chapter, you saw how to protect a document for comments, (that is how to prevent reviewers from doing anything except adding comments.) You can also protect a document for tracked changes. When you do, Word lets reviewers edit the document any way they want, but marks all the changes they make using the Track Changes feature—giving you an audit trail. Follow these steps to protect a document for Tracked Changes:

1. Choose Tools, Protect Document.
2. Choose Tracked Changes.
3. If you want to, enter a password.

4. Click OK.

5. If you entered a password, confirm it, and click OK again.

As with protecting a document for comments, if you don't use a password, users can turn off Track Changes by first choosing Tools, Unprotect Document.

Quick and Easy Tracking Changes with the Compare Documents Feature

Imagine you've asked someone to review a document, but you forgot to turn on Track Changes first. Have you forever lost the chance to see where changes were made and systematically resolve them? No! If you have a copy of the document in its original form (before the reviewer edited it), you can use Word's Compare Documents feature. When you're finished, you'll have a document that includes change marks wherever additions, deletions (and optionally, formatting changes) were made—just as if the edits were made with Track Changes enabled. Follow these steps:

1. Open the document where you want the change marks to appear.

2. Choose Tools, Track Changes, Compare Documents. The Select File to Compare with Current Document dialog box opens (see Figure 23.15).

3. Browse to select the file you want to compare with the one you already have open.

4. Click Open. Word now compares the two documents and inserts change marks wherever they differ.

FIG. 23.15

In this dialog box, you can browse to any local or networked location and choose a document to compare with the one you're using.

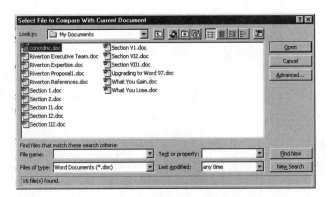

CAUTION

Compare Documents can occasionally deliver misleading results. For example, if you reorganize your document by moving large blocks of text, those will appear as large deletions and equally large insertions. Within those blocks of text, you won't have any way to tell whether additional copy edits were made. (You would have the same problem in a document you marked with Track Changes.)

Merging Revisions

You've already seen one scenario for reviewing a document; you send a file to one reviewer who makes changes and then forwards it to another reviewer who makes changes that are recorded in a different color, and so on. When everyone's finished, the changes are returned to you in one rainbow-colored document.

In today's fast-paced business world, however, you may not have time to wait for each person to review a document consecutively. You may have to send a separate copy of the document to each reviewer and receive a separate marked up copy in return. You can use Word's Merge Documents feature to integrate all those changes into a single document, where you can re-solve them all at once in an organized fashion.

Follow these steps to merge revisions from several documents into one:

1. Choose Tools, Merge Documents. The Select File to Merge Into Current Document dialog box opens (see Figure 23.16).

2. Browse to select the document you want to merge.

3. Click Open.

4. Repeat steps 1–3 for each additional document with revisions you want to incorporate.

FIG. 23.16

In this dialog box, you can choose a file that contains changes you want to merge into the document you already have open.

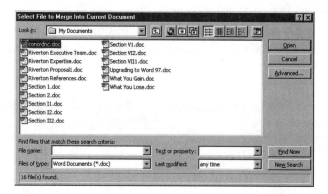

> **CAUTION**
>
> The Merge Documents feature only merges tracked changes; it does not integrate any other difference that may exist between two documents. If you want to merge the contents of two documents (other than tracked changes), use Insert, File.

Resolving Proposed Changes

No matter how you get change marks into your document, the real beauty of Word's Track Changes feature comes later, when you see how easy it is to resolve the changes your review-ers have proposed.

There are two ways to resolve proposed changes: using the Reviewing toolbar, or using the Accept or Reject Changes dialog box. In general, the Reviewing toolbar is a bit quicker. The dialog box gives you more choices and more information. In this section, you'll learn how to use both of them, starting with the Reviewing toolbar.

Resolving Changes from the Reviewing Toolbar

To start resolving changes with the Reviewing toolbar, first double-click the TRK button on the status bar to turn off Track Changes (so you aren't creating more changes as you work). Then choose View, Toolbars, Reviewing to display the Reviewing toolbar.

Now, click Next Change or Previous Change. Word moves forward or back in your document, selecting the first change it finds. After a change is selected, you can choose from the following options:

- *Identify* the change, by hovering the mouse pointer above it. A ScreenTip appears, identifying the reviewer and when they made the change (see Figure 23.17).

- *Reject* the change by pressing Delete or Backspace. or by clicking the Reject Change button on the Reviewing toolbar.

- *Accept* the change by clicking the Accept Change buttons on the Reviewing toolbar.

- *Modify* a suggested insertion by clicking Accept Change and then editing it in your document.

- *Undo* a change you just accepted, rejected, or edited by clicking the Undo button on the Standard toolbar.

Part
VI

Ch
23

FIG. 23.17

If you hover your mouse pointer above a tracked change, Word displays a ScreenTip containing the reviewer's name and whether the change consists of an insertion or a deletion.

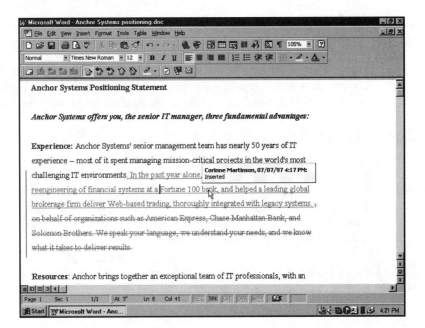

Resolving Changes from the Accept or Reject Changes Dialog Box

You can also accept or reject changes from a dialog box designed for the purpose. Choose Tools, Track Changes, Accept or Reject Changes, and the Accept or Reject Changes dialog box opens (see Figure 23.18). This dialog box gives you more control than the Reviewing toolbar does. For example, you can control how your document looks while you're reviewing changes. If you click the Changes with Highlighting button, you'll see all the change marks in your document. If you click Changes without Highlighting, you'll see the document as it would look if you accepted all the changes.

FIG. 23.18

With the Accept or Reject Changes dialog box open, you can move through your document, resolving one proposed revision at a time.

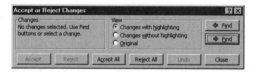

Accepting or Rejecting All Changes at the Same Time

It's unlikely, but you might occasionally be able to resolve all your revisions at the same time. Perhaps you (or your boss) makes an executive decision to disregard all the wrong-headed comments provided by someone in another department. With the Accept or Reject Changes dialog box open, click Reject All to reject them all at the same time. Your document now appears as though none of the comments had ever been made.

 If you think better of this, click Undo.

Conversely, one of your reviewers may be so smart—or so important—that it is immediately obvious you need to accept all of the comments. Click Accept All; the revision marks all disappear and the tracked changes slip seamlessly into your document as if they'd been there all along.

Accepting or Rejecting Changes One at a Time

As in the Reviewing toolbar, you can accept or reject changes one by one from the Accept or Reject Changes dialog box. To find the next change in a document, click → Find. To find the preceding change, click ← Find. To accept a change you've selected, click Accept. Word integrates it into your document and moves on to select the next change. To reject the change, click Reject; Word eliminates the change and moves on to select the next one. When you're finished working in this dialog box, click Close.

 You don't have to resolve all your changes at the same time; you can leave some unresolved until you get more information or speak to the right person. You might want to insert a comment reminding yourself why a change is still unresolved.

Using Word's New Versioning Feature

Many Word users are in the habit of using File, Save As to save a new copy of every new draft they create. By doing so, they not only make sure of having a recent backup in the event of disaster, they also create an audit trail that helps identify when a critical change was made in case it is questioned later.

Nothing has changed the need for storing backups, but Word now has a more convenient, reliable way of providing that audit trail. You can now store each new version of your document in the same file—so older versions can't easily get lost, misplaced, or confused with the current version. Follow these steps to save a new version of an existing file:

1. Choose File, Versions.
2. The Version dialog box opens (see Figure 23.19).
3. Click Save Now. The Save Version dialog box opens (see Figure 23.20).
4. Enter comments on the version, such as whose changes it reflects, or why the new version was created. (Don't worry about entering the current date and time, or your own name—Word has already done that for you.)
5. Click OK. Word saves a new version of the document in the same file as the original.

Part
VI

Ch
23

FIG. 23.19
Click Save Now in the Versions dialog box to save a new version of your document in the same file.

FIG. 23.20
In the Save Version dialog box, enter detailed comments about why this draft was created, or whose comments it reflects.

TIP You can also save a new version by choosing File, Save As, and choosing Save Version. The Save Version dialog box appears; enter your comments and click OK.

CAUTION

If you save a file containing multiple versions using a format other than Word 97, the older versions will be lost. Make sure to use File, Save As to save a new file. Then, you'll still have all the versions in your previous file.

N O T E   In a file containing multiple versions, Word's document statistics apply only to the current version. ■

Working with Multiple Versions of a File

After you've created one or more additional versions of a file, you can choose File, Versions to reopen the Versions dialog box and work with these files. In Figure 23.21, you can see how this dialog box looks after several versions have been created.

FIG. 23.21
The Versions dialog box provides several new options after you have versions from which to choose.

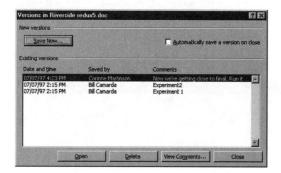

To open any version, select it and click Open. To delete an old version, select it and click Delete; Word asks you to confirm the deletion and reminds you that you can't undo this action.

 TIP   If you're planning to send a document out for review, you may want to delete all old versions to make sure reviewers only see the current one. (Or better yet, use File, Save As to create a new copy of the file and then delete the unwanted versions from the copy.)

In the Versions dialog box, you can already see the first few words of comments about the file; if you want to see more, click View Comments. You can't edit comments made about a version that was saved previously; the comments are read-only.

Saving a Version as a Separate File

When you open an older version of a file, Word displays the document in a separate editing window, which splits the screen as shown in Figure 23.22. Notice that the version you opened has a save date in its title bar—a gentle reminder that you're not working with the current version.

FIG. 23.22
If you open an older version, Word displays a new editing window and displays the version's creation date in the title bar.

The older version's name includes its creation date

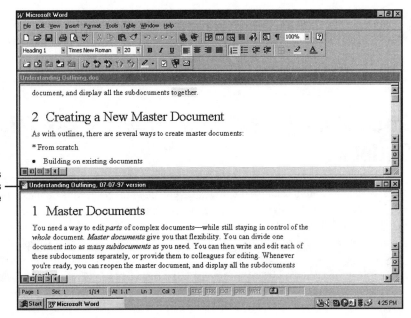

If you make changes to the older version, Word won't save it in the same file any longer. When you choose Save, Word displays the Save As dialog box, and shows the file name as it appears in the title bar with the version creation date. When you click Save, you get a new file containing only the version you edited.

 Unfortunately, you can't use Word's Compare Documents feature to compare two versions of a document within the same file. You can work around this limitation, however, by saving each version you want to compare as a separate file, and then choosing Tools, Track Changes, Compare Documents.

Automatically Saving New Versions

You may want to save a "snapshot" of your document each time another editor or reviewer finishes with it. Follow these steps to do so:

1. Choose File, Versions.

2. In the Versions dialog box, check the Automatically Save a Version on Close check box.

3. Choose Close.

CAUTION

This feature works best if you expect each reviewer to open the file once and close it once. If you or your colleagues expect to open and close the file several times before completing work on it, you're likely to find yourself with dozens of versions you don't really need.

T I P   Word offers another (also imperfect) way of tracking how much a document has been worked on. Choose File, Properties, Statistics to display the Statistics tab of the Properties dialog box. Here, you can see how long your document has been open, and how many times it has been saved. Of course, if you save a document often, you might get a revision number in the hundreds.

Streamlining the Review Process with Microsoft Outlook

Few things in life generate quite as many loose ends as reviewing a large document. To resolve an outstanding issue, you may realize you need to speak with a colleague, do some more research, check with the lawyers, run a search on the Web, or think something through in more detail. If you use the Microsoft Outlook personal information manager, it's very easy to create a new task associated with your current document and include it on your list of tasks to perform.

N O T E   Microsoft Outlook is included in Microsoft Office 97 Professional, Standard, and Small Business Editions, but not in stand-alone versions of Word 97 or in Microsoft Home Essentials. You can purchase Outlook separately if you want. ■

To create a new task list, first, save the file you're working on, and click your insertion point in the paragraph you're concerned about. Choose View, Toolbars, Reviewing to display the Reviewing toolbar. Then, click the Create Microsoft Outlook Task button. Microsoft Outlook's Task dialog box opens (see Figure 23.23).

FIG. 23.23
Using Outlook's Task window to create a new task associated with your document review.

Save and Close button
Name of task
Word document icon
Assign Task button
Editable description of task

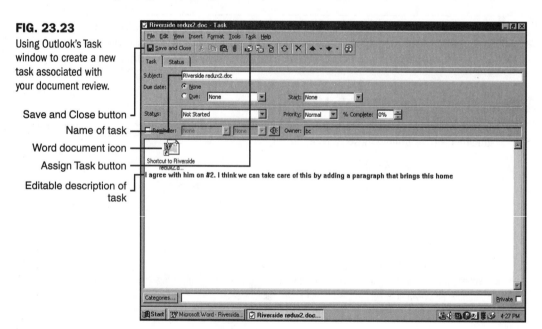

The following list points out some important elements of Outlook's dialog box and some of the ways you can use it:

■ The task is named after your Word file. You can edit the task name in the Subject text box.

■ You can set all kinds of information about your task, including a due date, start date, and reminder notification.

■ The large text box at the bottom of the Task dialog box contains the paragraph of text where you clicked your insertion point. The text gives you some context to help you remember what task you set up for yourself. You can edit the text to make it even clearer.

■ The text box also contains an icon representing your Word document. In the future, if you're working in Outlook, you can double-click the file icon any time you want to open the Word document.

When you're finished creating the task, click Save and Close; Word enters the task on your Task List (see Figure 23.24).

▶ **See** "Using Outlook With Word," **p. 767**

Part
VI

Ch
23

FIG. 23.24
The task you established by clicking Create Microsoft Outlook Task now appears in your Outlook Task List.

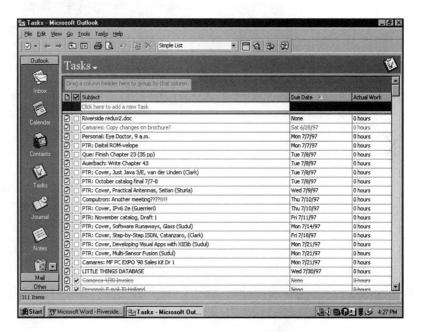

Assigning a Review Task to Someone Else

It's all well and good to assign a task to someone else, but it's equally likely that your review process will turn up tasks that someone else needs to perform.

If your colleagues also use Outlook, and you use a compatible e-mail system, such as Microsoft Exchange Server, you can easily transform the task you created into an e-mail message that can be sent to someone else. Because the task already includes a copy of your file, this is an exceptionally easy way to transmit a file for review. Start by saving your Word file, and if you want, clicking your insertion point in the paragraph with which you're concerned. (If you don't, Outlook will leave the description blank, but you can always add your own.) Click the Create Microsoft Outlook Task button on the Reviewing toolbar to display the Task dialog box (refer to Figure 23.23). Now, click Assign Task. Outlook changes the Task window to an e-mail window (see Figure 23.25).

FIG. 23.25

If you click Assign Task, Outlook displays this e-mail window, where you can delegate your problem to someone else.

Send button ─┘

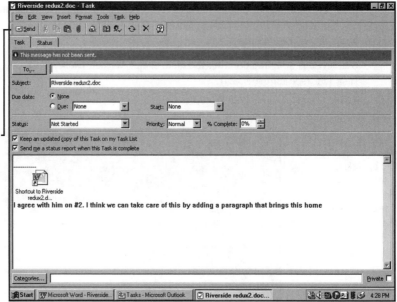

To choose a recipient from the Select Task Recipient dialog box, click To (see Figure 23.26). Select a recipient, and click To; this adds the task to your list of recipients. You can repeat the process to send the task to more than one recipient. Click OK when you're finished, and then click the Send button (refer to Figure 23.25) to deliver the message.

TROUBLESHOOTING

I'm reviewing tracked changes, but Word won't let me accept or reject any. Most likely, your document is still protected for tracked changes. If so, choose Tools, Unprotect Document. If you're asked for a password, enter it. If you don't have the password, you may not be authorized to accept or reject changes.

FIG. 23.26
This figure illustrates
selecting a recipient for
your task.

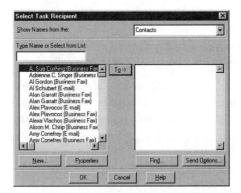

Part
VI

Ch
23

I've added tracked changes, but they're not showing up—and I've already checked to make sure the Highlight Changes on Screen check box is checked in the Highlight Changes dialog box. Your changes might be formatted in hidden text. Click the Show/Hide ¶ button on the Standard toolbar to check.

ScreenTips don't appear when I hover my mouse pointer over a comment or a tracked change. Choose Tools, Options, View and make sure the ScreenTips box is checked.

I tried to insert a comment at the beginning of a sentence or paragraph, but Word inserted it after the first word. This is a Word 97 bug. Until it's fixed, consider inserting comments at the end of sentences or paragraphs.

I used Word's Versioning feature, but Word crashes when I open an older version. If your file contains form fields (see Chapter 24, "Creating Electronic and Printed Forms"), you've just encountered another Word 97 bug. Use File, Save As to store each version in a separate file (just as you did before Word introduced Versioning).

I merged two files, but change marks didn't appear in the resulting file. Make sure you've turned on Highlight Changes on Screen in the Tools, Highlight Changes dialog box. If change marks don't appear, it's possible you forgot to turn on Track Changes. Starting from your original (unchanged) file, use the Compare Documents feature (Tools, Track Changes, Compare Documents) to mark all differences between your original and the file you sent out for review. Then use the Merge Documents feature (Tools, Merge Documents) to integrate each reviewer's set of changes into the original file, including the set of changes you just created using Compare Documents.

I saved my file to HTML, and my highlighting and comments are gone. Unfortunately, yes, they are. Word's HTML export filter doesn't preserve comments, and HTML itself doesn't support highlighting. If it's worth your time, you can copy your comments into the document text, save the file as HTML, and then (using Word's Web authoring tools) format the text in HTML Comments style. After you do, your comments will appear in your HTML text file, but won't display on the Web page unless someone chooses to view HTML source code.

From Here...

In this chapter, you've learned about many of Word's tools for streamlining the group review of a document. Now, learn more about using Word with your colleagues:

■ What kind of documents are virtually always shared with other people? Forms. In Chapter 24, "Creating Electronic and Printed Forms," you'll learn how to create electronic forms in Word that are faster to fill out and easier to manage.

■ In this chapter, you've taken a quick look at one way Word and Outlook can work together. In Chapter 27, "Integrating with Microsoft Office," take a closer look at how these two Office 97 siblings support each other.

■ Word's reviewing tools are just one way Word 97 can adapt itself to use in businesses and organizations. For a closer look at managing Word's many other workgroup and organizational capabilities, see Chapter 28, "Installing and Configuring Word in a Network Environment."

CHAPTER 24

Creating Electronic and Printed Forms

by Joe Lowery

In the previous chapter, you saw how Word could be used to collect comments and revisions; in this chapter you'll see how you can use Word to collect data as well. ■

Starting out with forms

This section includes an overview of what forms can do and the basics of how to use them. Word 97 dedicates an easy-to-use toolbar to the creation and maintenance of forms.

Enhancing your forms

Word 97 has added some very intriguing features to forms—features that can help you automate your document production with little or no programming necessary.

Activating an electronic form

You can use ActiveX controls in your forms, whether they are intended for the Internet, the intranet or just around the office.

Querying forms

Word 97 lets you set up your form so that it asks your user a series of questions and fills out the form for them.

Controlling form files

Forms require a little special care and handling. You'll find in this section specific techniques and methods for getting the most out of your form templates and form data.

Solving form problems

The unique nature of forms gives rise to some unique problems. Here's where you can turn for the appropriate solutions.

How You Can Use Word's Forms Feature

Interactivity has been a buzzword for so long you may have lost sight of the most basic interactive tool: the form. Word 97 lets you create the following kinds of forms:

- A protected electronic form where the user's answers are limited to specific areas and types of responses.
- A printed form that is intended to be completed with a pen.
- An online form where you can guide the user through a series of questions.

In addition to fairly obvious applications like questionnaires and surveys, forms can also be used in more traditional word processing functions like automated document production. Lawyers use forms to fill out contracts, while realtors use them to complete loan applications. Virtually any document that uses largely repetitive text and distinguishes itself from other documents like it by specific, detailed information can be generated by a form. You even have the options to save or print only the data from a form, which enables you to put the information into a database or fill out preprinted forms.

 TIP The term online refers to all manner of electronic forms: those that are used to automate documents as well as those created for use on the Internet.

When it comes to the World Wide Web, forms are definitely cutting-edge. Word 97 lets you gather a full range of feedback from your Web page visitors. You have the option of using traditional input forms like a text area, check box, or option button, or some of the more sophisticated ActiveX controls. After the form has been filled out, it is submitted—generally meaning that the form results are sent to the designated recipient for collection or further processing.

Creating the Skeleton of a Form

No matter what the end-result is for your form—hard-copy, computer file, or Web page—you first have to create the shell in which to place your form elements. You use all the regular text and drawing tools you normally would in making a document, but certain areas are reserved for your *form fields*. A form field is a placeholder, usually indicated by a shaded area, where a particular type of data is input.

Because they are meant to be completed by a number of different people over a period of time, forms generally start as templates. You can also decide to save a regular document as a template.

To create a new, blank template, follow these steps:

1. Choose File, New to open the New dialog box.
2. From the General tab, select the Blank Document file.
3. In the Create New section, click the Template option button.
4. Click OK.

If you were creating a Web page with a form, you could use the same procedure as previously outlined, but instead of the General tab, choose the Web Pages tab, and Blank Web Page instead of Blank Document.

TIP It's a good idea to lock your form prior to saving. To do this, choose Tools, Protect Document, and then click the Forms option button from the Protect dialog box. This topic is covered in more detail later in this chapter in the section titled "Protecting Forms from Unauthorized Change."

After you've built the skeleton for your form, make sure you save it as a template. By default, Word saves all templates in the Templates folder; saving your file here will make it appear in the General tab of the New dialog box. You can also save it in any of the Templates subfolders, such as Letters & Faxes, Memos, Publications, and so on, that correspond to the other tabs of the New dialog box. All templates are assigned a .dot file name extension instead of the regular .doc.

When it comes time to edit your form, you must open the template itself, not a document created from the template. To make sure that you're opening a template, you can change the Files of Type to Document Templates in the Open dialog box. If you've protected your document, you'll need to choose Tools, Unprotect Document before proceeding.

▶ **See** "Using Word's Built-In Template Library," **p. 171**

Working with the Forms Toolbar

Word 97 has grouped the essential commands for creating and editing a form together in the appropriately named Forms toolbar. Enable this toolbar as you would any other: choose View, Toolbars, and then choose Forms from the submenu. Like any other toolbar that initially "floats" on the screen, you can dock the Forms toolbar by dragging it to any screen edge. As you can see from Figure 24.1, there are nine buttons available:

- *Text Form Field* is used for general text entry.

- *Check Box Form Field* enables the user to select one or more options from a series of possibilities.

- *Drop-Down Form Field* lets the user choose one option from several listed possibilities.

- *Form Field Options* is used to specify the conditions for any form field.

- *Draw Table* enables the form designer to drag out a table.

- *Insert Table* puts a table in the form with a set number of columns and rows.

■ *Insert Frame* includes a free-floating box in the form for precise placement.

 ■ *Form Field Shading* makes form fields visible in a medium gray.

 ■ *Protect Form* locks the document from any change except entering information into form fields.

FIG. 24.1

When you're beginning to create a form, use the Forms toolbar to speed your work.

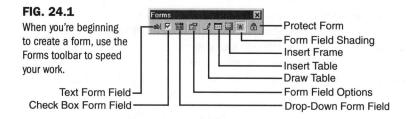

Protect Form
Form Field Shading
Insert Frame
Insert Table
Draw Table
Form Field Options
Drop-Down Form Field

Text Form Field
Check Box Form Field

Adding Text Form Fields

When it comes to basic forms, by far the most common type of entry is plain text. There are very few forms out there that do not, at a minimum, gather your name and address—and most require everything from your e-mail address to your hat size. Text form fields are the work-horses of forms.

To insert a text form field, first open the Forms toolbar. Make sure your insertion point is where you want the form field to appear and then click the Text Form Field button on the Forms toolbar. By default, you'll see a medium gray rectangle approximately ½" wide by one line high. This doesn't indicate how much text you can add; text form fields are initially open ended, meaning that you can insert any number of characters in them.

 If you find the gray shading obtrusive, you can turn it off by clicking the Form Field Shading button on the Forms toolbar. The shading disappears but your fields are still in place. However, unless you're using an alternative way to mark your fields (such as with an underline), it's a good idea to leave the shading enabled.

To remove a text form field from your document, first select it. The field turns a darker shade of gray than normal. Now, press Delete. If your document is protected, you can't delete the form field even though you can access it; you must first choose Tools, Unprotect Document or click the Protect Form button on the Forms toolbar.

Formatting Your Text Form Field   You can format your text form field just as you would any other text character—make it bold, italic, or underline, change the font name or size, and so on. The field itself retains the same gray shading; most formatting, especially anything font-related, isn't evident until some text is placed in the field.

T I P Adding some additional formatting to your text form fields is a good way to make the form more readable. Use bold rather than italic or a font change to make your text entries stand out.

As with any other editing, you have to add your formatting when the form is in its unprotected state. When the form is locked, you'll find that the entire Formatting toolbar is inactive.

ab| **Setting the Text Form Field Options**   Word 97 gives you a fair amount of flexibility over your text form field. You can set the type of text, determine how many characters can be input, make the field a particular case or format, and even set a default response. All of these characteristics and more are accessed through the Form Field Options button on the Forms toolbar.

As you can see from Figure 24.2, there are four major areas available to alter the appearance of the text form field:

- *Type.* Choose between the following options:

    Regular text—used to allow entry of any key. (Default)

    Number—restricts entry to numeric keys only. If non-numeric keys are used, the field is evaluated to zero when input is confirmed.

    Date—restricts entry to a valid date or time. An error message alerting the user to this restriction appears if an incorrect entry is made.

    Current Date—automatically inserts the current date when the document is opened.

    Current Time—automatically inserts the current time when the document is opened or printed.

    Calculation—sets the field to be equal to equation in the Default Text box.

- *Default text.* This displays the entered text, if any, initially in the text form field. The user can replace the default text with his or her own. This field is not available if either the Current Date or Current Time options are chosen. When Calculation is selected to be the field type, this box is titled "Expression" and starts with an equal sign.

- *Maximum Length.* This sets the number of characters that can be input into the text box. The default is Unlimited. Each click of the spinner arrows increases the character count by one.

- *Format Type.* This determines the formatting applied to the text form field. The options available depend on the Type chosen. If General Text is selected, you can choose between different cases; if Number or Calculation is chosen, the formats are restricted to standard, currency, and other accounting specific number formats; if any of the date or time options are selected, the options are limited to those formats.

CAUTION

When you're creating or editing your form, get in the habit of protecting your document before you test your changes. Otherwise, selecting the form field and then entering some text will potentially erase the field. To quickly lock and unlock your form, use the Protect Form button on the Forms toolbar.

FIG. 24.2
The Text Form Field Options dialog box lets you control a user's input.

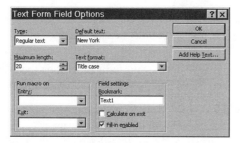

The more advanced features of the Text Form Field Options dialog box such as running macros and adding help text are covered for all the form field elements later in this chapter.

Adding Check Box Form Fields

Check boxes are a very clear and handy method of indicating a selection of one or more options that are not mutually exclusive. Instead of having to type a phrase like "Yes, I agree" or "No thanks, I'm not interested," check boxes let your user to quickly indicate preferences or—by omission—rejections among a series of elements. Check boxes are generally used when it doesn't matter how many of the items in a group your user can select. For example, a check box is the method of choice when you see the phrase "Check all that apply" as in a survey or questionnaire.

 To insert a check box, simply click the Check Box Form Field button on the Forms toolbar. By default, a square shaded box the same font size as the current line appears. To see the check box in action, first protect the form. If the check box is the only or first form element on the page, it is highlighted with a slightly thicker border. You check the box by either clicking it once with the mouse or pressing either the Spacebar or the X key; checking the box again by any of the previous methods removes the cross in the box.

Specific options for the check box are fairly limited. To see them, select your check box and then click the Form Field Options button on the Forms toolbar. In the dialog box, you can choose between having the size determined by its surrounding font (the default Auto option) or you can set it by clicking Exactly and setting the size using either the spinner buttons or by typing in a new point size. You can also determine whether the initial condition of the check box is Not Checked or Checked. by choosing the appropriate option button in the Default Value section.

Adding Drop-Down Form Fields

You see examples of drop-down form fields all the time; they're functionally identical to the menus across the top of Word and most other computer programs in use today. Drop-down form fields are used when you want to present your user with a variety of specific options from which only one selection can be made. You might use a drop-down form field in a human resources document where you're asking your applicants to choose between three different dental plans.

This form field is inserted in your document just like the others. Place your insertion point where you want the field to appear. Click the Drop-Down Form Field button from the Forms toolbar. To specify the items in your list, follow these steps:

1. Select the drop-down form field in your document with which you want to work.

 2. Click the Form Field Options button on the Forms toolbar.

3. In the Drop-Down Form Options dialog box shown in Figure 24.3, type the first item in your list in the Drop-Down Item box.

4. Click Add or press Enter.

5. Continue steps 3 and 4 until all items are entered.

6. To remove an item from the list, select it, and click the Remove button.

7. To edit an item in the list, select it, and click the Remove button. Make any necessary changes in the Item box and then click Add.

8. To move any item in the list, select the item, and click the up or down arrows to adjust its position.

9. Click OK when you are finished.

10. Click the Protect Form button to see your drop-down form field in action.

FIG. 24.3
Use the drop-down form field when you want the user to choose from a list of mutually exclusive items.

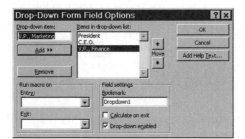

CAUTION
The Drop-Down Form field has a limit of 50 characters.

Advanced Form Field Features

Word 97 has enabled all the form fields with several enhanced features that can make your forms easier to use and help automate your work. One of these features lets you embed several degrees of guidance for each of your form fields. These can range from a simple message in the status bar like "Enter Your Social Security Number" to a more complex Help message that appears when the user presses the F1 key. Another feature enables you to run specific macros upon entering or exiting the form field, which is a great help when you are completing a document based on user responses! The final feature allows your fields to be calculated after the user has entered the information, which is much nicer than having to remember to press the F9 Update fields key all the time.

Adding Help to Your Forms

One of the most time-consuming tasks faced by any office is training. Whenever you introduce a new procedure that's intended to save time, you run the risk of spending even more time training people how to use it. That's why it's recommended that you always make some form of online help available when you are creating a new form to fill out.

Word 97 makes two levels of help available for every form field: Status Bar and Help Key. When enabled, the Status Bar help displays a line of context-sensitive guidance whenever a form field is entered. The Status Bar help can show up to 83 characters. The Help Key feature kicks in when the user presses the F1 key while on a specific form field. You can be much more explicit with the Help Key; you can enter up to 255 characters to be displayed.

Follow these steps to add help to your form fields:

1. Double-click the desired form field.
2. In the Form Field Options dialog box, click the Add Help Text button

    The Form Field Help Text dialog box opens as shown in Figure 24.4.
3. To have context-sensitive help appear in the status bar, click the Status Bar tab.
4. To use an existing phrase, click the AutoText Entry option button and select the entry from the drop-down list.
5. To create a phrase to be used, click the Type Your Own option button and type into the large text area.
6. To have context-sensitive help appear when the F1 key is pressed, click the Help Key (F1) tab and follow steps 4 and 5.
7. Click OK when you are finished.
8. Lock the form using the Protect Form button on the Forms toolbar.

The Help features can be used in conjunction with each other. For example, you might construct a travel reimbursement form. One form field's status bar might say "Enter total airline ticket cost—Press F1 for necessary departmental approvals"; in the same form field's Help Key section you could list the allowable travel expenses per department.

Running Macros from Form Fields

As your Word 97 use gets more sophisticated, you'll likely begin to use macros to automate your work. How do you use macros in a form, where the user could choose from several options? Each form field lets you assign a macro that is performed each time the field is entered or exited. This capability enables you to open additional options or fill out other parts of a form based on user input.

FIG. 24.4
Use the form field Help Key option to provide additional details for each field.

After your macro is written, linking it to a form field is very straight-forward. First, double-click the field to which you want to attach the macro. Second, in the Run Macro On section, choose between Entry or Exit (you can do different macros for each, if you like). Third, select the macro from those listed. Click OK and you're done. As always, make sure to lock the document using the Protect Form button on the Forms toolbar after you've made your modification.

The key to using macros in the form field is to make sure they are in your form template. As you may remember from Chapter 6, "Templates, Wizards, and Add-Ins," (and covered in greater depth in Chapter 30, "Recording and Running Visual Basic Macros"), different templates can store different macros. If the form template is open when you create your macro, choose its file name in the Store Macros In text box of the Record Macro dialog box (or if you're writing your own macro, use the Macro In text box of the Macros dialog box). If you want to use a macro previously written in another document, choose Tools, Templates and Add-Ins, and click the Organizer button. Copy the appropriate macro from one file to another using the Organizer dialog box as described in Chapter 6.

▶ **See** "Understanding Global Templates," **p. 179**

▶ **See** "Moving Macro Project Items Among Templates and Documents," **p. 856**

Calculating Form Input

If you've ever worked with a spreadsheet program like Excel and then had to do calculations in a Word table, you've probably wished that Word had an automatic function that would recalculate the formulas every time a value was changed. Well, sometimes wishes do come true. Normally, if you change any numbers in a Word table, you have to highlight the cell with the formula in it and press F9 to update the fields. With the New Calculate On Exit feature for form fields, you can easily set your Word table so that it automatically recalculates a formula anytime one of the values involved is changed.

The following is a step-by-step example of how you might use this feature:

1. Place text form fields where you want to enter your numbers by clicking the Text Form Field button on the Forms toolbar. Make sure you insert a form field for the total.

2. In all but the final form field (where the total is to appear) first change the Type from General Text to Number in the Text Form Field Options dialog box. Next, check the Calculate on Exit check box. If you like, you can also change the Number Format. Note the name of each form field in the Bookmark text box. (You can also change this to something other than Text1 .)

3. In the text form field that is to display the total, first change the Type to Calculation. Next, put your formula in the Expression text box. You refer to the other form field through their Bookmark name. A typical formula that adds the three form fields above it would read "=SUM(TEXT1,TEXT2,TEXT3)". Do not select the Calculate on Exit option for this final form field box.

> **CAUTION**
>
> The Calculate on Exit feature has no effect on a form field whose type is set to Calculation. This means that you can't use one field as a subtotal and then add another number to it to get a total. Microsoft has confirmed this to be a problem in Word 97 that they are researching.

4. After you've closed the text form field dialog boxes, lock the form by clicking the Protect Form button on the Forms toolbar.

Now any time you enter a number into your form fields the formula recalculates.

Creating Printed Forms

Turning your computer-based form into a printed form takes a little bit of work. One of the major problems comes from the Text Form field. Even though it enables your user to enter an unlimited number of characters, on-screen—and in print—the Text Form field is barely large enough for a two character state abbreviation. The Drop-Down Form field is another area that suffers in the translation from screen to hard copy.

Designing a printed form depends more on Word's drawing tools than on its form tools. A printed form must be laid out explicitly; the lines for an address block must be long enough and far enough apart to make it possible for the information to be properly entered. Any options normally put in a drop-down list must be stated one-by-one. The check box, which looks okay on the screen, might be too small on the printed form to be noticed.

Here are a number of pointers aimed at making your printed form design work faster and more smoothly:

■ If you're designing a form that is intended to be filled out by a typewriter, make the font size 12 or 10 points. The type elements for most typewriters are usually one of these two sizes and it makes aligning the responses much easier.

- Avoid the underscore character when creating multiple long lines. It is much more pleasing to the eye if the line lengths match and much harder to do with the underscore character. Use tabs with the underline attribute instead of the underscore character.

- The Drawing toolbar enables you to create a variety of shapes perfect for forms: straight lines, arrows, boxes, circles, and numerous AutoShapes. Moreover they can all be independently positioned and aligned.

- A table is an easy way to create a series of evenly spaced lines. You can turn off all but the bottom border and set the table height to be exactly a certain point size. The Forms toolbar has both Insert Table and Draw Table buttons.

- If you need to position a element of the form precisely, use a frame. Click the Insert Frame button on the Forms toolbar and drag out the size frame you want. You can specify the size and position by choosing Format, Frame.

- Create a quick list of check box items by choosing Format, Bullets and Numbering and selecting the Open check box bullet. You can select any other symbol as a check box by clicking the Customize button on the Bullets and Numbering dialog box and then selecting the Bullet button. Click the Font button to change the bullet's size. Turn off your check list by clicking the Bullet button on the Formatting toolbar.

Part
VI

Ch
24

Enhancing Your Form with ActiveX Controls

Microsoft has introduced a new technology called ActiveX that incorporates and extends the document-handling capabilities of Object Linking and Embedding (OLE). Word 97 comes with a series of ActiveX controls that greatly embellish what you can do with forms. There is, however, a much steeper learner curve that comes with the power of ActiveX controls. In order to take full advantage of all that they can do, you must become familiar with working with a control's properties and writing Visual Basic for Applications (VBA) code.

While much of the power of ActiveX is geared toward the Internet, you don't have to create a Web page to use these advanced controls. ActiveX controls, such as spin button, can be included in any form that you design. The overall process is the same as using elements from the Forms toolbar—open a new template and layout your new form. Instead of using the Forms toolbar, though, all ActiveX controls are accessed through the Control Toolbox.

Using the Control Toolbox

When it comes to forms, the Control Toolbox is ActiveX central. You insert, edit, code, and run any ActiveX control through the Control Toolbox. To open it, choose View, Toolbars, and then select Control Toolbox. This toolbar is divided into two main areas, one for overall design control and the other for inserting specific ActiveX controls. Table 24.1 gives you an overview of what each button does.

Table 24.1 The Control Toolbox Handles All ActiveX Control Operations

Icon	Name	Description
	Design Mode	A toggle that enables you to create or edit ActiveX controls. When selected, the Exit Design Mode window opens.
	Properties	Opens the Properties dialog box where you can change an ActiveX controls options.
	View Code	Switches to the Visual Basic Editor for creating and editing VBA code.
	Check Box	Inserts a check box with an attached label, generally used to indicate choices that are not mutually exclusive.
	Text Box	Inserts an input area for text.
	Command Button	Creates a user-definable command button for launching macros and VBA code.
	Option Button	Inserts an option button with an attached label, generally used to indicate choices that are mutually exclusive.
	List Box	Inserts a drop-down list where all the items are defined.
	Combo Box	Inserts a drop-down list combining defined items and user-definable items.
	Toggle Button	Inserts a toggle button that is used to control and indicate an on/off state.
	Spin Button	Inserts a spin button that lets the user increment or decrement numbers or items when associated with another control.
	Scroll Bar	Inserts a scroll bar that lets the user move up and down a list when associated with another control.
	Label	Inserts a text label on a form.
	Image	Inserts a picture on a form.
	More Controls	Opens list of additional ActiveX controls available in the system, if any.

To insert any ActiveX controls, you must be in Design mode. Click the Design Mode button to enter and leave this mode. Figure 24.5 shows some of the ActiveX controls prior to being modified. You modify your ActiveX control through the Properties button.

FIG. 24.5

ActiveX controls can greatly increase the flexibility of your forms.

Control Toolbox

Exit Design
Mode button

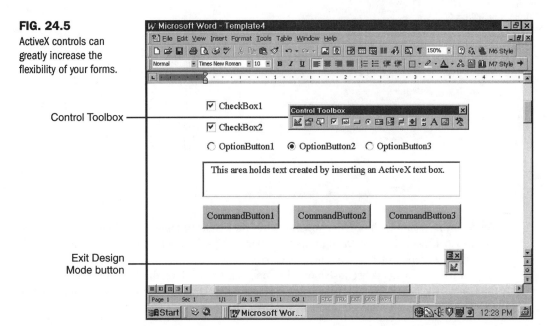

 TIP Clicking any of the ActiveX controls on the Control toolbox inserts the control in a floating frame, by default. To place a control in-line at your insertion point, press Shift when you click the control on the Control toolbox.

Changing a Control's Properties

You might find your first look at an ActiveX control's properties to be somewhat overwhelming. Instead of a dialog box with more or less understandable options, the Properties dialog box of an ActiveX control is a long table displaying a mixture of English and VBA code words. In fact, examining the properties of a control is one entry into the world of VBA programming.

You open the Properties dialog box for a particular ActiveX control by selecting it and then clicking the Properties button on the Control toolbox. As you can see in Figure 24.6, the Properties dialog box is divided into two sections. On the left is a listing of all the individual properties and on the right are their associated values. You can check the properties either alphabetically, by clicking the Alphabetic tab or grouped by category, by clicking the Categorized tab. You can change any property by clicking its value on the right and inputting a new value. Some properties have preset options; these appear with an arrow on the right side when the value box is clicked. Any altered values take effect when you confirm your edit by leaving the value box or pressing Enter.

Part
VI

Ch
24

FIG. 24.6

The Properties dialog box is where you can quickly alter an ActiveX control's appearance or action.

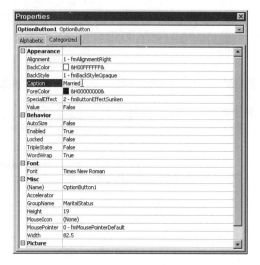

The following example shows how you might use the Properties dialog box to make some changes to a particular ActiveX control, the Option Button. Option Buttons are a useful ActiveX control; they enable you to put mutually exclusive choices on your form and make it impossible for your user to accidentally chose more than one. Start by clicking the Option Button icon on the Control toolbox. Each time you do this it places a new Option Button on your form. You can position your Option Buttons by clicking and dragging them.

When you create your first Option Button, Word appends the label OptionButton1 to it. Successive Option Buttons are labeled OptionButton2 and OptionButton3, and so on. Each button's label is one of its properties. To specify new, appropriate labels for each button, follow these steps:

1. Select the first Option Button.
2. Click the Properties button from the Control Toolbox.
3. On the Categorized tab, find the Appearance category.
4. Click in the right box next to Caption and double-click the current caption.
5. Type your new label and press Enter to confirm. The Caption property is updated and your new label appears next to the Option Button.
6. Click the remaining Option Buttons and follow steps 3-5. You don't have to close the Properties dialog box in between changing each Option Button.
7. Close the Properties dialog box by clicking its Close button in the upper-right corner.

 You can also select different ActiveX controls to edit by selecting their name from the Title text box at the top of the Properties dialog box. Click the arrow on the right to see a listing of available elements in your document.

One of the key features of the ActiveX Option Button is that it enables you to create groups where the choices are mutually exclusive. In order to use more than one group on your form—one for marital status, another for gender, and so on, you have to specify the name of each group and associate it to the proper Option Buttons. This is also handled through the Properties dialog box. You'll find GroupName under the Misc category. By default, there is no GroupName assigned and the value box is blank. Enter the same value in the GroupName property for each button in that group. If you don't differentiate the different groups, all the options buttons in your form are considered to be in the same no name group; your user can only choose one Option Button on the form.

 TIP Word includes a very extensive help system on VBA. To access it, open the ActiveX Control Properties dialog box, click one of the properties, and then press F1.

Writing ActiveX Code

Changing the properties of an ActiveX control will only take you so far. If you really want to activate your form, you need to write VBA code. When you click the View Code button in the Control toolbox, Microsoft Visual Basic opens. If you're unfamiliar with programming in general or Visual Basic in particular, you might want to look at Chapters 30 and 31 to understand the concepts a little better. Chapters 32 through 34 dig a little more deeply into the world of VBA. Extensive ActiveX VBA programming is beyond the scope of this chapter, but you will see how you can begin to input your code.

Some ActiveX controls require VBA programming to be initialized and have the proper values inserted when the form opens. The drop-down box is a good example. With the Forms toolbar, clicking the Drop-Down Form Field's options enables you to enter the items in the list. On the other hand, similar ActiveX controls, the List Box and the Combo Box, need to be initialized through VBA. Take a look at the Combo Box to see how it's done.

The Combo Box is a specialized version of the Drop-Down Form Field. In addition to giving the user a specific list of items to choose from, the Combo Box also enables the user to input his or her own option. Follow these steps to set up a Combo Box in a Form template:

1. Open or create your template form.
2. Insert an ActiveX Combo Box control by clicking the Combo Box button on the Control Toolbox.
3. Place your Combo Box by clicking and dragging it on the form. You can resize it by clicking and dragging its sizing handles.
4. Click the View Code button on the Control Toolbox to open the Visual Basic editor. You can also double-click the inserted control.

   In the Visual Basic editor, the default object and procedure appear on the right pane of the window.
5. Click the arrow in the Object drop-down list box above the code on the left to display other Visual Basic objects and select the Document object.

6. Click the arrow in the Procedure drop-down list box above the code on the right to display other Visual Basic procedures and select New.

A new subroutine, `Private Sub Document_New()`, appears in the code window.

7. In between the lines `Private Sub…` and `End Sub`, type the following code:

`AddItem.ComboBox1("Value")`

Substitute your value in the parenthesis. You can add as many items as you like. Place each AddItem command on a separate line.

8. Click the Save button on the Visual Basic editor toolbar.

9. Save and close your template form.

Figure 24.7 shows the code and the result when a document is opened based on the Form template created previously. When the Form template is saved the code actually becomes part of the modified control. This enables you to distribute your enhanced form without having to attach any macros as with the standard form fields.

FIG. 24.7
VBA code gives you complete control over your ActiveX objects.

Resulting example ————

Visual Basic editor ————

Example code for combo box ————

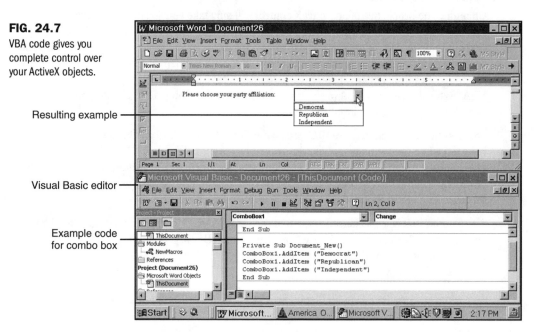

Working with Prompting Forms

Word 97 includes a new feature that enables you, as the form creator, to ask your form users a series of questions and then automatically fills out the form based on their answers. This technique is very useful when it comes to filling out a contract or other document that has a lot of boilerplate text surrounding a few changing entries.

Follow these steps to build a form that prompts the user:

1. Create or open a template that holds your form elements.

2. Place your insertion point where you want the form field response to appear.

3. Choose Insert, Field to open the Field dialog box.

4. From the Categories list, select Mail Merge.

5. From the Field Names list, select Fill-In.

6. Click in the box after the field code "FILLIN" and type the prompt you want the user to see. Be sure to include it in quotes.

7. To insert any default, placeholder text, click the Options button. From the Options dialog box, select \d; click the Add to Field, and type your default text, again in quotes. Click OK to close this dialog box.

8. If you want the formatting of your field to update when entered, clear the Preserve Formatting During Updates check box.

9. Click OK when you have finished.

10. Word displays an example of what your prompt will look like (see Figure 24.8). Click OK.

Part
VI

Ch
24

 T I P It's a good idea to use the \d option to put some default text in your form—even if the default "text" is a couple of spaces. Otherwise, the form field is zero characters wide and impossible to see. You might find it helpful to use the angle bracket characters to make your placeholding text really stand out, like this example shown in Figure 24.8.

FIG. 24.8
The Fill-In field lets you complete your form by answering prompted questions.

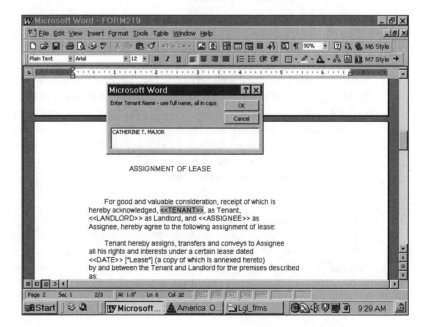

When you create a new form based on the protected and saved template, Word runs through the prompts one-by-one. When all the prompts have been answered, the text is inserted into the proper places and this part of your document is complete.

Protecting Your Form from Unauthorized Change

By now you're familiar with locking the document through the Protect Form button on the Forms toolbar. It is necessary to protect the form in order to activate many of the form functions such as check boxes and drop-down lists. In some situations, this level of protection is sufficient; however, there are circumstances where access to the form needs to be more rigorously controlled.

A more elaborate method of document protection is available by choosing Tools, Protect Document. From the Protect Document dialog box that opens, (see Figure 24.9) you can protect specifically for forms (or comments or tracked changes) and add a password. After the password is enabled, the document can't be unlocked without it.

FIG. 24.9

The Protect Document dialog box enables you to password-protect specific sections of your document.

Moreover, you can lock specific sections of a document and leave others unlocked. This technique works well when you want to use form fields in part of your document, but leave the remainder open for editing. You separate your document into sections by choosing Insert, Break and selecting Continuous Section Break. To protect a specific section, first choose Tools, Protect Document. Then, after you've clicked Forms in the Protect Document dialog box, click the Sections button. (If the Sections button is not available, either Forms is not selected or you don't have any continuous section breaks in the document). The Sections dialog box lists all available sections by number (Section 1, Section 2, and so on) with a check box next to the name. Check off all the sections to be protected. Click OK when you're done and OK again to close the Protect Document dialog box.

> **CAUTION**
>
> If you enter text in a form field when the form is protected, and then unprotect it and re-protect it, Word clears all form fields and the text is lost. You can preserve text in a field by selecting the field and pressing Ctrl+F11. This locks the selected Text Form field. This works only with Text Form fields.

Saving Your Form

It's essential to remember that forms are best based on templates. While you can make a form from a regular document, you would have to re-create the form each time you used it. If you want your users to be able to access the form by choosing File, New and opening the Template dialog box, you must save the form in the designated Template folder or one of its subfolders.

By default, document templates are stored in the Templates folder of the Microsoft Office (or Microsoft Word) folder. You can verify—and change—that by choosing Tools, Options and clicking the File Locations tab. You'll find the location listed next to the User Templates file type. To change the default template location, select User Templates and click the Modify button. Choose a new directory from the Modify Location dialog box and click OK. If you're on a network, you might also have the Workgroup Templates location set; only your network administrator can change this location.

Part
VI

Ch
24

Where do you save completed forms that are based on the template? Anywhere you like. These are considered to be normal Word documents and can be filed in any manner you see fit.

Saving Only the Data in a Form

One of the key reasons for using a form is to collect data. Data is best accessed through a database where it can be sorted, filtered, and output in various forms. Word 97 gives you an easy method to extract the information from a filled-out form without having to re-enter it into a database; you can save only the data in a form.

To save just the data from a form, follow these steps:

1. After your form has been filled out, click the Save button on the Standard toolbar.
2. Click the Options button on the Save As dialog box.
3. Check the Save Data Only for Forms check box and click OK.
4. Change the file type to Text Only.
5. Choose a file name and folder location for your file. Click OK.

 T I P If you want to save all your forms as data-only, you can choose Tools, Options, click the Save tab and then enable the Save Data Only for Forms check box.

When Word saves just the form data, it uses comma-delimited fields. You might be familiar with the concept of a comma-delimited field if you've worked with mail merges. The information from each field is placed in quotes and separated by commas. For example, one data file might look like this: "John", "Johnson", "123 Somter Street", "Avery", "SC", "29678".

This file format is used for both Text Form fields and Drop-Down Form fields. Information returned from a Check Box Form field is handled slightly differently. A checked box shows up as a 1 while an unchecked box is a 0. Neither are in quotes.

T I P You can also print just the data from the form; use this feature when you want your data to appear on preprinted forms. To set this up, choose Tools, Options and on the Print tab, check the box next to Print Data Only For Forms. The data prints in the same location on the page as it does on-screen.

After you have saved your forms as data, the information can be imported into an existing database in a program like Microsoft Access. Almost any database program can read comma-delimited fields saved in a text file. If you speak VBA (Visual Basic for Applications) you could write a macro to append the information in each form into one master file to make importing even easier.

Distributing Your Forms

Forms can be sent around pretty much like any file. You can copy them to a floppy, e-mail them as an attachment, or put them in a network folder accessible by your target audience. You can post them on a Web site so that the form can be filled out by anyone in the world—or you could post it on your company's intranet to keep its access in-house.

Naturally, you can also print them and distribute them the old fashioned way as well, by hand, complete with a number 2 sharpened pencil.

TROUBLESHOOTING

My form fields keep disappearing. What's going wrong? Always check to make sure your forms are locked. If the form isn't locked, selecting a form field for entry is just like highlighting a word or a block of text; the next character you enter erases whatever is selected. Always keep your Forms toolbar open and available when you are creating or editing a form. It's much easier to remember to click the Protect Form button than it is to choose Tools, Protect Document.

I can't find my form fields. Check your options (Tools, Options). Chances are you have the Field Codes box on the View tab enabled. This overrides the form fields and instead of text, check boxes, or drop-down form fields the user sees {FORMTEXT}, {FORMCHECKBOX}, or {FORMDROPDOWN}.

How do I get Word to tab through my form fields in the proper order? By default, the tabbing order is set by placement on the page. The tabs start in the form field closest to the top of the page and farthest left. From there it goes left-to-right and down. However, if you use the frames to precisely position your form fields, the tabs may not go in the order you desired. You can force Word to go where you want by using the On Exit Macro function.

To build the macro you need to know the bookmark name of the form field you are tabbing to. Double-click the form field and note the name in the Bookmark text box. Then choose Tools, Macro, Macros and select Create. Be sure to put the macro in the Form template on which you are working. Type the following code in the Visual Basic editor:

```
Selection.Goto What:=wdGoToBookmark, Name:="FormFieldName"
```

where "FormFieldName" is the bookmark name of your form field.

How can I include special characters in my forms? If you use the Fill-In field for prompting your users, you have to take extra steps to use certain characters in your prompt. For example, let's say you wanted your prompt to say: "Type "M" or "F" in the box." If you put that sentence next to the Fill-In field as is, Word sees only the first pair of quotes and your prompt would read: "Type." You must preface the quote with a backslash character to have it appear correctly. Therefore the proper form field line would read:

```
FILLIN "Type \"M\" or \"F\" in the box."
```

Notice that the backslash goes before each quote, not just each quote pair. Similarly, if you ever want to have a backslash appear in your Fill-In prompt, you must use a extra backslash before it. For example:

```
FILLIN "Name the file to be stored in c:\\Invoices\\1997"
```

 TIP When creating macros to alter the tabbing order, it's good to change the bookmark names of the form field so that they're meaningful. "MaritalStatusBox" is far easier to remember than "Checkbox97." Similarly, name your macros so that you can identify them by sight, for example, "GotoMaritalStatus" rather than "Macro103."

Part
VI

Ch
24

From Here...

In this chapter, you learned how to create basic forms as well as forms that prompt the user and forms that take advantage of ActiveX technology. Next, you might want to move on the following chapters:

- Take another look at how to manage templates as covered in Chapter 6, " Templates, Wizards, and Add-ins."

- Review how to use the drawing tools to create fancier forms. See Chapter 21, " Drawing in Word."

- Explore the potentials of working with macros. See Chapter 30, "Recording and Running Visual Basic Macros."

- Learn more about writing Visual Basic for Applications programs in Chapter 31, "Getting Started with VBA," and learn by example in Chapters 32-34.

CHAPTER 25

Automating Your Documents with Field Codes

by Joe Lowery

In the previous chapter you saw how forms could help speed document production. This chapter offers an in-depth look at the underlying mechanism for automating your document: field codes. ■

Starting out with fields

Fields are a great way to make the most of information already existing in your document. You'll learn the basic structure of fields and see which fields are already working for you.

Detailing field codes

There are nine different field code categories. This section gets into the nitty-gritty of working with field codes with syntax and descriptions of every field code.

Maintaining your fields

Fields need information to be useful. Here's how to ensure you have the most current data associated with your fields. You'll learn about linking, updating, and locking your document's fields, selectively or all at the same time.

Representing picture-perfect fields

What good is the automatic text insertion offered by fields, if it doesn't look the way you want it to? Word 97's text and numeric "picture switches" give your information exactly the right look.

Solving field problems

Is it a Field of Dreams? Or a mine field? Here's your map through the hot-spots highlighting some of the most common problems with fields.

What Fields Can Do for You and Your Organization

Here's the technical definition of a field: A field is a placeholder for data that Word automatically inserts in your document. Here's the real-world definition: a field is a time-saver. Word 97 automates your document production by placing existing information—whether input by yourself, someone else, or calculated by Word—into designated fields.

You could do everything required of you without ever touching a field, but who has that much time? Sure, you could update the page numbers by hand or retype the document author's name on every page, but there is no reason for you to do so—it's why fields were designed. The time invested in mastering even a few fields and their options is minuscule compared to the amount of time you save with each new document.

Fields are frequently the short answer to the often asked question, "How do I (fill-in-the-blank) in Word 97?" It's not that you have to memorize every field and all of their options. The best course is to familiarize yourself with the possibilities fields offer. Then, when you ask yourself the "how do I" question, you can respond, "Fields, of course." In fact, you'll see in the next section that you're probably already using fields and don't even know it.

Fields You May Already Be Using

One of the most common word processing functions is automatic page numbering. When you choose Insert, Page Number, just what does Word insert? You guessed it, a field. The same is true when you want to indicate the total number of pages in a document as well, such as "Page 1 of 23"—this format uses two fields, one for the current page number and one for the total number of pages.

Another common field used is the date field. When writing repetitive letters or time-stamping documents, it's amazing how much time you can save by letting Word put in the current date and time. Of course, it's essential that your computer be set for the right date and time. Luckily, most of today's computer systems have a built-in clock battery to keep the date current—and even correct for daylight savings time.

Perhaps the single largest application of field codes is the Mail Merge tool. Every merge field that you insert is a specialized field code, as are all of the word fields such as Next Record. Although you could insert all the field codes necessary to create a mail merge main document by hand, it's far simpler to choose Tools, Mail Merge and use the Mail Merge toolbar. However, there are field codes used in merges that can also be used in other ways, as you saw with the FILLIN field code in Chapter 22, "Using Microsoft Graph."

▶ **See** "An Overview of Word's Mail Merge," **p. 372**

Viewing Fields

What does a field code look like? Try this: open a document that uses Automatic Page Numbering. Make sure you're in Page Layout view to see the headers and footers and press Alt+F9.

Suddenly your innocuous "Page 3 of 17" is revealed to be something moderately incomprehensible like {PAGE *MERGEFORMAT} of {NUMPAGES *MERGEFORMAT}. Press Alt+F9 again to return to Normal view.

If you want to work with the field codes visible all the time, you can set your options to do so. Choose Tools, Options, and click the View tab of the Option dialog box. Check the Field Codes check box in the Show section. If you pressed Alt+F9 already and are currently showing the field codes in your document, you'll find the Field Codes box already checked.

When you insert a field code, the default is for it to be shaded a medium gray when selected. You can change this by first choosing Tools, Options, and then selecting the View tab. Click the arrow next to the Field Shading drop-down list box to see the other options, as shown in Figure 25.1. You can choose Never to eliminate field code shading entirely—which would mean that you could never distinguish your field codes from the rest of your document. You can choose Always to force the field code to continually show up on-screen (although it never prints).

FIG. 25.1

You set your field codes options in the View tab of the Options dialog box.

Part

VI

Ch

25

Inserting a Field

There are numerous specialized ways to insert a field—Insert Date, Insert Page Number, and the Mail Merge tools among them—but there's one place where you can find *all* the field codes and their options. By choosing Insert, Field to open the Field dialog box, you can see the field codes listed by category or alphabetically. The Field dialog box also provides prompts for each field code and their associated options.

Follow these steps to insert a field code into your document:

1. Choose Insert, Field. The Field dialog box opens as shown in Figure 25.2.
2. To choose a field code from an alphabetical list, select All in the Categories column.

3. To choose a field code from a specific kind, select one of the nine named options in the C̲ategories column.

4. Select a field code from the Field N̲ames list in the right column. The field code template is displayed next to F̲ield Codes with available options and switches.

5. Enter any needed text in the Field Code text box.

6. To add any switches, click the O̲ptions button.

7. Click OK when you're finished.

FIG. 25.2

Choose from over 75 field codes through the Field dialog box.

Elements of a Field

After you have inserted any field, press Alt+F9 to see it's inner workings. All field codes have three basic parts: the delimiters, the field name, and the instructions.

The delimiters are what allow Word to recognize the field code as a field code and they look like curly braces {}. However, the delimiters only look like curly braces—you can't type them in from the keyboard, add the field code information, and expect them to work. To insert a field code by hand, press Ctrl+F9. This places a pair of curly brace field code delimiters in a shaded area, ready for you to put in the other elements.

The second part of a field code is the field code name. Although it is not case sensitive if you misspell the name (you can put in "AutoNum", "AUTONUM" or "autonum", for example), the field won't work correctly. In fact, it won't work at all.

The instructions are the specifics for each field code. There are four different types of instructions:

■ *Bookmarks* give a field code a reference point in your document. For example, using {INCLUDETEXT *"Filename"* Bookmark} lets you include a bookmarked portion of a text from another file.

■ *Expressions* are the mathematical and relational connection to field codes. For example, using {=SubTotal+ShipCost} gives you the total of bookmarked subtotal and shipping cost figures. In this example, the equal sign is actually the field code name.

■ *Text* enables you to specify prompts or information to be placed in the document, verbatim. For example, using {FILLIN "Please enter your mother's maiden name."} displays the quoted text as a prompt in a dialog box.

■ *Switches* are the options for a field code. For example, using {PAGE * ROMAN} sets the page numbering command to use uppercase roman numerals (I, II, III, and so on) instead of the default Arabic numerals (1, 2, 3, and so on).

Of the four instructions, switches are by far the most complex. They are covered more extensively in the next section.

 It's a good habit to always put any needed text following the field code word in quotes. Single words and numbers can be entered without quotation marks, but if you put quotes around everything, you won't have to think about it.

Field Switches

Switches are optional instructions that let you customize a field code. Switches begin with a backslash, the (\) character, followed by a character or letter. What switches do depends entirely on the field code. A field code can have any number of switches or none at all. You can see which switches are available for each field code by selecting the field code and clicking the Option button in the Field dialog box. This opens the Field Option dialog box as shown in Figure 25.3. If the Option button does not become active that means that there are no switches for the selected field code.

FIG. 25.3

Use the Option button in the Field Options dialog box to implement various field code switches.

If you make a mistake when choosing your switches, Word lets you know after you confirm your options by closing the Form dialog box. Instead of inserting your field code, Word puts an error code in its place. For example, if you click two different date formats, you'll see `Error! Too many picture switches defined`. Click the Undo button to remove the error code (or highlight and delete it) and insert your field code again.

N O T E The field code options use the term *picture* when referring to any formatting option. You'll see the references to both Date-Time Picture Switches and Numeric Picture Switches. ■

Field Characters

Because switches use quotation marks and the backslash character for special functions, you have to take extra steps if you want to use either quotes or a backslash in your field code. The key is to use the backslash character as the escape character to indicate a special circumstance. Here's how it works:

■ To include quotation marks as part of a field code, place a backslash character before each quote mark. For example, if you want to prompt your users with a FILLIN field code to put their entries in a particular format, your entry in the Field Code text box would read as follows:

```
FILLIN "Please enter the expiration date in the \"MM-DD\" format."
```

■ To use the backslash character as part of a field code, place an additional backslash in front of the character. For example to include text with a specific file name, you must use the backslash character to create the path name, like this:

```
INCLUDETEXT "c:\\my documents\\business\\boilerplate1.doc"
```

Types of Fields

Field codes are organized according to their function. When you open the Field dialog box by choosing Insert, Field, you'll find nine different groupings in the Categories column. As previously noted, click any of the categories to bring up the corresponding entries in the Field Names column.

Date and Time Fields

As you would expect, the Date and Time fields let you insert the current date and time into your document. What you might not know, however, is that these fields can also tell you when a document was created, saved, printed—even the total amount of time spent editing it. These field codes are often used in headers and footers to differentiate different draft documents. Table 25.1 describes the field codes found under the Date and Time category.

Table 25.1 Date and Time Field Codes

Field Name	Format	Description
CreateDate	CreateDate [\@"Date-Time Picture"]	Inserts the date and time a document was created.
Date	Date [\@"Date-Time Picture"] [Switches]	Inserts the current date.
EditTime	EditTime	Inserts the total editing time in minutes.
PrintDate	PrintDate [\@"Date-Time Picture"]	Inserts the date and time the document was last printed.

Field Name	Format	Description
SaveDate	SaveDate [\@"Date-Time Picture"]	Inserts the date and time the document was last saved.
Time	Time [\@"Date-Time Picture"] [Switches]	Inserts the current time.

Document Automation Fields

The Document Automation fields bring a whole new level of embedded interactivity to your documents. A couple of the field codes (Compare and If) are used to facilitate programming-like branching within the document. Two others (GoToButton and MacroButton) enable you to place command-type buttons in your document. Another (DocVariable) provides a valuable link to VBA programming. Table 25.2 describes the Document Automation fields.

Table 25.2	Document Automation Fields	
Field Name	**Format**	**Description**
Compare	Compare Expression1 Operator Expression2	Compares the two values using the specified operator and returns 1 if true and 0 if false.
DocVariable	DocVariable "Name"	Inserts the value of the document variable named.
GoToButton	GoToButton Destination DisplayText	Jumps to a new location in the document.
If	If Expression1 Operator Expression2 TrueText FalseText	Compares two values and inserts the appropriate text.
MacroButton	MacroButton MacroName DisplayText	Runs the named macro.
Print	Print "PrintCommands"	Sends printer-control code characters to the selected printer.

Part
VI

Ch
25

In order to see the result from many of the field codes, including those in the Document Automation category, the document must be locked. As you may remember from Chapter 24, "Creating Electronic and Printed Forms," you do this by either selecting Tools, Protect Document, and choosing the Forms option or by clicking the Protect Form button on the Forms toolbar.

CAUTION

The Print field code works well with a PostScript printer, or a Hewlett-Packard LaserJet Series II or Series III printer, but it may not work properly with another type of laser printer. The Print field code works with a dot-matrix printer only if the printer supports the PassThrough command.

Document Information Fields

Word keeps track of a lot of information about each document. Some of the information requires your input through the Summary tab of the Properties dialog box, such as the Author's name. Other information, such as a document's word count, is calculated by Word and continually updated. All of it can be brought into play through the Document Information field codes.

The Document Information field codes are generally used to make obvious some facet of the document. Quite often a company requires that each document display its path and filename or other such information for easy retrieval. Information that gives a correct updated view of the current document, such as the word count, is also extremely useful. Table 25.3 describes the Document Information field codes.

Table 25.3   Document Information Fields

Field Name	Format	Description
Author	Author ["NewName"]	Inserts Author's name from the Properties dialog box, unless a new name is given.
Comments	Comments ["NewComments"]	Inserts the Comments from the Properties dialog box, unless new comments are given.
DocProperty	DocProperty "Name"	Inserts the value of the property chosen through the Options button.
FileName	FileName [Switches]	Inserts the name and/or path of the file.
FileSize	FileSize [Switches]	Inserts the file size of the current document.
Info	Info [InfoType] [Switches]	Inserts the value of the InfoType as chosen through the Options button.
Keywords	Keywords "NewKeywords"	Inserts the keywords from the Properties dialog box, unless new keywords are given.
LastSavedBy	LastSavedBy	Inserts the name of the last person who saved the current document.
NumChars	NumChars	Inserts the total number of characters in the document.
NumPages	NumPages	Inserts the total number of pages in the document.
NumWords	NumWords	Inserts the total number of words in the document.
Subject	Subject "NewSubject"	Inserts the subject from the Properties dialog box, unless a new subject is given.

Field Name	Format	Description
Template	Template [Switches]	Inserts the name and path of the template, if any, attached to the document.
Title	Title "NewTitle"	Inserts the title from the Properties dialog box, unless a new title is given.

CAUTION

There's a problem with the NumPages field code in Word 97. It doesn't automatically update when you open a previously saved file that includes the field code. If you use a "Page X of X" type footer, you'll get field results like "Page 3 of 1." To work around this problem, switch document views or print the document and the field code will update properly.

Equations and Formulas Fields

If you've ever used a table to calculate a column of numbers you've used one of the Equations and Formula field codes. When you choose Table, Formula, Word inserts a = (Formula) field code, often in the form "=SUM(ABOVE)". In addition, you can also use an Equations and Formula field code to insert a specialized math element like a fraction or a radical, or completely control the placement of some text.

Use the Equations and Formula field code when you're doing just a little math. If you're doing extensive calculations, you're probably better off building your table in Excel and importing or linking it. Likewise, for complex formula representation, use the Equation Editor.

▶ **See** "Using Equation Editor 3.0," **p. 780**

For straightforward table formulas or simple mathematical equation, however, these math specific fields codes are very quick and useful. Table 24.4 describes the Equations and Formula fields.

Table 25.4   Equation and Formula Fields

Field Name	Format	Description
= (Formula)	= Formula [Bookmark] [*Numeric-Picture]	Calculates a number using a mathematical expression.
Advance	Advance [Switches]	Offsets following text right, left, up, or down, or to a specific horizontal or vertical position.
Eq (Equation)	Eq Instructions	Inserts a mathematical expression.
Symbol	Symbol CharNum [Switches]	Inserts the character specified by the ANSI character number.

Part
VI

Ch
25

> **CAUTION**
>
> There's a bug in the = (Formula) field code that won't let you calculate numbers in more than 85 rows using the ABOVE or BELOW keywords. If, for example, your formula "=SUM(ABOVE)" or "=COUNT(BELOW)" refers to more than 85 numbers, the result will be incorrect. As a workaround, specify the cell range, like this "=SUM(A1:A87)".

Index and Tables Fields

By far the easiest way to create an index, table of contents, or table of authorities is through the Insert, Index and Tables menu option. What you may not realize is that when Word inserts an index or table of contents, it is actually inserting a field code. To verify this, press Alt+F9 while looking at a generated table of contents. All of your text disappears to be replaced by something like {TOC \O "1-4"} which is field code lingo for a table of contents created by looking at the outline styles and showing levels 1 through 4.

If you do a lot of work with indices, table of contents, or table of authorities, it's a good idea to familiarize yourself with their respective field codes. You can quickly change the field code without having to open the Index and Tables dialog box, make your modification and then re-insert the table of contents. If, for instance, you wanted to show only the first three levels in the previous example, all you have to do is press Alt+F9, change "1-4" to "1-3" and press F9. You'll get a dialog box asking if you want to update just the pages or the entire table. Choose Entire Table and click OK. The table regenerates.

Table 25.5 lists Index and Tables fields available to Word 97 users.

Table 25.5 Index and Tables Fields

Field Name	Format	Description
Index	Index [Switches]	Generates and inserts an index.
RD	RD "FileName"	Includes a file while creating an Index, TOC, or TOA.
TA	TA [Switches]	Marks a table of authorities entry.
TC	TC "Text" [Switches]	Marks a table of contents entry.
TOA	TOA [Switches]	Generates and inserts a table of authorities.
TOC	TOC [Switches]	Generates and inserts a table of contents.
XE	XE "Text" [Switches]	Marks an index entry.

 The TA, TC, and XE field codes are all formatted as hidden text. In order to reveal them, click the Show/Hide ¶ button.

Links and Reference Fields

When your document begins to connect with other documents or use internal cross-references, the Links and Reference fields come into play. These fields let you include text, pictures, or links—both from within the document and without—with an added level of flexibility. The AutoText field, for example, lets you insert an AutoText entry as a field rather than as retyped text. This means that if you edit your original AutoText entry and then update the document, all your AutoText fields will reflect the changes.

One of the most used of the Links and Reference fields is the Ref field. The Ref field is used to insert any text marked by a bookmark. For most bookmarks, you can use the abbreviated version of the command and just put the bookmark name in the field delimiters, like this: {Bookmark1}. However, for any bookmark with the same name as a Word field, you must use the Ref keyword. If, for example your bookmark name was "Author," you would have to use {Ref "Author"} to insert your text; otherwise Word inserts the text associated with the document property Author. Table 25.6 describes all the Links and Reference fields.

Table 25.6 Links and Reference Fields

Field Name	Format	Description
AutoText	AutoText AutoTextEntry	Inserts a predefined AutoText entry.
AutoTextList	AutoTextList "Literal Text"	Displays a list of AutoText entries for insertion.
Hyperlink	Hyperlink "Filename" [Switches]	Jumps to the specified file or place in document.
IncludePicture	IncludePicture "Filename" [Switches]	Inserts the named image.
IncludeText	IncludeText [Bookmark] "Filename" [Switches]	Inserts the named document or the bookmarked contents.
Link	Link ClassName "FileName" [PlaceReference] [Switches]	Set up a link with content from another application.
NoteRef	NoteRef Bookmark [Switches]	Inserts the number of a bookmarked footnote or endnote.
PageRef	PageRef Bookmark [Switches]	Inserts the page number of a bookmark.
Quote	Quote "Literal Text"	Inserts the indicated text into the document.
Ref	[Ref] Bookmark [Switches]	Inserts the contents of the named bookmark.
StyleRef	StyleRef StyleIdentifier [Switches]	Inserts text formatted with the specified style.

Part
VI

Ch
25

Two Links and Reference fields, new to Word 97, bring a World Wide Web-like interface to your documents. The AutoTextList field embeds an inline option list that enables the user to choose which AutoText entry to insert. As shown in Figure 25.4, the user right-clicks the field and a list of pertinent AutoText entries appears. The second new field is the Hyperlink field and is what Word 97 puts in your document when you choose Insert, Hyperlink. Hyperlinks let you jump to different places in a document, different documents, or even different Web sites.

▶ **See** "Using Hyperlinks," **p. 521**

FIG. 25.4

The AutoTextList field lets your users choose from a defined list of options.

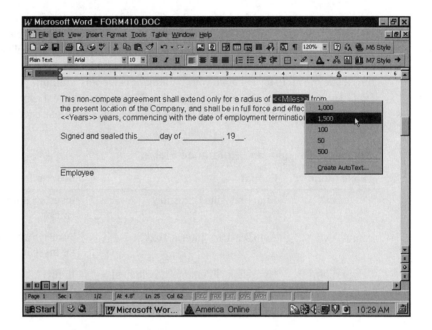

Mail Merge Fields

As with the Index and Tables field codes, the best way to use most of the Mail Merge field codes is through the tool designed for their use: the Mail Merge Helper. However, you may encounter situations where you need to tweak the codes inserted by Word to get the results you need. If you press Alt+F9 while looking at your main mail merge document, you'll see a host of field codes, all of which are categorized as Mail Merge field codes.

You saw in the previous chapter on forms how the Fill-In field could be used outside of a mail merge to automate your documents. This is true of another field, the Ask field. The Ask field puts up a dialog box requesting input like Fill-In, but instead of inserting it, the Ask field code assigns the answer to a bookmark. The bookmark can then be referenced, compared, and otherwise treated like a variable in programming. Another Mail Merge field code, Set, lets you assign bookmarks directly. A description of all the Mail Merge fields can be found in Table 25.7.

Table 25.7 Mail Merge Fields

Field Name	Format	Description
Ask	Ask Bookmark "Prompt" [Switches]	Displays a dialog box that prompts for text to be assigned to a bookmark.
Compare	Compare Expression1 Operator Expression2	Compares the two values using the specified operator and returns 1 if True and 0 if False.
Database	Database [Switches]	Inserts a Word table containing the result of a database query.
Fill-in	Fillin ["Prompt"] [Switches]	Displays a dialog box that prompts for text to be inserted into the document.
If	If Expression1 Operator Expression2 TrueText FalseText	Compares two values and inserts the appropriate text.
MergeField	MergeField FieldName	Merges data from the data source into the main document.
MergeRec	MergeRec	Inserts the number of the current data record.
MergeSec	MergeSec	Inserts the Number of successfully merged records.
Next	Next	Forces the next data record to be merged in the same document as the previous record.
NextIf	NextIf Expression1 Operator Expression2	Compares two values and merges the next data record in the same document if True.
Set	Set Bookmark "Text"	Assigns named text to a bookmark.
SkipIf	SkipIf Expression1 Operator Expression2	Compares two values and skips the next data record if True.

Part
VI

Ch
25

Numbering Fields

One of the most effective time-saving tools in Word 97's repertoire is automatic numbering. Whether you're working from an detailed outline, a legal document, or just an ordinary numbered list, being able to make your additions, deletions, and edits without having to renumber everything is almost worth the price of the program. The Numbering fields embrace and extend the capabilities found under the Numbering button on the Formatting toolbar. Table 25.8 describes the Numbering fields.

Table 25.8 Numbering Fields

Field Name	Format	Description
AutoNum	AutoNum	Automatically numbers paragraphs sequentially.
AutoNumLgl	AutoNumLgl	Automatically numbers paragraphs in legal outline format.
AutoNumOut	AutoNumOut	Automatically numbers paragraphs in standard outline format.
Barcode	Barcode \u "LiteralText " or Bookmark \b [Switches]	Inserts a bar code readable by the post office.
ListNum	ListNum ["Name"] [Switches]	Inserts the next number of a named item.
Page	Page [* Format Switch]	Inserts the current page number.
RevNum	RevNum	Inserts the number of document revisions which is equal to the number of times a document has been saved.
Section	Section	Inserts the current section number.
SectionPages	SectionPages	Inserts the number of pages in the current section.
Seq (Sequence)	Seq Identifier [Bookmark] [Switches]	Inserts the next sequential number for the named item.

New to Word 97's numbering features is the ListNum field. This field combines the functionality of the AutoNum, AutoNumLgl, AutoNumOut, and the Seq fields while adding a few new wrinkles of its own. ListNum enables you to create many different lists and keep track of the numbering for each of them, separately. For example, the same document could have separate lists of figures, illustrations, tables, and graphs.

Moreover, ListNum doesn't just number paragraphs; it lets you put numbers anywhere in a paragraph, like the Seq field. However, unlike the Seq field, ListNum lets you specify the level in the list. ListNum combines the sophisticated level-handling of an outline numbering system with flexible placement control. This is a boon to lawyers and any other business creating contracts where numbering references are essential.

User Information Fields

The User Information fields let you access the name, address, and initials of the currently registered Word 97 user. You can access this data by choosing Tools, Options and clicking the User Information tab as shown in Figure 25.5. Use these fields when you want to easily put your name on a Prepared by: line. Using these fields in templates is a good way to personalize the work of an entire office with just one file. The User Information fields are described in Table 25.9.

FIG. 25.5

The User Information fields pull data from the User Information tab of the Option dialog box.

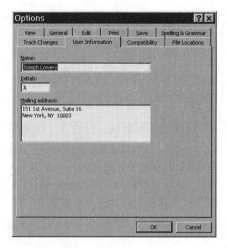

Table 25.9   User Information Fields

Field Name	Format	Description
UserAddress	UserAddress "NewAddress"	Inserts the user address.
UserInitials	UserInitials "NewInitials"	Inserts the user initials.
UserName	UserName "NewName"	Inserts the user name.

 You can override the User Information settings by putting new text following the field code. For example {UserName "Sherman Hornsworth"} inserts the new name in place of the one currently in the User Information settings.

Updating Fields

Word 97's field capabilities are really terrific; you can cross-reference, number, calculate editing time, and so much more. However, if you edit your document, only some changes are incorporated automatically. With few exceptions, fields have to be updated manually.

It's very simple to update a field. Select the field and press F9. To update all the fields in a document, choose Edit, Select All and then press F9. If you've used the Link field code to update information linked to another Word document, press Ctrl+Shift+F7.

CAUTION

Keep in mind that if you update all the fields in an entire document, you're updating any indexes, tables of contents, tables of authorities, and so on that might be in the document. Unfortunately, if you've tweaked the formatting of any of these items, the formatting is lost during the update. As you'll see in the next section, you can lock a field so that it doesn't update.

There's a way to make sure that you have the most current information anytime you plan to print your document. Choose Tools, Options and click the Print tab. In the Print Options tab, enable the Update Fields check box. This automatically updates all the fields in the document. While you're in the Print Options tab, if you have any outside files associated with the current document, you might also want to enable the Update Links check box.

Locking, Unlocking, and Unlinking Fields

There are times when you want to lock specific fields and leave others open. Word provides a facility for you to do just that. When you lock a field, you prevent any changes to the field results, not to the field. You can still delete or reformat the field, and even cut it and paste it somewhere else. A locked field is only prevented from being updated by Word.

You lock a field by selecting it and pressing Ctrl+F11. Of course, you can unlock a field to allow updates by pressing Ctrl+Shift+F11 again. Similarly, you can also unlink a field from its original source. Press Ctrl+Shift+F9 to unlink a selected field. However, after a field is unlinked, the current field result becomes regular text. Later, if you want to update the information, you must insert the field again and re-establish the link.

There's a special switch for locking field results. Adding "\!" to a field code prevents it from being updated (unless the field is moved). This Lock Result switch also prohibits any field from being included in the result of a Bookmark, IncludeText or Ref field. The Lock Result switch is often used when you want to be assured that your referenced or included text is identical to your original text and no codes, such as a date code, have been inadvertently updated.

Fields Shortcut Menu

There are numerous keyboard shortcuts devoted exclusively to fields. One group of shortcuts make it easier to insert commonly used fields, without having to go through the Insert menu; these shortcuts are listed in Table 25.10.

Table 25.10   Keyboard Shortcuts for Commonly Used Fields

Field to Insert	Keyboard Shortcut
Date field	Alt+Shift+D
ListNum Field	Alt+Ctrl+L
Page field	Alt+Shift+P
Time field	Alt+Shift+T
Empty field	Ctrl+F9

Another group of keyboard shortcuts apply to fields in general. Table 25.11 consolidates much of the information about field keyboard shortcuts found throughout this chapter.

Table 25.11   Keyboard Shortcuts for Fields in General

Action	Keyboard Shortcut
Update linked information in another Word document	Ctrl+Shift+F7
Update selected fields	F9
Unlink a field	Ctrl+Shift+F9
Switch between a field code and its result	Shift+F9
Switch between all field codes and their results	Alt+F9
Go to the next field	F11
Go to the previous field	Shift+F11
Lock a field	Ctrl+F11
Unlock a field	Ctrl+Shift+F11

Moving Among Fields

You may have noted in the previous listing of keyboard shortcuts that Word has a facility for moving from one field to the next. Pressing F11 moves you to the next field, and pressing Shift+F11 takes you to the previous one. Word can move from field to field whether or not the field codes are revealed.

You can also locate specific fields using either the Find or the Go To command. To search for a field using the Find command, you first must reveal the codes by pressing Alt+F9. Then choose Edit, Find and type ^19 in the Find What text box followed by the field code name—^19 is the special symbol for the opening field brace.

If you don't remember the exact spelling of the field code, it's easy to use the Go To command instead. Follow these steps:

1. Choose Edit, Go To.
2. From the Go to What list, choose Field, as shown in Figure 25.6.
3. Click the arrow next to the Enter Field Name text box and select a field from the drop-down list.
4. Click either the Next or Previous buttons to find your field in a specific direction.

Note that, unlike with the Find command, you don't have to reveal the field codes when you use the Go To method to locate a specific field.

Formatting Field Results

When it comes to formatting field results, you can affect both style and substance. You can format a field's style just as you would any character—changing its font and its font size, making it bold or italic, and even changing the spacing. Simply highlight the field and make your formatting changes, either through the Formatting toolbar or through the Format menu.

FIG. 25.6

You can "Go To" any field code in your document.

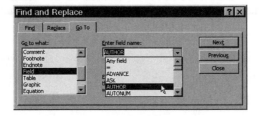

Word also offers another type of formatting through three different general switches. Depending on the type of field code, you can specify:

- The case of text (upper, lower, caps, and so on)
- The style of a number (Arabic, Roman numeral, hexadecimal, and so on)
- The representation of a number (used to specify leading zeros, decimals, and so on)
- The representation of a date or time (used to specify leading zeros, separators, and so on)

Format Switches

Both the text case and number style types of formatting use the Format switch (*) followed by a keyword. Table 25.12 describes all the options.

Table 25.12 Format Switches	
Instruction	**Description**
* caps	Converts the first character of each word to uppercase.
* firstcap	Converts the first character of the first word to uppercase.
* lower	Converts all characters to lowercase.
* upper	Converts all characters to uppercase.
* alphabetic	Converts a number result to lowercase alphabetic characters.
* ALPHABETIC	Converts a number result to uppercase alphabetic characters.
* arabic	Converts a number result to Arabic cardinal form.
* cardtext	Converts a number result to its cardinal text (for example, written word) form.
* dollartext	Converts a number result to cardinal text, inserts "and" at the decimal place and the first two decimals as Arabic numerators over 100 (for example, "Fifteen and $^{23}/_{100}$").
* hex	Converts a number result to hexadecimal numbers.
* ordinal	Converts a number result to Arabic ordinal form (for example, 30th).

Instruction	Description
* ordtext	Converts a number result to ordinal text form (for example, Seventh).
* roman	Converts a number result to lowercase Roman numerals.
* ROMAN	Converts a number result to uppercase Roman numerals.

Numeric Picture Switches

The Numeric and Date-Time switches are referred to as picture switches because you define a representation for the field result. If you've ever chosen a number format in Excel, you're familiar with picture switches. To represent a number with a dollar sign, a comma for a thousands separator and two decimals in it, a sample field code looks like this: {=SUM(ABOVE) \#
"$#,##0.00"}. Notice that a picture switch starts with a \# character combination.

TIP It's not necessary to surround a numeric picture switch with quotation marks unless the switch contains spaces.

Certain field codes, such as Seq, make the most common numeric picture switches available through the Options button. However, you can always create your own by using the Numeric Picture switches listed in Table 25.13.

Part
VI

Ch
25

Table 25.13   Numeric Picture Switches

Instruction	Description
0 (zero)	Required digit placeholder. If a digit is not in the result, a zero is displayed.
# (number sign)	Optional digit placeholder. Displays a digit only if the result requires it.
x (truncate)	Truncating digit placeholder. Drops any digit to the left of the placeholder and rounds up when placed to the right of the decimal point.
decimal point	Indicates decimal point placement. The decimal point must match the decimal character in system setting.
thousands separator	Enables thousands separator. Character used must match the thousands separator in system setting.
– (minus sign)	Inserts a minus sign if result is negative, or a space is result is positive or zero.
+ (plus sign)	Inserts a plus sign if the result is positive, a minus sign if it is negative, or a space if it is zero.
positive; negative	Denotes specific number formats for positive and negative numbers, separated by a semicolon.

continues

Table 25.13 Continued

Instruction	Description
positive; negative; zero	Denotes specific number formats for positive, negative, and zero results.
'text' (literal text)	Inserts verbatim text in the result. The text must be enclosed with single quotation marks.
`sequence`	Includes the current number in a sequence (previously defined by Seq). The sequence label must be enclosed in accent grave marks.
character	Inserts any character in the result, including percent signs, ampersands, and spaces.

Date-Time Picture Switches

The Date-Time picture switches work much like the Numeric picture switches: you combine certain instructions to get the date and time format you want. Indicate a Date-Time picture switch with a \@ before your format representation. For example, assuming you're in the last month of the year, the field code {Date \@ "MMMM 'yy"} returns December '97. Table 25.14 describes the Date-Time picture switches.

Table 25.14 Date-Time Picture Switches

Instruction	Description
M	Displays the month number without a leading zero.
MM	Displays the month number with a leading zero.
MMM	Displays the month as a three letter abbreviation.
MMMM	Displays the full name of the month.
d	Displays the day number without a leading zero for single digit days.
dd	Displays the day number with a leading zero for single digit days.
ddd	Displays the day as a three-letter abbreviation.
dddd	Displays the full name of the day.
yy	Displays the year as two digits with a leading zero for years 01 through 09.
yyyy	Displays the year as four digits.
h or H	Displays the hour without a leading zero for single-digit hours.
hh or HH	Displays the hour with a leading zero for single-digit hours.

Instruction	Description
m	Displays the minutes without a leading zero for single-digit minutes.
mm	Displays the minutes with a leading zero for single-digit minutes.
AM/PM	Displays AM or PM in uppercase.
am/pm	Displays am or pm in lowercase.
A/P	Displays abbreviated AM or PM in uppercase (for example, 8 A and 10 P).
a/p	Displays abbreviated AM or PM in lowercase (for example, 8 a and 10 p).
'text' (literal text)	Inserts verbatim text in the result. The text must be enclosed with single quotation marks.
`sequence`	Includes the current number in a sequence (previously defined by Seq). The sequence label must be enclosed in accent grave marks.
character	Inserts any character in the result, including colons, hyphens, and spaces.

 Unlike most of the switches, a couple of the Date-Time picture switches are case sensitive. You have to use an uppercase M to designate months and a lowercase m to indicate minutes. Similarly, when you are dealing with hours, an uppercase H signals a 24-hour clock while a lowercase h means a 12-hour clock.

TROUBLESHOOTING

What kind of trouble can fields lead to? With all the switches possible, both general formatting types and field specific ones, the everyday typo is a leading source of field-related headaches. Use the Option button whenever possible to have Word insert the proper command. If you are inputting some text with spaces, don't forget to enclose all the text with quotation marks.

My fields won't update. What do I do? As with forms, the mistakes most likely to occur with fields have to do with locking and unlocking. Keep in mind that locking a field only prohibits the result from being updated, it doesn't stop the field from being deleted or typed over. If you press Ctrl+Shift+F11 to unlock a field and it still doesn't update, press Alt+F9 to reveal the field code. You might find a Lock Result switch, \!, in the field; delete it and press F9 to update the field.

I am having trouble viewing my codes. The Word 97 document is composed of layers. There is the normal, inline text layer, and there is the drawing layer that many objects, including graphs, equations and charts, use. If you are having trouble viewing your codes, it could be because they are embedded in such an object which is floating over the text.

To view the field codes in an object, follow these steps:

1. Right-click the object.
2. From the Quick menu, click Format Object.

3. From the Format Object dialog box, click the Position tab.

4. Click the Float Over Text check box to clear it.

5. Click OK.

This makes your floating object an inline object and the fields should display properly.

When I try to number paragraphs in a table cell, I keep getting the number repeated. What's going on? Word exhibits some unexpected behavior when combining tables and the AutoNum field. If you attempt to automatically number several paragraphs within a table cell using AutoNum, Word inserts the same number for each line. The new field code, ListNum, doesn't have the same problem. However, you must remember to indicate a list name for the numbering to work properly, like this, {ListNum "Lots"}.

From Here...

In this chapter, you learned about the power of fields and how fields can help you work more efficiently. Details of all the Word 97 fields were covered with information on how to update, find, and format the fields in your document. Next you might want to read the following chapters:

■ Review how to use the everyday fields covered in Chapter 3, "More Day-to-Day Productivity Tools."

■ Look into how fields are automatically inserted through the mail merge process as examined in Chapter 13, "Using Mail Merge Effectively."

■ Learn more about hyperlinks and how you can use them to connect to other parts of the same document, other documents and, of course, the World Wide Web. See Chapter 18, "Footnotes, Bookmarks, Cross-References, and Hyperlinks."

■ See how to access some of the more specialized Office 97 functions to easily perform field-like functions, like the Equation Editor and Excel, in Chapter 27, "Integrating with Microsoft Office."

CHAPTER 26

Customizing Word

by Bill Comarda

Word is remarkably easy to personalize, and you can personalize it extensively—making your copy of Word look and feel very much different than the next person's. Judiciously applied customization can make Word more convenient, more comfortable, more productive, and even more fun.

If you use Word several hours a day, as you read this chapter think about the minor annoyances you've found in Word. Think about the tasks that seem to take longer than necessary, the toolbars that don't include the tasks you perform most, the automated actions you find yourself undoing. You might just be able to eliminate those annoyances.

If you're responsible for the way people in your company use Word, you can use many of the same customizations to create a word processing program that more closely serves the needs of your colleagues and your organization as a whole. ■

Starting Word automatically

Why bother double-clicking when Word can start automatically and even open a document at the same time?

Customizing toolbars

Get one-button access to any command, macro, font, style—just about anything in Word.

Adding new toolbars

How about a custom toolbar that brings together all the commands you use most?

Customizing menus

It's easy to add or remove commands from any Word menu. You can even add an entirely new menu!

Creating new keyboard shortcuts

You can create convenient keyboard shortcuts for any built-in Word command, macro, font, style, toolbar button, or menu item.

Changing Word options

Use the Options dialog box to make Word more convenient, more friendly, and more personal.

Starting Word Automatically

For millions of people, it's a given: when they turn on their computer in the morning, they'll be working in Word. If you're one of those people, you can set up Windows 95 or Windows NT to run Word automatically whenever you start your computer. You'll have a little more time to get coffee, and when you get back, Word will be all set for you to get started.

To run Word at startup:

1. Right-click an empty part of the Windows 95 or NT 4.0 taskbar (see Figure 26.1).

FIG. 26.1

To add Word to Windows' StartUp folder, start by choosing Properties from the Taskbar shortcut menu.

2. Choose Properties.

3. Click the Start Menu Programs tab (see Figure 26.2).

FIG. 26.2

From this tab, you can add or remove any program from Word's StartUp folder.

4. Click Add. The Create Shortcut dialog box opens.

5. If you know where Word is, enter the full path and file name in the Command line. Otherwise, choose Browse; then find and Open Winword.exe.

In a default installation, Word is usually found at

```
c:\Program Files\Microsoft Office\Office\Winword.exe
```

T I P   If you're working on a long-term project that involves the same document day in and day out, you can place a Word document in the StartUp folder. Then, whenever you start your computer, Word opens with that document already displayed.

6. Choose Next. The Select Program Folder dialog box opens (see Figure 26.3).

FIG. 26.3
To reach the StartUp folder, you'll probably have to scroll down.

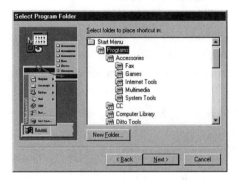

7. In the Select Folder to Place Shortcut In scroll box, double-click StartUp (*not* Start Menu). The Select a Title for the Program dialog box opens. You can leave the title that exists (Winword.exe). Or you can rename it Microsoft Word (or anything else).

8. Click Finish. Windows inserts a shortcut to Word 97 into its StartUp folder.

9. Click OK.

Starting Word with a Particular Task

You've already learned that you can automatically start Word when you start your computer and that you can open a document at the same time. But what if there are a few different documents you start with? Let's say that on Tuesday and Wednesday you usually work on correspondence; on Thursday and Friday you work on a book project. You can create one desktop shortcut that runs the Letter Wizard when Word starts; another that opens the master document where your book files are stored.

To create a desktop shortcut that loads Word with custom behavior, follow these steps:

1. In Windows Explorer, browse to and select Word 97's WINWORD.EXE file. In a default installation, this is stored in the c:\Program Files\Microsoft Office\Office\ folder.

2. Right-click the WINWORD.EXE icon to display the shortcut menu.

3. Choose Create Shortcut. A shortcut appears in the same folder.

4. Right-click the shortcut and choose Cut.

5. Show the Windows desktop by minimizing or exiting Windows Explorer and any other programs that might be in the way.

6. Right-click the Windows Desktop and choose Paste. You now have a standard Word shortcut. The next step is to customize it.

7. Right-click the shortcut, and choose Properties. The Properties dialog box opens.

8. Click the Shortcut tab.

Part
VI

Ch

26

9. In the <u>T</u>arget text box, within the quotation marks, enter the startup option switches you want to use. (See the options in Table 26.1.)

10. Choose OK.

11. From the Windows Desktop, click the shortcut name. Wait a moment; then Windows will display an editing cursor inside the name.

12. Enter a name that corresponds to the task the shortcut will perform, and press OK.

Table 26.1   Word 97 Startup Options

This Switch...	Does This...
/a	Loads Word without loading add-ins or global templates.
/l	Loads Word with a specific add-in. (Follow /l with the add-in's filename and complete path.)
/m	Loads Word without running any automatic macros (AutoExec, and so on). (Follow /m with a macro name, and Word runs that macro instead of AutoExec.)
/n	Starts Word without opening a blank document.
/t	Starts Word and opens a document as a template. (Follow /t with the name of the document.)

When might you use a startup option? You might run Word with the /a and /m options if you suspect you may have a macro virus infection. Or you might create a special desktop shortcut that runs Word and a specific custom macro which creates a unique editing environment for specific tasks. Figure 26.4 shows a Windows desktop with custom options for loading Word.

 To run a specific wizard at startup, record a macro that loads the wizard. Then create a desktop shortcut that runs this macro instead of any of Word's automatic macros. In the following example, the name of the macro is runwizard, and Word has been installed in the default location. You would enter the following in the <u>T</u>arget text box of the Shortcut tab:

```
c:\Program Files\Microsoft Office\Office\WINWORD.EXE /m runwizard
```

FIG. 26.4
At the far right of the Windows desktop are custom options for loading Word.

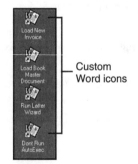

Custom
Word icons

Customizing Toolbars

By default, Word displays the Standard and Formatting toolbar, and enables you to display additional toolbars through the View, Toolbars menu commands. However, what if you want to add or remove buttons from a toolbar or create an entirely new toolbar with the buttons you need to perform specific tasks? Word makes it easy.

Before you learn how, *when* would you bother to do this? Many times. Think about creating new toolbar buttons if you or your colleagues often perform any of the following actions:

- Are forced to use dialog boxes to apply formatting, such as double-underlining or small caps, which doesn't appear on Word's formatting toolbar
- Run macros that don't have keyboard shortcuts you can easily remember
- Want easy, one-click shortcuts for basic Word commands, such as creating an envelope, sending a fax, or applying a heading style
- Want easy, one-click access to any style or built-in AutoText entry
- Want to customize your editing environment for the specific documents your company creates

Adding a Command to a Toolbar

The simplest way to customize a toolbar is to add a command to it. Here's how:

1. Choose Tools, Customize. The Customize dialog box opens (see Figure 26.5).

FIG. 26.5
In the Toolbars tab of the Customize dialog box, you can display any toolbar for customization—if it isn't already displayed.

Part
VI

Ch
26

2. If the toolbar you want to customize isn't already visible, choose the Toolbars tab, and check the box associated with that toolbar.

N O T E Under normal circumstances, several Word toolbars can't be displayed unless you are performing the tasks to which they relate. However, from the Toolbars tab, you can display any toolbar you want. ▇

3. If necessary, move the toolbar to a location that's more convenient. To do so, drag the title bar until the toolbar moves where you want it.

4. Choose the Commands tab (see Figure 26.6). You now have an enormous number of choices for the commands you can add to your toolbar. These are organized in Categories:

FIG. 26.6

From the Commands tab, you can select any command and drag it to a toolbar or to the menu bar.

- The categories *File, Edit, View, Insert, Format, Tools, Table*, and *Window and Help* correspond to Word's menus of the same names. However, they include many options that don't appear on standard Word menus. For example, the File category includes items like Close All and Save All—items that "didn't quite make the cut" to be displayed on the standard File menu.

- Several other categories, including *Web, Drawing, AutoShapes, Borders, Mail Merge, Forms*, and *Control Toolbox*, correspond to existing Word toolbars. Again, there are typically more options available in the Customize dialog box than on the default Word toolbars. From the Commands tab, you can add these buttons to any toolbar you want.

- The *All Commands* category lists more than 400 individual commands Word can perform—everything from ApplyHeading1 (format selected text with the Heading 1 style), to WordUnderline (apply underlining to all selected words, but not the spaces between them).

- The *Macros* category lists all currently available macros. In other words, you can create a toolbar button for any existing macro.

- The *Fonts* category lists all currently available fonts. In other words, you can create a toolbar button that automatically formats any selected text in any font on your system.

- The *AutoText* category lists all AutoText entries in all open templates. So you can create a toolbar button that inserts any AutoText entry you like.

- The *Styles* category lists all available styles, including any custom styles you've created. You can create a toolbar button that applies any style you like.

5. Choose the Category containing the element you want to add to your toolbar. The list of choices available within that category appears in the Commands scroll box.

6. In the Commands box, select the choice you want.

7. Now drag the command out of the Customize dialog box, and drop it on the toolbar you want, in the location where you want it to appear (see Figure 26.7). This is the most nonintuitive, surprising step in the process: nowhere else in Word do you actually drag a command outside the borders of a dialog box!

FIG. 26.7
The I-marker indicates where your new button will be placed.

I-marker indicates where the button will go

+ symbol indicates you can place the button here

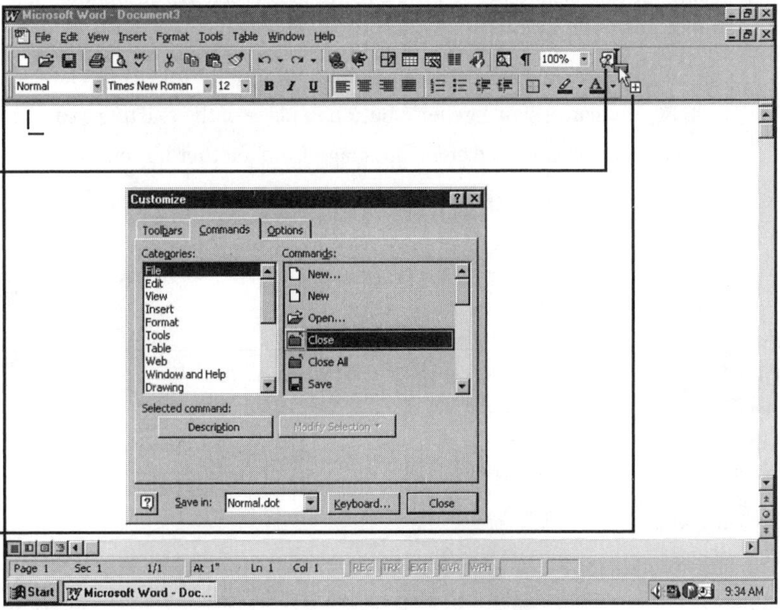

You now have a toolbar button that works like all the other toolbar buttons Word contains. After you close the Customize dialog box, click the button and it performs the task associated with it.

TIP Whenever the Customize dialog box is open, you can make changes to any toolbar or menu, not just the one on which you've been working.

In Word 97, menus and toolbars are interchangeable. You can add any built-in menu, or even an entirely new menu, to any toolbar you like. You also can easily add toolbar buttons to the menu bar.

To add a menu to a toolbar, do the following: In Step 5, instead of choosing one of the categories discussed previously, choose either Built-in Menus or New Menus. Then, in the following steps, choose the menu you want, and drag that to the toolbar. To add a toolbar button to the menu bar at the top of the screen, simply drag it there, instead of dragging it to a toolbar.

Part
VI

Ch
26

Modifying the Appearance of a Toolbar Button

Many of the commands you can add to a toolbar come with their own button icons. However, if you choose a command without its own icon, Word places the entire text of the command in the toolbar. In some cases, this text can be quite long; in fact, it may be so long that existing buttons are pushed beyond the edge of the screen. If you want to change the appearance of a toolbar button for this or any other reason, you have several options:

- You can edit the text in the toolbar button for brevity or clarity.
- You can assign a generic button in place of the existing text or image.
- You can copy and adapt an image from another button.
- You can create a button yourself, from scratch.

All these options, and others, are available from the Customize shortcut menu. To display it, make sure the Customize dialog box is open; then right-click the button you want to change (see Figure 26.8).

T I P You can change any button, not just the one you've inserted.

FIG. 26.8

You can change the appearance of a toolbar button with the Customize shortcut menu.

If you want to edit the text of a toolbar button, click in the Name text box on the shortcut menu, type the new name you want, and press Enter.

If you want to copy an image onto any toolbar button, follow these steps:

1. Right-click the toolbar button image you want to borrow or adapt.
2. Choose Copy Button Image.
3. Right-click the toolbar where you want to paste the image.
4. Choose Paste Button Image.

Follow these steps if you want to use one of Word's 42 generic buttons:

1. Right-click the button you want to change.
2. Choose Change Button Image (see Figure 26.9).

FIG. 26.9

You can assign one of Word's 42 generic toolbar button images to any button you want.

3. Select an image from the cascaded menu.

4. Press Enter.

Using the Windows Clipboard, you can copy any bitmapped image onto a toolbar button, including images created in programs such as Microsoft Paint.

1. Open the graphics program and create or open the image you want.

2. Select all or part of the image, and copy the selected image to the Clipboard.

3. Switch to Word and choose Tools, Customize.

4. Right-click the toolbar button where you want to use the image.

5. Choose Paste Button Image.

Be aware, however, that most images created elsewhere weren't designed for use on tiny, square toolbar buttons. You'll have best results with square images that have strong outlines and little internal detail.

If you're wondering where you can find more button images, here's a source you might not have thought of: Excel and PowerPoint. Each of these programs has its own Tools, Customize dialog box, largely identical to the one in Word. You can copy an image from a toolbar button in Excel or PowerPoint, and then paste it onto a toolbar button in Word.

If Word displays both the image and the text and you don't want to see the text, follow these steps:

1. Right-click the button.

2. Choose Default Style from the shortcut menu.

Editing Existing Button Images

It's possible you still don't have the right image for your custom toolbar button. In that case, you can create it yourself with Word's Button Editor—or better yet, adapt it from an existing image that's close, but not quite right.

If you have an image you can start from, make sure the Tools, Customize dialog box is open, and paste the image onto your button. Then, right-click the button, and choose Edit Button

Part

VI

Ch

26

Image from the shortcut menu. Word's Button Editor appears (see Figure 26.10). If you selected a button with an image, that image appears enlarged in the Picture box. If the button you selected had no image at all, the Picture box appears blank.

FIG. 26.10

In the Button Editor, you can color or erase individual pixels within your button to get the exact image you want.

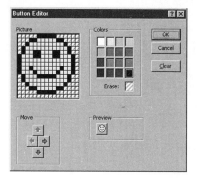

Now, you can add or erase lines and colors from the picture. To choose a color, click its square in the Colors area. To add color to the image, drag the mouse pointer across the individual pixels you want to color. To erase an existing part of the image, click the Erase square in the Colors area, and drag that across the individual pixels. As you work, the button in the Preview area shows how your button now appears. If you're not happy with the results, you can choose Clear to blank out the Picture box and try again.

This is painstaking work—which is why you're better off starting from a button image that can be adapted, rather than working from scratch.

Organizing Entire Toolbars

So far, you've learned how to add individual buttons to toolbars. Now step back a moment, and look at the toolbar itself. Does it contain the buttons you really need? Should you delete some buttons that you rarely use? Should you move or copy some button from other toolbars, regroup your buttons so they fit together more logically, or create an entirely new toolbar and copy buttons there?

When the Customize dialog box is open, you can do all these things and more.

Deleting Toolbar Buttons

Some buttons perform functions you might never use. For example, if you use Word solely to write poetry, it's conceivable that you could live without the Insert Microsoft Excel Worksheet button on your Standard toolbar. To delete a toolbar button, follow these steps:

1. Choose Tools, Customize.

2. Drag the toolbar button off the toolbar.

3. Click Close in the Customize dialog box.

TIP If you're responsible for managing Word in an organization, you might want to delete toolbar buttons associated with features you'd rather your colleagues didn't use. For example, if you want people to use Word's powerful Track Changes feature rather than simply highlighting text in documents they review, you might remove the Highlighter button from the Formatting toolbar.

It's best to plan for these kinds of changes before you deploy Word throughout your company, because you can create and install an official company template that reflects your additions and deletions to the Word interface, and you can train people based on your custom interface from the outset.

Copying or Moving Toolbar Buttons

You've already learned you can copy the image on a toolbar button, but what about the button itself?

■ To move a toolbar button, drag it from one toolbar to another.

■ To copy a toolbar button, press Ctrl while you drag the button from one toolbar to another.

■ To move a toolbar button within the same toolbar, drag it to its new location.

Widening Boxes in a Toolbar

If you add the Font, Font Size, Style, or (Web) Address command to a toolbar, Word doesn't insert a button; rather, it inserts a drop-down box, just like the Style drop-down box that appears on Word's Formatting toolbar. You might find the box too wide or narrow for your purposes. For example, you might be in the habit of using exceptionally long style names. Or you might want to squeeze a font box onto a toolbar with little extra space for it.

To change the width of a box on a toolbar, make sure the Customize dialog box is open. Then, place your mouse pointer on the left or right edge of the box, and drag it to the width you want (see Figure 26.11).

Part VI

Ch 26

FIG. 26.11
Dragging a font, font size, or style box to the width you want.

Dividing Toolbar Buttons Logically

Perhaps you've noticed that Word 97 buttons are grouped logically, and there is a 3-D *group separator line* between each group of buttons. You can add a group separator line of your own to make your custom toolbar buttons easier to understand and use. To do so, make sure the Customize dialog box appears. Then, follow these steps:

1. Right-click the button immediately to the right of where you want the separator to appear.

2. Choose Begin a Group from the shortcut menu. Word places a separator line between the two toolbar buttons (see Figure 26.12).

FIG. 26.12
A separator line inserted between two toolbar buttons.

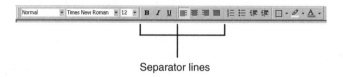

Separator lines

Adding a New Toolbar

Until now, you've worked on toolbars that already exist. However, one of the most common ways to customize toolbars is to create your own custom toolbar. That way, you can leave the existing toolbars alone and avoid confusing people who don't understand why they don't match the documentation. You can add sets of commands to custom toolbars associated with specific tasks or clients. You can even store them in custom templates, so they appear automatically when you create documents based on those templates. For example, you can do the following:

■ You can create a toolbar associated with invoicing, and attach it to your invoice template.

■ You can create a "long document" toolbar with buttons for inserting bookmarks, index entries, tables of contents, and other elements (see Figure 26.13).

■ In a law firm, you can create a toolbar containing AutoText entries that insert contract boilerplate and attach it to a contract template all your lawyers, paralegals, and legal secretaries use.

FIG. 26.13
A sample "long document" custom toolbar bringing together many of the features one typical user might need in creating a long document. Names have been edited to fit.

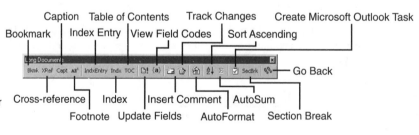

To create a new custom toolbar, first make sure the template where you want to store it is open. Then, follow these steps:

1. Choose Tools, Customize.

2. Choose the Toolbars tab.

3. Choose New. The New Toolbar dialog box appears (see Figure 26.14).

4. In the Toolbar Name text box, type the name of your new toolbar.

FIG. 26.14

Enter the name of your new toolbar in the New Toolbar dialog box.

5. In the Make Toolbar Available To drop-down list box, decide whether to store the toolbar in Normal.dot, where it will be available at all times, or in a different open template.

6. Click OK. Word displays a new, empty toolbar (see Figure 26.15). Now you can add any buttons you want, as you've already learned how to do.

FIG. 26.15

Word displays an empty toolbar; you can now move or copy buttons into it.

 If you later decide you want to move a toolbar from one template to another, you can do so, using the Toolbars tab of the Organizer dialog box. You can get there by choosing Tools, Templates and Add-Ins, clicking Organizer, and choosing the Toolbars tab.

▶ **See** "Keeping Track of Styles with the Organizer," **p. 157**

Renaming and Deleting Custom Toolbars

You can't rename or delete any of Word's built-in toolbars. However, you can rename or delete a toolbar you've created. To rename a toolbar, follow these steps:

1. Choose Tools, Customize.

2. Choose the Toolbars tab.

3. In the Toolbars scroll box, click the toolbar you want to rename.

4. Click Rename. The Rename Toolbar dialog box opens (see Figure 26.16).

5. Enter a new name and choose OK.

Part
VI

Ch
26

FIG. 26.16

You can change a toolbar's name in the Rename Toolbar dialog box.

To delete a toolbar, follow these steps:

1. Choose Tools, Customize.

2. Choose the Toolbars tab.

3. In the Toolbars scroll box, click the toolbar you want to rename.

4. Click Delete.

5. Click OK to confirm that you want to delete the toolbar.

Restoring Default Settings

If someone else has customized Word on your computer by adding or removing toolbar buttons from Word's built-in toolbars, and you do not want the same customizations, you can return each toolbar to its original settings as follows:

1. Choose Tools, Customize.

2. Choose the Toolbars tab.

3. In the Toolbars scroll box, click the toolbar you want to reset.

4. Click Reset. The Reset Toolbar dialog box opens (see Figure 26.17).

5. From the Reset Changes drop-down box, choose the template containing the toolbar you want to reset. When you reset a toolbar in Normal.dot, you reset it for all your documents.

FIG. 26.17
In the Reset Toolbar dialog box, specify the template containing the toolbar you want to reset.

 TIP A quick way to eliminate all of Word's custom settings is to move your Normal.dot template to another folder where Word doesn't know to look for it—in other words, a folder outside the paths for User Templates and Workgroup Templates that you have specified in the File Locations tab of the Options dialog box. Word generates a new Normal template based on its default settings, including default toolbars and menus.

Customizing Menus

In Word 97, customizing menus is extremely similar to customizing toolbars. Three aspects of customizing menus will seem very familiar if you've read the previous section about toolbars:

- You work from the Tools, Customize dialog box.
- You drag choices where you want them to appear.
- You can customize existing menus or create new ones.

The simplest case is adding a command to an existing menu.

Adding a Command to an Existing Menu

You might find there's a command you often use that should appear on a Word menu, but doesn't. For example, the File menu includes Save and Save As, but why not Save All? Then you could save all your open files at the same time. Why isn't the Print Preview command on the View menu? It's a view of a document, isn't it? Whatever you would like to change, here's how to do it:

1. Choose Tools, Customize.
2. Click the menu you want to change, to display it. Note that a black rectangle appears around whatever menu or menu item you select (see Figure 26.18).
3. In the Customize dialog box, display the Commands tab.
4. Choose the Category of the command you want to add. Word's categories of commands were discussed in detail earlier in this chapter.
5. In the Commands scroll box, choose the command you want to add.
6. Drag the command (see Figure 26.19) to the location on the menu where you want it.
7. Release the mouse pointer. The new command appears on the menu.

FIG. 26.18
Select the menu to which you want to add a command.

FIG. 26.19
Drag the desired command to the menu.

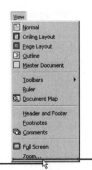

Mouse pointer ——————————— I-marker indicates where the menu item will go

Part
VI

Ch
26

> **CAUTION**
>
> Be careful not to drag built-in menu items off a menu, or to drag an entire menu off the menu bar by mistake. If you're not careful, it's easy to lose commands you really need. Remember, Undo doesn't work on actions you take with the Customize dialog box open. If you make an error, your best option is to exit Word and choose <u>N</u>o when you are asked to confirm changes to the Normal.dot template; all the changes you made will be abandoned.

Adding a Keyboard Shortcut to a Menu Item

In Word, every built-in menu command contains a letter designated as the shortcut key; for example, you can choose Save <u>A</u>s from the <u>F</u>ile menu by pressing Alt+F+A. You can add a shortcut key to a custom command as well.

In many cases, Word includes a shortcut key automatically when you drag the command to a menu. If that shortcut key isn't already in use on the same menu, there's little reason to change it. If it is the same, however, you'll almost certainly want to change it.

N O T E   If two commands on the same menu use the same shortcut key, when you enter the letter you get the command that appears closest to the top of the menu. If you enter the letter again, Word selects the other command that uses the same shortcut key. ▪

To add or change a shortcut key, follow these steps:

1. Choose <u>T</u>ools, <u>C</u>ustomize to open the Customize dialog box.
2. Display the menu containing the command you want to change.
3. Right-click the command you want to change. The shortcut menu appears (see Figure 26.20).

FIG. 26.20

Add (or move) the & symbol immediately before the letter you want to use as a shortcut key.

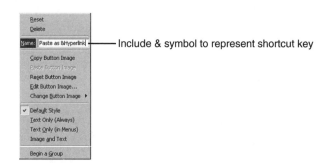

—— Include & symbol to represent shortcut key

4. In the <u>N</u>ame text box, insert the **&** symbol before the letter you want to be your shortcut key.
5. Press Enter.

 In the <u>N</u>ame text box on the shortcut menu, you can edit the name of a menu item any way you want. You can remove a keyboard shortcut by editing out the & symbol.

Adding a Separator

As with toolbars, you may want to set apart several custom menu items with a separator, just as Word itself does. This works virtually the same as it does for toolbars. Make sure the Customize dialog box is open. Then, follow these steps:

1. Select the menu containing the commands you want to organize.
2. Right-click the command immediately beneath where you want to insert a separator.
3. Choose Begin a <u>G</u>roup from the shortcut menu.

Removing a Command on a Menu

Some people find Word's menus cluttered; they like to remove menu items they know they'll never use. It's easy to do so. With the Customize dialog box open, follow these steps:

1. Select the menu containing the command you want to remove.
2. Drag the command off the menu.

 You can remove a menu command without opening the Customize dialog box. Press Alt+Ctrl–(Minus sign). The mouse pointer changes to a thick, horizontal line. Now, select the menu command you want to delete. Instead of performing the action, Word removes the menu item.

Part

VI

Ch

26

Adding Your Own Menus

One of the most useful ways to customize menus is to add a completely new menu for commands specific to your company. For example, as shown in Figure 26.21, you might create a unique Company menu that contains forms, useful documents, and macros associated with your organization.

FIG. 26.21

In this example, the custom Company menu contains important documents and macros, making them much easier to access.

To add a new menu, follow these steps:

1. Choose Tools, Customize.
2. In the Categories list, choose New Menu (the last item on the list).
3. If you want to store the menu in an open template other than Normal.dot, choose the template in the Save In drop-down box.
4. Drag the New Menu command from the Commands scroll box to where you want it to appear on the menu bar. It appears, bordered in black.
5. Right-click your new menu (or choose Modify Selection).
6. Enter a new name in the Name text box. Don't forget to include an **&** symbol before the letter you want to use as a shortcut.
7. Press Enter.

Restoring Default Menus

If you no longer want the customizations you've applied to a specific menu, you can restore the original settings. As usual, make sure the Customize dialog box is open. Then, right-click the menu you want to restore, and choose Reset from the shortcut menu.

Creating New Keyboard Shortcuts

You probably know that Word contains hundreds of keyboard shortcuts: Ctrl+F for Find, Alt+Shift+X to insert an index entry, and so on. If you want, you can change those keyboard shortcuts, or add new ones. When might you want to?

- When you're switching from another word processor whose keyboard shortcuts you're accustomed to
- When you often find yourself using a command or macro that doesn't come with a keyboard shortcut

Associating Keyboard Shortcuts with Current Menu Commands or Toolbar Buttons

If the keyboard shortcut you want to create corresponds to a toolbar button or menu item that already exists, here's how to add the shortcut:

1. Press Alt+Ctrl+(Plus sign). (This only works if you use the + symbol on the numeric keypad.) The mouse pointer changes to the Command symbol (see Figure 26.22).
2. Choose the menu item or click the toolbar button that corresponds to the command. The Customize Keyboard dialog box appears (see Figure 26.23).
3. Press the key combination you want to set as your shortcut. The combination appears in the Press New Shortcut Key text box.

FIG. 26.22
When the mouse pointer appears as shown in the figure, you can use it to assign a keyboard shortcut to an existing menu or toolbar.

Use this mouse pointer to assign keyboard shortcuts

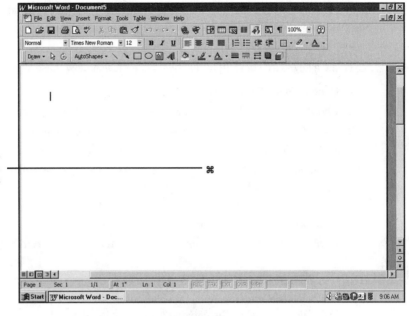

FIG. 26.23
In the Customize Keyboard dialog box, press a keyboard shortcut to associate it with the command you've chosen.

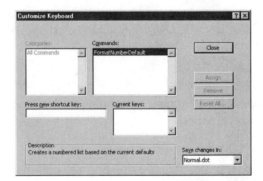

4. Look in the Currently Assigned To area; if the shortcut you've chosen is already in use, press backspace and try another one.

5. Click <u>A</u>ssign. You'll see the new key combination in the C<u>u</u>rrent Keys scroll box.

Associating Keyboard Shortcuts with Other Commands

You might be perfectly satisfied using toolbar buttons and menus for the commands that already have them. However, what about commands that don't? For example, you might create a keyboard shortcut to apply a specific font or style, or insert a specific AutoText entry. Maybe there's a foreign language accent mark or symbol you use regularly; rather than always opening the Symbol dialog box to access it, you would like to create a keyboard shortcut that enters the symbol. Or perhaps you recorded a macro that you didn't expect to use much, so you didn't bother to create a keyboard shortcut for it at the time. Now that you realize how useful your macro is, you would like an easier way to access it.

▶ **See** "Recording Your Macro," **p. 847**

To create a keyboard shortcut for elements like these, follow these steps:

1. Choose Tools, Customize.

2. Choose Keyboard. The Customize Keyboard dialog box appears.

3. In the Categories scroll box, choose the category containing the command you want.

4. In the Commands scroll box, choose the command you want.

5. Press the keyboard shortcut you want to set as your shortcut. The combination appears in the Press New Shortcut Key text box.

6. Look in the Currently Assigned To area; if the shortcut you've chosen is already in use, press backspace and try another one.

7. Click Assign. You'll see the new key combination in the Current Keys scroll box.

Resetting Keyboard Shortcuts

If you decide you no longer want one specific custom keyboard shortcut, display the Customize Keyboard dialog box, select the command and click Remove.

If you want to eliminate all custom keyboard shortcuts in the Normal template, display the Customize Keyboard dialog box, select the command and click Reset All. Word asks you to confirm this action; click Yes.

> **CAUTION**
>
> Resetting keyboard shortcuts eliminates all custom keyboard shortcuts stored in the Normal template, including those you may have created earlier when you recorded custom macros.

Changing Word Options

The Options dialog box (Tools, Options) brings together ten categories of Word behaviors that you can easily customize:

- ■ *View* options that control aspects of Word's appearance
- ■ *General* options that don't fit anywhere else
- ■ *Edit* options that control Word's behavior as you edit
- ■ *Print* options that control how and what Word prints (see Chapter 12, "Printing, Faxing, and E-Mail")
- ■ *Save* options that control how, what, and when Word saves files
- ■ *Spelling & Grammar* options that control how Word checks spelling and grammar (see Chapter 4, "Making the Most of Word's Proofing Tools")

- *Track Changes* options that control the formatting Word uses to represent revisions when it is tracking them (see Chapter 23, "Managing Revisions")

- *User Information* options that store the information Word uses whenever it needs your name, initials, and mailing address

- *Compatibility* options that make it easier to use documents created in other formats and work with the users who created those documents

- *File location* options that specify where Word looks for documents, images, templates, and other files it needs

Throughout this book, you've come across some of the options available here. In this section, you'll take a systematic look at the options that have been covered briefly (or not at all) elsewhere.

Changing View Options

In Chapter 1, "Word: Take the Controls," you learned about some ways to change Word's appearance. For example, you learned that you can choose View, Full Screen to hide all of Word's menus and toolbars except for a Close Full Screen button and see much more of your document. To control many other aspects of Word's appearance, choose Tools, Options, View. The default settings for View options are shown in Figure 26.24.

FIG. 26.24

The View tab of the Options dialog box brings together a variety of adjustments to Word's appearance.

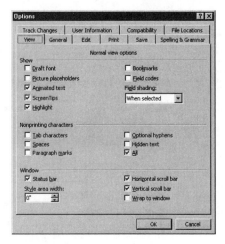

Part
VI

Ch
26

N O T E   The options available in the View tab will change depending on the view you're in. For example, Wrap to Window is unavailable in Page Layout view, which is intended to reflect the printed appearance of your document as closely as possible. Later in this section, you'll learn about options that only appear in the Page Layout and Online Layout views. ■

Adjusting What Appears On-Screen

The first category of View options cover a variety of options for what appears on-screen as you edit.

Draft Font enables you to display all the text in your document using a Windows 12-point system font, as shown in (see Figure 26.25). Italics and boldface are both shown as underlined text. Colored text retains its color; animation and some text effects are displayed. Spacing and paragraph indents are correct. If you have a slower computer, *Draft Font* may significantly improve Word's performance. You might consider using it for original writing; then turning it off when you need to work with formatting.

TIP   If you choose Page Layout or Online Layout view while Draft Font is turned on, Word displays all the correct fonts and formatting. But if you switch back to Normal view, the Draft font will be shown again. You can use this feature to quickly toggle back and forth between editing and formatting.

FIG. 26.25

This figure illustrates a document displayed in Word's Draft font.

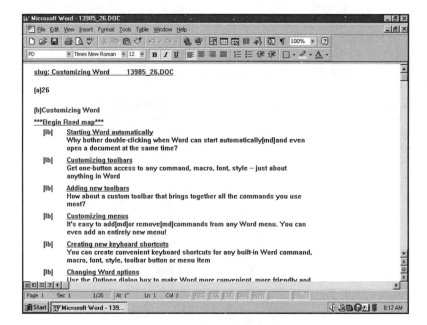

Picture Placeholders instructs Word to display an empty box wherever you've inserted an image. When this is turned off, Word spends time processing images for display, even if you're merely scrolling past them to another destination. The more images your document contains, the slower Word is. When you're focused on editing text instead of viewing images, consider turning on Picture Placeholders.

TIP   Because the placeholder boxes are the same size as the original images, you can use Picture placeholders in Page Layout view to evaluate layouts more quickly when you don't need to view the pictures themselves.

Animated Text allows Word to display animation created in the Animation tab of the Format, Font dialog box, such as sparkle text. When this box is cleared, the animation disappears and the text appears as it will when printed.

Clearing the *ScreenTips* check box turns off ScreenTips that appear when you hover the mouse pointer over a comment, tracked change, footnote, or endnote. Similarly, clearing *Highlight* prevents highlighting from appearing your document.

> **N O T E** To turn off the AutoComplete ScreenTips that appear when you start typing text that matches an AutoText entry, clear the Show AutoComplete Tip for AutoText entry check box in the AutoText tab of the AutoCorrect dialog box. To turn off ScreenTips that appear on toolbar buttons, choose Tools, Customize, Options, and clear the Show ScreenTips on Toolbars check box. ▪

Checking the *Bookmarks* check box adds gray brackets at the beginning and end of any text you've bookmarked. Checking the *Field Codes* check box displays field codes throughout your document instead of the results they generate. You might use this when you're troubleshooting fields, such as cross-references or index entries that aren't delivering the results you expect.

> **T I P** Whether you've checked the Field Codes box or not, you can still toggle field codes on and off by selecting them and pressing Shift+F9. However, as long as the check box is turned on, new fields you enter will appear as field codes rather than results.

In the *Field Shading* drop-down box, you can tell Word how to keep you posted about the presence of field codes in your document. The default option, when selected, tells Word to display field codes in gray only when you've selected or clicked within them. The Always option tells Word to show field codes and field results in gray *all* the time. Marking field codes in gray shows you where they begin and end and reminds you which information is being generated in your document automatically. However, you (or a colleague unfamiliar with Word field codes) might find the gray formatting distracting. If so, choose Never.

Part
VI

Ch
26

Controlling the Display of Nonprinting Characters

By default, when you click the Show/Hide Paragraph button on the Standard toolbar, Word displays much more than paragraph marks; it also shows tab characters, spaces, optional hyphenation marks that may or may not print, and hidden text.

At times, this may give you more information than you want. For example, you might want to see all the paragraph marks in your document, because you know they contain important paragraph formatting. However, you might not want to see an obtrusive dot between every single word on your page.

You can control which of Word's nonprinting characters appear when you toggle on the Show/Hide Paragraph button. To do so, make sure the All check box is cleared, and check the boxes of each nonprinting character you want to see: Tab characters, Spaces, Paragraph marks, Optional hyphens, and/or Hidden Text. If you do want to see all the nonprinting characters, choose All.

All supersedes any other check boxes. This is a convenience; you can set up Word to display the nonprinting characters you want to see most of the time, and then simply toggle All on or off when you need to see the rest of them, rather than adjusting each setting individually.

Controlling Word Interface Options

You can control five elements of Word's appearance from the Window area of the View tab. In three cases, Word gives you the option of turning off standard elements of the Word interface to make more room for editing. You can turn off the Horizontal scroll bar if you rarely work with documents that extend beyond the right edge of the screen. You can turn off the Vertical scroll bar as well, though you'll rarely if ever want to do so. Finally, if you never refer to the settings in the status bar, you can hide that as well.

You might find two additional options helpful. *Wrap to Window* tells Word to make sure all text appears within the width of your screen. While this slightly reduces the "what-you-see-is-what-you-get" accuracy of Word's display, it eliminates the annoying horizontal scrolling that sometimes accompanies documents that are slightly wider than normal. Because Wrap to Window tells Word to display widths inaccurately, it's unavailable in Page Layout and Online Layout views.

Finally, *Style Area Width* enables you to display the styles associated with each paragraph in a column to the left of your document text (see Figure 26.26). This makes it more convenient to identify and work with heavily styled documents. By default, this is set to 0"—in other words, no Style Area Width. If you set it to a higher number, such as 0.7", you'll see the style information.

FIG. 26.26

This figure shows a document displaying styles in use at the left edge of the editing window.

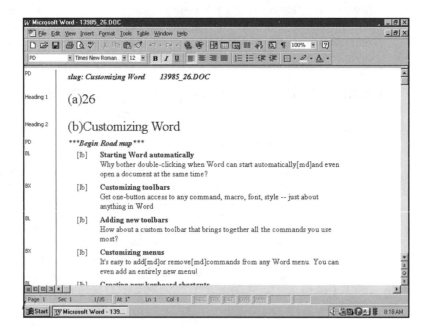

Different Options for Page Layout and Online Layout View

When you switch to Page Layout view or Online Layout view, some of the options discussed earlier, such as Wrap to Window, are no longer available. Others take their place:

■ *Clearing the Drawings* check box hides any drawings you may have created using Word's drawing tools. (These are already hidden when you work in Normal or Outline view.)

■ *Checking the Object Anchors* check box makes it possible to see object anchors that show an object attached to a specific paragraph. As with options like Spaces and Paragraph Marks, the object anchors only appear when you toggle the Show/Hide Paragraph button on.

■ *Checking Text Boundaries* tells Word to show dotted lines around margins, columns, and objects, giving you a little more visual feedback about where text can be placed.

■ In the Window section at the bottom of the tab, there's one more user-interface element you can turn on or off: *Vertical Ruler.*

■ In Online Layout view only, you have one more option. By default, Online Layout view enlarges fonts smaller than 12 point to make them more readable on-screen. In the Enlarge Fonts Less Than scroll box, you can raise or lower the font size Word uses as its threshold. For example, if you choose 10, Word enlarges all fonts smaller than 10 points, displaying them as 10 point type. This doesn't affect how the fonts actually print.

Changing General Options

Quite simply, the General tab of the Options dialog box is where Word collects the options that don't fit anywhere else. You can see its default settings in Figure 26.27.

FIG. 26.27

This figure shows the default settings for the General tab of the Options dialog box.

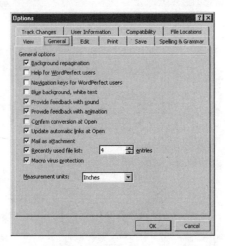

By default, *Background Repagination* keeps track of page numbering continuously while you work. Like all of Word's automatic, on-the-fly features, this one takes a little bit of processing power. So if you're finding that Word 97 runs too slowly on your computer, you might try turning off Background Repagination.

Background Pagination is always on in Page Layout view and Online Page Layout view. Otherwise, how could Word show true page layouts?

If your computer is running Word too slowly, try working more in Normal view and less in Page Layout view.

■ When *Help for WordPerfect* users is turned on, Word's parallel help system for users transitioning from WordPerfect for DOS is also enabled. When you type a keyboard combination that corresponds to a WordPerfect feature, WordPerfect Help tells you how to perform the same task in Word and in some cases, even demonstrates the feature.

▶ **See** "Setting WordPerfect Help Options," **p. 837**

■ When *Navigation Keys for WordPerfect Users* is turned on, Word's Page Up, Page Down, Home, End, and Esc keys start behaving the way they would if you were running WordPerfect. For example, Page Down moves the insertion point down six lines instead of a full page.

■ The next option, *Blue Background, White Text*, is also designed to help WordPerfect users feel at home. It displays text in white against a blue, WordPerfect for DOS-like background. Some people who have never used WordPerfect still find this to be softer on their eyes; it's a matter of personal taste. Figure 26.28 shows a sample, but it looks better on your monitor; try it for yourself.

FIG. 26.28

Some people, especially former WordPerfect for DOS users, find the Blue Background, White Text option more readable.

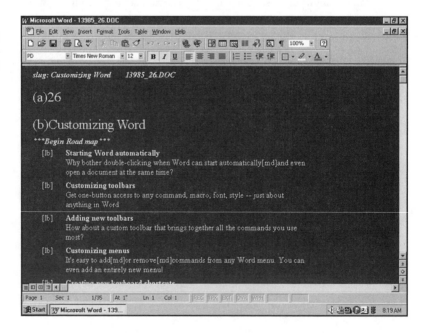

- *Provide Feedback with Sound* tells Word to play sounds in response to specific actions or events, such as error messages. You need three things to play sounds: a sound card, speakers, and the sound files themselves, which are not automatically installed as part of the Microsoft Office installation.

ON THE WEB

Sound files are stored in the Sounds folder of the Office 97 CD-ROM. If you don't have them, you can download them from Microsoft's Web site. They're currently located at **www.microsoft.com/ OfficeFreeStuff/download/sounds.EXE**—not at the Free Stuff location to which Microsoft directs you.

- *Provide Feedback with Animation,* turned on by default, uses special animated pointers to tell you that certain automated procedures are in progress, such as AutoFormatting, background saves, and background printing.

- *Confirm Conversion at Open* may come in handy if you often work with files in other formats. In general, Word is capable of recognizing the source of a document and using the appropriate converter. For example, Word recognizes WordPerfect 5.1 documents and uses the WordPerfect import filter, even if those documents have a Word-like .DOC extension. However, in rare instances Word may choose the wrong filter or you may want to choose the filter you use. If so, check this box. When you open a file in a different format, Word enables you to choose which converter to use.

- *Update Automatic Links at Open,* turned on by default, tells Word to automatically update any information in your document that is based on other files linked to your document. In general, you'll want to leave this enabled. However, if you prefer to see your document with the content it had the last time you worked with it, or if you suspect the source document is no longer available, you can clear this check box to turn off automatic updating.

- The next option, *Mail as Attachment,* relates to the way Word integrates with MAPI-compatible e-mail software that may be installed on your computer. With this option turned on, if you choose File, Send to, Mail Recipient, Word opens an e-mail message window and includes your file as an attachment. Unfortunately, some recipients may have e-mail systems that don't handle attachments correctly, and some can't handle Word-formatted documents in any event. If your recipients use incompatible e-mail systems like these, clear the Mail as Attachment check box. Word copies the unformatted text of your document into your e-mail editing window instead.

- By default, Word displays the last four files you worked on at the bottom of the File menu. If you work on a great many files, you may want to increase the number of files displayed in this *Recently Used File List.* Conversely, if you have added custom items to the File menu, you might not even have room for four files. To make a change, click in the Entries scroll box, and type a number from 1 to 9.

Part VI

Ch 26

TIP If you don't want any files listed in the Recently Used File List (possibly because you don't want others to know what you've been working on), clear the Recently Used File List check box.

■ The *Macro Virus Protection* check box tells Word to warn you whenever you open a document that contains macros, so you can determine whether those macros might possibly be infected with a macro virus. In general, you should almost certainly leave this enabled. You might conceivably turn it off if you never download or read documents from others who might be infected. You might turn it off temporarily if you're deliberately working with macros in templates you yourself created.

■ *Measurement Units* tells Word which measurement system to use in its rulers and in *some* of its dialog boxes: Inches, Centimeters, Points, or Picas. Note that not every measurement changes when you change this setting. For example, font size is still measured in points no matter which setting you choose.

In general, you can enter margins and similar information in any system you choose, by adding the appropriate prefix or suffix. For example, if you enter 1" as your top margin while Word is set to display centimeters, Word inserts the appropriate margin setting and converts it to 2.54 cm automatically. Conversely, if Word is set to inches, you can enter centimeters by adding **cm** after the number.

Changing Editing Options

If you've been working with Word for quite some time, you've probably become very comfortable with Word's default editing settings. If you're relatively new to Word, you may find some of them strange and want to change them. Editing behavior is controlled through the Edit tab of the Options dialog box (see Figure 26.29).

FIG. 26.29

The Edit tab controls how Word responds as you enter and edit text.

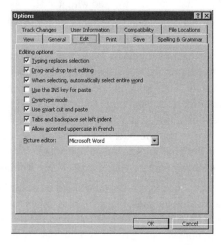

■ *Typing Replaces Selection,* which is on by default, means that you can replace text by selecting it and typing over it. That makes editing faster, and most people like it. Others find themselves deleting text they meant to keep. If you find that happening, clear the check box.

■ *Drag-and-Drop Text Editing,* also on by default, activates Windows' drag-and-drop feature. With this feature turned on (as it is by default), you can select text, right-click, and drag it to a new location. Some people find drag and drop an especially intuitive way of moving text. Others find that they accidentally move text when drag and drop is enabled. If you want to turn it off, clear the check box.

■ *When Selecting, Automatically Select Entire Word* is a shortcut designed to make it easier to select large blocks of text. You don't have to precisely start at the beginning of a word to select the whole word. Rather, as soon as you select the space after a word, the program assumes you intended to select the whole word. Some people don't like Word to make assumptions about what they intend to select. If that's you, clear the check box.

■ If you check *Use the INS Key for Paste,* the Insert key pastes text from your clipboard into your document. In previous versions of Word, INS normally toggled Overtype mode on and off, unless you checked this box. However, Microsoft has disabled that toggle in Word 97. As a result, checking this box gives you another convenient way to insert text without losing any capabilities that aren't already gone. In Insert mode, Word inserts text as you type and moves existing text to its right. In Overtype mode, Word instead replaces existing text, one character at a time, as you type "into it." You can turn on Overtype mode by double-clicking OVR in the status bar, or you can do it here by checking the Overtype Mode check box.

■ *Use Smart Cut and Paste* tells Word to eliminate any extra spaces you might leave when you delete text, or extra spaces you might insert when you paste text. In effect, Smart Cut and Paste makes sure there is exactly one space between each word in a sentence. It's another way in which Word acts as if it knows better than you do. The fact is, Word is almost always right, but some people find features like these a little presumptuous.

■ *Tabs and Backspace Set Left Indent* is turned on by default; it enables you to increase and decrease left indents at the beginning of a paragraph by pressing the Tab and Backspace keys.

■ The *Allow Accented Uppercase in French* option tells Word it can suggest accented uppercase characters as corrections when proofing, or as options in the Change Case dialog box. This only works for text formatted as French, and it only works if you have French proofing tools installed.

■ Finally, the *Picture Editor* drop-down box enables you to choose which drawing or image editing program will open when you double-click an image in your document. Typically, the choices are Microsoft Word (in other words, Word's built-in picture editing feature), or Microsoft Photo Editor 3.0 (if you have installed it). However, if you have installed the optional Microsoft Draw 97 applet, this choice will be listed, too. Other imaging tools registered as OLE applications might appear as well.

Part VI

Ch 26

Setting Save Options

In the Save tab of the Options dialog box (see Figure 26.30), you can control Word's behavior in saving files:

■ *Always Create Backup Copy* tells Word to rename the previous version of your document with a .BAK extension in the same folder as the new version it is saving.

- *Allow Fast Saves* enables Word to save time on most saves by recording all the changes to your document together instead of integrating them throughout your document.

- *Prompt for Document Properties* opens the Properties dialog box whenever you save a document for the first time.

- *Prompt to Save Normal Template* gives you a chance to abandon changes to default settings, AutoText entries, and macros before Word saves them to the Normal template at the end of your editing session.

FIG. 26.30

Use the Save tab of the Options dialog box to control Word's saving options.

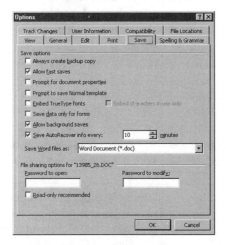

- *Embed TrueType Fonts* tells Word to embed the TrueType fonts you've used in your document. Check this box when you suspect your readers won't have access to the fonts you used to create your document. Keep a few things in mind, however. First of all, embedding fonts can dramatically increase font size. It's probably not a good option if your documents have many fonts and you're planning to send multiple copies across a network. Second, not all TrueType fonts can be embedded; font manufacturers have the power to prevent their fonts from being embedded as an antipiracy measure, and some companies such as Émigré have exercised that option. Third, PostScript fonts can't be embedded with this feature.

  Occasionally, you might want to embed a font you've used in only one or two document headlines. To save space, Word 97 now provides an option, *Embed Characters in Use Only*, which lets you embed up to 32 individual characters from a font without embedding the entire font. If you've used more characters than this, Word embeds the entire font. Stay away from this option if you expect your recipients to edit the headline, because they will not have access to other characters they may need.

 If you have a complex, heavily formatted document that you want others to read but not edit, consider using a program like Adobe Acrobat to save relatively compact versions of your file, which can then be read and printed with fonts and formatting largely intact.

■ *Save Data Only for Forms* means that, in electronic forms, Word will save only the text entered by the person filling out the form, not the surrounding form itself. This information will be stored in a tab-delimited, text-only format that is easy to import into databases.

■ *Allow Background Saves* lets Word save "in the background" as you work. While Word is saving, a pulsating disk icon is displayed in the status bar.

■ The *Save AutoRecover Info Every* scroll box tells Word how often to create a document recovery file. You can set intervals from 1 to 120 minutes.

■ *Save Word Files As* enables you to specify a default format other than Word 97 in which to save your files.

■ Finally, file sharing options allow you to specify a password users will need to open a document; or a password they will need to modify it. You can also use *Read-only Recommended* to discourage people from opening your document in a way that permits modification, without actually preventing them from doing so.

▶ **See** "Creating Automatic Backups," **p. 39**

▶ **See** "Saving Only the Data in a Form," **p. 691**

▶ **See** "Word Document Security," **p. 815**

▶ **See** "Displaying the Summary Tab Whenever a New File Is Saved," **p. 826**

Setting User Information

Word uses your name, initials and address in a variety of ways. It stores your name as the Author in the Properties dialog box of any new document you create. It includes your name automatically in letters and envelopes you create using Word's wizards and templates; your initials are also included in letters. It attaches your name and initials to any changes or comments you insert using Word's Track Changes or Comments features. To set or change your name, initials or address, display the User Information tab of the Options dialog box (see Figure 26.31). Enter your Name, Initials, and Mailing Address as you want them to appear when Word uses them. (For example, your initials don't have to correspond precisely to the name you enter in the name box—it's up to you.)

Part
VI

Ch
26

N O T E Word also tracks your Company Name as you entered it during installation, but this information cannot be permanently changed except through the Registry. ■

Setting Compatibility Options

You might be accustomed to working with a different version of Word, or a different brand of word processor, such as WordPerfect. Or you may have documents that originated on a different system, such as a Macintosh running Microsoft Word 5.1. These programs differ subtly in the ways they display text.

These subtleties are almost all minor, but they can occasionally cause significant problems. For example, Microsoft 5.1 for the Macintosh uses larger Small Caps than Word 97. This minor difference could conceivably affect where lines, or even pages, break—throwing off carefully created page layouts.

FIG. 26.31

Use the User Informa-
tion tab of the Options
dialog box to change
your personal informa-
tion settings.

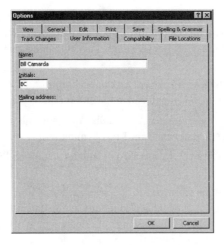

Using the Compatibility tab of the Options dialog box (see Figure 26.32), you can adjust Word
to display your document as it would look if opened in a different program.

FIG. 26.32

In the Compatibility tab,
you can adjust Word
97's behavior to match
that of older versions for
Windows, DOS, and
Macintosh, as well as
WordPerfect.

N O T E These Compatibility settings don't actually change the contents of an existing file. They
change only its appearance, so you can accurately format your document to reflect the
software and computer from which it will eventually be used and printed. ▪

If you know the program that created a file, the quickest way to ensure compatibility is to
choose that program name in the *Recommended Options For* drop-down list box. Word 97 has
built in options designed to reflect differences in appearance for the following:

- Word 6.0/95
- Word for Windows 1.0
- Word for Windows 2.0
- Word for the Macintosh 5.x
- Word for MS-DOS
- WordPerfect 5.x for DOS
- WordPerfect 6.x for Windows
- WordPerfect 6.0 for DOS

You can also choose Custom to create custom settings if you need them.

Using Font Substitution

If you've been asked to edit a file that was created with another word processing program, or on another type of computer, such as a Macintosh, you may find that you don't have all the fonts that were used in the original file. Word 97 automatically substitutes fonts it does have for those it can't find.

In some cases, these font substitutions are no-brainers. For example, many Macintosh documents are created with PostScript fonts such as Times Roman and Courier. On standard Windows PCs that don't have Adobe fonts installed, Word substitutes the TrueType equivalents, Times New Roman and Courier New.

Note that the substituted fonts are similar but not identical to the originals, so you might find unwelcome changes in line and page breaks. Also note that the original font names still appear in the Font drop-down box on the Formatting toolbar, so if you return the document to its source, the original fonts will automatically be in use.

Occasionally, you'll want to control the way Word substitutes fonts. For example, perhaps you've been handed a document formatted with the Eras Bold ITC font. You don't own Eras Bold ITC, and Word substitutes Lucida Sans Unicode, which looks quite different. However, you do have one of the many competitive "knockoff" fonts that resemble Eras Bold ITC. Your font has a name that Word doesn't recognize as being equivalent to Eras. You can tell Word to use that font instead of Lucida Sans Unicode whenever it comes across text formatted as Eras Bold ITC.

To use font substitution, choose Tools, Options, and click the Compatibility tab. Then, click Font Substitution to open the Font Substitution dialog box (see Figure 26.33).

N O T E If there are no substituted fonts in your document, Word won't display the Font Substitution dialog box. Rather, it displays a message telling you no font substitution is necessary. ■

The Font Substitution dialog box lists all the Missing Document Fonts it has found, and the fonts it has substituted. (In some cases, it simply substitutes a Default font, typically Times New Roman.) To change a font substitution, select the row containing the Missing Document

Part
VI

Ch
26

Font and the font Word has substituted. Then, in the <u>S</u>ubstituted Font drop-down box, select the font you want to use.

FIG. 26.33

In the Font Substitution dialog box, you can control which fonts are used when you don't have the ones with which your document was formatted.

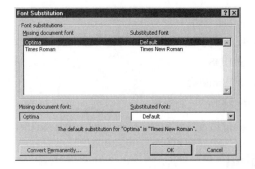

As you've already learned, when you substitute a font, Word displays and prints the document using the font you chose. However, the original font is still shown in the Font drop-down box. This is obviously welcome for documents that may be returned to their source. In other cases, however, it can be confusing. After all, the font you see on-screen no longer matches the font Word "says" the text has been formatted with.

It's easy to reformat the document using the fonts you've already chosen as substitutes. In the Font Substitution box, choose Convert <u>P</u>ermanently. Click OK to confirm the change. Wherever Word finds a substituted font in your document, it converts the document to call for the substituted font name instead of the original one.

Setting File Locations

There's one final Options tab, File Locations (see Figure 26.34), that specifies where Word looks for the files and documents it needs. By default, for example, Word looks for (and stores) documents in the C:\My Documents folder. You might find that you're piling up all sorts of documents in this folder, when most of the documents ultimately need to be moved to another folder. In this tab, you can tell Word to use a different default.

If you know you'll be working primarily in a specific folder for a week or two, change the documents location to that folder. When you start Word and display the Open dialog box, Word automatically displays the contents of that folder.

In the File Locations tab, you can also control where Word looks for clip art, templates, workgroup templates shared across a network, user options, AutoRecover files, tools, and templates or add-ins that should run at Startup.

▶ **See** "Using Workgroup Templates," **p. 800**

To change a <u>F</u>ile type, select the row containing the file type and location, and choose Modify. The Modify Location dialog box opens (see Figure 26.35). Browse to the folder you want, and choose OK twice.

FIG. 26.34
The File Locations tab enables you to change where Word looks for documents, templates, and tools.

FIG. 26.35
The Modify Location dialog box enables you to set a new location for whatever file type you've chosen.

From Here...

In this chapter, you've looked at many of the ways Word can be customized to your personal needs and tastes. Now, learn even more about extending Word to make it even more useful to you:

- Take advantage of Word's extensive integration with the other Microsoft Office applications, including Excel, PowerPoint, Access, and Outlook. Chapter 27, "Integrating with Microsoft Office," shows you how.

- As you've learned in this chapter, one of the most important reasons to customize Word is to build a word processing program that meets the specific needs of your organization. To learn more about using and managing Word in a business setting, see Chapter 29, "Sharing Files and Managing Word."

- Macros are the most powerful form of Word customization: they allow you to make Word do practically anything. In Chapter 30, "Recording and Running Visual Basic Macros," you'll learn the basics of recording macros. Then, in Chapters 31 through 34, you'll learn how to leverage Visual Basic for Applications to build practical, real-world solutions for yourself and your organization.

Part VI

Ch

26

CHAPTER 27

Integrating with Microsoft Office

by Joe Lowery

One of Word's strengths comes from its association with Office 97. Tight integration with sister programs like Excel, Access, and PowerPoint extend the power of both Word and the other programs. This chapter demonstrates techniques for making the most of Word in the Office environment. ■

Excel and Word Integration

See how to easily move between Excel and Word to get the most from their Office 97 integration.

Bring Access Data into Word

This section covers bringing both Access data and reports into Word.

Visualizing with PowerPoint

Learn how Word can make the preparation for your next presentation smooth with PowerPoint.

Managing your office with Outlook

More than an ordinary planner (scheduler, calander, and address book), Outlook's duties include e-mail, tracking your Word output in Journal, and more.

Using Binder

Make the most of Binders extensive formatting and other capabilities.

Opening the Microsoft Toolbox

See how programs like the Office Shortcut Bar, Photo Editor, Organization Chart, Equation Editor, and Camcorder can make your documents more professional and easier to use.

Integrating Excel and Word

Word 97 is a very powerful word processor with extensive add-on features that give it basic capabilities in a number of areas including simple calculations. However, it's not a dedicated spreadsheet program like Excel. Luckily, because of the tight integration among Office 97 products, you can easily have the best of both worlds. You can insert Excel spreadsheets or charts when you need the extra number-crunching power. Or perhaps you just want to take advantage of work already completed in one program and avoid having to redo it in another.

This integration between Word and Excel is a two-way street. Excel can display tremendous mathematical prowess, but it's not a document management system like Word. You can use Word to publish your Excel information into a coherent report format and take advantage of your Word 97 skills to format an Office-compatible document.

Moreover, the connection between Word and Excel is as lively as you want it to be. If, for example, you link your quarterly report to sales data kept in three different files (gathered by three different reps) on your company's network, every time you open or print the report, your numbers are updated. Just as importantly, you can also set the links to not update automatically.

There are a number of techniques for bringing Excel data into Word, none of them overly complicated and some of them down right simple. The next section shows you how to begin with a new worksheet when you just want to use Excel's mathematical capabilities in Word.

Inserting a New Excel Worksheet in a Word Document

In previous chapters, you've seen how you can use Word to add numbers in a table or insert a field that can calculate a formula anywhere in a document. That, however, is about the limit of Word's built-in math skills. There is a silver lining here though; you can easily tap Excel's functionality without ever leaving Word. Naturally, to make the most of this arrangement, you need to be spreadsheet savvy, but Word even makes that easy by keeping a consistent interface, thereby reducing the learning curve.

 There are two basic ways to insert a new Excel worksheet into a Word document. The first, the Insert Microsoft Excel Worksheet button on the toolbar, looks and works just like the Insert Table button. Follow these steps to insert an Excel Worksheet into your document:

1. Click your insertion point in your document where you want the worksheet to appear.

2. Click the Insert Microsoft Excel Worksheet button on the toolbar, which causes a grid to drop down.

3. Move your mouse over the grid to select the size of your worksheet. To expand beyond the initial 4×5 grid, move your mouse to the right or bottom edge. Click to confirm your choice. The worksheet is inserted in a frame at the insertion point and the standard Word menus and toolbars change to Excel menus and toolbars as shown in Figure 27.1.

4. Enter your data in the worksheet as you would in Excel.

5. Click anywhere outside the worksheet to return to editing your document in Word.

FIG. 27.1

Inserting an Excel Worksheet gives you Excel menus, toolbar, and layout.

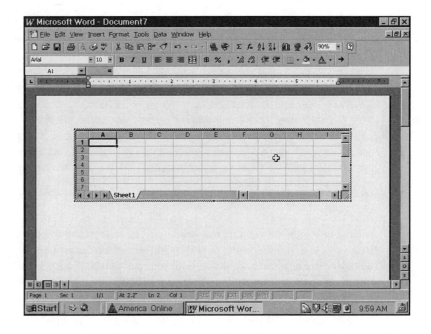

The other way to insert a new Excel worksheet is through the menus. Choose Insert, Object to open the Object dialog box. From the Create New tab, scroll down the Object Type list until you see Microsoft Excel Worksheet. Double-click it to insert the worksheet and close the dialog box. The default worksheet is 7 columns wide by 10 rows high.

There are two additional options when you insert an Excel Worksheet through the menus. First, you can elect to anchor your worksheet to the text rather than appear in a floating frame. To do this, from the Object dialog box as shown in Figure 27.2, clear the check mark in the Float over Text check box.

FIG. 27.2

The Object dialog box lets you select from a wide range of applications.

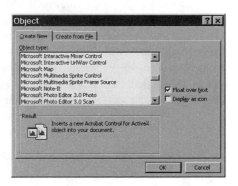

Second, if you find the worksheet distracting or redrawing too slowly on your screen, you can choose to have the object inserted as an icon. Enable this by checking the Display as Icon check box in the Object dialog box. When you double-click the embedded icon, the Excel

Worksheet opens up in a separate window for input and editing. Before you can view (or print) the worksheet as part of your Word document, you must convert it to an Excel object. Right-click the Excel icon and choose Worksheet Object, Convert. Be sure to clear the Display as Icon check box and have Convert To selected as well as Microsoft Excel Worksheet. Click OK. You may have to double-click to edit the worksheet and then resize it to the proper dimensions.

TIP While it's good to know approximately what size you want your spreadsheet to be, you can always resize the frame to include more (or fewer) cells. When you're in Excel mode, position your pointer over any of the sizing handles on the frame surrounding the Excel worksheet. Click and drag the frame to a new size. If you are in the regular Document mode and resize the frame, the number of cells stay the same, but size of the cells change.

After you've inserted your worksheet, you'll notice the typical Excel layout with alphabetic column headings and numeric row headings. You can resize the columns just like in Excel by moving your mouse pointer over the right side of a column boundary. Click and drag the boundary to a new width. Basically, until you click outside the Excel worksheet, all commands, menus, toolbars function as though you are in Excel. Anytime you want to edit the worksheet from within Word, just double-click the Excel Worksheet to enter the Excel mode.

To delete an Excel Worksheet from your Word document, first make sure you're in Word editing mode (if the Excel layout is active, click outside of the worksheet into the regular document). Next select the object by clicking it once and pressing Delete.

TIP The latest version of Excel supports multiple worksheets accessed by clicking one of the sheet tabs at the bottom of the Excel window. The default sheet is labeled Sheet1. Although you can add additional sheets to the Excel Worksheet you inserted in Word, only one sheet is visible at a time.

Importing Excel Objects

There are a lot of reasons you'd rather import Excel data into your Word document than open a new worksheet and input it by hand. First and foremost, you might be working with an existing Excel Workbook with information that you want to bring into your document. Second, you might need to share the worksheet information with someone who has Excel, but not Word. Saving an embedded Excel Worksheet in an Word document means that you can only open it in Word. Third, you might need to include data from different parts of your Excel Workbook, whether on the same worksheet or on multiple worksheets. Finally, you might just feel more comfortable keeping your Excel and Word environments separate and using the task bar buttons to go back and forth.

Whatever the reason, Word has plenty of ways to accommodate you and still give you control over your inserted Excel object. Here are your options:

- You can import a copy of an entire existing Excel Workbook.
- You can import a linked version of an existing Excel Workbook.
- You can insert a range of cells from Excel as a table in Word.

- You can insert a range of cells from Excel into Word and retain all the Excel formatting.
- You can insert a range of cells as a link from Excel to Word.

Importing an Entire Workbook You import an existing workbook through one of the same mechanisms that you used to open a new workbook. Choose Insert, Object again, but this time click the Select from File tab. Unless you know the file name, click the Browse button to select your file. Two options that are available on the Create New tab, Float over Text and Display as Icon, are offered here.

After you confirm your file choice by clicking OK in the Object dialog box, a copy of the entire Excel Workbook is inserted in your Word document as an object. More often than not, the workbook object is larger than your Word page. This forces the object's borders to extend to the edge of the page, and still some of your information could be off-screen. Figure 27.3 shows an example of this. Remember that if you use the object's sizing handles while in Word mode, the object shrinks or grows much like a picture. You must be in Excel mode to reveal more or less of workbook.

FIG 27.3
A newly inserted Excel Workbook may need to be resized to be viewed properly.

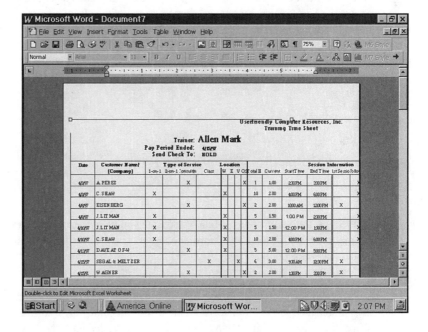

Part
VI

Ch
27

N O T E Note the difference between a worksheet and a workbook. A workbook can be composed of many separate worksheets, although only one is visible at a time in your Word document. The default Excel Workbook has 16 worksheets, which can seriously increase your Word document file size. Consider just inserting the range of cells that you need. ■

You also have the option of importing a linked version of your workbook. In the Object dialog box, from the Select from File tab, check off the Link to File check box. The difference here is that you are no longer working with a copy of the original file; you're working with the actual file. When you double-click the Excel object to edit it, Excel opens the workbook in another window and any changes you make are incorporated into the source file. Likewise, with a linked object, any changes you make in the source file are reflected in the linked version.

Inserting a workbook as a linked file is both a blessing and a curse. The good news is that all of your updates are centralized and you don't have to worry about making changes in both Excel and Word. On the other hand, sometimes you want to lock in your report data after a certain point. Luckily, Word 97 lets you have it both ways.

After you have embedded a linked object into your Word document, the Edit, Links option becomes active. Choosing this menu option opens the Links dialog box as seen in Figure 27.4. From here you can choose to update your link automatically, manually, or to completely lock the link. If the Manual option is chosen, you must select the object (or the entire document) and press F9 or click the Update Now button from the Links dialog box. Locking the link deactivates the Update Now button and prevents any updates from occurring until the link is unlocked, but your original Excel file can still be edited.

FIG. 27.4
You can modify a linked object's status at any time through the Links dialog box.

Inserting a Range of Cells   Most of the time you need to insert just a small portion of an overall Excel Workbook into a Word document. The process for doing this is one you're sure to be familiar with, Cut and Paste. As noted previously, there are three different results you can achieve when inserting a range of Excel cells: they can appear as a Word table, as an independent Excel object, or as a linked Excel object.

The simplest method of transferring data is to select and copy it from Excel and paste it into Word. If you have highlighted a range of cells, the pasted entry is converted into a Word table. Numbers are right-justified, and formulas become values. Most formatting is retained, with the exception of spanned columns, which can be simulated by selecting the cells in question and choosing Table, Merge Cells. Cutting and pasting is a good alternative for simple, fixed data where there is little or no chance of the former formulas needing to be recalculated.

N O T E When a range of Excel cells are copied and pasted into a Word document, the table that the data appears in is formatted with borders turned on for each cell and around the entire table, whether or not the selected cells have borders in Excel. To alter, you must select the table in Word and choose Format, Borders and Shading and select your options. ■

If you even think it's remotely possible that you'll need to update your numbers and recalculate your formulas, it's best to paste the Excel data as an object. The process is basically the same as regular cut and pasting with one little twist. Follow these steps to insert Excel information as an object:

1. From Excel, select the range of cells you want to insert.
2. Click the Copy button on the Standard toolbar.
3. Switch to your Word document.
4. Place the insertion point where you want the data to appear.
5. Choose Edit, Paste Special. The Paste Special dialog box opens as shown in Figure 27.5.
6. From the As list, select Microsoft Excel Worksheet Object.
7. Make sure that the Paste button is selected.
8. Click OK to confirm your choices.

FIG. 27.5

Paste Special lets you maintain all your Excel data's formulas and formatting.

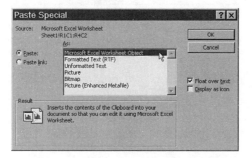

As with the insertion of an entire sheet, you have the following options for your data: Float over Text or Display as Icon. Just check the check box to enable the feature.

After you discover the Paste Special command, inserting your Excel data as a linked object is very straightforward. From the Paste Special dialog box, choose the Paste link option button instead of Paste.

Creating Maps and Charts in Excel

One of the things that Excel does well is create charts from existing data. Word has access to another charting program, Microsoft Graph 97 (covered in Chapter 22, "Using Microsoft Graph"), but if your charts are already built, you can insert them as easily as you can the range of cells from which they're derived. In fact, it's basically the same copy and paste operation, with the same Paste Special options that you used for inserting cells. There's only one slight difference: there is no Table option. Use the normal copy and pasting to insert a chart or map as a discrete object and use the Paste Special command to activate the Link function.

Both Word and Excel have access to a special program called Microsoft Map that enables you to chart data to a regional, national, or global map. To create your map, first select the data you want (make sure the labels indicate countries or states) and then click the Map button in the toolbar. After your map is drawn and selected, click the Copy button and switch to Word. Click the Paste button to insert the map into your Word document. Although you can double-click it to edit it as you expect, you can't link it to the data. Figure 27.6 shows a sample map created in Excel and imported into a Word report.

FIG. 27.6

You can import Excel charts and Maps into any Word document.

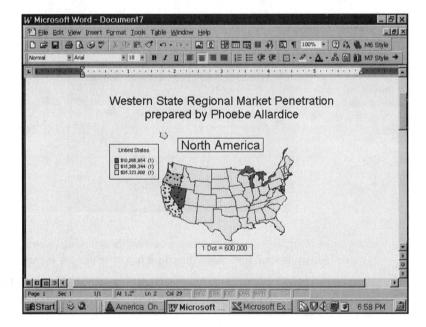

Working with Access and Word

Access is to data as Excel is to numbers and Word is to, well, words. Increasingly, much of an office's day-to-day business is keeping track of, and communicating with, the data. Take an overdue invoice notice, for example. Although the general letter is a word processing document, the key bits of information are data, such as the business name and address, invoice numbers, amount due, and so on. This type of data is best managed in a database program like Access. The tight integration of Access and Word enable you to produce an unlimited number of reports, letters, labels, and other documents based on the same data source.

The main connection between Word and Access is the Mail Merge tool. When you invoke the Mail Merge Helper, you'll find that Access is one of your choices when it comes to types of data with which Word can work. Although it's true that you can create a data source from within Word, when your business reaches a certain level of complexity, it's better to handle your data separately. Why? The primary benefit of using a separate database as your source for mail merges is data centralization. If all the related data is in one file, which you and your co-workers can access for a variety of purposes, there's only one place the data can be updated.

▶ **See** "An Overview of Word's Mail Merge," **p. 372**

Establishing Criteria for Importing Data

Although Word can automatically read Access files, it does require that certain elements be properly formatted. As a quick database jargon refresher, remember that a database is made up of many records, each of which represents one business, person, or transaction. The records, in turn, are composed of a number of different fields. Each field represents one unique aspect of a record, such as a first name, a last name, a street address, a ZIP code, and so on. Databases are often represented as tables with each column representing a different field and each row a different record. The first row of the table is reserved for the field names and is called the header row.

In Access, you can enter field names up to 64 characters with spaces and most special characters. However, if you're planning on using your database in Word, it's best to limit your field names to 20 characters or less and avoid spaces and any special characters outside of the underscore. Otherwise, when you link your Word document with your Access database while setting up a mail merge, Word truncates the field names to 20 characters and alters any spaces or special characters to the underscore character.

Word inserts your Access data just as it appears in Access. So if your AmountDue field isn't formatted to show dollars and cents in Access, it won't show up that way in Word. The same is true of date fields and text fields. One data entry trick many people use is to have the field automatically uppercase whatever is input so that they won't have to deal with pressing Shift for upper- and lowercase.

Exporting Access Reports to Word

Access has a fairly comprehensive system for building reports from the data stored in its tables and queries. However, there are times when you need to integrate the reports into your Word documents for reference or further formatting. Just as you can pull information from Access into Word through the Mail Merge tool, you can also publish reports from Access directly into Word. You can even make Word start automatically with the reports already loaded!

There are two methods for making a report from Access available to Word: one more automatic and the other more customizable. The first, more automatic, method takes your report, converts it, names it, saves it, and opens it in Word—all from one command. All you have to do is select the report from your Access database window and choose Tools, Office Links, Publish It with MS Word. Access first runs the report and then, essentially, prints it to a Rich Text Format (or .rtf file), which preserves the formatting. The new file is then saved under its report name with an .rtf extension in the same folder where Access is installed. Finally, if Word is not running, the program is started and the file is loaded.

Using the Publish It with MS Word command is the most efficient method for converting your Access report. However, you do trade some control for the expediency. The second method, exporting your report, gives you the same results but enables you to specify name, placement, and file type when it comes to saving the file. Follow these steps to export your report to Word:

1. Select the report in Access by highlighting it in the Database window.
2. Choose File, Save As/Export from the main Access menu.
3. From the Save As dialog box, check the box next to the To an External File or Database option. Click OK.
4. Select a folder, file name, and file type for your report from the Save Report In dialog box.
5. To have Word automatically load the converted report, check the AutoStart check box.

 TIP When do you use which method? Use the first one, Publish It with MS Word, when you want to immediately incorporate your report into a Word document. After it has opened into Word, you can cut and paste it into your document. Use the second method, Save As/Export, when you want to keep the report available as a separate document.

Using PowerPoint with Word

PowerPoint is traditionally referred to as a presentation program. Over the years it has developed into the multimedia center of Office 97. Not only can you incorporate text and images in a slide format, but you can also add animation, sound, and movies to teach, explain, and persuade through PowerPoint. Because both Word and PowerPoint are Office 97 family members you have a strong connection that lets you share information in both directions.

Here are just a few of the ways you can use PowerPoint and Word together:

- Draft your outlines in Word, and then you can import them into PowerPoint.
- Send a presentation's preset information from PowerPoint to Word, including outlines, notes, and handouts.
- Publish the notes, action items, and other information that occurs during a presentation in Word.
- Embed slides or an entire presentation into a Word document for inclusion in a report.

To learn about PowerPoint, start by looking at how you can use your work from Word as a basis for a PowerPoint multimedia presentation.

Using Word Outlines in PowerPoint

Quite often, the impetus for a PowerPoint presentation is a report drafted in Word. If you use Outline or Heading styles in Word, you can built your presentation effortlessly. Even if you haven't applied the styles, there's workaround that will still enable you to adapt your Word document to PowerPoint slides.

The trick to "no-brainer" Word-to-PowerPoint conversions is setting up your Word document using Heading or Outline styles. Each paragraph, or title, formatted with the Heading 1 style becomes the title of a new slide, while each paragraph, or subtitle, formatted with the Heading 2 style becomes the first level of text, and so on.

When transferring information back and forth, it's best to have both Word and PowerPoint open. In Word, open the document, choose File, Send To, and then click Microsoft PowerPoint. You'll see a brief progress bar and then the program switches to PowerPoint in Outline view with your Word text imported, as shown in Figure 27.7.

FIG. 27.7
Build your presentation's "talking points" by sending your Word outline to a PowerPoint presentation.

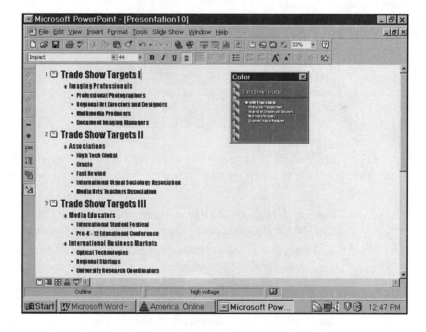

 TIP If you haven't used the Heading or Outline styles in Word, you can still bring your document into PowerPoint with a slight workaround. If your document uses tabs to indicate headings and subheadings, save it as a text file. In PowerPoint, switch to Outline view and choose Open. Change the file type to All Outlines and select your text file. The first paragraph not indented becomes the slide title; the paragraph indented once becomes the first level of text and so forth.

Exporting PowerPoint Files to Word

The slides are the flashy part of a PowerPoint presentation, but there's also a lot of supporting material: an outline, speaker notes, and handouts to name a few. PowerPoint makes it easy for you to export all of this information and more to Word where you can further modify it or incorporate it into an existing document. Moreover, through PowerPoint's Meeting Minder utility, you can take notes during your presentation and even assign tasks or actions. Naturally, you can export these items to Word as well.

When giving a presentation, it's extremely useful to have a hard copy of your talk that tells you what slide comes when and what to say about it. After you've created your slide show, you can export it to Word so that you can further develop your speakers notes. From PowerPoint's main menu, choose <u>F</u>ile, Send To, Microsoft <u>W</u>ord. This opens the Write-Up dialog box as shown in Figure 27.8.

FIG. 27.8

You can send your entire slide presentation along with any speaker notes to Word for further editing through the Write-Up dialog box.

The Write-Up dialog box comes with various layout options that not only govern how your Write-Up will look, but also what you are actually exporting. You can choose from the following options:

- *Notes <u>N</u>ext to Slides* creates a three-column table showing slide number, a small image of the slide, and speaker notes. Figure 27.9 shows an example of this selection.

- *Bl<u>a</u>nk Lines Next to Slides* creates a three-column table showing slide number, a small image of the slide, and a series of underscored lines for speaker notes.

- *Notes <u>B</u>elow Slides* puts each slide on its own page with a slide number, and the speaker text.

- *Blan<u>k</u> Lines Below Slides* puts each slide on its own page with a slide number, and a series of underscored lines for speaker text.

- *<u>O</u>utline Only* sends just the outline for the presentation with no slide representation in Rich Text Format.

FIG. 27.9

Exporting your presentation to Word lets you easily edit and revise your speaker notes.

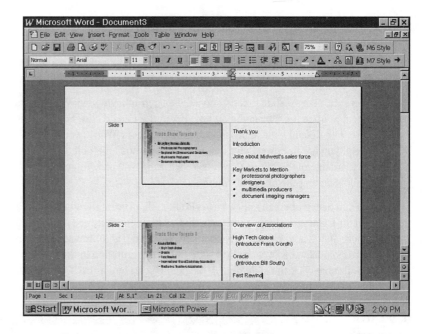

You'll notice that there are Paste and Paste Link options for all but the Outline Only selection. As with all embedded objects in Word, choosing Paste Link causes the document to be updated whenever changes are made to the source material, in this case a slide or presentation.

Meeting Minder is a PowerPoint utility that enables the presenter to take notes or keep minutes during the presentation. Right-click the slide during any presentation and select Meeting Minder. There are two tabs to the Meeting Minder dialog box: Meeting Minutes and Action Items. Meeting Minutes is an open-ended text area. Action Items are task oriented to-do items. Clicking the Export and then the Export Now buttons sends the current Meeting Minder to a Word document. It's best to only export these items once at the end of the session as Word creates a new document each time the information is sent.

Part
VI

Ch
27

Embedding PowerPoint Slides in Word

PowerPoint comes with a great number of templates and designs to give your message a professional edge. Word gives you full access to them to include in a report or any hard-copy presentation, without creating a slide show, electronic or otherwise.

To create a single slide that can be used as a graphic in your Word document, choose Insert, Object to open the Object dialog box. From the Create New tab, choose Microsoft PowerPoint Slide. The default slide appears as an object in your Word document. While you are within the object, you are in PowerPoint mode and the menus and toolbars reflect PowerPoint options. Click outside of the object to return to working in Word. You can edit your document by double-clicking the object at any time.

You can also embed an entire PowerPoint slide presentation in a Word document. This works well for training and other manuals that would benefit from a multimedia presence. From the Object dialog box, choose the Create from File tab and browse to your existing presentation. Word normally displays the first slide of the presentation in the document. To run the presentation, double-click the slide object. As can be seen by Figure 27.10, a special menu strip appears that enables the viewer to stay in Word and see the entire slide show.

FIG. 27.10

You can embed an entire presentation in your displayed Word document with just a double-click.

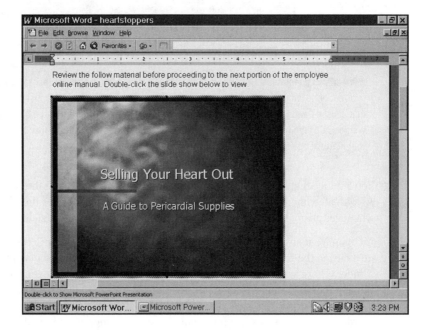

Of course you can also incorporate any existing PowerPoint slide by using the Copy and Paste features. As with Excel and other objects, you can either put a plain copy of your slide straight into your document by clicking the Paste button on the Standard toolbar. You also can put a linked copy of the slide by choosing Edit, Paste Special, selecting Microsoft PowerPoint Slide Object from the list, and then selecting the Paste Link option before you click the OK button.

Now, whenever you update your PowerPoint slide, your Word document is also updated.

 T I P If you want to copy the entire PowerPoint slide to paste in your Word document, be sure you're in the PowerPoint Slide Sorter view (choose View, Slide Sorter). If you are in Slide view, only the selected portion of your slide will be copied and pasted.

Using Outlook with Word

Outlook's role as the Office manager both supports and relies on Word's word processing expertise. Outlook gives you an edge by allowing you to incorporate Word's output in any message (e-mail or fax) either as an attached file or as part of the message itself. Furthermore, you can check your Word documents from the detached point of view of Outlook's Journal to track your progress with a particular project or overall.

Outlook makes strong use of Word in the integral E-Mail function. You can opt to have Word act as Outlook's e-mail editor and take advantage both of Word's copious features and familiarity. As you saw in Chapter 13, "Using Mail Merge Effectively," you can also access your Outlook address book to perform a mail merge. The more you investigate Outlook, the more you can benefit from its ties to Word.

Working with Word Files in Outlook

The first way that you can work with Word files in Outlook is to include any Word file (or portion of a file) with an Outlook message. You can attach the entire file to your message, use Copy and Paste to incorporate Word text into the body of your message, or you can include the Word text as a linked object. The method you choose depends on the effect you are trying to achieve.

The simplest way to include a Word file with your e-mail message is to insert it. After you're in the body of a new message in Outlook, the Insert File button (the paper clip) becomes active on the toolbar. When selected, the Insert File button opens a dialog box so that you can browse for the file. After you've selected it, an icon representing the file appears in your message as seen in Figure 27.11. You can insert as many different files as you like.

Part VI Ch 27

> **CAUTION**
>
> If you attach a file to your Outlook message, be sure the recipient's system can read the type of file you're sending. For example, Word 6.0 (for Windows 95) can't read Word 97 files directly without a converter. You can, however, save files in the Word 6.0/95 format. See Chapter 29, "Sharing Files and Managing Word."

If you just want to include a portion of your document, use Copy and Paste. Select your text in Word, and click the Copy button on the toolbar. Switch to Outlook, place your insertion point where you want the text to appear in your message and click the Paste button.

FIG. 27.11

Use the Insert File button to attach any Word document, or other file, to your Outlook message.

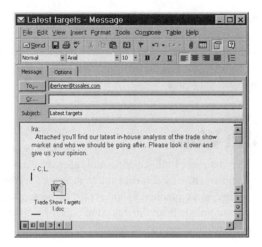

TIP While it's perfectly acceptable to use the Cut feature rather than the Copy one, you're less likely to accidentally delete a needed portion of your document if you routinely use Copy.

The other method of including text from a Word document creates a link between the existing document and the message. Use this method only if your original information in the Word document could possibly be updated before you send your message through Outlook.

To paste a linked passage from Word, follow these steps:

1. Select the text you want to copy in your Word document.

2. Click the Copy button.

3. Switch to Outlook.

4. Place the insertion point in the body of the message where you want the text to appear.

5. Choose Edit, Paste Special from the Outlook menu.

6. From the Paste Special dialog box, choose Microsoft Word Document Object in the As section.

7. Select the Paste Link option and click OK. The text is inserted into your message in a bounding box that visible when selected.

Tracking Word Progress in the Outlook Journal

Did you ever wonder how much time you spent on a particular document over a series of days? Or maybe you're looking for a particular file you worked on sometime last Wednesday in the afternoon, but now you can't find it or remember its name. Outlook's Journal function can keep track of all of your Word (and other types of files) output, detailing what your worked on when and for how long.

To see which entries are currently in your Journal, click the Journal folder in the Outlook bar on the left side of the screen. You'll see timeline items that are currently selected to be tracked in your Journal. If you don't see any items, or the items you want to see aren't there, choose Options, Tools and click the Journal tab. Put a check mark next to any of the Outlook items or Office 97 program files you want to track in the dialog box shown in Figure 27.12.

FIG. 27.12
You can opt to track Word and other program files through the Journal.

You can choose between a daily, weekly, or monthly timeline by clicking the appropriate toolbar button. Figure 27.13 shows a daily view. Each icon has a Duration bar above it to show when and for how long the document was open. If you double-click the icon, you can get an exact readout of the duration in minutes and get access to a shortcut to the file for immediate retrieval.

Using Word as Outlook's E-Mail Editor

You can add a great deal of functionality, not to mention ease-of-use, by choosing Word as your e-mail editor in Outlook. Take a look at the features you can add:

- *AutoCorrect* automatically corrects typos on-the-fly.
- *Bullets and Numbering* adds bullets and numbering to note important points.
- *Document Map* navigates and organizes e-mail messages quickly. Word creates a map, via hyperlinks, to each message.
- *E-Mail Name and Internet Address Conversion* automatically converts e-mail names and Internet addresses to hyperlinks.
- *Highlighter* uses color to emphasize the key points in a message.
- *Spell It* checks your spelling while you work.
- *Tables* uses tables to present your information in an organized fashion. All table formatting is preserved, including shading and borders.

FIG. 27.13
The Journal shows how long you worked on a document and when.

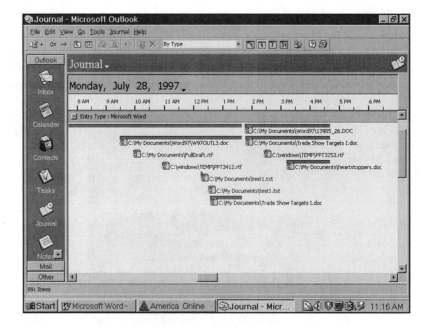

To enable Word as your e-mail editor, choose Tools, Options and click the E-Mail tab. Check the box next to the option, Use Microsoft Word as the E-Mail Editor.

You can also choose from a variety of e-mail templates to convey different messages. To select a new template, choose New, Choose Template. Double-click your choice from the templates displayed in the dialog box. Figure 27.14 shows the While You Were Out template.

FIG. 27.14
You can vary the e-mail template you use depending on the purpose of the message.

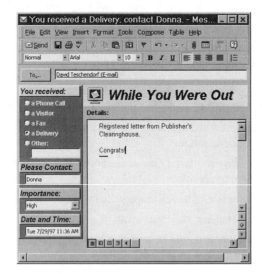

If you use Word as your e-mail editor, you can still send e-mail messages to people who do not use Word. However, features unique to Word change to plain text. For example, a table converts to tab-delimited text, and Internet addresses do not act as clickable links.

Using Binders to Combine Multiple Documents

An office doesn't survive on single Word documents alone. Reports can include numerous documents, spreadsheets, and presentations created separately by different individuals in different departments, if not different states. Office 97 includes a terrific program aimed at gathering together disparate material into one cohesive publication. This program, appropriately named Binder, is far more than its metaphoric binder clip. Binder can combine Word documents, Excel workbooks, and PowerPoint presentations into one easily transportable file. Moreover, Binder can print the entire file with consecutive page numbers and consistent headers and footers for all included documents.

After you've grouped your varied documents in a Binder file, you can edit them through the same overall interface while working with the native application menus, toolbars, and even macros. This means that you can switch between a Word document and an Excel workbook from within Binder without having to learn a whole new set of procedures or commands. It truly is the best of both worlds.

Each document in a Binder is in its own section. You can rearrange the sections at any time, as well as duplicate and delete them. A Binder can consist of any combination of existing documents and new documents. You could, for example, pull together the last four, already published, quarterly reports and create a new Excel chart that depicts the big picture especially for the Binder. You can even put multiple Binders together.

Working with Binders

To include documents in a binder, you need to start with a Binder file. You can start Binder in a number of ways. One way is to click the Start button on the Windows 95 task bar and choose Microsoft Binder from the Programs submenu. If enabled, you could also click the Binder icon (a binder clip) from the Office Shortcut Bar. You could also right-click the Desktop and choose New, Microsoft Binder from the Quick menu.

However you do start Binder, it automatically creates a new, blank file. To insert an existing file as a new Binder section, choose Section, Add from File and then select your file from the subsequent dialog box. If you're creating an original document for the binder, choose Section, Add. This opens the Add Section dialog box, which enables you to choose from any installed Office 97 template, including the ones for blank documents.

Figure 27.15 shows that the Binder window is divided into two parts or panes. The left pane is known as the *Contents pane* and shows an icon for each document in your binder. You can hide (and show) the contents pane by clicking the double-headed arrow to the left of the File menu. Whenever one of the icons in the Contents pane is activated, a right pointing arrow appears next to the icon and the document appears in the right or *Document pane*. Clicking different

Part
VI

Ch
27

types of documents invokes different menus and toolbars over the Document pane. The menus are a blend of the application menus and the Binder menu. Any operation that would affect an individual section, such as rearranging or hiding, is found under the new Section menu. Binder-wide commands such as Print or Page Setup are located under the File menu.

FIG. 27.15
The Binder window shows included sections on the left and the currently active document on the right.

Show/Hide Left pane
Section menu
Contents pane
Document pane
Word and Binder menus merged

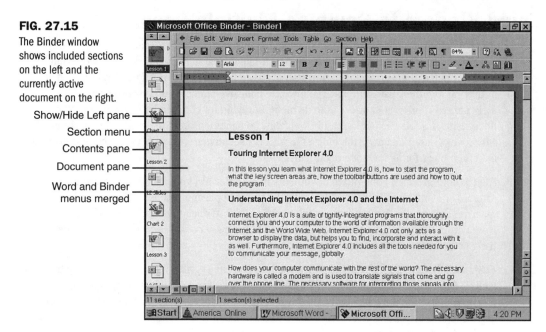

It's important to note that whenever you add a file to your binder, a copy of that file is added, not the original. Unlike Office 97 embedded objects, you don't have an option to link the original and binder file.

 TIP You can merge two or more Binder files together. Choose Section, Add from File and pick an existing Binder file. The documents contained in the existing binder are copied to the new Binder file.

Editing Your Binder Sections

You have two choices when it comes to editing a section in the Binder. You can either edit it from within the Binder or you can edit it in its native application and return to the Binder when you are finished. For any work that spans more than one section, it is best to edit within the Binder and take advantage of all the tools, like Binder-wide printing, available. You'll still have a complete set of menus, toolbars, and shortcut keys available to you to make your editing relatively straightforward.

If you need to do extensive editing within one of the sections, you can work in the application window as you normally would. Follow these steps to edit a document outside of the Binder:

1. Select the document you want to edit.

2. Choose Section, View Outside from the Binder menu.

3. A new application window opens with your document.

4. After you've completed your edits, click the Document Close button or choose File, Close & Return to Binder menu option.

 Naturally, you can cut, copy, and paste between sections of a binder, but you can also drag and drop as well. Highlight the text you want to move (or copy) in the Document pane of one section. Click and drag it over to another section in the Contents pane and press the Alt key while continuing to hold down the mouse button. The selected document is activated and now you can drag and drop your text wherever you like. You can copy the material by holding down Ctrl as with a regular drag-and-drop procedure.

Managing Your Binder

The Section menu has controls that enable you to move, delete, duplicate, rename, and hide the individual sections, among other commands. You can also access most of the management type commands by right-clicking the Section icon in the Contents pane.

 You can act on more than one document at a time by using the extended selection technique. Click the first document in the Contents Pane and then press Ctrl and click the other documents to add to the selection.

Rearranging Files in a Binder   You can move a section before or after any other section by choosing Section, Rearrange. This opens the Rearrange dialog box shown in Figure 27.16. Select the section you want to move, and then click the Move Up or the Move Down buttons to adjust the section's position in the Binder. Click OK when you have finished.

FIG. 27.16

You can rearrange your sections to any position in the Binder.

Part
VI

Ch
27

 You can also rearrange the sections by clicking and dragging the icons in the Contents Pane.

Duplicating Your Sections   There are times when you want to duplicate certain sections in your Binder. For example, you might want to put a PowerPoint slide as a transition between every major section of your Binder. Select the section to copy and then choose Section, Duplicate. The Duplicate dialog box opens and enables you to specify the section you would like the copy to follow. Highlight that section and click OK.

Hiding Sections When you hide a section of a binder, its icon is removed from the Contents Pane so that it can't be activated or printed as part of the overall Binder. Select the section (or sections) you want to hide and choose Section, Hide. To retrieve hidden sections, choose Section, Unhide Sections. A dialog box opens listing the hidden sections in the Binder; double-click and the document re-appears.

Saving Individual Sections As you would expect, saving the Binder is handled by clicking the Save button on the toolbar or choosing File, Save. However, what if you want to save an individual section? Choose Section, Save as File to open a standard Save file dialog box. This option comes in handy when you've made extensive changes to a copy of an existing file or when you want to isolate an original file prepared for the Binder.

Printing a Binder One of the major benefits to using Binders is that you can print a collection of documents as though they are one large report. Continuous page numbers and consistent headers and footers go a long way towards transforming a diverse group of documents into a cohesive publication. Follow these steps to set up the pages for the entire Binder:

1. Choose File, Binder Page Setup.
2. From the Header/Footer tab of the Binder Page Setup dialog box, choose the All Supported Sections option or select the individual sections to affect (see Figure 27.17).
3. To add a preset header or footer, choose from one of the options by clicking the arrow on the right of the Header or Footer box.
4. To add a custom header or footer, click the respective Custom button.

   From the Custom dialog box, put your text in the Left, Center, or Right sections. You can insert field codes for page number, section number, number of sections, binder name, date, or time.
5. Click OK when you've finished or click the Print button to open the Print dialog box.

After you've completed your binder page setup and before you print it, it's a good idea to choose File, Binder Print Preview. Previewing the file is helpful for spotting unnecessary or incorrect page breaks. When in Print Preview mode, you'll have an option to skip from one section to the next.

When you're ready to print, choose File, Print Binder. The Print Binder dialog box is similar to the regular Word Print dialog box, but there are a couple of exceptions. In the Print What section, you can choose to print all the available sections or only those selected in the left (Contents) pane. In the Numbering section, you can either make the page numbers consecutive or restart the numbers with each section.

FIG. 27.17
Binder Page Setup lets
you establish headers
and footers for the
entire Binder.

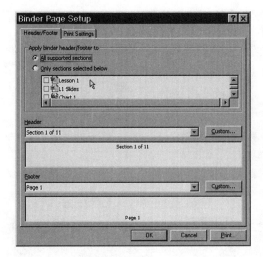

Using the Microsoft Office Shortcut Bar

The Office Shortcut Bar is one of the true work horses of Office 97. The Office Shortcut Bar is a completely customizable toolbar that enables you open the following items:

- A wide range of types of documents, from Word templates to Outlook messages
- Any folder or application on your Desktop, or in any frequently accessed location
- Any Office 97 application
- Any application at all

Moving the Office Shortcut Bar

You can set the Office Shortcut Bar to dock along any edge of the screen, ready to appear at the touch of a mouse. Or you can park it unobtrusively on the Desktop. To move the Office Shortcut Bar just click any areas not occupied by a button and drag the bar. When you get close to the top, bottom, left, or right edges of the screen, the bar snaps into position. Figure 27.18 shows a typical Office Shortcut Bar floating on the Desktop, customized to stay on top of any application.

N O T E Some editions of Office 97 don't automatically install the Office Shortcut Bar. To set it up, open the Add/Remove Programs utility in the Control Panel and click the Windows Setup tab. You'll find the Microsoft Office Shortcut Bar under Office Tools.

Part
VI

Ch
27

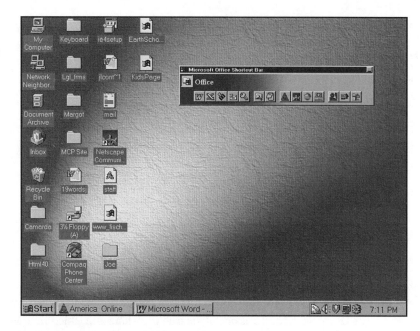

Customizing the Office Shortcut Bar

To get the most out of your Office Shortcut Bar, it is essential that you customize it. After you discover how useful and adjustable the Office Shortcut Bar is, you'll find yourself updating it at the drop of a hat. To begin the personalization of your Office Shortcut Bar, right-click the background of the toolbar (anywhere unoccupied by buttons). From the Quick menu, choose Customize. This opens the Customize dialog box with its four tabs: View, Buttons, Toolbars, and Settings.

The View tab of the Customize dialog box, shown in Figure 27.19, controls the overall settings for the Office Shortcut Bar. You can select the color for any of the available toolbars in the Color section. The Options section enables you to control the following options:

FIG. 27.19
You can completely personalize your Office Shortcut Bar through the Customize dialog box.

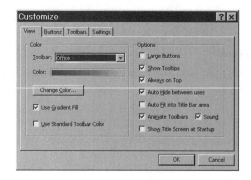

- *Large Buttons* controls the size of the buttons in the toolbar.
- *Show ToolTips* displays the name of the toolbar when touched by the mouse pointer.
- *Always on Top* keeps the Office Shortcut Bar always visible.
- *Auto Hide Between Uses* makes the Office Shortcut Bar disappear unless the mouse is near it.
- *Auto Fit into Title Bar Area* puts the Office Shortcut Bar in the title bar area of an application. This option has no effect if the Office Shortcut Bar is docked on either side of the screen.
- *Animate Toolbars* makes the Office Shortcut Bar slide out.
- *Sound* associates a sound effect with the Office Shortcut Bar's appearance.
- *Show Title Screen at Startup* displays the Microsoft Office title screen when the Office Shortcut Bar starts.

The Buttons tab of the Office Shortcut Bar is where you select the various programs and applications that appear on the toolbar. Check any existing entry in the scrolling list or add a new one by clicking the Add File or Add Folder button. You can also control the order of the toolbar buttons by using the Move Up and Move Down buttons. Finally, you can rename or delete any button by selecting it and clicking the appropriate command.

You're not limited to only one toolbar on the Office Shortcut Bar. Add additional toolbars, either preset or custom, by clicking the Toolbars tab. After the toolbars are enabled here, you can further customize them on the View and Buttons tab.

The Settings tab enables you to choose the location of the template folder used by the Office Shortcut Bar. The templates available are the ones used by the generic document buttons when you click the Open Office Document button.

Using Microsoft Photo Editor

Office 97 includes a program for retouching and altering photographs called the Microsoft Photo Editor. You can use the Photo Editor to acquire a scanned image or to edit one already digitized. The editing controls are quite elaborate. In addition to the regular cropping and resizing options, the Photo Editor has a wide range of special effects that let you do everything from enlarging your image to poster size to converting it with a stained glass effect.

If you have a scanner, you can choose Insert, Picture, From Scanner to begin digitizing an image; this also starts the Photo Editor. Otherwise, start the Photo Editor by choosing Insert, Object and then selecting Microsoft Photo Editor Photo from the list on the Create New tab or choosing a digitized photograph from your system on the Create from File tab. (Figure 27.20 shows an image in the Photo Editor.)

Part

VI

Ch

27

FIG. 27.20

The Microsoft Photo Editor is useful for cropping and touching up photographs within Word.

After the image is loaded into the Photo Editor, you have numerous options. The basic resizing, cropping, and rotation commands are found under the Image menu as are the color balancing and Autobalance commands. The Effects menu offers 14 different possibilities that can affect the entire picture. Each effect, such as the Chalk and Charcoal shown in Figure 27.21, has a number of parameters. You can apply the same effect several times for varied results. Here, experimentation and copious use of the Undo button are your best tools when discovering what is possible.

FIG. 27.21

Chalk and Charcoal is just one of 14 effects in Photo Editor.

When you've finished editing the picture, click the Close button or choose File, Exit and Return from the Photo Editor menu. You can return for further editing by double-clicking the image at any time.

Using Microsoft Organization Chart 2.0

One of the most dreaded assignments any secretary can get is to draw up a new org chart. Trying to keep all the boxes and lines straight with Word's regular drawing tools is a very difficult process. Office 97 includes a program aimed at the problem: Organization Chart 2.0. Aside from organization charts, you can also use the program to create any diagram that requires a hierarchical structure.

Choose Insert, Object and then choose MS Organization Chart 2.0 to begin the process. Figure 27.22 shows the opening screen of the program with its beginning template. Highlight any text and replace it to begin constructing your chart. When you click in any of the existing boxes, you'll see two additional comment areas.

FIG. 27.22

Organization Chart 2.0 starts with a predefined template.

Select tool

Enter Text tool

Zoom

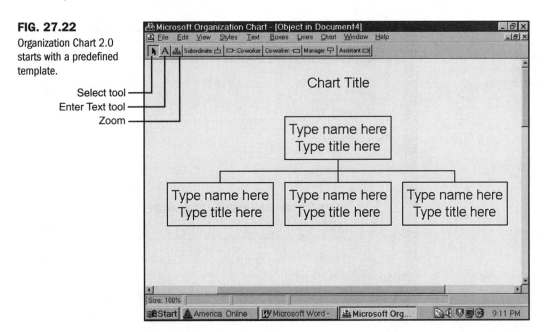

You add additional elements to the org chart by first choosing the Select tool from the toolbar. Then pick the appropriate member button on the toolbar (Subordinate, Co-worker, Manager, or Assistant) and click the box to which you want to add. You can choose from eight different chart styles as well as a number of different box and line styles and colors.

If you need to move a box, choose the Select tool and then click and drag your box. Drop it onto any other box to connect to it. The relationship between the two boxes is determined by where you position the box prior to dropping it.

To add text, click the Enter Text tool and click anywhere in the chart. You can modify a text's font, color, and alignment by first selecting your text and then making your choice from the Text menu.

Part

VI

Ch

27

When you've finished creating your org chart, choose File, Exit and Return from the Organizational Chart 2.0 menu. As with other embedded objects, you can edit the chart by double-clicking it.

Using Equation Editor 3.0

The Equation Editor is useful for creating extended mathematical expressions. A variety of mathematical symbols and templates simplify the process of constructing the most complex formulas. Begin by choosing Insert, Object and selecting Microsoft Equation Editor from the option list. A working area, surrounded by a dotted box, opens on your screen as does the Equation toolbar shown in Figure 27.23.

FIG. 27.23
Use the Equation Editor
for inserting complex
formulas in your Word
document.

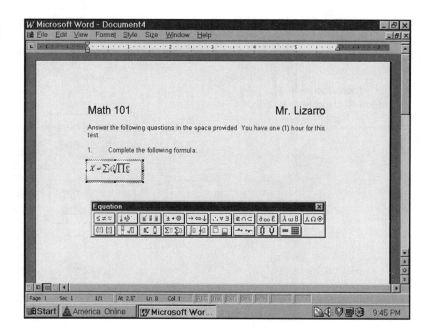

Numbers, variables, and ordinary mathematical operators (such as =, +, -) can be typed directly from the keyboard. To enter an operator or symbol not available from the keyboard, click the appropriate button on the top row of the Equation toolbar and select from one of the options that appear in the drop-down menu. Complex expressions such as fractions, square roots, or integrals can be added by clicking the appropriate button on the bottom row of the Equation toolbar and choosing one of the drop-down options. Depending on the choice, an expression has one or more outlined boxes for inserting numbers or other symbols.

The relative spacing for the formula is handled through the Format, Spacing menu option. This opens the Spacing dialog box (see Figure 27.24) where you can control the line spacing, matrix row and column spacing, superscript height, subscript depth, and the limit height between symbols.

FIG. 7.24

You can control a formula's overall spacing through the Spacing dialog box.

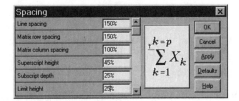

Using Microsoft Camcorder

Microsoft Camcorder is used to record actions, procedures, and sounds that take place on your computer. The recording can be saved as a movie that can be played in Camcorder, or saved as a stand-alone program that can be played by others without a Camcorder. A typical use for Camcorder is to create a computer training session or a demonstration.

Start Camcorder by clicking the Start button on the Windows 95 task bar and selecting Microsoft Camcorder from the Programs submenu. A small window, shown in Figure 27.25 controls the Camcorder process. You can set preferences for movies that you record, such as the keys to use to stop recording a movie, the quality of the sound you record, and whether to show Camcorder in front of open programs.

FIG. 27.25

You can use the Microsoft Camcorder program to record and playback all of your actions on a computer.

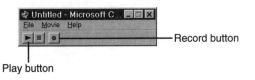

Record button

Play button

Start the recording by clicking the red Record button. You can record mouse movements as well as keystrokes. When you've finished the actions you want to record, press Esc (or the key set in Camcorder preferences to be the Stop Key). You can play back the movie by clicking the Play button. Save the file by choosing File, Save As or File, Create Standalone Movie.

> **CAUTION**
>
> Recording a movie can take a lot of memory and disk space. If you find that Camcorder warns you about low memory conditions when you attempt to record, try reducing your screen size or resolution as well as closing any open programs before proceeding.

Part
VI

Ch
27

From Here...

In this chapter you saw how you could begin to integrate Word with the other members of the Microsoft Office 97 family: Excel, Access, PowerPoint, Outlook, and the various Microsoft tools. Here's where you might want to go next:

- Delve deeper into the potential of mail merge by checking out Chapter 13, " Using Mail Merge Effectively."

- Review another of Word's special focus tools, Microsoft Graph, in Chapter 22, "Using Microsoft Graph."

- See how Word can be used to its fullest advantage in an overall corporate environment in Chapter 28, "Installing and Configuring Word in a Network Environment," and Chapter 29, "Sharing Files and Managing Word."

- Take the next step of integration and automation by investigating the power of Visual Basic for Application in Chapter 31, "Getting Started with VBA."

Installing and Configuring Word in a Network Environment

by Bill Camarda

Word is increasingly designed to meet the needs of large organizations and the individuals within those organizations who are responsible for its use. Whether you are an office manager, IT manager, help desk professional, or simply the leader of a workgroup team, you'll find these capabilities can make your organization significantly more productive.

In this chapter, you'll learn how to plan your Word 97/ Office 97 deployment and how to make important choices about installation. You'll also learn how to use global templates to customize Word's behavior to the needs of your teams and your organization. Then, in Chapter 29, "Sharing Files and Managing Word," you'll learn how to handle many of the issues that arise in managing Word on a day-to-day basis, after it's up and running.

Let's start at the beginning: planning for—and installing— Word 97. ■

Planning to deploy Word 97 throughout your organization

Careful planning makes the difference between happy users and outright chaos.

Centralizing installations through a network server

Save time by allowing all users to install from a single networked location.

Customizing installations with Setup scripts

Take complete control over how Word and Office install.

Using system policies, Registry options, and the Zero Administration Kit

Take complete control over how Word and Office operate.

Using workgroup templates

Provide a central location for the templates you want everyone to share.

Issues in Deploying Word 97 Enterprise-Wide

This chapter is written from the perspective of the manager or professional responsible for managing or supporting Word 97 in an organization. However, many of the features covered in this chapter, such as using Document Properties and converting files for use with older versions of Word, will be of interest to most Word users.

ON THE WEB

The best source for additional information on many of the topics covered in this chapter is the Microsoft Office 97 Resource Kit, available in print, or on the Web at **www.microsoft.com/office/ork/**.

As you decide whether (and how) to deploy Word 97 and Office 97 throughout your organization, carefully consider the costs and benefits listed in Table 28.1.

Table 28.1   Costs and Benefits of Deploying Word 97 and Office 97

Potential Costs	Potential Benefits
Cost of software upgrades	Access to new Internet/intranet authoring tools
Potential cost of hardware upgrades	Access to new VBA development environment; ability to leverage other in-house Visual Basic skills and resources
New training for end-users	Long-term potential for lower support costs due to increased integration among Office applications; new Office Assistant
New training for help desk professionals	Access to improved team-based editing tools, such as versioning
Installation time	Potentially lower third-party software costs (Office 97 includes Outlook and several applets, such as Microsoft Photo Editor.); access to enhanced productivity features, such as improved drawing tools and AutoText boilerplate tools
	Opportunity for superior management (compared with Word 6) through Windows 95/NT 4.0 system policies

You might choose to roll out Word and Office 97 incrementally, as you roll out new hardware, or upgrade to either Windows 95 or Windows NT Workstation. Or you might identify selected departments and organizations that can benefit from Word 97 and Office 97 features first—such as content developers for your corporate intranet. Yet another option is to begin deploying Office 97 when you have completed development of custom VBA applications that build on it.

Planning for Deployment

If you are planning to upgrade a large number of users to Word 97 and Office 97, careful preparation will be critical to your success. Preparation for deploying Word 97 in a large organization typically involves the following:

- *Organizing a project team.* In addition to technical people who understand your computing and networking infrastructure, make sure you include training and help desk staff, as well as representatives of the end-user organizations who will be expected to be productive with Word 97.

- *Taking inventory of current hardware and software.* Which systems are most widespread throughout your organization and will be appropriate test beds for Word 97? Which hardware will need upgrades? Does your installed base already run a compatible operating system, such as Windows 95 or Windows NT Workstation 4.0? If not, which existing systems are worth upgrading, and which aren't?

- *Testing Word 97 and your custom applications.* After you know the computer model(s) that are most widely used in your organization, create a miniature network that simulates the way Word and Office 97 will be run after you deploy them. Make sure e-mail is up and running as well, using the same mail system you're actually running in the organization.

  Make sure all your test computers are virus free and that the operating systems on these systems are working properly. Make preliminary decisions about which optional Word and Office features you expect to install. If you plan to automate your installation, create your installation script. Then install Word and Office and start testing.

> **CAUTION**
>
> Be especially careful to test your custom applications. Keep in mind that older 16-bit custom applications that make Windows 3.x API calls will need updating. Also remember that Word 97 updates all WordBasic macros to Visual Basic for Applications. Most macros come through the transformation just fine, but you should give them a workout just to make sure.

In addition to testing reliability and compatibility, pay especially close attention to new features that may offer opportunities for improving your processes but will require additional training. Equally important, carefully evaluate performance: will your systems run Word 97 quickly enough to satisfy your users?

- *Run a trial roll out.* Identify a small organization or a large workgroup that could benefit from Word 97—and isn't under exceptionally bad deadline pressure at the moment. Ensure that sufficient training and support resources are in place to assist the new users. Inform the pilot organization in whatever way works best in your organization. Then install Word and Office, using whatever scripts and methods you developed in the lab. Track how long everything takes so you can scale your estimates in planning your full-scale roll out. Most importantly, make sure you get as much user feedback as possible. You should seek user feedback regarding performance, reliability, the quality of your support, and how much disruption the upgrade caused them. Now is the time to make adjustments before you inflict the same mistakes on everyone else!

■ *Perform the final roll out.* You've purchased any upgrades or new systems you need. You've updated your company and IT (Information Technology) policies. You have the approvals you need. Now you're ready to go.

If you're planning to install from network servers, run an administrative Setup on each server you intend to use (this is discussed in more detail later in this chapter). Make sure your users know what's about to happen, and what's expected of them. For example, if they will need to run a batch file to install Office 97, tell them how. If Office 97 will install automatically the next time they turn on the computer, warn them. If they'll come in the next morning and find Office 97 waiting for them, warn them of that, too. If users need training, make sure they get at least some of it before they're called on to be productive with Word and Office 97.

Perform full backups on all of the client computers that store important data. Make sure your technicians have access to any client computers that may cause problems. Then run the installation.

Controlling the Way Word and Office Install

By now, it's common knowledge that you can install most Microsoft desktop applications by running Setup from within Windows. However, it's not as widely known that you have many options for running Setup, many of which are available as command-line parameters (switches) from the Setup program.

You can run Setup from the command line by choosing Start, Run from the Windows 95 or Windows NT taskbar. Then, enter the Setup command, in the Run dialog box along with the parameters, as shown in Figure 28.1.

FIG. 28.1

This figure illustrates running Setup from the Run dialog box.

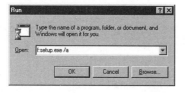

The parameters you can choose from are listed in Table 28.2.

Table 28.2 Parameters for Customizing Setup Behavior	
Parameter	**What It Does**
/a	Runs an administrative install that prepares a network server for client installations
/b	Skips unnecessary Setup dialog boxes:
	/b1 automatically runs a typical install

Parameter	What It Does
	/b2 automatically runs a custom install
	/b3 automatically runs a Run from CD or a Run from Network Server Install
/c	Skips the Product ID dialog box; enter the OEM Certificate of Authorization 20-character Product ID after the parameter
/f	Creates all Office files using 8.3 file names, not long file names
/g	Creates a log file; adds and appends log file information to an existing log file instead of overwriting it
/gc	Increases the detail in a log file by recording calls and returns from custom actions; adds and appends log file information to an existing log file instead of overwriting it
/k	Skips the 11-digit Product ID dialog box; enter the 11-digit CD-ROM key after /k
/l	Overwrites a default Setup.lst file with one you specify
/m	Specifies Microsoft License Pack (MLP) licensing information for floppy disks; follow /m with a number indicating how many MLP licenses you've purchased
/n " "	Prompts for a user name if one cannot be found in the Windows Registry
/n	Specifies a user name in the event one cannot be found in the Windows Registry; insert the user name following /n
/o	Specifies an organization name if one cannot be found in the Windows Registry; insert the organization name following /o
/q	Controls the role of the user in a batch mode installation:
	/q0 hides all dialog boxes except the last one; this is the default setting
	/q1 hides all dialog boxes, including the last one
	/t hides all setup user interface elements
/qn	Same as /q but does not reboot the computer when finished:
	/qn1 hides all dialog boxes except the last one; this is the default setting /qnt hides all setup user interface elements
/r	Reinstalls an application (for maintenance mode)

continues

Part

VI

Ch

28

Table 28.2   Continued

Parameter	What It Does
/s	Specifies a folder to look for an STF file containing detailed Setup directions include the folder name after /s
/u	Uninstalls Office:
	Adding a removes shared components without asking the user's permission
/x	Establishes a network installation log file for one administrative installation point; include the file name after /x
/y	Simulates an install, copying all appropriate entries to the Registry, but not copying files to hard disk; a troubleshooting aid

Choosing the Type of Installation to Perform

As you probably know from installing Word or Office on a stand-alone system, you can choose how much of Word and Office you actually want to install. Like stand-alone installations, network client installations may be one of the following types:

- *Typical*, in which the Setup program installs the features Microsoft expects most users will need.

- *Custom*, in which you specify which components of Word and/or Office are installed. You might use this option if there are some standard components you've decided not to install, such as applets like Photo Editor; or if there are some nonstandard components you *do* want to install, such as unusual file converters.

If you decide to have your users install from a network server, you have a third choice:

- *Run from Network Server*, in which relatively little of Word and Office are copied to the user's hard drive; during a session, most of the files are retrieved from the network. (For a stand-alone installation, the equivalent option would be *Run From CD-ROM*.) Run from Network Server typically leads to slower application performance, but it uses local hard disk space more efficiently. It simplifies and centralizes maintenance; however, if the network goes down, users lose access to their applications.

Choosing Where to Install From

If you decide to install Word 97 or Office 97 on client workstations using original CD-ROMs or floppy disks, you will have to be physically present at each computer during the installation process. If you install from a network server, you don't necessarily have to be physically present, but someone in your organization will certainly have to be available in the event of problems.

Later in this chapter, you'll walk through creating an *administrative installation point*—the network location from which client workstations can install Word and Office.

Controlling the User's Level of Involvement

As you may have noticed in Table 28.2, you have a good deal of control over the role individual users play in the setup process. Your users can run Setup the conventional way, by double-clicking the Setup icon to install from a CD-ROM, floppy drive, or network server.

N O T E Later, you'll learn how to create a custom script that runs in place of the standard script that the Setup program normally refers to when a user runs Setup. ▧

If you prefer, you can tell users to run Setup using a command line, such as

```
setup.exe /q1 /b1
```

This tells Setup to run a typical installation without any intervention from the user.

If you really want to keep people out of the loop, you can add your Setup command line to each user's system logon script. Then Setup runs automatically the next time the user logs on.

Centralizing Installations Through a Network Server

If you are upgrading many computers to run Word 97 and/or Office 97, you'll probably want to centralize as much of the process as possible. The first step toward centralizing installation is to enable each client workstation to install Word and Office from one (or a few) centralized network locations.

To do this, you must run an *administrative installation* on your network server. This creates an *administrative installation point*: two folders containing the files and instructions needed for installation on individual client computers. After you've created the administrative installation point, individual users can run Setup from their own workstations, accessing the files and instructions on the network share you're creating. As you'll learn later, you can customize which files the Setup program installs by writing a custom Setup script.

Preparing for an Administrative Install

In this section, you'll walk through the process of running an administrative installation. Before you start, make sure of the following items:

- You have enough disk space available on your server: at least 280M for Office 97 Standard and at least 325M for Office 97 Professional.

■ You have full permissions for all of the folders you intend to use, and you have set those folders up to provide read-only access to your users. Later, you'll learn that users will need read/write access to many of Word's folders if they run the program from a network server. However, for purposes of installation from a network server, they only need read-only access.

■ There are no previous versions of Office on the same drive.

■ You've logged all users off the server and prevented them from accessing the folders where you will install Office 97.

■ You've disabled your virus detection software.

Now start the administrative installation. Load the Office 97 CD-ROM in your network server. Choose Start, Run.

In the Run dialog box, enter the CD-ROM's drive name, along with the Setup command and the /a parameter (refer to Figure 28.1). The welcome screen of the Office installation program appears. Click OK. The Microsoft Office Setup window appears, providing more instructions about an administrative installation (see Figure 28.2). Click OK again.

FIG. 28.2

Before you move forward, Setup offers a little more advice.

In the Organization Information dialog box (see Figure 28.3), enter the name of your organization if it is not already recorded in the Windows Registry. If it is already there, you won't be able to change it through Setup—you'll have to change it directly in the Registry. Click OK, and click OK again to confirm the information you provided.

FIG. 28.3

The Organization Information dialog box uses organization information already stored in the Registry, if it finds any.

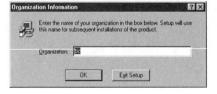

Enter your 11-digit CD registration key (see Figure 28.4), click OK, and click OK again to confirm the registration key. Setup now recommends a destination folder for the core Office 97 files (see Figure 28.5). If this is the right folder, click OK. Setup creates the folder if it does not exist. If you want a different folder, click Change Folder; browse to and select the folder, choose Open, and choose OK.

FIG. 28.4

Enter your 11-digit CD registration key from the back of the Office 97 CD-ROM jewel case.

FIG. 28.5

Setup recommends a folder for the core Office files; this folder is typically named MSOffice.

Next, the Setup program offers to install shared applications in the destination folder it believes you want (see Figure 28.6); by default, this is the \MSApps folder on the same disk as the \MSOffice folder you just created. Again, you can accept the selection or click Change Folder to set a different location.

FIG. 28.6

Setup recommends a folder for the shared applications that come with Microsoft Office files; this folder is typically named MSApps.

Part

VI

Ch

28

You're now asked to enter or confirm the server and path name where users should connect to install Word and Office (see Figure 28.7). You can choose whether to connect to this server using Server Name or Drive Letter. When you're finished, click Continue. Next, you can decide whether shared files should be stored on the Server or Local hard drive—or whether that should be the User's Choice (see Figure 28.8). When you're finished, click OK.

FIG. 28.7

In this dialog box, you can confirm or establish the name and path of the server from which users will be installing.

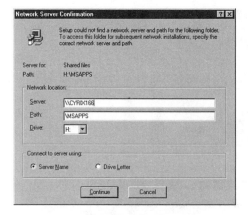

FIG. 28.8

Next, decide where to store Office shared files.

In the last step before you're ready to start copying files, you can select English language dictionaries and sample files optimized for the United States, Great Britain, or Australia (see Figure 28.9). Make a choice and click OK. Setup checks for disk space, and if you have enough, it immediately starts copying files.

FIG. 28.9

Last but not least, choose U.S., English, or Australian dictionaries and sample documents.

Customizing Installations with a Setup Script

After you run an administrative install, you can customize the Setup script you've just copied onto your server's hard drive. To do so, use the Network Installation Wizard (see Figure 28.10), a special tool included on the CD-ROM that comes with the Microsoft Office 97 Resource Kit.

FIG. 28.10
The Network Installation Wizard walks you through the process of customizing a Setup script.

ON THE WEB
You can also download this (and other) Office Resource Kit tools from the Web at **www.microsoft.com/office/ork/appa/appa.htm**.

The Network Installation Wizard can customize most aspects of how the Office Setup program runs, including the following:

- Which components of Word and Office are installed
- Which folder is established as the default folder for storing new documents
- Where shared files should be placed
- Which shortcuts should be added to the Start menu or Desktop

After you run the Network Installation Wizard to customize your scripts, your settings appear as the defaults. However, if you allow users to run Setup interactively, they can change these settings. Alternatively, as discussed earlier, you can use a command line, such as

```
setup.exe /q1 /b2
```

which installs Word and Office invisibly—in Quiet mode—just as you've specified. You can use the Network Installation Wizard to install additional files you may have created, such as custom templates and dictionaries.

Part
VI

Ch
28

N O T E   The Network Installation Wizard places a relatively benign front end on a relatively complex, delicate process: editing the .STF and .INF files that Office 97 depends upon extensively throughout the setup process.

If you are customizing Office 97 Standard Edition, the Network Installation Wizard modifies Off97std.stf and Off97Std.inf. If you are customizing Office 97 Professional Edition, the Network Installation Wizard modifies Off97pro.stf and Off97pro.inf.

To use the Network Installation Wizard, you need to know about one more file: Setup.lst, which the wizard will ask you to locate. This file contains the names of the .STF and .INF files the wizard should use, along with installation parameters. ■

Installation via System Management Server

If you are rolling out Word and Office on a network built around Windows NT Server, you have another installation option. You can use Microsoft System Management Server (SMS), an optional product designed to help organizations manage their software resources more effectively.

In the simplest case, you can use SMS to automatically run a Typical or Custom installation on a set of user computers you define. Follow these steps:

1. Create an administrative installation point by running Setup using the SETUP /A command.

2. From the dialog box shown in Figure 28.11, create a *package*, the SMS term for a folder containing all of the Office files that need to be installed, along with a Package Definition File (PDF) that contains the appropriate Setup commands. Microsoft includes eight sample PDF files as part of the Office Resource Kit. Of special interest are:

File Name	Description
Off97pro.pdf	Office 97 Professional Edition PDF file
Off97std.pdf	Office 97 Standard Edition PDF file
Word97.pdf	Word 97 stand-alone PDF file

N O T E   These .PDF files should not be confused with the Adobe Acrobat .PDF files that are widely used to exchange formatted documents. ■

FIG. 28.11

The Package Properties dialog box in Microsoft Systems Management Server enables you to select a PDF file and specify your administrative installation point.

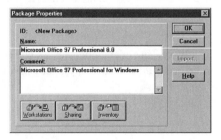

3. From the Job Details dialog box, create a list of client computers on which you want to install Word and/or Office.

4. Create a job consisting of the package and the list of target computers.

5. Run the job.

Using System Policy Editor and Policy Templates

You can still control the way users work with Word and Office 97 even after you've installed these programs. You exercise that control through *system policies*, which are files that control aspects of a program's behavior. The Microsoft Office 97 Resource Kit includes a set of sample system policies for Office 97, along with an updated version of the System Policy Editor used to manage them.

 TIP Windows 95 and Windows NT Workstation can also be controlled by system policies.

You can use the System Policy Editor to customize policy files for:

▪ All users

▪ Groups of users

▪ Specific computers

▪ Specific users on specific computers

When a user identifies him or herself to the network at logon, the network server downloads his or her system policy files. After this occurs, the settings in the local user's Registry are edited to correspond to the requirements or limitations established in the policy files. System Policies work with both Windows 95 and Windows NT 4.0 (but not Windows NT 3.51).

N O T E In Windows NT Server-based networks, a client workstation's primary network logon must be Client for Microsoft Networks in order for System Policies to work. In NetWare-based networks, Microsoft Client for NetWare must be the primary logon client. ▪

To create policy files, start with policy templates. The relationship between files and templates is no different than in Word. You open a new policy file based on a policy template. Next, you make the changes you want. Finally, you save the file.

In Windows 95, Microsoft's sample policy template for Office 97 is named Off97w95.adm; the Windows NT 4.0 version is called Off97nt4.adm. Follow these steps to use one of these templates as the basis for your own system policies:

1. Install the System Policy Editor by double-clicking the POLSETUP.EXE file provided with the Office Resource Kit.

2. Copy the .ADM policy template file you want to use into the appropriate folder—typically \Windows\Inf in Windows 95, or \Winnt\Inf in Windows NT 4.0.

Part
VI

Ch

28

3. Run the System Policy Editor (see Figure 28.12).

4. Choose Policy Template from the Options menu (see Figure 28.13).

5. Click Add to display the Open Template File menu (see Figure 28.14).

6. Double-click the policy template you want to use; then click OK. Windows loads the policy template.

7. Choose New Policy from the File menu. Two icons appear in the main window: Default Computer and Default User (see Figure 28.15). Double-click either one to edit the policy template settings associated with it.

N O T E   Default Computer controls the relatively small number of Word and Office settings that apply to entire computers. These include where to look for custom dictionaries, AutoCorrect files, and additional Office Assistant "personalities."

Default User controls the larger number of settings that are attached to individual users, not computers. These include settings for the Options dialog box, AutoFormat settings, and a variety of Internet and Web Page Authoring settings. ▨

8. In the Default User Properties dialog box (see Figure 28.16) or the Default Computer Properties dialog box, edit the policies you want to change. For each policy, you have three choices:

Checked means the policy is always in effect whenever a user logs on.

Cleared means the policy is never in effect, even if a local user wants it to be.

Grayed means whatever local settings the user has established are left alone.

9. When you're finished editing settings, click OK.

FIG. 28.12

The System Policy Editor.

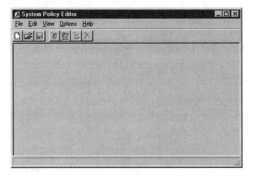

FIG. 28.13

How to add a policy template on which you can base your new policy file.

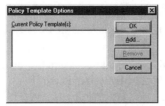

FIG. 28.14

Use the Open Template File menu to browse to the policy template you want to use.

FIG. 28.15

Choose Default User to set policies associated with users; choose Default Computer to set policies associated with computers.

FIG. 28.16

The Default User Properties dialog box controls a wide variety of Word behaviors.

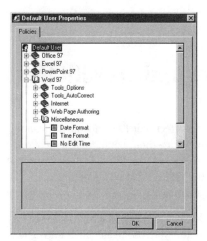

Now it's time to discuss a few of the ways you might use System Policy Editor to change Word's behavior. In the following list, the text in parentheses indicates the categories, subcategories, and names of the corresponding settings.

In *Default User,* you might...

■ Define standard locations for Workgroup Templates that all of your users can share (Office 97/Common/Workgroup Templates)

Part

VI

Ch

28

- Quiet the office by turning off audio feedback in all Office applications (Office 97/ Common/Sound)

- Add an FTP site that all Office applications will recognize, such as an FTP site connected to your intranet (Office 97/Internet/Add FTP Sites)

- Require all your users to turn on Word's macro virus protection (Word 97/ Tools_Options/General/Macro Virus Protection)

- Make Word 6.0/95 format (instead of Word 97 format) the default for all new file saves (Word 97/Tools_Options/Save/Default Save)

- Improve performance on slow systems by turning off Background Spelling and Background Grammar (Word 97/Tools_Options/Spelling & Grammar/Background Spelling and Background Grammar)

- Specify where to look for standard elements of your Web pages (Word 97/Web Page Authoring)

- Specify a default date format (Word 97/Miscellaneous/Date Format)

In *Default Computer,* you might...

- Change where Setup looks for the information it needs to uninstall Office 97 (Office 97/ Uninstall)

- Establish a path to a new AutoCorrect file (Word 97/Spelling Advanced/Default AutoCorrect File)

- Establish a path to additional clip art databases for Clip Art Gallery 3.0 to use (Clip Art Gallery 3.0/Concurrent Database #1)

Setting Local Registry Options with the RegOptions Macro

Many settings, including some that affect Word's performance, cannot be edited from the Office97.adm policy template. To change these settings, you must edit the Registry. To make this somewhat more convenient and less risky, Word 97 provides a macro, RegOptions, stored in the Support8.dot template in the \Office\Macros folder.

▶ **See** "Running the Sample Macros in Macros8.DOT and Support8.DOT," **p. 859**

After you've installed Support8.dot, select Tools, Macro, Macros to display all of your active macros. Choose RegOptions from the Macros list and click Run. The Set Registry Options dialog box opens (see Figure 28.17).

You can use Set Registry Options to make changes to default file storage locations, the Equation editor, and the proofing tools. Two settings in the Word 8.0 Options tab can improve performance in some situations. If you work with many documents that are graphics-heavy, you can increase the setting for BitMapMemory to enlarge Word's built-in bitmap cache, which can increase the performance of Word documents that include many graphics. Similarly, you can increase Word's CacheSize setting beyond the default 64K. On some systems, this improves file I/O and other aspects of Word's performance.

 T I P If you're careful, you can control even more aspects of Word's behavior using the Registry Editor.

FIG. 28.17
The Set Registry Options dialog box gives you control over additional aspects of Word's behavior and performance.

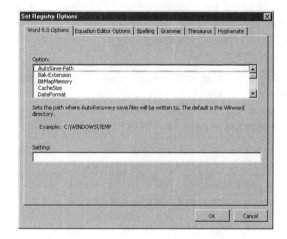

Word 97 and the Zero Administration Kit for Windows Initiative

In response to the market's demand for lower total cost of ownership, Microsoft has developed the Zero Administration Kit (ZAK) for Windows, which offers network administrators a faster way of achieving many of the same results that are possible with the System Policy Editor. ZAK is available now for Windows NT Workstation; it will be available shortly for Windows 95. Microsoft intends to provide additional Zero Administration features in Windows 98.

Microsoft describes ZAK as "a set of tools, methodologies, and guidelines designed to help corporate administrators install and configure Windows computers that are centrally administered." At the heart of ZAK are two options for configuring a workstation: Taskstation mode and Appstation mode. Both modes have much in common:

■ They assume that documents will be stored centrally on a server.

■ They limit the Start menu to only the options the user has been given (see Figure 28.18).

■ They store the user's "state" on the server. No matter what workstation users log on from, they will see the desktop you have created for them.

FIG. 28.18

In Taskstation or Appstation mode, a user has access to the options the administrator permits.

Taskstation mode is designed for workstations used by individuals who only run one or a very few programs. The built-in Taskstation mode assumes users will only run Microsoft Internet Explorer. It might be changed, however, to set Word 97 as the default program for those who only perform word processing tasks.

By default, Appstation mode is set up to run all installed Microsoft Office applications, as well as Internet Explorer. You can limit the Office applications that run or add custom applications. Increasingly, custom applications will use a Web browser as a front end, so they can be run through Internet Explorer (assuming it has been installed).

> **CAUTION**
>
> Many early users of the Zero Administration Kit have found it necessary to loosen the predefined constraints of the Taskstation and Appstation modes in order to provide access to all the Microsoft Office files their users need.

Using Workgroup Templates

One of the best ways to keep your entire workgroup or organization in sync is to use *workgroup templates*. You've already learned how templates enable you to create custom editing environments for specific clients, projects, or companies. You've learned that you can store all of the tools you need to edit specific documents in a custom template.

▶ **See** "Using Templates to Build Custom Editing Environments," **p. 170**

All of the templates you learned about in Chapter 6, "Templates, Wizards, and Add-Ins" are typically stored on your local hard disk. Word also enables you to provide for workgroup templates that are stored centrally on a network server. All of your users can share access to these templates at the same time. Better yet, you can centrally update and manage workgroup templates—eliminating the need to provide individual copies of your critical templates to every user.

Here are some of the ways you can use workgroup templates:

- Centrally store the AutoText boilerplate you want everyone to use
- Provide a library of standardized documents built around the needs of your department or company
- Update everyone's user interface at the same time

You can create a workgroup template the same way you create any other template. You can then store it in a folder that each user's computer recognizes as the location for workgroup templates. It usually makes sense to mark workgroup templates as read-only, to prevent inadvertent or unauthorized customizations that affect everyone who uses them. To ensure that unauthorized individuals don't have access to them, consider storing them on a server with limited permissions.

Follow these steps to specify a workgroup template location on a specific computer:

1. Choose Tools, Options.
2. Choose the File Locations tab (see Figure 28.19).
3. In the File types scroll box, click Workgroup Templates. (By default, no location is associated with workgroup templates.)
4. Click Modify. The Modify Location dialog box opens (see Figure 28.20).
5. Browse and select the folder you want to use.
6. Click OK twice.

FIG. 28.19

You can establish or change the workgroup templates folder in the File Locations tab of the Options dialog box.

FIG. 28.20

In the Modify Location dialog box, choose the folder you want to use.

Part
VI

Ch
28

The procedure just described sets a workgroup template location for a single workstation. You can, however, specify a workgroup template location through the System Policy Editor so that it applies to all users who are subject to the policies you create. Or you can specify it as part of a custom installation script.

After you establish a workgroup template folder, any templates you save there automatically appear in the General tab of the New dialog box when users open a new file, just as if they were stored locally.

CAUTION

If the workgroup template folder is temporarily inaccessible, the templates stored there will be absent when a user creates a new file. Of course, this means that users will be dependent on your network to create documents based on those templates.

From Here...

In this chapter, you've learned what you need to know to set up Word for use in a networked environment. Here are some chapters you may want to look at next:

- Learn what you need to know about managing Word on a day-to-day basis in Chapter 29, "Sharing Files and Managing Word." You'll learn how to cope with multiple file formats, manage document security, use document properties to make it easier to keep track of your organization's documents, and migrate WordPerfect users to Word.

- Discover how you can extend Word to meet your company's specific needs using Visual Basic for Applications. Chapter 30, "Recording and Running Visual Basic Macros" introduces the basics of recording macros. Chapters 31-33 introduce you to the Visual Basic language and walk you through building a real-world sample application.

CHAPTER 29

Sharing Files and Managing Word

by Bill Camarda

Word is increasingly designed to meet the needs of large organizations and the individuals within those organizations who are responsible for its use. Whether you are an office manager, IT manager, help desk professional, or simply the leader of a workgroup team, you'll find these capabilities can make your organization significantly more productive.

In this chapter, you'll learn how to manage the tricky issues that accompany Word 97's new file formats. You'll also learn how to maximize security using Word's encryption and file protection features; how to reduce the risk of macro viruses; and how to make it easier to find files on a network or intranet. You'll even learn how to use Word's built-in features to convert your organization from WordPerfect. ■

Manage mixed Word 97 and Word 6/95 file formats

Help Word 97 and Word 6/95 users work together more productively.

Improve Word's document security

Use encryption, document protection, and your operating system to customize security for your sensitive documents.

Use document properties to manage documents more effectively

With built-in and custom properties, you can make it easy to find documents wherever they are.

Converting from WordPerfect

If you're finally making the move, Word offers all the help you'll need.

Supporting Word in a global environment

Unicode support, international dictionaries, and other features make Word truly global in reach.

Working with Colleagues Using Word 6 or Word 95

In the original release of Word 97, if you attempt to save a file using the Word 6.0/95 (DOC) format, the file will be named with a .DOC extension but will actually be saved in Rich Text Format (RTF). If opened in Word 6 or Word 95, the file is automatically converted for display on-screen. However, if a Word 6 or Word 95 user chooses <u>F</u>ile, Save <u>A</u>s to save the file under a new name or in a different location, Word will list the file as an RTF file, as shown in Figure 29.1.

FIG. 29.1

If you save a file to Word 6/95 format, and then attempt to resave it from Word 6, the file will be exposed for what it really is: an RTF file.

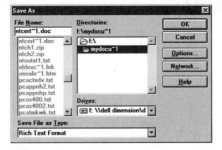

At best, this is extremely confusing. At worst, this feature can cause files to be misplaced or lost altogether. RTF conversion can cause problems with some Word features, notably graphics and frames. Even worse, if you try to import a file saved in RTF format into a third-party program that expects the Word 6 format, you may find yourself unable to do so. Among the programs that cannot import RTF files disguised as Word documents are Corel WordPerfect, Adobe PageMaker, and Quark XPress. The problem is so serious that many organizations postponed upgrading to Word 97 until it was resolved.

Now it has been. In June, 1997, Microsoft released the Word 6.0/95 Binary Converter for Word 97. This converter is available on a stand-alone basis, or as part of Service Release 1, which is discussed later in this chapter. After you install this converter, Word 97 actually saves in the true Word 6.0/95 format when you choose this option in the Files of <u>T</u>ype drop-down box in the Save <u>A</u>s dialog box.

ON THE WEB

You can download the updated converter from Microsoft's Web site at the following address:
www.microsoft.com/officefreestuff/word/dlpages/wrd6ex32.htm.

The Wrd6ex32.exe converter is designed to work with most international versions of Word. It is not necessary for Arabic, Hebrew, Thai, and Vietnamese versions of Word 97, which already ship with the updated converter. It does not work with Japanese, Korean, Simplified Chinese, and Traditional Chinese versions of Word, which utilize the double-byte character set. Microsoft says it will make a version of the converter available for these versions of Word by the end of 1997.

CAUTION

Of course, whether you save to RTF or to Word 6/95 format, you lose data or formatting that isn't supported by previous versions of Word. Some of the lost formatting is minor; for example, animated text is not supported by previous versions of Word. Some may be more significant. For example, if you plan to integrate Word as part of your intranet, be aware that hyperlinks are lost when you save back to an earlier format.

Worse, if you plan to password-protect your document—or use protection for tracked changes, comments, or forms, such documents will lose their protection when saved back to Word 6/95 format (even though Word 6 and 95 have comparable features).

Installing the updated converter goes a long way toward eliminating file compatibility problems between users of Word 6.0/95 and users of Word 97, but not all the way. You may want to standardize users on the Word 6.0/95 format until your entire organization is ready to start using Word 97 files. To make Word 6.0/95 format the default setting for an individual computer, do the following:

1. Choose Tools, Options.
2. Choose the Save tab (see Figure 29.2).
3. In the Save Word Files As drop-down box, choose Word 6.0/95 (*.DOC).
4. Click OK.

FIG. 29.2
In the Save tab of the Options dialog box, you can specify Word 6/95 as your default file format.

After you set Word 6.0/95 as a default file format, when a user saves a file for the first time, the Office Assistant opens (see Figure 29.3). It displays three choices: The user can choose the recommended format, choose another format, or view a list of the document and formatting elements that might be lost when the file is saved to the older format.

FIG. 29.3

After you specify Word 6.0/95 as the default file save setting, users see the following message when they save a file for the first time.

Choosing See What Might Be Lost opens the Word Help system and displays information about features that are lost when you save to the older format (see Figure 29.4).

FIG. 29.4

From this Help screen, users learn what will happen to their files if they save to Word 6.0/95 (or WordPerfect 5.x) format.

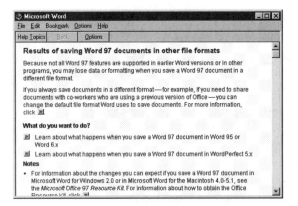

Using the Word 97 Converter for Word 6.0/95

Even if you upgrade Word 97 so that it can save files in true Word 6.0/95 format, you've only done half the job of ensuring file compatibility. You need to make sure Word 6.0/95 users have access to files stored in Word 97 format—either because those files came from outside sources, or because they use Word 97-specific features. For this purpose, Microsoft provides the Word 97 Converter for Word 6.0/95. You can find this file in the ValuPack folder of Office 97.

ON THE WEB

You can also download the Word 97 Convertor from Microsoft's Web site at **www.microsoft.com/ word/freestuff/converters/wrd97cnv.htm**.

To install the converter, double-click wrd97cnv.exe. If you are running Word 6, the installer recognizes this and installs the converter Msword8.cnv. If you are running Word 95, Word installs Mswrd832.cnv instead.

After the converter is installed, Word 6 or 95 can open Word 97 files. However, if you save a Word 97 file in Word 6 or Word 95, you still lose the Word 97-specific features. Wherever possible, use File, Save As to make a separate copy for editing, so you can at least retain the Word 97 features in the original file.

TIP In some cases, it may be possible to re-integrate the two files later in Word 97, using Tools, Track Changes, Compare Documents.

Displaying Word 97 Files on Computers Without Any Version of Word

Some of your workstations may have no version of Word installed at all. For example, individuals primarily responsible for a few specific tasks may use them. If these tasks rarely involve word processing, you may not want to invest in Word or Office software licenses for these workstations. Moreover, these individuals may be using older workstations, such as 80386-based systems, which cannot run Word 97.

As time passes, you may discover that these people can benefit from access to existing Word documents. For example, your corporate intranet may include manuals or sales guides written in Word. Giving customer service representatives access to these resources may help them solve customer problems more effectively.

For situations like this, Microsoft has released the Microsoft Word Viewer, a freeware application that can be freely copied and distributed. This small program enables any Windows user to view and print any Word 97 document. It supports many, though not all, Word 97 features. For example, it supports Page Layout view, Outline view, Online Layout view, Document Map, zooming, headers, footers, footnotes, comments, and hyperlinks—but not toolbars.

You can't edit text in Word Viewer (or fill out online forms). However, you can copy the text into other applications through the Windows Clipboard.

You can think of Word Viewer as Microsoft's answer to Adobe Acrobat Reader. It has one major advantage compared with Acrobat Reader: Anyone who owns Word can author documents that can be read with Word Viewer.

It also has two major disadvantages, which limit its value as an Internet solution for distributing Word documents. First, it only works in Windows environments (not Macintosh or UNIX). Second, it isn't nearly as widely used as Adobe Acrobat has become because webmasters can't count on sophisticated users having Word Viewer as much as they can count on the presence of Adobe Acrobat.

TIP The Word Viewer can be used as a helper application for viewing Word documents downloaded from the Internet. Word Viewer can also make it a little easier to work with customer and vendor organizations that have standardized on a different word processing platform.

The original release of Microsoft Office 97 came with a version of Word Viewer that worked only with files saved in RTF, Word 6.0/95, or Word 2.0 format. It was also limited to running under Windows 95 (and Windows NT 3.51 or higher). Two new versions of Word Viewer have since become available:

- Word Viewer 97, which displays Word 97 files on any Windows 95 or Windows NT 3.51, 4.0, or higher system
- Word Viewer 97 for Windows 16-bit Operating Systems, which displays Word 97 files on any Windows 3.x

Each of these viewers runs on virtually any computer that meets the minimum hardware requirements of the version of Windows it is already running. You can download either or both of them at **www.microsoft.com/word/internet/viewer/default.htm**. If you prefer, you can get a set of disks from Microsoft at the cost of shipping and handling by calling 1-800-360-7561.

CAUTION

Although Word Viewer can coexist with Word on the same computer, it works best on computers where Word isn't installed. Even though the Word Viewer Setup program is designed to ask which application should be the default for opening Word files, you may sometimes find that the wrong application loads if they are both installed.

This is especially annoying if you are trying to use Word as your e-mail editor in Outlook because Word Viewer is obviously incapable of editing e-mail.

Batch File Conversions

If you are upgrading your entire organization to Word 97 at the same time, you may find it convenient to convert your collection of Word 6/95 files to Word 97 format all at the same time. However, that's not the only time you may want to convert many files at the same time. For example:

- You may be migrating from an older version of WordPerfect, and want to convert your WordPerfect files for use in Word 97
- You may be creating an intranet and want to convert your Word 97 files to HTML
- You might be migrating from Macintosh to Windows, and want to convert older Macintosh Word 5.1 files for use in Word 97

Word 97 provides a batch conversion utility, the Conversion Wizard, for all these purposes. With the Conversion Wizard, you can create Word 97 documents from files in the following formats:

- HTML
- Lotus 1-2-3
- Microsoft Excel
- MS-DOS Text with Layout
- Outlook Address Book
- Personal Address Book
- Rich Text Format (RTF)
- Schedule+ Contacts
- Microsoft Word Template
- Text
- Text with Layout
- Unicode Text
- Windows Write
- Word (Asian Versions) 6.0/95
- Word 4.0-5.1 for Macintosh
- WordPerfect 5.x
- WordPerfect 6.x
- Microsoft Works 3.0 for Windows
- Microsoft Works 4.0 for Windows

Similarly, you can convert documents from Word 97 to the following formats:

- HTML
- MS-DOS Text, MS-DOS Text with Line Breaks, or MS-DOS Text with Layout
- Rich Text Format (RTF)
- Word 97 Template
- Text Only, Text with Layout, or Text with Line Breaks
- Unicode Text
- Windows Write
- Word 2.x for Windows
- Word 4.0 for Macintosh
- Word 5.0 for Macintosh

- Word 5.1 for Macintosh
- Word 6.0/95
- WordPerfect 5.0 (including Secondary Files)
- WordPerfect 5.1 for DOS
- WordPerfect 5.1 or 5.2 Secondary File
- WordPerfect 5.x for Windows
- Microsoft Works 3.0 or 4.0

The Conversion Wizard can convert all files in a specific folder. Before you use it, either place all the files you want to convert in the same folder; or if you want to convert files in their current folders, list the folders you want to convert, and run the Conversion Wizard separately in each folder.

> **CAUTION**
>
> Test out your file conversions on a few sample documents before performing them en masse and putting the resulting documents into production. You may find it necessary to tweak the settings of your conversion filter to get the results you want. In rare instances, if you find the converted documents unworkable, you might consider trying a third-party filter, such as those included in Conversions Plus for Windows (DataViz, 1-800-733-0030, **www.dataviz.com**).

To run the Conversion Wizard, follow these steps:

1. Click the Open button on the Standard toolbar. The Open dialog box appears.
2. In the Files of Type drop-down box, choose All Files.
3. Browse to the folder containing the Conversion Wizard. In default installations, this is the C:\Program Files\Microsoft Office\Office\Macros folder.
4. Double-click CONVERT8.WIZ. Word displays the Warning window that reminds you this file contains macros.

TIP If you plan to use the Conversion Wizard often, select the file and click the Add to Favorites button in the Open dialog box. Then, you can access it directly from the Favorites folder.

5. Click Enable Macros.
6. The preliminary Conversion Wizard dialog box appears (see Figure 29.5). Click the button next to A Batch Conversion of Files.

TIP If you will only use this dialog box to perform batch conversions, and never to edit converter or filter options, check the I Always Want to Perform Batch Conversions check box.

7. The Conversion Wizard opens. Click Next. The From/To screen appears (see Figure 29.6).

FIG. 29.5

The preliminary Conversion Wizard dialog box.

FIG. 29.6

On the From/To page of the Conversion Wizard, you specify which format you want to convert your file to (or from).

8. If you want to convert files stored in another format into Word 97 files, click Convert from Another Format to Word; then choose the format from the highlighted drop-down box. If you want to convert Word 97 files into another format, click Convert from Word to Another Format. A drop-down box becomes active beneath this button. From this drop-down box, select the format you want.

9. If you want to adjust conversion options, click Options. The Edit Converter and Filter Options dialog box appears (see Figure 29.7). You can now edit specific aspects of how the file converter works. Click OK when you're finished.

FIG. 29.7

In this dialog box, you can edit some aspects of how of Word's converters behave.

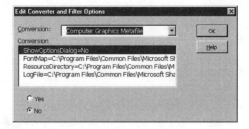

10. Click Next to move to the next window.

11. From the Folder Selection window (see Figure 29.8), click Browse (next to Source Folder) to specify the folder where your existing files are.

12. The Browse for Folder dialog box appears (see Figure 29.9). Select a folder, and click OK.

FIG. 29.8

From the Folder Selection dialog box, you can choose both a source and a destination folder.

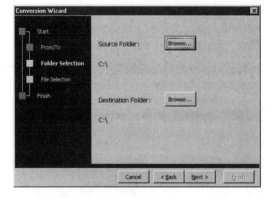

FIG. 29.9

From the Browse for Folder dialog box, you can choose a specific folder as either your source or destination folder.

13. Next to Destination Folder, click Browse again.

14. In the Browse to Folder dialog box, select a Destination Folder, and click OK.

15. Click Next to display the File Selection window (see Figure 29.10). From here, you can select the specific files you want to convert.

16. To convert all the files in the folder you selected, click Select All. All the files now appear in the To Convert box.

TIP If no files appear in the Available box, click the arrow next to the Type drop-down box to choose a different file extension.

For example, if you are converting HTML files to Word, the Conversion Wizard expects those files to use the extension .HTML. But many HTML files use the extension .HTM instead, and those choices don't appear unless you select *.htm from the Type drop-down box.

17. To prevent a file from being converted, double-click it in the To Convert box.

18. When you've finished selected files, choose Next.

FIG. 29.10

In the File Selection window, you can choose to convert all, or only some, files in a folder.

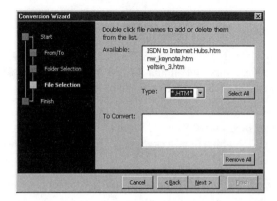

19. Click Finish to perform the file conversions. A progress bar appears on-screen showing how far along the Conversion Wizard is in the conversion process. When the process finishes, the Conversion Wizard offers you an opportunity to run another conversion (see Figure 29.11). If you click Yes, the wizard runs again.

FIG. 29.11

When the conversion process is complete, the Conversion Wizard asks if you would like to convert additional files.

N O T E   Don't assume the entire process will run unattended: check in every few minutes. The conversion process may occasionally stop to report an error message or, in some cases, to attempt to load a Web page included in a file being converted. ▪

Microsoft Office 97 Service Release 1

The Word 6.0/95 Binary Converter for Word 97 described earlier in this chapter is one of the most important elements of the Microsoft Office 97 Service Release 1, released by Microsoft in July 1997. If you are using the original version of Office 97, it will generally make sense to deploy the entire service release, rather than the converter alone.

ON THE WEB

In the United States, you can download Service Release 1 from Microsoft's Web site at **www.microsoft.com/Office/Office97/ServiceRelease**.

Double-click the .EXE file and follow the instructions to install it; you will not have to reinstall Word or Office. Outside the United States, check to make sure the appropriate localized service release is available; Microsoft expects to roll out updates throughout the fourth quarter of 1997.

Service Release 1 includes several bug fixes to Word and other Office programs, as well as the following new capabilities:

OfficeArt Support for MMX. If you use Office 97's graphics tools on an MMX computer (for example, most recent Pentiums, all Pentium IIs, AMD-K6, or Cyrix 6x86MX-based systems), these tools will now run faster. In particular, you'll be able to load and work with JPEG files more efficiently.

Better Internet Support in Microsoft Outlook. Service Release 1 includes the Internet Mail Enhancement Patch (IMEP), which improves the way Microsoft Outlook works with POP3 and SMTP Internet e-mail.

Microsoft Access Snapshot Technology. If you are running Microsoft Access 97, you will now be able to take a "snapshot" of your database and send it via e-mail or other methods. This allows others to see the electronic reports you want them to see, while protecting the confidentiality of the rest of your database.

This feature also allows you to e-mail much smaller files, improving network performance. Recipients don't need to be running Microsoft Access 97 to view these snapshots; all they need is the new Snapshot Viewer, which is free. Of course, this capability is only useful if you have purchased Microsoft Office 97 Professional Edition or Developer's Edition; other editions don't include Access.

If you have purchased Office 97 in Fall 1997 or later, you may already have a version that includes Service Release 1 patches. Or you may find that a workstation has already been upgraded with these patches. To check whether the service release has already been installed, choose Help, About Microsoft Word (see Fig. 29.12). If the product name appears as Microsoft® Word 97 SR-1, Service Release 1 has already been applied.

FIG. 29.12

This About Microsoft Word screen indicates that the Service Release has already been applied.

 Microsoft has made available two versions of the Service Release: a smaller version available on its Web site, and a more comprehensive update called the Enterprise Update, available only by calling Microsoft and providing the CD-key that verifies your ownership.

Word Document Security

Companies are increasingly concerned about the security of their documents. To this end, Word provides a number of features that offer varying levels of security. If you store your documents on network servers, you can combine Word's security features with the access restrictions built into your network operating system to tailor a security approach that meets the needs of your organization.

Word's security features include:

- Password-protected, 40-bit encryption
- Document protection that limits the changes that can be made to a document
- Limited macro virus protection

Using and Managing Word Encryption

Word makes it easy for users to encrypt documents using 40-bit encryption, the strongest encryption that may be legally exported. Follow these steps to encrypt and password-protect a document:

1. Choose File, Save As.
2. In the Save As dialog box, click Options. The Save dialog box opens (see Figure 29.13).
3. In the Password to Open text box, enter a password. Passwords can be up to 15 characters long, and can contain symbols and numerals as well as letters. For security reasons, Word displays asterisks on-screen as you type your password.
4. Choose OK. Word displays the Confirm Password dialog box (see Figure 29.14).
5. Re-enter the password exactly as you typed it the first time. (Use the same capitalization: passwords are case-sensitive.)
6. Choose OK.
7. Choose Save. Word saves the file.

FIG. 29.13
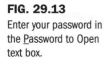
Enter your password in the Password to Open text box.

FIG. 29.14

Confirm your password in the Confirm Password dialog box.

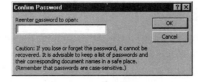

CAUTION

If you save to any format other than Word 97, every form of password protection is lost.

If you still have Word 6 or Word 95 on your system, you can save a file to Word 6.0/95 format, and then open one of those programs and add password protection there. (Word 97 can open documents encrypted by Word 6 and Word 95, as long as you have the password.)

CAUTION

After documents are encrypted, Word contains no feature for decrypting them without a password. Manage encryption very carefully, or you may find that you've lost access to business-critical documents.

 40-bit encryption is moderately strong, but it is far from unbreakable. If you are sending especially sensitive Word and Office files via e-mail—especially over the public Internet—you may be interested in stronger security. One option is PGPmail 4.5 from Pretty Good Privacy, Inc., which can encrypt e-mail sent from Microsoft Exchange and other major e-mail systems using 128-bit encryption, which is exceptionally difficult to break using today's computers.

TROUBLESHOOTING

I received a password-protected document, but when I tried to open it, I received the message "This document has been password protected with an encryption scheme not available in this region. Word cannot open this document." You may have set the Regional Settings on your Windows system to French. By French law, French systems are not permitted to use encryption as strong as Word's standard encryption. Do the following:

1. Choose Start, Settings, Control Panel.

2. Double-click the Regional Settings icon.

3. In the Regional Settings tab, click English (United States).

4. Choose OK.

5. Restart your computer.

Removing Password Protection from a File

After a file contains password protection, you can only remove the protection from within the file. To do so, follow these steps:

1. Open the file, and type the password when prompted.
2. Choose File, Save As.
3. Choose Options.
4. In the Password to Open box, delete the asterisks corresponding to the existing password.
5. Choose OK.
6. Choose Save.

Setting a File as Read-Only

You can allow users to read a document but not change it unless they have the appropriate password. To do so, set the file to read-only as follows:

1. Choose File, Save As.
2. In the Save As dialog box, click Options.
3. In the Password to Modify text box, enter a password.
4. Choose OK. Word displays the Confirm Password dialog box.
5. Re-enter the password.
6. Choose OK.
7. Choose Save.

 TIP You can also apply read-only status to a file from outside Word, by setting the Read-Only attribute in the file's Properties dialog box. In Windows Explorer, right-click the file's icon, and choose Properties from the shortcut menu. Then, click the Read-only check box.

You can't apply password protection this way, though the permissions you've set up on your network could prevent a user from altering the file's attributes.

CAUTION

Nothing (other, perhaps, than limited network permissions) prevents a user from opening a read-only file, saving it under a new name, and changing it. The user can then close the new file, reopen it, and save it using the original file's name—thereby deleting the original file. The result is the same as it would be if the file had never been password-protected at all.

"Recommending" Read-Only Status

You've just seen that you can password-protect a file as Read-Only, allowing users to read a file without a password, but making it more difficult for them to edit it. Word provides an even weaker form of protection that might be useful in circumstances where you would prefer that a file not be edited, but recognize that it may have to be. You can set a file as Read-Only Recommended.

When you set a file as Read-Only Recommended, if a user tries to open it, he or she sees a dialog box like that shown in Figure 29.15.

FIG. 29.15

In this dialog box, Word discourages—but doesn't prevent—users from editing a document.

If the user chooses Yes, the file opens as read-only. If the user chooses No, the file opens normally, and the user can edit it.

Limiting the Changes Users Can Make

You may want to allow a document to be edited, but limit the types of changes that can be made—thereby making it easier to review or use the document later. With Word's Protect Document feature, you can limit users to any one of the following:

- *Tracked changes*. Users can only make revisions that are tracked by Word's Track Changes feature.
- *Comments*. Users can only add comments to a document, using Word's comments tool.
- *Forms*. Users can only fill in the blanks in electronic forms, but cannot change any other aspects of the form.

To protect a document for any of these elements, follow these steps:

1. Choose Tools, Protect Document (see Figure 29.16).
2. Select the element you want to protect for.
3. If you want, type and confirm a password.
4. Choose OK.

If you protect a document, any user can make the limited edits you've allowed without having the password. However, a user needs the password to make any other edits. Follow these steps to remove protection from a document for additional editing:

1. Choose Tools, Unprotect Document.
2. If there is no password protection, the document is automatically unprotected. If password protection exists, enter the password in the Unprotect Document dialog box
3. Choose OK.

FIG. 29.16
In the Protect Document dialog box, you can protect a document for Tracked Changes, Comments, or Forms and add a password, if you choose.

Other Methods for Securing Documents

You have a few other options for securing Word documents, which depend on the features of the underlying operating system you are running. For example, follow these steps to hide a file so it does not appear in the Windows Explorer file lists:

1. Open Windows Explorer or Windows NT Explorer.
2. Select and right-click the file you want to hide. The shortcut menu appears.
3. Choose Properties from the shortcut menu.
4. In the General tab (see Figure 29.17), check the Hidden box.
5. Click OK.

FIG. 29.17
The General tab of the File's properties dialog box.

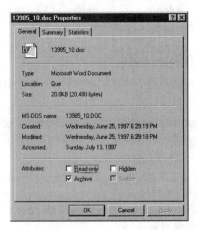

If the file is still visible in the Explorer list, follow these steps:

1. Choose View, Options (see Figure 29.18).
2. Click the Hide Files of These Types button.
3. Choose Hidden Files.
4. Click OK.

FIG. 29.18

Choosing View Options in Windows Explorer.

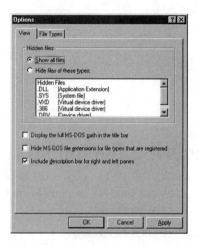

> **CAUTION**
>
> A hidden file may be exposed by choosing Show all Files in the View tab.

When a file is hidden in Windows Explorer, it is also hidden in Word's Open dialog box. However, you can open it by typing its file name in the Open dialog box.

Windows NT NTFS File-Level Security

If you maintain files on a network served by a Windows NT Server system, you can control access to both folders and files.

Folder-level permissions are similar to those that have long existed in other operating systems: *No Access*, *Read* (which let you view files as read-only), *Change*, and *Full Control* (which lets you change file and folder permissions as well as make edits to individual files).

If your server contains an NT File System (NTFS) partition, you can also set these four permissions for individual files stored on the NTFS partition. You have two more options as well: *Change Permissions*, which lets users change their rights to a file, and *Take Ownership*, which enables users to reassign permissions at will.

In practice, this means you can set general security for individual folders, but tighten security beyond that for specific, sensitive files within those folders. (However, you cannot set tight security for a folder and loosen it for an individual file.)

N O T E As Word 97 and other Office 97 programs run, they need read/write access to a variety of files and folders. Therefore, in order for users to run Word successfully from a networked NTFS partition, users must have read/write permissions to the same files and folders. The following folders require read/write permissions:

C:\

C:\Temp

C:\Winnt

C:\Winnt\Forms

C:\Winnt\System32

C:\Program Files\Microsoft Office

C:\Program Files\Microsoft Office\Office

C:\Program Files\Microsoft Office\Xlstart

C:\Program Files\Microsoft Office\Templates

The following additional files require read/write permission:

C:\Ffastun.ffa

C:\Ffastun.ffl

C:\Ffastun.ffo

C:\Ffastun.ffx

C:\Winnt\Artgalry.cag

C:\Winnt\<LogonID>.acl

C:\Winnt\<LogonID>8.xlb

C:\Winnt\<LogonID>.fav

C:\Winnt\Mso97.acl

C:\Winnt\Msoprefs.232

C:\Winnt\Outlook.fav

C:\Winnt\Outlook.prf

C:\Winnt\Outlook.prt

C:\Winnt\Forms\Frmcache.dat

C:\Winnt\System32\Ffastlog.txt

C:\Winnt\System32\Msforms.twd

Where <LogonID> is included in the file name, it corresponds to each user's logon ID. ▥

Part
VI

Ch
29

Preventing and Controlling Word Viruses

Macro viruses have become an unfortunate fact of life for millions of Word users. Whether you are responsible for Word running only on your computer, or for an entire workgroup or organization, you need to be aware of them, and you need to take precautions to minimize the risk of becoming infected.

Macro viruses are viruses written in a Word macro language—traditionally, WordBasic, but increasingly Visual Basic for Applications. Like other computer viruses, they have the ability to reproduce themselves and spread to other computers that share files. Like other computer viruses, some macro viruses are merely annoying while others can cause serious data loss.

Macro viruses take advantage of the remarkable flexibility provided by Word's architecture and macro languages. The classic macro virus, Concept, established a pattern followed by most macro viruses since. When you open a file infected with Concept, the macro virus copies itself into the Normal.dot template, and from there copies itself into new files. Because Word 6 and Word 95 could only store files as templates, files infected with Concept could themselves only be stored as templates—a clear giveaway that you were probably infected.

N O T E Because Word 97 can store macros with files as well as templates, you won't be able to count on this behavior in the future. ■

Concept added three macros to your list of macros: AAAZAO, AAAZFS, and Payload. Macro viruses since Concept have been more insidious; they have used macro names identical to common Word features such as FileSaveAs. As a result, if you attempted to save a file, you would instead run the macro virus program. The last step of the virus program might be to save your file normally. As a result, you might never know you were infected.

It's also common for macro viruses to use the automatic virus names built into Word, such as AutoNew and AutoOpen. A macro virus named AutoNew, for example, will run every time you create a new document—and almost certainly infect that document.

To give you a sense of how serious the problem has become, according to the National Center for Supercomputing Applications 1997 Virus Prevalence Survey, 80 percent of new virus infections are macro viruses.

Now that you understand what macro viruses are—and how serious they are—how can you prevent your computer from becoming infected? Start with the same common sense precautions that smart computer users have always known: *Only open documents that come from sources you trust*. In the age of the Internet, this is more of a challenge than ever—and more important than ever.

In addition, there are three types of technical precautions you can take:

■ Built-in Word features that deliver modest protection

■ Add-on Word features that deliver somewhat more protection

■ Excellent third-party virus protection software

Word's Modest Built-In Anti-Virus Features   Word 6 and the first release of Word 95 shipped with no virus protection at all. Word 97 is somewhat improved in this respect. When you run a macro stored in a Word 6 or 95 template, Word converts the macro to Visual Basic. If it recognizes the macro as a virus, it neuters the virus by failing to convert the parts that are infectious.

Most Word 6/95 viruses are caught this way. However, a few have slipped through. In two cases, a virus mutated by being translated from WordBasic to Visual Basic in a beta version of Word that didn't yet include macro recognition features.

Word's Warnings that a Macro is Present   Word offers one more built-in protection: If you open a document or template that contains a macro of any kind, Word can warn you of the macro's presence (see Figure 29.19). Sometimes, the macro will be perfectly benign—Word can't tell the difference. However, you're likely to receive some documents from people who don't normally embed macros in their files intentionally. In this case, you can contact them to see if the macro is legitimate. In the meantime, you can choose to open the document without activating the macros—or simply refuse to open it at all.

FIG. 29.19

Word can warn you about the presence of macros in documents and templates.

To make sure this level of macro protection is turned on, follow these steps:

1. Choose Tools, Options.
2. Choose the General tab.
3. Make sure the Macro Virus Protection check box is checked.
4. Choose OK.

Protection Against Changes to the Normal.dot Template   Because most macros make changes in the Normal.dot template, Microsoft has created a patch to Word which prevents macros from writing VBA code to Normal.dot. If you install this patch, you'll have to enter a password every time you create new macros in Normal.dot.

You can download this patch from **www.microsoft.com/office/antivirus/word/ normaldot.htm**. There are a few more things you need to know about it. If you enter the password to create or edit a macro, your protection is turned off for the remainder of your Word editing session. In fact, Microsoft recommends restarting Windows itself, not just exiting and restarting Word, before opening documents that might be infected.

Third-Party Virus Prevention   None of the Microsoft virus protection solutions are foolproof. Quite simply, you need a third-party anti-virus program—preferably one that is updated regularly to reflect the growing number of new viruses out there. The following are among the best third-party anti-virus software packages:

- Norton AntiVirus (**www.symantec.com**)
- McAfee VirusScan (**www.mcafee.com**)
- IBM AntiVirus (**www.av.ibm.com**)
- Dr. Solomon's Anti-Virus Toolkit (**www.drsolomon.com**)

Many of these companies now have packages designed specially for corporate use.

Using Document Properties to Simplify Document Management

In Chapter 1, "Word: Take the Controls," you learned about Word's powerful capabilities for finding files through the Open and Advanced Find dialog boxes. You may recall that one of the ways Word can search for files is by document property. In this section, you'll take a closer look at document properties and learn how to use them to your advantage—whether you're responsible for one desktop or many.

To work with document properties, choose File, Properties. The Properties dialog box opens (see Figure 29.20). It contains five tabs:

FIG. 29.20

You can review a document's properties (and edit many of them) by displaying the Properties dialog box.

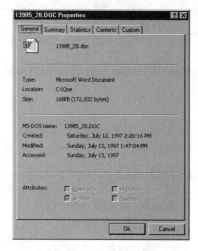

- *General*, which includes information Word automatically stores about every document, including when it was created; how large it is; and where it is stored
- *Summary*, which includes the document's title, COMMENTS, author, keywords, and other important document information
- *Statistics*, which includes information Word compiles about the size and contents of a document, as well as how long it has been open, and how many times it has been saved

- *Contents*, which includes major parts of a document file
- *Custom*, which enables you to create your own document properties or choose from 30 optional document properties Word can provide

General Information Stored in the Properties Dialog Box

Display the General tab of the Properties dialog box when you want to know basic information about your Word document, including its current size, its MS-DOS "short" (8.3) file name; when the file was created, last modified, and last accessed.

Most of the items in the General tab are self-evident, but a couple are worth calling your attention to:

- *Type* is typically a Microsoft Word document. Note that Word gets this information from the file extension. This means the Properties dialog box can't tell Word 97 documents from Word 6 documents. Nor can it tell Word 97 documents from templates that have been renamed with .DOC extensions (as some Word macro viruses have been known to do).
- *Modified* is especially useful information if Word or Windows crashes on you. It'll tell you when the file was last saved, so you can tell if your edits are likely to be reflected.
- *MS-DOS Name* is the old-fashioned 8.3 short file name stored with every file in Windows 95 and Windows NT—the name that stays with your file even if you send it to a Windows 3.x or Macintosh system that doesn't support Windows long file names.

No General information is stored with a file until you save it for the first time.

Working with Summary Information

Chances are, the Properties tab you'll use most is the Summary tab (see Figure 29.21). Here, you insert editable information about your file—including the categories you're most likely to search for in Word's Open and Advanced Find dialog boxes, such as Author, Comments, or Keywords.

If you've set up Word properly, much of this information can be entered for you automatically. Word will enter a title based on the first line of text in your document—commonly a document's title. Word enters the Author based on the name stored in the User Information tab of the Tools, Options dialog box. If you ever run AutoSummarize, Word will automatically copy the list of keywords it generates into the Keywords box. Finally, you can include Manager, Company, Category, and other information along with templates, so they are automatically included in every document built with those templates.

One more item on this tab is worth pointing out: Save Preview Picture. If you check this check box, the next time you save your document, Word copies its current headings into the Contents tab of the Properties dialog box. If you check this box, Word displays a thumbnail of the first page in the Preview pane, reflecting formatting. If you do not check the box, you can scroll through the text of the entire document in the Preview pane.

FIG. 29.21

For most people, the Summary tab will be the workhorse of the Properties dialog box.

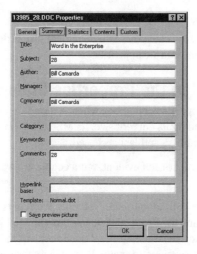

 TIP If nothing else, you might add your company name to the Summary tab of the Properties dialog box in Normal.dot. This provides a small added measure of security by showing who owns the computer on which your documents were created. It's easy to remove this information—but many Word users won't even realize it's there.

N O T E   The name specified in the Author box won't change if you forward the file to a colleague for editing on his or her computer. However, the Last Saved By name in the Statistics tab will change when your colleague saves the file. ■

Displaying the Summary Tab Whenever a New File is Saved

If you are responsible for the documents created by an entire workgroup or organization, consider requiring (or at least actively encouraging) them to include Summary information along with their document. One way to do this is to have Word display the Summary tab of the Properties dialog box whenever a user saves a file for the first time. Follow these steps to do so:

1. Choose Tools, Options.
2. Choose the Save tab.
3. Check the Prompt for Document Properties check box.
4. Choose OK.

Understanding and Using Document Statistics

The Statistics tab (see Figure 29.22) compiles several useful statistics about your document. You can see when your document was created, modified, and accessed—the same information you already saw in the General tab. Here, however, you can also see when your document was last printed. You can see who saved it last, even if it was saved by someone other than the author.

FIG. 29.22
The Statistics tab gives you a quick look at the most important statistics associated with your document.

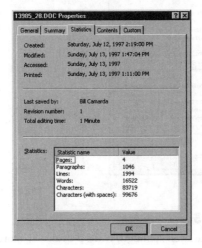

Revision Number tells you how many times you've saved the file. Because you may save a file every few minutes, it's easy to generate hundreds of revisions. If you want a true draft number, you can write a Visual Basic macro that requests the current draft number and stores it in another Properties box, such as Comments. You can name the macro AutoClose so it runs whenever you save a file associated with the template where the macro is stored.

The Statistics tab also reports Total editing time, which is actually the amount of time the document has been open. Of course, several other documents, or for that matter several different applications, may be open at the same time. Word doesn't care; it assumes you're editing a document whenever it's open.

 TIP See Chapter 30, "Recording and Running Visual Basic Macros," to learn how you can get even more detailed statistics about a document by using the SuperDocStatistics macro contained in Word's Sample Macros template (MACROS8.DOT).

▶ **See** "Using SuperDocStatistics," **p. 861**

Using Contents Information

As you saw earlier, if you check the Save Preview Picture check box in the Summary tab, the next time you save your file, Word stores its headings in the Contents tab. You can see an example in Figure 29.23.

NOTE Unfortunately, several document elements you might reasonably expect to find here are not included. For example, Document Contents does not report on multiple document versions stored in the same file; or macro modules stored with a file; or embedded graphics. ■

FIG. 29.23

The Contents tab shows the document's title and can also display all the headings in your document.

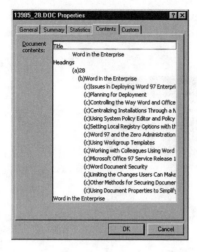

Creating Custom Properties

If the properties you've seen so far aren't enough, Word provides 27 more custom properties you can assign at will—or you can create your own. To work with custom properties, choose File, Properties, and display the Custom tab (see Figure 29.24). Follow these steps to add a new category:

1. Choose a name for your custom property in the Name scroll box, or type a name of your own.

2. In the Type box, specify the kind of information you want your property to contain: text, a date, a number, or a Yes/No choice.

3. In the Value text box, enter the value you want your custom property to start out with. For example, if you've created a Date Completed property, you might enter the date 11/1/97. The Value you insert must be in a format compatible with the Type you've just chosen.

4. When you are finished, click Add. The custom property, its type, and its value now appear in the Properties scroll box.

After the property has been created, you can modify it by selecting it in the Properties scroll box, entering a new Value or Type, and choosing Modify. Or you can delete it by selecting it and choosing Delete.

N O T E   You can't create a custom property without including a Value; in other words, you can't create an empty custom property. If you want to include a custom property in your document or template, insert a "dummy" value that users can later replace with a real one. ■

FIG. 29.24

If you need a property that Word doesn't provide, you can add it in the Custom tab of the Properties dialog box.

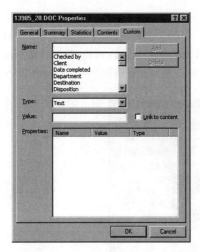

Creating Custom Properties That Update Themselves

You can create a custom property that knows how to update itself, based on changing information in your document.

Let's say every division in your company sends you a monthly executive summary reporting new sales activity. Your reporting template includes a table; that table contains a cell listing the total value of all new customer sales made that month. You might want to search all those documents, quickly identifying the divisions where sales exceeded $10,000,000. However, you have dozens of divisions and you would rather not open each file individually to see the value stored in the table: you only want to know the performers who have exceeded a certain threshold, so you can learn why.

To accomplish this, you first create a bookmark associated with the text in your document that you want to attach to your property:

1. In your template, select the formula field that will contain the calculation of total profits.

2. Choose Insert, Bookmark.

3. Type a bookmark name and click OK.

Next, you create a custom property based on that bookmark:

1. Choose File, Properties.

2. Choose the Custom tab.

3. Check the Link to Content check box. (This box will be grayed out unless your document contains at least one bookmark.)

4. In the Name text box, enter or select a name for your new Custom Property.

5. Notice that the Value box has turned into a drop-down box named Source. In the Source drop-down box, choose the bookmark to which you want to link your custom property.

6. Click Add. The new custom property appears in the Properties list. A Link icon appears next to it, indicating this custom property is linked to a bookmark (see Figure 29.25).

FIG. 29.25

You can create a custom property linked to bookmarked text in your document.

Link to bookmark in document

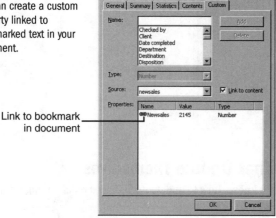

Using Properties Information with Fields

Many of the elements stored in the Properties dialog box can be placed in your document automatically, using fields. For example, you might want to create a cover sheet that prints with each of your documents. In the example shown in Figure 29.26, the cover sheet includes the following information:

- The name of the document's author
- The name of the author's manager
- Who saved the file last
- When the file was printed
- How many pages the file contains
- The file's name and path (where it is currently stored)

Figure 29.27 shows the fields that were used to create this cover sheet.

Table 29.1 lists the fields that utilize information stored in the Properties dialog box. Of course, any time you update your fields, any changes in the corresponding Properties boxes will be reflected in them.

FIG. 29.26
It's easy to create a
cover sheet that
automatically includes
all this information with
every document.

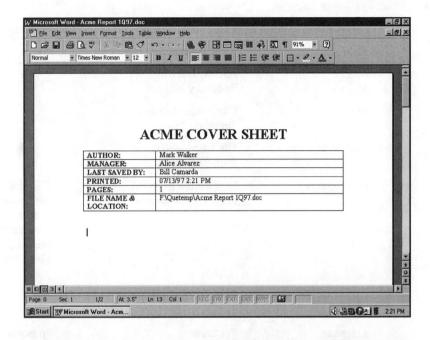

FIG. 29.27
The fields underlying
the cover sheet shown
in the previous figure.

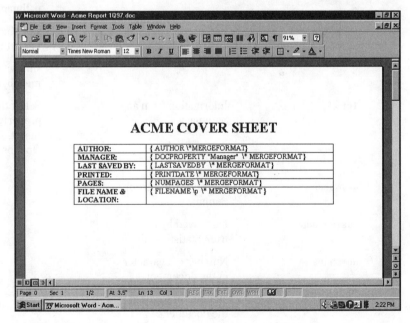

Table 29.1 Fields that Use Information Stored in the Properties Dialog Box

Field	What It Displays	Notes
Author	Author data from Summary tab.	
Comments	Comments data from Summary tab.	
CreateDate	File creation date from Generaltab.	
DocProperty	Information from any property you choose.	Can also work with custom properties after you create them. Select the property in Insert, Field, Options.
EditTime	Editing time from Statistics tab.	
FileName	File name.	\p switch adds full pathname.
FileSize	File size.	\k switch specifies kilobytes.
		\m switch specifies megabytes.
Info	Information from any Summary.	Select the property of your choice in Insert, Field, Options.
Keywords	Keywords data from Summary tab.	
LastSavedBy	Last saved by data from Statistics tab.	
NumChars	Number of characters in the document.	
NumPages	Number of pages in the document.	
NumWords	Number of words in the document.	

Field	What It Displays	Notes
PrintDate	Print date from the Statistics tab.	
SaveDate	Last saved date from General tab.	
Comments	Comments data from Summary tab.	
Template	Template currently attached to document.	\p switch adds full pathname of template.
Title	Title data from Summary tab.	

▶ **See** "Inserting a Field," **p. 697**

Using Windows 95/NT 4.0 Find Fast to Accelerate Searches for Properties

As already mentioned (and covered in detail in Chapter 1, "Word: Take the Controls"), you can often find documents more quickly by searching for their properties in the Open or Advanced Find dialog boxes. However, if you have a great many documents on your hard drive, you may find even Find searches for properties to be slow. That's when Microsoft Office's Find Fast feature is useful.

When you install Microsoft Office 97, you have the option of installing the Find Fast applet in the Windows 95 or Windows NT Control Panel. Find Fast makes searches faster, by regularly indexing all the Office documents stored on your hard disk(s). Word (and other Office programs) can then refer to the index when they perform their searches, instead of having to look in every single document. To see whether Find Fast is at work, choose Start, Settings, Control Panel (see Figure 29.28).

If Find Fast is present, double-click it. Find Fast opens (see Figure 29.29), displaying any indexes that already exist and whether they are being updated automatically.

If no indexes are present, you can choose Index, Create Index to create one. The Create Index dialog box opens. By default, Fast Find indexes all Office and Web documents. In the In and Below text box, enter the top level of your folder structure that you want indexed. In most cases, the following command indexes your entire computer:

```
c:\Windows\Desktop
```

Choose OK, and Fast Find creates the index.

FIG. 29.28

If you installed Find Fast with Office, it appears in the Windows 95 or NT 4.0 Control Panel.

FIG 29.29

From the main Find Fast dialog box, you can see which indexes already exist and whether they are being updated automatically.

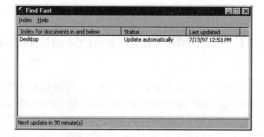

 TIP By default, Find Fast only indexes your local hard drives. However, you can use Index, Create Index to build additional indexes that cover network drives you use especially often.

N O T E Microsoft says the version of Find Fast included with Office 97 is far more efficient than the one which came with Office 95 and is far less likely to reduce system performance while it updates your files. ▓

CAUTION

If you are using Find Fast on a network, make sure that users have the same permissions for the index as they do for the documents being indexed. If users can access the index even though they do not have rights to the document, they can perform word association searches that determine which key words are included in a document even though they are not permitted to read the document itself.

TIP If you purchased the Microsoft Office 97 Professional Edition CD-ROM, you received the Office Server Pack, which includes a special Windows NT Server version of Find Fast. If your network is based on Windows NT Server, this version can run as a Windows NT Service. It can also be customized to work with Web pages as a search index. This lets you build an Internet or intranet Web site that uses Find Fast as its search engine.

Viewing Document Properties from Outside Word

All Windows 95 and Windows NT 4.0 files have a Properties dialog box; Word's is simply more extensive than most. So it's not surprising that you can view many of a document's properties from outside Word.

Right-click the document in either Windows Explorer or any folder window (or on the desktop itself, if you've created an icon associated with a specific document). The shortcut menu appears; select Properties. A truncated version of Word's Properties dialog box appears (refer to Figure 29.18).

Not all the same information is present: for example, you won't see Company and Manager in the Summary tab, and you won't see Total Editing Time in the Statistics tab. However, when you're outside Word, you can change the read-only, archive or hidden attributes of a file—something you can't do from the Properties dialog box within Word.

Converting from WordPerfect

If your company is converting from WordPerfect—especially WordPerfect 5.1 for DOS, the word processing software that dominated the market several years ago—Word comes with several features designed to make the transition especially easy. To access these features, double-click the WPH box in the status bar, or choose Help, WordPerfect Help. The Help for WordPerfect users dialog box opens (see Figure 29.30).

The Command keys scroll box includes a list of WordPerfect for DOS Command keys. When you select a Command key, Word displays a description of how to accomplish the same task in Word 97. Where Word offers additional help for WordPerfect Command key submenus, the Command key is followed by an ellipsis. You can view the additional information by clicking Help Text. When you've drilled down to the bottom level of information, you can click Help Text again, and Word displays the help information above your editing window, so you can view the information and perform the task at the same time (see Figure 29.31).

If Word has a demo available, and you want to watch the task performed, click Demo or Demo Now. Word displays your current document, and performs the action at your current insertion point. In some cases (see Figure 29.32), Word opens a dialog box and shows you what to do next.

FIG. 29.30

With the Help for WordPerfect Users dialog box open, people making the transition from WordPerfect can get detailed explanations of how Word features compare with WordPerfect for DOS.

Ellipses indicate additional information

Double-arrows indicate demos

WPH box in status bar

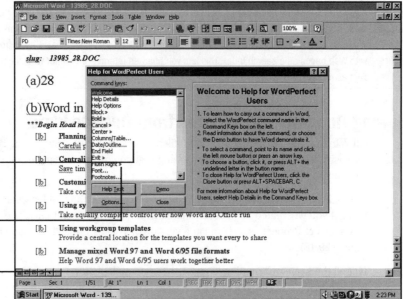

FIG. 29.31

From this dialog box, you can see the WordPerfect Help and work in the document at the same time.

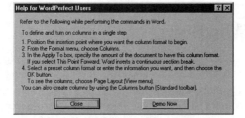

FIG. 29.32

Word opens the appropriate dialog box and tells you exactly where to insert information.

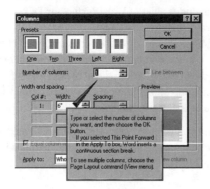

 T I P If WordPerfect Help performs an action you didn't intend, click Undo.

Setting WordPerfect Help Options

Word gives you options about how to use WordPerfect Help, based on how far along you and your users have come in transitioning from WordPerfect and DOS. To use these options, choose Help, WordPerfect Help, and choose Options. The Help Options dialog box appears (see Figure 29.33).

FIG. 29.33
You can control exactly how WordPerfect Help behaves.

If you check the Help for WordPerfect Users check box, Word displays or demonstrates instructions whenever you press a WordPerfect for DOS key combination. The WPH box in the status bar will be highlighted while this box is checked. If you check the Navigation Keys for WordPerfect Users check box, Word changes the way its Page Up, Page Down, Home, End, and Esc keys behave to match the way they work in WordPerfect for DOS.

Depending on the speed of your computer, you may find Word's feature demonstrations run too quickly—or too slowly. You can change their speed by choosing Fast, Medium, or Slow from the Demo Speed drop-down box.

 If you or your users miss WordPerfect's Reveal Codes feature, remember that even though Word doesn't have equivalent formatting codes, you can get detailed information about the formatting associated with any text. Use Word's What's This? feature, as follows:

1. Press Shift+F1.
2. Click the text you're interested in.
3. When you're finished, press Esc.

One more idea for converting from WordPerfect for DOS: if your WordPerfect documents contain line drawings or equations, the Microsoft Office 97 Resource Kit includes five special fonts you can use to make them translate to Word more accurately. You can download these fonts from **www.microsoft.com/OfficeFreeStuff/download/Fonts.exe**.

Supporting Word in an International Environment

Increasingly, you may find yourself supporting Word in an international environment. For the first time, Word 97 supports Unicode, a standard character set that includes all the commonly-used characters in virtually all of the world's major languages, including Asian languages. This makes it much easier to create documents that are entirely, or partially, in languages other than English.

Unicode support means you may not have to use language-specific fonts to display nonEnglish alphabets; you can use international fonts that work in many languages. For example, Microsoft's Windows Glyph List 4 (WGL4) font standard includes 652 characters required in languages from Western, Central, and Eastern Europe; Greece, and Turkey. Arial, Courier, and Times New Roman have been expanded to support this standard.

Both Windows 95 and Windows NT 4.0 can work with Unicode. However, NT 4.0 includes stronger support for Unicode and is especially preferred if you plan to work with Asian text.

In order to take advantage of Unicode in Windows 95, you must install the optional Multilanguage Support feature. First, insert the Windows 95 CD-ROM or disk. Then, follow these steps:

1. Choose Start, Settings, Control Panel.
2. Double-click the Add/Remove Programs icon.
3. Click Windows Setup.
4. Check Multilanguage Support.
5. Click Details to specify the alphabets and languages you want to use.
6. Click OK twice.

After Multilanguage Support is installed, there are two ways to enter text in another language, depending on the language you want to use:

▓ If you are using a Western European language, for example, German or French, choose Tools, Language, Set Language. The Language dialog box appears (see Figure 29.34). Choose the language you want, and choose OK. If you want to make this language the default language for all documents based on the Normal template, click Default and OK.

TROUBLESHOOTING

I'm using special Unicode symbol characters, but my printer won't print them properly. Many printer drivers do not support Unicode properly. These include the following:

● Canon BubbleJet BJ-C600, 4000, 4200, 4500, 4550, v 3.40

● Canon Multipass 2500 3.40

● Epson Color 500

● Epson Stylus Color, v 2.x

● Epson Stylus Pro / XL v. 2.11BE

● HP Color LaserJet 5 PCL, printer driver version F 1.300

● HP DeskJet 1600C, printer driver version 4.20

● HP LaserJet 4 PCL, printer driver version 3.78

- HP LaserJet 6P, standard printer driver

- Okidata 4 laser printer

The best solution is to see if your printer manufacturer has a newer printer driver that does support Unicode. Failing that, you may have to edit the Windows Registry to reset your printer driver so that it uses ANSI character layout functions instead of Unicode character layout functions. Detailed instructions for doing so may be found in the Microsoft Knowledge Base article Q159418.

FIG. 29.34

Setting a new language that uses a Western European character set.

If you are using a language that works with a different character set, you need to change your keyboard layout. In Windows 95, choose Start, Settings, Control Panel. Double-click the Keyboard icon. Choose the Language tab (see Figure 29.35). (In Windows NT 4.0, this tab is named Input Locales.) Click Add. The Add Language dialog box opens; choose a language and click OK. In the Language tab, check the Enable indicator on taskbar check box; this adds an indicator to the Windows 95/NT 4.0 taskbar showing which keyboard layout is currently in use. You can double-click this indicator to display all the available layouts and change the one in use.

FIG. 29.35

Adding a new keyboard layout through the Keyboard Control Panel applet.

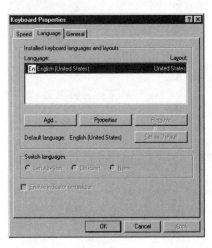

Getting Foreign Language Dictionaries in the U.S.

You've already learned that you can use the Set Language dialog box to specify which language you are using to enter text. However, you won't be able to proof foreign language text unless you have the appropriate dictionary. International versions of Word are available from Microsoft's subsidiaries in each country. In the United States, foreign language dictionaries for Word 97 are available from Alki Software Corporation (**www.alki.com**), 1-800-669-9673. Table 29.2 lists the dictionaries that are available now or will be shortly. An "X" appears next to each of the features available for each language.

Table 29.2 Foreign Language Dictionaries Available Through Alki Software

Language	Spelling	Hyphenation	Thesaurus	Grammar
Basque	X	X		
Bulgarian	X	X		
Catalan	X	X	X	
Croatian	X	X		
Czech	X	X	X	
Danish	X	X	X	
Dutch	X	X	X	X
English, Australian	X	X	X	X
English,UK	X	X	X	X
English,US	X	X	X	X
Estonian	X	X	X	
Finnish	X	X	X	
French (European& Canadian)	X	X	X	X
German&Swiss German	X	X	X	X
Greek	X	X		
Hungarian	X	X	X	X
Italian	X	X	X	X
Latvian	X	X		

Language	Spelling	Hyphenation	Thesaurus	Grammar
Lithuanian	X	X		
Norwegian (Bokmål& Nynorsk)	X	X	X	
Polish	X	X	X	
Portuguese (European& Brazilian)	X	X	X	
Romanian	X	X	X	
Russian	X	X	X	X
Serbian	X	X		
Slovak	X	X	X	
Slovenian	X	X	X	
Spanish	X	X	X	X
Swedish	X	X	X	
Turkish	X	X	X	

From Here...

In this chapter, you've learned a variety of techniques for managing Word, including ways to cope with Word's new file format; techniques for improving file security; tools for transitioning WordPerfect users; and how to use Word's internationalization features. Now, you'll move on to the piece de resistance for extending Word's capabilities: Visual Basic for Applications.

■ Even without macros, you can customize Word further—changing toolbars, menus, and many other aspects of the program's behavior. To learn how, refer back to Chapter 26, "Customizing Word."

■ In Chapter 30, "Recording and Running Visual Basic Macros," you'll see how far you can get with macros through simply recording the tasks you perform. Then, in Chapters 31–33, you'll take a closer look at Visual Basic and watch how practical, time-saving applications can be constructed with it.

The Power of Visual Basic for Applications

Recording and Running Visual Basic Macros

by Bill Camarda

To many people, macros mean *programming*, and programming isn't what they have in mind when they fire up Word in the morning. However, you don't have to be a programmer to take advantage of macros. You can save an enormous amount of time by simply *recording* macros, which is not much harder than running a tape player.

In this chapter, you'll learn how to record a macro, use the Macro toolbar, decide what to record, and assign a keyboard shortcut or toolbar button to your macro. You'll also learn how to run a macro you've recorded, and how to create macros that run automatically. Finally, you'll learn about the built-in macros that come with Word—where to find them, how to install them, and what they can do for you. ■

Understanding macros

Learn what kinds of tasks are most easily recorded and automated and just how much time you can save.

Planning to record your macro

Think through your macro so you can get it right the first time.

Creating toolbar and keyboard shortcuts for your macro

Set up your macro so it's always easy to run when you need it.

Running your macros

Learn three ways to run a macro and what to do if it doesn't work properly.

Moving and renaming macros and project items

It's easy to rename and reorganize macro modules. It's not quite so easy to move individual Word 97 macros, but you'll learn how.

Running Word's built-in macros

Office 97 comes with hard-to-find macros that can make your life a lot easier if you know about them.

Creating macros that run automatically

You can create macros that run automatically when you open or exit Word, when you create a document, or when you open or close an existing document.

Macros: The Basics

A *macro* is a set of procedures that Word can run automatically with a single keyboard shortcut or button click. Nearly anything you can do with Word can be automated with a macro, because every Word command has an equivalent macro command. There are three ways to create macros:

- You can record them by turning on the macro recorder and actually performing the procedure you want to store as a macro. That's the focus of this chapter.

- You can write them from scratch, using the Visual Basic language covered in Chapters 31 through 34.

- You can do some of both: record those steps that can be recorded, and then add intelligence and user input to your macros by writing Visual Basic code.

N O T E After you are comfortable with recorded macros and see the power that's available to you through macros, you may be ready to learn how to develop your own from scratch. If so, Chapter 31, "Getting Started with VBA," introduces the basics of Microsoft's Visual Basic macro programming language, and Chapters 32 through 34 walk you through three detailed, real-world applications.

What Tasks Should You Automate with a Macro?

Many experienced Word users have never given any thought to recording macros; they perceive it as too complicated. After they get past the psychological hurdle, they suddenly realize there are dozens of macros they could easily record—eliminating much of the day-to-day repetitive work they've been performing for years. Everyone performs different tasks, but here are some ideas to help you get started thinking about which macros might help you. Consider creating macros to automate (or at least streamline) the following tasks:

- Complex formatting tasks you perform repeatedly, such as formatting text as small caps, creating special indents, borders, and shading.

- Tasks that take several steps, such as running a mail merge, or compiling indexes or tables of contents that use heavily customized settings.

- "Cleaning up" long documents you import from elsewhere. Such documents often need to have repetitive Find and Replaces run on them to eliminate extra spaces, fix errors in product names, change formatting, and so on.

- Running routine file management tasks, such as saving a file to floppy instead of hard drive, or closing all open files.

- Changing one or more Word settings that may be buried in obscure dialog boxes. For example, if you want to add SmartQuotes to a document that doesn't have them, you can record a macro that turns off all of Word's AutoFormat options except SmartQuotes, runs AutoFormat, and then sets the options back the way you like them.

Planning to Record Your Macro

Before you actually record your macro, spend a few moments thinking about the task that you are planning to record. You might want to run a rehearsal—actually walking through the steps you expect to take, and noting any surprises or small details you might have forgotten. In particular, follow these guidelines:

- Check to ensure that you've set up your document to be in the same condition that it will be in when you run the macro later. For instance, if you're planning to record a macro that selects and reformats a paragraph, make sure your selection point is within the paragraph. Otherwise, you'll have to record steps to move there—steps that might cause problems when you run the macro later.

- If possible, take precautions to make sure the documents you run your finished macro on later will react appropriately to it. For example, if you're creating a macro that inserts text at the beginning of the document, the first step you record should be a command that moves to the beginning of the document. That way, the macro will work correctly no matter where your cursor is located in the document.

- Think about how to avoid error messages. For example, when you close a document that contains changes, Word displays a message asking if you want to save the document. To avoid seeing this message, record a File, Save command before you record the File, Close command.

- Make the macro as generic as possible; the steps you record shouldn't depend on the presence of text that only exists in the document you have open now. The more generic your macro, the more places you can use it.

- Consider keyboard shortcuts for navigation and text selection. While Word macros can record mouse toolbar button clicks and menu selections, they can't record mouse navigation and text selection. You have to use keyboard shortcuts instead. (For example, Ctrl+Home moves to the top of a document; Ctrl+End moves to the bottom.)

- If you're recording macros that use Word's Find and Replace feature, use the Search All option to make sure Word searches the entire document, no matter where your insertion point is currently located.

Part VII
Ch
30

Recording Your Macro

The quickest way to start recording a macro is to double-click the REC button on the status bar. Alternatively, you can choose Tools, Macro, Record New Macro. The Record Macro dialog box opens (see Figure 30.1).

Now, you have some decisions to make, including naming your macro, deciding where to store it, and whether to attach a toolbar or keyboard shortcut to it.

FIG. 30.1

In the Record Macro dialog box, you can name a macro, describe it, decide where to store it, and decide whether to give it a toolbar button or keyboard shortcut.

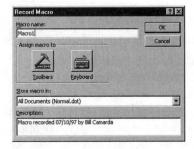

 TIP If you're creating a temporary macro that you probably won't use for more than a few hours, don't bother naming or describing it: just record it using Word's default name (for example, Macro1), use it, and delete it when you're finished.

Naming Your Macro

If you're planning to keep your macro around awhile, you'll first have to decide what to name it. Use a name that's as descriptive as possible, subject to the following constraints:

- Don't include spaces. (You can use underscore characters to simulate them, however.)
- You must start with a letter of the alphabet, though you can use numbers afterward.
- Names can consist of up to 80 letters and numbers; symbols and punctuation marks are generally unacceptable.

 TIP Use both upper- and lowercase letters to help make names clearer, as in the following example:

AddAsterisksToTextFile

Also, consider grouping all related macros together with names that start the same. If several macros relate to Acme Corporation, name them using a pattern like this:

ACMEAddAsterisksToTextFile

Deciding Where to Store Your Macro

Unless you specify otherwise, Word stores new macros in the Normal.dot template, where they are available to all your documents. If you prefer, however, you can store the macro in any open template. Word 97 gives you another new choice as well: you can store your macro with your document. When should you use each option?

- If your macro will be usable in many different kinds of documents, store it in Normal.dot.
- If you expect to use a macro only in specialized situations and you have a template associated with those situations, store it there. For example, if you have a template for generating sales proposals, that's where you should store a macro that inserts boilerplate scheduling and pricing information you only use in proposals.

■ Store the macro in your document if you intend to distribute the document to colleges, clients, or suppliers who won't have access to your templates.

TIP Later in this chapter, you'll learn how to move macros among templates and documents using the Organizer.

Describing Your Macro

The Record Macro dialog box includes a Description text box where you can insert information about the macro. Word already places two pieces of information there for you: who recorded the macro, and when. It's important to add specific information about what the macro does, especially because you're likely to create more than one macro with similar (but not identical) functions and names. Your total description can be as long as 255 characters.

TIP If you're already sure which keyboard shortcut or toolbar button you want to assign to the macro, enter that information here. By doing so, you'll make it much easier to find that information later when you need it.

You can edit the name and description of your macro later, in the Visual Basic Editor. The name and description appear at the top of the macro, in green text, on lines that begin with an apostrophe (indicating that they represent comments, not code to be run).

▶ **See** "Understanding the VBA Integrated Development Environment (IDE)," **p. 869**

Toolbar or Keyboard Shortcut?

Word now gives you an opportunity to assign a macro to either a toolbar or a keyboard shortcut.

It's not essential that you assign your macro to either a toolbar or a keyboard shortcut. You might plan to use the macro only on rare occasions; in that case, you can run it from the list of macros Word displays when you choose Tools, Macro, Macros. If you are recording the macro with the intention of copying it into a VBA program later, you might never run the macro on a stand-alone basis after you're sure it works properly.

However, if you plan to use the macro often, you should assign a toolbar or a keyboard shortcut. The next question is: which one? There are a few approaches to take:

■ You can add your macro to a toolbar that's always open, such as the Standard or Formatting toolbar. This works best if you use a screen resolution higher than 640×480 (for example, 800×600, 1024×768, and so on), because at 640×480 there's no extra room available on these toolbars. The advantage of adding a macro to the Standard or Formatting toolbar is that it will virtually always be visible to your users; they won't have to be reminded that it exists.

■ You can add your macro to a specialized toolbar, or one you create yourself. Then it will only be available when that toolbar is visible. This has two advantages. You don't have to worry about finding available space on the Standard or Formatting toolbars, and you can cluster related macros together on the same toolbar. The disadvantage is that your screen will be more cluttered and your editing window will be smaller. Some users just don't care for any more toolbar buttons than necessary.

■ You can create a keyboard shortcut associated with your macro. Keyboard shortcuts, of course, take up no space on your desktop. They're quick and easy to use. However, you'll need to make sure your users know about them. Consider creating a list of custom key assignments and distribute it to everyone who will have access to the macros you are creating.

If you want to print out a list of all key assignments associated with a specific template, follow these steps:

1. Choose File, Print.

2. In the Print What drop-down box, choose Key Assignments.

3. Click OK.

Assigning a Keyboard Shortcut   If you've decided to assign a keyboard shortcut to your macro, make sure the Record Macro dialog box is open, and that you've entered a macro name and description, and decided where to store your macro. (If the dialog box is not yet open, you can open it by double-clicking REC in the status bar.) Then follow these steps:

1. Choose Keyboard. The Customize Keyboard dialog box opens (see Figure 30.2).

2. Press the keyboard combination you're thinking about using (don't type the combination—just press the keys). The combination will appear in the Press New Shortcut Key text box. If that combination is already in use, Word tells you which function is assigned to that combination.

3. If you find that the keyboard combination is already in use, try another one. (While you have the option of overwriting the existing keyboard combination, you'll rarely want to do so. You might want to overwrite the existing combination if the existing combination is too hard to remember and you want to replace it with an easier option.

4. When you're satisfied, click Close. The dialog box closes, and the Stop Recording toolbar opens. You can now record your macro.

Assigning a Toolbar Button   If you chose to assign the macro to a toolbar button, follow these steps:

1. Choose Toolbar.

2. The Customize dialog box opens, showing the Commands tab.

3. If the toolbar in which you want to add the macro is already displayed, click the name of the macro in the Commands scroll box, and drag the macro the toolbar. The macro's name—including the template and module in which it is contained—now appear in a toolbar button.

FIG. 30.2

The Customize
Keyboard dialog box
lets you try out
keyboard shortcuts and
see if they're already in
use by other Word
features or macros.

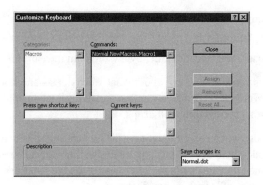

4. If the toolbar you want is not already displayed, choose the Toolbars tab. In the Toolbars list box, check the Toolbar you want to use. The Toolbar appears on-screen. Follow Step 3.

5. To edit the name into something less cumbersome, right-click the new toolbar button. A shortcut menu appears allowing you to type the new name in the Name text box.

6. Click Close. The dialog box closes, and the Macro toolbar opens. You can now record your macro.

   ▶ **See** "Customizing Toolbars," **p. 721**

If you want to create a toolbar shortcut based on a macro after you've created the macro, you can. Simply follow these steps:

1. Choose Tools, Customize.

2. In the Toolbars tab, check the toolbar where you want to place the shortcut (if it isn't already displayed).

3. Choose the Commands tab.

4. In the Categories scroll box, choose Macros.

5. In the Commands box, select the macro you want.

6. Drag the macro to the toolbar.

7. Click Close.

Recording the Steps for Your Macro

After you've chosen a toolbar or keyboard shortcut and clicked Close, Word displays the Stop Recording toolbar, as shown in Figure 30.3. You can now record the steps associated with your macro. These might include the following:

- Entering or deleting text
- Selecting text with keyboard shortcuts
- Opening dialog boxes and selecting options
- Navigating the document with keyboard shortcuts

- Saving or opening files
- Clicking toolbar buttons
- Changing the user interface, document view, or zoom measurement

There are a few things you should know about what Word does—and doesn't—record. You've already learned that Word can't record navigation and text selection you've done using the mouse. Similarly, it won't record drag and drops.

The macro recorder also won't record opening a dialog box unless you also click OK to apply the settings in that dialog box. This means, for example, that you can't record a macro that opens the Save As dialog box and waits for you to name the file. On the other hand, you can record a macro that saves a file with a specific name.

FIG. 30.3

The Stop Recording toolbar has two buttons: one to pause recording, and one to end recording.

Stop Recording

Pause Recording

> **N O T E** Unfortunately, Word 97 eliminates two convenient macro recording capabilities that existed in previous versions. You can no longer click Undo to reverse a command you just recorded. You now must delete it in the Visual Basic Editor. You also can no longer run one of Word's built-in commands through the Tools, Macro dialog box to record it as part of your macro. If you want to add a command that isn't available through a menu, toolbar, or keyboard shortcut, you have to use the Visual Basic Editor. ▓

When you record settings you establish in a dialog box, Word records all the settings in the tab you displayed, not just the settings you've changed. Then, when you run the macro, it applies all the settings. Make sure you don't inadvertently record settings that will be inappropriate for some of the documents with which you'll use the macro.

> **T I P** If some of the dialog box settings you record in a macro are irrelevant to the task at hand, you can open the Visual Basic Editor and delete those unnecessary settings—leaving only the ones you need. You'll learn how to do so in Chapter 31, "Getting Started with VBA."

If you click a toggle button to turn it on, Word only records the fact that you changed the setting. If the toggle button is already turned on when you run the macro later, Word will turn it off.

Occasionally, you might want to pause recording. (You might just want to think about what to do next, or you might want to do something you don't want recorded in the macro. For instance, you might want to navigate the document, copy text into the Find and Replace dialog box, or display Help.) To pause recording without ending the macro, click the Pause Recording button on the Stop Recording toolbar. Word won't start recording again until you click Pause Recording again.

When you've finished all the steps you want to record, click Stop Recording. Word ends the macro. It's immediately available for you to run.

If you click the Close button at the top right of the toolbar, the Stop Recording toolbar disappears, but Word keeps recording the steps you're taking. To stop recording when the Stop Recording toolbar isn't visible, double-click the highlighted REC button on the status bar.

CAUTION

When you choose to store a macro in the Normal.dot template, even though it's immediately available after you create it, it isn't permanently saved until the Normal.dot template is saved. Typically, this happens whenever you exit Word. However, if your session is interrupted before you do so (by a system crash or power failure, for example), you could lose macros you've recorded during the current session.

Creating Macros That Run Automatically

You may create a macro that you want to run automatically every time you perform a specific task, such as starting Word, opening a file, or closing a file. Word supports five special macro names, which it recognizes and runs at appropriate times. The macro names and the tasks they correspond to are shown in Table 30.1.

Table 30.1	Macros that Run Automatically in Word
Macro Name	**Runs When...**
AutoExec	Runs when Word starts
AutoNew	Runs when you create a new file
AutoOpen	Runs when you open a file that already exists
AutoClose	Runs when you close a file
AutoExit	Runs when you exit Word

You can also run these automatic macros any time you want—the same way you run any other macro. If you haven't created a toolbar or keyboard shortcut for them, choose Tools, Macro, Macros; select the macro and click Run. When might you use some of these automatic macro names?

- You might use AutoExec to display a dialog box that offers a specific set of options for the user when Word starts. For example, the macro might display a dialog box asking which kind of document the user wants to create; when he or she chooses, a new document is opened using the appropriate template. You'll learn a little about requesting user input through dialog boxes later in this chapter; you'll learn much more in Chapter 31, "Getting Started with VBA."

■ Another use for AutoExec is a macro that automatically opens the last file you were working on in your last session. This is a one-command macro. With the macro recorder turned on, choose the first file in the Most Recently Used file list (1). Then turn off the macro recorder.

■ You might use AutoNew to offer similar options that only apply to certain kinds of documents. For example, you can attach an AutoNew macro to a pricing letter template; the macro might display a dialog box asking whether the project you're pricing is on a standard or rush schedule. Depending on which type of schedule the user chooses, the macro places different AutoText boilerplate language in the document. Another AutoNew macro might display a fill-in field or an { ASK } input box requesting specific text from the user.

■ You might use AutoOpen to run a macro that updates all fields whenever a document opens because Word doesn't automatically do so. This is an easy macro to record: simply start the Macro Recorder, press Ctrl+A, press F9, and turn off the macro recorder.

■ You might use AutoClose to open the Spell Check dialog box whenever a user chooses to close a file, thereby making sure the user spell checks the document—or is at least reminded to do so. An even simpler method is to start the start the Macro Recorder, click the Spelling and Grammar button on the Standard toolbar, and turn off the macro recorder. You might also record an AutoClose memo that saves a duplicate copy of whatever file you're closing to a backup location.

■ You might use AutoExit to restore settings that have been changed during a session, but shouldn't be changed permanently. For example, if you share your computer with colleagues who insert their names and initials in the User Information dialog box, you could write an AutoExit macro that opens Tools, Options, User Information tab, and re-enters your own name and initials.

While AutoExec and AutoExit are stored only in Normal.dot template, you can create separate AutoNew, AutoOpen, and AutoClose macros for each template. That way, Word can provide different tools, dialog boxes, or guidance based on the type of document with which you are working.

If you want to start Word without running an AutoExec macro at the same time, press and hold the Shift key as Word starts.

Running Your Macro

Now that you've created your macro, the next step is to see if it works the way you intended. Open a document comparable to the documents with which you plan to use the macro. Then get the document "in the same condition" it should be when the macro is run. For example, if the macro applies formatting to text, select some text. If the macro inserts an AutoText entry, click the insertion point where the text should go.

Now, run the macro. If you have a keyboard shortcut, press it. If you have a toolbar button, click it. If you have neither, run the macro as follows:

1. Choose Tools, Macro, Macros. The Macros dialog box opens (see Figure 30.4).

2. In the Macro Name scroll box, select the macro you want to run.

3. Click Run. The macro runs.

FIG. 30.4

You can select and run a macro from the Macros dialog box.

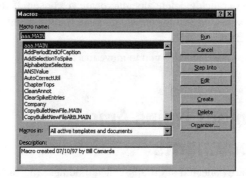

If a macro goes awry and starts doing things you don't want it to do, press Esc to stop it.

Viewing Only Macros Associated with One Template or Document

You'll notice a few other options available to you in the Macros dialog box. By default, Word displays a list of all the macros available in all your active templates and documents. If you record many macros, this might be a very long list. You can view only the macros associated with your current document, or those associated with a specific custom template that's already open. Click the Macros in the drop-down box, and make your selection there.

If you want to run a macro stored in a template that isn't open, you can open it as follows:

1. Choose Tools, Templates and Add-Ins.

2. Click Add.

3. In the Add Templates dialog box, select another template to be added as a global template.

4. Click OK twice.

Three other choices, Step Into, Edit, and Create, are associated with writing or debugging macros using the Visual Basic Editor. You'll learn more about each of these in Chapter 31, but these choices are outlined briefly as follows:

- Step Into opens the macro in the Visual Basic Editor, and runs the first line. You can keep running your macro one line at a time; if you run into a line that Word can't interpret, Visual Basic Editor stops and highlights the problem in red.

- Create opens the Visual Basic Editor, where you can write a new macro from scratch.

- Edit opens the Visual Basic Editor, displaying the macro you've chosen, so you can make changes to it.

- Delete enables you to quickly delete any macro you've chosen. If you click Delete, Word displays a dialog box asking you to confirm that you want to delete the macro; click OK and the macro is deleted.

- Organizer, discussed next, enables you to move macros between templates or documents.

Moving Macro Project Items Among Templates and Documents

In Word 97, new macros are collected in groups, called modules. You can move or copy these modules among templates and documents using Word's Organizer (see Figure 30.5). Simply follow these steps::

1. Choose Tools, Macro, Macros.

2. Click Organizer. The macro project items in Normal.dot are listed in the right-hand scroll box; any macros already stored in your document are listed in the left-hand scroll box.

3. To move a macro from Normal.dot to your document, select it in the right-hand scroll box, and click Copy.

4. To move a macro from your document to Normal.dot, select it in the left-hand scroll box and click Copy.

5. When you're finished moving macros, click Close.

To move a macro from Normal.dot to a different template:

1. Follow steps 1 and 2 in the previous list.

2. Choose Close File beneath the left-hand scroll box.

3. Click Open File. The Templates dialog box opens.

4. Browse to, and select the template you want to open. (If you want to open a document instead of a template, choose Word Documents in the Files of Type drop-down box.)

5. Click Open.

6. In the right-hand scroll box, click the macro or macro project item you want to open, and click Copy. This copies the macro or macro project item to the template or document you just opened.

7. When you're finished moving macros, click Close.

FIG. 30.5

You can use the Organizer to move macros between templates—and in Word 97, you can also use it to store macros with individual documents.

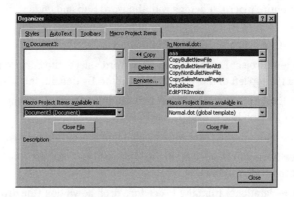

By default, macros placed in documents and templates are stored in modules named New Macros. If you copy a New Macros module from one template or document to another that already contains such a module, you'll overwrite the module already stored there, deleting those macros.

To avoid the problem, rename the module before you copy it. First, open the Macro Project Items tab of the Organizer dialog box, as follows: choose Tools, Macro, Macros; then click Organizer. With this tab open, follow these steps:

1. Select the module (Macro Project Item) you want to rename.

2. Click Rename.

3. In the Rename text box, enter a new name.

4. Press OK.

TIP You can still use the Organizer to copy individual macros created in previous versions of Word, which you've imported into Word 97.

If you need to simply must copy a single Word 97 macro rather than an entire module, you'll have to venture into the Visual Basic Editor. This long series of steps essentially does the following: it copies a block of code from one module to another in the Visual Basic Editor.

1. Open the template or document containing the macro you want to copy.

2. Open the template or document into which you want to copy the macro.

3. Choose Tools, Macro, Macros.

4. In the Macros in list, choose the template or document containing the macro you plan to copy.

5. In the list of macros, select the macro.

6. Click Edit. The Visual Basic Editor opens.

7. Select the entire macro. It begins with the word Sub and ends with the words End Sub. (Make sure to choose the macro with the correct name.)

8. Press Ctrl+C to copy the contents of the macro.

9. Choose View, Project Explorer. Note that Word selects the current module in the Project window at the top left of the Visual Basic Editor. By default, this is named New Macros.

10. In Project Explorer, click the Project and Module you want to copy the macro. By default, once again, the module is called New Macros.

11. Click in the code window (the window containing program listings).

12. Make sure (General) is selected in the Object drop-down box (the drop-down box at the top left of the code window).

13. Choose (Declarations) from the Procedure drop-down box (the drop-down box at the top right of the code window).

14. In the code window, scroll to the end of the code listings, and click the insertion point there.

15. Press Ctrl+V to paste the macro there.

16. Press Ctrl+S to save the project, including the macro you've copied there.

17. Choose File, Close and Return to Microsoft Word.

Running Word Commands: Word's 400+ Built-in, One-Step Macros

Word has more than 400 "one-step" macros built in. Every single command you can perform in Word can be run as a one-step macro—or included in a longer macro you write from scratch. You'll find many of these commands perform useful tasks to which you might appreciate having quick access. Some have equivalent toolbar buttons somewhere in Word; others don't. Here are a few examples:

- *FilePrintSetup.* Displays the Print Setup dialog box so you can switch between the printers you have available.

- *FileSaveAll.* Saves the contents of every file you have open, all at the same time.

- *Hidden.* Formats selected text as hidden text.

- *TableSortAToZ.* Alphabetizes a list of text—whether in a table or not.

- *ToolsCreateDirectory.* Lets you create a new folder in your current folder without opening the File, Save As dialog box.

To run one of these macros,

1. Choose Tools, Macro, Macros.

2. Choose Word Commands from the Macros In drop-down box.

3. Choose the command you want to run.

4. Click Run.

Running the Sample Macros in MACROS8.DOT and SUPPORT8.DOT

The Office 97 CD-ROM contains two files with sample Word macros. The macros stored in MACROS8.DOT help fix some of the minor annoyances that drive many experienced Word users batty. The two macros stored in SUPPORT8.DOT provide control over some technical aspects of Word and are primarily designed for support personnel. Both MACROS8.DOT and SUPPORT8.DOT can be found on the Office 97 CD-ROM, in the \Office\Macros folder. Word doesn't install either file by default, even if you perform a full installation.

▶ **See** "Setting Local Registry Options with the RegOptions Macro," **p. 798**

To install these macros, first copy them to your Word templates folder, typically C:\Program Files\Microsoft Office\Templates. You might prefer to copy them to a subfolder within this folder, such as Other Documents.

Next, load the MACROS8.DOT template as a global template. Choose Tools, Templates and Add-Ins; click Add. Browse to, and then select MACROS8.DOT. Click OK. You might want to install SUPPORT8.DOT while you're at it. If so, click Add again, then select SUPPORT8.DOT and click OK again.

These macros may give you some good ideas about the kinds of macros you might create with Visual Basic once you know how. If you want to view the code contained in them, do the following:

1. Create and save a new template based on the MACROS8.DOT template.

2. Choose Tools, Macro, Visual Basic Editor.

3. In the Project box, double-click the TemplateProject line associated with your new template file.

4. Click a macro stored in the Modules section to view its code.

After you load MACROS8.DOT as a global template, Word displays a one-button toolbar, Sample Macros, (see Figure 30.6). Now, you can click the Sample Macros button to run any sample macro you choose.

In the rest of this section, you'll find brief explanations of each of Word's Sample Macros.

FIG. 30.6

The Sample Macros toolbar provides access to all the sample macros in the MACROS8.DOT template.

Running the ANSI Value Macro   To use a symbol, it sometimes helps to know that symbol's position in the ANSI character set. Each character in the standard ANSI character set has a number, but Word doesn't provide an easy to way to find that number.

ANSI Value responds to this minor annoyance. Select one or more characters, and choose ANSI Value from the Sample Macros toolbar. The ANSI Value dialog box displays the ANSI numbers of each character you selected (see Figure 30.8).

FIG. 30.7

The ANSI Value dialog box displays the ANSI values associated with any character(s) you select.

Running the AutoCorrect Utility   *AutoCorrect Utility* (see Figure 30.9) enables you to create a backup document that includes a Word table with all the entries stored in your AutoCorrect dialog box. After you've created an AutoCorrect backup document, you can copy those entries for Word to use on another computer.

FIG. 30.8

You can use the AutoCorrect Utility to back up and restore AutoCorrect files.

Running Find Symbol   *Find Symbol* (see Figure 30.10) is like a Find and Replace dialog box engineered specifically for symbols. You can use it to search for characters in symbol fonts and replace those with other Symbols or with text. To do so, follow these steps:

1. Click Symbol in the Find What area. The Symbol dialog box opens.

2. Choose the symbol you want, and click Insert. The Find Symbol dialog box reappears.

3. If you want to replace the symbol with another symbol, click Symbol in the Replace With area; then choose the symbol and click Insert. If you want to replace the symbol with text instead, enter the replacement it in the Text box.

4. To search the whole document, click the Entire Document button; to search only text you've selected, click Selection.

5. To replace the next occurrence of the symbol, click Replace. To replace all occurrences, click Replace All.

FIG. 30.9
You can use Find Symbol to search and replace symbols formatted in Wingdings, Webdings, and other symbol fonts.

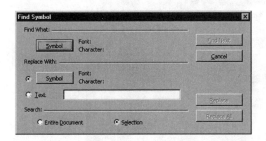

Part
VII

Ch
30

N O T E Find Symbol only works with fonts containing special characters, such as Symbol or Wingdings. It doesn't work with normal text fonts. ■

Running Table Cell Helper *Table Cell Helper* (see Figure 30.11) solves another of Word's minor annoyances, this one related to building formulas in tables. Like Excel, Word tables use cell addresses. For example, cell B8 corresponds to the second column, eighth row. However, unlike Excel, Word tables don't have column and row headings; in fact, there's no easy way to know what cell you're in, short of placing your finger on the screen and counting.

That's where Table Cell Helper comes in. Select a cell (or cells) within a table, choose Sample Macros, Table Cell Helper, and Word displays a dialog box telling you the cell or range name you've selected.

FIG. 30.10
Table Cell Helper makes it easier to create formulas in tables by identifying cell addresses for you.

▶ **See** "Calculating With Tables," **p. 248**

Using SuperDocStatistics SuperDocStatistics (see Figure 30.12) generates a breathtaking amount of information about your document, compiles detailed printed reports, and even contains a Go To function that makes it easy to go to the first usage of a field, style, or other document element.

FIG. 30.11

SuperDocStatistics
compiles detailed
information about any
document on which you
are working.

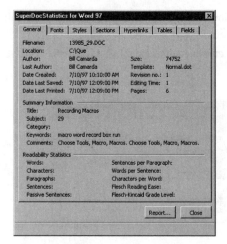

Using NormalViewHeaderFooter   NormalViewHeaderFooter (see Figure 30.13) resurrects
the old Word 2 Normal view header and footer panes that many long-time Word users prefer.
To use NormalViewHeaderFooter, follow these steps:

1. Choose NormalViewHeaderFooter from the Sample Macros toolbar.

2. Specify whether you want to see a header or footer. (You can also use this dialog box to
   set different headers and footers for first, odd and even pages, and to insert Page
   Numbers.)

3. Click OK.

FIG. 30.12

The Normal View Header
Footer dialog box
enables long-time Word
users to keep the
header and footer
panes they learned to
like.

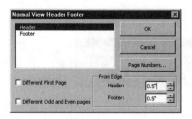

You can see a sample header window in Figure 30.14.

FIG. 30.13

A header window,
displayed via the
NormalViewHeaderFooter
macro.

Using Copy Spike   In Chapter 1, "Word: Take the Controls," you learned about Word's Spike, which lets you paste multiple blocks of text into the same location. The drawback of Spike has always been that it required you to cut text from its previous position. Word has never enabled you to copy text into the Spike—you've had to remove it from its previous location. The Copy Spike macro solves the problem, and makes Spike more convenient in some other ways, too.

When you choose Copy Spike from the Sample Macros toolbar, a cascaded menu appears, containing four options:

- *Add Selection to Spike*. Copies the text you've selected into the Spike without deleting it. (More precisely, it deletes and repastes the text, so you never notice a difference.)

- *Insert Spike*. Contents inserts the contents of the Spike at your insertion point. It's the equivalent of using the Spike AutoText entry.

- *Clear Spike Contents*. Empties the Spike.

- *Preview Spike*. Opens a dialog box (see Figure 30.15) that opens the first 256 characters of the Spike's current contents, in Rich Text Format.

FIG. 30.14
You can see what's in your Spike by choosing Sample Macros, Copy Spike, Preview Spike.

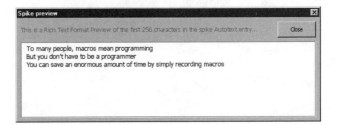

TROUBLESHOOTING

My macro displayed an error message when I ran it. Your macro may depend on specific settings that were present when you recorded it. For example, your macro might need to select text that was visible when you wrote the macro, but is hidden now. In Chapter 31, you'll learn more about debugging macros in the Visual Basic development environment.

In some of my documents, I can't record, edit, or run a macro. Those documents might be Read-only. Either get the password that gives you full permission to change the file, or save the file under a new name and record the macros in the new file.

I'm asked for a password when I try to record a macro. You or a colleague may have installed Word's add-on macro virus protection software, which prevents a macro from changing your templates without permission.

From Here...

In this chapter, you've learned all you need to know to record macros and to use the ones that Word provides. Now, you're ready to start working with Visual Basic for Applications, Microsoft Word's powerful new macro language.

■ Macros are an invaluable tool for improving the productivity of your entire workgroup or organization. You can get more ideas for managing Word for maximum productivity in Chapter 29, "Sharing Files and Managing Word."

■ In Chapter 31, "Getting Started with VBA," you'll start learning the basic concepts you need to understand to write VBA programs successfully. You'll also take a tour of the VBA development environment that comes with Microsoft Word 97.

■ After you're familiar with the basics of VBA, Chapter 32, "Taking More Control of Your Macros," shows you how to build more intelligence into your recorded macros by adding control structures, message boxes, and input boxes. Then, in Chapter 33, "Building a Real-World Solution with VBA and Word," you'll walk through the construction of a full-fledged VBA business application.

CHAPTER 31

Getting Started with VBA

by Bill Camarda

In Chapter 30, "Recording and Running Visual Basic Macros," you learned that Word enables you to record macros—automated sets of procedures that can be run at any time with a single keyboard shortcut or button click. When you record and save a macro, Word is actually creating and storing a computer program, written in a full-fledged programming language called Visual Basic for Applications (VBA).

This chapter will introduce you to VBA. Using extremely simple recorded macros, you'll start becoming comfortable writing VBA code with the Visual Basic Editor, Word's new macro editing environment. In Chapter 32, "Taking More Control Over Your Macros," you'll build on this, discovering basic VBA techniques for making your applications more intelligent—in other words, allowing them to react flexibly to circumstances, and take actions based on user input. Finally, in Chapter 33, "Building a Real-World Solution with VBA and Word," you'll walk through the construction of a real-world application.

Three chapters won't transform you into an expert VBA programmer. You'll need a whole book for that—at least! (You might consider Que's *Special Edition, Using Visual Basic for Applications 5*, by Paul Sanna.)

What is Visual Basic for Applications (VBA)?

Word comes with a state-of-the-art programming language. Learn how to take advantage of it.

When to use VBA

Sometimes recorded macros are all you need. Other times you need the full power of VBA.

Reading the code you've recorded

The best way to start learning VBA is to record a macro and read the statements VBA has written.

Working with the Visual Basic Editor

The Visual Basic Editor brings together everything you need to read, write, edit, debug, and manage your macros.

Understanding objects

In VBA, practically everything's an object—even Word itself.

Letting the Visual Basic Editor help you

Discover the Visual Basic Editor features that help you prevent errors and get more done.

Understanding modules and projects

How to find the macro you need to get the job done.

However, these chapters will introduce basic techniques you can use to supercharge your recorded macros—making them dramatically more useful to you and your colleagues. If you've never programmed before, hopefully these chapters will show you that it isn't quite as difficult as you might have imagined, and, just maybe, these chapters will whet your appetite to go even further.

N O T E The more you work with VBA, the more elegance and efficiency you'll learn to build into your code. These three chapters focus on getting the job done as easily as possible, leveraging the Word editing, formatting, and macro recording skills you already have. ■

What Is Visual Basic for Applications?

Visual Basic for Applications is the latest in a long family of programming languages that trace their descent to BASIC—the Beginner's All-Purpose Symbolic Instruction Code invented to teach programming to novice students. Versions of BASIC have been written for virtually every type of computer created since. In fact, Bill Gates first became well-known for writing a version of BASIC for the primitive Altair microcomputer seven years before anyone heard of an IBM PC, much less Microsoft Windows.

Several years ago, Microsoft took another important step toward making BASIC easier to use. Microsoft created a mouse-driven, point-and-click, graphical environment for writing BASIC programs. That product, Visual Basic, revolutionized programming by making it much more intuitive. Instead of programming every element and coordinate of a dialog box, for example, you could simply draw the dialog box, and Visual Basic would create the code for you.

N O T E As you'll see in Chapter 33, "Building a Real-World Solution with VBA and Word," you still have to program the events that take place whenever someone makes choices in the dialog box. Visual Basic doesn't do that for you, and neither does VBA. ■

VBA is Microsoft's adaptation of Visual Basic to the specific capabilities of Microsoft Word, Excel, PowerPoint, and Access. With Office 97, for the first time, the same programming language is available to virtually all Office applications. In fact, several other applications use VBA as well, including Microsoft Project, and the popular Visio business graphics program. As powerful as VBA is, it still shares one design goal with the earliest versions of BASIC—to be as easy to use as possible. To that end, VBA's syntax resembles English wherever possible.

N O T E Microsoft Outlook uses the Visual Basic Scripting Edition, another variant of Visual Basic. ■

Having a common language makes it easier for expert programmers to build applications that draw upon the capabilities of more than one program. Even if you're not an expert programmer, however, a common programming language has many benefits. After you've learned to work with VBA in Word, you'll know the fundamentals of automating Excel worksheets, streamlining PowerPoint presentations, or writing macros for any Windows program that uses VBA.

N O T E VBA uses the terms macro and procedure interchangeably, and you'll encounter both terms in this chapter. They mean the same thing, though the term procedure tends to be used more in connection with VBA programs that involve hand-coding in the Visual Basic Editor. ▪

How VBA Relates to WordBasic

For Word users, VBA replaces a macro programming language named WordBasic, which was included with previous versions of Word. If you have macros written in WordBasic, don't worry; in nearly all cases, your macros will still run. The first time you open a Word 6 or Word 95 template in Word 97, your macros are automatically revised to be compatible with VBA. Some lines of code don't need to be changed at all. In other cases, Word adds the text

WordBasic.

to the beginning of each statement that needs to be changed.

If you happen to already be familiar with WordBasic, this gives you a short-term crutch to fall back on. You can keep using much of the syntax you already know, as long as you use the same WordBasic "prefix." However, to take full advantage of Visual Basic, you really should learn Visual Basic syntax as quickly as possible.

Part
VII

Ch
31

> **CAUTION**
> After you convert macros to VBA, they can no longer be understood by WordBasic. If you expect to use a previous version of Word again, copy your templates before you open them in Word 97.

When To Use VBA

In the previous chapter, you saw that you can do quite a lot by simply recording macros. However, recorded macros can't do everything. If the macro you want to write has any of the following characteristics, you'll most likely have to supplement your recorded instructions with VBA code:

- The macro calls for user input.
- The macro must make decisions on its own. For example, you might want to create a macro that formats some tables but not others, or sends one letter to salespeople who have met their quotas and a different letter to those who haven't.
- The macro must work in a wide variety of situations.
- The macro will be used by others and requires careful testing.

■ The macro must work with other programs that use VBA.

■ The macro must work with open documents other than the document that is currently active.

■ The macro is complex and must be designed to work as efficiently as possible.

Editing VBA code also comes in handy when you need to fix an error you made while recording a macro. Finally, even if your recorded instructions do everything you need to accomplish, the VBA environment gives you tools for testing it.

Reading Code You've Recorded

The easiest way to begin working with Visual Basic is to record a macro of your own, and then read the "program" Word has constructed to match the commands you recorded. Follow these steps to record a macro that formats a block of text as 14-point bold:

1. Select text to be formatted.

2. Double-click the REC button on the status bar. The Record Macro dialog box opens.

3. Enter a name for the macro in the Macro Name text box. (For purposes of this example, name the macro **Bold14**, and skip the steps involved in assigning the macro to a toolbar button or keyboard shortcut.)

4. Choose OK.

5. Click the Bold button on the Formatting toolbar.

6. Choose 14 from the Font Size box on the Formatting toolbar.

7. Double-click the REC button on the status bar again to stop recording.

TIP   Yet another way to record a macro is with the Visual Basic toolbar. Follow these steps:

1.   Choose View, Toolbars.

2.   Select Visual Basic from the cascaded menu.

3.   Click the Record Macro button.

You now have a macro to inspect. Open the Visual Basic Editor as follows:

1. Choose Tools, Macro, Macros to display the Macros dialog box.

2. In the Macro Name box, select the macro you just recorded (Bold14).

3. Choose Edit. The Visual Basic Editor opens (see Figure 31.1).

TIP   The procedure you just used opens the Visual Basic Editor with a specific macro already displayed. When you're comfortable navigating the Visual Basic Editor, you might find it quicker to avoid the Macros dialog box. You can open the editor directly by pressing Alt+F11 or choosing Tools, Macro, Visual Basic Editor.

FIG. 31.1

The Visual Basic Editor brings together comprehensive tools for editing and managing macros.

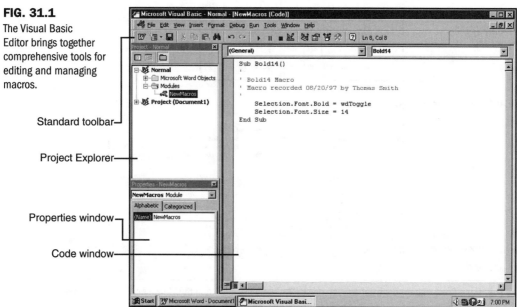

Standard toolbar

Project Explorer

Properties window

Code window

Part
VII

Ch
31

Understanding the VBA Integrated Development Environment (IDE)

If you've never programmed, chances are you'll find the Visual Basic Editor environment to be quite unfamiliar the first few times you see it. Microsoft calls the Visual Basic Editor an Integrated Development Environment, which means that it brings together all the tools a programmer needs to get the job done. These include tools for the following:

- Writing and editing programs
- Designing dialog boxes and other user-interface elements
- Running programs
- Testing and debugging programs
- Tracking all the elements of individual programs
- Tracking VBA programs stored in different locations

Rather than introducing every element of this editing environment up front, this chapter will introduce you to Visual Basic Editor features only as you need to understand them.

Working with the Code Window

For the moment, there's only one element you need to know about: the large window at the right side of the screen. This is called the Code window, and it's where the Visual Basic Editor displays the code it has recorded. You can take a closer look at the Code window in Figure 31.2.

FIG. 31.2

A closer look at the
Code window.

Object box —

Procedure box —

Border between macros —

Full module view —
Procedure view —

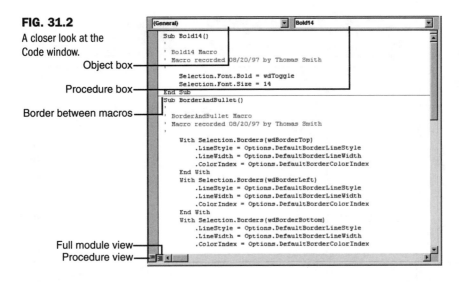

```
(General)                                      ▼    Bold14                          ▼
    Sub Bold14()
    '
    ' Bold14 Macro
    ' Macro recorded 08/20/97 by Thomas Smith
    '
        Selection.Font.Bold = wdToggle
        Selection.Font.Size = 14
    End Sub
    Sub BorderAndBullet()
    '
    ' BorderAndBullet Macro
    ' Macro recorded 08/20/97 by Thomas Smith
    '
        With Selection.Borders(wdBorderTop)
            .LineStyle = Options.DefaultBorderLineStyle
            .LineWidth = Options.DefaultBorderLineWidth
            .ColorIndex = Options.DefaultBorderColorIndex
        End With
        With Selection.Borders(wdBorderLeft)
            .LineStyle = Options.DefaultBorderLineStyle
            .LineWidth = Options.DefaultBorderLineWidth
            .ColorIndex = Options.DefaultBorderColorIndex
        End With
        With Selection.Borders(wdBorderBottom)
            .LineStyle = Options.DefaultBorderLineStyle
            .LineWidth = Options.DefaultBorderLineWidth
            .ColorIndex = Options.DefaultBorderColorIndex
```

  T I P   If the Code window does not appear, press F7 or choose <u>C</u>ode from the <u>V</u>iew menu. If several Code
windows appear cascaded, maximize the one you want to use.

If you've recorded more than one macro, the Code window provides some tools to make it easy
to focus on one specific macro. You can choose a specific procedure to view by selecting it from
the Procedure drop-down box at the upper-right of the Code window. You can also switch from
viewing multiple procedures to just one by clicking it and then clicking the Procedure View
button at the lower-left of the Code window.

Identifying the Beginning and End of a Macro

Now, take a closer look at the macro you've just recorded. All recorded macros, and most
macros written from scratch, begin with the word Sub (for subroutine) and end with the words
End Sub. The first line also includes the macro's name, as in the following example:

```
Sub Bold14()
```

This line is called the *declaration* because it's the way the macro declares its existence to VBA.

N O T E   Sub and End Sub are examples of keywords—words that have a specific meaning in VBA
and generally shouldn't be used for other purposes. ■

If you want to change the name of a macro, you can edit this line to reflect the new name. Later,
when you choose <u>T</u>ools, <u>M</u>acro, <u>M</u>acros to view your list of macros, the new name will be reflected there.

The Visual Basic Editor follows the same rules as the macro recorder you learned about in the previous chapter: macro names can be up to 80 characters long, must start with a letter, and can't contain any spaces, punctuation, or the following characters:

$ @ # ! & %

If you violate the rules, Visual Basic Editor won't stop you, but if you try to run the macro, it will halt immediately and display a syntax error message.

> **N O T E** You probably noticed the empty parentheses after the macro name. These parentheses can contain *arguments* that retrieve information from other macros. None of the macros you'll learn about in these three chapters will use arguments this way, but they can be extremely useful in more advanced programming. ▪

Editing Within the Visual Basic Editor

Editing in the Visual Basic Editor's Code window works the same way as it does in Word. You can enter text by typing it. You can also cut and paste, using the same keyboard shortcuts available in Word (Ctrl+X to cut, Ctrl+C to copy, Ctrl+V to paste). In addition, the Visual Basic Editor includes its own Standard toolbar, which contains Cut, Copy, Paste, Undo, and Redo buttons that work just as they do in Word. The Standard toolbar is shown in Figure 31.3. Its editing tools are marked, along with some additional buttons you'll learn about later in this chapter.

FIG. 31.3

The Visual Basic Editor's Standard toolbar includes a variety of editing tools that will be familiar to Word users.

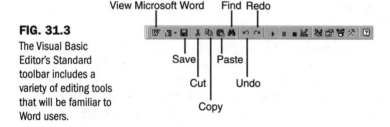

You'll also notice a Find button that displays a Find dialog box customized to the needs of VBA programmers (see Figure 31.4). When your macros are simple, you might not need the Find dialog box; you can find what you need by simply looking at your code. However, macros tend to grow quickly, and as they do, the Find dialog box becomes extremely helpful.

> **N O T E** You can also reach the Find dialog box by pressing Ctrl+F. If you expect to replace text, press Ctrl+H. If you want to find the next location where text is used without reopening the Find dialog box, press F3. Note that this is different from Word's keyboard shortcut to perform the same task (Shift+F4). ▪

FIG. 31.4

The VBA Find dialog box makes it easy to search for and replace text in your macros.

Identifying and Using Comment Lines

After the Sub line that includes the name of your macro, the following four lines of the macro you recorded each start with an apostrophe. This identifies them as comments that VBA should not try to process:

```
'
' Bold14 Macro
' Macro recorded 08/19/97 by Thomas Smith
'
```

The first and last lines are there simply to make the macro code easier to understand. They separate the comment lines from the actual code you want VBA to run. The third line consists of the information Word automatically entered in the Description text box when you recorded the macro. You can edit this or any other comment line. If you did not write a description of your macro when you recorded it, now is a good time to do so.

You can also add new comment lines or add new lines anywhere in the program. In fact, the more complicated your macro becomes, the more important it is to do so. You'll be surprised to discover how easy it is to forget what you were trying to accomplish when you return to a macro after a few months.

Programmers often place an apostrophe at the beginning of a line of code to temporarily disable a line of code from running. This is called *commenting out* the line. It can be a valuable troubleshooting tool. It can also help if you're working on a complicated command and you don't have the syntax quite right yet. If you comment out the line until it's working correctly, you may still be able to use the rest of the macro without generating error messages.

 TIP If you're not sure whether a property is important, try commenting it out and running the macro to see if it works properly.

It's easy enough to enter or delete apostrophes manually, but if you expect to add (or remove) several comments, the Visual Basic Editor provides a convenient shortcut. Select the text you want to comment. Then, choose View, Toolbars, Edit to display the Edit toolbar. (If it's in your way, you can drag it up until it docks just under the Standard toolbar.) Now, click the Comment Block button to add apostrophes to all the lines you've selected. If you want to remove the apostrophe, select the lines, and click the Uncomment Block button.

Figure 31.5 displays the Edit toolbar, with several other useful buttons marked; these buttons will be discussed later in this chapter. Keyboard shortcuts for several of the more helpful buttons are listed in parentheses.

Complete Word   Indent   Uncomment
(Ctrl+Space)   (Tab)   Block

FIG. 31.5
The Visual Basic
Editor's Edit toolbar.

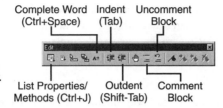

List Properties/   Outdent   Comment
Methods (Ctrl+J)   (Shift-Tab)   Block

 T I P   In addition to the Edit toolbar and the Standard toolbar, the Visual Basic Editor provides separate toolbars for debugging and creating dialog boxes (see UserForms, covered in Chapter 33, "Building a Real-World Solution with VBA and Word").

Understanding Statements

The next two lines of code are each *statements*:

```
Selection.Font.Bold = wdToggle
Selection.Font.Size = 14
```

A statement is a single action that VBA can take. Statements are the building blocks of VBA programs, so in order to write VBA programs successfully, you have to clearly understand them. To do so, you must also understand one crucial fact about VBA that sets it apart from many traditional programming languages: its extensive use of objects.

Understanding Objects, Properties, and Methods   In VBA, virtually everything is an *object*. Much of VBA programming consists of accessing these objects, setting their properties, and performing tasks with those objects. Documents are objects. Paragraphs are objects. As you'll see in a moment, a selection of text is also an object, called the Selection object. Even Word itself is an object, called the Application object.

N O T E   All these objects are organized in the Word Object Model, a hierarchical framework in which the Application object sits at the top, and all the other objects are stored within it. You don't have to become all that familiar with the Word Object Model to start getting results with VBA; the code you record already takes it into account. For now, it's enough to know that the Word Object Model represents a logical structure that VBA can use to organize and control all of Word's features. ▪

Objects have attributes, which VBA calls *properties*. For example, a Paragraph object might have an Alignment object that determines whether paragraphs are left-aligned, centered, right-aligned, or justified. The Word Application object has properties that affect Word as a whole, such as a property that sets the default format Word uses to save files.

Part

VII

Ch

31

Many objects can also perform tasks. In VBA, these tasks are called *methods*. For example, the `ActiveDocument` object has a method named `Close`, which closes any active document when the macro runs. If you record a one-line macro that closes a document, you get the following statement:

```
ActiveDocument.Close
```

The statement begins with the object, and follows with the method, separated by a period. This is the basic format of many VBA statements: first the object, then a period, then either a method or property, or in some cases both.

Analyzing a Statement   Now you're ready to understand the two statements you recorded in your Bold14 macro. Here they are again:

```
Selection.Font.Bold = wdToggle
Selection.Font.Size = 14
```

In both statements, you recorded actions that changed a text selection, so VBA uses the `Selection` object. You'll probably find that many (if not most) of the macros you record use the `Selection` object because many macros change the formatting or contents of selected text. Both of these statements also change Font formatting, so both use the `Font` property of the `Selection` object. However, it's not enough to specify the `Font` property; VBA must also specify the formatting you want to change, and how you want to change it. That's where `Bold = wdToggle` comes in.

This instruction tells Word, in effect, to click the Bold button. If the selected text is not Bold, the statement will change it to bold. If the text is already bold, the statement will clear the boldface formatting, just as it would have if you clicked the Bold button on Word's Formatting toolbar.

Most of the time, however, you click the Bold button because you want to format text as bold, not "not bold." Is there a way to make sure that this statement always works that way? Yes, you can edit it. The following statement makes sure your text selection is formatted as Bold, no matter how it looked before the macro ran:

```
Selection.Font.Bold = True
```

This is a simple example of why you might want to use the Visual Basic Editor to double-check a recorded macro even if it seems to be working well. You might notice some minor tuning that could help improve your macro's reliability when it runs under circumstances different from when you recorded it.

N O T E   You could modify this statement in a variety of ways. For example, if you decided to use italic instead of boldface, you could edit the statement to:

```
Selection.Font.Italic = True
```

Of course, you might then want to change the name of the macro as well. ■

Using the Properties/Methods List

You may be wondering: out of all the millions of ways you can edit a statement like this, how do you know which ones will work? Fortunately, the Visual Basic Editor can tell you. If the Edit toolbar is displayed, click the insertion point on the part of the statement you want to edit and then click the List Properties/Methods button. If the Edit toolbar is not displayed, press Ctrl+J. Alternatively, right-click where you want to edit. A shortcut menu appears (see Figure 31.6). Choose List Properties/Methods.

FIG. 31.6

For beginners, one of the most useful options in the Code window's shortcut menu is List Properties/Methods.

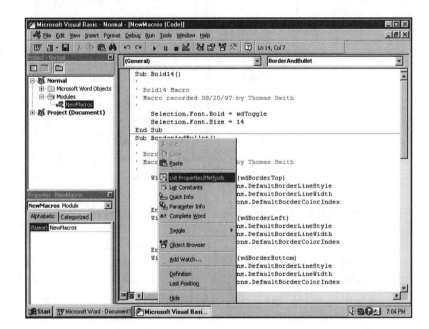

In either case, Visual Basic Editor displays a list of all the options that apply to the object or property you're currently using (see Figure 31.7). Your choices may include properties, methods, and in some cases, other options as well. Make a choice, and the Editor enters it, replacing any property, method, or other code element that needs to be removed. Although this feature certainly doesn't prevent errors completely, it does eliminate many of the keyboard and syntax errors you might make.

Working with the Properties/Methods List offers VBA programmers a bonus benefit. It can be difficult for beginners to tell properties from methods or other elements of a VBA statement. To help, the Properties/Methods List displays an icon that tells you what each option is. Some of the icons you'll encounter most often are listed in Table 31.1.

FIG. 31.7
You can choose any of the properties, methods, or other elements listed in the Properties/ Methods List, and the Visual Basic Editor will enter it in your statement accurately.

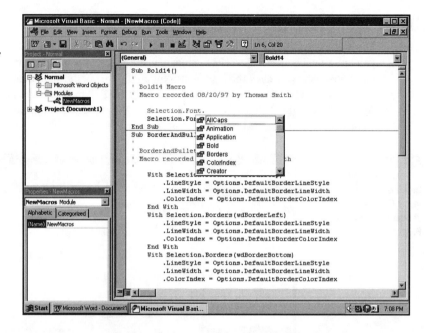

Table 31.1   Selected Icons That Appear in the Properties/Methods List

This icon...	Represents...
	Property
	Default property
	Method
	Default method
	Constant
	Module
	Built-in keyword or type

Using Complete Word to Ensure Accurate Spelling

If you start typing an element of code and you're not sure of the precise spelling, Visual Basic Editor's Complete Word feature can help you complete it accurately. Click the code element and then press Ctrl+Space. (You can also click the Complete Word button on the Edit toolbar, or choose Complete Word from the shortcut menu.) The Visual Basic Editor displays the word it thinks you're trying to type, along with other options spelled similarly (see Figure 31.8). If there's only one choice that fits the characters you've already typed, the editor enters it.

FIG. 31.8
Using the Complete Word feature to spell the elements of a statement accurately.

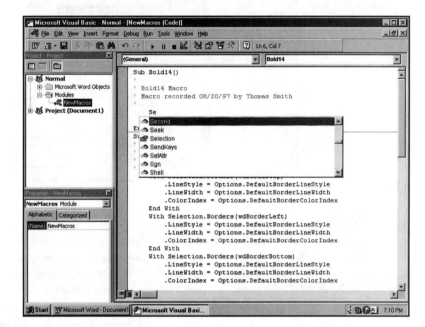

Part
VII

Ch
31

Using Automatic Syntax Checking

Nothing on this earth will eliminate program bugs entirely, but the Visual Basic Editor offers one more tool to help reduce the number of error messages you get as you run your programs. It's called Automatic Syntax Checking, and it's turned on by default. With this feature, the Visual Basic Editor automatically checks the syntax of your statement as soon as you press Enter to start another statement. If the statement is incorrect, it turns red, and a message box appears to tell you what's wrong. For example, in Figure 31.9, Automatic Syntax Checking has flagged a statement that is incomplete because it is missing an expression that states a font size. If you're not sure what's wrong, you can click Help in the message box to get more information from the VBA Help system. You won't always understand VBA's recommendations, but they're usually the best place to start in troubleshooting a problem.

FIG. 31.9

VBA's Automatic Syntax Checker flags syntax errors in a message box as soon as you press Enter on a line that is incorrect.

Syntax Error (displayed in red)

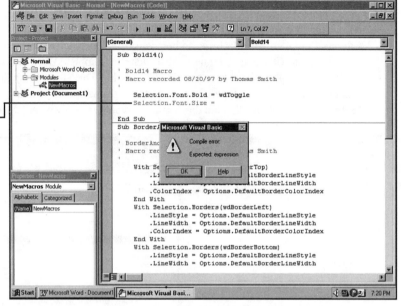

CAUTION

Program errors are a bit like DNA mutations. Many simply prevent the program (or organism) from running. Those kinds of errors are easy to spot and often relatively easy to fix. The really frustrating errors are often those that don't prevent a program from running but instead deliver inaccurate results, sometimes sporadically. These types of errors are sometimes called program logic errors.

Arguably, the macro you recorded earlier in this chapter contained a program logic error. It worked perfectly when boldfacing normal text, but delivered a (possibly) unexpected result when applied to text that was already boldfaced. That's because the program logic was wrong; it specified toggling Bold on or off, rather than making sure the text would always be formatted as boldface.

If Automatic Syntax Checking isn't working, you may have to turn it on. To do so, choose Tools, Options in the Visual Basic Editor, and display the Editor tab (see Figure 31.10). Click to enable the Auto Syntax Check check box and then choose OK.

N O T E   Some programmers like to leave some lines unfinished and fix all the problems at the same time before running the code. If that's your style, you might want to turn off Auto Syntax Checking by clearing the check box. ■

FIG. 31.10

You can turn on Auto Syntax Checking in the Editor tab of Visual Basic Editor's Options dialog box.

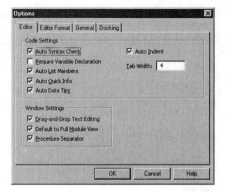

Recording New Statements to Use in Your VBA Macro

VBA is profoundly integrated with Word, and it knows more about Word than any of us ever will. As a result, it can be full of surprises. For example, look again at that statement you recorded awhile ago:

```
Selection.Font.Bold = WdToggle
```

Editing that statement to toggle italic instead of boldface would be very easy:

```
Selection.Font.Italic = WdToggle
```

But what if you tried it with underlining?

```
Selection.Font.Underline = WdToggle
```

Zap! Instant syntax error. Worse, you might spend hours trying to figure out why. (The answer is that Word provides nine different types of underlining, so you can't simply toggle underlining on. VBA needs you to specify which type of underlining to apply.) Instead of scratching your head, you'll find it much easier to record the step you want, see the code VBA creates, and copy it into your macro. To do so, follow these steps:

1. Click the View Microsoft Word button on the Standard toolbar in the Visual Basic Editor. This displays Microsoft Word.

2. Follow the steps required to record the macro.

3. Click Microsoft Visual Basic in the Windows taskbar to return to the Visual Basic Editor. The new macro appears at the bottom of the Code window.

The underlining macro appears in Figure 31.11. You'll see that the statement is more complicated than the ones you've seen so far. You'll learn about *If...Then* statements in Chapter 32, but briefly, this statement does the following:

- Checks the selected text to see if it is currently underlined
- If it is not underlined, applies a single underline
- If it is underlined (using any type of underlining), removes the underline

FIG. 31.11

The underlining macro you just recorded contains an If...Then statement to determine whether selected text is already underlined.

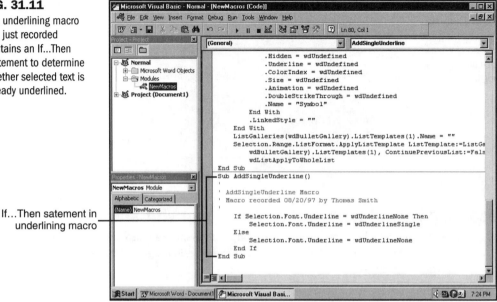

If...Then satement in underlining macro

> ▶ **See** "Using *If...Then...Else* Control Structure," **p. 901**

Assuming this statement does what you intended, you can select it and copy it into your previous macro. However, as you create more and more macros and store them in different locations, it can become difficult to find the macro you're seeking. Now is a good time to talk about how the Visual Basic Editor organizes and stores macros.

Understanding Modules and Projects

As you learned in Chapter 30, "Recording and Running Visual Basic Macros," Word can store recorded macros with either your current document or any template that is open when you record them. When you record a macro, it is placed in a section of the Word file or template called a module. By default, your macros are stored in a module named NewMacros. Every file or template can have its own NewMacros module, although it's likely you'll work most with the macros in the Normal.dot template. A module can contain as many modules as you want, except that it is limited to 4,000 lines of code. A file or template can store as many modules as you like.

N O T E   When Word converts old WordBasic macros stored in Word 6 or Word 95 templates, each macro is assigned its own module. ■

The Visual Basic Editor provides a window where you can choose which modules you want to work with: the Project Explorer window (see Figure 31.12). The Project Explorer window is organized hierarchically, a bit like Windows Explorer. To see all the modules in the Normal.dot template, double-click Normal (typically at the top of the window). Then, double-click the Modules folder (if it isn't already open). You'll see a list of all the modules available to you. Double-click a module to see the macros contained in that module.

FIG. 31.12

The Project Explorer lists all modules and other objects associated with macro projects. (The Properties window has been closed, to reveal more Project Explorer listings.)

Part

VII

Ch

31

 T I P   Sometimes, the Project Explorer window may not appear. If this occurs, press Ctrl+R, or choose Project Explorer from the View menu.

Double-click the module you want, and its contents appear in the Code window. You can then choose the procedure you want to edit in the Procedure drop-down box, as shown in (see Figure 31.13).

N O T E   In the Visual Basic Editor, each Word template or document corresponds to a project. Projects can contain other objects along with modules. For instance, they can include the UserForms that contain the custom dialog boxes you can add to your procedures. For now, however, you're concerned only with modules. ■

FIG. 31.13

You can use the Procedures drop-down box to select a procedure from the current module.

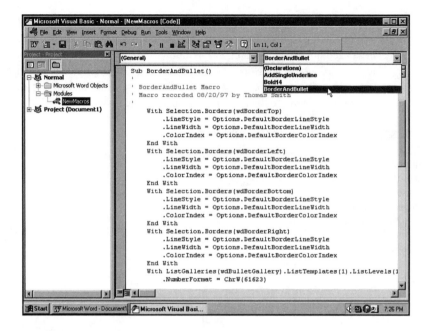

Saving Changes to Macros

By now, you're probably already sensitive to the importance of saving your documents regularly. If anything, it's even more important to save your macros often. If you've spent a great deal of effort to get a statement just right, you won't be pleased if a system crash occurs with your macro edits unsaved.

Fortunately, it's easy to save your macros. Press Ctrl+S, or click the Save button on the Visual Basic Editor standard toolbar. This saves all the macros in the module you are currently using.

> **CAUTION**
>
> You need to save changes to each module separately. Pressing Ctrl+S saves only the changes to the module in which you're currently working. To save the current project, including all modules associated with it, press Ctrl+5.

Recording Dialog Boxes and "With" Statements

In this chapter, you've spent a good deal of time with a very simple recorded macro that formatted text as 14-point Bold, using toolbar buttons. As it turns out, there's another way to get the same result—by recording the selections you make in Word's dialog boxes. There are two reasons you'll probably use this approach quite often:

- First, many of the actions you'll want to record may not have toolbar buttons. You'll have no choice but to use dialog boxes.

- Second, by using dialog boxes, you can create many settings at the same time, translating them all into object properties at once.

However, as you'll see, macros you record using Word dialog boxes look and work somewhat differently from what you've seen so far, and you'll need to know some things about editing them.

Follow these steps to record a macro that uses the Font dialog box to format selected text as 14-point Bold:

1. Select text to be formatted.
2. Double-click the REC button on the status bar. The Record Macro dialog box opens.
3. Enter a name for the macro in the Macro Name text box. (For purposes of this example, name the macro **Bold14Dialog**. As before, don't bother to assign the macro to a toolbar button or keyboard shortcut.)
4. Choose OK.
5. Choose Format, Font.
6. In the Font Style scroll box, choose Bold.
7. In the Size scroll box, choose 14.
8. Choose OK.
9. Double-click the REC button again to stop recording.

Part
VII

Ch
31

Now, open the Visual Basic Editor again:

1. Choose Tools, Macro, Macros.
2. In the Macro Name box, select the Bold14Dialog macro.
3. Choose Edit.

The macro you just recorded is shown in Figure 31.14. You've just recorded all the settings in the dialog box you just used.

There's a lot of code here, but only one statement. The first line begins with `With`, and includes the object and property you intend to manipulate (`Selection.Font`). The last line, `End With`, tells VBA the statement ends here. In between, each indented line represents a separate property, corresponding to separate settings in the Font dialog box. You can quickly see the two properties you added:

```
.Size = 14
.Bold = True
```

FIG. 31.14

In a single With statement, this macro captures all the settings in the Font tab of the Font dialog box.

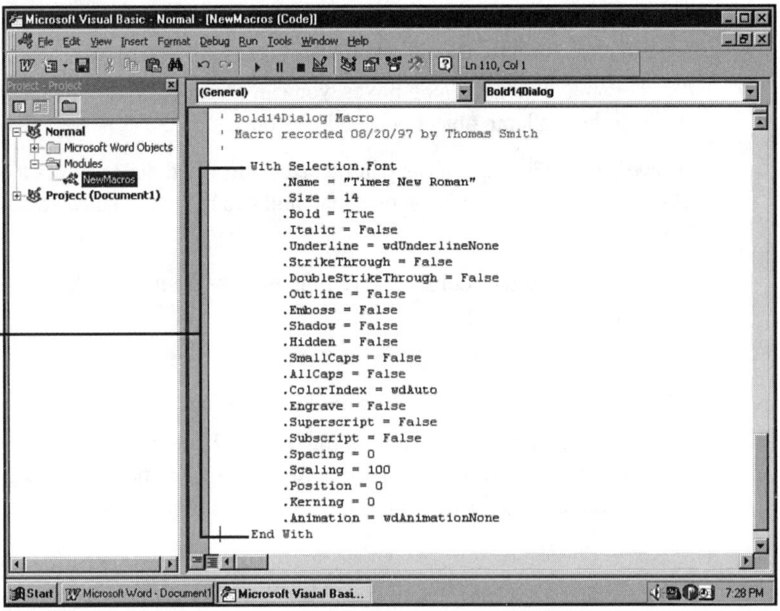

With Statement

What about all those other settings? VBA has no way of knowing which ones you intended to include and which ones you didn't, so it captures all of them, and when you run this macro, it applies all of them. Let's say you run this macro on text formatted with the Arial font. Not only will that text be reformatted as 14-point Bold, it will also be reformatted as Times New Roman, because your macro includes the line

```
.Name = "Times New Roman"
```

The solution is to simply edit out the properties you don't need. The statement you really need looks like this:

```
With Selection.Font
        .Size = 14
        .Bold = True
End With
```

When you run a macro containing that statement, VBA reformats the selected text as 14-point Bold and leaves all the other properties alone.

Notice that the lines between With and End With are all indented. VBA doesn't care whether you indent or not, but the indentation makes it much easier for human beings to read the statement.

Earlier, you saw that VBA adds extra blank comment lines at the beginning of a macro to make it more readable. The more complex your macros become, the more you'll want to use both spaces and indents to enhance readability.

To increase the indentation of one or more lines of code, select them and press Tab (or choose Indent from Visual Basic Editor's Edit toolbar). To reduce the indent of one or more lines of code, select them and press Shift+Tab (or choose Outdent from Visual Basic Editor's Edit toolbar).

Be careful not to delete lines you intend to keep. If you're not sure what a line is there for, click inside it and press F1. In most cases, Visual Basic Editor will display a Help window describing the property in more detail, as shown in Figure 31.15.

FIG. 31.15

If you're not sure what a property is for, click it and press F1. In most cases, VBA will display a Help screen.

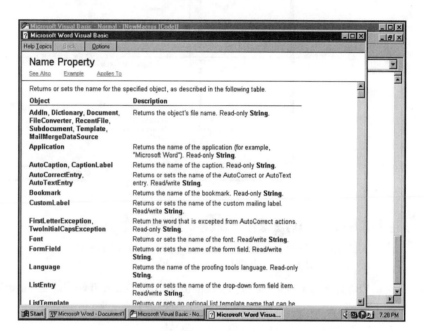

Part
VII

Ch
31

Using Quick Info

Sometimes you don't need full-fledged help, but you would like to know the syntax VBA expects you to use along with a given statement or method. Click the code you want to learn more about, and press Ctrl+I to display Quick Info (see Figure 31.16). A ToolTip appears above the code, providing syntax information (or in some cases, information about parameters currently in use).

FIG. 31.16
Quick Info provides syntax information that can sometimes help you complete a statement.

Quick Info ——

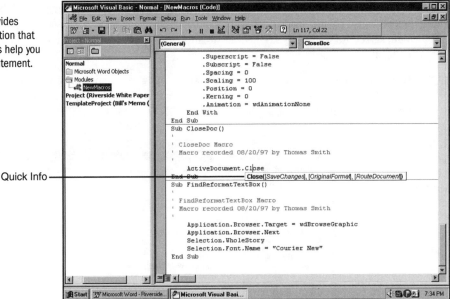

Understanding the VBA Help System

You've already encountered some examples of how VBA tries to help programmers make fewer mistakes and get the job done more quickly.

VBA Help is an optional component of Word or Office. If you haven't installed it, you can do so as follows:

1. Insert the Word or Office CD-ROM.
2. Choose Start, Settings, Control Panel from the Windows taskbar.
3. Double-click the Add Remove Programs icon.
4. Select Microsoft Office 97, and click Add/Remove. The Word or Office Setup installation maintenance program runs.
5. Choose Add/Remove.
6. Select Microsoft Word.
7. Click Change Option.
8. Select Help.
9. Click Change Option.
10. Check the Help for Visual Basic check box.
11. Choose OK twice.
12. Choose Continue. Setup installs the file.
13. Choose OK.

First, and most obvious, there's Office Assistant, the same Clippit paperclip or other character you've gotten to know in Word. Press F1, or click the Office Assistant toolbar button on the Visual Basic Editor's Standard toolbar, and the Office Assistant appears (see Figure 31.17).

FIG. 31.17
Office Assistant works in the Visual Basic Editor, too.

If you prefer, you can enter the Help system directly, by choosing Help, Contents and Index. You'll probably find the following areas of Help information most valuable:

- User interface help (Assistance with the Visual Basic Editor menu commands, toolbar buttons, keyboard shortcuts, and other interface elements)

- How-to topics (Guidance on specific tasks that VBA programmers use most)

- Language reference (Detailed information on syntax, objects, methods, properties, and other VBA elements)

- Conceptual topics (Ideas for avoiding problems and working more effectively)

- Microsoft Word Visual Basic Reference (Specific, detailed information on Word objects, properties, and methods)

From Here...

In this chapter, you've gotten your feet wet with VBA and the Visual Basic Editor. Now it's time to start writing useful macros:

- If you'd like a refresher on recording macros, skip back to Chapter 30, "Recording and Running Visual Basic Macros," which shows just how much you can accomplish even without Visual Basic Editor.

- In Chapter 32, "Taking More Control of Your Macros," you'll learn how to use VBA control structures to build macros that can make intelligent decisions. You'll also learn how to use message boxes and input boxes to build macros that can reflect user input.

- Then, in Chapter 33, "Building a Real-World Solution with VBA and Word," you'll walk step by step through the construction and testing of a practical application, mixing and matching recorded and hand-coded statements to get the job done as quickly as possible.

Part
VII

Ch
31

CHAPTER 32

Taking More Control of Your Macros

by Bill Camarda

In Chapter 31, "Getting Started with VBA," you began exploring the VBA programming environment, reading simple recorded macros, and slightly enhancing them. You've gotten your feet wet, but you haven't done much that couldn't be done with the Macro Recorder, given some patience and care. In this chapter, you will. You'll start building intelligence into your macros.

You'll learn about VBA variables and control structures that enable you to tell VBA not just what to do, but when and how to do it. After that, you'll learn two easy ways to reflect user input in your macros: message boxes and input boxes. Then, in Chapter 33, "Building a Real-World Solution with VBA and Word," you'll go further—creating custom dialog boxes as part of the development of a complete application. ■

Understanding variables

Variables are cubbyholes where VBA stores data that can be updated.

Working with control structures

Learn how `For...Next` loops, `Do...While` loops, and `If...Then` statements help you to build intelligence into your macros.

Enhancing the macros you record

Record five practical macros and then use VBA code to make them do even more.

Create message boxes and input boxes

In one line of code, you can make your macros interactive with impressive message and input boxes.

"Wiring" your message and input boxes

Learn how to attach your message and input boxes to actions your macro can perform.

Understanding Variables

Many of the techniques you're about to learn depend upon the use of *variables*. A variable is simply a cubbyhole in memory where VBA stores information that might change as the program runs. There are many kinds of variables; you'll see a number of them at work in this chapter.

One thing beginners especially like about VBA is that it enables them to create a variable with very little trouble. All you have to do is enter the name of the variable and give it a starting value. VBA declares the variable implicitly, creating a generic variable that can contain any kind of information you want. Conceptually, the statement you create looks like this:

```
Variable = Whatever you like
```

As long as the name you've chosen isn't already reserved by VBA for something else, and meets VBA's syntax requirements, it'll work. (The syntax requirements roughly boil down to this: use alphanumeric characters, and don't use spaces. Underscores are OK, but many other nonalphanumeric characters are not, because VBA uses them for other purposes.)

In the following example, you create a variable named `Inventory` and set it to `50,000`:

```
Inventory = 50000
```

After you have the `Inventory` variable, you can specify the variable wherever you need to perform a calculation based on the current number of items in inventory.

Variables can store many different kinds of data, called *data types*. For example, string variables contain text that can't be used for calculations, integer variables contain whole numbers between –32,767 and +32,767, and Boolean variables can be set only to True or False. Beginning programmers don't have to worry much about these distinctions because variables that have been declared implicitly can store any kind of data. However, advanced programmers generally prefer to declare their variables explicitly, primarily for these two reasons:

- *Performance*. When you declare a variable explicitly, VBA sets aside only as much memory as it needs for the variable, and it doesn't have to waste processing time translating a generic "Variant" variable into the specific data type it needs.

- *Accuracy*. Declaring variables explicitly also helps to improve the accuracy of your code. If you inadvertently misspell the name of a variable, VBA displays an error message because you haven't already declared the variable. Otherwise, VBA simply assumes you're creating a new variable, and your program won't work right.

There are several ways to create a variable explicitly; the most common is to use a `Dim` statement that declares the variable and specifies its type. (`Dim` stands for dimension: from VBA's standpoint, you're establishing the dimension of the space in memory that needs to be set aside.) In the following example, a `Dim` statement is used to declare a variable named `ProjectDue`, and tell VBA to store only dates there:

```
Dim ProjectDue as Date
```

Many programmers like to declare all their variables up front, so it's easy to keep track of them, especially when problems arise. Again, however, if you're planning to record only very simple macros, you don't have to worry about `Dim` statements. Just let VBA handle your variables implicitly, and you'll be fine.

Understanding VBA Control Structures

It's no small accomplishment to write a macro that runs smoothly from beginning to end, starting at the first line and working its way a line at a time to the last line, `End Sub`. Macros like that can do quite a lot, but they're not very flexible. For example, what if you want to write a macro that does any of the following:

- Enters different text or adds different formatting based on what it finds in your document
- Repeats one or more tasks several times, and then moves on
- Knows enough to stop processing when it reaches the end of your document
- Checks to make sure that all the values in a table are within certain parameters

You can't record a macro to do any of those things, but with a little VBA code, they're all quite easy.

In this chapter, you'll learn about VBA control structures by example. First, you'll record a macro that's reasonably useful all by itself. Then, you'll go into the Visual Basic Editor and add a control structure that makes it even more useful.

N O T E As mentioned in Chapter 31, "Getting Started with VBA," when you become more familiar with VBA, you may find more efficient ways to write some of the code that the Macro Recorder records. In this chapter, however, you'll focus simply on extending the Macro Recorder's code and getting the job done. ▨

Example #1: Recording a "Cleanup" Macro

One of the most common uses for macros is to clean up extra characters, spaces, or paragraph marks left in a document by another program, or perhaps retrieved from the Web. It's especially common for people who were weaned on typewriters to insert two spaces after each sentence. Nowadays, because most documents are printed on laser printers using high-quality fonts, the new accepted standard is to place one space between sentences, just as typesetters always have. The macro you'll record will use Find and Replace to solve two problems at the same time:

- It will search documents for two consecutive spaces and replace them with one.

- It will strip out stray paragraph marks.

 TIP

Many of the most useful macros you'll create will make liberal use of Find and Replace.

Of course, you won't want to strip out *all* the paragraph marks in your document. Many of them are obviously necessary. In fact, in some documents, there are places where you may want to leave two consecutive paragraph marks. (For instance, in documents that do not use styles with extra spacing before or after paragraphs, a second paragraph mark is often used to leave extra space between paragraphs.) Therefore, the macro you'll record will search for three paragraph marks and replace them with two. To record the macro, follow these steps:

1. Double-click the REC button on the status bar. The Record Macro dialog box opens.

2. Enter a name for the macro in the Macro Name text box. (For purposes of this example, name the macro StripSpacePara, and skip the steps involved in assigning the macro to a toolbar button or keyboard shortcut.)

3. Choose OK.

4. Press Ctrl+H to open the Replace tab of the Find and Replace dialog box.

5. In the Find What text box, enter the following: **^p^p^p** (this instruction tells Word to search for three consecutive paragraph marks).

6. In the Replace With text box, enter **^p^p** to search for two consecutive paragraph marks.

7. In the Find What text box, enter two spaces.

8. In the Replace With text box, enter one space.

9. Click Replace All. Word searches the entire document and tells you how many replacements it has made.

10. Click OK.

11. Click Replace All.

12. Click OK and Close.

13. Double-click REC on the status bar to stop recording.

Now, look at the macro you just recorded:

1. Choose Tools, Macro, Macros to display the Macros dialog box.

2. In the Macro Name scroll box, select the macro you just recorded (StripSpacePara).

3. Choose Edit. The Visual Basic Editor opens (see Figure 32.1).

FIG. 32.1
The StripSpacePara macro makes heavy use of With statements.

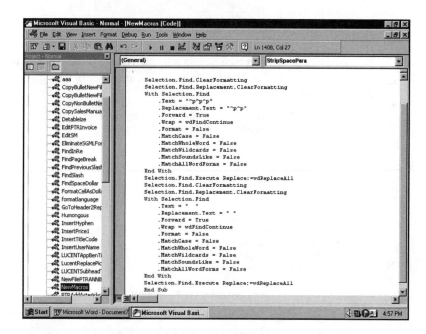

There's quite a bit of code here. In fact, there's so much code that it was necessary to shrink the text in the Code window to show it all.

N O T E Here's how you can shrink (or enlarge) text in the Code window:

1. In the Visual Basic Editor, choose Tools, Options.

2. Choose the Editor Format tab (see Figure 32.2).

3. Choose a type size from the Size drop-down box.

4. Choose OK.

FIG. 32.2

The Editor Format tab of
the Visual Basic Editor
Options dialog box.

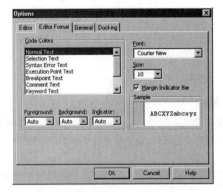

Because you'll probably record quite a few "Find-and-Replace" macros, it's worth spending a
few moments to take a look at this one. Let's focus on one of the actions you recorded, replacing three paragraph marks with two:

```
Selection.Find.ClearFormatting
Selection.Find.Replacement.ClearFormatting
With Selection.Find
    .Text = "^p^p^p"
    .Replacement.Text = "^p^p"
    .Forward = True
    .Wrap = wdFindContinue
    .Format = False
    .MatchCase = False
    .MatchWholeWord = False
    .MatchWildcards = False
    .MatchSoundsLike = False
    .MatchAllWordForms = False
End With
Selection.Find.Execute Replace:=wdReplaceAll
```

The first two statements do something very important: they tell VBA to remove any formatting
you may have included in a previous search. In other words, if you run this macro immediately
after you replaced a batch of Heading 2 styles with Heading 1 styles, these statements make
sure those styles are not part of your new search. Without these statements, your macro would
almost certainly not find all the text you want to replace, and when it made replacements, it
would probably insert formatting you don't want.

```
Selection.Find.ClearFormatting
Selection.Find.Replacement.ClearFormatting
```

The bulk of the macro consists of a `With` statement much like the one you saw in Chapter 31.
As you learned there, each indented line between `With` and `End With` corresponds to a property, and the properties correspond to settings in the Replace tab. For example,

```
.Text = "^p^p^p"
```

corresponds to the entry you placed in the Fi_nd What text box, and

```
.Replacement.Text = "^p^p"
```

describes the entry you placed in the Replace With text box. The next two properties are also important:

```
.Forward = True
.Wrap = wdFindContinue
```

.Forward = True tells Word to start searching at the insertion point and search in the direction of the end of the document. .Wrap = wdFindContinue tells Word that when it reaches the end, it should go to the beginning of the document and keep searching until it reaches the insertion point. In other words, these statements make sure that Word searches the entire document.

The next six properties (.Format, .MatchCase, .MatchWholeWord, .MatchWildcards, .MatchSoundsLike, and .MatchAllWordForms) are not relevant to this macro, so they can be removed.

As you've already learned, this statement ends with End With. But the macro doesn't end there. There's one more statement:

```
Selection.Find.Execute Replace:=wdReplaceAll
```

This tells VBA to actually go ahead and perform the Find and Replace. (Remember, you might have chosen simply to close the Find and Replace dialog box without executing the search.)

After you get rid of what you don't need, your revised macro appears as shown in Figure 32.3. Notice that the ClearFormatting statements at the beginning of the macro only need to appear once. No formatting is added later in the macro, so none has to be removed again.

Part
VII

Ch
32

FIG. 32.3

The finished StripSpacePara2 macro, with excess code edited out.

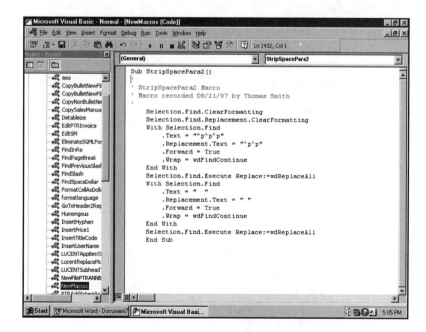

This macro is fairly useful, but you may have noticed a problem: this macro only searches for extra paragraph marks once. If someone left five straight paragraph marks in your document, four of them will still be there when the macro finishes. You could simply record the same steps over and over again—and in some quick-and-dirty macros, there's no reason not to do it that way. However, a more efficient and flexible approach is to use a For...Next loop.

Understanding *For...Next* Loops

In a For...Next loop, you tell VBA how many times you want to perform a task. You also create a counter variable that keeps track of how many times you've already performed the task.

Each time your program performs the task, it asks, in effect, "am I done yet?" If not, VBA returns to the beginning of the loop and runs the task again. If, however, the program discovers it has run the task as many times as you told it to, it stops looping and moves on to the next statement in the macro.

In the following generic example, you create a counter variable that performs an action 10 times:

```
For x = 1 to 10
     Stuff you want to do
Next x
```

The first line establishes the counter variable, names it "x," and tells the program you want the loop to run 10 times. The indented line represents the task you want. The final line tells the program to increment the counter variable and then to determine whether it should run the loop again.

Here's how to use a For...Next loop in the StripSpacePara macro you've just recorded and edited. In this example, you'll only run the loop five times; that should be enough to catch most stray paragraph marks.

```
Sub StripSpacePara()
    For x = 1 to 5
        Selection.Find.ClearFormatting
        Selection.Find.Replacement.ClearFormatting
        With Selection.Find
            .Text = "^p^p^p"
            .Replacement.Text = "^p^p"
            .Forward = True
            .Wrap = wdFindContinue
        End With
        Selection.Find.Execute Replace:=wdReplaceAll
        With Selection.Find
            .Text = "   "
            .Replacement.Text = " "
            .Forward = True
            .Wrap = wdFindContinue
        End With
        Selection.Find.Execute Replace:=wdReplaceAll
    Next x
End Sub
```

TIP Note that all the contents of the `For...Next` loop are indented for easy readability. Remember that you can quickly indent several lines at once by selecting them and pressing Tab.

Why use a `For...Next` loop rather than simply recording steps over and over again?

- Your code runs faster. This isn't much of an issue in small macros running on fast computers, but as your macros get larger, performance will matter.
- Your code is easier to understand.
- It's easier to make changes. For example, what if you suddenly start coming across documents with 20 consecutive paragraph marks? All you have to do is change the `For` statement to run 20 times instead of five.
- It's easier to fix problems. What if you discover the search you created isn't quite working right? You only have to edit it in one location, not repeatedly.

N O T E Later, you'll learn about the `.Find.Found` property, which can help you extend this macro even further. With `.Find.Found`, you can write a StripSpacePara macro that keeps looping until it finds no more changes to make. ■

TROUBLESHOOTING

If your procedure hangs, you may have inadvertently created an *infinite loop*—a loop where a program continually looks for a specific event in order to move on, but that event never occurs. Often, this happens when a variable is set to a value outside the range of values the loop is designed to expect. To fix the infinite loop, edit it to make sure that the condition the program is looking for can actually happen.

Part
VII

Ch
32

Example #2: Reformatting Tables

Word's formatting features are powerful, but there can still be quite a bit of repetitive work involved in using them. That's where macros come in handy. In this section, you'll record a macro that searches for the next table in a document and reformats it using one of Word's built-in Table AutoFormatting formats. After you've done so, you'll build on the statements you've recorded, adding a control structure that reformats one table after another until it reaches the end of your document.

First, create a document that contains at least one table, with space above and beneath it. Then, follow these steps to record the macro:

1. Double-click the REC button on the status bar. The Record Macro dialog box opens.
2. Enter a name for the macro in the Macro Name text box. (For purposes of this example, name the macro FormatTableContemporary, and skip the steps involved in assigning the macro to a toolbar button or keyboard shortcut.)

3. Choose OK.

4. Press Ctrl+Home to go to the beginning of the document. This ensures that when the macro is run, all tables will be reformatted no matter where the user left his or her insertion point.

5. Click Select Browse Object beneath the horizontal scroll bar.

6. Choose Browse by Table. Word moves the insertion point to the first cell of the next table in the document.

7. Choose Table, Select Table. Word selects the entire table.

8. Choose Table, AutoFormat. Word displays the Table AutoFormat dialog box.

9. In the Formats list box, choose Contemporary.

10. Choose OK.

11. Press the down arrow key to move the insertion point beyond the table. This prepares the macro to find the next table.

12. Double-click the REC button on the status bar to stop the Macro Recorder.

You now have a macro that will search for the next table and AutoFormat it using the Contemporary style. Figure 32.4 shows the macro displayed in the Visual Basic Editor; the Project Explorer and Project window have been closed to accommodate its width.

FIG. 32.4

The FormatTableContemporary macro searches for the next table in a document and AutoFormats it.

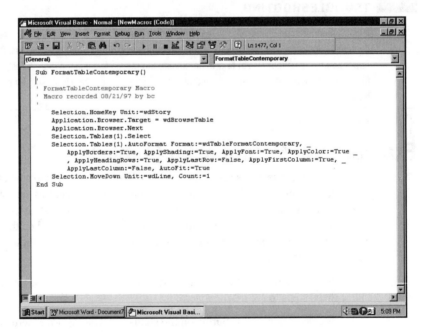

A few elements are worth noting. In the first line:

```
Selection.HomeKey Unit:=wdStory
```

HomeKey is a method associated with the Selection object, which means, as you may recall, that it is an action that can be performed on the Selection object. The action in this case is "go to the beginning of the unit." The unit, in this case, is wdStory, which is VBA's way of referring to all the body text in the document, excluding headers, footers, footnotes, and other document elements.

In the following two lines, VBA is using the Browser property of the Application object. The first line sets the Browser to search for tables. The second line actually performs the search, placing the insertion point in the first cell of the first table it finds.

```
Application.Browser.Target = wdBrowseTable
Application.Browser.Next
```

Now that you're in a table, the following line selects the entire table. Here, you're using an object, a property, and a method all at once. Selection is the object Tables is the property of the object and Select is the method—the action being taken.

```
Selection.Tables(1).Select
```

The following line applies AutoFormatting to the table. Notice that since the code extends beyond a single line, VBA places underscore (_) *continuation characters* at the end of each line. All lines connected by continuation characters are processed as if they fit on a single line.

```
Selection.Tables(1).AutoFormat Format:=wdTableFormatContemporary, _
    ApplyBorders:=True, ApplyShading:=True, ApplyFont:=True, ApplyColor:=True _
    , ApplyHeadingRows:=True, ApplyLastRow:=False, ApplyFirstColumn:=True, _
    ApplyLastColumn:=False, AutoFit:=True
```

Finally, the last statement moves the insertion point down one line:

```
Selection.MoveDown Unit:=wdLine, Count:=1
```

You now have a fairly powerful macro, but you can make it more powerful. You've already learned how to create a For...Next loop that runs a specific number of times. Now, you'll learn how to adapt the macro to keep running until it reaches the end of the document and then stop.

Using *Do...While* Loops

You don't need to do anything with the first two lines of your macro:

```
Selection.HomeKey Unit:=wdStory
Application.Browser.Target = wdBrowseTable
```

Beyond this, however, you do need to make some changes. First, you need to create a Boolean variable, which can only return one of two values: *True* (equal to –1), or *False* (equal to 0). The Boolean variable you'll add to this macro will be named EndOfDoc, and its value will depend on whether the insertion point is at the end of the document or not. The value of True (-1) will be returned if the insertion point is at the end of the active document; otherwise, 0 will be returned.

```
EndOfDoc = (Selection.End = ActiveDocument.Content.End - 1)
```

Next, you need to create a `Do...While` loop. This is a loop that performs an action as long as a condition is met. When the condition is no longer met, the loop ends, and the program continues to the next statement. Conceptually, a `Do...While` loop looks like this:

```
Do While Condition Exists
    Tasks you want to perform
Loop
```

In the current example, you want the loop to keep running as long as `MoreTables = True`, in other words, as long as the program can still find more tables in the document. When the program can't find any more tables, it moves to the next statement, which is `End Sub`—the end of the program.

Each time the program moves to a new table, it then tries to select the entire table. However, if there are no more tables in the document, an error occurs. The `On Error Resume Next` statement prevents the error from stopping the execution of the program. If the program couldn't find a table, the `Err` system object contains a value of `5941`. Testing for this value tells you whether to set the value of `MoreTables` to `False`.

```
On Error Resume Next
Selection.Tables(1).Select
If Err = 1594 Then
    MoreTables = False
Else
    ...
End If
```

The finished code looks like this:

```
Sub FormatTableContemporary()

    Selection.HomeKey Unit:=wdStory
    Application.Browser.Target = wdBrowseTable
    MoreTables = True
    Do While MoreTables = True
        Application.Browser.Next
        On Error Resume Next
        Selection.Tables(1).Select
        If Err = 1594 Then
            MoreTables = False
        Else
            Selection.Tables(1).AutoFormat Format:=wdTableFormatContemporary, _
            ApplyBorders:=True, ApplyShading:=True, ApplyFont:=True, _
➥ApplyColor:=True _
            , ApplyHeadingRows:=True, ApplyLastRow:=False, _
➥ApplyFirstColumn:=True, _
            ApplyLastColumn:=False, AutoFit:=True
            Selection.MoveDown Unit:=wdLine, Count:=1
    Loop
End Sub
```

Not bad, but you can do even better. What if you have more than one kind of a table in your document, and you only want to apply the AutoFormat to a specific kind of table? In the next couple of pages, you'll learn how to do just that—using the most popular control structure of all, the `If...Then` statement.

There are other kinds of `Do...While` structures.

- `Do...Loop While` runs the loop at least once, even if the condition has not been met. If the condition has been met, it keeps running until the condition is no longer met.

- `Do...Until` loops only run when the condition is not met and stop immediately when it is met.

- `Do...Loop Until` loops combine the two previous structures. They run once whether the condition is met or not. Then, they only keep running as long as the condition is not met.

Using the *If...Then...Else* Control Structure

Think about all the times you make a decision about what to do next in Word:

- If someone meets their sales quota, you send them a letter of congratulations; if not, you send them a letter exhorting them to do better.

- You format your document one way if it's going to senior management and another if it's a rough first draft for use at a team meeting.

- You print on the expensive color printer when you're presenting to customers and on the cheaper laser printer the rest of the time.

Part
VII

Ch
32

VBA can help you automate some of these decisions. In some cases, the information VBA needs to make the decision might already be in your document. For example, your document might contain a table listing the sales made by each of your salespeople, and your macro might be able to use that information to determine whether to send a congratulatory letter.

In other situations, as you'll learn later, you can provide the information through a message box or input box. In either case, `If...Then...Else` gives you the tools you need to make sure your program acts appropriately based on the input it receives.

The simplest versions of `If...Then...Else` fit on a single line. Conceptually, they look like this:

```
If ConditionIsMet Then DoThis Else DoThat
```

When your program runs, it tests the condition by looking in your document, checking the contents of a variable, or in a number of other possible ways. If the condition is met, the program does what `Then` tells it to do. If the condition is not met, the program does what `Else` tells it to do. In the following example, you have already created a variable named `Income`:

```
If Income >96900 Then TaxRate = 0.31 Else TaxRate = 0.28
```

In this example, you have a variable named `WordCount` that stores the document's word count. If the word count is greater than 200, the program runs the Spell Check.

```
If WordCount > 200 Then ActiveDocument.CheckSpelling
```

Note that the previous statement doesn't include `Else` at all. If the program finds that the document's word count is less than 200, it simply moves on to the next statement.

These are very simple uses of `If...Then...Else`. However, it's likely that you'll have a series of statements that should be performed if the condition is met. For these situations, use an `If...Then block` statement, which looks like this:

```
If ConditionIsMet Then
     DoThis
     AndThis
     AndThisToo
Else
     DoThat
     AndTheOtherThing
End If
```

Some commands you can record are actually `If...Then...Else` statements. For example, you might remember this from the section "Recording New Statements to Use in Your VBA Macro" in Chapter 31. It's the code VBA records when you click the Underline button on the Standard toolbar:

```
If Selection.Font.Underline = wdUnderlineNone Then
    Selection.Font.Underline = wdUnderlineSingle
Else
    Selection.Font.Underline = wdUnderlineNone
End If
```

Similarly, when you record clicking the Spelling and Grammar button, VBA records the following:

```
If Options.CheckGrammarWithSpelling = True Then
    ActiveDocument.CheckGrammar
Else
    ActiveDocument.CheckSpelling
End If
```

Again, you don't even have to provide statements underneath `Else`; if you don't, your program will simply continue on to the statement after `End If`.

Example #3: Reformatting Only Tables That Meet Certain Criteria

Now that you understand `If...Then` statements, return to the macro you were about to create. You already have a macro that applies AutoFormatting to every table in a document and stops when it reaches the end of the document. Now, you want to modify that macro so it only AutoFormats tables which contain quarterly results. You happen to know that all those tables contain the headings Q1, Q2, Q3, Q4. The plan is to build code that will do the following:

- Search for Q1 inside each table.
- If Q1 is found, reformat the table.
- If Q1 is not found, go on to the next table and look for it there.

You can start with the code you already have. You won't need to change anything outside the `Do...While` loop you already created. All the new action takes place inside that loop, which means the program will still stop running when it reaches the end of the document, just as you want. In fact, the first two lines inside the loop don't change either, because you still want to find the next table and select it:

```
Application.Browser.Next
Selection.Tables(1).Select
```

Because all the tables you want to reformat contain the text Q1, the next block of code searches for Q1. Although you could record this code, you would have to make significant changes in what you record.

```
Selection.Find.ClearFormatting
With Selection.Find
    .Execute FindText:="Q1", Forward:=True, Wrap:=wdFindContinue
    If .Found = True Then
        Selection.Tables(1).Select
        Selection.Tables(1).AutoFormat Format:=wdTableFormatContemporary,
➥ApplyBorders _
            :=True, ApplyShading:=True, ApplyFont:=True, ApplyColor:=True, _
            ApplyHeadingRows:=True, ApplyLastRow:=False,
➥ApplyFirstColumn:=True, _
            ApplyLastColumn:=False, AutoFit:=True
    Else
    End If
End With
```

For example, as you saw earlier, the macro recorder would create a separate statement to execute the search, such as `Selection.Find.Execute`. However, you need to execute the search as part of your `With` statement, because you'll need to embed an `If...Then` control structure later, within the same statement.

The following lines set up `.Find` the way you need it. Notice the compact syntax used with the `.Execute` method, which details the `Find` object properties that should be executed:

```
Selection.Find.ClearFormatting
With Selection.Find
    .Execute FindText:="Q1", Forward:=True, Wrap:=wdFindContinue
End With
```

Now, your `If...Then...Else` statement can snuggle in neatly, immediately after the `.Execute` line:

```
If .Found = True Then
        Selection.Tables(1).Select
        Selection.Tables(1).AutoFormat Format:=wdTableFormatContemporary,
➥ApplyBorders _
```

Part
VII

Ch
32

```
            :=True, ApplyShading:=True, ApplyFont:=True, ApplyColor:=True, _
            ApplyHeadingRows:=True, ApplyLastRow:=False,
➥ApplyFirstColumn:=True, _
            ApplyLastColumn:=False, AutoFit:=True
      Else
      End If
```

You've seen most of that code before, in the AutoFormatting macro you recorded earlier, but the first line is interesting:

```
If .Found = True Then
```

This makes use of the .Found property of the Find object, which reports whether a Find and Replace action actually found anything. This is a terrific convenience. For example, imagine writing a macro that searches your document for index entries. (First, you would have to record a step to toggle field codes so they were visible in your document.) You could then use an If...Then statement to insert an index only if an index entry was found.

VBA provides another control structure, Select...Case, which can be used if you have several options to chose from, not just two. For example, you might use Select...Case to pick the right federal tax rate from a tax table. The generic syntax for Select...Case is as follows:

```
Select Case expression
    Case Result1
        DoThis
        AndThat
    Case Result2
        DoThisInstead
        AndThatInstead
    Case Result3
        TryThis
        AndTryThat
    Case Else
        OrDoThis
        AndDoThat
End Select
```

You can choose among as many values as you want. For example, you might use Select Case to draw upon a library of ZIP codes in your local area, simplifying mailings.

Providing for User Input

Of course the most powerful kind of control is the kind human beings can exercise. In the remainder of this chapter, you'll learn to make your programs respond to the needs of real users. There are three ways to do so:

- With message boxes that give the user information and ask for a response, typically a Yes or No response
- With input boxes that ask for one line of information
- With dialog boxes that work just like other Word dialog boxes, enabling users to establish many settings at the same time

Message boxes and input boxes are covered in this chapter; dialog boxes are covered in Chapter 33, "Building a Real World Solution with VBA and Word." Again, in each case, you'll start by recording a macro and then learn how to adapt it using VBA.

Example #4: Opening a New Memo Document

Imagine that you spend most of your time creating memos. You might create an AutoExec macro that automatically opens a new memo document whenever you start Word. To do so, follow these steps:

1. Double-click the REC button on the status bar. The Record Macro dialog box opens.
2. Enter the name AutoExec in the Macro Name text box, and choose OK to start recording the macro.
3. Choose File, New.
4. Click the Memos tab.
5. Double-click the Contemporary Memo icon to display a new document based on the Contemporary Memo template.
6. Double-click the REC button again to stop the macro recorder.

The macro you've just recorded appears in Figure 32.5. It's short and to the point. The macro applies the Add method to the Document object; in other words, it creates a new document. It sets the Template property, specifying the complete path and file name of the template to be used. Finally, it sets the property NewTemplate to False, which simply means that you are creating a new document, not another template.

Part
VII

Ch
32

FIG. 32.5

This AutoExec macro opens a new document based on the Contemporary Memo template.

All well and good, but there are those occasional days when you start your PC intending to write something other than a memo. What then? In the following sections, you'll learn how to adapt this macro in two ways:

- You'll add a message box that asks whether you want to create a memo.
- You'll write code that takes the user's response and uses it to determine whether to create a memo.

Creating a Message Box

Creating the message box is the easy part. The simplest possible message box includes only the MsgBox function and the text you want to appear in the message, surrounded by quotation marks:

```
MsgBox("The macro has completed successfully")
```

When you run this statement, you see the message box shown in Figure 32.6.

FIG. 32.6
The simplest possible
message box offers only
an OK button.

This is the type of message box you might provide when you simply want to notify a user of something. There's little doubt that people will see this message box, but that's about all the interactivity it gives you. However, there are five other types of message boxes, and they give you quite a few more options. These message boxes are listed in Table 32.1.

Table 32.1 Types of VBA Message Boxes

Type of Message Box	Value	Constant
OK, Cancel	1	vbOKCancel
Abort, Retry, Ignore	2	vbAbortRetryIgnore
Yes, No, Cancel	3	vbYesNoCancel
Yes, No	4	vbYesNo
Retry, Cancel	5	vbRetryCancel

To use one of these message boxes, you need to specify which one you want. You also need to rework the statement a bit, creating a variable that stores the answer your user gives you. Conceptually, here's what it should look like:

```
variable = MsgBox("Question to user", TypeOfBox)
```

Now, apply that to the macro created in the previous section. Your goal is to ask whether to create a memo or not. All you need to do this is a simple Yes/No message box. In this example, you'll store the result in a variable named memo:

```
memo = MsgBox("Do you want to create a memo?", 4)
```

You can see the finished message box in Figure 32.7. By the way, you can get the same result by using the constant in Table 32.1 instead of the value. It takes longer to type, but you'll find it easier to understand if you need to work on the macro later:

```
memo = MsgBox("Do you want to create a memo?", vbYesNo)
```

FIG. 32.7

A Yes/No message box that asks whether you want to create a memo.

Understanding Functions and Constants

Two important terms need to be defined here. First, VBA statements such as memo = MsgBox("Do you want to continue?", vbYesNoCancel) are called *functions*. A function is any statement that, when run, gives you a value. As you work with VBA more and more, you'll begin to find functions extremely helpful. VBA has a lengthy series of built-in math and financial functions that handle the hard work of calculations for you. For example, the NPV function calculates the net present value of an investment, based on cash flow and discount rate information you give it.

The second term mentioned previously is *constant*. In a sense, a constant is the flip side of a variable. You create a variable when you need to store a value that is likely to change. You create a constant when you need to store a value that cannot change. In the previous statement, vbYesNoCancel is the constant. VBA always displays a Yes, No, Cancel dialog box when this statement runs, never some other kind of a dialog box.

Whenever you see a term in a VBA statement that starts with vb, you're looking at a constant that is available throughout Visual Basic for Applications. Whenever you see a term that starts with wd, such as wdStory, you're looking at a constant that is available only in Word.

When the user makes a choice, information is stored in the variable you created. This information is stored in two forms: as a value, and as a constant. Table 32.2 shows you both:

Part
VII

Ch
32

Table 32.2   How Message Box Button Clicks Are Stored in a Variable

Button click	Value	Constant
OK	1	vbOK
Cancel	2	vbCancel
Abort	3	vbAbort
Retry	4	vbRetry
Ignore	5	vbIgnore
Yes	6	vbYes
No	7	vbNo

So, in the macro you've been working on, the user will have two options: Yes (equal to 6 or vbYes), or No (equal to 7 or vbNo).

Optional Syntax for Message Boxes

There's some optional syntax you might want to use with your message boxes. For example, you can include a title in quotation marks; this will appear in the title bar of your message box, so that users will immediately recognize what they'll be called upon to do. For example, the following statement sets up a Yes/No message box named Employee Identification:

```
EmployeeName = MsgBox ("Are you an authorized employee?", vbYesNo,_
"Employee Identification")
```

You might also want to use one of the standard icons you sometimes see in message boxes: stop signs, question marks, exclamation points, or information icons. You can add a constant that adds one of these icons. The constants are shown in Table 32.3. Place a plus sign before the constant.

Table 32.3   Icons You Can Include in Your Message Boxes

Icon	Value	Constant
Stop sign	16	vbCritical
Question mark	32	vbQuestion
Exclamation point	48	vbExclamation
Information icon	64	vbInformation

The following example creates the message box shown in Figure 32.8:

```
EmployeeName = MsgBox ("Are you an authorized employee?",_
vbYesNo + vbQuestion, "Employee Identification")
```

FIG. 32.8

A message box containing a custom title bar and a Question Mark icon.

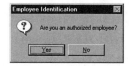

Reflecting the User's Response in Your Program

Imagine that you're running a macro containing the `MsgBox` statement just discussed. You click the Yes button. Now what? There's a "Yes" (actually, a value of 6 or a constant of vbYes) floating around in your computer somewhere. However, it's not attached to anything. It doesn't lead the program to do anything. So nothing happens; the program simply moves on the next statement. You have to wire your program to take action based on the user's input.

You've already learned one easy way to do so: use an `If...Then` statement. You can tell the program: *if the user clicked Yes, do one thing; if the user clicked No, do something different.* In this example, you'll set things up so that when users click Yes, they get a new memo document based on the Contemporary Memo template. When users click No, they get a blank document. As you'll see, the `If...Then` statement in this macro uses the variable values you just learned about.

Here's the AutoExec macro, appropriately revised:

```
Sub AutoExec()
'
' AutoExec Macro
' Macro recorded 08/21/97 by Thomas Smith
'

    memo = MsgBox("Do you want to create a memo?", 4)
    If memo = 6 Then
        Documents.Add Template:= _
        "C:\Program Files\Microsoft Office\Templates\Memos\_
➥Contemporary Memo.dot" _
        , NewTemplate:=False
    Else
        Documents.Add
    End If
End Sub
```

Notice one other line has been added, after `Else`:

```
Documents.Add
```

This line tells the program to open a blank document if the user clicks No. Without this line, Word wouldn't open any document at all.

N O T E You could record that `Documents.Add` statement and copy it into your macro. However, by now, you might be getting comfortable enough with VBA to type it in yourself. ■

Example #5: Sharing a Computer Among Several Users

Imagine that several people in your office share the same computer: Bob uses it on Tuesday, Mary on Wednesday, and so on. You want to keep track of everyone's work. The easiest way is to make sure every document they create contains their names in the Author text box in the Properties dialog box. However, you know that your users will never remember to change User Information in the Options dialog box every morning when they start working, and if they don't, new documents won't capture the correct Author names.

The solution is another AutoExec macro. In this section, you'll record a macro statement that changes the User Information in the Options tab. You'll then adapt that macro statement so it retrieves user input from an *input box* and places that input in the User Information tab.

N O T E In Word, you can only have one AutoExec macro at a time. However, you can write an AutoExec macro that performs more than one task. ■

The first step is to record the macro by following these steps:

1. Double-click the REC button on the status bar. The Record Macro dialog box opens.
2. Enter the name AutoExec in the Macro Name text box, and choose OK to start recording the macro.
3. Choose Tools, Options.
4. Click the User Information tab.
5. Enter your name in the Name text box.
6. Clear any entry in the Initials box.
7. Click OK.
8. Double-click the REC button again to stop the macro recorder.

In the following code, you can see the macro you just recorded. It's a start, but there's a big problem: this macro inserts your name in the User Information tab.

```
Sub AutoExec()
'
' AutoExec Macro
' Macro recorded 08/22/97 by Thomas Smith
'
    Application.UserName = "Thomas Smith"
    Application.UserInitials = ""
    Application.UserAddress = ""
End Sub
```

You'll need to do two things to change that: create an input box, and tell the program to place the information it retrieves in the User Information tab.

Understanding Input Boxes

Input boxes are quite similar to message boxes, except that they provide a text box where users can enter a line of text. OK and Cancel buttons are standard with input boxes; you don't have to worry about specifying them.

As with message boxes, you create a function that stores information in a variable; you also provide text that tells the user what information to enter. Conceptually, the statement looks like this:

```
variable =  InputBox("Question to user")
```

As an example, to create a variable named EmployeeName that stores whatever name the user types in the input box, use the following statement:

```
EmployeeName = InputBox("What is your name?")
```

The macro can now capture the user's name information, using the dialog box shown in Figure 32.9.

FIG. 32.9

An input box requesting a user's name.

As you've already learned, that's not enough; you have to tell the program what to do with the user's name. Fortunately, this requires only a slight edit to the program. Take a look at this line you already recorded:

```
Application.UserName = "Thomas Smith"
```

The information between the quotation marks is called a *string*, which simply means that it is being stored as text for some purpose. In this case, of course, the information is there to be placed in the User Information tab of the Options dialog box. A string could just as easily be used to include text in a letter, or to store an e-mail address in a macro that automatically sends messages.

Information stored "as text" in a string can't be used, for example, in a formula, even if the information is in numeric form. You can, however, convert strings to values, and vice versa. For example, you might write a program that copies a quantity from a purchase requisition, storing it in a string. You might then need to create formulas that utilize that quantity. You can use the Val function, followed by the string name in parentheses. In the following example, a string named Quantity is converted to a value:

```
Val(Quantity)
```

Conversely, you might have a value stored in a variable, and you need to display that value in a message box. VBA requires you to convert it to a string first. You can do so with the `Str` function. The following example converts a variable named `Cash` to a text string:

```
Str(Cash)
```

In any event, you don't want this string here. Instead, you want the contents of the `EmployeeName` variable. When the program is run, by the time this statement is reached, `EmployeeName` should contain the name the user typed into the input box. Edit the statement as follows:

```
Application.UserName = EmployeeName
```

Notice that you've removed the quotation marks. If you don't, VBA will assume this is simply another string. Now, when the program reaches this statement, it searches for the contents of the `EmployeeName` variable, and places them in the User Information tab of the Options dialog box. The final program looks like this:

```
Sub AutoExec()
'
' AutoExec Macro
' Macro recorded 08/22/97 by Thomas Smith
'
    EmployeeName = InputBox("What is your name?")
    Application.UserName = EmployeeName
    Application.UserInitials = ""
    Application.UserAddress = ""
End Sub
```

 TIP You can add titles to input boxes the same way you add them to message boxes.

From Here...

You now have a grounding in many of the basic techniques you'll need to build powerful VBA applications. You've learned the basics of working with control structures, message boxes and input boxes, and variables. You've gained more experience working with VBA objects, methods, and properties. Now you're ready to do even more.

- In Chapter 33, "Building a Real-World Solution with VBA and Word," you'll mix-and-match recorded commands and VBA statements to build a complete business application. Along the way, you'll learn how to provide even more user input, by creating full-fledged dialog boxes using VBA's UserForm feature.

- If you would like to revisit basic macro recording, skip back to Chapter 31, "Getting Started with VBA."

- Finally, for some ideas on customizing Word's user interface to give people easier access to your macros, see Chapter 26, "Customizing Word."

Building a Real-World Solution with VBA and Word

by Bill Ray

You've already learned that the power of Visual Basic for Applications macros to automate your word processing applications goes far beyond the capability to record and play back individual macros. By creating an integrated solution, involving template design, custom forms, and advanced VBA programming techniques, you can completely customize the process of creating documents required by your organization.

To use VBA most effectively, you need to use all the skills you've learned about in this book, such as template design, using field codes, bookmarks, and hyperlinks, and customizing toolbars and menus. The more you make use of the built-in features of Word, the less VBA programming you'll have to do.

This chapter shows you how to design, build, and deploy the automated production of one of the most common documents produced by any organization—the memo. ■

Designing an application

Learn how to evaluate the requirements of an automated word processing application and plan a strategy for implementing a solution in Word 97.

Designing the user interface

Create the input forms, toolbars, and menus that enable the user to interact with your automated template.

Writing the VBA code

Create the VBA macro code to display the forms and update the documents according to the requirements of the application.

Deploying your application

Learn how to distribute your application in both networked and stand-alone environments.

Planning an Automated Solution in Word 97

Before you begin to create an automated solution to building a Word document, you must understand the requirements of that document and the benefits that automation can bring to the process. You must evaluate these requirements to determine the degree of automation you need and the approach your design will take. Some of the important aspects of document design that you should evaluate are as follows:

- *Document layout.* What are the requirements for paper size, orientation (portrait or landscape), margins, headers, footers, and page numbers?
- *Formatting and styles.* What fonts are used in the document? What are all the different paragraph styles, including indenting, topic headings, numbering, bullets, or any other distinctive formatting?
- *Special elements.* Are there any characteristic items, including graphics, repetitive text, tables, or any other elements that occur on a predictable basis in this type of document?
- *User input.* What text is entered by the user? Can the user type text wherever he wants to, or must some items be entered in designated locations or in an ordered sequence?

Identifying and documenting these characteristics of the document you are automating will have a lot to do with your approach to designing a solution. For example, if you are very particular about the page layout and formatting rules, but you don't have any specific requirements about what text is entered, or where it is entered in the document, you will probably want to create a template to contain the formatting, with little or no VBA macro code required. On the other hand, if your data entry requirements are very specific and inflexible, your application may benefit from the design of custom forms to allow the user to input data, and from VBA code that enters the data in the desired locations.

One of the key elements of designing an automated solution in Word is to let Word do as much of the work as possible, before you create your first line of VBA code. Taking this approach lets you focus your programming efforts on those items that require automation, reducing the overall amount of code that you have to write, and making your application easier to maintain and to modify as your requirements change.

Understanding the Role of Templates

After you have identified the requirements of your application, you will often begin the development process by creating a document template. The template contains the formatting and layout characteristics of your application, and contains the macro code and custom forms that you will use in your solution.

Every Word document is based upon a template. It is easy to take this simple rule for granted if you base most of your documents on the global template, which is named Normal.dot. The global template is useful for capturing your general preferences, and general purpose macros, but specific document templates can contain the distinct characteristics of any special document, such as a letter, fax cover, office form, or a sales proposal.

Much of the design of the application can be built into the template, without writing unnecessary VBA code. The elements of your design process that can be captured in the template design are as follows:

- *Page layout*. Set the paper size, margins, and other overall document layout requirements of your application. If necessary, divide the document into sections to accommodate settings that change throughout the document.

- *Styles*. Translate the font and paragraph formatting requirements of your application into the styles that are built into the template.

- *Text and graphics*. Many applications contain text that appears in a consistent location in every document, such as memo headings, letterhead, or office forms. This also might include graphic elements, such as a company logo. You can enter text and graphics into the template, so that it will be reproduced for each document created by the template.

- *AutoText*. Your application might contain passages of text that the user can enter into the document, but at a location that is not predetermined. This could be anything from long passages of legal text to product names, addresses, or even single characters such as mathematical symbols or foreign language characters. Saving these elements as AutoText entries in the template makes them available both to the user, through interactive insertion of the AutoText entries, and to your application, which might automatically insert the AutoText entries at a later time.

- *Bookmarks*. You can identify special locations in the template through the addition of bookmarks. You can use a bookmark to identify a location where text items must be entered, such as the headings of a memo, or boxes on an office form. You can also use bookmarks to identify entire passages of text, which may be targets for copying or deleting by your VBA code.

- *VBA code and customizations*. After you have completed the basic design of the template, you can create the VBA code and other customizations that are specific to this application. Those customizations include custom forms, menus, toolbars, and shortcut keys. By storing these elements in the template, they are unique to this application, and will not interfere with the customizations in any other applications you create.

Now, consider the design of a template that can be used to create a memo, the most common document for many organizations.

Consider the case of ABC Corporation. The employees of ABC Corporation, like those in many companies, are required to create a lot of office memos. In the absence of a template for the ABC memo, employees are expected to create memos from scratch. Even though ABC Corporation has published a set of rules for creating memos, there are several problems with the current state of affairs in memo creation at this organization.

- *Inconsistency*. Not everyone follows the rules for creating the ABC memo, either because they don't want to bother, or because they aren't really skilled enough in the features of Word. Some employees choose the wrong fonts, margins, or paragraph styles. Other users omit some of the required elements of the memo, such as the carbon copy list, or place them in the wrong location on the page.

- ▓ *Wasted time*. Most users must recreate the design of the memo each time they want to create a new memo. This results in performing the same set of actions repetitively. This repetition is not only wasteful of time, but is also a further source of inconsistency. Some of the more adventurous users have recorded some or all of the process into macros or AutoText entries, but most of them have limited skills in creating and modifying macros, so the solutions are not often as effective as they could be.

- ▓ *Costs*. The current state of affairs results in a variety of costs to the company. An obvious cost is the cost of the wasted time we mentioned. Additional costs are found in support calls from users who are trying to create memos, corrective action that must be performed for users who can't successfully create the memos, and lots of paper wasted during test printings as memos are being revised and reformatted.

The office memo is a classic example of an application that can benefit from template design and automation. Memos must be created by users of all skill levels, and can occupy a large amount of the time and effort of many employees. The benefits of correcting the problems listed previously will be felt throughout an organization. Additionally, the result of this automation—a consistent, attractive memo layout—will be appreciated by everyone who has to write or read a memo.

An example of the memo layout that is used in the ABC Corporation memo is shown in Figure 33.1. There are a few items that we must take into account in designing the template for this memo:

- ▓ The banner at the top of the memo must reflect the purpose of the memo. For example, it may be an InterOffice Memorandum, Personnel Memorandum, or Confidential Memorandum.

- ▓ The headings for To, From, Date, and Subject must be aligned consistently, and the information entered to the right of each heading must be aligned properly.

- ▓ The date should be entered automatically, but the user should be able to edit the date.

- ▓ The cc list is optional. If there are no cc's, the cc label should not appear.

- ▓ The standard font is Arial, 12 point. Paragraphs are left-aligned, with a space after each paragraph.

You can begin creating a template by starting with a normal document, or a document based upon a similar template. Enter any text, graphics, tables, or other document elements into your new template.

Figure 33.2 shows the layout of the ABC memo template during the design phase. The elements that make up the memo headings have been entered into a table, with the widths of the table columns adjusted to meet the requirements of the template. The area for entering the cc list has been created by merging three cells to create a larger area for the list.

FIG. 33.1

The ABC Corporation memo layout will be used to create and print memos.

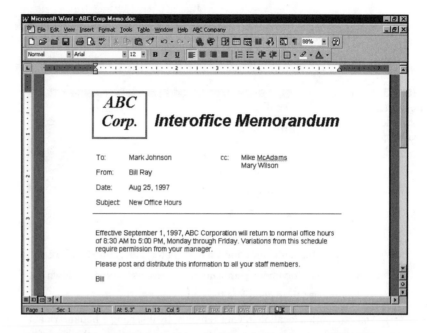

FIG. 33.2

The ABC memo template uses a table to align the memo headings and provide a space for user input.

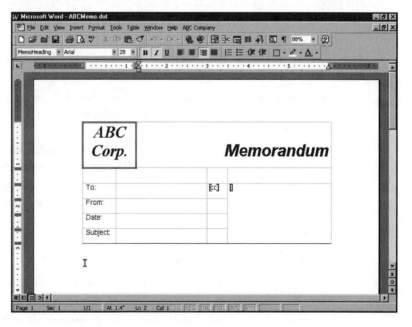

The border lines at the top and bottom of the table are part of the table formatting, and the Memorandum text is right-aligned to leave room for the customized headings for the different memo types the user will select.

After you have created the basic layout, it's a good idea to save your work. Remember to save the work you've done as a template:

1. Choose File, Save As. The Save As dialog box appears, as shown in Figure 33.3.

FIG. 33.3

Use the Save As command to create your template.

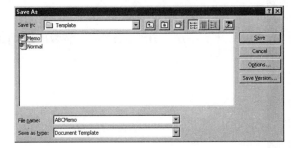

2. Enter the name for your template in the File Name text box.
3. Choose Document Template in the Save as Type drop-down list.
4. Choose OK to complete the command.

You can mark a location in your template by inserting a bookmark at the location. Bookmarks give your VBA code an easy way to move the selection to the bookmarked location, quickly and reliably. This lets you perform any action on the selection, such as typing text, applying formatting, or leaving the insertion point where you want the user to type.

Figure 33.4 shows the ABC memo template with the three bookmarks that are required for our macros:

- The *ccLabel* bookmark identifies the location of the label next to the cc list. If the user decides not to use a cc list, you don't need to display this label. The bookmark will make it easy to select this text for deletion.

- The *ccText* bookmark is in the location where the cc list will be entered, using a DocVariable field code. This field code will be deleted by the macro if the user decides not to use a cc list.

- The *Body* bookmark provides the location where the insertion point will be left at the conclusion of the macro. This is where the user will begin typing the content of the memo.

To create a bookmark in your template, follow these steps:

1. Select the location for the bookmark. The location can either be an insertion point, or some selected text.
2. Choose Insert, Bookmark. The Bookmark dialog box appears, as shown in Figure 33.5.

FIG. 33.4
Bookmarks identify the key locations that the macro needs for automation.

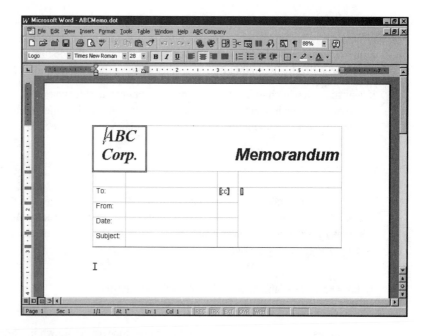

FIG. 33.5
The Bookmark dialog box is used for adding and deleting book-marks in a document or template.

Part VII

Ch 33

3. Type a name for the bookmark in the Bookmark Name text box.

4. Choose Add to add the bookmark.

The user of your template will use a custom form to enter the text for the memo headings that are required by the ABC Memo template. The macro needs a reliable way to move this text from the form to the desired location in the document.

DocVariable field codes provide a convenient and reliable way to display the text that the user has entered in the custom form. Instead of having the macro type the text directly into the document, the macro stores the text in document variables. Document variables can only be used by your macro code, and can't be modified by the user unless she writes her own macro to do so. There is no way for the user to accidentally delete the document variables, by acciden-tally selecting them or typing over them.

The DocVariable field codes are used to display the values of the document variables, at the locations you desire. You can refer to an individual document variable as many times as you want, by placing additional DocVariable codes throughout the document. Each code can be formatted individually, so that its appearance reflects the text around it.

If your macro code changes the value of a document variable, you don't need to modify the DocVariable codes in your document at all. Because the codes refer to the variables, they automatically reflect the modified value of the document variables the next time the field codes are updated.

> **CAUTION**
>
> Field codes do not update themselves automatically, so there is no guarantee that the DocVariable field codes reflect the latest value of the document variables. As with any field code in Word, you can update a DocVariable field code by selecting it and pressing F9. In the VBA code developed later in this chapter, the macro code automatically performs this function.

To insert a DocVariable field code, follow these steps:

1. Select the location in the document or template where you want the field code to appear.
2. Choose Insert, Field. The Field dialog box appears, as shown in Figure 33.6.

FIG. 33.6

The Field dialog box is used to insert field codes in a document or template.

3. Choose Document Automation in the Categories list, and then select DocVariable in the Field Names list.
4. Add the name of the variable you want to display by typing it between quotation marks in the Field codes text box. In Figure 33.6, Author is the name of the document variable that will be displayed in the document.
5. Choose OK to complete the command and insert the field code into the document at the location of the insertion point.

When you insert the field code, it may appear at first as though nothing was inserted. This is the result of the fact that the document variable doesn't yet have a value, so there is nothing to display. How do you know the code was inserted correctly?

At any time you are working with a Word document, you can switch between displaying the results of the field codes in your document, or displaying the codes themselves. To do so, follow these steps:

1. Press Alt+F9 to turn on the display of field codes.

2. Press Alt+F9 again to turn off the display of field codes, displaying the results of the field codes.

Figure 33.7 shows the ABC Memo template, with field codes displayed, after entering DocVariable field codes for the information that will be entered by the user.

FIG. 33.7

DocVariable field codes mark the locations of the data that will be entered by the users of the ABC Memo template.

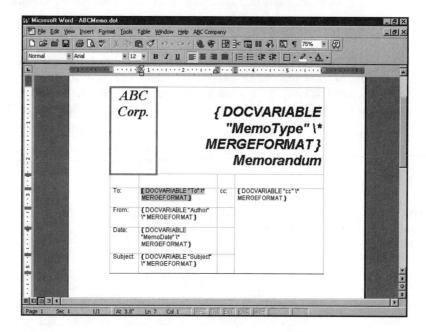

N O T E When you switch to field code display by pressing F9, the document is reformatted to allow enough room to display the contents of the field codes. This may distort the layout of the document. This distortion is temporary, and will be eliminated when you return to Result display by pressing F9 again. To display the field code for only one code at a time, select the field code, then press Shift+F9. ■

Designing the User Interface

After you have designed your template, it's time to begin creating the code for your application. As you can see, you will often invest quite a bit of design time on the template itself, before writing your first line of code.

The VBA programming environment has a custom form design tools that you can use to create your own dialog boxes to get information from the user. Custom dialog boxes have several advantages over allowing the user to enter the text directly into the document:

- Your VBA code will be able the user to enter the input text in the correct location, or better yet, to use document variables to store the text securely.

- You can give the user assistance in entering data by providing list boxes, check boxes, options buttons, and other controls in your forms.

- You can write VBA code that validates the data entry, checking for appropriate entries, and making sure that all required entries are made, before allowing the user to proceed.

- Data entry will be faster, more accurate, and more pleasant for the user as the result of using a well-designed custom form.

Custom dialog boxes, also known as *forms*, are developed using the Visual Basic Editor, or VBE. You customize the forms you create in the VBE by adding *controls*, such as text boxes, command buttons, check boxes, and list boxes. The VBE contains a variety of controls, and can be customized by installing additional controls that are commercially available.

Before using the VBE to design your form, you should plan the form by considering the information you need to gather and the types of controls that should appear on the form. Figure 33.8 shows the form that is used by the ABC Memo template to gather information from the user.

FIG. 33.8

The ABC Corp. Memo dialog box lets the user enter the information that will appear in the memo.

This dialog box contains several types of controls:

- *Text boxes* are used for the To, From, Date, Subject, and cc List data. Text boxes let the user enter text directly.

- A *combo box* is used to select the Memo Type. The user can click the arrow at the right end of the control to display the list.

- A *check box* is used for the Include cc list selection. The user can click the control to make the check box appear, indicating a True value, or disappear, indicating a False value.

- *Command buttons* are used for the OK and Cancel buttons. Clicking these buttons will indicate that the user has completed the data entry, or has decided not to create a memo at this time.

■ *Label* controls are used to display text on the form. Labels often appear next to other controls, to help the user know where to enter data.

The first step in designing the form is to add a form to the template's VBA project. To do so, follow these steps:

1. With your template open, activate the VBE by pressing Alt+F11.
2. Open the Project Explorer window, if it is not already open.
3. Select the TemplateProject item corresponding to the template you are working on.
4. Choose Insert, UserForm. A new form is added to the project and is opened for editing.

You'll probably want to change some properties of the form before adding any controls to the form. To do so, follow these steps:

1. If the Properties window is not displayed, choose View, Properties Window, or press F4.
2. Select the property you want to modify and enter a new value for the property.

There are two properties you should set for each form when you begin your design:

■ The Name property identifies the form in your VBA code. You should supply a descriptive name for the form, to make your code easier to understand. In the ABC Memo template, the form is named *MemoForm*.

■ The Caption property contains the text that appears in the title bar of the form. This should be text that will identify the dialog box to the user.

Figure 33.9 shows a new form after modifying the Name and Caption properties.

FIG. 33.9
The Properties window is used to set the properties of a form or the controls on a form.

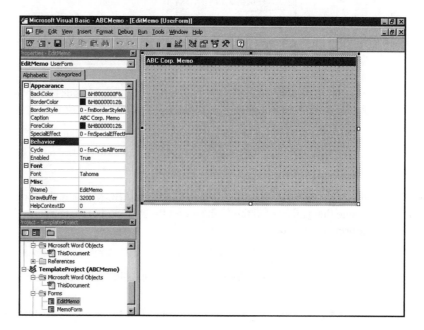

In the case of the ABC Memo form, change the following properties:

■ Set the Name property of the form to *MemoForm*.

■ Set the Caption property of the form to *ABC Corp. Memo*.

Adding Controls to the Form

The toolbox is used to add controls to a form. If the toolbox is not displayed, choose View, Toolbox to show it. The toolbox is shown in Figure 33.10.

FIG. 33.10

The toolbox is used to add controls to a custom form in the VBE.

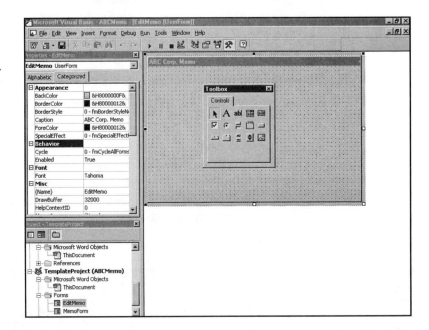

After you have selected the types of controls you need for your form, you can use the toolbox to place the controls on the form. To do so, follow these steps:

1. Click the Toolbox on the control you want to add to your form.

2. Click the form at the location where you want the control to appear.

3. Drag the control to position and size it.

Let's apply these steps to the construction of the ABC Memo dialog box. The following steps assume that you created the form and set the Name and Caption properties, as you learned in the previous section.

The first control you'll place on the form is the label for the combo box.

1. Click on the form to select it. If the Toolbox is not visible, choose View, Toolbox to display it.

2. Using the mouse, click the Label control on the Toolbox, as shown in Figure 33.11.

FIG. 33.11

The user is selecting the Label control before adding it to the form.

3. Point to the location on the form, where you want the label to appear. The appearance of the mouse pointer changes to a crosshair, as shown in Figure 33.12.

FIG. 33.12

The user points to the location where the label will be placed on the form.

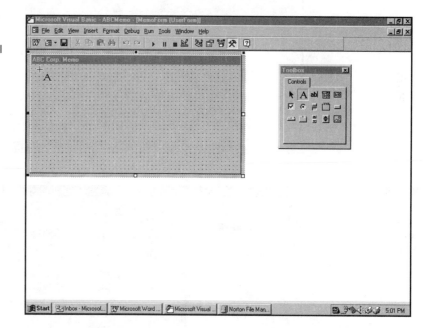

4. Click the form at the desired location. The control is placed on the form.

5. Use the mouse to adjust the size and position of the control. Use the *sizing handles*, which are the boxes that appear around the control, to stretch or shrink it, as shown in Figure 33.13.

6. Now you can change the caption of the label. If the Properties window is not open, press F4 to display it, as shown in Figure 33.14.

Part
VII

Ch
33

FIG. 33.13

Use the sizing handles to adjust the height and width of the control on the form.

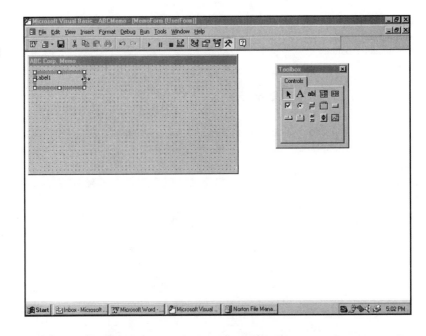

FIG. 33.14

Use the Properties window to change the Caption property of the Label control.

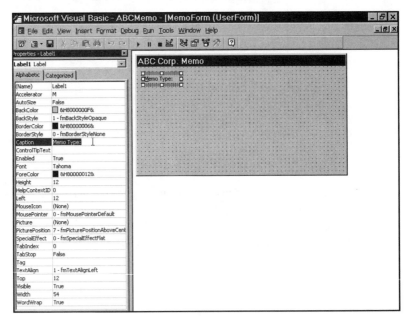

7. Make sure the label is still selected, then edit the Caption property of the label. Change the caption to *Memo Type:*.

The next control you'll add to the form is a combo box for selecting the memo type.

1. Click the form to select it, and display the toolbox.

2. Using the mouse, click the ComboBox control on the toolbox, as shown in Figure 33.15.

3. Point to the location on the form where you want the combo box to appear. The appearance of the mouse pointer changes to a crosshair.

4. Click the form at the desired location. The control is placed on the form.

5. Use the mouse to adjust the size and position of the control.

6. Now you can change the name of the combo box. If the Properties window is not open, press F4 to display it.

7. Make sure the combo box is still selected, then edit the Name property of the label. Change the name to *cmbxMemoType*.

Now you can add another label, which will identify the text box for whom you're sending the memo to.

1. Add another label control immediately under the label you previously placed on the form.

2. Change the Caption property of the label to *To:*.

Next, add the text box that you can use to enter the name to the person you're sending the memo to.

1. Click the form to select it. If the toolbox is not visible, choose <u>V</u>iew, Toolbo<u>x</u> to display it.

2. Using the mouse, click the TextBox control on the toolbox, as shown in Figure 33.16.

3. Point to the location on the form where you want the text box to appear. The appearance of the mouse pointer changes to a crosshair.

4. Click the form at the desired location. The control is placed on the form.

5. Use the mouse to adjust the size and position of the control.

6. Now you can change the Name property of the text box. If the Properties window is not open, press F4 to display it.

7. Make sure the text box is still selected, then edit the Name property of the text box. Change the name to *txtTo*.

FIG. 33.16

The user is selecting the TextBox control before adding it to the form.

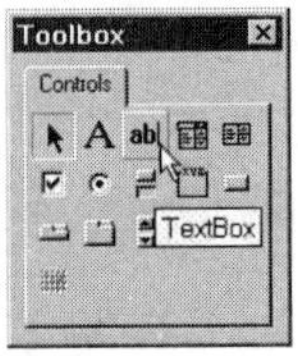

Now you can add some additional labels and text boxes for gathering additional information from the user.

1. Add a label beneath the previous label, and change its Caption property to *From:*.
2. Add a text box beneath the previous text box, and change its Name property to *txtFrom*.
3. Add a label beneath the previous label, and change its Caption property to *Date:*.
4. Add a text box beneath the previous text box, and change its Name property to *txtDate*.
5. Add a label beneath the previous label, and change its Caption property to *Subject:*.
6. Add a text box beneath the previous text box, and change its Name property to *txtSubject*.

Next, you'll use a check box to indicate whether the user wants to include a carbon copy list in the memo. Since a check box control has its own caption, you don't need to add a label control.

1. Click the form to select it, and display the toolbox.
2. Using the mouse, click the CheckBox control on the toolbox, as shown in Figure 33.17.

FIG. 33.17

The user is selecting the CheckBox control before adding it to the form.

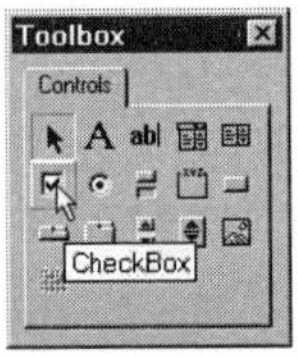

3. Point to the location on the form where you want the check box to appear. The appearance of the mouse pointer changes to a crosshair.
4. Click the form at the desired location. The control is placed on the form.
5. Use the mouse to adjust the size and position of the control.
6. Now you can change the caption of the check box. If the Properties window is not open, press F4 to display it.
7. Make sure the check box is still selected, then edit the Caption property of the label. Change the caption to *Include cc List:*.
8. Change the Name property of the check box to *chkIncludeCC*.

Now you can add the last label and text box to the form.

1. Add a label beneath the check box, and change its Caption property to *cc list:*.

2. Add a text box beneath the label you just added, and change the text box's Name property to *txtCCList*.

3. Because several names might be entered in this text box, adjust the height of the text box to make it tall enough for several names.

4. To allow multiple lines of text to be entered into the text box, change its MultiLine property to *True*.

The last two controls on the form are the command buttons. The user can click one of the buttons to indicate that he or she has completed the entries in the dialog box.

1. Click on the form to select it, and display the toolbox.

2. Using the mouse, click on the CommandButton control on the toolbox, as shown in Figure 33.18.

FIG. 33.18

The user is selecting the CommandButton control before adding it to the form.

3. Point to the location on the form where you want the command button to appear. The appearance of the mouse pointer changes to a crosshair.

4. Click the form at the desired location. The control is placed on the form.

5. Use the mouse to adjust the size and position of the control.

6. Set the Name property of the command button to *OkButton*, and the Caption property to *Ok*.

   Repeat steps 1 through 5 to add a second command button.

7. Set the Name property of the second command button to *CancelButton*, and its Caption property to *Cancel*.

Figure 33.19 shows the results of placing the desired controls on the MemoForm. The text box for receiving the *To* information is selected. The Name properties that you have set for the controls will be used in the VBA code that you will write to automate the form.

Writing the VBA Code

Now that you've designed a template and a form, it's finally time to write some VBA code. You will create several different VBA procedures to display and control a form:

■ A *macro* to display the form. In the ABC Memo template, this will be the event procedure that runs when a new document is created.

■ A *procedure* to dismiss the form. This is usually an event procedure of one of the command buttons on the form.

Part
VII

Ch
33

FIG. 33.19

The ABC Memo template uses the MemoForm to get data from the user.

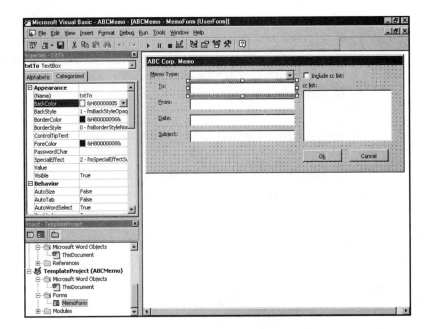

- *Event procedures* will respond to events that occur while the form is open. These events include the initialization of the form, entering data in a control, clicking a control, and many others.

Each template contains a module named ThisDocument, which is a member of the Microsoft Word Objects folder in the Project Explorer window. Double-click ThisDocument to open the document module, which contains the event procedures for the document. There are three event procedures for each document:

- *Document_New* is executed each time a new document is created from this template.

- *Document_Open* is executed each time a document based upon this template is opened.

- *Document_Close* is executed before a document based upon this template is closed.

To display a form you call the Show method of the form. Because the ABC Memo template's dialog box should appear every time a new document is created, Listing 33.1 is entered in the Document_New procedure of the ThisDocument module. The single statement calls the Show method of the form named MemoForm.

Listing 33.1   ABCMEMO.DOT—The *Document_New* Procedure Runs Every Time a New Memo Is Created

```
Private Sub Document_New()

    MemoForm.Show
End Sub
```

Responding to Events of the Form

While a form is displayed, you might want to run some VBA code to perform actions based on events that occur on the form. These events include initializing the form, changing the data of a control, moving from one control to another, or closing the form.

The procedures for responding to these events are created automatically by VBA when you create the form and its controls. All you have to do is to enter the code for any actions you want to take place in response to these events.

Each form that you add to a project contains its own module for storing VBA code. The form module is mainly used for storing the even procedures for responding to the events of the form.

To open the form module for a form, display the Project Explorer window, and select the form whose code you want to edit. Either double-click the form's name, or choose View, Code.

The Initialize event of a form is executed each time the form is loaded. This event is useful for carrying out any actions that you want to happen before the form is actually displayed. To edit this event procedure, follow these steps:

1. Display the form's Code window.
2. In the Code window's Object list, select UserForm.
3. In the Code window's Procedure list, select Initialize. The UserForm_Initialize procedure is displayed.

Listing 33.2 shows the code that you can enter into the UserForm_Initialize procedure, to automatically execute each time the ABC Memo dialog box is displayed. This code performs several functions:

- The AddItem method of the combo box is called five times to supply the list data for the drop-down list.
- The Text property of the combo box is set to an initial value.
- The To, From, and Subject text boxes are initially set to be blank.
- The Date text box is initialized to the current date, and formatted in a particular date format.
- The chkIncludeCC check box is set to False, and the txtCCList and lblCCList controls are made invisible. If the user checks the box later, these controls will be displayed.

Part
VII

Ch
33

Listing 33.2   ABCMEMO.DOT—The *UserForm_Initialze* Procedure Runs When the Form Is First Displayed

```
Private Sub UserForm_Initialize()
    Me.cmbxMemoType.AddItem "Interoffice"
    Me.cmbxMemoType.AddItem "Personnel"
    Me.cmbxMemoType.AddItem "Finance"
    Me.cmbxMemoType.AddItem "Management"
    Me.cmbxMemoType.AddItem "Confidential"
    Me.cmbxMemoType.Text = "InterOffice"
    Me.txtTo.Text = ""
    Me.txtDate.Text = Format(Date, "mmm d, yyyy")
    Me.txtFrom.Text = ""
    Me.txtSubject.Text = ""
    Me.chkIncludeCC = False
    Me.lblCCList.Visible = False
    Me.txtCCList.Visible = False
    Me.txtCCList.Text = ""
End Sub
```

When the user clicks the chkIncludeCC check box, the VBA code needs to make the corresponding label and text box visible. Clicking the check box again should hide the list. Notice that when the check box becomes True, the SetFocus method of the txtCCList text box is called. This moves the insertion point into the text box automatically.

The VBA code to perform these actions is entered into the Click event procedure for the check box. To edit this procedure, follow these steps:

1. Display the form's Code window.

2. In the Code window's Object list, select chkIncludeCC.

3. In the Code window's Procedure list, select Click. The chkIncludeCC_Click procedure is displayed.

Listing 33.3 shows the event processing code for this control.

Listing 33.3   ABCMEMO.DOT—The *chIncludeCC_Click* Procedure Displays or Hides the Label and Text Box for Entering the cc List

```
Private Sub chkIncludeCC_Click()
    If Me.chkIncludeCC = True Then
        Me.lblCCList.Visible = True
        Me.txtCCList.Visible = True
        Me.txtCCList.SetFocus
    Else
        Me.lblCCList.Visible = False
        Me.txtCCList.Visible = False
    End If
End Sub
```

Using the Form's Data in a Document

To update the ABC Memo document with the data from the Custom dialog box, your VBA code must respond to the closing of the dialog box. Because the OkButton and CancelButton controls are used to close the dialog box, you can put the code to control the closing process in these two buttons. Additionally, the initial routine that displayed the form will be modified to complete the updating operation.

The code in the OkButton control can also be used to validate the user input. You can check to see that all required entries have been made before allowing the form to be closed. Listing 33.4 shows the code for the OkButton control.

The procedure begins by setting an integer variable, OkToClose, to True. This sets the assumption that you are going to allow the form to close. Next the Len function is used to check the length of the text entered into the To, From, Date, and Subject text boxes. If any of the text boxes are empty, the OkToClose variable is set to False.

If OkToClose is still True, the Hide method is called to make the form invisible, and the global variable CreateMemo is set to True. Otherwise, a message is displayed reminding the user to finish the data entry before continuing.

The VBA code to perform these actions is stored in the Click event procedure of the OkButton control. Follow these steps to edit this procedure:

1. Display the form's Code window.
2. In the Code window's Object list, select OkButton.
3. In the Code window's Procedure list, select Click. The OkButton_Click procedure is displayed.

Listing 33.4 ABCMEMO.DOT—The *OkButton_Click* Code Checks to See Whether All Required Entries Have Been Made Before Closing the Form

```
Private Sub OKButton_Click()
    Dim OkToClose As Integer

    OkToClose = True
    If Len(Me.txtTo.Text) = 0 Then OkToClose = False
    If Len(Me.txtFrom.Text) = 0 Then OkToClose = False
    If Len(Me.txtDate.Text) = 0 Then OkToClose = False
    If Len(Me.txtSubject.Text) = 0 Then OkToClose = False
    If OkToClose = True Then
        Me.Hide
        CreateMemo = True
    Else
        MsgBox "Data entry error! All fields must be filled in.", _
            vbOKOnly + vbExclamation, "ABC Memo Error"
    End If
End Sub
```

Listing 33.5 shows the code for the Cancel Button, which simply hides the form and sets the CreateMemo variable to False.

The VBA code to perform these actions is stored in the Click event procedure of the CancelButton control. Follow these steps to edit this procedure:

1. Display the form's Code window.

2. In the Code window's Object list, select CancelButton.

3. In the Code window's Procedure list, select Click. The CancelButton_Click procedure is displayed.

Listing 33.5   ABCMEMO.DOT—The *CancelButton_Click* Procedure Closes the Form

```
Private Sub CancelButton_Click()
    Me.Hide
    CreateMemo = False
End Sub
```

The global variable CreateMemo is used to determine whether the user clicked the OkButton or the CancelButton to close the form. To make the variable global to the template, the following line of code is entered into a standard module in the template.

```
Public CreateMemo As Integer
```

Now that the document has been dismissed, you can use the data from the form to update the document. The Document_New procedure has been modified as shown in Listing 33.6, to update the document.

After calling the Show method of the form, the procedure waits until the form has been dismissed before continuing its execution. At this point the procedure checks the value of the CreateMemo variable to determine which button was used to dismiss the dialog box. If the value is True, the memo will be created, but if the value is False, the active document is closed without being saved.

If the user selected the OkButton, the following actions are carried out by the VBA code:

1. The document variables corresponding to the DocVariable field codes are updated with the values from the form. For example, the following line of code sets the "To" variable with the contents of the Text property of the txtTo control:

   ```
   ActiveDocument.Variables("To") = MemoForm.txtTo.Text
   ```

2. The code checks the value of the chkIncludeCC check box. If it is True, the "CC" document variable is updated. If the check box is False, the procedure selects the "ccLabel" and "ccText" bookmarks, and deletes their contents.

3. All the fields in the document are updated, so the current results are displayed.

4. The "Body" bookmark is selected, so the user can begin typing.

5. Several display properties are set, so the users will get a consistent screen appearance each time the macro runs.

Listing 33.6   ABCMEMO.DOT—The *Document_New* Procedure Displays the Form and Responds to the Entries in the Form

```
Private Sub Document_New()
    Dim fld As Field

    MemoForm.Show
    If CreateMemo = True Then
        MemoForm.Hide
        ActiveDocument.Variables("MemoType") = MemoForm.cmbxMemoType.Text
        ActiveDocument.Variables("To") = MemoForm.txtTo.Text
        ActiveDocument.Variables("Author") = MemoForm.txtFrom.Text
        ActiveDocument.Variables("MemoDate") = MemoForm.txtDate.Text
        ActiveDocument.Variables("Subject") = MemoForm.txtSubject.Text
        If MemoForm.chkIncludeCC = True Then
            ActiveDocument.Variables("cc") = MemoForm.txtCCList.Text
        Else
            ActiveDocument.Bookmarks("ccLabel").Select
            Selection.Delete
            ActiveDocument.Bookmarks("ccText").Select
            Selection.Delete
        End If
        For Each fld In ActiveDocument.Fields
            fld.Update
        Next
        ActiveDocument.Bookmarks("Body").Select
        ActiveWindow.View.TableGridlines = False
        ActiveWindow.ActivePane.View.ShowAll = False
        ActiveWindow.View.ShowFieldCodes = False
        ActiveWindow.View.ShowBookmarks = False
        Unload MemoForm
    Else
        'User cancelled the dialog, so close the document
        ' without saving.
        Unload MemoForm
        ActiveDocument.Close SaveChanges:=False
    End If
End Sub
```

Part
VII

Ch

33

Deploying the Application

Automated solutions, such as the ABC Memo template that is demonstrated in this chapter, can be distributed throughout an organization. The applications and customizations that you create for Word can be installed on a network file server, minimizing the administrative work associated with installing and maintaining the applications for many users. The applications can also be installed on stand-alone computers, an important option for laptop computer users or for organizations that don't use a network. The key to designing your installation strategy efficiently is a thorough understanding of how Word works with templates.

Installing Global and Document Templates

Because your macros are stored in templates, it's important to know where you should install your templates for easiest installation and support, for networked and stand-alone systems. First, you must understand the three different categories of templates that are recognized by Word. The easiest way to categorize the types of templates is by examining the File Locations settings as shown in Figure 33.20. You can display this dialog box by choosing Tools, Options, then selecting the File Locations tab.

FIG. 33.20

Use the File Locations tab of the Options dialog box to customize your installation.

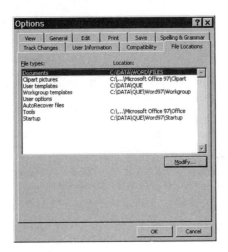

There are four settings in the File Locations settings that are important to understand in order to design your installation:

- *Documents.* This is the default directory for saving new documents created by the user. This directory is often set as a private directory on a network, or a local hard drive directory.

- *User templates.* This is the directory that contains the Normal.dot template, and any other templates created by each user. This directory should be a private directory on the network, or a local hard drive directory.

CAUTION

The User Templates directory should not be a shared directory, and it is not recommended that you attempt to share the Normal.dot template. Word is designed to let each user save his or her macros in a unique Normal template, which requires write-access to the file. If you need to share global macros among all your users, you can store them in a global template that is stored in the Startup directory, as described in the bullets that follow.

■ *Workgroup templates.* This directory contains the templates that you design for specific applications, such as the ABC Memo template. On a network, you can make this a shared directory, to which the users have read-only access. This enables you to make the application widely available, without the risk of the users accidentally making changes to the templates. Of course, you can always set the Workgroup Templates directory to a local directory on the user's hard drive, which is necessary for laptop and other stand-alone users.

 If you have a lot of templates to store in your User and Workgroup Template directories, you might want to create additional directories to keep the templates separated by category. If you create sub-directories immediately beneath the User or Workgroup template directories, these directories are represented as additional tabs on the New dialog box that appears when you choose the File, New command, as shown in Figure 33.21.

FIG. 33.21
The New dialog box displays tabs representing subdirectories of the User and Workgroup Template directories.

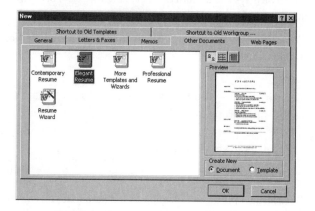

■ *Startup.* This directory can be used to store templates that you want to load automatically at the time that Word is started. Templates in this directory are loaded invisibly and in read-only mode, but the macros, menus, and toolbars in the templates are available for use. These templates are sometimes referred to as "other global templates," in contrast to the Normal template, which is known as the "global template" for each user. On a network, the Startup directory can be a shared, read-only directory, to minimize the number of copies of these templates that you need to distribute.

 Global templates that you place in the Startup directory provide the most efficient method for sharing general-purpose macros, menu customizations, and toolbars among all your users. Because the templates are loaded in read-only mode, the users can't accidentally change the macros in these templates, but they still have full write-access to their own Normal templates.

Part
VII

Ch
33

Creating Custom Toolbars and Menus

The automated ABC Memo template you created in this chapter is designed to run automatically, every time you create a new document based upon the template. The user can create a new ABC memo by choosing the File, New command and selecting the ABC Memo template. However, by creating custom menus or toolbars you can make it even easier for the user to create a new memo.

The custom menus or toolbars that you create are used to run a simple macro that creates a new ABC Memo. This macro is shown in Listing 33.7. The macro creates a new document by adding a document to the collection of open documents, basing the new document upon the indicated template.

Because the new document is based upon the ABCMemo template, the Document_New procedure in that template runs automatically when the new document is created. The Document_New procedure, in turn, displays the MemoForm, causing the UserForm_Initialize procedure to run. This chain of events is typical of the programming process in VBA.

The NewABCMemo macro can be stored in any module in the user's Normal template, or in any module in a global template.

Listing 33.7   ABC.DOT—The NewABCMemo Macro Creates a New Document Based upon the ABCMemo Template

```
Sub NewABCMemo()
    Documents.Add Template:="ABCMemo"
End Sub
```

The NewABCMemo macro is a good example of a macro that you can store in a global template. In the ABC Corporation example, you can create a template called ABC.DOT, saving the new template in your Startup directory. Then create the new macro in the ABC template.

Toolbars and Menus are actually two special cases of the Command Bars that have been added to Office 97 applications, including Word 97. You can customize both toolbars and menus by using the same process.

1. Open the template in which you want to make customizations to the menus and toolbars.

2. Choose Tools, Customize. The Customize dialog box appears, as shown in Figure 33.22.

3. Click to activate the check box for any toolbars you want to have open for customization. The Menu Bar item refers to the menu at the top of the application window.

4. Select the Commands tab to activate the panel that lets you select commands and macros to be added to the toolbars and menus. The Commands tab is displayed in Figure 33.23.

FIG. 33.22

The Customize command lets you select the toolbars that are displayed in Word.

FIG. 33.23

The Commands tab of the Customize dialog box is used to add buttons to toolbars and menus.

5. Select Macros in the Categories list, and then in the Commands list select the macro you want to add to a toolbar or menu.

N O T E Unfortunately, the Commands list in the Customize dialog box is not wide enough to display most long macro names. It's a good idea to keep a list of the macros you have created, so you can select the correct macro from the alphabetical list. ▨

6. Make sure to select the template where you want to store your customizations in the Save In tab.

7. Drag the macro name from its position in the Commands list to the position in the toolbar or menu where you want the customization to appear. Figure 33.24 shows the NewABCMemo macro command being dragged on the Standard toolbar. Figure 33.25 shows the new command as it appears on the toolbar, after releasing the mouse pointer.

FIG. 33.24

The NewABCMemo macro command is being dragged onto the Standard toolbar.

Location of the new ABC Memo button

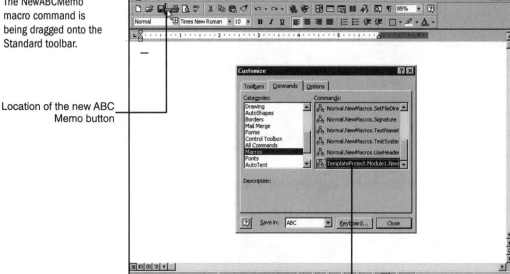

Macro name that is placed on the toolbar

Now you can use the new toolbar button to run your macro, creating a new memo document. You could stop here, but chances are, you'll want to improve the appearance of the toolbar button. You can edit the toolbar button so that it displays text, a button image, or both. To do so, follow these steps:

1. If the Customize dialog is not open choose Tools, Customize.

2. Right-click the button you want to modify. The context menu appears, as shown in Figure 33.25.

3. Select the command you want to use to change the button's appearance:

   - Click next to the Name command to edit the text that appears on the button.

   - Choose Change Button Image to select from a collection of pre-designed button images.

   - Choose Edit Button Image to display a graphical editor for drawing or modifying the button image.

   - Choose Default Style to display the button as an image on a toolbar, or as text and image on a menu.

   - Choose Text Only (Always) to display text only on either menus or toolbars.

   - Choose Text Only (in Menus) to display text only on a menu.

- Choose Image and Text to display both an image and text, on both toolbars and menus.

- Choose Begin a Group to place a separator immediately before the current button or menu command.

4. Choose Close in the Customize dialog box to complete the customizations and return to normal operation.

FIG. 33.25

The context menu for customizing toolbar buttons lets you change the appearance of the button face.

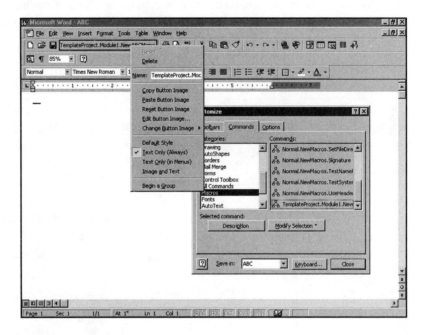

Figure 33.26 shows the Standard toolbar after the ABC Memo button has been set to display both an image and text. Figure 33.27 shows the File menu after it has been customized with a new command that creates a new ABC Memo.

TROUBLESHOOTING

There are several lines of code that I'd like to skip over while I'm testing my code, but I'll need to restore the lines later. Is there a quick way to do this? Yes. In the VBE, display the Edit toolbar, which has a pair of buttons named Comment Block and Uncomment Block. Select the lines you want to skip over, and click the Comment Block button to put comment characters at the beginning of every line that you have selected. To remove the comments, select the lines that you previously commented, and click the Uncomment Block button.

continues

continued

I set the value of a variable in my VBA code, and I'd like to use that value the next time I run the macro. This doesn't seem to work, since VBA doesn't store the value of the variable once the macro stops running. Is there a way around this? Yes. As the question infers, VBA doesn't store the value of a variable between executions of a macro or procedure. You can use a document variable to store the value of a VBA variable for later use.

Suppose you have a variable called UserName, containing a string value. To store the value in a document variable, assign the contents of the variable to a member of the Variables collection.

```
ActiveDocument.Variables("UserName") = UserName
```

To retrieve the value the next time the macro runs, just reverse the assignment.

```
UserName = ActiveDocument.Variables("UserName")
```

FIG. 33.26
The ABC Memo button is always available, whenever you want to create a new memo.

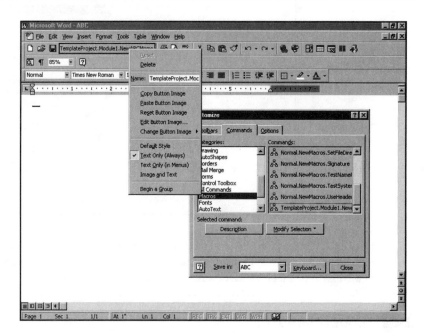

FIG. 33.27
The File menu has been customized with a new ABC Memo command.

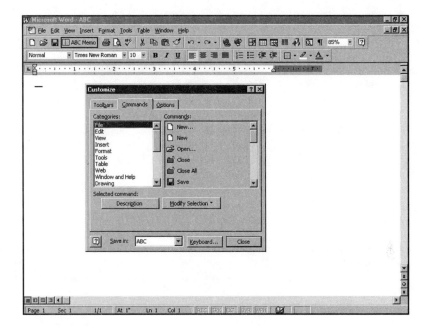

From Here...

In this chapter, you designed a complete automated application in Word, taking advantage of template design, custom dialog boxes, VBA code, and custom toolbars and menus.

Part
VII

Ch
33

Appendixes

Business Sites on the Web

by Joe Lowery

This appendix is a listing of business resources you can find on the Internet. Whether you're just in the planning and startup phase of your business, involved in international trade, need legal or accounting assistance, or interested in the latest trade shows and conferences, you'll find a Web site that can help you find answers. ■

Business Startup and Planning

America's Brightest

http://www.americasbrightest.com/

This Santa Monica-based organization describes itself as the "one-stop shop" for small businesses and working professionals. A subscription-based service with a one-month free trial, America's Brightest offers giveaways and a wide range of discussion groups.

Big Dreams

http://vanbc.wimsey.com/~duncans/

Big Dreams is an online newsletter dedicated to individuals starting their own business. Visit the site and play the Business Game to ask yourself key questions about your new business, or take a look through current and archived issues for topical articles.

BizTalk

http://www.biztalk.com/

BizTalk is an electronic magazine devoted to small business. Departments include news, finance, law, politics, technology and more. *BizTalk* runs contests to provide seed money for start-ups.

Business Plan Resource File

http://www.aifr.com/startup.html

Sponsored by the American Institute for Financial Research, this site is designed to help emerging business with their first business plan. A full compendium of general advice is offered in addition to having information on interactive business plan software.

Business Research Lab

http://spider.netropolis.net/brl/brl1.htm

This site is dedicated to the development of market research, an essential element for start-ups. Filled with tips and articles on conducting surveys and focus groups, the site also has a large number of sample surveys on file.

BuyersZone

http://www.buyerszone.com/index.html

BuyersZone is an online buyer's guide for businesses. It includes articles on what to look for in everything from 401(k) plans to voice mail systems. Also featured is The Inside Scoop, which offers the latest tips and stories of "buying disasters."

CCH Business Owner's Toolkit

http://www.toolkit.cch.com/

CCH (Commerce Clearing House) features articles on Small Office, Home Office (SOHO) guides to everyday business, coupled with a comprehensive listing of business tools, including model business forms, financial templates, and checklists.

Education, Training, and Development Resource Center for Business and Industry

http://www.tasl.com/tasl/home.html

This page, sponsored by Training and Seminar Locators Inc., offers help in finding business education resources. An index of qualified training providers and information about products and services is included.

Internal Revenue Service

http://www.irs.ustreas.gov/

An important step in planning your business is to establish your tax status and potential responsibilities. The new IRS site has a special "Tax Info for Business" section with many helpful tax guides, including the Tax Calendar to keep track of special deadlines; a Business Tax Kit, a downloadable package of forms and publications; and the interactive Tax Trails for Business.

LinkExchange

http://www.linkexchange.com/

LinkExchange is an online advertising network that claims more than 100,000 members. If you have a Web site to promote, you can join for free; you then display ads for other members, and they display ads for you. There are also low-cost paid services.

Marketing Resource Center

http://www.marketingsource.com/

A free service of Concept Marketing Group, Inc., the Marketing Resource Center has an extensive articles library on planning your business, marketing tools and contacts, a database of industry associations, and links to online business magazines.

Marketshares

http://www.marketshares.com/

Marketshares tracks the best commercial and corporate Web sites. You can use their built-in search engine or browse their categories including Arts & Entertainment, Business & Technology, Finance & Money, and Travel & Transportation. Most links include a paragraph describing the site.

PRONET

http://www.pronett.com/

PRONET is a Multilingual Interactive Business Centre: The corporate philosophy is to help small- to medium-sized businesses grow by helping them use the Internet as a natural extension of their communications and marketing programs.

Occupational Safety and Health Administration

http://www.osha.gov/

Aside from a wealth of information on health and safety regulations and statistics, the OSHA site features software advisors that you can download on confined space standards, and asbestos regulations to help you figure out your requirements.

Small Business Advisor

http://www.isquare.com/

A terrific collection of articles for the new businessperson forms the core of this site. Example titles include "Don't Make these Business Mistakes," "Getting Paid," and "Government Small Business Resources." You'll also find tax advice and a glossary of business terms.

Small Business Workshop

http://www.sb.gov.bc.ca:80/smallbus/workshop/workshop.html

Sponsored by the Canadian government, this site has a host of articles for any business around the world. Areas include Starting Your Business, Marketing Basics, Planning Fundamentals, Financing Your Business, and Basic Regulations.

Tax Planning

http://www.hooked.net/cpa/plan/index.html

"An ounce of prevention…" is certainly worth more than a pound when it comes to taxes. This site specializes in information on tax planning—for individuals, businesses, and even an IRS audit. Take the tax challenge to find out how much you don't know about taxes.

Tax Prophet

http://www.taxprophet.com/

Hosted by Robert Sommers, the tax columnist for the *San Francisco Examiner*, the Tax Prophet has a number of FAQ files on tax issues and tax information for foreigners living in the U.S. The Interactive Tax Applications is very informative; try the Independent Contractor versus Employee Flowchart to check your job status.

U.S. Small Business Administration

http://www.sbaonline.sba.gov/

SBA Online is your online resource to government assistance for the small businessman. The site is organized into special areas on Starting, Financing, and Expanding Your Business as well as other information on SCORE, PRONET, and local SBA links.

Business Financing

Angel Capital Electronic Network

http://www.sbaonline.sba.gov/ADVO/acenet.html

Angel Capital Electronic Network, or ACE-Net, is an Internet-based network sponsored by the SBA's Office of Advocacy. The site gives new options for small companies seeking investments in the range of $250,000 to $5 million.

America Business Funding Directory

http://www.businessfinance.com/

America Business Funding Directory is the first search engine dedicated to finding business capital. You can search categories ranging from venture capital to equipment lending to real estate, as well as a private capital network of accredited investors.

Bankruptcy FAQs

http://site206125.primehost.com/faqs.html

Sponsored by Gold & Stanley, P.C., commercial bankruptcy lawyers, this site answers many basic questions about the ins-and-outs of bankruptcy from all perspectives. Topics include "How to Recover Money" and "10 Things to Do when a Bankruptcy Is Filed."

Closing Bell

http://www.merc.com/cb/cgi/cb_merc.cgi

Closing Bell provides a daily e-mail message containing closing prices and news for a personalized portfolio of market indices, mutual funds, and securities from the three major U.S. exchanges. Visitors can also sign up for news alerts during the day for followed companies.

Computer Loan Network

http://www.clnet.com/

Borrowers can use this Web site to add a loan Request for Proposal (RFP) directly to the CLN MortgageNet mortgage multiple listing service. Mortgage brokers, lenders, banks, and secondary marketers will search the system, locate your RFP, and then find ways to offer you a lower note rate than your currently quoted rate, if possible.

Currency Converter

http://www.oanda.com/cgi-bin/ncc

An interactive Web page designed to allow you to see current conversions for 164 currencies. Convert your U.S. dollars to everything from the Albanian lek ($1 = 155 leks) to the Zambian kwacha ($1 = 1,310 kwacha). You can also check the previous day's rates or download a customizable currency converter.

EDGAR Database

http://www.sec.gov/edgarhp.htm

EDGAR, the Electronic Data Gathering, Analysis, and Retrieval system, performs automated collection, validation, indexing, acceptance, and forwarding of submissions by companies and others who are required by law to file forms with the U.S. Securities and Exchange Commission (SEC). Its primary purpose is to increase the efficiency and fairness of the securities market for the benefit of investors, corporations, and the economy. EDGAR is also a great resource of filing examples.

Export-Import Bank of the U.S.

http://www.exim.gov/

The Export-Import Bank offers programs on loans and guarantees, working capital, and export credit insurance. All the necessary application forms can be found online here with additional literature on importing from and exporting to various countries around the world.

FinanceNet

http://www.financenet.gov/

FinanceNet was established by Vice President Al Gore's National Performance Review in Washington, D.C. in 1994 and is operated by the National Science Foundation. This site features a listing of government asset sales including a subscription to daily sales.

Financial Women International

http://www.fwi.org/

Founded in 1921, Financial Women International serves women in the financial services industry who seek to expand their personal and professional capabilities through self-directed growth in a supportive environment. FWI's vision is to empower women in the financial services industry to attain their professional, economic, and personal goals, and to influence the future shape of the industry.

National Credit Counseling Service

http://www.nccs.org/

The National Credit Counseling Service's Web site features news about its Debt Management Program for businesses and individuals, as well a full range of information on credit, budgeting, and financial planning.

Prospect Street

http://www.prospectstreet.com/

Prospect Street is a venture capital firm specializing in resources for high-tech entrepreneurs: information technology, software, the Internet, and wireless communications. Its site has links to investment, stock, and technical research sources.

Securities and Exchange Commission

http://www.sec.gov/smbus1.htm

This page of the SEC site opens its small business area where you can find information on taking your small business public. In addition to a complete Q&A, you'll also find current and pending initiatives of interest.

U.S. Tax Code On-Line

http://www.fourmilab.ch/ustax/ustax.html

This Web page allows access to the complete text of the U.S. Internal Revenue Title 26 of the Code (26 U.S.C.). To make cross-referencing easy, hyperlinks are embedded throughout the text.

International Business and Trade

Asia-Pacific Economic Cooperation

http://www.apecsec.org.sg/

Based in Singapore, this organization's Web site carries information on the economies of its 18 member countries, information on intellectual property rights overseas, and a financial procedures guidebook with government procurement outlines.

Bureau of Export Administration

http://www.bxa.doc.gov/

A key element of this site is the EAR Marketplace, a one-stop source for timely Export Administration Regulations data, including a current, searchable copy of the Export Administration Regulations online. You can also find current information on U.S. encryption policy here.

Central and Eastern Europe Business Information Center

http://www.itaiep.doc.gov/eebic/ceebic.html

CEEBIC is a primary information source for doing business in the emerging markets of central and eastern Europe. Each country has a full profile that includes market research and business and trade opportunities. A recently added page features tax and VAT rates for the area.

Contact! The Canadian Management Network

http://strategis.ic.gc.ca/sc_mangb/contact/engdoc/homepage.html

This bilingual (English and French) site features links to more than 1,500 Canadian small business support organizations. Here you'll also find a small business handbook on doing business in Canada and information on cross-cultural business strategies.

The Electronic Embassy

http://www.embassy.org/

The Electronic Embassy provides information on embassies for every country with special attention to those on the Internet. There is also an International Business Center that spotlights commercial and nonprofit organizations providing goods, services, or opportunities to international markets.

ExporTutor

http://web.miep.org/tutor/index.html

Is your business export ready? Follow this site's 10-Step Road Map to Success in Foreign Markets, developed by Michigan State University's International Business Center, to find out. There's also a Quick Consultant with valuable information on everything from Accounting to Value Chain Analysis.

India Market Place

http://www.indiaintl.com/

Here you'll find in-depth information on doing business in India, Indian business news updated every business day, extensive information about trade shows being held in India and links to India-based business management resources, directories and databases, and associations.

TrADE-Net Italy

http://www.tradenet.it/

Italy is filled with small- to medium-sized companies known for their quality and desire to export. TrADE-Net Italy has a searchable industry directory organized by category—perfect for finding your company just the right import item.

Venture Web—Japan

http://www.venture-web.or.jp/

Searching for a Japanese connection? Whether you're looking for a partner in Japan or marketing your availability to the Japanese market, you can submit your request for posting on the site. Other areas of the site have information on export/import regulations and human resource links.

Web of Culture

http://www.worldculture.com/index.html

The Web of Culture is an wonderful site to visit before working with or going to a new country. The site includes information on business, religion, resources, and holidays. There's even a very visual page about gestures and their meanings in different countries.

Job Opportunities and Labor Resources

AFL-CIO

http://www.aflcio.org/

The AFL-CIO Web site focuses on information on unionization and other labor-related issues. New sections include an Executive Pay Watch, Ergonomics, Working Women, and Summer Jobs for Seniors.

America's Job Bank

http://www.ajb.dni.us/

A multi-state project of the public Employment Service, America's Job Bank is for both employers and employees. A section on Occupational Employment trends offers in interactive outlook handbook and answers to many surveys such as, "What's the fastest growing occupation?"

Computer Register

http://www.computerregister.com/

If you're in the market for computer consultants or related services, check out these extensive advertisements, including employment. Classifieds are provided for both job seekers and employers.

CareerPath.com

http://www.careerpath.com/

CareerPath.com posts more than 400,000 new jobs on the Internet every month, and is updated daily by newspapers across the U.S. You can search their help wanted database by category, newspaper, and keyword.

Department of Labor

http://www.dol.gov/

The government site has information on minimum wage regulations, labor protections and welfare reform, and small business retirement solutions. Visitors can access "America's Job Bank" as well as such for regulatory and statutory information.

Ernst & Young's Virtual HR Office

http://www.idirect.com/hroffice/

This site is a resource center for the human resource professional which includes a chat room, bulletin board, newsletter and links to other HR sites in both the U.S. and Canada.

E-Span

http://www.espan.com/

Connecting the right person with the right job is what E-Span is all about. Visitors can access a resume database, a reference and resource library, and information on career fairs.

JobWeb

http://www.jobweb.org/

Run by the National Associations of Colleges and Employers, JobWeb lists jobs, employer profiles, and career planning resources. One resource, the Catapult, offers a variety of career assessment tools.

National Center for Employee Ownership

http://www.nceo.org/

The National Center for Employee Ownership (NCEO) is a private nonprofit organization. The NCEO site is a leading source of information on employee stock ownership plans (ESOPs), stock options, and other forms of employee ownership.

Telecommuting, Teleworking, and Alternative Officing

http://www.gilgordon.com/

This site features telecommuting information from around the world, and from many different perspectives, on the subjects of telecommuting, teleworking, the virtual office, and related topics. Includes a FAQ section and listing of upcoming events.

Legal and Regulatory

American Law Source Online (ALSO)

http://www.lawsource.com/also/

This site is notable because it has links to all American online legal systems, including the Federal judiciary and all 50 states and territories. ALSO has equally far-reaching coverage of Canadian and Mexican law.

Business Law Site

http://members.aol.com/bmethven/index.html

Sponsored by Methven & Associates, the Business Law Site covers federal and state statutes, and legal research sites for both business and high-tech law. You can also find a full compendium of tax forms, information on international law, and a listing of legal research sites.

Corporate Counselor

http://www.ljx.com/corpcounselor/index.html

The Corporate Counselor has resources including daily news, columns, and articles on employment law, securities, antitrust, and other business issues.

Department of Labor Poster Page

http://www.dol.gov/dol/osbp/public/sbrefa/poster.htm

A fixture in every American workplace finds its online equivalent: the Department of Labor mandatory notices. So far, you can download posters for the minimum wage requirements, OSHA, the Family Leave Act, and the Equal Opportunity Act. All posters are in PDF format; you'll need a PDF reader like Adobe Acrobat (http://www.adobe.com).

International Trade Law

http://itl.irv.uit.no/trade_law/

Sponsored by the Law Department at Norway's University of Tromsø, you can search this site for virtually any subject related to international trade law. Typical topics include Dispute Resolution, Customs, Protection of Intellectual Property, GATT, and other free trade treaties.

The Legal Information Institute

http://www.law.cornell.edu/

Sponsored by Cornell University, the Legal Information Institute Web site houses its collection of recent and historic Supreme Court decisions, hypertext versions of the full U.S. Code, U.S. Constitution, Federal Rules of Evidence and Civil Procedure, and recent opinions of the New York Court of Appeals complete with commentary. Fully indexed and searchable.

QuickForms Online

http://www.quickforms.com/

QuickForms is an easy-to-use interactive system that drafts sophisticated agreements automatically weighted in your favor. Answer a view questions online, and you have your draft agreement in 10 minutes. A wide range of contracts are available.

Magazines Online

Advertising Age

http://www.adage.com/

All the information you could ever need about the movers and shakers of advertising. The site features a section on getting the most out of your Web site called NetMarketing as well as the DataPlace, featuring industry reports and statistics.

Barron's Online

http://www.barrons.com/

In addition to complete contents of their weekly publication, *Barron's Online* features the ability to examine most companies mentioned in their articles through the Barron Dossiers. *Barron's Online* requires a free registration.

BusinessWeek

http://www.businessweek.com/

BusinessWeek's online-only content includes Maven, the interactive computer shopper, and BW Plus with listings of the best business schools, business book reviews, and articles on the computer industry and the Information Age. You can also access BW Radio—hourly market reports in RealAudio format.

Disgruntled

http://www.disgruntled.com/

Describing itself as "The Business Magazine for People Who Work for a Living," *Disgruntled* provides an irreverent look at being employed. There's even a Boss Button on every page which takes you to a proper-looking spreadsheet when the boss is looking over your shoulder.

Entrepreneurial Edge Online

http://www.edgeonline.com/

Articles aimed at the innovative entrepreneur fill this site. You also find a Pointers from the Pros section, a SmallBizNet (with a full digital library), and the Interactive Toolbox, a series of self-calculating worksheets and benchmarking and assessment tools.

Fast Company

http://www.fastcompany.com/

A new edge business magazine with a host of "how-to" articles: how to make a group decision like a tribe, how to deal with the issues of dating and sexual harassment on the job, how to choose a career counselor, how to disagree (without being disagreeable), and more.

Financial Times

http://www.usa.ft.com/

The online edition of the *Financial Times* is divided into three sections: News & Comment, with "tastes" of articles from the newspaper as well as stock market information updated every 30 minutes; Themes & Topics, for categorized articles; and Connect & Respond, where online visitors can find services, such as recruitment advertising and library of annual reports.

Forbes Digital Tool

http://www.forbes.com/

In addition to current and archived articles from Forbes, this Web site features the Toolbox, a collection of reports and indices; ASAP, Forbes' supplement on the Information Age; Angles, a section on media and politics; and access to a free Investment Monitor.

Fortune

http://www.pathfinder.com/fortune/

Can't wait to see if you made the 500 this year? Check out the digital version of the famous survey as well as online areas dedicated to the stock market, mobile computing, managing your money, and information technology. You'll also find a special Fortune Forum for exchanging views on investing and related matters.

Hispanic Business Magazine

http://www.hispanstar.com/

This site covers information for business owners and professional with a Hispanic interest. There is also a national resume referral service, a market research area focusing on the U.S. Hispanic economic market, and a special events department that provides a calendar of events.

Inc. Online

http://www.inc.com/

Self-described as the "Web site for Growing Companies," *Inc. Online* is actually several minisites, including Inc. itself, with articles and archives; Business & Technology, with statistics to benchmark your business; and Local Business News, where you can choose from more than 25 U.S. cities for local business news and resources.

MoneyWorld Online

http://www.money-world.net/

MoneyWorld Online features investing information and tips on the most promising investment opportunities. *MoneyWorld* offers "hot-pick" IPOs, a series of long and short picks and growth industry surveys.

Red Herring

http://www.herring.com/mag/home.html

Red Herring provides business information for the technology and entertainment industries with a special focus on emerging markets. Their online site features an Entrepreneurs Resource Center with workshops on the unique challenges facing business startups.

Success Magazine

http://www.SuccessMagazine.com/

The *Success* site includes a searchable archive of past articles, a survey of the best 100 franchises (with links), and the Source, a compendium of business-related links, organized by subject.

The Wall Street Journal—Small Business Suite

http://update.wsj.com/public/current/summaries/small.htm

Although the interactive *Wall Street Journal* is a subscription service ($49 per year), this service is free. Articles of interest to small business are the primary feature here along with a series of discussion groups, Web resources, and a business locator.

Marketing and Market Research

American Demographics/Marketing Tools

http://www.marketingtools.com/

At the American Demographics/Marketing Tools Web site, you can check out consumer trends, tactics and techniques for information marketers, or access *Forecast*, a newsletter of demographic trends and market forecasts.

American Marketing Association

http://www.ama.org/

AMA is a national organization of marketing professionals. Their Web site features a special section on Internet marketing ethics as well as a calendar of events, publications, and information on regional chapters.

Business Intelligence Center

http://future.sri.com/

What type of person is your customer? The Values and Lifestyles (VALS) program at SRI Consulting, hosts of this site, studies consumers by asking questions about their attitudes and values. You can answer an online questionnaire to determine your VALS type—and see how you fit with other consumers.

Business Wire

http://www.businesswire.com/

Business Wire is a leading source of news on major U.S. corporations, including Fortune 1000 and NASDAQ companies. You can look up a company, category, keyword, or region and find all the pertinent business news. You can sign up for their service online.

Commando Guide to Unconventional Marketing and Advertising Tactics

http://199.44.114.223/mktg/

This online reference covers such topics as how to market survey your competition, doing your own professional marketing and business plan, referral systems, barter exchanges, print advetorials, and telemarketing.

First Steps: Marketing and Design Daily

http://www.interbiznet.com/nomad.html

Developed by the Internet Business Network, First Steps contains a rich source of articles on market research and industry analysis regarding business to business transactions. Much of the marketing and design work is Internet-oriented.

International Public Relations

http://www.iprex.com/

IPREX specializes in international public relations. Its areas of expertise include business-to-business, crisis management, energy and environment, and technology. Its news section has valuable information on public relation trends.

Market Facts and Statistics

http://www.mightymall.com/sevenseas/facts.html

This 1996 survey covers the countries of the world's population, gross national product, and growth rate. Each country has a small paragraph on its economy and markets. The information is organized by major regions: Asia, Western Europe, Central Europe, Middle East, Atlantic, and West Indies.

Marketing Resource Center

http://www.marketingsource.com/

Sponsored by the Concept Marketing Group, the Marketing Resource Center maintains an articles archive with more than 250 business-related articles. Their Tools of the Trade section links to an association database and software for general business and project management.

Retail Futures

http://e1.com/RF/

Sponsored by the Institute for Retail and Merchandising Innovation, this site carries information on tracking customer preferences, category and brand management, regional marketing, and store and product design issues.

Sales Leads USA

http://www.abii.com/

This site is run by American Business Information, Inc. which specializes in generating company profiles. Free services include searching for businesses or people by name with American Directory Assistance or searching by type of business with American Yellow Pages.

Selling.com

http://www.selling.com/

This site is dedicated to salespeople and their needs. Here, you'll find a collection of selling concepts and exercises written by salespeople, for salespeople.

Sharrow Advertising & Marketing Resource Center

http://www.dnai.com/~sharrow/register.html

You have to register at first to visit this site, but it's well worth it; the Advertising Parody section is worth the time by itself. The BizInfo Resource Center has an overview of database marketing, a direct mail profit spreadsheet, and information on approaches to integrated marketing.

Top Marketing Tips, Tricks, and Techniques

http://www.disclosure.com/marketing/toptricks.html

What's the inside scoop? Check out this site, sponsored by Disclosure, Inc., for all the skinny on advertising, direct marketing, marketing law, marketing management, promotions, public relations, trade shows, and telemarketing.

U.S. Census Bureau

http://www.census.gov/

The Census Bureau is a great site to gather social, demographic, and economic information. The site has more than 1,000 Census Bureau publications featuring statistical information on such topics as the nation's population, housing, business and manufacturing activity, international trade, farming, and state and local governments.

World Business Solution

http://thesolution.com/

The World Business Solution is a free marketing manual available from TheSolution.com. There's also a section devoted to downloadable or lined handy forms and reference.

Nonprofit Information

Charity Village

http://www.charityvillage.com/cvhome.html

The Charity Village contains hundreds of pages of news, jobs, resources, and links for the Canadian nonprofit community. Sponsored by Hilborn Interactive, Inc., this site is updated daily in both French ("Rue Principale") and English ("Main Street").

Council on Foundations

http://www.cof.org/index.html

The Council of Foundations is an association of foundations and corporations gathered to promote responsible and effective philanthropy. You'll find information on the various types of foundations as well as a Community Foundation Locator service.

The George Lucas Educational Foundation

http://glef.org/welcome.html

The George Lucas Educational Foundation, a tax-exempt, charitable organization based in Nicasio, California, was established to facilitate the innovative uses of multimedia technologies to enhance teaching and learning. The site has frequently updated information about innovative efforts to change education.

The Gen-X Group

http://www.globalserve.net/~genxgrp/

The Gen–X Group is a not-for-profit Christian organization promoting charities and nonprofit organizations on the Internet. The site features a short course on how and why nonprofit organizations can get on the Web.

The Grantsmanship Center

http://www.tgci.com/

The Grantsmanship Center specializes in training for grant-writing and fundraising. Much of the site is designed to support their courses around the country. The site also contains a cross-referenced database of state and federal funding.

IdeaList

http://www.contact.org/

This site features a global directory of nonprofits with links to more than 10,000 sites in 110 countries. There is also an online library of tools for nonprofits, with information about fundraising and volunteering, accounting and management, legal issues, and nonprofit support organizations.

Nonprofit Resources Catalog

http://www.clark.net/pub/pwalker/

A personal project by the head of United Way Online, this site features meta-links (links to pages of links) dedicated to Interlink sites that benefit nonprofits. Categories include Fundraising and Giving, General Nonprofit Resources, and United Ways on the Internet.

Patents, Trademarks, and Copyrights

Basic Patent Information

http://www.fplc.edu/tfield/ipbasics.htm

Sponsored by the Franklin Law Center, this compendium of resources offers beginning information for artists, independent inventors, Internet authors and artists, programmers, and small business owners, including information on how to avoid being burned by fraudulent invention promotion schemes.

Copyright Clearance Center

http://www.copyright.com/

Copyright Clearance Center (CCC) is a not-for-profit organization created at the suggestion of Congress to help organizations comply with U.S. copyright law. CCC offers a number of catalogs that you can search to see if a work is registered.

Copyright Website

http://www.benedict.com/index.html

This lively site provides real world, practical, and relevant copyright information including a look at famous copyright infringement cases, copyright fundamentals, and distribution of copyright information over the Web.

Intellectual Property Center

http://www.ipcenter.com/

News and information on intellectual property issues dominate this site. Government statutes and decisions are highlighted, along with memos from law firms on intellectual property issues.

Nerd World: Copyrights & Patents

http://www.nerdworld.com/users/dstein/nw427.html

This site provides a resource of links to many patent attorneys and intellectual property law firms from around the world. A recent survey showed many contacts in the U.S., Canada, and Japan.

Patent Application Drafting

http://w3.gwis.com/~sarbar/patapp01.htm

This Web site gives an overview of the steps necessary for writing a patent application, section by section. Aside from covering the statutory legal requirements, Intellectual Property Attorney R. Lawrence Sahr gives insightful comments on the target audience for your patent: the patent office itself.

Patent Pending Resource

http://silkpresence.com/patents/

Sponsored by the patent law firm of Ogram & Teplitz, this site covers new patents law, a FAQ on provisional patent application that allows the "Patent Pending" label to be used. There are also online forms that ask a patent attorney's questions before you schedule a visit.

U.S. Patent Office

http://www.uspto.gov/

The home page for the U.S. Patent Office gives you access to downloadable patent application forms and searchable databases. These include both the U.S. Patent Bibliographic Database (U.S. patents issued from January 1, 1976 to July 8, 1997), and the AIDS Patent Database (full text and images of AIDS-related patents issued by the U.S., Japanese, and European patent offices).

Procurement and Contracting

Acquisition Reform Network

http://www-far.npr.gov/

The Acquisition Reform Network (ARNet) provides services to members of the government acquisition community, both public and private sector. Its resource center, the Federal Acquisition Virtual Library, provides links to numerous other federal acquisition resources on the World Wide Web. Numerous opportunities are also listed.

BidCast

http://www.bidcast.com/

BidCast is a subscription service that allows you to browse and search thousands of U.S. federal government bids. You can sign up the e-mail service for personal notification. There is a free trial section that allows you to look at Commerce Business Daily listings.

Business Information and Development Services (BIDS)

http://www.bidservices.com/newindex.html

BIDS is an electronic publishing and consulting firm which informs small businesses about upcoming government contract opportunities and provides assistance in the procurement process. Their site offers information from both the Commerce Business Daily (U.S.) and Supply and Services Open Bidding Service (Canada).

Commerce Business Daily

http://www.govcon.com/public/CBD/

A sophisticated search engine for finding government procurement opportunities. You can search for a procurement or award under a specific category, by contract value or by a search phrase. You can even specify the level of "fuzzyness" the engine uses to find items bearing a close similarity to your search criteria.

Electronic Commerce Program Office (ECPO)

http://www.arnet.gov/ecapmo/

The Electronic Commerce Program Office (ECPO) is a multi-agency group assembled under the co-leadership of the General Services Administration and the Department of Defense to implement Electronic Commerce/Electronic Data Interchange (EC/EDI) for the federal acquisition programs. An online tutorial can help you get started.

Electronic Commerce Resource Center

http://www.ecrc.ctc.com/

The ECRC Program promotes awareness and implementation of Electronic Commerce and related technologies into the U.S.-integrated civil-military industrial base. Downloadable products can be found in the Electronic Commerce Testbed.

Environmental Protection Agency Procurement

http://www.epa.gov/epahome/Contracts.html

Visit this site for a full listing of business opportunities and EPA acquisition resources. In addition to covering policy and procedure, you can also find an acquisition forecast and a special section devoted to small business opportunities.

FAA Acquisition Center

http://www.faa.gov/asu/asu100/acq-reform/acq_home.htm

After you've checked out the FAQ page on supplying to the Federal Aviation Administration, visit FAST, the FAA Acquisition System Toolset. FAST is a interactive databank designed to guide users through the FAA's new Acquisition Management System (AMS); it contains examples, templates, instructions, tips, policy documents, and other automated tools.

Federal Acquisition Institute

http://www.gsa.gov/fai/

Trying to find your way through the maze of federal acquisition? Pay a visit to the Federal Acquisition Institute, a one-stop acquisition training shop. Here you can sign-up for the FAI Online University or download a Contract Pricing Reference Guide.

General Services Agency

http://www.gsa.gov/

The GSA's mission is to provide expertly managed space, supplies, services, and solutions at the best value to Federal employees. In addition to full information on buying practices, you can also visit its online shopping service, GAO Advantage.

Government Accounting Office

http://www.gao.gov/

The U.S. General Accounting Office (GAO) is a nonpartisan agency that conducts audits, surveys, investigations, and evaluations of federal programs. You can sign up for daily reports through the GAO Daybook service or visit the GAO FraudNET for allegations of fraud, waste, abuse, or mismanagement of federal funds.

Government Contractors Glossary

http://www.kcilink.com/govcon/contractor/gcterms.html

An excellent resource for finding your way through the verbiage of government contracts. A special Acronym Table appears at the end of this guide to enable you to identify the full meaning of the most common government acronyms.

National Technology Transfer Center

http://www.nttc.edu/

The National Technology Transfer Center's task is to take technologies off laboratory shelves and put them to work in U.S. businesses and industries where taxpayers get even more benefits from their investments. Full database services, a training center, and links to other business assistance sites are hallmarks of this Web site.

State and Local Procurement Jumpstation

http://www.fedmarket.com/statejump.html

This invaluable Web page gives you links to procurement sources for all 50 states, not to mention Washington, D.C. and Guam. Most states also have some local listings for specific cities as well as economic development links supplying market data.

U.S. Business Center

http://www.business.gov/

This one-stop shop is designed to streamline interactions between businesses and the government. Common questions and answers are organized by subject, and an expert tool area gives you forms and guidance in everything from Disaster Assistance to Finding a Zip Code.

U.S. Post Office

http://www.usps.gov/business/

The Post Office wants to give you the business! This Web site provides an overview of doing business with the USPS and even tells you how to submit an unsolicited bid. You can download the Procurement Manual, as well as check out business opportunities.

U.S. Veteran Affairs

http://www.va.gov/osdbu/

The online Department of Veteran Affairs site promotes increased use of small and disadvantaged businesses, including acquisition opportunities. A focus of this site is the VA's 1997 Forecast which supplies marketing information useful to the small business person in selling their goods and services, both to the VA and to the VA's large prime contractors.

Small Office/Home Office

America's Small Business Finance Center

http://www.netearnings.com/

Sponsored by Net Earnings, Inc., this one-stop shop offers business advice on insurance policies and prices, and on applying for loans and credit cards. You can also sign up for online payroll service here.

American Express Small Business Exchange

http://www.americanexpress.com/smallbusiness/

The American Express Small Business Exchange offers online classifieds (buying and selling); expert advice where you can ask a specific question, browse the categories, or check out the tip of the month; and business planning and resources with information on starting, managing, or expanding your business.

Bathrobe 'til 10

http://www.slip.net/~sfwave/

This guide for the home professional offers articles and information for the solo self-employed. Concerned about word use? Pay a visit to the Grammar Queen to clear up those business correspondence blues.

Biz$hop

http://www.bizshop.com/

Biz$hop is a virtual company specializing in helping entrepreneurs achieve success in their own businesses. There are numerous reports and free business resources available—be sure to download the free "First 25 Business Decisions" report.

BizResource.com

http://www.bizresource.com/

Dedicated to encouraging small businesses and entrepreneurs, BizResource offers an on-going series of business tips (both via e-mail and archived online), a business chat area, and a series of audio, video, and computer resources.

Business@Home

http://www.gohome.com/

An electronic magazine dedicated to the working-from-home community, Business@Home includes articles on opportunity, marketing, and technology. Its Cool Tools department reviews recent hardware and software important to the general home office worker, while the Consultant's Corner focuses on the consultant's work experience.

Business Resource Center

http://www.morebusiness.com/

This site hosts an excellent four-part primer with advice and activities to get you thinking about your business, its customers, development, and marketing. In addition, you can find templates and worksheets here for press releases and business plans.

Business Start Page

http://www.wp.com/fredfish/

Here's a great place to start your business day. This site offers a virtual desktop where you can find everything at your fingertips: Yellow, Blue, and International page telephone directories, links to shipping companies, a reference library, and a series of tips and tricks.

Center for Family Business

http://199.103.128.199/fambiznc/cntprovs/orgs/necfb/

Run by Northeastern University, this site features an on-going series of articles on running a family business (both home and office- or store-based). These family business issues include generational change, sibling rivalries, and how to balance family and business priorities.

EGOPHER—The Entrepreneur Gopher

http://www.slu.edu/eweb/egopher.html

Sponsored by St. Louis University, EGOPHER is designed for people and organizations interested in new, small, or entrepreneurial businesses. A variety of Top 10 lists for entrepreneurs is available along with topical business resources and access to core research journal in entrepreneurship.

Electronic Money Tree

http://www.soos.com/$tree/

Aimed at the Internet savvy (or those who want to be) entrepreneurs, the Electronic Money Tree consists primarily of a digest of articles. Sample articles include "Can SOHO Really Compete?" "Biz Tips," "Better Press Releases," and "Time Management."

Entrepreneur's Bookstore

http://kwicsys.com/books/

There are more than 600 information reports offered at this site, most from $1 to $2 each. The reports are categorized. Sample topic areas include Mail Order, Multilevel Marketing, Legal, and Direct Response TV.

Entrepreneur Magazine's BizSquare

http://www.entrepreneurmag.com/

This site is chock-full of information for the SOHO businessperson. Visit the Resource Center to check out the online Franchise 500 and Business Opportunity 500 lists. Then go to the SOHO Mall for all your business-related software, books, magazines, and audio or videocassettes.

EntreWorld

http://www.entreworld.org/

The EntreWorld site is organized by business level. Visit the Starting Your Business area for information on business planning, finding the right people, or creating products that win loyalty. Running Your Business is devoted to later stage companies with information on expanding your customer base and exit strategies.

FranInfo

http://www.frannet.com/

Thinking about franchising? Visit FranInfo's site to find information on buying a franchise or franchising your own business. The site has several self-tests to determine if you're ready for franchising, as well as listing of franchises for sale.

Guide to the Small Business Administration

http://www.geocities.com/WallStreet/2172/

Before you dive into the SBA bureaucracy, you might want to visit this site first. There's lots of details covering the various SBA programs available with information to help you find just the right one for your business.

Heath's Computer and Telecommunication Acronym Reference

http://www.sbri.com/acro2.htm

Visit this site before your next cocktail party where you want to impress others with statements like, "My GOSIP is about to go LUNI on Harv's LANE." Or maybe when you just want to find out what all those jargonese initials mean.

Home Office Association of America

http://www.hoaa.com/

There's power in numbers—even if you're working alone. The Home Office Association of America offers group health insurance, a long-distance calling plan, a debt collection service, home business and equipment insurance, and more. Be sure to visit their 50 Great Home Office Startup Ideas page.

Home Office Links

http://www.ro.com/small_business/homebased.html

A full compendium of Web links for small and home-based offices including franchises, business opportunities, reference material, newsgroups, searching tools, and services for small business. Links to just about anything related to small- and home-based business can be found here.

Home Office Mall

http://www.the-office.com/

A centralized location for products and services catering to the home office professional. Find everything from computers for rent to computer furniture, to networks for female executives.

Home Realtors Information Network

http://www.realtors.com/

About the only thing all home business have in common is the home. This Web site, sponsored by the National Association of Realtors, has almost 900,000 listings of homes around the country—and, of course, a search engine to help you find your dream office.

NetMarquee Family Business NetCenter

http://nmq.com/

This site supplies news and information for owners and executives in family-owned businesses. There is a calendar of events, weekly articles, and a listserve for on-going discussion related to family businesses.

Offshore Entrepreneur

http://www.au.com/offshore/

With the motto, "Neither profit, nor opportunity, have any borders," the Offshore Entrepreneur takes you through the promise, pitfalls, and profit of basing your business in another country. The site offers abundant information on tax-planning and forming an offshore corporation.

Opportunities for Women in Small Business

http://www.mindspring.com/~higley/project.htm

One path around the glass ceiling is to open your own business. This site is dedicated to helping women choose and run a business. There are profiles of successful women, as well as financial and legal advice and tips on how to avoid failure.

Resource Center for Home-Based Businesses

http://www.masseypub.com/

Learn from someone who made the home-based business dream come true. Featuring information on self-published brochures, this site offers a FAQ section, details on seminars, and an area devoted to mail order scams.

Retail Business Resource Center

http://www.retailadvz.com/

Looking for a site where you can learn from the experts? The Retail Business Resource Center offers theme-oriented live business chats, live workshops, and even a business therapist offering real-world solutions to real-world problems.

Small Business Innovative Research

http://www.sbir.dsu.edu/

Small Business Innovative Research is a federally supported program aimed at funding small businesses with money from Federal agency and department's R&D divisions. This site assists small companies in applying for that funding by answering questions and providing online tests.

SOHO America

http://www.soho.org/

SOHO America is a small business benefits association. In addition to news of interest to the small office/home office market, this site offers a comprehensive list of health benefits, business tools, and personal discounts available to members.

Your Small Office

http://www.smalloffice.com/

This site is the online presence of *Small Office Computing* and *Home Office Computing* magazines and features articles from their magazines. The Web site visitor will find a great number of reviews of network, computer, and office equipment as well as a full "How To" department covering everything from Startup to Sales and Marketing.

U.S. Chamber of Commerce Small Business Institute

http://www.uschamber.org/programs/sbi/index.html

The U.S. Chamber of Commerce runs a Small Business Institute with a variety of resources both for free and for sale. There are self-study programs on Mastering Your Business on the Internet and the Small Business Institute Series, as well as information on the SOHO Conference.

Travel and Transportation

Airlines of the Web

http://w2.itn.net/airlines/

Where can you find a listing of *all* the airlines, both passenger and cargo? At the Airlines of the Web site, of course. Passenger airlines are categorized by region, and you can also find airline-related information like 800 numbers and a link to a real-time reservation service.

American Airlines

http://www.americanair.com/aa_home.htm

The American Access Web site takes a full-service approach. Here, you can plan your travel, check out AAdvantage frequent flier miles, take advantage of the NetSaver fares, and download Personal Access, American's Windows-based software program that brings you dedicated AAdvantage information, travel planning, and up-to-the-minute information and specials.

American Movers Conference

http://www.amconf.org/

The American Movers Conference is an association of 3,000 professional moving companies in the U.S. Their site has information on how to prepare your move, how much a "self-haul" might cost, and listings of movers across the country.

Continental Airlines

http://www.flycontinental.com:80/index.html

Continental On-Line's main claim to fame is its C.O.O.L. Travel Assistant which can be used to schedule and book airline travel on Continental, Continental Express, and Continental Micronesia as well as more than 40 rental car companies and 26,000 hotels around the world.

FedEX

http://www.fedex.com/

Not only can you now track your overnight package online, but you can also use their interactive rate finder, and even ship packages via the Internet to more than 160 countries from the U.S. and Canada. There's also a searchable database of drop-off locations and downloadable software for managing your shipping, including the airbill printing.

HomeBuyer's Fair

http://www.homefair.com/home/

While most of this site is dedicated to helping you buy or sell your home, the HomeBuyer's Fair has some amazing interactive tools in its Popular Exhibits area. There's a Salary

Calculator for comparing the cost of living in hundreds of U.S. and international cities, a Moving Calculator for figuring the cost of a move, and a Relocation Crime Lab for comparing crime statistics.

InterKnowledge Travel Network

http://www.interknowledge.com/

When your business takes you to an exotic locale—meaning you've never been there before—stop by the InterKnowledge Travel Network site first. The site is characterized by beautiful images and full details on geography, culture, and climate.

Northwest Airlines

http://www.nwa.com/

This Northwest Airlines site has information on CyberSavers, their online low-cost tickets, as well as regular travel and frequent flier information. A full slate of vacation packages rounds out the site.

U.S. Air

http://www.usair.com/

Tune into the U.S. Air Web site to schedule and book a flight or check your frequent flyer miles. An extensive area of the site is devoted to its U.S. Airways Cargo service where you can use the software to track shipments with real-time information from airport drop-off to pickup.

United Parcel Service

http://www.ups.com/

Interactive functions featured at the UPS site include package tracking, cost-estimating, a drop-off locator, and pick-up scheduling. UPS also makes available free software for all of these functions as well as up-to-the-minute zone and rate charts.

Trade Shows and Conferences

EXPOguide

http://www.expoguide.com/

If you're thinking about selling your product through a trade show, stop by this site first. It has a full listing of trade shows, conferences, and exhibitions as well as comprehensive coverage of show services and associations. Although primarily intended for trade show managers, there's still plenty of information here for exhibiting companies.

CD Information

http://www.cd-info.com/CDIC/Industry/TradeShows.html

Today, much of computing and information storage and retrieval revolves around the CD-ROM. This site is CD-centric and lists many upcoming exhibition, conferences, seminars, and workshops in a month-by-month format.

Guide to Unique Meeting Facilities

http://www.theguide.com/

A terrific resource for meeting planners, The Guide to Unique Meeting Facilities covers colleges and universities, retreat centers, camps and lodges, and cultural and historical venues, as well as traditional conference centers. There is also a Hot Date/Cool Rate area to highlight facilities with open, economical dates.

Major Trade Shows In Asia

http://www.tdb.gov.sg/trshow/tr_menu.html

You can start your search for Asian trade shows here, either by country, industry or by date. Fourteen countries, including Brunei, China, Japan, South Korea, and Vietnam, and more than 25 different industries are covered.

Trade Show Central

http://www.tscentral.com/

Sponsored by the International Association for Exhibition Management, Trade Show Central gives you easy access to information on more than 30,000 trade shows. Its searchable database links to an e-mail notification service where you can request more information. Its AudioNet connection broadcasts and archives keynote speeches from major events.

Wall Street Directory

http://www.wsdinc.com/index.html

Wall Street Directory offers a wide range of information for traders and investors. To see its up-to-the-minute conference information, select the Seminars-Shows-Conventions category and click the Search by Category button.

Small Business Administration Upcoming Events

http://www.sbaonline.sba.gov/gc/events.html

Organized on a monthly basis, the SBA keeps a listing of many business-related seminars and conferences. Although not hot-linked, all conferences have telephone contact information. Free seminars are prominently noted.

EventWeb

http://www.eventweb.com/

A free mailing list service for meeting, conference, and trade show promoters. Sample articles include "How to Exhibit at a Virtual Trade Show," "Expanding Educational Horizons in the Online World," and "Promote Your Speakers—Inexpensively!"

Tradeshow News Network

http://www.tsnn.com/

The Tradeshow News Network allows you to search for a trade show in the U.S. by location, date, or industry. Its Trade Show Education department offers tips on both exhibiting and attending, as well as an Ask the Expert section.

Virtual Online Trade Show

http://www.volts.com/

This site promotes the Virtual Trade Show concept, and is aimed at both exhibition managers and exhibitors. Exhibitors can see how they can save money, broaden their exposure, and communicate with their customers. ●

What's on the CD?

The contents of the CD-ROM are easily viewed and navigated through with any Web browser. If you do not have a browser, you can use Internet Explorer 3.02, which is provided. The contents of the CD are organized into the following categories: Electronic Books, Software, Business Sites on the Web, and Source Code and samples from the book.

Detailed instructions on CD use and operation can be found in the README.DOC file on the CD-ROM. ■

Electronic Books

This CD is packed with several electronic (Web-based) versions of Que's leading titles. Some of these titles include:

Office 97 Quick References

- ■ *Office 97*
- ■ *Word 97*
- ■ *Excel 97*
- ■ *Access 97*

Operating Systems

- ■ *Platinum Edition Using Windows 95*
- ■ *Special Edition Using Windows NT Workstation 4.0*

Internet

- ■ *Special Edition Using Internet Explorer 3.0*
- ■ *Special Edition Using FrontPage 97*

Software

The CD-ROM includes many full as well as trial-version software products and utilities to make your Office 97 computing experience more productive and exciting. All of the software can be installed directly from the CD-ROM.

Office 97 Add-Ins and Tools

Village Software FastStart Sampler Excel Solutions   The Village Software FastStart Sampler includes 12 ready-made Excel templates to provide spreadsheet solutions for common business and personal needs. These templates were hand-selected as a special sample package from Village Software's FastStart's product line.

ActiveOffice   ActiveOffice, the "Essential Graphics Companion to Microsoft Office," instantly transforms text and numbers into compelling graphics that effectively communicate the key ideas, trends, and relationships in all of your documents, spreadsheets, and presentations.

ActivePresenter   ActivePresenter gives you all of the tools you need to deliver high-impact, low-cost presentations on the Web.ActivePresenter—which features SPC's revolutionary Intelligent Formatting technology—includes everything you need to create, publish, and present in one powerful, simple-to-use solution.

Office Toys 97   Office Toys 97 is an add-in for Microsoft Word 97, which creates a toolbar filled with many great Word utilities. These utilities provide you with a quicker and smarter way to use Word 97 and the files you create. Some of the powerful utilities and functions include the following: Office Navigator, Project Manager, More Proofing Tools!, Formatting tools!, Auto-backup, Virus Alert!, Smart printing tools!, Style Management!, and much more.

Microsoft Office 97 Viewers   Microsoft provides distributable viewers for three of their Office products. These viewers enable you to share Word, Excel, and PowerPoint documents with individuals who have not installed Microsoft Office applications on their computer systems.

Business and Professional

App

B

Pagis Pro97   Pagis Pro97 is a fully featured scanning application that allows you to scan documents (one or multiple pages) into your Windows 95/NT 4.0 desktop. With a color, grayscale, or binary scanner, you can easily scan documents into your PC and then file, copy, print, send or use them with your favorite application by simply "dragging and dropping" them onto the application icon.

GoldMine   GoldMine is the number one Workgroup Contact Manager. It is designed to automate business professionals—whether they work remotely in the field, alone on a desktop PC, or with others in networked offices. It combines contact management, day and time planning, sales automation, and mail list management with group calendaring, database design, data synchronization, and e-mail messaging.

WinFax Pro   WinFax Pro gives you hassle-free faxing anywhere, anytime. Why waste time printing documents and feeding a fax machine? Fax right from your computer. WinFax Pro is easy to install and use—step-by-step wizards show you exactly what to do.

Paint Shop Pro   Paint Shop Pro—a powerful and easy-to-use image viewing, editing, and conversion program—supports more than 30 image formats. With numerous drawing and painting tools, this might be the only graphics program you will ever need!

Internet

EarthLink Total Access   Total Access offers a quick-start tool for connecting to the Internet. EarthLink Network specializes in providing inexpensive Internet access throughout the United States.

Microsoft Internet Explorer 3.02   Microsoft Internet Explorer is a must-have application for Web viewing. With the explosion of the Web, many companies, organizations, and individuals are generating Web-based documents. In order to view these documents, you need a Web browser. Even if you already have Netscape installed on your computer, many sites optimize their Web pages for Internet Explorer. The version that is provided runs on both Windows 95 and NT.

Adobe Acrobat Reader with Search 3.01   The free Adobe Acrobat Reader enables you to view, navigate, and print PDF files across all major computing platforms. Adobe has created two flavors of Acrobat Reader 3.01, Acrobat Reader and Acrobat Reader with Search. Reader with Search includes additions that allow the user to search within a collection of PDF files on a hard disk, CD, or local area network (for which an index file has been created with the Acrobat Catalog tool).

CuteFTP   CuteFTP is a Windows-based Internet application that allows you to use the capabilities of FTP without having to know all the details about the protocol itself. It simplifies FTP by offering a user-friendly, graphical interface instead of a cumbersome command-line utility.

WinZip   WinZip brings the convenience of Windows to the use of Zip files. It requires neither PKZIP nor PKUNZIP. The new WinZip Wizard makes unzipping easier than ever. WinZip features built-in support for popular Internet file formats, including TAR, gzip, UNIX compress, UUEncode, BinHex, and MIME. ARJ, LZH, and ARC files are supported via external programs. WinZip interfaces to most virus scanners.

WebPrinter 4-Pack   WebPrinter instantly turns your valuable Internet, CD-ROM, and Windows data into attractive booklets with WebPrinter. With only two clicks, sports stats, custom travel itineraries, financial how-to guides, product literature, maps, and even photos are transformed into convenient, double-sided booklets.

PointCast Network   Through personal news profiles, viewers are enabled to customize the information they receive. Viewers specify news topics of interest, and the PointCast Network delivers current news to their desktops. They can modify personal news profiles at any time.

Business Sites on the Web

The CD includes a hyperlinked version of Appendix A, "Business Sites on the Web." To take advantage of Web publishing, click the hyperlink of any business site and go directly to their Web site. ●

Index

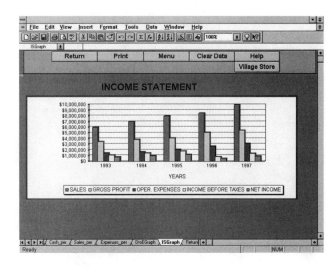

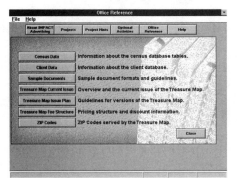

Complete and Return this Card
for a *FREE* Computer Book Catalog

Thank you for purchasing this book! You have purchased a superior computer book written expressly for your needs. To continue to provide the kind of up-to-date, pertinent coverage you've come to expect from us, we need to hear from you. Please take a minute to complete and return this self-addressed, postage-paid form. In return, we'll send you a free catalog of all our computer books on topics ranging from word processing to programming and the internet.

Mr. ☐   Mrs. ☐   Ms. ☐   Dr. ☐

Name (first) [ ] (M.I.) [ ] (last) [ ]

Address [ ]

City [ ] State [ ] Zip [ ]

Phone [ ] Fax [ ]

Company Name [ ]

E-mail address [ ]

1. Please check at least (3) influencing factors for purchasing this book.

Front or back cover information on book .... ☐
Special approach to the content .... ☐
Completeness of content .... ☐
Author's reputation .... ☐
Publisher's reputation .... ☐
Book cover design or layout .... ☐
Index or table of contents of book .... ☐
Price of book .... ☐
Special effects, graphics, illustrations .... ☐
Other (Please specify): _____ ☐

2. How did you first learn about this book?

Saw in Macmillan Computer Publishing catalog .... ☐
Recommended by store personnel .... ☐
Saw the book on bookshelf at store .... ☐
Recommended by a friend .... ☐
Received advertisement in the mail .... ☐
Saw an advertisement in: _____ ☐
Read book review in: _____ ☐
Other (Please specify): _____ ☐

3. How many computer books have you purchased in the last six months?

This book only .... ☐   3 to 5 books .... ☐
2 books .... ☐   More than 5 .... ☐

4. Where did you purchase this book?

Bookstore .... ☐
Computer Store .... ☐
Consumer Electronics Store .... ☐
Department Store .... ☐
Office Club .... ☐
Warehouse Club .... ☐
Mail Order .... ☐
Direct from Publisher .... ☐
Internet site .... ☐
Other (Please specify): _____ ☐

5. How long have you been using a computer?

☐ Less than 6 months   ☐ 6 months to a year
☐ 1 to 3 years   ☐ More than 3 years

6. What is your level of experience with personal computers and with the subject of this book?

	With PCs	With subject of book
New	☐	☐
Casual	☐	☐
Accomplished	☐	☐
Expert	☐	☐

Source Code ISBN: 0-07897-1398-5

7. Which of the following best describes your job title?

Administrative Assistant .... ☐
Coordinator .... ☐
Manager/Supervisor .... ☐
Director .... ☐
Vice President .... ☐
President/CEO/COO .... ☐
Lawyer/Doctor/Medical Professional .... ☐
Teacher/Educator/Trainer .... ☐
Engineer/Technician .... ☐
Consultant .... ☐
Not employed/Student/Retired .... ☐
Other (Please specify): _____ ☐

8. Which of the following best describes the area of the company your job title falls under?

Accounting .... ☐
Engineering .... ☐
Manufacturing .... ☐
Operations .... ☐
Marketing .... ☐
Sales .... ☐
Other (Please specify): _____ ☐

9. What is your age?

Under 20 .... ☐
21-29 .... ☐
30-39 .... ☐
40-49 .... ☐
50-59 .... ☐
60-over .... ☐

10. Are you:

Male .... ☐
Female .... ☐

11. Which computer publications do you read regularly? (Please list)

_____
_____
_____
_____
_____
_____
_____
_____
_____
_____

Comments: _____
_____
_____

Fold here and scotch-tape to mail.

Check out Que® Books on the World Wide Web
http://www.quecorp.com

As the biggest software release in computer history, Windows 95 continues to redefine the computer industry. Click here for the latest info on our Windows 95 books

Make computing quick and easy with these products designed exclusively for new and casual users

Examine the latest releases in word processing, spreadsheets, operating systems, and suites

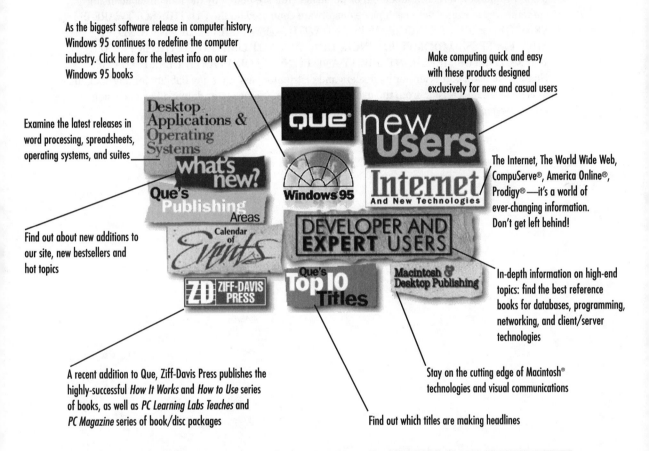

The Internet, The World Wide Web, CompuServe®, America Online®, Prodigy®—it's a world of ever-changing information. Don't get left behind!

Find out about new additions to our site, new bestsellers and hot topics

In-depth information on high-end topics: find the best reference books for databases, programming, networking, and client/server technologies

A recent addition to Que, Ziff-Davis Press publishes the highly-successful *How It Works* and *How to Use* series of books, as well as *PC Learning Labs Teaches* and *PC Magazine* series of book/disc packages

Stay on the cutting edge of Macintosh® technologies and visual communications

Find out which titles are making headlines

With 6 separate publishing groups, Que develops products for many specific market segments and areas of computer technology. Explore our Web Site and you'll find information on best-selling titles, newly published titles, upcoming products, authors, and much more.

- Stay informed on the latest industry trends and products available
- Visit our online bookstore for the latest information and editions
- Download software from Que's library of the best shareware and freeware

Licensing Agreement

By opening this package, you are agreeing to be bound by the following: